1,000,000 Books

are available to read at

Forgotten Books

www.ForgottenBooks.com

Read online
Download PDF
Purchase in print

ISBN 978-1-5276-1092-7
PIBN 10876504

This book is a reproduction of an important historical work. Forgotten Books uses state-of-the-art technology to digitally reconstruct the work, preserving the original format whilst repairing imperfections present in the aged copy. In rare cases, an imperfection in the original, such as a blemish or missing page, may be replicated in our edition. We do, however, repair the vast majority of imperfections successfully; any imperfections that remain are intentionally left to preserve the state of such historical works.

Forgotten Books is a registered trademark of FB &c Ltd.
Copyright © 2018 FB &c Ltd.
FB &c Ltd, Dalton House, 60 Windsor Avenue, London, SW19 2RR.
Company number 08720141. Registered in England and Wales.

For support please visit www.forgottenbooks.com

1 MONTH OF FREE READING

at
www.ForgottenBooks.com

By purchasing this book you are eligible for one month membership to ForgottenBooks.com, giving you unlimited access to our entire collection of over 1,000,000 titles via our web site and mobile apps.

To claim your free month visit:
www.forgottenbooks.com/free876504

* Offer is valid for 45 days from date of purchase. Terms and conditions apply.

English
Français
Deutsche
Italiano
Español
Português

www.forgottenbooks.com

Mythology Photography **Fiction** Fishing Christianity **Art** Cooking Essays Buddhism Freemasonry Medicine **Biology** Music **Ancient Egypt** Evolution Carpentry Physics Dance Geology **Mathematics** Fitness Shakespeare **Folklore** Yoga Marketing **Confidence** Immortality Biographies Poetry **Psychology** Witchcraft Electronics Chemistry History **Law** Accounting **Philosophy** Anthropology Alchemy Drama Quantum Mechanics Atheism Sexual Health **Ancient History** **Entrepreneurship** Languages Sport Paleontology Needlework Islam **Metaphysics** Investment Archaeology Parenting Statistics Criminology **Motivational**

THE

ANNUAL REGISTER,

OR A VIEW OF THE

HISTORY,
POLITICS,

AND

LITERATURE,

FOR THE YEAR
1770.

THE SIXTH EDITION.

LONDON:
Printed (by Assignment from the Executors of the late Mr. James Dodsley)

FOR W. OTRIDGE & SON; R. FAULDER; CUTHELL & MARTIN; OGILVY & SON; R. LEA; J. NUNN; J. WALKER; LACKINGTON, ALLEN, & CO.; E. JEFFERY; AND VERNOR AND HOOD;

By Knight and Compton, Middle Street, Cloth Fair.

1803.

PREFACE.

THE year we treat of afforded much matter for History, and perhaps still more for Speculation. Though fruitful in great and extraordinary events, it seemed to threaten more than it expresly told. A war which desolated a great part of Europe, and might in its consequences have affected the political system of the whole, appeared at this time as little more than a secondary object of consideration. Battles and sieges, the destruction of armies and fleets, and the ruin of countries, however distant the scene of action, would, in times of less business and importance, have nearly superseded all other matter, and have been considered as the only objects that demanded the care of the Writer, or that claimed the attention of the Public.

In the present instance it has been otherwise; and however interesting these subjects of observation or discussion may be, others have arisen nearer home, by which, as a nation, we are more immediately affected. The extraordinary movements of some of our great neighbours, and the hostile appearances for some time, on the side, at least, of one of them, were more than objects of curiosity; and though the storm seems for the present blown over, it has afforded sufficient cause for reflection. The issue of the present convulsions in France, whether they terminate in increasing the despotism of the Monarch, or in regaining or enlarging the rights or liberties of the People, must be to us a matter of great importance. Fortunate, we should think it, if in this precarious and critical state of affairs, when almost every part of Europe presents an ample field for discussion, our own domestic concerns were in so happy a situation, as not to furnish the Patriot and Politician with the most just and serious anxiety for the welfare of his own country.

We

PREFACE.

We hope that so much matter and such various subjects of discussion, as have swelled our History beyond the limits usually assigned to it, will sufficiently plead with the Public for our being later this year than we intended; and that if, upon the whole, we have endeavoured to give the clearest and most impartial account of foreign and domestic transactions, which the limited and imperfect information that can be obtained so near the time of their being acted will admit of, we shall still continue to meet with that indulgence which we have hitherto so happily experienced.

THE ANNUAL REGISTER,

For the YEAR 1770.

THE HISTORY OF EUROPE.

CHAP. I.

State of the Belligerent Powers. Russia. Conduct of the Neutral Powers. Probable consequences of the war. Turky. Firmness of the Grand Signior. Probability of a peace. Spain. Falkland's Islands. Great Britain. Portugal.

THE great successes of the Russians in the two last campaigns, though flattering and brilliant, have not been productive of those immediate advantages which would have attended conquests of the same nature in other parts of the world. The fertile and extensive provinces between the Danube and the Niester, if they had been situated in the cultivated parts of Europe or Asia, and subject only to the well-regulated rapine of a disciplined army under an able general, would in themselves have nearly provided for the support of the war.

In the present instance, the conquered countries are in so ruined a state, that instead of contributing to defray the expences of the war, they cannot supply the common articles of subsistence; and forage is the principal, if not the only aid, which they can afford to their defenders or assailants.

The Russians will, however, derive great advantages in the future opera-

operations of the war from this accession of territory; and being in possession of all the fortresses, and the Turks driven totally beyond the Danube, this state of security, as well as that arising from the submission of the Budziac Tartars, will encourage the remaining natives to cultivate their lands and rebuild their houses, and the fugitives to return to their country. Nor will the Turks find it easy now to renew the war on this side of the Danube; an attempt, in which they will experience many of the same difficulties, which we had formerly shewn, would attend the progress of the Russians, if they were to extend their operations into Bulgaria. In either case the river will be found a very important barrier.

Though the Tartars of the Crim and Little Tartary, as well as those of Oczacow, have hitherto continued firm in their attachment to the Porte, and have despised all the offers as well as threats, which have been used to detach them from it; yet it can scarcely be conceived by the present appearance of affairs, that without the intervention of some other power, or some extraordinary and unexpected good fortune on the side of the Turks, they can be able to withstand the power of Russia for another campaign. The Turkish operations on the Danube can be considered as little more than a diversion in their favour, and in the present wretched state of their marine, the support by the Black Sea must be weak and uncertain. Nor is any extraordinary defence to be expected from the fortress of Oczacow; single and exposed as it is, without support, and the dreadful fate of Bender before its eyes.

While the Russians triumph upon the Danube and the Niester; by their expedition to the Mediterranean, they seem to have enclosed all Europe, from the bottom of the Baltic, to the Streights of the Dardanelles, within the line of their hostility. Extraordinary events are seldom brought about, without a singular concurrence of circumstances to facilitate their execution; and it may perhaps be found, that most of the great revolutions which have taken place in the history of mankind, would have failed, if they had been attempted at any other time than that precise æra, which seemed calculated for their completion, and to have removed or smoothed every obstacle to their success. This expedition is one of those remarkable events which could have as little taken place, as the attempt could have been believed or foreseen, at any period of time prior to the present.

It had become the policy of the great European commercial powers, long before Russia was mistress of a ship, to suffer no new maritime state to spring up amongst them; nor did the antiquity of the republic of Genoa protect her from the jealousy of Lewis the Fourteenth, when she, who had before aspired to be a rival for the commerce of the world, was restrained from building ships in her own docks; and even restricted as to the possession of more than a specified number. Arbitrary precedents of the same nature were not unknown in antiquity and it is no wonder that the modern European states, whose avidity for commerce, as soon as they had tasted her sweets, was beyond all former example, and involv them in continual wars amon themselves for the share they shoul posse possess in her favour, should eagerly convert such precedents to their own advantage, and behold every new rival for it with the extremest jealousy.

Peter the Great's efforts to create sailors and a navy, were beheld with admiration as a novelty, and as the extraordinary attempts of an extraordinary man. His great ships and his land admirals were amusing to himself and to others in the Baltic, and destructive to Sweden in the declining state of that kingdom. Such a naval force as could be formed in such a sea, and locked up within it, was of little consequence to the great commercial states; and it was the strict policy of these, as well as of later times, that it should be confined to those limits.

The particular jealousy with which the Mediterranean powers have at all times regarded every intrusion on that sea, which being surrounded by their dominions, they seem in some measure to consider as their peculiar property, would in any other circumstances of public affairs, have proved an insuperable bar to this enterprize. Nor is this attempt more repugnant to the principles adopted by the commercial states, than it is to the general political system of Europe, which has been so long and so eagerly pursued, and which to preserve a due equilibrium is totally averse to the making of great conquests, or to the formation of a new dominion. To all these standing impediments to an attempt of this nature, may be added, the general dread entertained of the over-grown power of Russia, and a conviction of the consequences that have already ensued from that supreme ascendant which she has acquired, and which she so arbitrarily displays in all the affairs of the north.

Such, however, are the peculiar circumstances of the present times, and such the extraordinary fortune of the Empress Catherine, that with a very moderate naval force, ill found and ill provided, and manned with raw and unexperienced sailors, she has sent fire and sword into the shores of Greece, and the isles of the Archipelago.

Great Britain, indeed, beheld without uneasiness, the aggrandizement of a power, in whose alliance she is to look for a balance to the family compact. France does not chuse to interfere in a quarrel which might bring into the Mediterranean an English, to the aid of a Russian fleet. The distress which the Levant trade suffers, is more felt by France than by Great Britain; and Great Britain profits more by the prosperity of the Russian arms and empire, than she suffers by a temporary suspension of her commerce in that part of the world, where our dealings are not near so extensive as those of France. If the progress of the Russian arms should meet any check, it must be owing to the intervention of Prussia and Austria: neither of which powers can see, without a rational alarm, Russia becoming the mistress of Poland, and the total destroyer of the Turkish empire; out of whose ruins something truly formidable might arise in time.

This Mediterranean expedition has however hitherto answered more the purpose of damage to the enemy, than of direct benefit to Russia. The passage of the Dardanelles has not been made good, nor does there seem any great probability, as it was not effected during the first surprize and confusion, that it should succeed,

succeed, after the Turks have had so long a time, under the conduct of able engineers, to prepare for its defence. Neither have the Russians been able to possess themselves of an island or port in the Archipelago, of any consequence, during the whole summer. This expedition, however, contributed to embarrass and distract the councils of the Porte, to keep back some of their best troops and officers from the Danube, and by cutting off the supply of provisions by sea, to increase the tumults and disorder at Constantinople. It is also probable that it encouraged, in a considerable degree, the rebellion that has broken out in Egypt.

None of these consequences, except the destruction of the Turkish fleet, seem equivalent to the vast expences that have attended it, and which at present are ill adapted to the state of the Russian finances. It may also perhaps be doubted, whether they have not been counterbalanced by the ruin and slaughter of the Greeks, who seem by some fatality to be devoted to inevitable destruction, wherever the Russians appear in their favour.

This consequence was however to have been expected, from the excessive ignorance of the Greeks, and the inability of the Russians to support them with effect. It does not indeed appear to have been good policy in Russia, to have made so fatal and useless a trial of the disposition of these unhappy people. It was natural enough that they should wish for a deliverance from their oppressors, and that, vain of their antient national glory, they should think themselves possessed of the virtue of their ancestors: their ignorance of geography, of the state of Europe, and even of the ability of Russia to assist them, would sufficiently account for any act of madness that they were capable of committing. The Russians are, however, too well informed to imagine that a people immersed in a corruption of two thousand years, broken by long slavery, and sunk through every state of degradation; whose depravity, and total insensibility of condition, were become proverbial, and whose imaginary bravery only depended upon their having never seen the face of an enemy, should all at once do more than inherit the valour of their ancestors, and, without discipline or knowledge of any thing martial, not only encounter regular forces, but subdue those conquerors to whom they had basely submitted when they were yet a people, and the remains of a great empire. It would seem that this trial should at least have been reserved for a better opportunity; when they could have landed a sufficient body of forces to have kept the field independently of the Greeks, whom they were to consider only as feeble auxiliaries, but willing subjects.

Upon the whole, this war has placed the military character of Russia in a very high point of view. And while their armies have gained the greatest honours in the field, their sailors have learned to traverse new seas, and to navigate and fight under the direction of English officers. An admiral of our nation of high note, and of superior knowledge in all the parts of his profession, has gone lately into their service; and there is little room to doubt under his tuition, and from his acknowledged judgment in the construction of ships, but their marine

rine will soon make a very respectable figure.

In other respects there is no doubt but Russia will obtain the most solid advantages, in consequence of her success in this war; among which the establishment of such a barrier, as will secure her whole European frontier from the future insults of the Tartars, may be considered as an object of great importance: as besides their depopulating and preventing the cultivation of her finest provinces, she was at the expence of employing 50,000 men in peace and war, in guarding the lines upon that long extent of frontier. It is also little to be doubted in the present circumstances, that the court of Petersburgh will gain the grand and favourite point which has been so long and so eagerly coveted, of establishing a port, or perhaps more than one, upon the Black Sea; and it is as probable that it will urge, to the utmost extent, the obtaining a liberty to trade upon it in Russian bottoms.

The renewing of the fortifications of Azoph, which were destroyed in pursuance of the treaty of the year 1739; or even the restoring of the port of Troitza, or the Trinity, would not answer all the purposes, nor at present gratify the ambition, of the court of Petersburgh. This city, which is the metropolis of the Cuban Tartary, lies on the Asiatic shore of the antient Tanais, now called the Don, a few miles from its junction with the eastern extremity of the Palus Meotis, which now takes its name from the city. Though the harbour of Azoph was capable of receiving vessels of considerable size, yet from some shoals that crossed the river near the mouth, those of a certain burthen could not fall down to the sea, without taking out their heavy loading and guns. For this reason, the Russians built the port of Troitza, a few miles lower down, but immediately on the sea, where they had a good harbour, capable of building and receiving ships of any burthen. The Streights of Caffa are the only navigable communication between the Black Sea and this of Azoph; and as the Turks are masters on both sides, by erecting proper fortifications at Jenicola in Crim Tartary, and on the opposite shore of the island of Taman, which form the Streight, they might command the navigation of it. Notwithstanding these impediments, Azoph has always been considered as a place of the greatest importance to Russia, and was accordingly the first object that attracted the ambition of Peter the Great; who, as soon as he found himself sole master by the death of his brother, and that the Turks were engaged in a losing war with the Emperor and Venice, took that opportunity, in the year 1696, to besiege and take it. The bad state of the Turkish affairs, together with his being included as an ally by the other hostile powers, obliged them to cede it to him by the treaty of Carlowitz; and nothing but the imminent danger in which both he and his army were involved many years after upon the banks of the Pruth, could have obliged him to restore it.

Ports that lie immediately on the Black Sea, are the least that it can be expected will now content Russia; and those of Oczacow and Kimburn, situated on either side of the mouth of the great river Borysthenes or Nieper, are ready to drop into their hands. These fortresses, together with Bender,

[*A*] 3

der, and Bialgorod, both on the Niester, and which are already in their possession, would, besides a sufficient length of sea-coast, and a great extent of country, give them the sole command of these great rivers, and shut in the remaining Tartars in such a manner, as would totally prevent their future incursions.

Another part of the great primary design formed by the court of Petersburgh, still remains for completion; and is a matter of such importance, as to render its issue much more doubtful than those we have already mentioned. The obtaining of a free right of trade to and from the Mediterranean, directly through the Streights of the Dardanelles, is an innovation of such a nature, and pregnant with such consequences, as cannot fail to be seriously alarming to most of the commercial states of Europe. Without pretending to enter into the motives which may operate upon the present ruling system of policy, it is certain that in the war of the year 1739, the ministers of the maritime powers at Constantinople, though their respective courts were directly adverse in all other politics to that of Versailles, in this instance coincided with it, and equally opposed the Russians obtaining any share of the Levant or Mediterranean trade. Nor is it to be thought that any thing but the most extreme necessity, and every other hope of preserving a temporary existence being at an end, can ever bring the Porte to submit to so fatal a concession. The Turkish empire no longer exists, when Russia becomes mistress of the Black Sea.

We take these to be the outlines of the great purposes, which the court of Petersburgh wishes to accomplish, in consequence of its success in this war. To secure for the future, with little expence, an almost unbounded length of frontier, which has been hitherto badly maintained by lines, and an endless chain of forts; to gain, along with security, a large accession of new territory and new subjects; to acquire a great and extensive commerce; and to become a first-rate maritime power, are objects adequate to such success.

The Grand Signior has borne with amazing firmness, the heavy losses and misfortunes of the war; nor have his licentious soldiers, nor tumultuous subjects, gone to those extremities, which past experience of their conduct would have given room to expect, under such a series of calamities. Neither have these mighty evils, nor the dangers with which he is surrounded, disturbed the equanimity of this prince's mind, or precipitated him in the manner of his ancestors, to acts of injustice, violence, and cruelty; on the contrary, we see, that with a lenity before unheard of at the Porte, the most unfortunate of his commanders (except in the single instance of the capetan-pacha or high-admiral) not only escape with their lives, but without any other punishment than their removal to other departments, from those offices, in which they were unfortunate. The same moderation is observable to his Christian subjects; and notwithstanding the rebellion of the Greeks and the unheard-of violences and barbarities they committed, we hear of no vengeance that he has taken, either upon the persons or goods of their inoffending brethren. The villanies committed by the sailors and deserters, or the mischiefs occasioned ed by the rage of the populace in great cities, are out of the question; they being equally outrages to government as to the sufferers, and as such, severely punished at different times. Such enormities, in less trying and less heating circumstances, have been too often practised in countries where a more perfect form of government and a purer religion were boasted.

Whatever the consequences of the war may be, this prince has not hitherto departed from his proper dignity to avoid them; and if he has not a confidence in some support with which the public are unacquainted, his constancy in this instance is truly remarkable. We find, notwithstanding the unparalleled losses of the present year, that he is making every preparation to support the war, and to carry on the ensuing campaign with vigour; and it has been rumoured that he intended to command the grand army in person.

The Turks are, however, no longer the same; and it would require more than the abilities of the Czar Peter to make them again great; as it is much easier to civilize the savage and instruct the ignorant, than to reclaim the degenerate from rivetted ill habits. This vast, ill founded, and unwieldy empire, seems indeed nodding to its fall, and nothing but its situation could support it much longer. Its European possessions bring it, in a considerable degree, within the system of the great European republic; a happy circumstance at present to the Ottomans.

The noble provinces of Greece, the Asiatic Turky, and Egypt, together with the numerous Mediterranean islands, the Signory of the Black Sea, and its adjoining provinces, from situation, products, and numberless other advantages, might become in any other hands, and any other form of government, the center of commerce, riches, and power; and the greatest empire perhaps in the world. Even a division of the spoil would totally change the face of affairs in Europe; and perhaps cause as great a revolution in riches, power, and commerce, as the discovery of America did. While the indolence, religious principles, and wretched policy of the Turks, prevent their making a proper use of those blessings, which fortune has so fruitlessly bestowed upon them, it is the general interest of the rest of Europe, that they should continue in such improvident hands. In any other, such powers would have been dangerous, if not fatal.

It may perhaps be worth remembrance, that within little more than two hundred years, a bold pirate, with only the scum and outcasts of the Levant, became sovereign of the sea, destroyed and founded kingdoms, and made half the shores of Europe tremble. The military genius and knowledge of the Turks are now extinct. They are no longer terrible; and besides the safety that arises from their weakness, and from their ignorance in maritime affairs, the commercial states carry on an advantageous trade for and with them; and through their want of industry, have the additional benefit of freight, for conveying their commodities from one part of the empire to the other.

Such seems to be the present state of the belligerent powers; and notwithstanding the great successes of Russia, we cannot think that peace, upon such advantageous

ous terms as she may equitably require, can be an undesirable object to her. The expences of so complicated a war, carried on by sea and land at such a distance from her dominions, are far beyond what her finances can bear. Recruiting, in Russia, from the vast distance of the provinces, the length of time taken, and the difficulties that occur in traversing such boundless and inhospitable deserts as lie between them, and above all from the mortal aversion to the service which possesses the people, is attended with greater loss and difficulty, than in any other country in the world. For though the districts are obliged to furnish their quotas of men, they must be strictly and strongly guarded by a superior force, from thence to the place of their destination, so that the number of troops employed upon this business is almost incredible; and notwithstanding the utmost care that can be taken, they frequently lose half the recruits, before they join their regiments; which can be easily conceived from the numberless opportunities of escape that must present, in a journey perhaps of three or four thousand miles, and which frequently lasts for several months: nor does the evil rest here, for as the deserters (from the particular form of the government) can never return to their homes, nor mix again with the community, they are obliged to retire to the woods, where they herd in considerable bodies, and continue for the rest of their lives in the most savage state, subsisting by robbery, and committing innumerable murders.

It is also observable, that the Russians, though bred in a northern climate, and naturally robust and of strong bodies, lose more men by sickness in a campaign than any other armies in the world: this, in a great measure, may be imputed to the constant habit of the extreme hot vapour baths, which they use regularly twice a week when at home, and thereby cause a most violent perspiration; and with which it is impossible they should be supplied in a camp. The severity of their lents, which take up more than half the year, contribute also to this mortality; for though the clergy not only dispense with their keeping them when on service, but by order of the court have taken great pains to recommend the contrary, they are, notwithstanding, so superstitiously attached to them, that they will endure any thing, even death, sooner than be guilty of the smallest violation of the rules.

Depopulation is the bane of Russia; and the loss of lives in this war must be prodigious, and for the length of time greatly exceed that of any former period. How sensible she is of the heavy expences of the war, is evident from the large loans which she has negociated at Amsterdam and other places, and which she had attempted at Venice, till the reverse of fortune in the Morea damped the spirits of the lenders.

As to an intention of pushing her conquests much farther, or even an obstinate determination of retaining the Danubian provinces, it is probably no part of the present system of Russia. Such a conduct

duct might give too much umbrage to her great and jealous neighbours, who though silent spectators stand ready armed, watchfully attentive to all the events of the war. She has the balance now in her hands: the consequences that may attend a perseverance in the war must be very uncertain; but no peace can be proposed in her present superiority, that will not add highly to her power, splendour, and advantage.

On the other hand, the great losses which the Porte has sustained, the hopelessness of being able to recover them in the present state of their armies, the danger to which their islands are subject from the inability of the marine to protect them, and the revolution in Egypt, which requires to be speedily checked, before Ali Bey extends his conquests, and has time to establish his government; all these causes make peace much to be wished for at Constantinople, and worth the purchase, at any price, almost, which it can be supposed Russia will think it prudent to fix upon it. Upon the whole, from the present appearances on both sides, we should imagine peace not to be at a great distance.

While the rage of war was laying waste the countries from the north-east to the south of Europe, its calamities were very near being extended to the west and center, and might possibly in its consequences have nearly involved the whole. The violent act of hostility committed by Spain, in dispossessing England by force of its settlement in Falkland's islands, accompanied with a new and unheard-of insult offered to the British flag, by the forcible detention of a King's frigate for twenty days, and the taking off of her rudder, in time of profound peace between the two nations, was an injury of such a nature, as scarcely left room for a hope that these evils could have been averted.

An accommodation has, however, taken place since the end of the year, which, for the present, has in some degree skinned over the sore, without removing the causes from which it proceeded. The continuation of the general repose seems, indeed, principally owing to accidental or unforeseen events: of these, may principally be considered the calamities of the people in France, proceeding from civil distractions, from tempests, torrents, an earthquake which nearly ruined the island of St. Domingo, and a famine at home from the inclemency of the seasons; to all which may be added the almost total loss of public credit, from the extraordinary measures taken last year, and pursued in this, in regard to their funds: to these causes we are probably only to look for the preservation of the general tranquillity, as it cannot be imagined that Spain would have ventured upon the commission of so daring an act of hostility, against a nation whose power she had so lately and so fatally experienced, if she had not a full assurance at the time that it was resolved on, of being effectually supported by all the other branches of the Bourbon line. Nor was the object of contention in any degree of sufficient worth to authorize the risque of a war, if it had not been blended with other matters; if the ill disposition of that family to Great Britain, and the jealousy arising from the progress of the Russians in the Levant, had not operated with superior force.

The whole attention of the court of Spain has accordingly been taken up during the present year in preparations for a war. We have formerly observed, that no pains or expence had been spared, for some years past, in putting their West-India possessions in a most respectable state of defence: this has been continued with redoubled diligence, while large bodies of troops have been successively embarked from Europe for that quarter, and a very formidable naval force was preparing at the Havanna.

At home every thing bore the face of war. Levies were made with the greatest industry; all young men above the age of fifteen were enrolled; the troops were marched from the interior provinces to the sea-coasts, where great quantities of heavy artillery and stores were also sent, to put the fortresses there in the best state of defence. The city and port of Cadiz were particularly attended to, and such speedy measures taken for its defence, as sufficiently indicated the apprehension of an attack. The navy was already in such a state, as shewed that the present event was by no means unexpected. A strong fleet was formed at Ferrol, and there were considerable squadrons stationed both at Carthagena and at Cadiz. Every thing both at sea and land seemed to threaten an immediate attack upon Gibraltar, which was but weakly garrisoned, and could have expected no timely assistance from home for its protection. A similar design seemed to be formed in the West-Indies against the island of Jamaica, which seemed to be in equal circumstances of danger, as there was no naval force in that quarter that could have prevented its taking place. Upon the whole, whatever the circumstances were that prevented a war at the present juncture, they seem to have been highly fortunate to England, as, through some unaccountable negligence, we were totally unprepared, both at home and abroad, for an event which all Europe expected to take place; and our navy was far from being in that immediate state of service, which it should always be in a great maritime country like this, whose power and security depend in so great a degree upon its marine.

The same weak and cruel system, which has so long disgraced the government of Portugal, becomes every day more glaring and dreadful in it effects, and seems finally to threaten the total ruin of that country. Real or pretended conspiracies, with all the cruel consequences peculiar to that government, are now so common as to excite neither surprize nor pity. At the same time, private executions, without any form or pretence of trial, the most dreadful and abhorred by mankind, of all the vices of despotism, are said to be the present favourite mode of removing the obnoxious, and may be considered as the completion of this system. The prime minister, the principal actor in the tragedy, does not seem to be much more at his ease than the spectators; and has arrived at that ultimate perfection of tyranny, the fear of being seen by his fellow-citizens, without a strong military guard

guard as a protection against their resentment.

We have frequently had occasion to observe with regret, the unfriendly treatment which the English have for some years met with, in the course of their commerce with this country; and which has been continually increasing, ever since the despotism of the present minister had been fully established. Great hopes had been formed at different times, upon the appointment of new ministers to that court, that they were endued with such powers, and would have pursued such measures, as by reinstating matters upon their natural basis, and recurring to the spirit of the treaties subsisting between the two nations, would have finally terminated all disputes, and have guarded effectually for the future, against those oppressions and continued causes of complaint, under which the British merchants and factory had so long laboured. The public, besides being deeply interested, were the more sanguine in these expectations, as it seemed to require no great depth of argument, nor any very specious colouring, to convince the court of Portugal how conducive it was to its interest, and how necessary even to its safety, to cultivate the friendship of Great Britain, and to preserve inviolably those treaties, which had been founded upon the wisest policy, for the mutual benefit of both nations. Besides, no new claim was set up, no right nor privilege demanded, but what had been established by mutual concurrence, and confirmed by the uninterrupted usage of a long succession of years: and it could be easily proved, that the advantages arising from the alliance and friendship subsisting between the two nations, were to the full as much in favour of Portugal as England.

CHAP. II.

War on the Danube. State of the armies during the winter. Account of the countries that were the seat of war. Battle at the river Larga, in which the Kan of the Tartars is defeated. Grand Vizir crosses the Danube. Great battle fought between the Pruth and the Cahul, in which General Romanzow gained a complete victory. The Turks pursued to the Danube, and obliged to cross that river with great loss.

THE new grand vizir Halil Bey did not arrive at the camp near the Danube till the latter end of the year, though he had used the utmost expedition for that purpose, as the disorders committed by the Janizaries and other soldiers, became every day more alarming. The restoring of any degree of order and subordination, among such licentious and mutinous troops, who had long indulged themselves in the most intolerable excesses, and had already massacred several of their principal officers, and were more disposed to sheath their swords in each others' breasts than to face an enemy, presented such difficulties as perhaps neither the courage nor abilities of the vizir could have surmounted, if he had not taken the prudent precaution, of
being

being attended by fourscore mules, loaded with gold and silver coin. A proper distribution of this money had however its effect, and enabled him, in some degree, to bring about a reformation that was so much wanted.

As the provinces of Moldavia and Walachia were objects of the greatest importance to the Porte, the vizir determined, if possible, to profit, during the winter, of the distance of General Romanzow's army, and however contrary to the genius of his troops, to triumph for once over the inclemency of the season. This project was the more capable of success, as the Turks were not only masters of the Danube, but were still possessed of Ibrailow, and some other fortresses in Walachia. The design was worthy of a commander, and if it succeeded to its full extent, the vizir would have had the honour to have retrieved during the winter the fatal miscarriages of Moldovangi Ali Pacha, and the campaign would again have been opened on the banks of the Niester.

In consequence of this determination, the Russians, who were stationed in the conquered provinces, found that neither the season, nor the successes of the late campaign, were sufficient to procure them rest or safety in their quarters. A continued and cruel war was carried on during the long ensuing winter and spring, in which a number of small but bloody engagements were fought, of which we have but few particulars, and those that are given very imperfect, and contradictory in every circumstance of place, time, and event.

Upon the whole, these actions were not productive of any consequence of great moment; at the same time that they were attended with the loss of a great number of men, and the troops were harassed and ruined on both sides. The Russians were in general successful in the field; which indeed may be concluded, as well from the succeeding as the preceding fortune and conduct of the war. Thus the grand vizir's design did not take place in its full extent, which was to drive the Russians beyond the Niester, and make that river, so far as the fortress of Choczim would admit, once more the line between the two armies at the opening of the campaign: it however succeeded in part, and if every thing else had been equal between them, the consequences might have been very considerable: having it in his power to throw fresh troops whenever he pleased over the Danube, he not only removed the enemy totally from the borders of that river, but he by degrees so straitened them in their quarters, and they were so weakened by fatigue and the continued loss of men, that he recovered the whole province of Walachia, and the lower part of Moldavia, and thereby opened the communication again by land with Bessarabia and the Tartars.

In the mean time the country presented a scene of the most dreadful desolation; every thing was destroyed: such of the wretched inhabitants as had not the fortune to escape to the neighbouring countries, naked and destitute of every thing, became either slaves to the Tartars, or victims to the revenge and fury of the Turks. At length, having compleated the reduction of the province, the vizir appointed Monalechi, a Greek of great courage

age and ability, to be Hospodar of it, in the room of Gregorio Giko, who was then at Petersburgh, and was charged with betraying the country to the Russians. The Turkish revenge being also sated, it was too late considered, that a country without inhabitants could be of little use to the possessor, and the vizir issued an ineffectual proclamation, to assure the Greeks of protection, and to encourage the fugitives to return to their country.

The Russian generals were not much more at ease, though in service of less danger, who were employed during the winter upon the long extended frontier of Poland and the Ukraine, than those who were stationed in the Danubian provinces. Here the Tartars renewed their customary ravages, and though these incursions were attended with various success, and that they were sometimes severely chastised, their route, whether victors or vanquished, is generally fatal to the inhabitants of the countries through which they pass.

The Russian troops dispersed in different parts of Poland were as fully employed by the confederates, who seemed to increase in courage and boldness, if not in numbers, by their continued losses. Thus the army under the command of General Romanzow on the banks of the Niester, was the only part of the Russian forces that could enjoy any rest during the winter, and that was exempt from the fatigues and dangers of the war.

Great preparations were made on both sides for the opening of the campaign; and the Porte seemed to strain every nerve to retrieve its past losses. It was reported that the grand vizir's army would have amounted to two hundred thousand men; and it is probable that if the Tartars are included as a part of it, and the different detachments taken in, it may not fall short of that number. It was however very sickly; malignant fevers of the most dangerous kind, which finally terminated in the plague, having through the whole course of the year made a dreadful havock in it. The war in the Morea contributed to lessen its numbers considerably, and its force much more, as the Albanians and Epirots, who were employed upon that service, are among the bravest soldiers in the Turkish empire.

We have seen no authentic list of the Russian forces that were on actual service in this campaign. By the best accounts that have been published of the state of this empire, it appears that Russia cannot by any means support above 130,000 regular forces, for any considerable length of time out of the country; and that the armies employed in her former wars were generally much short of that number. As to the irregular troops, of which she can employ such amazing numbers, they are only of use in such wilds as are generally the scene of their operations, and against such enemies as the Tartars: if they were to act against regular forces, and in an inclosed country, they would ruin their friends instead of their enemies. Whatever the numbers were, they were this campaign divided into many parts: the grand army was commanded by General Romanzow, another on the side of Bender by Count Panin. General Prosorowski advanced towards Oczacow, at the head of a considerable body

of

part of the river, which, so far as we can comprehend the account, seems to have been nearly parallel to Bender, from which it was distant about 120 miles. In the mean time a considerable army of Turks and Tartars marched along on the same side of the river to meet them. When the two armies came in sight, the Turks immediately, and with great judgment, changed their position, and took possession of a most advantageous camp, which they as suddenly fortified in the strongest manner.

June 25th.

This army was commanded by Capian Ghieri, Kan of the Crimea; a mark to him of the greatest honour, and of uncommon confidence in the Porte; for as these Kans are heirs to the empire, in failure of issue in the Ottoman line, it has been the constant policy of that family not to entrust them with the supreme command of a Turkish army. This prince had three bashas under his command, and the army was said to consist of about 80,000 men. The ground on which they encamped was a steep, rocky, and almost inaccessible eminence, which the Russian account calls a mountain, covered on one side by the Pruth, and on the other by the little river Larga.

This camp was so well chosen, and the ground so difficult, that notwithstanding the repeated efforts of General Romanzow to bring on an engagement, it was above three weeks before he could hazard a general attack. The Turks not being inured to that strict discipline, nor tempered by that long service, which enables veteran soldiers to bear with patience the fight and continued insults of an enemy, twenty thousand of their bravest partizans descended from their strong camp, and attacked the Russians with great resolution; but were repulsed, and beaten back to their camp with considerable loss.

At length, some difficulties having been probably removed, or some favourable circumstances occurred, with which we are not acquainted, the Russians, three days after this engagement, mounted the hills at the dawn of the morning, where they found four great and strong entrenchments, covered with a numerous artillery; these they attacked with great resolution, and met with as obstinate a defence. The Russians however triumphed over all opposition, and beat them successively out of the four entrenchments, after which the Turks abandoned their camp, and fled in the greatest disorder. The victors became possessed of a great booty upon this occasion, besides thirty-eight pieces of brass cannon, and several other trophies.

July 8th.

No account is given of the loss on either side, in killed, wounded, or prisoners, in this engagement; it is only said that of the Russians was moderate, considering the length and importance of the action. We are as much in the dark as to the manner in which the retreat was conducted, and whether there was any pursuit: even the route which the Turks took after the battle is only to be discovered by comparing other circumstances, which had no immediate relation to this action. In a word, the account given of this battle, though attributed to General Romanzow, is so inaccurate, that it is only by deduction, from the former and subsequent conduct

conduct of the campaign, that the side of the Pruth on which it happened could be ascertained, as by one part of it the Turkish camp seems to have been upon the right, and by another on the left of that river.

The victory at the river Larga was only a prelude to, and contributed to accelerate, one much greater; which at the same time that it does the greatest honour to the military abilities of General Romanzow, establishes the infinite superiority of the Russian troops beyond a doubt; and evinces almost to a demonstration, that in the present style of arms, and discipline among the Turks, there is scarce a possibility of their being able to cope with them.

The Kan of the Tartars having retreated towards the Danube, the Grand Vizir thought proper to cross that river at Isakka, at the head of the grand army to support him. General Romanzow in the mean time pursued his march along the Pruth, towards its confluence with the Danube. The two armies came in sight of each other in the evening, and at eight o'clock the Turks encamped at about 4 miles distance from the Russians, both armies lying between the Pruth and the river Cahul. The Tartars formed a separate corps on the left of the Russians, but afterwards spread themselves in their rear, to cut off a great detachment which General Romanzow had made for the escort of a convoy of provisions. In certain situations boldness is prudence; it is in these that great genius is distinguished from common abilities: the present was one of them, and General Romanzow did not want discernment to perceive it. A more cautious commander might have hesitated till he had lost his army.

The Russian army was greatly weakened by making this detachment; and the inequality of numbers was such, as in common cases would have made it inexcusable to have risked a battle. The General, however, having duly weighed the goodness of his troops, the confidence with which they were inspired from a long course of success, and the consequences that might result from the dangerous design formed by the Tartars, resolved boldly to attack the enemy next morning. The Russian army was accordingly in motion before light, and began its march at the break of day. An unexpected incident which took place in the night would have staggered a mind of less firmness, and damped the courage of any but veteran troops. As soon as the morning had cleared up, the General perceived, to his great astonishment, that the Turks, notwithstanding their prodigious numbers, and the daring countenance they bore in the evening, had fortified their camp during the night with no less than three great and strong entrenchments, superior to those which he had lately forced in the Kan's camp, and defended by a host, which, as to number and appearance, should have despised any other protection than what their arms and their valour gave them.

The die was however cast, and the General bravely persevered in his resolution. His situation was truly critical, for a defeat must have been attended with the total loss of the army; nor would Count Panin have found it easy, in that case, to have retired in safety from Bender,

Bender, even with the loss of his artillery and stores. In a word, the whole fate of the war seemed to hang upon this day.

Aug. 2d.

The Turks did not however wait to be attacked in their entrenchments: these were only intended as the last resort, and the Russians found themselves almost surrounded, at a considerable distance from the camp, by several large bodies of troops, who attacked them in front and flank with the greatest bravery. A desperate engagement ensued, in which the close order and excellent discipline of the Russians still prevailed, and they continually gained ground on the enemy. As they advanced nearer the entrenchments, which were covered with a prodigious artillery, the battle grew every instant more terrible: at length the Grand Vizir made a sally in person, at the head of the Janizaries and all the bravest troops in the army. The conflict now became dreadful, and was supported with the most determined resolution and obstinacy on both sides. After a continued fire of artillery and small arms, which lasted for five hours without intermission, the Russians, by the united force of their bayonets, penetrated to the first entrenchment, which they carried by a desperate assault.

A pause then ensued, which was only preparatory to a new engagement, between the entrenchments, if possible more furious than the first. In this the Turks used every possible effort to retrieve the fortune of the day; one body still coming on and renewing the engagement with fresh ardor as another was defeated. At length, seeing that the bravest corps of their Janizaries, and all the other best bodies of their infantry, were successively defeated, and unable to withstand the closeness of the Russian array, the continued weight of their fire, and the irresistible force of their bayonets, they lost all hope and courage, and the second and third entrenchments were successively carried. The rout then became general; and the Grand Vizir seeing every thing lost, made the best of his way, together with his principal officers and the celebrated Count Potocki, to the Danube, which was about twenty miles from the field of battle.

The whole camp, tents, equipage, a vast quantity of ammunition, 143 pieces of brass cannon, and above 7,000 carriages loaded with provisions, became a prey to the conquerors. The fugitives were pursued to the Danube, where the crowds were so great as to render the passage very difficult and dangerous, and some bodies of horse, it is said, were obliged to swim over; others crossed the Pruth, and directed their course to Ibrailow, and other parts of Walachia. It is said that above 7,000 Turks were killed on the field of battle, and that the roads to the Danube were covered with dead bodies; a great number of prisoners, among whom were many of considerable rank, were also taken. Some accounts make the loss amount to 40,000 men, and say that the Grand Vizir's army consisted of 150,000: General Romanzow, in his letter to the Empress, does not give the numbers that engaged, nor the loss on either side; he however takes notice of the great inferiority of his own army. The loss of

HISTORY OF EUROPE.

of men in such a battle must undoubtedly be very great, and in its consequences much greater.

Nothing could be more decisive than this battle, nor more glorious to General Romanzow and to the troops that he commanded. It might be said in the language of poetry, that the genius of Russia particularly predominated upon this occasion, and had chosen the Pruth as the scene of victory, to wipe off the disgrace which Peter the Great had formerly met with on the banks of that river. The General acknowledges in his letter to the Empress, that the Turks behaved with great bravery, and says that the Russians were never engaged in any battle that was more obstinately disputed. The great superiority of the Russians may be attributed to their quickness and dexterity in the management of the artillery, in which they are particularly excellent, and scarcely rivalled by any other nation; to the constant and regular fire of their small arms, in which the Turks are very deficient; and to their charging with screwed bayonets, against which the sabre can scarcely be considered as a weapon. In other respects, there seems to have been no fault in the conduct of the Turkish Generals; and it is evident that there was no want of resolution in their troops.

The Tartars had engaged the convoy without success during the battle, the event of which perhaps had an effect upon their conduct; they were however totally separated from the Turkish army, and being at a great distance from the Crimea, and the Russians in possession of the intermediate countries, it was a long time before they could make their way home, after having been reduced to great straits, and suffering very considerable losses. We do not hear of the cavalry having been engaged on either side in this battle: it is probable that the greater part of the Russians had been detached to escort the convoy, and perhaps the nature of the ground did not admit of the Turks making use of their's.

It would seem that the Turks have not known in any part of this war how to make a proper use of their cavalry. Their European horse were long esteemed among the best in the world: they have still great courage, able bodies, good horses, are excellent horsemen, and know the use of the sabre from their infancy: an army of foot without discipline is worth nothing; but a body of horse with these qualifications would, if properly conducted, be at all times formidable. The extensive plains, vast wastes, and inexhaustible growth of herbage, in the countries that are the seat of the war, point them out as the proper scene of action for such troops, and where they might undoubtedly be employed with very great effect. As to the Turkish infantry, it is evident, that, unless they adopt the improvements in arms and discipline made by the European nations, they never will be able to make any figure against them in the field.

CHAP. III.

Bender besieged by Count Panin. Brave defence made by the garrison and inhabitants. The Governor in a fit of despair poisons himself; another chosen by the garrison in his room. Globe of compression; a kind of mine so called by the Russians. The place taken by storm, and burned; a great slaughter made. Budziac Tartars conclude a treaty with the Russians. General Romanzow fixes his head quarters at Calpouk, near the Danube. Ibrailow besieged. Kilia Nova taken. Bialogrod taken by Baron Inglestrom. Turks abandon the citadel of Ibrailow, after a long siege. The Turks being entirely driven beyond the Danube, the Russian armies go into winter quarters. War in Georgia.

WHILE the arms of Russia were thus victorious on the Pruth, under General Romanzow, Count Panin was not less industrious in prosecuting their success on the Niester. He had for some time invested Bender, and was expediting all the necessary preparations for besieging it in form. Bender was situated upon the Niester, about 180 miles to the south-east of Choczim, and 100 north-west of Bialogrod or Ackirman, which lies at the mouth of the river; and was from size, strength, situation, and the number of its inhabitants, a place of the greatest consideration in these countries.

We have already seen that General Proforowski had been detached early in the campaign, to scour the country between the Niester and the Nieper or Boristhenes, thereby to keep the Budziac Tartars in awe, and prevent their impeding the operations of Count Panin. This service he performed with great effect, having laid waste and ruined the country, taken a great booty in cattle, delivered several thousands of the poor Walachians who had been carried into slavery, and proceeded successfully with his incursions to the very gates of Oczakow, which lies at the mouth of the Nieper, about 130 miles to the south-east of Bender.

This success greatly facilitated the operations of Count Panin, who divided his army into two parts, to besiege the fortress effectually; a measure which could not have been attempted with safety, if the enemy had any army in the field to take advantage of the separation made by so large a river. Every thing being at length prepared, the trenches were July 30th. opened on both sides of the river at the same time, and the garrison next day set fire to the suburbs; after which a furious cannonade and bombardment was begun from all quarters, and vigorously returned by the town. The fortress was very strong, and the garrison very numerous; who, besides the Governor, were headed by several Bashas and officers of rank, so that the place was defended with the greatest bravery.

In sixteen days from the opening of the trenches, the garrison made seven desperate sallies, in which, though they lost a great number of men, they gave sufficient proofs of their

their refolution: and though the town was twice on fire in that time, they were neither difcouraged nor difconcerted by it. The Serafkier, Mahomet Wafa Waliffi, who was Governor of the place, was fo overcome with grief and defpair upon receiving an account of the lofs of the two late battles, that he put an end to his life by taking a dofe of poifon. Another Bafha was killed by the falling of a bomb: the garrifon however were not difcouraged, and appointed Demin, a Bafha of three tails, and a brave man, who had more fortitude in oppofing ill fortune than his predeceffor, to be their Governor.

In this manner was the fiege carried on for near two months, with the greateft labour, induftry, and refolution on the one fide, and an obftinate courage not fhort of defperation on the other; as the garrifon and inhabitants were in that unhappy fituation, which from the beginning fcarcely admitted of a hope of relief or deliverance. Continual fallies were made, with little advantage, but great lofs on both fides. The Burghers and inhabitants, who were very numerous, had from the beginning gone through all the hardfhips and dangers of the fiege, which they bore with the fame conftancy and intrepidity that the foldiers did: they fought like men wedded to the old dwellings and habitations in which their anceftors had lived for a long fucceffion of years, in which they firft drew breath themfelves, and who were determined to perifh along with them.

In the mean time the Ruffians were pufhing on their mines with indefatigable induftry; particularly one of an extraordinary conftruction, in which they placed great confidence, and which from the pedantry of a modern French Engineer, who was either the inventor or improver of it, received the ridiculous appellation of globe of compreffion, terms that convey no ideas either of its conftruction or powers. In this mine, or rather complicated labyrinth of mines, interwoven and inclofed one within the other, it was pretended that a given quantity of gunpowder would caufe a greater explofion, and throw up a greater quantity of earth, than in any other method. This excited all the eagernefs and expectation that naturally attend the refult of an untried fyftem; it however generally appears, that the greateft operations are produced by very fimple means.

Count Panin had made feveral overtures during the fiege to induce the garrifon to treat of a capitulation, to which they obftinately refufed to liften. At length the globe of compreffion being brought to its due ftate for fervice, and charged with the amazing quantity of 400 poeds of gunpowder, each poed amounting to about forty pounds weight, every thing being befides prepared for a ftorm, and the army ftrengthened by the arrival of a reinforcement from General Romanzow, Count Panin once more fummoned the Governor to furrender, which was again peremptorily refufed.

Every thing was then prepared to make the affault that night; Sep. 27. the troops deftined to that fervice were divided into three columns, and marched to their refpective ftations with the greateft filence. The firing of the globe of compreffion was to be the signal for the attack, which they hoped, besides ruining the outworks, might shake down, or make a breach in some of the principal walls of the town, and at the same time bury the defenders, either under the ruins, or the mountains of earth which it was expected would have been thrown up. The Russians themselves were apprehensive of the consequences of this dreadful mine, as it was not easy to define how far the effects of such an enormous mass of gunpowder might extend; and the troops who were to make the attack in that quarter were accordingly stationed at a considerable distance, with orders to advance with the utmost expedition as soon as the mine had sprung. To be prepared for all events, the troops were provided with petards for bursting the gates, as well as with ladders for scaling the walls; and while one part were thus employed, another was to throw up entrenchments with the greatest speed on the glacis, so as to secure a lodgment there, if every thing else should fail. False attacks were to be made at the same time to divert and distract the attention of the garrison, and the whole army was ranged upon the wings of the first parallel, ready to support the assault, none being left in the camp but the sick and wounded.

The globe was blown up at ten o'clock at night, with a most horrible concussion, which shook the whole circumjacent country; and during the astonishment and confusion excited by this dreadful phenomenon, the three attacks were instantly begun, and carried on with the greatest vigour. It being soon perceived in the army, by the direction of the fire and the cries of the soldiers, where the assault was taking place with greatest effect, several of the most distinguished officers, and a number of others who wanted to signalize themselves, desired leave of the General to grant them an equal share of the honour and danger with those that were already engaged, which he readily granted, and gave them four companies of chosen grenadiers to attend them upon that service.

This select detachment having eagerly joined the foremost troops, the example they gave, and the emulation they excited, soon became irresistible. Nothing was able to withstand their impetuosity. The double ditches at the foot of the glacis were instantly passed and filled up; the double palisadoes before the covered way were as soon surmounted or destroyed; a great ditch with a convette, two fathom deep and six wide, was no longer an obstacle, and an outward wall was not able to stop their career.

The ardour of the troops kept pace with the rapidity of their success, and the body of the fortress was the next object of their impetuosity. The gates were tried in vain, for they were so closely and firmly plated with iron, that the petards had no effect. Scaling ladders were every where applied, and if they had not a sufficient number of their own, those they took from the enemy would have sufficed, who disputed every inch of the ground with the most obstinate bravery, and had used the ladders to get over the works, but seldom survived to carry them off.

The

HISTORY OF EUROPE.

The Russians at length got every where over the walls; and now a new and dreadful fight began in the dark, on and amongst the fortifications, in the streets, lanes, and passages, and from the houses. The conflict became so doubtful, so extensive, and so dangerous, that the Russians were under a necessity of setting fire to the town, which they did in several parts at the same time: the flames raged every where, but not with greater fury than the combatants; and the burning houses increased the horrors of the night, by shewing its calamities. Every street and lane the Russians gained was by dint of fire and bayonet; and at the next turning, the defendants rallied, and renewed the fight with all their former obstinacy and desperation.

This dreadful scene of rage, cruelty, bloodshed, and horror, continued the whole night; presenting to view every scene of calamity and distress that human nature is capable of undergoing, and every spectacle that is shocking and terrible to it. The gardens, the fortifications, the streets, and the houses, reeked with blood, and were covered with dead bodies, while the flames still pointed out fresh objects of revenge to the survivors.

At length, after ten hours' continued fight, the flames and the assailants seemed to have vanquished every opposition, and at eight in the morning the soldiers began to shout and cry out victory. The Seraskier, who commanded the town, with most of those that survived, had by this time retired to the castle, where they found the flames had already reached. A select body of 1,500 cavalry, and 500 infantry, sensible that the castle could afford but a very temporary protection, took the nobler resolution of cutting their way through the enemy, or of perishing in the attempt. They accordingly made a desperate sally from the town, on the side near the river, and cut their way through the Russian troops for some time with great fury, and seemed to have a fair prospect of effecting their purpose. Fortune, so generally the friend to courage, was, however, at this time wayward, and deserted it in its extremest need. A Russian Colonel of the Corps de Reserve, with a considerable body of cavalry, happened by chance to come full in their way, in the course they had intended to take, which was to gain the road towards Ackirman, and make their escape that way. This casual rencounter having checked their impetuosity, the neighbouring troops had time to recover from their first surprize, and, gathering round, attacked them furiously on all sides. All hopes of safety and escape being now at an end, they determined upon a cruel revenge, and by a sudden motion made their way to that quarter of the Russian camp, where the sick and wounded were lodged upon several eminences, for their security and better accommodation.

Count Panin perceived the danger, and immediately dispatched several generals, with all the troops that could be gathered in the hurry from the fortress and suburbs, to prevent it, while he himself followed, and the whole army

army was every where in motion. The Turks were soon surrounded, and attacked on every side by troops of every denomination: cavalry, infantry, cossacks, and hunters, fell on promiscuously as they came up; and made a noble defence; and the General was obliged to order the artillery to be brought up from the hindmost parallel to play upon them; they, however, still fought it out with the greatest intrepidity, and were almost totally cut to pieces.

On the General's return from this engagement, he met a deputation from the Seraskier, who demanded a capitulation; this being refused, and the castle at that time all in flames, he was obliged to surrender himself and his garrison prisoners of war; the fire being so urgent, that the Russians were obliged to remove them immediately to the camp for their preservation.

The total number of prisoners, including the inhabitants of all ages, amounted to 11,749, of whom 5,554 were Janizaries and Spahis, with their commanders, besides the Seraskier and two Bashas. The number of souls in the town, at the beginning of the siege, were computed at 30,000, of whom one half were soldiers. The Russian accounts, which are the only ones we have, say, that the defenders of the town were, at the beginning of the last assault, near one-third superior in number to the whole army that besieged it. Such representations, calculated to answer particular purposes, are more or less adopted by all nations, and should be received with many restrictions. In the present instance, this account of the numbers, as well as of the small loss said to be sustained by the victors, tally very badly with the acknowledgments that are made of the desperate valour and resolution shewn by the Turks; as well as with the natural and inevitable consequences that must attend one of the most cruel and desperate engagements that we have almost any account of in modern history; supported for so long a time, and involved, along with the darkness of the night, in all the intricacy, confusion, and danger, which such a variety of ground, and so many different situations, among walls, ditches, narrow streets, and burning or falling houses, were capable of producing; where judgment and discipline were nearly out of the question, and every thing seemed committed to chance, fury, rage, and despair.

The fire continued for three days, and could not be restrained till it had consumed every thing. Thus fell, and totally perished, the celebrated town of Bender; famous, among other things, for the hospitable reception and protection which it afforded to Charles the XIIth of Sweden, as well as for his long residence in it after the fatal battle of Pultowa. As it was from its strength and situation the grand magazine of the Turks for their northern provinces, the Russians found a vast quantity of arms, bombs, granades, gunpowder, and other military stores; besides above two hundred pieces of brass cannon, and eighty-five brass mortars: they also took four horse tails, fourteen batons of command, and forty pair of colours.

The country of the Budziac Tartars had suffered all the calamities of the war from its first breaking out; which affected them the

more

more fenfibly, as they led domeftic lives, were rich in flocks and herds, and cultivated the country in a confiderable degree. Their difpofition being to dwell in open pleafant villages rather than in towns, they were entirely at the mercy of any enemy that became mafter in the field; or if they efcaped barely with their lives, their property was totally loft. This year had been particularly fatal to them: General Proforowfki had cruelly ravaged the country between the Niefter and the Bog: the upper part of Beffarabia fuffered in the fame manner from the army under Count Panin; and the lower part of the province, near the Black-fea, was experiencing the fame treatment from the troops under Baron Ingleftrom, who was fent by General Romanzow after the late victory, to lay fiege to Bialogrod, or Ackirman, at the mouth of the Niefter.

In this fituation, totally abandoned, and not a hope left of any timely relief from the Porte, feveral of their Mirzas or chiefs, to prevent the total ruin of their country, entered into a negociation, during the fiege of Bender, with the Ruffians, and at length concluded a treaty, by which they renounced all connection and alliance with the Turks, and fubmitted themfelves to be under the protection of Ruffia, on condition of enjoying their religion, and all their antient rights, liberties, and immunities.

General Romanzow, after the great victory of the 2d of Auguft, fixed his head quarters at Calpouk, which lies between the confluence of the Pruth and the Danube, and the Black-fea; from whence he fent large detachments over the former, to diflodge the Turks from their pofts in Walachia: this was eafily effected, except at Ibrailow, which made an obftinate defence, and to which General Glebow laid fiege in form.

Kilia Nova, a ftrong town, fituated on the moft northern branch of the Danube, not far from its entrance into the Black-fea, was befieged by another detachment of this army, and furrendered in the beginning of September, after eight days open trenches, on condition that the garrifon, confifting of 4,000 men, and commanded by a Bafha of three tails, fhould be tranfported to the other fide of the Danube; that fuch of the inhabitants as chofe to go fhould have the fame benefit, and in any cafe that their private property fhould be fecure.

Bialogrod, held to be the capital of Beffarabia, though Bender was a place of much greater note and importance, furrendered in the fame manner, in the beginning of October, to Baron Ingleftrom, after a fiege of only ten days: the inhabitants confifting of about 6,000 people, and the garrifon of 2,000, were with all their moveables tranfported to the other fide of the Danube.

The citadel of Ibrailow made a long and brave defence, the garrifon being continually reinforced by the Grand Vizir with frefh troops from the other fide of the Danube; and it was not till the latter end of November that all their defences being nearly deftroyed, and the fortrefs reduced almoft to a heap of rubbifh, the garrifon took the refolution of abandoning it by night, and making their

their escape over the Danube. Several other posts upon that river have been since taken by the Russians, and they are now masters of all the northern banks of it, and some of their hunters made a successful incursion even to the other side.

The Grand Vizir continued at Isatfka till the middle of November, at which time he retired farther into the country of Bulgaria. General Romanzow took up his head quarters, for the winter, in Jassy; his army being partly cantoned in that neighbourhood, and partly stationed on the borders of the Danube, and in the newly taken fortresses. General Count Panin, after putting things into the best condition at Bender (that the ruined state of the place would admit of), and having left a considerable body of troops for its security, retired with the rest of his army into the Ukraine; whither General Berg also returned, after committing some devastations on the borders of Crim Tartary.

We are much in the dark as to the operations of Count Tottleben, on the side of Georgia: while the Russian accounts crown him with great success, the Turkish tell us quite the contrary; nor have any consequences appeared that at all confirm the former. It seems pretty certain, that, being joined by a considerable number of Georgians, he descended into Armenia, and laid siege to Erzerum, the capital of that country: here the Turks say he was totally defeated by the neighbouring Bashas, and drove back to the mountains, with the loss of several thousands of his men. This account must in part be true, as he undoubtedly quitted Armenia, and no other cause has been assigned for it: at the same time it is said, that, instead of wasting time at the siege of Erzerum, if he had marched directly to Trebisonde, which is situated on the Black-sea, was in no posture of defence, and not above 140 miles distance, he could not have failed of success, and as the Russians have now a number of small vessels on that sea, might have been supported with effect.

However this might be, we find this General has since been engaged in a kind of civil and petty war in Georgia, where the Princes and Chieftains seem divided among themselves, and either the Russians, or those with whom they have acted, have changed sides, at least once. The celebrated Prince Heraclius, who it was supposed first encouraged this expedition, has since been called a deceiver, and spoken of as an enemy; and a Prince Solomon, who at first opposed them, has lately been severely chastised by the Turks for acting in concert with them. In the mean time, the Russian accounts give a pompous list of conquered places, as if taken from the Turks, though they are most of them places of no consequence and unknown, or else that belonged to the Georgians. It is probable that the principal end of this expedition was to gain a thorough knowledge of the country; to foment dissensions among the princes and great men; and by degrees, under the colour of friendship and religion, to prepare that slavery for the bravest nation in Asia, which the avowed enmity of the Turks and Persians was never able fully to accomplish.

CHAP.

HISTORY OF EUROPE.

CHAP. IV.

Russian expedition to the Mediterranean. Count Orlow arrives in the Morea. Insurrection of the Greeks; cruelties committed by them. Mifitra, Arcadia, and other places taken. Messalongi taken. Coron besieged. Navarino taken. Patras taken, and the castle besieged. Several other places ineffectually besieged. Greeks massacred at Patras, and the city burnt. Mainotes defeated. Turkish army arrives in the Morea. Execution of several of the principal Greeks. Modon besieged by sea and land; actions between the besiegers and a body of Turks and Albanians; the siege finally raised. Russians and Greeks totally separate; the latter retire to Novarino, and soon after abandon the Peninsula. Admiral Elphinstone's squadron arrives from England. Engagements at sea. Turkish fleet destroyed in the harbour of Cifme. Captain Pacha beheaded. Levant Trade ruined. Smyrna in danger. Castle of Lemnos besieged; relieved by Hassan Bey. Enormities committed by the runaway sailors and deserters. Plague at Constantinople. Revolution in Egypt. Aly Bey.

THE misfortunes of the Turks were not confined to the Niester or the Danube: the most southerly as well as the most northern parts of their European dominions were now doomed to bear all the rigors of war, and the sea as well as the land to be a witness of their disgrace. The time seemed at length arrived, when the wretched administration and conduct of their government, which they had for so long a time totally neglected, and suffered their military departments by sea and land to languish and run to ruin, should now be exemplarily punished on both these elements: an error into which all the great empires of the world have, at a certain period of their existence, successively fallen; which has as constantly and fatally brought its own punishment along with it, and which has, notwithstanding, been continually adopted by their successors, when they arrived at the same zenith of power, riches, and seeming security.

The Russian fleet, which had left England in the latter part of the preceding year, notwithstanding the great and friendly assistance it had met with in this country, arrived at Port Mahon, where it wintered, shattered and sickly.— The same kind offices being, however, repeated there, and the same powerful and masterly assistance which characterises the English nation in every thing relative to maritime affairs being again freely given, the ships were put into as good condition as the state they were in could admit of; and the men, from the benefits of a fine climate, and plenty of fresh fruits and provisions, recovered their health very fast.

In the mean time, application had been made to the different Italian States to know the degrees of friendship and succour that might

might be expected from them, upon such occasions as should induce or oblige the Russian ships to put into their ports. These states, in general, shewed a considerable degree of reserve upon this occasion, and precisely restricted the number of ships that should be admitted into one port at a time, and the length of their continuance in it; and in the dominions of Naples, the quantity of provisions with which each ship was allowed to be furnished was particularly specified: at the same time, the garrisons in the seaports were strengthened, the batteries mounted with cannon, and every other measure taken, which, if not sufficient to prevent surprize or danger, were fully so, to express an affected apprehension, and, a jealous caution and dislike. We have formerly seen, that the Venetians absolutely refused admittance to the Russians in any of their ports or islands: this resolution they have firmly adhered to, and severely punished by confiscation of lands and goods, and every other method in their power, such of their subjects in Cephalonia and other islands as either fitted out ships, or went simply as volunteers to assist them. At the same time, they fitted out a considerable fleet to guard the Adriatic, and to protect their islands and coasts. The Grand Master of Malta was invited by the Russians to take an active share in the war, and a requisition made, that they might be admitted to make use of the port of Malta, as a place of general rendezvous for their fleets, and for the equipment and fitting out of their ships. These proposals the Grand Master did not think fit to comply with: he totally refused taking any share in the war, and limited to three, the number of their ships that should at any one time be admitted in the harbour of Malta.

Some Russian officers of rank had been employed, in the course of the preceding year, to carry on a negociation with the Greeks, which was easily effected, not only from the intercourse and mixed boundaries of the Venetian and Ottoman territories on that side, but partly through the remissness, and partly the mildness, of the Turkish government. The garrisons were thin and negligent; the ports and duties slackly attended to; the Greeks were in possession of the trade and the shipping; were almost the only inhabitants in the open country, and had a great majority upon the coasts, and even in the cities and towns. If to all this we add the want of a necessary communication by post, and the taciturnity, reserve, supineness, and indolence of the Turks, we must conceive their opportunities of information very imperfect, and that it must principally come through or from the christians.

We accordingly find, that the Russian officers not only carried on a negociation in the country, in time of open war, with the greatest safety, but sent ships to the coasts, freighted with arms and ammunition, which were landed and distributed with equal facility, long before the arrival of their fleet in the Mediterranean. The hopes excited by these means were raised to the highest pitch of extravagance and enthusiasm, as soon as it was certainly known that the fleet had arrived at Minorca; and the phrenzy of the Greeks upon this occasion can only, perhaps, be

equalled

equalled by that heretofore shewn by the Jews, upon the appearance of a pretended Messiah among them.

The Russian fleet departed from Minorca in the beginning of February, and shaped its course for the Morea; but having met with some storms by the way, was separated, and much the greater number of the ships obliged to take refuge in different parts of Italy, Sicily, and Sardinia, in which several of them were obliged to continue a considerable time, to refit, and repair the damages they had sustained. Count Orlow, who was commander in chief of the whole armament, however arrived at Cape Metapan, the antient promontory of Tenarus, in the Morea, and the southern extremity of the peninsula, on the last of February, with only three ships of the line, and two others.

This country, the antient Peloponnesus, the seat once of poets, heroes, and philosophers, being all classical ground, is too well known to require any description; nor has the curiosity of modern travellers suffered even its misfortunes, or present wretchedness, to lie in obscurity. The Count having debarked such land forces as he had with him at Maina, which lies a little to the westward of Cape Metapan, and about 50 miles to the south-west of Misitra, the antient Sparta; the Mainotes, the descendants of the Lacedemonians, and who still possessed the country of their ancestors, under subjection to the Turks, immediately flew to their arms in every quarter, and joined them by thousands. The other Greeks immediately followed their example, or rather only waited to hear of the arrival of the Russians, to do what they had long intended; and the whole Morea seemed every where in motion.

The open country was quickly over-run, and Misitra, Arcadia, and several other places, as speedily taken: the Russian ships that had been separated, or that put into Italy, arrived successively, and landed their men in different quarters, where every small detachment soon swelled to a little army, and the Turks were every where attacked or intercepted. In the mean time a dreadful massacre was carried on, and the Greeks gave a loose to the most base and effeminate revenge: the Turks were every where slaughtered without mercy; every act of shameful and horrid cruelty committed; while, to the disgrace of humanity and the christian religion, neither age, sex, acquaintance, or connection, were a defence against their savage barbarity. The governor of Messalongi, finding himself unable to defend the fortress any longer, and expecting no mercy from the assailants, put his person into the hands of the Greek Syndic of the town, who, from acquaintance and connection, he expected should either have protected or concealed him; but the villanous Syndic, as soon as he was in his power, murdered him. It is said, that the commander of the Greeks hanged the Syndic; and it may be wished to be a truth.

The rage and fury with which the inhabitants of the continent were seized extended itself to the islands: the desire of novelty, hope of plunder, and animosity to the Turks, operated every where, and produced every where similar effects; repeated acts of the most barbarous

barous cruelty, and of the blindest folly. Three Turkish ships that were collecting recruits for the army, having put in at the small island of Micone, one of the Cyclades, the greatest part of their crews being on shore, were all murdered by the inhabitants; and those that remained on board, as well as the ships, only saved by a timely flight: an order was said to be issued to massacre all the inhabitants, but we have not heard of its being put in execution. The Venetian islands, notwithstanding the strictness of the government, and the severity of the proclamations that were issued to prevent it, were in a great measure deserted by their inhabitants, each hurrying to have a share in the spoil and the carnage. At Cephalonia, Count Metaxa, and several others, fitted out ships at their own expence, and joined the Russian fleet; and the inhabitants, who shewed themselves as well disposed for a revolt as those in the Turkish territories, had an open engagement with the troops stationed in the island; in which, though they were routed and dispersed, a considerable number were slain on both sides.

Count Orlow, upon his arrival at Maina, had published a manifesto in the name of the Empress, in which she declared, that she looked upon it as a religious duty, to free the Greeks from the Turkish slavery; she at the same time promised protection and rewards to those who should join her army, and the severest punishments to those who refused. It is a singularity, perhaps not unworthy of remark, and shews how strong national habits will inadvertently appear, even where there seems no cause to call them forth, that as fear is the operating principle throughout the whole Russian empire, from the highest noble to the lowest peasant, their public acts are tinged by it, though the matters they relate to are foreign, and out of their own dominions; and as sure as a favour or reward is offered in a Russian proclamation, it is clogged on the other hand by an opposite threat of extreme punishment.

From Maina, the Russian commander proceeded with the fleet to Coron, which was invested by sea and land. This city and castle stands on the western side of the peninsula, about forty miles to the north-west of Maina, on a fine bay of the same name, and were formerly places of great strength; but, like most of the other fortresses in the Turkish dominions, have been long neglected, and suffered to go to ruin. The Basha of the Morea had, during these transactions, collected such troops as he could hastily get together, which being few in number, were overpowered and defeated in several small engagements by the Russians and Greeks, and he was at length obliged to retire with such as remained to Napoli de Romania, a great and strong city and port on the eastern side of the peninsula. In the mean time the Russians made themselves masters of Navarino, a considerable city, with an excellent harbour and two castles, about 28 miles to the west of Coron; which, from the goodness of the harbour, situation, and other advantageous circumstances, they made the general place of arms.

Patras was taken in the latter end of March, a very flourishing city, in which the Turkish inhabitants were

were more numerous than in most others of the Morea; it was the metropolis of the province of Clarentia, and situated on the north-west extremity of the peninsula, on the arm of the sea which separates it from Livadia, now called the gulph of Lepanto, about 20 miles south of Lepanto, which lies on the opposite shore, 60 west of Corinth, and 120 north-west of Misitra. This city, from the circumstances that attended it, seems to have been taken by surprize, and a most cruel and inhuman slaughter was made of the Turks, without regard to age or sex: the garrison, and such others as could escape, retired into the castle, which was immediately besieged.

As the Turks were unable to appear in the field, such of them as survived the first effects of the revolt made the best of their way to the nearest fortresses; and the insurgents were now so numerous, that they laid siege to Corinth, Napoli de Romania, Modon, and Trippolizza; besides Coron and the castle of Patras, which we have already mentioned. This was a service, however, to which the Greeks were very unequal; and the small number of the Russian land forces, which probably did not much exceed two thousand, did not allow of their supplying the deficiency. The Turks, besides, made every where a brave defence: at Trippolizza, the besiegers were totally ruined, and every Russian upon that service, except two, killed, by the continual and successful sallies made by the garrison. It did not happen better at Coron, where the Greek inhabitants being more numerous than the garrison, and the latter worn down with the continual danger and fatigue of guarding against a double enemy, within the walls and without, abandoned the city, (which was immediately taken possession of by the besiegers) and retired within the castle. The garrison afterwards found means to set fire to the oil magazines in the city, with such success, that they reduced it totally to ashes, and, making a sally during the confusion caused by the fire, made such a slaughter, both among the besiegers and inhabitants, that the survivors were glad to make the best of their way to Navarino. Their success was little better in other places; and though it was said that they defeated a body of Turks who attempted to pass the isthmus of Corinth, we find immediately after that they had retired from that quarter.

The siege of the castle of Patras still continued: in the mean time a body of Turks and Albanians having passed the isthmus, marched to its relief, and attacked the besiegers at April 13th. break of day. The governor of the castle at the same time made a general sally with his garrison; the city was set on fire in the conflict, and a dreadful carnage ensued. The Turks now retaliated all the cruelties of the Greeks, with the same barbarous spirit which had before inspired them: every thing became a victim to their ungovernable fury, and the city was burned to its foundations.

The foreign consuls had fortunately escaped to Zante: the son of the English consul, from some error, or imprudence, run a great risk of his life, and was most remarkably delivered. This young gentleman had shut himself up in his

his hotel, with his own family, two Neapolitan travellers, and several ladies of the best families, and greatest distinction in the city, whom he had taken under his protection; his whole suite amounting to about seventy persons. A body of Albanians came with axes to force his gates in the heighth of the confusion; but he representing to them, that his nation was in alliance with the Porte, the Albanians, with a temper and humanity which in the same circumstances and heat of blood would have done honour to more civilized and better disciplined soldiers, took him and all that were along with him under their protection, and conveyed them safely to the castle.

Here however their fear, as well as their danger, was redoubled. Upon their entrance into the fortress, the first thing that presented, was the dreadful spectacle of a number of dead bodies lying round in heaps, and the executioners busily employed, according to the Turkish summary method, in cutting off the heads of the principal Greeks; as they were taken and sent in from the action. As these ministers, whether of justice or tyranny, are little used to listen either to arguments or supplications, the unfortunate young gentleman and his companions were only delayed till it came to their turn to undergo the same operation. Most happily for him and them, the governor arrived in the interim; immediately recollected the consul's son, took them all under his protection, and sent them to his own apartments for their greater convenience and safety. They had the good fortune the same night to meet with an opportunity of being all safely conveyed to Zante.

Every thing went wrong with the Greeks after the destruction of Patras. The Turks and Albanians had scarcely compleated that service, when they received intelligence, that a large body of Mainotes were advancing towards the isthmus of Corinth, with an intention of penetrating into Achaia. This they immediately marched to prevent, and totally routed the Mainotes, after killing above two thousand of them.

The Morea still continued a scene of the greatest bloodshed and cruelty. The carnage at Patras gave a new whet, which was not at all wanted, to the barbarous and sanguinary revenge of the Greeks; which, together with the cruelties they were originally guilty of, seemed to give a sanction to the Turks for taking that vengeance to which they were naturally too much disposed. It is, in many instances, painful to treat or to read of the transactions of the present war, as it has through all its parts been sullied and disgraced with acts of ferocity, oppression, and cruelty, which are happily but little known in the western and middle parts of Europe. The enmities of these polished nations are tempered by a generosity and humanity which alleviate, and in a great measure conceal, the deformity and horrors of war; and a list of the killed and wounded after a battle, when attended with no circumstances to excite horror or disgust, causes little more emotion than the sight of an adjutant's roll would before it.

The Seraskier, Basha of Bosnia, arrived

arrived in the Morea at the head of 30,000 men, most Albanians and Epirotes, soon after the defeat of the Mainotes. This officer, who had much distinguished himself in the course of the present war, recovered all the northern part of the peninsula, as soon as he appeared in it; and all the Greeks that were found with arms, or out of their villages, were instantly put to death: at the same time the archbishop of Trippolizza, and some other Greeks of distinction, who were charged with being the principal instigators of the revolt, were executed.

The principal force of the Russians and Greeks was now employed in the siege of Modon, which was vigorously carried on by sea and land. As this city, which lies about 120 miles to the south-west of Corinth, is well fortified, has a very strong castle and a fine haven, it was an object of great importance to the Russians, as, under the protection of their fleet, they might have supported a garrison there, and by that means preserved a footing in the peninsula, until by the arrival of reinforcements they might once more be enabled to dispute the possession of it. Its remoteness afforded a prospect of succeeding before it could be relieved; and it was the only hope now left, and was accordingly the last effort they made.

A body of Turks and Albanians however traversed the peninsula, and attacked the besiegers with great fury in their camp, at one o'clock in the morning; and were well supported by the Governor, who made a vigorous sally at the same time. It now appeared evidently, that the spirit of the antient

May 17th.

Spartans had totally forsaken their posterity. The Mainotes, sunk and dispirited by the late actions, which taught them the difference, severely, between massacreing a defenceless people, and engaging an enemy openly in the field, abandoned their posts almost as soon as they were attacked, and were cut to pieces, almost without resistance. The Russians however made a noble stand, and fought most courageously; they did all men could do, to protect their dastardly friends, who, if they had acted with only a common degree of resolution, would undoubtedly have gained a compleat victory. They were at length however overpowered by numbers, and having lost a great many men, and their commanders the young Count Orlow, and Prince Dolgoroucki, being both wounded, they were obliged to abandon their camp, together with a battery of twenty pieces of cannon, and retire to the shore under the protection of their ships.

The Albanians now having no enemy to contend with, in the true spirit of irregular troops, fell to plunder the camp with such greediness, that they were soon in great disorder; a fault not to be committed with impunity in the face of their veteran enemies, who immediately took the advantage, and, being joined by a detachment from the ships, attacked them in turn with great fury, and routed them in such a manner, that they again recovered their camp and their battery. This success brought together the scattered Mainotes, and the siege was again renewed. The Russians now saw, that their only hope of success depended upon expedition, and upon taking the place before the arrival of fresh succours: they

they had a recent experience that the Greeks were of no use against an equal enemy; but a confidence in their numbers might make them useful in an attack upon an inferior. The ships accordingly drew nearer the fortress to second the attack, and a general assault was made; but the garrison behaved with such resolution, that they were repulsed with great loss. The Mainotes had now lost all hope as well as spirit, and, separating themselves totally from the Russians, withdrew to the fastnesses of their native mountains. The latter retired to Navarino, which they kept for some time longer in their hands; but nothing remarkable happened after this, till they entirely abandoned the peninsula.

During these transactions in the Morea, the Russian fleet was reinforced, about the middle of April, by the arrival from England of the squadron under Admiral Elphinston. In the month of May, the Turkish fleet also arrived in those seas, and some engagements of no great consequence happened soon after between them. The Turks, however, seem to have had the worst, as they retired to the Archipelago; and the Russians having taken on board the remains of their land forces in the Morea, pursued them. The two fleets came in sight in the channel of Scio, which divides that island from Natolia, or the Lesser Asia, where the Turks were at anchor in a very advantageous situation, their rear and flanks being covered by some islands and rocks that lay contiguous to the continent. The Turkish fleet was considerably superior in force, consisting of 15 ships of the line, from 60 to 90 guns, besides a number of chebecs and galleys, amounting in the whole to near 30 sail; the Russians had only ten ships of the line, and five frigates. Some of the ships engaged with great resolution, whilst others on both sides found various causes for not approaching near enough. The Russian Admiral, Spiritoff, encountered the Captain Pacha in the Sultana of 90 guns, yard-arm and yard-arm: they both fought with the greatest fury, and at length run so close, that they locked themselves together with grappling irons and other tackling. In this situation the Russians, by throwing hand grenades from the tops, set the Turkish ship on fire, and as they could not now be disentangled, both ships were in a little time equally in flames. Thus dreadfully circumstanced, without a possibility of succour, they both at length blew up with a most terrible explosion. The commanders and principal officers on both sides were mostly saved; but the crews were nearly totally lost.

The dreadful fate of these ships, as well as the danger to those that were near them, produced a kind of pause on both sides; after which the action was renewed, and continued till night, without any material advantage on either side. As soon as it was dark, the Turkish ships cut their cables, and run into a little bay on the coast of Natolia, near a small town called Cisme: this fatal measure was owing to the ignorance, obstinacy, and probably want of resolution, of the Captain Pacha, who persisted in the execution of it, notwithstanding the remonstrances of Zaffer, and Hassan Bey, and others of the bravest and most experienced officers, who foresaw

July 5th.

HISTORY OF EUROPE. [35

saw and pointed out all the dangers with which it was attended.

The Turks erected some batteries to cover the entrance of this little harbour, which was so confined, that several of the ships received great damage, and some stuck fast in the sands for want of water. Thus enclosed, and huddled together like birds under a net, the Russian fleet surrounded the mouth of the harbour next morning, and cast anchor within cannon shot of them; at the same time, Admiral Elphinston was immediately employed in the preparation of four fire-ships, whose operations were intended to take effect that night. This however being a service with which the Russians were not acquainted, it appeared very terrible, and they shewed a great backwardness in undertaking it: an English lieutenant, who had quitted the service of his country upon some disgust, boldly undertook the conduct and management of the fire-ships, and Commodore Greig, another officer of the same nation, with equal spirit took the command of the ships that were to cover them.

At twelve o'clock at night, Commodore Greig, with four ships of the line and two frigates, having approached to the mouth of the harbour, engaged the enemy within 400 yards, and an incessant cannonade and bombardment ensued: about one o'clock a signal was made to Lieutenant Dugdale to run in with the fire-ships, which he readily performed, and bore down himself upon the weathermost ship, one of his consorts upon the next in the line, and the two others he ordered to fall on board the two leewardmost of the Turkish fleet: at the same time a fortunate shot having set the rigging of one of the ships in the center on fire, it added much to the confusion and danger, in a place where they had so little room to act. The sailors on board the lieutenant's fire-ship were so overpowered by the horrors of the night, and dreaded so much the result of an operation which they did not comprehend, that it was only by dint of sword' and pistol he could keep them on board when he approached the enemy; and at length, when within a few yards, he being obliged to run forward to take a closer view, the man at the helm immediately deserted it, and with the whole crew jumped into the boat, and totally abandoned him. The lieutenant bravely lashed the helm, and seeing a boat full of Turks ready to board him, before he had quite reached the ship, he with the same intrepidity fired the fuzee with his pistol, and though he was nearly blown up, and terribly burnt, by some loose gunpowder that lay on the deck, he ran forward, and hooked the cable of the Turkish ship, so that the fire was immediately communicated to her. The lieutenant after this brave exploit jumped into the sea, and was with great difficulty saved.

The fire took place so effectually, that in five hours the whole fleet, except one man of war and a few galleys that were towed off by the Russians, was totally destroyed; after which they entered the harbour, and bombarded and cannonaded the town, and a castle that protected it, with such success, that a lucky shot having blown up the powder magazine in the latter, both were reduced to a heap of rubbish. Thus, through the fatal mis-

[C] 2

misconduct of a commander, there was scarcely a vestige left, at nine o'clock, of a town, a castle, and a fine fleet, which had been all in existence, at one, the same morning.

It is said that the Turks lost 6,000 men upon this occasion, which does not however seem probable, considering the nearness of the ships to the shore, and the number of boats that the fleet as well as the port must have afforded. The run-away sailors filled the whole coasts of the Levant with slaughter and confusion, murdering the Greeks wherever they met them, and endeavouring to burn the towns and cities. At Smyrna, these ruffians massacred several hundreds of the Greeks, and it was with the greatest difficulty that the Janizaries prevented them from treating the other Europeans and foreign merchants in the same manner, as well as from burning and plundering the city, which they several times endeavoured; nor was tranquillity thoroughly restored till the arrival of Cara Osman Oglou, a Turkish nobleman of great power and riches in that country, who came with all the pomp of a prince, at the head of 3,000 of his vassals and followers, and having made some examples, and corrected the mal-conduct of some of the civil officers, dispersed these incendiaries. In the mean time, the unfortunate Captain Pacha, who was wounded in the engagement, and who notwithstanding bore the total blame of this fatal misfortune, was beheaded by order of the Grand Signior, and Zaffer Bey appointed Captain Pacha in his place.

The Russians, by this great and unexpected success, became undisturbed masters of the sea, and having blocked up the Streights of the Dardanelles, intercepted and totally ruined the trade of the Levant. Count Orlow rewarded the brave lieutenant, who had conducted the fire-ships, with the command of the Turkish man of war that had been saved, and which carried 62 brass cannon; he also gave Commodore Greig the rank and title of Admiral, with an assurance that it should be realized to him, as soon as an express could return from the Empress.

In the mean time they over-run the neighbouring islands, and being joined by great numbers of the Greek inhabitants, as well as by those who had followed their fortunes from the Morea, they laid siege to the castle of Lemnos; the possession of which, from its vicinity to the Dardanelles, and having a good harbour, was an object of great importance to them. While some of the Greeks were employed in this siege, a much greater part betook, after the example of their ancestors, to piracy, plundering indiscriminately, under the pretended sanction of the Russian flag, both friend and foe, and filled the Archipelago with their robberies and cruelties.

The once celebrated and still great and trading city of Smyrna was now in a most critical situation; its domestic dangers seemed at least equal to its powers of defence; and an attack from the Russians, which was every day expected, seemed to threaten its utter destruction. The inhabitants were accordingly in the greatest consternation; but the apprehension of such an event was more particularly dreadful to the foreign factories, and

and the great number of European merchants constantly resident, to whom it would probably have proved fatal in the first instance, as they had nothing less to expect than to become victims to the fury and violence of the populace. A deputation to Count Orlow, it was hoped, might prevent such a design, if it was formed, from being carried into execution: to this, however, the jealousies which the Turks must entertain of any communication or intercourse between the resident Christians, and an enemy so near and so dangerous of their own profession, seemed to present insurmountable difficulties.

The usual jealousy of the Turks remitted upon this occasion, and gave place to the common safety: they embarked in this measure with as much eagerness as the proposers, and furnished a small vessel with a flag of truce, for the deputy, as well as some Janizaries, to protect him on his course, from their own people. An English merchant was prevailed upon to undertake this hazardous office, as it was thought, from the great friendship subsisting between the two nations, that he was more likely than any other to succeed in the negociation: the same reasons, however, doubled the danger to him and his countrymen, if any misfortune had followed. This Gentleman, after running great risks in his voyage from the pirates on both sides, found Count Orlow busily engaged in the siege of Lemnos, who received him with great distinction, and shewed every mark of respect and regard for his country. The Count informed him, that neither his instructions nor inclinations led him to offer any injury to the Christians of any nation; that the English in particular were held by the Empress in the highest degree of esteem and friendship, and that he should think himself happy, in every occasion that offered, of fulfilling her friendly intentions, and expressing his own affection to them. The Count then observed, that it was a thing unheard of in the process of a war, to let an enemy know what was, or was not, within the intended line of operation; that it was besides beyond his knowledge, as such operations must in a great measure depend upon intervening circumstances, as well as upon the exclusive will of the Sovereign.

This was the general answer to the deputation; but Count Orlow at the same time treated the Gentleman with such uncommon marks of friendship and attention, and gave him such assurances that nothing but the utmost necessity could induce his mistress to order, or him to take any step that might prejudice his nation, as fully removed his apprehensions, and convinced him that he had met with the desired success. The Count at parting gave him several Turkish prisoners to take along with him, and told them they owed their liberty only to that Gentleman, and to the country which he belonged to, and desired himself to attribute every particular satisfaction he had received to the same cause. This favourable reception of the deputy restored quiet to the inhabitants of Smyrna, and safety to the strangers.

It would be an injustice to the character of Count Orlow not to take notice of the extraordinary humanity and generosity, with which

which he, upon every occasion, treated the Turkish prisoners that fell into his hands, in the course of this naval war. Among other noble instances of this nature, the Lady of an officer of high rank was taken on her passage from the coast of Syria, together with her daughter, a fine child of about nine years old: the Count immediately ordered them to be removed from the cruizer on board his own ship, where they were lodged and treated with every degree of respect, attended by their own people without the smallest restraint, and all their rich baggage and effects returned. With the same spirit of generosity, he, in conformity with the Turkish manners, abstained from seeing the Lady; but treated the child, when she chose to come to see him, with all the tenderness of a parent, and made her several valuable and curious presents. At length, the first opportunity that presented, he sent the whole family, at his own expence, on board a neutral ship, to the husband and father at Constantinople. Such actions should not be forgotten, and require no praise but the relating.

The siege of the castle of Lemnos went on but slowly, and continued a long time: the Greeks, who were almost the only land forces that the Russians now had, were languid operators in a service that required patience, labour, and discipline, and which presented no immediate, nor raised no golden hopes of plunder. At length Hassan Bey, whom we had occasion to mention in the late sea-fight, crossed over by night from the continent of Romania with 3,000 men, and conducted matters so well, that the besiegers never heard of his being in the island, till he attacked them suddenly before day in their camp. The consequence was, that the Russians were routed, and the survivors obliged to take shelter in their ships; and the Greeks were almost totally cut to pieces: the few that escaped, and the inhabitants of the island that assisted the Russians, were hanged without mercy wherever they were caught.

Later accounts say, that the Russians returned to the island, and not only recovered their former footing in it, but obliged Hassan Bey and his troops to experience all the severities which they had before inflicted on the Greeks. These accounts, though there has been more than sufficient time for it, have not, however, been properly authenticated. The Russians have made several attempts to force their way through the Dardanelles, but without effect; and notwithstanding the unparalleled fortune that attended them in destroying the Turkish fleet, the consequences have not hitherto been equal to what might have been expected from so extraordinary an event.

During this state of extreme loss and misfortune, the Turkish empire seemed convulsed in all its parts: order, submission, and respect to government, seemed totally at an end; massacre and confusion took place; and to fill up the measure of calamity, the plague made the most cruel ravages, above a thousand persons dying daily, in Constantinople only, for several weeks. The destruction of their fleet was better known in that metropolis, and was in itself more immediately alarming, than any other misfortune that could have happened;

happened; and as if the dangers from without were not sufficiently terrible, the run-away sailors filled it with slaughter and confusion, and actually, set fire to the city and suburbs at several times: at length these miscreants were so strengthened by the accession of vagabonds and villains of all sorts, particularly by the crowds of deserters from the Danube, who had nothing to subsist on but plunder, that they came to an open engagement with the Janizaries in the suburbs of Pera, where some thousands of them were deservedly cut to pieces, and the rest dispersed.

In the mean time, every immediate measure was taken for the security of the Dardanelles, and all the remaining ships and galleys were fitted out with the greatest expedition to assist in defending the passage. The late Vizir, Moldavangi Ali Pacha, was recalled from his exile, and sent at the head of 15,000 men for the same purpose; where the first enemies he had to encounter were the rebellious sailors, who landed in a body in spite of the Captain Pacha, and, making zeal for their religion a cloak for their avarice and licentiousness, intended to have plundered and burnt the city of Gallipoli, and to have massacred the Greeks: they were however happily disappointed in this cruel design by the vigour and resolution of the late Vizir, who severely chastised their profligacy, and, after killing a great number of them, reduced the remainder to order. The Chevalier Tot, a French Gentleman who had been consul in Tartary, and is said to be an engineer of the first rank, together with several others of his countrymen, were also procured, to erect new batteries on the streights, and to put the castles into a proper state of defence. By these means, together with the uncertainty of the winds and currents necessary to facilitate such an enterprize, all the attempts of the Russians to force their passage have hitherto proved fruitless.

Nor has the revolution in Egypt, nor the intercepting of the trade from the Lesser Asia and Syria by the Russians, been attended with the fatal consequences to the metropolis that were expected, as amidst all its calamities it has been constantly and plentifully supplied with provisions; a felicity for which it is principally indebted to the long extent of sea-coast from the mouth of the Hellespont to the Black-sea. In the mean time, the winter season having obliged the Russians to quit their station near the Dardanelles, the trade through the streights has again been opened.

While the Porte has thus fatally experienced all the vicissitudes and havock of war, the calamities of pestilence, and the headlong destructive evils of anarchy, in their European dominions, the same ruinous system of policy, and weakness and relaxation of government, have extended their effects into other parts of this great empire, and have produced a new and extraordinary revolution in Egypt. The celebrated Ali Bey, who has so long made a distinguished figure among the factions that for some years have torn that country to pieces, has at length thrown by the mask, and, taking advantage of the present state of distress and danger, has boldly mounted the throne

throne of the antient Sultans of that kingdom.

It appears that the Ottomans have from the beginning made but a lax use of their authority in the government of Egypt. The distance and climate made it difficult to support any considerable number of troops there; while from its peculiar situation, and the number of barbarous nations on its borders, who would naturally join the natives, or at least afford them shelter and protection if overcome, nothing less than an army could enforce a very strict obedience. Satisfied with the great benefits that resulted from its being a granary to Constantinople and other parts of their dominions, as it had formerly been to antient Rome, the Turks were content with a very moderate tribute, not above one-third of which came into the treasury. A garrison of Janizaries was kept at Cairo, where a Basha with the title of Governor, but with little more power than what the great men of the country chose to allow him, constantly resided. The Princes and Grandees of the country had absolute power in their respective territories, and held a general assembly or council every year at Cairo, where they settled the payment of the revenues, and debated upon such other national matters as demanded consideration. To prevent any restraint from the Governor, or their being overawed by the Janizaries, as well as from the continual quarrels among themselves, they all came attended by their armed vassals. Such assemblies, among so barbarous a people, naturally factious and treacherous, presented continual scenes of bloodshed and confusion; while the Governors, by occasionally supporting one party against the other, endeavoured to derive that power and consequence from their dissensions which the authority of office was incapable of procuring.

Ali Bey, who seems to be a man of strong natural parts, and considerable abilities, appears to have improved upon the line of policy struck out by the Governors, and by dexterously shifting for a number of years from one side to another, and destroying by degrees such parties as were obnoxious to him, he at length formed one great one, which like Aaron's rod swallowed up all the others. Not content with the kingdom of Egypt, he has laid claim to Syria, Palestine, and the part of Arabia that had belonged to the antient Sultans. The usurper accordingly marched at the head of an army to support these pretensions, and has actually subdued some of the neighbouring provinces both of Arabia and Syria.

At the same time that he is engaged in these ambitious pursuits, he is not less attentive to the establishing of a regular form of government, and of introducing order into a country that has been so long the seat of anarchy and confusion. His views are equally extended to commerce, for which purpose he has given great encouragement to the Christian traders, and has taken off some shameful restraints and indignities to which they were subject in that barbarous country; he also wrote a letter to the republic of Venice, with the greatest assurances of his friendship, and that their merchants should meet with every degree

gree of protection and safety. His great design is said to be, to make himself master of the Red-sea; to open the port of Suez to all nations, but particularly to the Europeans; and to make Egypt once more the great center of commerce.

Though this conduct and these views shew an extent of thought and ability that indicate nothing of the barbarian, and bespeak a mind equal to the founding of an empire, yet if the Porte can conclude a tolerable peace with Russia, there seems no great probability that this new government will be lasting. The people over whom Ali Bey has assumed the rule, are effeminate, cruel, treacherous, and dastardly; who, for a long succession of ages, have been the easy prey of every barbarous invader, and corrupted with every vice that debases human nature. If it could be imagined that such a people would act like men in the defence of their rights, their own malice and treachery would probably afterwards execute what the enemy was incapable of effecting in the field. It could be only the total subversion of the Ottoman empire that could afford a prospect of success to this undertaking.

CHAP. V.

Unhappy state of Poland; the plague breaks out in that country. Germany. Conduct of the Emperor. Of the King of Prussia. Prussian troops enter the territories of Dantzick. Changes in the Ministry at Copenhagen. Danish expedition against Algiers. Sweden. Difference between the States of Holland and the Elector Palatine.

POLAND still continues to groan under all the calamities of a war, in which her share is only to suffer. While labouring under the yoke of foreign cruelty and oppression, and convulsed in every part by the domestic rage of her citizens, these complicated evils have this year been increased by the addition of that most dreadful scourge the pestilence. This distemper broke out in some villages on the frontiers of Turkey, from whence it soon spread into the adjoining provinces of Poland, and made the most cruel ravages in Podolia, Volhinia, and the Ukraine. Having penetrated into the strong frontier city of Kaminieck, where it made great havock among the garrison as well as the inhabitants, the survivors totally abandoned that important fortress, which continued exposed and deserted for several months, neither Russians nor natives venturing to take possession of it. All the peasants of a village belonging to Prince Czartoriski were swept off in one day, and nine monasteries were left without an inhabitant.

It would seem that this fatal scourge of mankind, in the present lawless state of that country, continually scoured by independent or opposite bodies of armed men, together with the constant communication occasioned by the taking of prisoners and plunder, and the carrying off provisions, could not by any human means have been restrained in its progress. The lines

lines however that were drawn, and the great care taken to prevent its spreading, have providentially succeeded, and confined its rage to those provinces where it first began, where it is said to have swept off 250,000 of the people. By the latest accounts, the severe cold of the winter has effectually checked its fury: happy if the returning heat of the summer, operating upon the misery and distresses of the people, does not again call forth its latent seeds into action.

The continued losses of the confederates have by no means lessened their exorbitances, nor even in appearance their numbers; on the contrary, they seem to multiply and acquire new strength by repeated destruction, are in possession of several provinces, and that extensive country presents nothing but endless scenes of ruin and desolation. If we are surprized at the astonishing perseverance which still produces confederacies, we cannot be less so, that the country should in any manner be capable of supporting them: it might be imagined that in such a state of insecurity and anarchy, where there is so little hope of enjoying the future crop, the husbandmen would wholly abandon the cultivation of the earth. It appears by a calculation said to be accurate, that the confederates had exacted above a year ago, from the inhabitants of the province of Great Poland only, since the first commencement of hostilities, above 16 millions of florins: to which, if we add the provisions and forage furnished to the Russians, the plunder and ruin of private families, and the loss sustained from the great number of exiles, who carried off their most valuable moveables, some idea may be formed of the deplorable state of the country.

The great Germanic powers still observe the same mysterious conduct with respect to the affairs of Poland, and the events of the present war, which we have before more than once taken notice of. The breaking out of the plague has afforded an opportunity to the Emperor as well as the King of Prussia to form lines composed of great bodies of troops along the frontiers of that country. The close connection that at present subsists between these Princes, the mutual completion of their forces, the attention they pay to their respective military departments, and the excellent condition of their armies, seem to indicate some great design in view.

The Emperor, in pursuance of his former conduct at Milan, the good effects of which had been so happily experienced by the inhabitants of that dutchy, has set apart one day in the week at Vienna for receiving petitions and complaints from all his subjects, without any the smallest distinction as to birth or rank; and the officers of the court have express orders not to turn away any person whatever who may come to implore his protection, let their condition be ever so low. He at the same time nobly declared, that it behoved him to do justice, and that it was his invariable intention to render it to all the world, without respect of persons.

The camp and grand review this year at Neustad, in Moravia, seemed calculated for the entertainment and reception of the King of Prussia, who paid a visit to the Emperor at that place. The meeting between these great monarchs was in Sept. 3. appearance

appearance so cordial and affectionate as greatly to affect the beholders, particularly the troops, many of whom remembered, and had experienced, the fatal consequences of the animosity that had so long subsisted between the two families.

The people were disposed to imagine, that other causes besides pleasure or curiosity had conduced to the late visits between these Princes; and that the war between the neighbouring powers, to which neither of them could be indifferent, was the ultimate object of them. The visit paid by Prince Henry of Prussia to the court of Petersburgh seemed in some degree to countenance this opinion; and made it not appear impossible, that such a partition of territory might be agreed upon between the three courts, as would be highly advantageous to them, and which in the present circumstances must have been submitted to as well by the Porte as the republic of Poland. The city of Dantzick, and regal Prussia, were objects of the most important and alluring nature to one of the parties; nor were the provinces of Moldavia and Walachia less so to another; while Russia might have been amply compensated on the side of Tartary and the coasts of the Black-sea.

However this may be, states that have great power seldom want ambition; and the Emperor is now said to have the finest and best disciplined army that ever the house of Austria was possessed of. With this force, and the affections of the people, which he so eminently possesses, he may well be supposed to form great designs; and the present situation of affairs seems in a particular manner to afford an opportunity for their completion.

The city of Dantzick had an occasion this year of experiencing one of the many misfortunes to which a small state, which has great and formidable neighbours, is frequently exposed. A body of Prussian troops made a sudden Sept. 29. irruption at two o'clock in the morning into the territories of that city, where they surprized several of the out-posts, seized the cannon, and made the men prisoners. They were afterwards reinforced to the number of five thousand, and encamped about four miles from the city, where they continued some weeks, but observed an exact discipline.

This violent transaction could not fail of being sufficiently alarming to the Dantzickers, who, having secured their gates, applied to all the foreign Ministers to write to their respective courts to implore their protection, or intercession in their favour. It seems that the Magistrates had forbidden the Prussian recruiting officers to levy men within their free city; and the Postmaster had refused to pass some casks of silver, which came for the Prussian resident, without examination. The complaint founded on the last of these causes was the more groundless, as the post office belongs to the King of Poland, and the Magistrates have no manner of authority over it.

The consequence was, that in about a month, the city, upon agreeing to pay 75,000 ducats, and subscribing to certain conditions, was admitted to depute two counsellors to make a submission to his Prussian Majesty. The conditions were: 1st. That they should settle and pay without delay all the demands made by the King's subjects on the city or burghers:—2d. That the Prussians

Prussians should have liberty to enlist recruits, agreeable to the treaty of Whelavar:—3d. That they shall not harbour any Prussian deserters:—4th. That the money consigned to the Prussian resident shall not be liable to inspection:—and, 5th. That the inhabitants shall comport themselves in such a manner as not to give any future cause of complaint to his Prussian Majesty.

At the same time all the Prussian subjects that were residents of Dantzick were peremptorily ordered to return to their respective countries. Nothing could be more arbitrary, nor attended with circumstances of greater cruelty than this act. Many of these people had married, had formed all their connections, had acquired considerable fortunes, and had spent the principal part of their lives in that great trading city: so that this order carried along with it all the pungent stings of banishment from a native country, at the most critical periods, and in the most interesting situations of life.

Several quick and unexpected revolutions have taken place this year in the Danish ministry. Count Holke, the great favourite of the King, and supposed to possess an unbounded ascendency over him, was suddenly, to the surprize of the world, without any motives publicly assigned, degraded from all his employments, and banished the court. Several other great changes as rapidly, and almost as unexpectedly, have since taken place at this court: the Counts Moltke, Thott, Reventlau, and M. de Rosencrantz, have been dismissed from their employments, without a pension, or other mark of favour to any of them, except M. Rosencrantz. General Philosophow, the Russian Minister, quitted this court abruptly, and without taking leave, immediately upon these last changes, which took place just at the close of the year.

The cause of these movements has not yet transpired. It is said that the French interest has of late gained ground considerably at Copenhagen; and from the sudden departure of the Russian Minister, it might not seem unwarrantable to hazard a conjecture, that the intrigues of that busy court had some share in this change of Ministers. The King, however, continues the same patriotic conduct towards his people which has hitherto distinguished his reign; as a new proof of which, as well as of his disposition to the encouragement of arts, sciences, and learning, he has this year freed the press from all restraints, and by a rescript dated at the castle of Hirscholm, exempts all books published in his dominions from any kind of censure.

The ill success of the expedition which the Danes undertook this year against Algiers, is a recent instance that large ships, heavy cannon, and a number of sailors, will not constitute an useful and effectual navy, without that military bravery and skill which is only to be acquired in actual service. The squadron sent upon this expedition was conducted by Admiral Kaas, and consisted of four ships of the line, two frigates, two bomb-vessels, and a fire-ship. The Admiral having anchored in the road of Algiers, hoisted a white flag, after which he entered into a fruitless negociation with the Dey, who was so much displeased with a letter he had received from him, that he ordered the Algerine colours to be hoisted, and several cannon shot

Aug. 3.

to

to be fired at the Danes; but they being at such a distance as to be out of all danger, still continued in the same pacific disposition, without returning a single shot, and the white flag flying.

This strange appearance of war and peace, of avowed threat and of real inaction, continued on the side of the Danes for five whole days, though the Algerines fired at them several times with great fury, but without effect, as they were never within reach of their shot. In the mean time the Algerines fitted out six galleys and galliots, who made a bold attempt, in the night, to bring off the Danish bomb-vessels, in which, however, they failed of success. The inhabitants of the city were notwithstanding in great confusion, as the longer the cloud was gathering, the more dreadful they apprehended would be its effects when it burst; they accordingly deserted the place in great numbers, and retired with their most valuable moveables to the woods and mountains.

On the 6th morning, the Admiral hoisted the bloody flag, and the cannonade and bombardment at length began, which was immediately answered with great briskness by all the castles and forts about the city, and continued all day, but without a single shot having taken place on either side. In the evening, the Admiral again hung out the white flag; and the Algerine galleys made another attempt in the night, with great resolution, to bring off the bomb-vessels, but were overpowered by the superior fire of the fleet, which continued till morning. This sort of engagement was carried on to the 12th day, during which time the barbarians made several spirited though ineffectual attempts, as well by their galleys, as by a raft, or floating battery, which they constructed, to have made the Danes repent of their visit.

On that day, the Admiral hung out a white flag, and sent a sloop towards the shore, under the same peaceable ensign, which was met by the Captain of the port, in a bark, who came to know the cause of its approach. A letter from the Admiral was then delivered to the Captain, which he was charged to deliver into the Dey's own hands, but which he soon after brought back, with an account that the Dey refused to receive it. The Danes lingered two days longer, during which time, the Algerines were struggling with the weather, though it blew a storm, to endeavour to bring the raft to bear upon them. At length, on the 15th day, the fleet weighed anchor in the morning, and put an end to this unaccountable expedition.

Sweden has been productive of nothing very interesting this year: a sum of money having been allotted by the states to enable the Princes of Sweden to gratify their curiosity of making a tour to see the principal nations of Europe, the Prince Royal, and his next brother Adolphus Frederick, set out in the latter end of the year upon that laudable design.

A new ordinance relative to pomp and luxury has been issued, by which the severity of the former, of 1765, has been much relaxed. All wines, however, except those of France, the Rhine, and Portugal, as well as punch, still continue to be prohibited; as are worked ruffles, velvets, and silk laces upon liveries.

The

The use of coffee, tea, and chocolate, is permitted; but every family that use them must pay for a licence in proportion to their rank and number. The importation of window-glass from England and France is permitted, but subject to a duty of 25 *per cent*. By another regulation, the expence of funerals is limited, and oak coffins are prohibited; as are heyducs and running footmen.

The death of the King, which happened since the close of the year, and the accession of a young active Prince, nearly allied to the King of Prussia, and who does not seem deficient in ability, may probably cause great alterations in the internal government as well as in the general political system of this country. We have seen upon former occasions that the court have a very great party in the country: and a young Prince, if he has only common abilities, will find a disposition very favourable to his augmenting the number of his friends.

A misunderstanding, which happened this year between the States of Holland and the Elector Palatine, relative to the navigation of the Rhine, and the payment of certain duties claimed by the former, had for a time the appearance of being attended with serious consequences. The Elector, upon this dispute, stopped some vessels belonging to the republic at Dusseldorp, and the latter published an interdiction of the navigation on the Rhine to his subjects, and prohibited all commerce and communication between the two states. This was resented so warmly by the Elector, that his troops received orders to be ready to march at the shortest warning; whereupon the states issued an order for fifteen battalions to reinforce the garrisons of Maestricht, Vauloj and Urava, and a number of vessels were prepared to convey artillery and warlike stores to those places. The courts of Vienna and Berlin, and the Elector of Triers, however, interfered upon this occasion, and by their friendly mediation, affairs were amicably adjusted, July 19th. and the navigation on the Rhine again opened.

CHAP.

CHAP. VI.

France. Sufferings of M. de Chalotais. Profecution commenced againft the Duke de Aiguillon, at Verfailles. A bed of juftice held, at which the King puts a ftop to the profecution by his Letters Patent. Conduct of the Princes of the blood. Arret of the Parliament of Paris againft the Duke. The King iffues an arret, by which that of the parliament is annulled. Grand deputation from the parliament to Verfailles; the King's anfwer. Conduct of the other parliaments. Deputation from the parliament of Britany; two of its members fent to prifon. The King arrives fuddenly at Paris, and holds a bed of juftice, at which all the papers relative to the profecution are feized, and the decrees of the parliament erafed from the Regifters. Violent meafures taken with the other parliaments. Arret from the King's council of ftate. Diftreffes of the people from the fcarcity of provifions. Corfica: Expedition to Tunis. State of Italy.

WHILE war has been laying wafte one part of Europe, and has been hardly withheld from the other, that reftlefs active fpirit in France, which has fo often urged its influence among her neighbours, feems now, perhaps, happily for them, to find domeftic matter fufficient to give it full employment. The partiality and obftinacy fhewn by the King in behalf of his favourite, the Duke de Aiguillon, being oppofed by the intrepid refolution of the parliaments in defence of the eftablifhed and legal government, has already effected in part, and feems finally to threaten, fome extraordinary alteration in the conftitution of that country.

This Duke, who has occafioned fo much confufion in his native country, was feveral years Governor of the province of Britany, and acquired fome credit in the laft war, from his having the command of the regular forces and militia, who attacked our rear in the wellknown affair of St. Cas. Whatever degree of merit he might derive from that action, the adminiftration of his government was fuch, as to bring upon him a great degree of the odium of the people whom he governed: till at length a public profecution was commenced againft him by the parliament of the province for crimes of the deepeft and blackeft die. Whatever foundation there might have been for thefe charges, there muft have been fomething very alarming and extraordinary in his conduct that could induce the whole nation to unite againft one man, with as much fervor as the particular members of the province that he governed. Nor was this a popular odium only, founded upon the fympathy of the people, or proceeding from the veneration they owed to their parliaments: we fee that the Princes of the blood, and fuch of the Peers as were not under immediate influence, though the natural fupporters of the crown, were upon this occafion on the fame fide, and as sanguine as the people, and ventured to encounter all the rage of an arbitrary monarch, in their endeavours to bring him to justice.

Among many other charges brought against the Duke de Aiguillon by the parliament of Britany, those relative to the prosecution which he had carried on for four years, with unremitting vengeance, against the celebrated and unfortunate M. de Chalotais, their attorney-general, were the most affecting to the public. This venerable gentleman was 74 years of age, and is described as a person, who for genius, learning, integrity, and goodness of heart, was an honour to human nature. These qualities made him the more sensible to the mal-administration of the D. of Aiguillon, and urged him with all the resolution as well as indignation of a virtuous magistrate, to exert himself to the utmost in opposition to it. The consequence was natural, from such a man as the governor is represented to be: he had great interest at court, which he made effectual use of for the removal of so great an eye-sore, and misrepresented his conduct in such a manner, as to procure an order for his banishment.

Thus, at the age of seventy and upwards, was a worthy man torn from all the ease and comfort necessary at that time of life; from the aids of friendship, the pleasures of society, and the endearing connections of blood and family, to be dragged about from prison to prison, from dungeon to dungeon, only for daring to be honest, and for fulfilling his duty to God and his country. In this situation, we find facts of so horrid a nature, that, if they had not composed a part of the charge, which was brought and supported by the parliament, we should not have thought proper to mention them; observing at the same time, that we do not vouch for their authenticity, but relate them as charges not yet refuted. Ineffectual attempts having been made to take away the life of Monsr. de Chalotais with poison, the unhappy sufferer was at length sent to the Castle of Morlaix, where, by the subornation of false witnesses, and the management of some profligate creatures (whom his enemies had appointed to be his judges), a pretended form of trial was hurried through, and a sentence as speedily as privately passed for his execution.

At this critical period, when every thing seemed hastening to a fatal conclusion, the parliament of Britany had the fortune to obtain such lights, as enabled them to develope some of the most hidden parts of this complicated scene of iniquity; which they immediately laid before the Duke de Choiseul, who with great humanity interfered, and his order in favour of M. de Chalotais arrived time enough at Morlaix to stay the hand of the executioner; the scaffold having been then just finished in the castle.

The parliament, having now obtained what it deemed sufficient proofs against the Duke de Aiguillon, his trial was commenced in the presence of the King, at Versailles, in the month of April; the Princes of the blood and the Peers, amounting to about sixty, and the parliament of Paris, of which they com-

compose a part, being his proper judges: the prosecution was managed and carried on by the Attorney-general of the parliament of Paris, assisted by the attornies of the parliament of Britany; the whole nation waiting in suspense for the decision; while one of the parties, from his virtue and sufferings, was as much the object of their love and admiration, as his enemy was of their utmost detestation and abhorrence. At this trial, the written proceedings carried on against M. de Chatolais in the Castle of Morlaix came of course to be laid before the King and Peers, and, it is said, disclosed such a scene of cruelty and iniquity, as not only justified the charges already made, but exceeded whatever could have been surmised.

In this midst, however, of these proceedings, the King thought proper, by a violent exertion of power, to put a total stop to the due course of justice, and to all farther inquiries into the Duke de Aiguillon's conduct. He accordingly held a bed of justice at Versailles, and obliged letters patent to be registered in the presence of all the Princes and Peers, by which a stop was put to the trial, the charges were suppressed, and all persons prohibited from taking any farther notice of them.

June 27th.

Upon this occasion, the Duke of Orleans, first Prince of the blood, told the Chancellor, in the King's presence, that although he had not been bound by the resolutions of parliament, in which he had before concurred, yet he could not, in conscience, give an opinion where votes were not free, concerning letters patent, which were as contrary to the laws and maxims of the kingdom, as to the honour of the peerage. The King said to the Duke of Orleans, " In case that my Parliament should convoke the Princes and Peers, I forbid you to go to the House. I charge you to signify this to the other Princes of the blood." To which the Duke answered, " Sire, the other Princes of the blood are here: this order will become your mouth much better than mine. Besides, I beg to be excused." The King then turned to the other princes, and said to them, " Gentlemen, you hear." To which the Prince of Conti replied, " Yes, Sire, we hear something very contrary to the rights of the peerage, and very little to the advantage of the Duke de Aiguillon."

Notwithstanding the disapprobation shewn by the Princes and Peers, the King, as a proof of his entire satisfaction in the conduct of the Duke de Aiguillon, took him along with him on a party to Marli, immediately after this transaction. The royal countenance was not, however, sufficient to protect him from the general indignation of the people, nor from the legal though determined resolution of the parliaments in their proceedings against him. That of Paris immediately assembled, and published a thundering arret, whereby the Duke was forbid to take his seat again in parliament, or to exercise any of the functions of the peerage, till the blots upon his honour and character were wiped off by a legal trial. This arret was immediately succeeded by a counter one, passed by the King in council, which annulled that of the par-

July 2d.

50] ANNUAL REGISTER, 1770.

parliament, declared it to be an infringement of the royal authority, and commanded the Duke to take his place among the Peers.

This arret was followed by strong representations from the Princes and Peers, complaining not only of the illegal proceedings at the late bed of justice, which annihilated the undoubted rights, at the same time that it sacrificed the honour of the peerage; but also of the King's arbitrary mandate, which forbade them to deliberate upon a subject in which their most essential interests and most valuable privileges were involved. Representations of the same nature were made by the parliament of Paris, who sent a grand deputation of forty-two of their members to Versailles, headed by the First President, to whom the King returned the following answer:

"After the decree you gave on the 2d of this month, which I have annulled, I ought not to listen to your representations: I will never permit any opposition to the execution of my letters patent of the 27th of last month; and I forbid you, under the pains of disobedience, to throw any obstacle in the way of the Duke de Aiguillon's enjoyment of all the rights of Peerage in your Assembly." The peremptoriness of this command had, however, no effect upon the conduct of the parliament; who, having met next day in full assembly, confirmed all their former decrees and resolutions, and only deliberated what were the proper measures next to be taken in consequence of it.

The other parliaments were not behind hand in vigour or resolution with that of Paris. They declared the late transactions to be illegal, and as subversive of the King's authority, which was founded upon the laws, as they were destructive to justice, and to the rights and privileges of the peerage and people.

Arret followed arret from the parliaments of Bourdeaux and Toulouse, by which the duchy of Aiguillon was stripped of all the rights and privileges of peerage, until the Duke should be acquitted, by due course of law, of all the charges laid against him. The parliament of Rennes returned unopened the King's letters patent, which were sent to annul one of their arrets. They also burnt, by the common hangman, two printed memorials in favour of the Duke de Aiguillon, which they declared to contain the most detestable tenets, totally subversive of the constitution, of the rights, liberties, and franchises of the people; and founded upon principles that tend to overturn all legal government, and to loosen every band that unites mankind in a state of society.

The King's council being sent to court by the parliament of Paris to know what day it would please his Majesty to receive their remonstrances, were answered by the Chancellor, "That his Majesty would neither *see* nor *hear* his parliament." The Council were, however, blamed, upon the assembling of the chambers to receive the report, for not delivering their message personally to the King, and for accepting any answer from the Chancellor.

A deputation of nineteen members from the parliament of Britany received leave to wait upon the

the King at Compeigne; but were forbid to pass through Paris, either going or coming back.

Aug. 20th. The King did not suffer them to speak a sentence; told them that his letters patent should have imposed a most absolute silence on them; that their conduct was of too serious a nature to pass unpunished; but that he would content himself with punishing two of them, which he hoped would be sufficient to keep the rest to their duty. Two of the members were accordingly seized, and sent prisoners to the Castle of Vincennes.

Notwithstanding the ill success which had hitherto attended the parliament of Paris in all its applications to the King, it still persevered in sending repeated deputations and remonstrances to him; and though the season of the year for their vacation was arrived, resolved not to adjourn, while the laws and constitution of their country were in so critical a situation.

Sep. 3d. At length the King arrived suddenly at Paris, in the morning, attended by his guards, who having immediately surrounded the parliament house, he entered it, and held a bed of justice, at which it is said he reproached the members in the severest terms; he then told the Chambers of Inquests and Requests, that he had no need of them, and they might retire; after which all the decrees, acts, and proceedings, against the Duke de Aiguillon were called for and delivered, and ordered to be erased from their registers. The Chancellor then made a speech, in the King's name, in which he told them, among many other things, "That their example had been the principal cause of still more irregular proceedings in some other parliaments; that the King now imposed the most absolute silence, and forbid all deliberations upon those subjects. That he forewarned them, that he should look upon all correspondence with the other parliaments as a criminal confederacy against his person and authority. He ordered all his first presidents, and all other presidents and officers of the parliament, who should preside in his absence, to break up all assemblies wherein any proposal should be made for deliberating upon objects concerning which he has imposed silence, as well as upon any letters or dispatches they should receive from other parliaments." Thus ended this extraordinary bed of justice, which had thrown the whole city of Paris into the utmost terror and dismay; and which was farther increased by the profound silence that had been commanded, and was for some time observed, in every thing relative to the transactions of this day.

The parliament however had resolution enough to meet again, and issued an arret, in which they observed, talking of this matter, that the many acts of arbitrary power, exercised against both the spirit and letter of the constitution of the French monarchy, and indeed against the solemn vow of the King, leave no room to doubt of a premeditated design to change the form of government; they however professed their firm intentions to persevere in carrying truth to the foot of the throne, and postponed the farther consideration of what passed at the late bed of justice to the following December.

[D] 2 In

In the mean time violent measures were pursued with several of the other parliaments. The parliament of Britany, besides the injuries it had already sustained, particularly in the loss of two of its members, carried off from the King's presence, though making part of a deputation that had the sanction of his leave for its protection, and whose situation seemed the more deplorable, as their fate was unknown, was now surprized by the intrusion of the Count de Gayon, a Major General, who brought the King's letters patent for them to register, and an order to erase their own arrets. Though the parliament declared they could not deliberate in his presence, he notwithstanding refused to withdraw; upon which all the members quitted the house, except the First President, Solicitor General, and Register, to whom he produced letters de cachet, and who were accordingly obliged to attend him till one in the morning, at which time the business was finished. The parliament however issued a very strong protest against this act of power, which they shewed in the highest degree to be arbitrary and illegal, and declared it to be null and void in every part.

At Metz, Marshal d'Armentieres entered the parliament house, at the head of eight companies of grenadiers, and, after tearing to pieces an arret of their's, banished several of their members to Vizoul. And at Besançon, the parliament having committed the King's Attorney there into confinement, Marshal de Lorges went at the head of a detachment, forced open the prison, and set the Attorney at liberty.

The parliament of Rouen, which has always had the honour to distinguish itself in support of the constitution, against the despotic will of the monarch, without regard to these violences, with its usual spirit, prepared a very strong remonstrance; and in consequence of its breaking up, charged the court of vacation with its delivery, as well as with the using all possible means to further its intention. The court of aids in Paris did the same, and presented it; but the King refused to hear or accept it. This remonstrance was written with great energy, and, to the amazement as well as anger of the court, was printed and published the next day.

In the mean time an arret of the King's council of state was issued, to annul the resolutions of the parliament of Bourdeaux against the Duke de Aiguillon. In this arret, among several others, the following are laid down as maxims not to be controverted: "That the whole administration of the public power resides in the King's person alone, and that he is accountable for that administration to God only; that it is from him alone that the magistrates hold their power; that they are and can be nothing more than the officers of his Majesty, charged with the execution of his will; that if, for the good of his people, he grants them leave to represent to him what they think conducive to his service, and advantageous to his subjects, it is their duty to do it only with the respect due to his sacred person; that it is never allowed to oppose the execution of his orders, but only to make the most respectful representations; and that, when his Majesty does not think proper to condescend, obedience is a duty imposed by all the laws;
that

that his Majesty is sole legislator in his kingdom, independent and undivided; that he alone has a right of putting the antient laws in execution, of interpreting them, of abolishing them, and of making new ones."

As the disputes between the King and the parliament of Paris entered into the ensuing year, in which they were finally terminated by the total dissolution of the latter, and the establishment of a new and extraordinary tribunal in its room, we must therefore defer our account of the conclusion of them till it appears in its proper place in our next volume. By that time, some of the consequences of the extraordinary measures pursued by the King may possibly begin to appear, and new lights be probably thrown upon the causes that led to these measures: at any rate, we may then have more accurate accounts than can be obtained at present.

During these transactions the kingdom was in a state of the greatest dissatisfaction and confusion; and notwithstanding the strong powers of government in that country, so little was prudence able to restrain public discontent, that the Bastille and other state prisons were filled with unhappy offenders. The patriotism and heroic firmness of the parliaments, who, at the expence of fortune and personal safety, persevered to the last in defence of the laws and constitution of their country, wedded all mankind to them, and every order, from the prince of the blood to the peasant, was on their side. Indeed, if we consider the temper shewn by the people, it is not to be conceived, that any thing but the immense standing army, which with an iron hand has so long ruled that country, could have hitherto prevented the most extraordinary consequences from taking place. How long this destructive power may continue to desolate the country, or whether, as has frequently been the case, it may at length fall by its own enormous weight, must be left to time to disclose.

We have already taken notice of the scarcity of provisions which prevailed this year in France. The distresses of the people were so excessive, that it is said 4,000 persons perished by famine in Limosin and the Marche only; and in Normandy, the most fruitful province of France, barley bread sold at above two-pence a pound. This misery produced numberless riots and insurrections in different parts, in which much mischief was done, and many lives lost. The ports were opened, and liberty given to foreigners as well as natives to import corn, to store it, and to export it whenever they pleased upon paying the customary duties, without any retrospect as to the price for which it might have been sold at any time during its continuance in the ports. Upon the whole, this country is at present far from being in an enviable situation with respect to its domestic affairs; nor could a stronger instance perhaps be given of its internal ill government, than that, since the death of King Stanislaus, notwithstanding every means being used to prevent it, above 2,000 families, it is computed, have emigrated from the city of Nancy in Lorrain, which had been in so flourishing a state during that Prince's administration.

Corsica has in no degree gratified the rapacity of its conquerors, if that can be called a conquest where

where the people are upon every occasion in a state of defiance, as soon as the weakness of the invader or the nature of the country admits the smallest hope of success; where the French are afraid to stir without their walls for fear of being massacred; and where the Governor was this summer obliged to make a kind of campaign at the head of 5,000 men, to restrain the fury of the supposed subjects. Indeed, the Count de Marbeuf gained no great honour by this kind of campaign; a great many examples of cruelty, and a few perhaps of justice, were made. The real insurgents fled to their native and inaccessible fastnesses; they had no intention of engaging the French in the field, and they knew they would not follow them. As there was no doubt but their friends and countrymen, who dwelt in more exposed places, held a correspondence with them, and would aid and assist them, when it could be done with safety, it was thought necessary to strike a terror by numerous executions. A number of these poor people have also been sent in chains to France, from whence they are to be transported to the West-Indies: in this the French seem to have adopted the eastern policy, of securing the conquest by removing the inhabitants to distant parts of the world.

The French, however, from the heat of the weather and the unhealthiness of the country, have paid dear for this summer expedition; and it would seem, that while the present invincible aversion of the natives to their government continues, it cannot cost them less, unless they totally exterminate them, than 18 or 20 battalions to keep possession of the island. At an assembly of the states convened this year by the Count de Marbeuf, the following are said to have been their demands: "That France shall have the supreme dominion of the kingdom of Corsica, but that the government shall be republican; that the public employments, churches, and benefices, shall be at the disposal of the Corsicans; that the people shall have a Speaker, to deliver whatever they may have to lay before the King; that all public acts shall be in the Italian language; and that they shall retain the privileges of salt, and of the mint."

A small squadron which was sent from France to bring the Tunisians to reason, succeeded much better in that enterprize than the Danes did in their's against Algiers. It appears that regency had concluded a treaty with the Corsicans, while they were yet a free people, and seem never to have approved of the invasion of that island: since the conquest of it, they took all Corsican barks that they met under French colours, and made slaves of the crews: they also drove the French African Company from a valuable coral fishery, which they possessed on their coasts. When the French squadron, which consisted only of two ships of the line, together with some frigates, bombs, and Maltese galleys, appeared before Tunis, their demands were so high, being 800,000 livres for the expence of the expedition, and 200,000 for the loss of the coral fishery, that the Bey equivocated for some days without giving a direct answer.

M. Broves, the French commander, did not however chuse to be trifled with; and after drawing the inhabitants of his nation out of the city, who were suffered to depart

part with their effects, without the least molestation, or the receiving even an insult from the populace, he left some frigates to cruize at the mouth of the harbour, and sailed with the rest of the squadron to bombard Biserta. This port, which is in the kingdom of Tunis, lies about 40 miles north of the capital, and is built near the site, and probably out of the ruins, of the antient Utica: the French bombarded it with vigour, and threw in between 2 and 300 bombs; some galliots were burnt, and some other mischief done, but not very considerable. From thence they proceeded to Susa, and some other places on the coast; but as the design of the expedition was only to obtain satisfaction, and security for the future, and the Bey was averse to war, matters were easily compromised. A treaty was accordingly concluded, the principal articles of which were, the restoration of the Corsican slaves with their effects; an acknowledgment of that island's being now the property of France, and the coral fishery to be again put upon its former footing.

Italy, which has been so often the theatre of war, now happily enjoys all the blessings of peace and repose; an advantage which is not lost to her, as the different states seem to vie in improving their country, increasing their commerce, and cherishing those arts that properly appertain to peace. Without that violence that generally attends the first efforts of reformation, and which the Jesuits so lately experienced in France, Spain, and Portugal, the Italian powers seem unanimous in the general intention of reducing the exorbitant power of the clergy, contracting their numbers, and lessening their riches; they do this, however, with such a degree of moderation, and so strict a regard to justice, as to refrain from all acts of inhumanity, and from the ruin of helpless and unfortunate individuals. By this means the reformation will be effectually and almost imperceptibly brought about, with the greatest advantage to the state, and with less clamour or discontent.

The present Pope, by his moderation, good sense, and the peculiar happiness of his temper, has conciliated all those powers who were so adverse to the court of Rome in the time of his predecessor. By this means, enmity has died away, good humour takes place, and he will owe to kindness what his predecessor lost by a rigid, and perhaps harsh, perseverance in defence of what he deemed his rights. The breach with Portugal, which seemed irreparable, is already made up, and a papal nuncio received at that court; France has almost resigned Avignon, and the territories seised and claims made by the King of Naples will probably follow.

CHAP.

CHAP. VII.

State of affairs previous to the meeting of parliament. General discontent upon the determination on the Middlesex election. Addresses: Petitions the consequence of the addresses. Parliament meets. Speech from the throne. Debates. Amendment proposed to the address: Affair of the petitions violently agitated: Amendment rejected. Resignations. Motion tending to define the jurisdictions in cases of contested elections; amendment to the motion. Motion in the House of Lords. Protest.

THE general discontent excited by the proceedings on the Middlesex election, particularly by the final decision given upon the petition presented by some freeholders of that county, at the close of the last session of parliament, did not at all subside during the summer. On the contrary, the remotest counties caught the alarm, and the body of freeholders, in general, throughout the kingdom, thought themselves wounded in the most vital part. It is, however, to be doubted, whether they would so soon have adopted the method of expressing their feelings by petitions to the throne, if it had not been for some well meant though probably not well judged measures, that were taken some time previous to the ultimate decision on the Right of Election.

Addresses from great bodies or communities, that give a plaudit to the public management and conduct of affairs, must be very flattering to all ministers. They have frequently desired them, when any difficult conjuncture in affairs, foreign or domestic, has made it necessary to take along with them the collective sense of the people. At this particular time, when public discontents ran higher, and public measures were more freely and loudly censured, than at any other late period, such testimonies of popular approbation, if they could be pretty generally obtained, would not only have been pleasing, but highly useful. They would have made it appear, at a time when a question of the most delicate and important nature was on the point of being agitated, that such censures were groundless, and proceeded either from interested views, or the particular animosity of a few; while the measures on which they were founded were well received, and satisfactory to the nation at large.

Upon this principle, measures were taken at the spring assizes to feel the temper of the counties; and as addresses, in their general acceptation, are considered as little more than matters of compliment and good humour, and that the Judges, Lieutenants of the counties, and Sheriffs, have great influence at these meetings, it was not doubted but a considerable number, if not a majority, might have been induced to present them, especially as moderate men, even when far from being satisfied with the measures of government, will seldom

hazard

hazard a refusal, which, however unjustly, the party that happen then to be warm in outward professions of loyalty will always construe into an instance of disaffection. Whatever probability appeared on the side of these reasons in speculation, the design answered but indifferently, when it came to be brought into execution; and if the event could have been perceived in time, by remotely trying the public disposition, which does not appear impossible, it would seem much more prudent to have laid the measure totally by for the present, than, by an obstinate perseverance, to shew a weakness which would have been otherwise unknown, or which, at least, must have continued a matter of doubt.

Essex, Kent, Surry, and Salop, were the only counties from which such addresses were obtained. The management used to get some, even of this small number, in a great degree frustrated the end that was proposed: management, in a divided county, perhaps necessary, and which, in a popular cause, would have been easily overlooked. The Universities addressed on this occasion. A considerable opposition was made to the measure at Oxford; at Cambridge, the interest of the Duke of Grafton carried it with less difficulty. The cities of Bristol and Coventry, and the corporation of Liverpool, with a few other places of less note, presented addresses. An address was also presented, which, purporting to be from the Merchants, principal Traders, and Inhabitants of the city of London, was intended to contradict the sentiments and counteract the proceedings of the corporate body of this great metropolis, in which the party of the court was extremely weak. The manner in which this address was said to have been obtained, and the riot that ensued upon the delivery of it, our reader will see in the Chronicle, and its Appendix, for the former year.

The spirit of addressing could be carried no farther in England. It was invidiously observed, that Scotland was much more ready in expressing the most perfect satisfaction in the conduct and character of the Ministers. Addresses, which filled the Gazette for several weeks, came from every town, and from almost every village in that part of the kingdom.

The style of many of these addresses was not altogether proper: they were unnecessarily overloaded with professions of loyalty, which are needlessly repeated, except in cases of great doubt, or real danger, when they carry much the more weight for not being in common use. By representing the people to be in little less than a state of rebellion, they threw an oblique and alarming imputation upon a considerable part of the nation. It seemed to many, that they were called upon to justify their discontent, by shewing, in some manner, equally strong and public, that their opposition to the court was not taken upon false or trivial ground. The final decision of the Middlesex election, whilst the nation was in a ferment from other causes, furnished a favourable opportunity.

Petitions were therefore set on foot, in many places, for the redress of grievances, for the removal of bad ministers, and for the banishment from the royal presence,

sence, for ever, of those evil counsellors, who, the petitioners asserted, had endeavoured to alienate the affections of the subjects, and to deprive them of their dearest and most essential rights. The county of Middlesex, as the most immediately affected, took the lead upon this occasion, and presented a petition, which, it was generally thought, would have had greater force, if it had not been clogged with a verbose and tedious detail of all the real and supposed grievances that had been complained of for the last six or seven years.

The city of London succeeded to the county of Middlesex: this petition was pretty nearly in the same strain with the former. Although the discontent spread fast and widely, and was even stronger in some remote places than in the neighbourhood of the metropolis, the course of petitioning seemed for some time to be at a stand: several doubts arose in the minds even of those who were most animated against the conduct of the ministry; some questioned the legality of a petition to the crown against a decision of the House of Commons in matter of election, and did not see, though the complaint were legal, how it was in the power of the crown to give redress; others were disgusted with the pattern of the first petitions, which were filled with a variety of matters, some of which they considered either as stale, or frivolous, or doubtful.

These difficulties were removed in several places by the activity of the opposition, who, it must be owned, exerted very great powers with equal industry. They argued, that the imprudent matter or expressions of any petition formed no objection to the measure itself. That if the right of election was important, the violation was flagrant; and no remedy was to be expected for that flagrant violation of an important right, from the very body which had been guilty of the violation. The crown could not, indeed, rescind the act of the House of Commons; but the crown could send that House of Commons to their constituents; and these might chuse a House disposed to redress the grievance complained of. In this manner the crown might administer a remedy: the legality of an application for it could not be denied, since the House of Commons had, by express resolution, admitted a right in the subject to petition the crown for the dissolving as well as the calling and sitting of parliaments.

These arguments prevailed in about seventeen counties, and several cities and boroughs. The petitions were said to be signed by upwards of 60,000 of the electors. Some of the petitions were principally confined to the violated right of election; others were more diffuse: Yorkshire, Westminster, and some others, prayed in express terms for a dissolution of parliament; some only insinuated it; while a good many prescribed no particular mode of redress.

Such was the state of affairs previous to the meeting of parliament. The nation had been in a great ferment during the whole summer——the like had scarcely been ever remembered. Many fast friends of administration having found, that, whether from the nature ers of the act, or the dexterity of misrepresentation, the power of declaring incapacities in the House of Commons was extremely and universally unpopular, thought it would be wise to give way to the general disposition, and that it would be no disgrace to rescind in one session their own resolution of another; that they would thereby immediately remove that fatal source of discontent, the Middlesex election, let what would else remain behind, and prevent its being any longer a matter seriously alarming to the most moderate and dispassionate part of the nation, while it was used as a means by the turbulent and ambitious of bringing themselves into consequence.

On the other hand, several of the court party cried out for measures of severity. The authority of parliament had been trampled upon. The K—— had been insulted on his throne by proceedings at once the most absurd and provoking,— insolent petitions. A dissolution of parliament was desired from the King; and on what ground? because that parliament had complied with the ministers whom the King himself had appointed. How could he expect to be obeyed in those great critical emergencies, that must necessarily occur in any plan for aggrandizing the crown, when the ministers who formed such plans were given up, and the P——, who had acted under their influence, was dissolved? To support the ministers effectually, it was not only necessary to adhere to their grand measure in the Middlesex election, as a perpetual rule of policy, but to punish the contraveners, who, otherwise, might continually keep alive that matter of complaint. Besides, if the subjects were suffered to proceed in this method of remonstrating to the crown in their natural capacity, not only without but against their representatives, a majority in parliament would become ineffectual to the support of government; and so no ministry could be safe, except in courting the popular opinion to the manifest detriment of the service of the sovereign. They would therefore have these petitions considered as acts little less than treasonable, and to be examined and punished as crimes of the greatest magnitude.

The minds of all men were occupied on the one side and the other with these considerations, and great expectations were formed concerning the manner in which these great points would be handled in the speech Jan. 9th. from the throne. The speech began by taking notice of a distemper that had broke out among the horned cattle; touched some topics concerning foreign affairs, and the distractions of America, and concluded with the usual recommendation to unanimity. No notice whatsoever was taken of the great domestic movements which had brought on or followed the petitions.

The public were much surprized at the silence concerning the petitions, and at the solemn mention of the horned cattle, which filled the place of that important business. It became even a subject of too general ridicule, especially as the existence of the distemper, or at least the extent or danger, did not dispose the people to more serious thoughts.

The

The opposition, however, did not copy the reserve of the speech. Upon reading the address, a motion was made for the following amendment, to assure his Majesty, that they would immediately enquire into the causes of the discontents that prevail in every part of his Majesty's dominions. This motion occasioned long debates, which were carried on with a warmth and acrimony of expression before unknown in that assembly, and in the course of which the severest animadversions were made upon different parts of the speech.

The affair of the petitions was violently agitated; and while, on one side, the grievances and discontents of the people were urged as the strongest reasons for the proposed amendment, some of the gentlemen on the other side denied the existence of either grievances or discontents: another more moderate and smaller part of those who supported administration did not deny but there might be some grievances, though much exaggerated; they acknowledged the discontents, and they declared themselves willing to consider them at a proper time, as well as to re-consider the Middlesex affair, though they were still of opinion that they had acted right in it, upon the principles of the law as it stood when they made the decision: these principles, they allowed, might bear hard on the rights of the electors, especially in parliaments continued beyond the session: they said they were willing to listen to methods of redress soberly proposed, and at a time of leisure; but they objected to the motion, as it would be to criminate themselves; to assure his Majesty, that, by an abuse of power, they had been the cause of all the prevailing discontents, and in effect to join in a prayer for their own dissolution.

The far greater number, however, on this side of the question, admitting the discontents, entirely charged them, as well as the petitions, to the gentlemen in opposition, through whose influence and industry the people were persuaded to imagine the one, and to sign the other; while the only cause for either was the ill will of their leaders to administration. They observed, that the majority of gentlemen of large fortunes, of the justices of peace, and of the clergy, in some of the counties, had not signed the petitions; that a majority of the counties had not petitioned; that the inferior freeholders were not capable of understanding what they signed; that the farmers and weavers in Yorkshire and Cumberland could neither know nor take any interest in what befel the freeholders of Middlesex, if they had not been set on by seditious and factious men, by grievance-hunters and petition-mongers; that by these people, meetings were advertised, speeches made, writings published, government vilified, the parliament abused, and the people inflamed; that all this was done only to distress government; but that, if even a majority of such freeholders had signed petitions, without any influence or solicitation, they were only to be considered as the acts of a rabble, and of an ignorant multitude, incapable of judging.

Such

Such was the language, besides many opprobrious epithets, that it had been wiser not to use, drawn out by the violence of party, and the heat and eagerness of debate. These charges drew from the gentlemen in opposition a spirited avowal of the part they had taken in respect to the petitions, and of the sentiments which they delivered to their constituents: they contended that they were bound to render to their constituents an account of their conduct in parliament; to give them their advice and opinion, when asked in any thing that related to their interests; and to give them the earliest notice of any measures that were subversive of their rights, or dangerous to the constitution. That in the present instance, they did not hunt after petitions or petitioners; the petitioners sought them; for the instant that the unprecedented decision of the majority on the Middlesex election was known, every independent freeholder in the kingdom was struck with the most alarming apprehensions. Several freely acknowledged, that they went to the meetings of the freeholders whenever they were invited, and thought it their duty so to do, and to give them every legal assistance in their power to obtain a redress of the injury done to them. In consequence of some violent threats that were thrown out by the other side, they boldly avowed the signing the petitions, and dared their opponents to put the threats in execution.

The charges of meeting, and writing, and speaking, which had been mentioned by a great lawyer as a sinister method, were ridiculed; and it was asked, in what other method people communicate their sentiments? It was observed, that it had been insinuated, that our grievances are imaginary, because they are such as the peasants or artificers of Devonshire and Yorkshire would not immediately feel, nor perhaps discover, till they felt. But if those who see oppression in its distant though certain approach; if those who see the subversion of liberty in its cause, are always few, does it follow that there are never approaches to oppression, or remote causes of the subversion of liberty? If the few who can and do discover effects in their causes open the eyes of others; if those who see the rights of election invaded in Middlesex, acquaint the graziers and clothiers, in remote counties, with their interest in the event, and its consequences, are they for that reason leaders of a faction, and actuated by personal and selfish views?

As to the majority of gentlemen of large fortune not having signed the petitions, the fact was disproved in some instances in which it had been asserted: it was besides observed, that many gentlemen were much influenced; that the justices of peace were immediately appointed by the crown; and that no body of men could be under greater influence than the clergy, yet that some of these even had signed the petitions. It was asked, if the bulk of the freeholders were of no account? if their opinion was of no weight? and it was asserted, that they were that respectable body of men who alone were superior to all menace, all fear, and all influence.

It was said, that the petitioning counties, cities, and towns, were, in in respect to opulence and number of inhabitants, far superior to those that had not petitioned; and that they contributed more to the land-tax, which was now a test of freehold property in this country, than the rest of the united kingdom. That it was well known what steps were taken in several other counties to prevent their petitioning; that in some they wanted leaders; in others great men, who were easily influenced themselves, had such power that nobody dared to oppose it; that it was much in the sheriff's power to prevent or damp the meeting of a county, which power had been exerted upon several occasions; and that, where the disposition appeared prevalent, hasty measures had been taken at some of the assizes to prevent the grand jury from deliberating as a body.

But was it to be brought as a proof that there was no discontent, because all the counties did not petition? What must that government be, against which every member of the community lodges a complaint? That, indeed, the present complaints, along with being more general, were marked with particular circumstances, which sufficiently distinguished them from all others, and shewed they were the general voice of the people, as well of those who had expressed their sentiments publicly as of those who had not. That at other periods, and some of the most critical in this country, petitions militated against petitions; the whigs petitioning one thing, the tories against it; two parties always opposing one another; but in the present instance, neither the whole weight of power, nor the influence of the great, had been able to produce one opposite petition or address from the time the first was delivered. Some gentlemen coming from counties that had not petitioned, declared that even there the discontent was general.

Many other matters, foreign and domestic, were brought on in the course of the debates of this day: the conduct observed in regard to the colonies was particularly scrutinized; and the decision on the Middlesex election was largely entered into: both these will come in course before our readers in their proper place. Other matters were of a temporary nature, but all served abundantly to vent that ill humour which so strongly predominated on both sides.

The first Lord of the Admiralty was called upon to declare, whether France did not threaten a war, because some concessions were refused which would have been derogatory to the honour of the British flag, if complied with. To this it was answered, that a French frigate, bearing a royal commission, arrived, and cast anchor in the Downs, in the same road where some of his Majesty's ships then were, without paying the usual salute. That the Lieutenant who commanded a sloop of war of twenty guns, sent an officer on board to demand the customary respect, which the Captain of the French vessel refused: having, as he said, no orders to pay it, and not being sufficiently informed of the right to demand it, he could not nor would not risque the honour of his nation in a point of so great consequence. The Lieutenant returned for answer, that his pretended ignorance should not exempt

exempt him from paying that act of obedience to the British flag which his nation had ever paid to it in the narrow seas; and with a firmness becoming the dignity of a British officer, declared he would sink him if he obstinately refused. The French Captain was peremptory, and the Lieutenant drew up along-side of his vessel, and fired a shot into her; at the same time he sent the officer, who had carried the message, to strike the flag, which the French Captain thought proper to suffer to remain in the same situation during his stay.

That this was the nature of the present dispute: the French ministry had complained of this act, but seemed by no means disposed to carry things to extremities in support of their demand of redress, as they found no disposition in our court to relax in the claim to that ceremonial of submission, the exacting of which was the occasion of the dispute.

After long debates, the proposed amendment was rejected by a great majority, and the address passed in the usual form. The King observed, in the answer to the Address, "That his interest and those of his people must ever be the same; and that, in pursuing such measures as are most conducive to their real happiness, they would give to him the truest and most acceptable testimony of their attachment to his person and government."

Among other particulars that distinguished the debates of this day, the Marquis of Granby, commander in chief of the forces, made a public recantation of the opinion which he had formerly given on the Middlesex election: he said, that it was for want of considering the nice distinction between expulsion and incapacitation, that he had given his vote for the sitting of a member who was not returned in the last session of parliament: and that he should always lament that vote as the greatest misfortune of his life. That he now saw he was in an error, and was not ashamed to make that public declaration of it, and to give his vote for the amendment.

A few days after the opening of the session, a great number of resignations took place: Lord Camden resigned the Seals; the Marquis of Granby all his places, except the regiment of blues; the Duke of Beaufort, his place of Master of the Horse to the Queen; the Duke of Manchester, and Earl of Coventry, of Lords of the Bedchamber; the Earl of Huntingdon, his place of Groom of the Stole; and Mr. James Grenville, his office of one of the Vice-Treasurers of Ireland. Mr. Dunning, the Solicitor-General, also resigned that employment. Jan. 17.

The whole of administration seemed to be falling to pieces. A violent panic prevailed; but the court, resolute in its purposes of governing by men who had no popular views or connections, was determined to fight the battle, notwithstanding this desertion of so many of its principal commanders. Mr. Charles Yorke was with much difficulty prevailed upon to accept the Seals. He died three days after. Every thing seemed to conspire against the court.

Sir John Cust resigned his office of Speaker of the House of Commons, through his ill state of health, and was succeeded by Sir Fletcher Jan. 22.

cher Norton. This gentleman was proposed by the Minister, who was supposed to conduct the affairs of government in the House of Commons, and another was proposed by the gentlemen in opposition: this brought on, by a division, a new trial of the force on both sides, in which, however, the former had a majority of near two to one.

Jan. 28. A few days after, to the general astonishment of the nation, the Duke of Grafton resigned his office of first Lord of the Treasury, and was succeeded by Lord North, who was already Chancellor of the Exchequer.

Various causes were assigned, or rather surmises formed, upon the motives of this resignation. Some imagined that he had been over-ruled on various occasions in the cabinet, and did not chuse to make himself any longer responsible for measures which he did not entirely approve. Others attributed it to the pure effects of fear: they said that a violent opposition was foreseen in both Houses; that the murmurs and discontents of the people were become truly alarming; that impeachments were talked of, and even threatened; and concluded, that he had not hardiness enough to stand the shock of these different encounters. However this might be, the writers on the side of government at that time, after the repeated praises which they had bestowed on his public conduct, particularly his firmness, now suddenly changed their tone, and reproached him with a cowardly desertion in the time of danger. His Grace however publicly declared, that he would still continue to support the measures of administration: a promise which he punctually fulfilled upon every occasion.

As the decision on the Middlesex election was the grievance, of all others, which the people principally complained of, and what appeared to the gentlemen in opposition as a measure more dangerous to the constitution than any that had been adopted for many years, so it became during this session the principal subject of debate in both Houses, and was, as well within as out of doors, the great object of public attention. Though it was soon found that there was no prospect of rescinding the former vote of exclusion, it was still thought that some concession would have been made to quiet the minds of the people; and that, whatever reasons might particularly determine a perseverance in support of that single act, as the principle on which it was founded was (whether right or wrong) deemed so alarming an invasion of the rights of the freeholders, it would be either effectually guarded against, or totally given up, for the future.

Jan. 30. The House having resolved itself into a grand committee on the state of the nation, a motion was made, That in the exercise of its jurisdiction, it ought to judge of elections by the law of the land, and by the custom and practice of parliament, which is part of that law. This was understood to be the leading proposition to a string of resolutions that were to lead to a condemnation of the principles of the determination in the Middlesex election. The manner of putting this beginning was full of parliamentary skill; the question being conducted by an experienced and able Member, Mr. Dowdeswell,

HISTORY OF EUROPE.

well. If the truth of the proposition was denied, a monstrous and alarming power would be assumed in parliament. If it was admitted, other propositions reflecting on the determination of the House would follow, connected with this, and perhaps equally hard to be evaded. If got rid of for the present by a previous question, it might return again to torment them daily.

They, therefore, after admitting the truth, denied the necessity of coming to such a resolution, which standing alone might suppose that the House reflected on its own acts: and then moved an amendment, which should at once put an end to all hopes of their ever changing their ground, or giving way to the opposition; which was, that the following words should be added to the motion. And that the judgment of this House in the case of John Wilkes was agreeable to the law of the land, and fully authorized by the practice of parliament. As this amendment was totally subversive of the principles upon which the motion was founded, it was accordingly opposed with great vigour, and the debates renewed with fresh warmth, till at length, upon a division, the numbers being 224 to 180, the question with the amendment was carried; and being now passed into a public resolution, and thereby become a full confirmation of the former decision on the Middlesex election, it put a final end to the hopes of those who still expected that the former determination upon that subject would have been rescinded.

The majority upon this question was not however so great as it had been lately upon other occasions; and a motion was made in the same committee next day—That by the law of the land, and the known law and customs of parliament, no person, eligible by common right, can be incapacitated by vote or resolution of that House, but by act of parliament only. In the course of the debates upon this question, a motion was made to adjourn the committee; but this proposal not being seconded was dropped; other matters were however called up which interrupted the debate, and it was passed over without coming to a division.

Nor was the affair of the Middlesex election less agitated in the House of Lords, where a great debate arose upon it at the opening of the session. Upon this occasion, a great law Lord, as well as high officer of state, whose opinion had been long wished for, and was held in much estimation by the public, pronounced it decisively against the measures pursued upon that election. This public disapprobation, besides the great weight it carried, from the particular circumstances of station and character, was rendered more effective, at least out of doors, by the uncommon energy of the terms in which it was delivered. He declared, that he considered the decision upon that affair as a direct attack upon the first principles of the constitution; and that if, in the judicial exercise of his office, he was to pay any regard to that or to any other such vote, passed in opposition to the known and established laws of the land, he should look upon himself as a traitor to his trust, and as an enemy to his country.

This public avowal of an opinion so contrary to the conduct, if not to the views, of administration, was

Vol. XIII. [*E*] considered

considered as a total defection, and resented as a desertion from that side. It had however been preceded, on the same day, by a similar declaration relative to the Middlesex business, on the part of the Earl of Chatham, who now seemed disposed to recover that almost boundless popularity which he once possessed, and which, in consequence of a subsequent conduct, he had in a great measure lost. We have before seen the neglect and indifference with which this nobleman had been treated by that administration which was generally supposed to have owed its existence to him; and in consequence of which, and of his finding that the line of public conduct which he had laid down was broken through, and his opinion continually over-ruled, he first retired from public business, and, upon an additional cause of disgust, at length totally resigned.

He now emerged from that retirement which was but ill suited either to his habit of life or disposition, and seemed, in spite of infirmity, to have recovered his former vigour and spirit. The incapacitating power assumed by the House of Commons was loudly and totally condemned by him, and the whole management in the affair of the Middlesex election severely censured. The censures upon this subject were not however more heavily placed than those which he soon afterwards passed upon the general conduct, measures, and views of administration, which he condemned in the strongest terms, and has since sealed his disapprobation by a constant and uniform opposition to them. Such a defection and opposition, in the present tottering and disjointed state of administration, seemed to carry a most threatening aspect towards it: nor could any ministry perhaps have subsisted, in equal circumstances, at almost any other period.

A motion was made some time after, (by a noble Marquis, who had lately presided at the head of public affairs) similar to that which we have just recited to have been the subject of debate in the other House; the design of which was to procure a declaratory resolution, that the law of the land, and the established customs of parliament, were the sole rule of determination in all cases of election.

Long debates ensued upon this question, in the course of which much of the same ground was gone over on both sides which we have formerly shewn to have been taken upon this subject; and the motion was at length over-ruled by a large majority. The opposers of the question, having obtained this proof of their strength, were resolved to exert it to advantage; and upon the same principle that produced the amendment to the late motion in the other House, determined to pass such a resolution as would preclude all further attempts of the same nature in this. A motion was accordingly made late at night, That any resolution directly or indirectly impeaching a judgment of the House of Commons in a matter where their jurisdiction is competent, final, and conclusive, would be a violation of the constitutional right of the commons, tends to make a breach between the two houses of parliament, and leads to a general confusion.

The astonishment excited by the hardiness that ventured upon a measure of so extraordinary tendency

dency seemed for a time to absorb all the powers of opposition. It was said, that this motion included a surrender of their most undoubted, legal, necessary, and sacred rights; a surrender as injurious to the collective body of the people, to their representatives, and to the crown, as it was totally subversive of the authority and dignity of that House. That the surrender of rights and powers which were not given for their own particular advantage, but merely as a constitutional trust, to be exercised for the benefit of the people, and the preservation of their laws and liberties, would be an act of treachery to the constitution. That it would be in effect a declaration, that if the House of Commons were guilty of the greatest exorbitancies, were to trample upon all the rights of the people, and to subvert the whole law of election; that even in such a critical emergency of the constitution, the people are to despair of any relief whatsoever, from any mode of direct or indirect interference of the Lords. That though it is generally true, that neither House ought lightly and wantonly to interpose even an opinion upon matters which the constitution has entrusted to the jurisdiction of the other, it is no less true, that where, under colour of a judicial proceeding, either House arrogates to itself the powers of the whole legislature, and makes the law, which it professes to declare, the other not only may, but ought, to assert its own rights, and those of the people. That by the present resolution, this constitutional controul would be given up, which that House, as appears by antient and modern precedents, had always claimed and exercised; which had been also exercised by the other upon critical occasions, and for the purpose of which the legislature had been divided into separate branches, that they might operate as mutual checks, and each be restrained from exorbitance by the interposition of the others.

That the discontents of the people, which are alledged as a motive for this measure, arise from the injuries they have received, and should be the strongest reason to induce the Peers, who are the hereditary guardians of their rights, to shew their constant attention to their welfare by a timely interposition in their favour; thus by their healing mediation to make up the unhappy differences between them and their representatives, and restore that harmony and confidence which are absolutely necessary for the public happiness and safety. That by this resolution, they not only refuse to stand by the people at present, and renounce the power of doing it hereafter, even if they were to suffer the most grievous injuries, but they also abdicate their antient and unquestioned province and duty of being the hereditary council of the crown, rendering themselves unable to give their advice in a point in which, of all others, the crown may stand most in need of the wisdom and authority of that House. And that it was as derogatory to their dignity, as it was contrary to their duty and interest, to make such a surrender of their rights, without at least the holding of a previous conference with the other, to discover whether they were inclined to admit a correspondent immunity from interposition on their parts, in matters within the jurisdiction of the Peers.

[*E*]2   Great

Great objections were made to the time and manner of introducing and conducting this question. That a resolution new in matter, wide in extent, weighty in importance, involved in law and parliamentary precedents, should be moved at midnight, after they were spent with the fatigue of a former long debate; that an adjournment of only two days, to enable the Lords to consult the journals on so important a matter, should be refused; and that an immediate division should be pressed, were represented as proceedings altogether unparliamentary and unjust; by which every possibility of debate is precluded, and all argument and fair discussion suppressed.

The principal stress, in support of the motion, was laid upon the necessity of preserving a good understanding between the two Houses. This was enforced by the licentiousness of the people, and the seditious spirit of the times. It was said that, in the present circumstances, it particularly behoved all the legislature to draw together in the closest manner; as nothing less than their most cordial and intimate union could support legal government, and prevent the madness of the people from precipitating themselves into a state of anarchy and confusion.

The right of interference was called in question, or denied. It was said, that it was unusual and irregular in either House of parliament to examine into the judicial proceedings of the other; and that, as these decisions cannot be called into question by appeal, they are to be submitted to without any examination elsewhere of the principles on which they are founded. That in the present instance such an interference would be a real and most alarming invasion of the rights of the people, who are too jealous of their privileges to suffer the Peers to meddle with them: and that, as the Peers are not even allowed to interpose in the election of a single representative, under what colour of pretence can they assume a power of sitting in judgment upon the whole body of representatives, and pronouncing on the choice of every elector in the kingdom?

The question being repeatedly and eagerly called for, an end was put to the debate by a division, and the motion carried by about the same majority that had rejected the former. These two questions were productive of two of the strongest and most remarkable protests that we have met with, which were signed by forty-two Lords. In the last of these, the protesting Lords pledge themselves to the public, that they will avail themselves, as far as in them lies, of every right and every power with which the constitution has armed them for the good of the whole, in order to obtain full relief for the injured electors of Great Britain.

CHAP.

CHAP. VIII.

Motion for disqualifying certain officers of the revenue from voting for the election of members of parliament: opposition to it: the motion overruled. Civil list. Repeal of part of the late revenue act, for imposing duties in the colonies: duty upon tea continued. Act for regulating the proceedings on controverted elections. London remonstrance: great debates: Address to his Majesty.

DURING the fitting of the committee on the state of the nation, a motion was made to bring in a bill for disqualifying certain officers of the revenue from voting for members of parliament. The gentlemen who supported this motion set out by shewing the small produce of the customs and excise at the time of the revolution, together with the little probability that then appeared of its swelling to the present enormous amount of six millions sterling: to this they attributed the inattention of the patriots of that day, who, if they had foreseen the unconstitutional weight that must have been thrown into the scale on the side of the crown by the appointment of officers for the collection of so vast a revenue, would, undoubtedly, have taken proper and effectual measures to prevent the dangerous influence which it must afford in the election of representatives for the people.

It was observed, that the chief officers in the collection of these revenues had been disqualified by act of parliament from fitting in the House of Commons; and that the very same reasons held for disqualifying the inferior officers from returning members to sit there. The danger arising from the influence must be the same in both cases. It was declared, that the motion was not made to distress or weaken administration; and those who now supported it said they would do the same in office as well as out. They said, that the great object of a minister in this country was not so much the procuring of the voice within doors, as it was to gain the confidence and opinion of the people without; that he may shuffle on for a little time by the aid of a majority in his favour there; but if the majority of the people were against him, he could never obtain power with permanence and honour; he could neither be respectable abroad, nor useful at home. The proposed measure would, therefore, instead of weakening administration, give it the most effective strength; and a majority in the House would be a pledge of a majority in the nation: if the minister's measures were good, they would meet with a most effectual support; and if bad, no friend to his country could wish that they were supported at all. No minister that professes to have the public

good

good in view can pretend, consistently with such profession, that any measure tending to produce a real representation of the people can impede his designs; therefore those who oppose this motion must profess to adopt measures which a free representation would not approve.

It was said, that it became absolutely necessary to take some measures to quiet the minds of the people; that there was no doubt but the proceedings of last year, which had caused so much uneasiness throughout the nation, were, by this time, sufficiently regretted on both sides of the House; and that a measure that led to an equal representation was, in the present circumstances, peculiarly calculated to restore quiet and good humour among the people; but that, independent of every other consideration, the influence of the crown upon the electors in their choice of representatives had the most alarming and fatal tendency; and that, if Charles the First had had the same power in his hands to manage and govern the boroughs, he must have succeeded in his design of enslaving the nation.

Objections having been made to the disfranchising of so great a number of people, it was answered, that it would not be the taking away of a franchise; it would only be a suspension of it: let him that prefers his franchise to his place quit his place, and his franchise will return. Can it be pretended that officers will not be found for the customs and excise, because such officers are deprived of the franchise in question? The right of sitting in parliament is as valuable a franchise as the right of voting for a member to sit there. Many offices disqualify for a seat in parliament, yet are these offices sought for with such earnestness, that members frequently even go out of parliament to obtain them. Can it, then, be pretended that it is unjust to separate the possession of a franchise from the possession of a place? or, that a man, who knowingly and voluntarily accepts a place from which a franchise is separated, has a right to complain for not bringing his franchise into place along with him? That the influence of the crown, in the present instance, was so glaring, that it did not admit of a question; that there could be no influence so dangerous; and that there were many boroughs in which the officers of the revenue had a very great share in the elections; and it was too much to expect that they would follow their free opinion, or their natural affection, against the will of a minister, on whom they were dependant for their daily bread. Members elected by custom-house officers are therefore the representatives of the minister, not of the people; and are representatives that will certainly adhere to the interest and obey the instructions of their constituent.

On the other side it was said, that the bill which was the object of the present motion was wholly unnecessary. That, as the law stands at present, no person in the customs, excise, or post-office, can intermeddle by persuasion or dissuasion in the voting for representatives in parliament, under very heavy penalties. The cruelty of depriving so great a number of people of their franchises was expatiated

patiated upon; that it was a matter that required great consideration, and that they were not now ready for such a motion; that it seemed in its consequences to strike at the liberty of the subject, and that no man could tell where bills of disqualification might stop.

That, besides, the motion itself seemed to be irregular: prior resolutions should have been proposed in the committee to warrant such a proceeding, and to shew its expediency, in the nature of heads of a bill, so as that the matter and design of it might have been fully understood; but, as it stood at present, the motion might perhaps extend to officers in the army and navy; that no evidence had yet been brought of the undue influence of the crown; and that insinuations and proofs were to be considered as very different matters.

The debates upon this occasion, as had usually been the case of late, were carried on with great warmth, and were branched out into a number of other subjects. Those distinguished by the name of Tories, or Country Gentlemen, who had been for some time regularly engaged in support of administration, were reproved for their opposition to this bill, as inconsistent with all their professions. It was affirmed, that the party had formerly brought in and supported a bill of a similar tendency, if not the very same, with that which they now opposed. On their part, they reproached the Whigs with taking such measures as tended to public confusion, and that in supporting this ministry they supported government itself. The question being at length put, the motion was rejected by a very considerable majority.

We have seen last year, that, upon the grant made for the discharge of the large debt contracted by the civil list establishment, a promise had been obtained from administration, that as it was too late in the session to prepare the papers and accounts then required for the inspection of the House, relative to the expences of that department, and the debts incurred by it, they should, however, be prepared and ready to be laid before it at the ensuing meeting. Some of these papers being now before the House, a motion was made for an account of 28th. the civil list expences, from the 5th of January, 1769, to the 5th of January, 1770.

It was said, in support of this motion, that the civil list revenue, if misapplied, instead of maintaining the dignity of the crown, served only to besiege it with parasites; and in the place of promoting industry, or arts, to subvert the freedom of the people. That though the funds allotted for this purpose were fully adequate not only to every necessary but to every liberal expence that was requisite to support the dignity of the regal character, yet neither the greatness of the fund, nor the known œconomy of the present times, were sufficient to prevent an enormous debt from being contracted, and the people from being applied to for more money, at a time when all the thinking men in the kingdom were of opinion that they had granted too much already.

That necessary expences must have been much more considerable in the late reign than at the present time; that the Royal Family was then grown up, and consequently demanded larger allowances; the journies to the continent, however expedient, were frequent, and at all times expensive; and no body would pretend to say, that magnificence was not as well understood and perhaps better supported than at present; yet the late King not only lived within the limits of the civil list, but left a sum of 170,000l. at his decease, which came to his present Majesty, and had been wholly saved from that revenue.

That as the people are now liable, from the lately established precedent, to be called upon for every occasional deficiency in the civil list, it was therefore necessary to know the expences of the last year, and in what manner the public money had been disposed. That it was neither intended nor wished to limit the crown to a stipend inadequate to its real dignity and greatness. On the contrary, if it appears, upon enquiry, that the money has been expended in the advancement of useful arts, or the encouragement of liberal sciences; if it has been given to relieve the wants of the truly necessitous, or applied to reward the merits of the truly deserving, the promoters of the enquiry will be the first to admire and applaud such noble acts of benevolence, and real magnificence.—But if, on the contrary, it has been lavished upon the profligate; if it has been squandered upon those parricides who are seeking the ruin of the unhappy country, whose generosity poured it forth for nobler purposes; if, while resulting from the virtues, it has been employed to destroy the happiness of the people; it was their duty to remark with severity upon so scandalous a misapplication, and to prevent it, if possible, for the future. That, if it has been properly disposed of, there can be no reason to fear an enquiry into the manner: if improperly, it becomes doubly a duty to make the discovery, because the honour of the crown is not only concerned, but, what is of still greater importance, the prosperity of the nation.

To this it was answered, that if an application had been now made for an additional sum of money to make good any deficiency in the civil list establishment, an enquiry into the causes of it would be natural and justifiable, and it would be but reasonable that the Minister, in such a circumstance, should give satisfaction as to the excess, and shew the reasons why the provision was not sufficient; but that, until such a requisition was made, it would be ultimately improper, disrespectful to the crown, and unjust, to enter into any examination of the royal expences. That a certain specified sum of money is allotted annually for the support of the civil list, and that it is not even pretended, that while the expences are confined within the stipulated sum, there can be the minutest pretence for scrutinizing the disbursements. How, then, is it known that there has been the smallest excess in the course of the past year? how is it known that a shilling of it has been improperly applied? or how is it even known that there may not have been a considerable saving made in the expenditures?

That

That the argument brought on the other side to prove the necessity of an enquiry, because a large sum had been voted last year to supply a deficiency, had quite a different effect from what it was intended for; that as it had been then granted freely, without any enquiry, it was a proof of such confidence in the House, and of its being convinced as well that the demand was reasonable, as that the money would have been properly applied, that it precluded every motive that could be urged for an enquiry at present. That it was now become the popular mode of language to charge, or insinuate, every act to be the effect of corruption, and to arraign the principles, or call in question the independency, of the representatives; but that, however the spreading of these notions may answer the purposes of party, or of particular men, no person, in his sober senses, could imagine, that the H—— of C——s could be guilty of a perfidy to its constituents, or would wantonly lavish away those treasures to destroy, which are notoriously collected to promote, the happiness of the people.

That upon the whole, as the civil list is entirely the revenue of the crown, the crown has a right to dispose of it at will. If future applications are made for additional supplies, the expenditure may then be examined with propriety. That there are, nine years' accounts now lying upon the table, and the account now demanded, even if voted to be brought in, being necessarily made up, not for a quarter day, but for an unusual time, could not possibly be ready for inspection this session. It was therefore hoped that the motion would be rejected, and that all enquiries into the civil list expences should be waved, till future aids were appplied for.

The Minister, who had been called upon to pledge himself that in his time the expenditure of the crown should not exceed its income, refused to engage absolutely; but promised, that he would advise the greatest economy to be used in every department, and that the disbursements should be so cautiously attended to, as not to exceed the stated revenue, except where the utility of the excess would be so evident as to make it certain of approbation. This motion of opposition had the fate of the rest,

Nothing had yet been done in the affairs of the colonies; but a petition having been now presented by the American merchants, setting forth the great losses they sustained, and the fatal effects of the late laws, which, for the purpose of raising a revenue in the colonies, had imposed duties upon goods exported from Great Britain thither; the ministry March 5. thought it proper to bring in a bill for the repeal of so much of the late act, passed in the seventh of his present Majesty, as related to the imposing of a duty on paper, painters' colours, and glass; the tax upon tea, which was laid on by the same act, being still to be continued.

The motives assigned for the bringing in of this bill were the dangerous combinations which these duties had given birth to beyond the Atlantic, and the dissatisfaction they had created at home,

home, among the merchants who traded to the colonies, which made this matter an object of the most serious consideration. It was remarkable, upon this occasion, that the Minister condemned these duties in the gross, and the law by which they were founded, as so absurd and preposterous, that it must astonish every reasonable man how they could have originated in a British legislature; yet, notwithstanding this decisive sentence, proposed a repeal of but a part of the law; had still continued the duty upon tea, lest they should be thought to give way to the American ideas, and to take away the impositions, as having been contrary to the rights of the colonies.

On the other side, it was moved to amend the motion, and that the act which laid on these duties should be totally repealed. To this it was objected, that the colonies, instead of deserving additional instances of tenderness, did not deserve the instance then shewn, for their resolutions became more violent than ever; that their associations, instead of supplicating, proceeded to dictate, and grew at last to such a height of temerity, that administration could not, for its own credit, go as far as it might incline, to gratify their expectations; that was the tax under consideration to be wholly abolished, it would not either excite their gratitude or re-establish their tranquillity: they would set the abolition to the account, not of the goodness, but of the fears of government; and, upon a supposition that we were to be terrified into any concession, they would make fresh demands, and rise in their turbulence, instead of returning to their duty. Experience, fatal experience, has proved this to be their disposition. We repealed the stamp-act to comply with their desires; and what has been the consequence? Has the repeal taught them obedience? Has our lenity inspired them with moderation? On the contrary, that very lenity has encouraged them to insult our authority, to dispute our rights, and to aim at independent government.

Can it then be proper, in such circumstances, while they deny our legal power to tax them, to acquiesce in the argument of illegality, and by the repeal of the whole law to give up that power? Thus, to betray ourselves out of compliment to them, and through a wish of rendering more than justice to America, resign the controuling supremacy of England— By no means: the properest time to exert our right of taxation, is, when the right is refused. To temporize is to yield, and the authority of the mother-country, if it is now unsupported, will, in reality, be relinquished for ever.

It was said, that there was great stress laid, both within and without doors, upon the advantages of our traffic with America, and that the least interruption of the customary intercourse was held up in the most terrifying colours to the kingdom; but that there were the best reasons to believe, that the associations not to buy British goods would speedily destroy themselves; for the Americans, to distress us, would not long persevere

severe in injuring themselves: they are already weary of giving an advanced price for the commodities they are obliged to purchase; and after all the hardships under which they say their commerce groans, it is still obviously their interest not to commence manufacturers. It was allowed to be true, that our exports to America had fallen very much of late; and that in the year 1768 they exceeded those of 1769 by the prodigious sum of 744,000l. they amounting in the former to 2,378,000l. and in the latter only to 1,634,000l. but this great disproportion was accounted for, by supposing, that the non-importation which ensued, being then foreseen by the importers, they prepared for it by laying in a double quantity of goods.

As to the particular duty to be continued upon tea, it was said, that the Americans had no reason to find fault; because when that was laid, another was taken off, which obliged them to pay near a shilling in the pound upon an average, whereas the present only imposes three-pence; therefore, as America in this article feels an ease of nine-pence per pound, she cannot properly accuse us of oppression, especially as every session has of late been productive of material advantages to her, either in bounties, free-ports, or other considerable indulgences.

On the other side, many of the general arguments which we have formerly given upon this subject, both as to the right and the expediency of our levying taxes, were again repeated, and the whole proceedings with regard to America were reiterated, and became the subject of the severest animadversion. The Minister observed, that the taxes were absurd—How came he to support the administration that imposed them? How came he not to have discovered this absurdity earlier? All the world had been sensible of it, and the repeal of the act had been frequently proposed. That repeal was refused, as they were resolved not to relax in favour of America, whilst America denied the right. Has America acknowledged it? Have they yet departed from their combination? The ministers (said they) condemn the concessions of their predecessors; yet they begin themselves by concession; with this only difference, that their's is without grace, benignity, or policy; and that they yield after a vexatious struggle. That every reason given for the repeal of a part of this act must extend not only with equal but with greater force to the whole. That the only cause assigned for not repealing the whole was to preserve the preamble, because it maintains the right of taxing the Americans; an argument totally futile and ridiculous, as there are two positive laws declaratory of that right, and there are many other taxes at this moment existing in exercise of the right; so that, as the mischiefs occasioned by the act in question have at length been acknowledged by the other side, no absurdity can be more glaring than their pretence for making only a partial repeal.

That a partial repeal, instead of producing any benefit to the mother-country, will be a real grievance; a certain expence to ourselves, as well as a source of perpetual discontent to the colonies. By continuing the trifling tax upon tea,

tea, while we take off the duties upon painters' colours, paper, and glass, we keep up the whole establishment of the custom-houses in America, with their long hydra-headed trains of dependants, and yet cut off the very channels through which their voracious appetites are to be glutted. In fact, the tea duty will by no means answer the charge of collecting it, and the deficiencies must naturally be made up out of the coffers of this country; so that this wise measure of a partial repeal is to plunder ourselves, while it oppresses our fellow-subjects, and all for the mere purpose of preserving a paltry preamble, which is utterly useless and unnecessary.

That parliament had plighted its faith to the East India Company, to remove the duty of 25 per cent. from teas, in order that the company might be enabled to sell them upon terms equally low with the Dutch, whose moderation in price constantly obtained a preference at every market. That the 25 per cent. was indeed taken off accordingly, but what was done with one hand was undone by the other: a fresh duty was laid on the commodity, and laid in such a manner, that it must operate as an absolute prohibition to the sale of their teas through every part of the extensive continent of English America, where they were before in general estimation. That, as a proof of this assertion, the teas sent to America in the year 1768 amounted to no less than 132,000l. whereas in 1769 they amounted to no more than 44,000l. and probably this year they will not exceed a quarter of that sum, as the proceedings here are hourly becoming more and more repugnant to the minds of the colonies, and as agreements have been lately entered into for the absolute difuse of that article. In justice therefore to the East-India Company, who have so considerable a stake in the national welfare, and pay so liberally to the support of government, the promise made to them ought to be discharged with the most punctual fidelity: that a discontinuance of the 25 per cent. on their teas was not a discharge of that promise; it was only to be discharged by enabling them to sell upon terms as reasonable as the Dutch.

It was added, that as it seemed probable that a rupture between England and her old enemies was at no great distance, it would be acting wisely in administration to reconcile our domestic divisions, and to regain the confidence of our colonies, before such an event took place. That at the same time that the act in question was diametrically repugnant to all the principles of commerce, there was not the smallest plea of utility to be urged in its defence; that even upon the principle of a spendthrift, if immediate profit was only to be considered, and all other consequences laid by, it had not that sordid recommendation: its whole produce, in its utmost extent, not exceeding 16,000l. a year, which was no more than sufficient to bear the expences that attended it. Let us then dismiss this pitiful *preamble* tax, and make the repeal total, unless the ministers would convince us, that a provision for their new custom-house instruments, beyond the Atlantic, is the only motive for this shameful profusion of the public treasure.

Such were some of the arguments upon

upon this interesting question; and it was remarkable upon this occasion, that several gentlemen in office opposed the motion even as it originally stood. The reasons given for this conduct were chiefly these: of consistency on the part of parliament; the general obstinacy of the Americans; and the violences committed in different parts of that continent, particularly at Boston. The question for the amendment being put, it was rejected by a considerable majority, the numbers being 204 to 142: the original motion was afterwards carried without a division.

In the midst of this season of heat and discussion, which in a greater or lesser degree was extended to every part of the kingdom, a bill of the greatest benefit to the constitution, and importance to the nation, was brought into the House of Commons by a leading member of the opposition; and though chiefly conducted by those adverse to administration, yet was also received by many who had always supported that system, and therefore happily passed into a law. This bill was entitled, *An Act for regulating the proceedings of the House of Commons on controverted elections*, and is generally known by the name of the Grenville Bill, from the late Mr. George Grenville, who brought it into the house. The Minister opposed this bill, with some other persons who used to be very prevalent: in this instance, however, they were unsuccessful.

March 7.

It will be proper to lay before our readers a few of the causes that were assigned for the bringing in, or that made it necessary to pass, such a bill, by which they will be the better enabled to judge of its utility.

Formerly, it was alledged that the trials of contested elections had been always by a select committee chiefly composed of the most learned and experienced of the House; and whilst this custom continued, the litigant parties, and the nation at large, were generally well satisfied with the decisions; but by degrees the committees of elections having been enlarged, and all who came having voices, a shameful partiality prevailed, so that for a remedy, during the time that Mr. Onslow was speaker, the admirable order with which he conducted business induced such as wished for a candid trial to be heard at the bar of the House.

This method of determining contested elections was, however, found to be very defective and faulty in numberless instances, which was principally owing to the extraordinary number of the judges, there not being so numerous a judicature in the world; and these not being bound by any tie, either by the giving of their oath, or their honour, to prevent any secret bias from operating on them, were led by friendship or party connection, contrary to the rules of equity and right, and to the making of the most partial decisions. Such an unlimited discretionary power must always be subject to numberless abuses; but, in this particular instance, the greatness of the number gave a sanction to partiality and injustice; for they not only kept one another in countenance, but the crime was supposed to be divided into so many shares, that while they were encouraged by the force of example to oppose the

sense

sense of their conviction, they looked upon their injustice to be diminished in proportion to their numbers, and each, at length, thought his share of the guilt to be so inconsiderable, as scarcely to cost him a reflection.

By this means, the suffrages of the people were wantonly sported with, and their most important and sacred birth-right, that of chusing their representatives, violated with impunity, and without a possibility of redress. At the same time, the method of trying these questions at the bar made them an insuperable obstruction to all other public business; and especially in the first session of a new parliament, they took up so much time, that it was almost a matter of surprize how the House could attend to any thing else: nor could any thing be more irksome to the members in general than this mode of decision in election matters, as they were continually teazed by applications from the contending parties for their attendance; and though their attendance was all that was avowedly required, the application tacitly included a requisition of their vote and interest: so that whatever part they took, even though they absented themselves, and gave no opinion, which was generally done when there was no immediate connection, still it was a source of dislike, if not of enmity: besides, though custom and example had given a sanction to the acting contrary to conviction, and it was become so general, that there was frequently a kind of real necessity for going along with a particular party or connection in opinion, the mind must, notwithstanding, frequently revolt at it, and regret that there was any occasion for such a necessity. To all which may be added, that as it is always supposed that a minister cannot subsist in this country without a majority to support him in parliament, so in every case of contested election (and such cases might be multiplied in any degree that was thought proper) the representation must finally come into his hands; and instead of the members being returned by the free voice of the people, they would be eventually appointed by administration.

The plan of this bill was excellent, and was laid down upon the constitutional idea of trials by jury. Upon a petition being presented, and a day appointed to hear the merits, and for the petitioners, witnesses, and counsel, to attend, the House on that day is to be counted; and if one hundred members are not present, it is to adjourn until so many are assembled, at which time the names of the members in the House are to be put into six boxes or glasses, to be drawn alternately, and read by the speaker, till forty nine are drawn: the sitting members and petitioners may also nominate one each. Lists of the forty-nine are then to be given to the sitting member, the petitioners, their counsel, agents, &c. who, with the clerk, are to withdraw, and to strike off one alternately, beginning on the part of the petitioners, till the number be reduced to thirteen; who, with the two nominees, are to be sworn a select committee to determine the matter in dispute. This select committee is impowered to send for persons, papers, and records; to examine witnesses, and to determine finally: and the House thereupon

upon is to confirm or alter the return, or issue a new writ for a new election.

An event which took place a few days after, as it renewed all the heat and debate within doors, so it added new force to the ill humour and discontent without, and became a general subject of discussion throughout the kingdom. This was the address, remonstrance, and petition of the livery and corporation of the city of London, in common-hall assembled, to the King; praying for the dissolution of parliament, and the removal of evil ministers. A piece as remarkable for the freedom and boldness of the sentiments which it conveyed, as for the extraordinary terms in which they were expressed; and which had like, in its consequences, to have been productive of the most violent, and perhaps dangerous, measures.

Among other passages in this remonstrance, it was asserted, that the only judge removeable at the pleasure of the crown had been dismissed from his high office for defending in parliament the laws and the constitution. That under the same secret and malign influence, which through each successive administration had defeated every good and suggested every bad intention, the majority of the H―― of C――s had deprived the people of their dearest rights. That the decision on the Middlesex election was a deed more ruinous in its consequences than the levying of ship money by Charles the First, or the dispensing power assumed by James the Second; a deed, which must vitiate all the proceedings of this p――t; for the acts of the legislature itself can no more be valid without a legal H―― of C―― than without a legal Prince upon the throne. That representatives of the people are essential to the making of laws; and there is a time when it is morally demonstrable that men cease to be representatives. That time is now arrived; the present H―― of C――s do not represent the people.

It was said, in the answer, which has been deemed by some to have been uncommonly harsh, that the contents of the remonstrance could not but be considered as disrespectful to Majesty, injurious to the parliament, and irreconcileable to the principles of the constitution. The remonstrance was delivered by the Lord Mayor, who who attended by the sheriffs and other city officers in their formalities, together with a few of the aldermen, and a great body of the common-council; the cavalcade of coaches being attended by a prodigious concourse of people to St. James's, whose shouts of approbation nearly shook the adjoining streets: a circumstance that did not lessen the indignation and animosity of those, who, being thoroughly satisfied with the measures of government themselves, considered the whole proceeding as the effect of faction, riot, and licentiousness.

A motion was made on the following day for an address, that a copy of the remonstrance, as well as of March 15. his Majesty's answer, should be laid before the House. This motion was vigorously opposed. The debate was long and violent, and strong threats were made use of on one side, and as daringly urged to the execution by the other. Upon this occasion, the late Mr. Beckford,

Beckford, who was then Lord Mayor, avowed the part which he had taken in the remonstrance, which he not only justified, but seemed to glory in. He said, it was he who put the question in the court of common-council and common-hall; and, though he had authority to put a negative upon the court of aldermen, in that case he would not do it. He was the great criminal, he said, and stood forth from the rest: the p———t was charged with corruption; the remonstrance said so: the fact was now to be proved, and he was ready to abide the issue. He was seconded by the sheriffs, and one of the city members, who justified the remonstrance, and acknowledged the share they had in it: said, that though they were the persons most immediately interested in any censure that might be passed upon it, they did not want to shelter themselves in concealment; they were ready and willing to enter into the merits of the remonstrance, either then, or at any other time; and were no less satisfied with regard to the justice than the expediency of the measure.

Many other gentlemen who opposed the motion went upon different ground, and several of the most moderate in opposition, who thought the principles right upon which the remonstrance was founded, highly disapproved of the terms in which it was conveyed. It was said, that the House of Commons being accused in the remonstrance, the motion tended to put the criminal in the place of the judge. That it was irregular to call for the remonstrance without calling for the petitions, the neglect of which gave rise to it. That the House was not competent in the case, because it had no power but what it derived from its constituents.

The injustice of censuring any part of the people for the exercise of a right in which they are warranted by the constitution, which is supported by the dictates of reason, the authority of precedents, and the positive declaration of our laws, was largely entered upon. Our sole consideration is simply, whether the people have or have not a right to petition; whether they are or are not legally authorized to lay their grievances before the throne, wherever they imagine themselves oppressed; and whether all prosecutions at law for the exercise of this privilege is not expressly prohibited in that palladium of public liberty, the Bill of Rights.

Among the many blessings arising to the kingdom from the revolution, the privilege of complaining to the throne, asserted, not acquired at that time, without the danger of punishment, is one of the noblest; the people in this respect are the sole judges of the necessity for petitioning.—It is as much a part of their right as it is a part of the royal prerogative to assemble parliaments, or to exercise any other power warranted by the constitution. As this is truly the case, with what shadow of propriety, with what colour of reason, do we arrogate a liberty of examining their proceedings? with what countenance do we fly in the face of the laws, and confidently assert that they shall be punished for what the laws peremptorily declare that they shall not even undergo a prosecution? Even admitting, on the present question, that the people have been mistaken,

that

that they have erred, that there are in reality no grievances to complain of, and that the manner of their remonstrance is as disrespectful as the matter of it is unjust, still, as the laws positively pronounce their right of petitioning, and their exemption from consequent prosecution, we are precluded from every enquiry into their conduct. They may be indiscreet, they may be warm, they may be turbulent; but let us not be rash, unwarrantable, and arbitrary. Let us not, while we are so nicely attentive to the errors of others, rush into palpable illegalities ourselves. Our power is great; but the power of the laws is much greater.

If they were to credit report, and they had nothing else now before them for any part of the proceeding, the answer to the remonstrance from the throne did not so much condemn any indecency in the remonstrance as it seemed to strike at the right of petitioning itself, and supposed that the granting such petitions would be ruinous to the constitution, which went not to the mode but to the substance of all such petitions: this evidently left the subject without any hope of redress; and consequently the right of petitioning for a dissolution of parliament, recognized by the House, becomes in effect a dead letter.

It was observed, that one of the capital errors of James the Second's reign was his punishment of the seven Bishops for petitioning. — Similar causes must always produce similar effects. The people may bear injury and oppression for a long time; but they will prefer annihilation to chains. The present measures shew, that the principle upon which the rights of the people were violated in the Middlesex election is to be supported in all its consequences, and carried to its utmost extent. The same spirit which violated the freedom of election now invades the declaration and bill of rights, and threatens to punish the subject for exercising a privilege hitherto undisputed of petitioning the crown. The grievances of the people are aggravated by insults; their complaints not merely disregarded, but checked by authority; and every one of those acts against which they remonstrated confirmed in the final resort by a decisive approbation. In such circumstances, what are they to do? or rather, what is not to be dreaded from their desperation?

The inexpediency, and perhaps danger, of still increasing the public ill-humour and discontent, by taking violent measures against so respectable a body as the corporation and citizens of London, was particularly insisted upon, and the apprehended consequences painted in the strongest colours. It was said, that great city had, upon numberless occasions, and in the most trying circumstances, proved herself the true friend to freedom, the undaunted supporter of justice, and the invincible champion of our glorious constitution.—A measure of this nature would at any time be extremely injudicious; but in a period like the present, was big with a thousand dangers. The metropolis is composed of the wealthiest citizens in the British dominions; their number is great, their influence prodigious, and their proceedings are, in general, the rules of action for all the inferior corporations in the kingdom. To brand them, therefore, at any time with a mark of obloquy, logy, would be to render an extensive share of the people dissatisfied either with the equity or moderation of government. It is to make that very part of the community, to which in the hour of public exigence we fly for assistance, from which we supplicate our loans, and obtain the essential sinews of political strength, our declared and confirmed enemies; and, out of a blind resentment to them, to commit a manifest outrage upon ourselves.

This would at any time be the consequence of offending the city of London: but in the present case the evils are infinitely more complicated and alarming. To censure the citizens for what nine-tenths of the whole empire consider as an act of the most exalted virtue, is to rouze the indignation of every honest subject in the British empire. It is to aggravate the fury of a discontent, already too pregnant with danger, and to open a scene of horror that will not close, perhaps, but on the total overthrow of the constitution. How, then, is it possible, that while the minds of the people are agitated almost to madness, any gentlemen can persevere in a continued succession of inflammatory measures, and hourly pour oil on the flame of that discord, which already blazes but too fiercely in this unfortunate country?

It was said on the other side, that though the right of petitioning was undoubted, law, reason, and necessity, required that the petitioners should be under the restriction of certain salutary limitations; that they should be influenced by truth, and guided by decency; that the matter of the petitions should be real, and the manner respectful to the sovereign. That, without these restrictions, the most treasonable matter, the most virulent libel upon the crown, or the constitution, might be covered by the specious name of petition; while Majesty, under that pretence, was liable to be hourly insulted, and obliged to submit to the most groundless censures, and to suffer the most shameful reproaches. That under this licence our foreign foes, or our domestic enemies, may at any time stir up a multitude to complain of grievances that never existed, and to make requisitions of the most extraordinary or most dangerous tendency. That they may humbly beseech the Prince to abdicate, and pray that he may be graciously pleased to transfer, his sceptre to the expelled family; or, if the sovereign should happen to catch their prejudices, and thereby acquire a considerable share of popularity, they may perhaps wish, in the headlong vehemence of their zeal, to see him seated on an arbitrary throne; and in a constitutional remonstrance, like the present object of debate, patriotically desire him not only to dissolve but to annihilate his parliaments.

Thus our constitution may be totally destroyed, because there is no law to punish, no authority to restrain, and no power whatever of withholding the licentiousness of petitioners; yet such must be the consequences in a state like our's, if every thing in the form of a petition was sanctified from the examination of the laws, and, on account of its form, to be admitted as a constitutional act of propriety.

It was said that moderation had been much talked of, and recommended; but that the numberless indignities which the House had of late experienced proceeded from an excess of lenity and moderation; that because they would not punish, the enemies of order supposed that they dared not: hence in proportion to lenity on the one hand, licentiousness grew audacious on the other. That they were hourly abused in the public prints, which formerly trembled at the bare apprehension of their resentment, and the press teemed with the grossest libels on their determinations. Thus sedition was at length rendered so courageous, that the livery of London, with the chief magistrate at their head, had now the temerity not only to solicit their dissolution, but to declare, in direct positive terms, that they are not the representatives of the people. That moderation in such circumstances was out of the question; that in times of infinitely more danger than the present, instead of supposing that the maintenance of its own dignity was a dangerous measure, that House looked upon a spirited exertion of its authority to be not only the most noble but the most politic conduct it could pursue. That if they submit to the present daring insult, and crouch under an outrage of so dangerous a nature, not only their own dignity will be at an end, but the constitution destroyed, the whole body of the people deprived at once of their representatives, and every act which has been passed since the time of election must be utterly without force.

That the sole question now was, whether they were a parliament, or not; if they were, what time could be so particularly necessary to shew their authority as the present, when the livery of London had confidently declared at the throne that they were not.. That if they were a House, they must prove themselves respectable; if they were not, they had no right to deliberate: their assembling must have been illegal. That much had been said about the danger of irritating the people; but these gentlemen did not recollect, that the people of England were at present comprized within them walls, and until their legal dissolution could have no real existence as a body any where without them: that the nation had chosen them as its agents for a term of years; that during that term they were virtually the nation. If they betrayed their trust, or proved unworthy of farther confidence, the people may discard them indignantly at the expiration of the term; but while they sat there, they were bound by and answerable for their acts.

That with regard to what had been thrown out about the seven Bishops in James the Second's reign, the case was not at all applicable. Their petition was entirely upon the point of religion, was couched in terms the most respectful to the throne, and delivered with as much privacy as possible to the sovereign; whereas the remonstrance in question denies the authority of parliament, insults the throne, and is delivered with all the circumstances of tumultuous parade, that can be calculated to terrify the minds of the peaceable, and inflame the passions of every misguided member of the community.

After long debates, the motion was carried by a majority of considerably more than two to one. The papers being laid before the House, and the journals and other records examined, fresh debates arose upon a motion being made for

for an address to his Majesty, and another for the concurrence of the House of Lords to the address. These motions met with great opposition, and very long debates ensued. The legality of petitioning for a dissolution of parliament was much discussed; and it was insisted, that it could not be illegal to recommend the doing of a legal act.

The censure contained in this address, they alledged, was conformable neither to the equity nor dignity of parliament; not conformable to equity, because no body of men could be competent to pass a censure on those who accused them; and that if those who presented the remonstrance were not punishable at common law, they were not criminal, and if not criminal ought not to be censured: the address was not conformable to the dignity of parliament, because it imputed an heavy crime, and proposed no sort of punishment; which was to shew a weak and feminine resentment, altogether unworthy of their situation, and miserably short of the arguments that were used to support that measure.

To the application for the concurrence of the Lords, it was objected, that such an act would preclude them from being judges, if any impeachment should afterwards come before them. Both the motions were however carried by a prodigious majority; and the address having received the concurrence of the Lords, at a conference, was accordingly jointly presented.

23d.

Great indignation was expressed in the address at the contents of the remonstrance, which was charged with being expressed in terms contrary to that grateful and affectionate respect due to his Majesty; with aspersing and calumniating one of the branches of the legislature, and expresly denying the legality of the present parliament, and the validity of its proceedings.

The presenting of petitions to the throne was asserted to have been at all times an undoubted right, the free enjoyment of which was restored at the revolution and continued since; and it was with the deepest concern that the exercise of so important and valuable a right was now seen so grosly perverted, by being applied to the purpose not of preserving, but of overturning the constitution; and of propagating doctrines, which, if generally adopted, must be fatal to the peace of the kingdom, and which tend to the subversion of all lawful authority. Thanks were returned for the answer made to the remonstrance, which was represented as a fresh proof of a determined perseverance in adhering to the principles of the constitution. Some censures were thrown out against the insidious suggestions of ill-designing men, and the unjustifiable excesses of a few misguided persons, who were in this instance seduced from their duty; and the confidence placed in the people in general was applauded and justified.

CHAP.

HISTORY OF EUROPE.

CHAP. IX.

State of affairs in Ireland, at the meeting of the new parliament. Augmentation bill passed. Privy-Council money bill rejected. Supplies raised in the usual manner. Lord Lieutenant's speech and protest; parliament prorogued. Consequences thereof. Motion made here for the Irish papers; rejected. Motion, and resolutions, relative to American affairs; over-ruled. Bill for reversing the adjudications relative to the Middlesex election. Debates on the answer to the remonstrance of the city of London. Resolutions proposed in the House of Lords relative to the colonies. King's speech. Parliament breaks up.

SOME late transactions in Ireland having thrown that country into a state of general disorder and discontent, occasioned a proposal on this side for a parliamentary enquiry into the causes and nature of them. We have before seen the sanguine hopes and expectations that were formed in that kingdom upon the passing of the octennial bill, and the degree of popularity which the present deputy had gained upon the strength of that favourite measure.

The great expences which attended the general election had somewhat however abated their satisfaction. The persons who held power for many years there thought the constant and unusual residence of the Lord Lieutenant was intended solely for the destruction of their power and influence. A strong opposition was prepared. But things still wore a placid outward form; and nothing appeared on the meeting of the new parliament but what promised harmony and good humour. The Houses seemed to vie with each other in their expressions of duty and gratitude to the throne, and of respect and regard to the Lord Lieutenant. This season of sunshine was rightly judged to be the proper time for the making of another experiment to carry into execution the bill for the augmentation of the forces, which had failed of success at the breaking up of the last parliament.

Oct. 17 1769.

A message was accordingly sent, recommending this measure in the strongest terms from the throne, as a matter which his Majesty had extremely at heart, not only as necessary for the honour of the crown, but for the peace and security of that kingdom. This message likewise contained a promise from the throne, that, if the augmentation took place, a number of effective troops, not less than 12,000 men, officers included, should at all times, except in cases of invasion or rebellion in Great Britain, be kept within the kingdom for its better defence.

The proposed augmentation was from 12,000, the former establishment, to 15,245 men, officers included: the strictest œconomy was promised to be observed in this service. The augmentation was to be made by an increase of the common men, without any additional corps or greater number of officers: and it was farther proposed, that, as the several general officers who now composed the military staff in that country should happen to die or be provided for, the number should be reduced, and consist of no more afterwards than a commander in chief, and five general officers. This promise was the more usefully applied, as the staff upon that military establishment was excessively loaded, and amounted nearly to 30,000l. a year, and besides being encumbered with an unnecessary number of general officers, most of these were absentees, who did no duty; and the number resident in the kingdom were scarcely sufficient to hold boards, and to go through the other necessary parts of the service.

A good many persevered in the opposition by which this augmentation had been lost in the former parliament. They said, that such a requisition seemed unusual and unnecessary in a time of profound peace. That the military establishment in that kingdom had been long and justly complained of, for being conducted upon a most expensive, ineffective, and ruinous system. The nation was already loaded with the enormous annual expence of near half a million sterling, for the support of a nominal body of troops of 12,000 men, of which almost one-fourth were commissioned and non-commissioned officers; the number of regiments having been gradually increased from 25 to 42, with a prodigious increase of expence, without any addition to the number of effective men, or of efficacy to the military establishment. Notwithstanding this vast expence, which should at least have effectually provided for the security of the nation, what with the regiments that were employed abroad upon garrison duty, and the great deficiencies in the number at home, the internal force scarcely amounted to 8,000 men.

Such a misapplication of the public money (it was said by those who opposed the measure) called therefore much more loudly for enquiry and redress than for a new grant. The public expences in that country, loaded besides with a debt, for their circumstances heavy, and incumbered with pensions to the amount of near 100,000l. annually, were already an intolerable burden to the people, and much more than they can afford, while the discouragements under which their commerce labours are continued. Such however was the favourable disposition of the majority at this time to government, or such their sense of the necessity of the measure towards the common defence, that notwithstanding a strong opposition within, and its being rather unpopular without doors, the Augmentation Bill was carried through, and passed in a very few days.

This apparent union of sentiments, good humour, and harmony, between the governor and governed was soon interrupted. A money-bill, which had originated and been framed in the Privy-council, was brought to the House of Commons; a measure, which, though in strictness legal, had been always a matter of violent altercation at the beginning of every parliament, at which time only it was used, in order to keep up a right claimed by the council under an act of Henry the VIIth, called Poyning's law, by which no bills are to pass in Ireland which have not been first certified from the Privy-council there,

there. It was asserted, that besides the antient practice, the very last parliament had passed such a bill, as well as the long parliament which had preceded it: that it was not a bill of any serious supply, but a mere matter of form; and that by the original law, no difference was made in the power of the council between money-bills and others. But by the opposition, now grown to a majority, it was represented as so flagrant a violation of their most essential and inherent rights, that it could not possibly be admitted without a total sacrifice of them. It was evident, they said, that if the granting of money as a free gift for the support of government was not vested in the Commons, they could no longer be considered as representatives of the people; and that the power of conferring favours on the crown, and obtaining benefits for the latter, being thus totally at an end, they could no longer act as a medium to preserve the connection, or support the confidence between them. That the framers of a money-bill are to be considered as the givers of the money; and that the reserving only an affirmative or negative to the Commons would be reducing them simply to the state of registers of the edicts of the Privy-council. That the Privy-council represent no man, nor body of men, and, consequently, cannot tax the people; that they themselves are represented in parliament, where all taxes must originate, and where they are equally bound with all others, and by the same authority.

Nov. 21. The bill was accordingly rejected; and in the vote for the rejection, the reason assigned was, its not having originated in the House of Commons. This objection did not impede the national supply; another money-bill was passed in the usual form, in the most liberal manner, and with the greatest unanimity.

The cordiality and unanimity shewn upon this occasion, by which they trusted solely to the honour of government, and provided fully for all its necessities, before they proceeded to any part of the national business, greatly, as they said, enhanced the merit of the act. The rejected bill provided only for the expenditure of three months, the present for the expences of two years, and the supply granted amounted to 2,168,681 l.; no inconsiderable sum, if we consider the circumstances of the country as they are commonly represented.

These two great points of government being obtained, in the augmentation of the army and the grant of the supplies, it was then thought the proper time to shew a resentment of the rejection of the money-bill; an affront which had been (prudently, as was said by one side; meanly and fraudulently by the other) dissembled, until government was got on solid ground.

The Lord Lieutenant, in a speech which he Dec. 26. made to both Houses, after the greatest acknowledgments for the liberality with which they had so effectually supported government, suddenly changed his style, and condemned, in the strongest terms, the rejection of the Privy-Council money-bill in the House of Commons, which he represented to be intrenching upon the rights of the crown, and entered a formal protest in the House of Lords

[*f*] 4 against

against that act of the House of Commons; and to preclude all debate upon the subject, or the possibility of passing resolutions against this measure, as suddenly prorogued the parliament to a long day.

Some notice of this design having been received before it was put in execution, a motion had been made in the House of Lords a few days before, that directions should be given to the Speaker not to suffer any protest of any persons whatsoever to be entered in the journals, who was not a Lord of Parliament, and a Member of that House, and which was not relative to some business that had been previously before the House, and wherein the protesting Lord had taken part with the minority, either in person or by proxy. This question being over-ruled by a great majority, a strong protest was entered by the minority, which attempted to shew that the only two cases in point, which were those of the Earl of Strafford, and Lord Sidney, were either transacted in such times, or attended with such circumstances, as totally voided their being drawn into precedent, and that every such act was contrary to the rights and derogatory to the dignity of the Peers. The House of Commons, before their breaking up, forbid the Lord Lieutenant's speech from being entered on their journals.

In this manner were the sanguine hopes blasted which had been formed upon the first meeting of the first limited parliament. No business had passed but a compliance with the requisitions of government; all the national business was undone; the temporary laws which are renewed or altered at every sessions, whether relative to agriculture, to trade, to the supplying of the capital with provisions, to the preservation of the public security, or the support of the public charities, were all expired. The consternation, distress, and discontent that followed, were great, and the whole kingdom was in a state of universal confusion and disorder.

This being a matter of too much importance to escape the notice of opposition in the British parliament, a motion was accordingly made, that the instructions to the Lord Lieutenant of that kingdom, by which he prorogued the parliament, might be laid before the House. This motion was not only seconded, but proposed to be extended, by moving that all the papers relative to the Irish Augmentation Bill should be also laid before them.

In the debates upon this subject, many parts of the late conduct of government in the administration of the affairs of that country underwent the severest strictures. It was said, that, having cajoled the parliament of Ireland out of a large sum of money, for the purposes of a military augmentation in a time of profound peace, and thought it perfectly constitutional then to receive it from the representatives of the people, the money was no sooner received, than they abridged the right of the Commons in granting it, and insisted that the power of originating money-bills belonged entirely to the Privy-Council; that, admitting for a moment their own principle, government had not a right to take the money, if parliament had not a right to give it, and they should either refuse the supply, or have acqui-

acquiesced in the legality of the grant. That the more the conduct of administration in this respect is examined, the more it will be found perplexed, inconsistent, and tyrannical: the Deputy, having obtained the money, returns thanks to the two Houses for their liberality; and after he has politely complimented their munificence, he enters a protest upon the journals of the Lords, and informs the whole world that they were not authorized to exert it.

That the laws of Great Britain had been violated, and its dignity sacrificed, to deceive our fellow-subjects in the sister nation out of their property; for that the promise which the chief governor had made to the Irish House of Commons, to induce them to consent to the augmentation, viz. that 12,000 men shall be constantly stationed among them, was not only giving up the prerogative of the crown, but was also directly repugnant to two English statutes, by which the *disposition* as well as the command of all the land and sea forces are made inherent in the crown; but that, by this promise, the spirit and obvious meaning of these laws is defeated, and the disposal of the 12,000 troops is not virtually in the sovereign, but actually in the Irish parliament. That in whatever light this matter was considered, whether as diminishing the royal prerogative for the purpose of artifice, or defeating the design of English acts of parliament for the shameful end of deluding the fellow-subjects in Ireland out of a supply, in either case it was a matter that merited the strictest enquiry.

It was contended, that the law called Poyning's is no authority for this violent procedure. That law gives to the Privy-Council the privilege of certifying parliamentary bills to this kingdom; but the privilege of certifying by no means includes the just authority of originating.

The conduct of a ministerial officer, who had declared in the Irish House of Commons that the Privy-Council money bill was a fine for the renewal of parliament, was severely animadverted upon. It was said, that this was an avowal of oppression and despotism in the extreme: that it was at once laying by the mask, and confidently telling the subject, that he shall not possess his absolute right, unless he pays the minister for indulging him with it.

Upon the whole, it was said, that they were called upon by every motive to enquire into the causes of the present deplorable state of their sister and neighbouring island; and, as they were endowed with a coercive power over ministers in every part of the British dominions, to give that redress to the people of Ireland which their own parliament could not grant; and that they were even led by their interest to pursue those measures which were at the same time evidently dictated by their justice.

On the other side, the necessity of preserving a due subordination in every part of the empire was enlarged upon; that a controuling power must be lodged somewhere; that the vast body of the British territories cannot subsist without a head; and that it is fitter for the various

various dependencies, which we have protected for so long a series of years, to obey our laws, than to think of dictating to their protectors. That it is amusing as well as surprising to see the very measures which are taken for maintaining the authority of this kingdom pointed out by the opposition as a degradation of its honour, and a sacrifice of the royal prerogative.

That the reason of the parliamentary prorogation was the solicitude of the very ministers who are now reviled, to preserve the dependance of Ireland upon this kingdom. That the Irish House of Commons entered into resolutions contrary to Poyning's Law; into resolutions which consequently shook the foundation of our authority over Ireland, and therefore the parliament was prorogued; and that the manner of the prorogation was warranted no less by precedent than justified by reason. That the prorogation was unavoidable, and the Minister would highly merit an impeachment, if he had not urged the expediency and necessity of it.

That the charges of violating the laws of England, and relinquishing the royal prerogative, by the promise given to the Irish parliament, was equally groundless. That the crown has, certainly, a right of disposing of the land and sea forces as it pleases; and the crown, therefore, stations 12,000 men constantly in Ireland, agreeable to this right: yet the exercise of the right, and the actual execution of the English laws, is now said to be repugnant to two English acts of parliament, and a relinquishment of the royal prerogative.

Great complaint having been made, that, among the other laws of public utility which had expired in Ireland in consequence of the late prorogation, the tax upon hawkers and pedlars, which was appropriated to the society for the building and maintaining of Protestant Charter Schools, had also ceased, by which that excellent institution would be totally and irretrievably ruined, the Minister, upon this occasion, pledged himself, that any loss resulting to the incorporated society from that measure should be made good from the privy purse. The question being at length put, the motion was rejected by a majority of more than two to one.

The state of affairs in America, had not yet been entered into, though they had been particularly recommended by the speech from the throne, and seemed to be one of the great objects which required the utmost attention and maturest consideration of parliament. The account which had been received of the late alarming riot in Boston, between the soldiers and town's people, and the consequence that followed, of the two regiments that were stationed in the barracks there being under a compulsatory necessity of retiring from the town, and going to Castle William, without any order from government for so doing, seemed to make this matter so urgent, as not to admit of any delay, before some conclusive measures were taken upon it; and the time pressed the more immediately, as a speedy prorogation was the natural consequence of the season.

The ministry, however, were very shy and tender upon this head, and

and seemed to wish rather to trust to a temporizing conduct with the colonies, and the hope of profiting by their disunion or necessity, than to lay open a series of discordant measures, which, however the separate parts might be defended by the immediate plea of expediency at the time, could bear no critical test of enquiry, when compared and examined upon the whole.

However this might have been, the principle upon which American affairs were suffered hitherto to lie dormant, notwithstanding the recommendation from the throne, it was by no means satisfactory to those who had opposed every part of the conduct of administration with regard to America.

May 8th. A motion was accordingly made for an address to the throne, setting forth the disputes that had arisen among the several governors and commanders, in almost all the colonies, since the appointment of a commander in chief; that the colonies have been for some time, and are still, from this and other causes, in a state of the greatest disorder and confusion; that the people of America complain of the establishment of an army there, as setting up a military government over the civil; and therefore praying that all these matters may be reconsidered, and such measures taken as would replace things there upon a constitutional footing.

This motion was introduced by observing, that, in the present critical situation of affairs, they were expressly called upon to enquire how the ministers here, no less than their officers there, have managed so unfortunately, as to kindle the present flame of dissension between the mother-country and her colonies. That, in fulfilling this duty, they must not only consider the matter of fact, but the right of things; not only the turbulence of the Americans, but the cause of that turbulence; and not only the power of the crown, but the equity with which that power had been exercised.

This motion had the usual fate of those made by the minority. It did not, however, prevent other steps upon the same subject. A set of resolutions were proposed, by which the whole ministerial system for several years past, with relation to America, was taken into consideration. All the contradictory instructions to the governors were canvassed, and their inconsistency and ill effects pointed out. Taxes imposed—repealed—imposed again, and repealed again. Assemblies dissolved—called again; and suffered to sit and proceed to business without disavowing or discountenancing the measures which had procured the former dissolution. Promises made to the assemblies, that certain duties should be repealed, and taxes taken off, which were unwarrantable, of dangerous consequence, and a high breach of privilege; and that it was equally derogatory from the honour of the crown, and the freedom of parliamentary deliberations, to have its faith pledged to the performance of such promises. Troops sent—driven out—violence and submission alternately made use of.—Treasons charged, adopted by parliament, not proved, nor attempted to be proved; or, if existing, not attempted to be detected and punished; an insult on the dignity

of

of parliament, and tending to bring either a reflection on its wisdom and justice, or to encourage treasons, and treasonable practices, by not carrying into execution the measures recommended by parliament.

All these resolutions, which may be seen in the Votes of the House of Commons, were rejected by a great majority; nor did administration enter much into a discussion or refutation of the matter or charges which they contained. The general arguments of the turbulence of the Americans, the disposition of the colonies to disclaim all dependance on the mother-country, the necessity of supporting its authority and the dignity of government, and the right of the crown to station the troops in any part of the dominions, together with the necessity of their being employed to support the laws, where the people were in little less than a state of rebellion, were those principally made use of. There was nothing pleasant in the view of the conduct of American affairs; and administration aimed at getting rid of the discussion as soon as possible, and put a negative on, or postponed by previous questions, all these resolutions.

About the same time, a bill was brought into the House of Lords by the Earl of Chatham, and read once, for reversing the adjudications of the House of Commons, whereby John Wilkes, Esq. has been judged incapable of being elected a member to serve in the present parliament; and the freeholders of the county of Middlesex have been deprived of one of their legal representatives.

The history of the transactions alluded to, and some of the strongest arguments against them, were included in the preamble of this bill, which, besides the general arguments that we have already seen upon this subject, was supported upon the new ground, that the mode of informality before objected to upon this question, of its not being properly before the House, could no longer have any weight, as it was now introduced by a bill.

Much law and many precedents were discussed, in the course of the debates upon this bill. Those who opposed the bill founded their objections chiefly upon the competency, the exclusive and inherent right of the House of Commons in its adjudications in all matters of that nature; and that their own late resolution had already decided the point, and confirmed the final right of determination to the other House. That, however, exclusive of that resolution, such a measure would be illegal and unprecedented. That the whole time of both Houses had been nearly taken up during the session with this subject; and that, as every determination had been against it, nothing could be more extraordinary than to find it again agitated.

Precedents were brought on the other side, to shew that such an interference had been practised by both Houses; and the expediency and even necessity of it, in some cases, was urged upon the same principles which we have before taken notice of in the debates upon the motion relative to this subject. The question was repeatedly called for, and being at length put, the bill was rejected by a great majority. A protest, signed by 33 Lords, upon the same ground as the former,

mer, was the consequence of this rejection.

A motion was made a few days after by the same nobleman, for a resolution to declare, that the advice which induced the late answer to be given from the throne to the remonstrance, &c. from the city of London is of a most dangerous tendency, as thereby the exercise of the clearest rights of the subject to petition the throne for redress of grievances, to complain of the violation of the freedom of election, to pray a dissolution of parliament, to point out mal-practices in administration, and to urge the removal of evil ministers, has, under pretence of reproving certain parts of the said remonstrance and petition, by the generality of one compendious word, *Contents*, been indiscriminately checked with reprimand; and the afflicted citizens of London have heard from the throne itself, that the contents of their humble address, remonstrance, and petition, laying their complaints and injuries at the feet of their sovereign, as father of his people, is considered as disrespectful to himself, injurious to his parliament, and irreconcileable to the principles of the constitution.

To this motion it was objected, that both Houses had already addressed the throne with their thanks, for the very answer which it was now proposed to them to condemn; that such a proceeding would not only be repugnant to order, but repugnant to common sense; that the answer given to the city upon this occasion was conformable to the answers given in several former reigns, which were specified, in similar cases; and that no cause could now be assigned in support of this measure, which did not equally subsist at the time that this question had been agitated before.

On the other side it was said, that as infallibility was not the lot of human nature, so it was no imputation on their understanding, nor degradation of dignity, to acknowledge an error: the constitution did not suppose their resolutions perfect; and experience continually shewed, that acts which were planned with the utmost circumspection in one session were absolutely necessary to be repealed in the next; yet this alteration in opinion is never considered as injurious either to the accuracy of their judgments, or to the probity of their hearts. That it had been advanced with triumph, that the answer in question was similar to the answers given in the reigns of the Stuarts, to similar applications of their subjects for redress of grievances: but are these the princes that are to be held up as patterns to posterity? And are there no precedents suited to the present times to be found but in their reigns? There was a precedent at hand adapted to the present question, which, however, it had not been thought proper to recollect; a precedent worthy of the man who established it. This was the case of the Kentish petition; in compliance with which, King William dissolved the parliament, to let the nation see he had no double game to play; and to shew, that, as he had no interest separate from the interest of his subjects, all parliaments were alike acceptable to him that were agreeable to the wishes of the kingdom. But, at present, government seems delighted in opposing the wishes of the people. Ireland, after its money is taken

away,

away, is deprived of its parliament, though the nation is unanimous for its sitting; and England, where the general voice calls out for a dissolution, is to be bleft, against its will, by a continuance of its representatives.

The Ministers were remarkably silent in the course of this day's debate; and though repeatedly called upon, and urged by the most provoking taunts, to vindicate their measures, abstained from all discussion, and repeatedly called for the question. They said in general, that all these bills, addresses, and resolutions, were substantially the same which the House had frequently well considered and rejected; and that it would be only encouraging a disposition to endless cavils to enter into debate upon the same matter, as often as ingenious people could give it a new shape. Many points, not immediately connected with the subject, were introduced; many charges made, and a secret and undue influence much complained of: the question was over-ruled by about the usual majority.

A motion for an address to the throne, for a dissolution of the present parliament, was made a few days after, and brought on long debates, in which all the public grievances and discontents were reiterated, and the great necessity, in the present situation of foreign and domestic affairs, of restoring harmony between the people and their representatives, and their having a parliament in whom they could place a thorough confidence, was enforced. This met with the same fate as the former.

May 18. Near the close of the session, a number of resolutions relative to the American affairs were proposed by the Duke of Richmond, nearly similar to those which we took notice of in the House of Commons, but upon a larger scale, and in which a greater number of objects of enquiry were particularized; all of which led to the heaviest censures, as well upon the measures prescribed at home, as the conduct pursued in the execution of them in the colonies. These resolutions were introduced by severe observations on the conduct of administration, who, having particularly recommended the American affairs to their attention in the speech from the throne, and acknowledged them to be of the utmost importance, yet the session has been spent, and this great business been totally neglected; not so much as a motion has been made of it: on the contrary, when the repeal of the frivolous and trifling revenue acts was brought before the House, every enquiry was artfully evaded that could lead to the smallest knowledge of the subject.

The nobleman who presided at the head of the American department being particularly involved in these censures, it was naturally expected that he would have entered largely into the business, and have endeavoured to explain and vindicate his own conduct. This, however, was not the case; and with an acknowledged conviction that he was particularly called upon, declined entering into any discussion of that nature; but confined himself to the present expediency of leaving this business to the consideration of the ministry, who might form some plan during the recess for accommodating these matters. The Ministers began to be

HISTORY OF EUROPE. [95*

be sensible that matters of this nature had been recommended to parliament rather prematurely, before any regular scheme had been formed. They were resolved, therefore, to avoid all retrospect: and accordingly the Lord in question of himself moved for an adjournment.

This could not fail to draw out many cutting observations and severe censures from the other side. It was observed, that though American affairs had, for these two years, been a standing subject of recommendation from the throne, yet every measure relative to them had originated in parliament, while the Ministers shrunk back appalled, at every breath that seemed to whisper an enquiry into them; that in all that time they had formed no plan, nor acted upon any system, but seemed to stumble upon wretched expediencies and absurdities, as they accidently arose in their way, while every new measure led to greater disorder and confusion than the former. That for the person who was particularly accused to evade an enquiry into his own conduct, by moving for an adjournment, was a manifest violation and mockery of justice, and such a prostitution of parliament as deserved a heavier punishment than any censure could convey.

The ministry refused to answer, or to take any notice of the proposed resolutions: the question was repeatedly called for an adjournment, and being at length put, was carried as usual.

Thus ended this session of parliament; the proro- May 19. gation having taken place next day. In the speech from the throne, the temper which had conducted all the proceedings of parliament was greatly approved; and the happiest effects expected from the firmness, as well as the moderation, which they had manifested in the very critical circumstances which attended their late deliberations. An assurance was given, that, in all events, it should be made the first and constant object of care to watch over the interests, and to preserve undiminished the rights of the people. And it was earnestly recommended to exert in their respective counties the same zeal and prudence which they had shewn in parliament for promoting the peace and welfare of the kingdom: that nothing can be so favourable to the wishes of those who look with jealousy on the strength and prosperity of this country as the prevalence of animosities and dissensions amongst ourselves; and to make it, therefore, their care to discountenance every attempt to infuse groundless suspicions and discontent into the minds of their fellow-subjects.

CHRO-

96*

CHRONICLE.

JANUARY.

5th. THE Cornish petition was presented to his Majesty by the High-sheriff, attended by Sir John St. Aubyn, and Sir John Molesworth, Barts. knights of the shire, Mr. Serj. Glynn, Thomas Pitt, Christopher Harris, and William Ellis, Esqrs.

The same day the Yorkshire, Worcestershire, Somersetshire, Northumberland, Cornwall, Newcastle, and Bristol petitions, were presented to his Majesty, at St. James's, together with a protest of the corporation of Liverpool, against the petition procured from that city, and all others.

8th. Wm. Williams, of Landovery, mercer, together with twelve other persons, disguised in waggoners' frocks, and armed with pistols, swords, cutlasses, and cased tucks, came to the dwelling house of William Powell, of Glanareth, in the county of Carmarthen, Esq. and knocked at the back door. Upon its being opened, William Williams, and two of the other villains, rushed into the parlour (whilst others stood centry) where Mr. Powell was sitting with three of his neighbours, and immediately stabbed him in nine different parts of his body, till his bowels came out, cut off his nose, and almost one of his hands. The people who were with him were so frightened, that they made no resistance, but immediately ran out: the assassins then retreated, without attempting to hurt any other person. The following day several persons followed their footsteps in the snow, and took particular notice of the impression and size of their shoes. The villains avoided all houses and paths, and went over bogs, morasses, and mountains, for about four computed miles, till they came to the house of one Charles David Morgan; but being tracked no farther, he was taken up, and brought before the coroner, where he gave a fair account of himself; but one of his shoes being taken off, and agreeing in size with one of the impressions taken notice of in the snow, he was committed on suspicion, and soon after confessed the fact, and discovered six of the accomplices; whereupon Sir William Mansel, Bart. and other gentlemen, immediately armed, and went with their servants in pursuit, and took five of them. One of the villains confessed that they were thirteen in number; and they were all hired by Williams to murder Powell, and not to rob the house. This Williams, in August, 1768, went with Mr. Powell's wife, and took her and her children from the boarding-school to London; and Mr. Powell was obliged to apply to the court of King's-Bench for a ha-

beas

beas corpus to get at his children; and by the recommendation of the court, allowed her 100l. a year for a feparate maintenance. Williams laid feveral fchemes in order to take away Mr. Powell's life, and attempted to fhoot him feveral times. The villains met, on the 7th inftant, in Charles David Morgan's houfe, and continued there till they went the following evening to murder Mr. Powell. One of the villains was difpatched by Williams that very night to inform Mr. Powell's brother with what was done, and ordering him to come and take poffeffion of the eftate. But Mr. Powell having made a will, and appointed guardians over his children, their fcheme was defeated.

About fix o'clock this morning, a moft dreadful fire broke out at Meffrs Johnfon and Payne, bookfellers, in Paternofter-Row, which totally confumed the faid houfe, Mr. Cock's, printer, Mrs. Bateman's, and Mr. Upton's, an auctioneer, (late the Caftle Tavern) backward; in which laft-mentioned houfe was kept the bibles, common-prayers, &c. belonging to the proprietors of the Oxford prefs, to the amount of 10,000l. and upward, together with a number of books belonging to Mr. Crowder, bookfeller, adjoining, whofe houfe is alfo damaged, as were many others.

9th. This day his Majefty went to the Houfe of Peers, and having opened the parliament with the ufual folemnity, made a moft gracious fpeech, from the throne, to both Houfes..For the fpeech, &c. fee the article of State Papers.

10th. Petitions from the following places were prefented to his Majefty at St. James's, viz. from Devonfhire, by Sir Richard Warwick Bamfylde, Bart. and John Parker, Efq. members for the county; from Derbyfhire, by Lord George Cavendifh, member for the county; from Gloucefterfhire, by Sir William Codrington, Bart.; from Wiltfhire, by Edward Popham, and Thomas Goddard, Efqrs. members for that county; from Herefordfhire, by Thomas Foley, jun. Efq. member for the county.

The houfe of two wealthy old men, brothers, on the fea-coaft in Somerfetfhire, was broke open and robbed of 1200l.

At the Guild of Merchants in Dublin the following refolutions were agreed to:

Refolved unanimoufly, That it is not only the undoubted right, but highly becoming, and of public utility, for all members of a free ftate, and more efpecially bodies corporate, to attend to, and occafionally declare, their fenfe of public meafures.

Refolved unanimoufly, That it is the duty of the conftituents to inftruct their reprefentatives in every matter of national concern.

Refolved, That the late fudden prorogation of the parliament of this kingdom was untimely, in as much as it has impeded the progrefs of many new and prevented the revival of many old laws, for the benefit, advantage, and better fecurity of the internal police, commerce, trade, and manufactures of this kingdom.

Refolved, That this corporation do inftruct their reprefentatives in parliament on the prefent calamitous fituation of this city and kingdom; and that fuch expedients as may be judged neceffary to prevent the like diftrefs hereafter be

fug-suggested to them for their future government.

11th. About 7 o'clock in the evening, Newbottle-abbey, the seat of the Most Hon. the Marquis of Lothian, was discovered to be on fire. It made its first appearance in the north-east wing, toward the parks, but had got to such a height before it was discovered, that there was no possibility of saving all that part of the house. The fire burnt with prodigious violence till about two in the morning, when its fury was stopped by a strong party-wall, which gave an opportunity of saving part of the house. The family were in the house at the time: they staid till about two, when my Lord and Lady came to town. The loss on this occasion must be very great. The fine pictures in the great gallery were all pulled down, and tossed over the windows, and suffered great damage; the library, the rich furniture of the principal apartments, and indeed almost every thing else, either suffered the same fate, or were consumed by the fire.

During the fire, the following melancholy accident happened. One of the millers of Newbottle-mills, on hearing the bell, ran to give his assistance. His wife, who was valetudinary, having gone to bed, he locked the door of his house after him. On his return he found her dead, lying in the chimney. It would appear she had got up; that her fright had thrown her into a fit, to which she was often subject; and that unfortunately she had fallen into the fire, where she was burnt to death.

17th. The Duke of Beaufort resigned his post of master of the horse to the Queen.

The Earl of Coventry has resigned his post of one of the lords of the bed-chamber to his Majesty.

The Marquis of Granby resigned all his places, except his regiment of blues.

The Duke of Manchester resigned his employment as one of the lords of the bed-chamber.

The Earl of Huntingdon his place of groom of the stole.

The Right Hon. James Grenville resigned his post of one of the vice-treasurers of Ireland.

About five o'clock yesterday, the Lord Chancellor received a message from the secretary of state's office, desiring, in his Majesty's name, that he would deliver up the seals that evening at seven o'clock: his Lordship accordingly, attended with a proper regalia, waited on his Majesty at the Queen's palace, and delivered them into his own hands.

Mr. Dunning, Solicitor-general to his Majesty, resigned that employment, but continues to officiate till another is appointed.

The petition of the freemen and principal inhabitants of Liverpool was presented to his Majesty by their worthy members Sir William Meredith, and Richard Pennant, Esq. This petition is said to be signed by near 1000 freemen, &c.; the protest of the corporation by not more than 450.

A Russian man of war of 80 guns was brought into Portsmouth dock, to be cut down to a third rate, as at present she is so crank she cannot carry sail.

The seals were this day delivered in council, by his Majesty, to the Right Hon. Charles Yorke, Esq. who was also created Lord Morden.

The

The Right Hon. Sir John Cust resigned his office of Speaker of the House of Commons, on account of his ill state of health.

20th. The sessions ended at the Old-Bailey, when eleven prisoners received sentence of death: twenty-five were ordered to be transported for seven years, and one for fourteen years; two branded in the hand, two to be privately whipped, and eighteen discharged by proclamation.

This evening, at five o'clock, died the Right Hon. Charles Yorke, Lord Morden, Baron of Morden, in the county of Cambridge, and Lord Chancellor of Great Britain, in the 48th year of his age. He was son to the late Lord Chancellor, the Earl of Hardwicke; and had enjoyed his place for so short a time, that the patent for his peerage could not have been made out. His eminent abilities are well known. It is said his Lordship's death was occasioned by the bursting of a blood-vessel.

The society for encouragement of arts, manufactures, and commerce, gave a gold medal, engraved by Mr. Pingo, to Mr. James English, for the cultivation of rhubarb in England.

21st. Sir Sidney Stafford Smythe, the Hon. Henry Bathurst, and Sir Richard Aston, were this day, by his Majesty in council, appointed commissioners for the custody of the Great Seal, and received the Great Seal accordingly, after having taken the usual oaths.

22d. By a letter from York, we are informed, that this night, about eleven, a large ball of luminous matter, in appearance a ball of fire, was observed in the S. E. part of the horizon of Malton, which appeared to fall towards the earth, in an oblique direction, for above half a minute, burning as it fell, and had in appearance a long fiery tail. During that time, the hemisphere was illuminated to such a degree, that you might have perceived a pin on the ground. After this phænomenon had disappeared, an uncommon loud rumbling noise was heard, much like the falling of a building, or a clap of thunder; but as the horizon was at that time remarkably clear, it was the general opinion there that it was an earthquake, as several windows were shaken. The aurora borealis appeared remarkably luminous all the evening.

About the same time, this phænomenon was seen by several persons in that city, who also heard a rumbling noise, and felt a tremor of the earth.

Lord Mansfield, who had, by virtue of a commission under the Great Seal, been appointed to supply the place of Lord Chancellor, or Lord Keeper, in the House of Peers, took his place accordingly.

A fire, occasioned by the negligence of the stable-keeper, broke out in the stables of his Grace the Duke of Norfolk, at Workfop Manor, in Nottinghamshire, which entirely consumed the same. Two horses were so burned, that they are since dead, and the rest were with great difficulty preserved.

23d. His Majesty came to the House of Peers; and being seated on the throne, commanded Sir Francis Molyneux, Gentleman Usher of the Black Rod, to let the Commons know, it is his Majesty's pleasure they attend him immediately. Who being come, Sir Fletcher Norton was presented, as their

their Speaker, to his Majesty, who was graciously pleased to approve their choice.

24th. A great mortality prevails among the Russian sailors at Portsmouth, where many of them have been on board four months, and now begin to sicken so fast, that it has been determined to land them by turns: and Hilsey barracks are allowed them for that purpose. It is said, that no less than ten die daily.

26th. About half an hour after ten, a fire broke out in the flax warehouse belonging to Mr. Thomas Steele, on Bennet's-hill, near Paul's-wharf, opposite the place where the dreadful fire happened, at the oil warehouse in Thames-street, a few months ago. The flames were so rapid, that it entirely consumed the warehouse, with several dwelling houses between that and St. Peter's-hill; St. Peter's Church also caught fire several times, but was preserved by the activity of the firemen; and the whole fire was got under by one o'clock, there being luckily plenty of water, and great assistance instantly ready. As few persons were in bed when the fire broke out, happily also no lives were lost.

28th. His Grace the Duke of Grafton resigned his post of first lord of the treasury, to the astonishment of the whole nation. The cause is variously reported: some say, to avoid being responsible for measures he might not wholly approve; others, that a great personage was displeased with the hasty dismission of Lord C———n, before another fit person was thought on to succeed him. Be that as it may, Lord North was immediately appointed in his room; and his Grace continues steady in support of the measures of government.

The river-Rhone, in France, swelled higher than has been known in the memory of man.

29th. His Majesty went to the House of Peers, attended by his Grace the Duke of Ancaster, and Lord Bruce, and gave the royal assent to the bills which were prepared.

Dr. Musgrave was heard before the H. of C———ns relative to the information he had to produce on the score of the late peace; and what he then delivered was voted in the highest degree frivolous and unworthy of credit.

This night it lightened so surprizingly in this city, that the oldest persons living do not remember their ever having seen it equalled before, even in the hottest season.

31st. This day a petition from the city of Coventry was presented to his Majesty.

An earthquake, in the island of St. Maura, in Greece, has lately destroyed 700 houses: most of the inhabitants were buried under the ruins.

From St. Christopher's we learn, that, on the 24th of October, seven members of the General Assembly of that island having, on some debate, quitted the house in an abrupt and indecent manner, were ordered into the custody of the serjeant at arms: that, on their refusal to make submission to the house, they were committed to the common goal, where they were confined; five days after which they were expelled the House, and discharged from their imprisonment: that, on their coming out of prison, a great concourse of people assembled

bled in the pasture, where a large bonfire was made, in which they burnt two effigies: and that on the 17th of November came on the election of four members for the parish of St. George's, Basseterre, in the room of the expelled members, when the same gentlemen were re-elected without opposition, to the great joy of the freeholders, who gave an elegant entertainment on the occasion.

The General Assembly of North Carolina was dissolved three days after its meeting in November last, by his Excellency William Tryon, Esq. the Governor.

The distemper among the horses rages with great violence; in the neighbourhood of Camberwell, Peckham, Dulwich, &c. no less than 50 have lately died. The distemper among the horned cattle has only been heard of in and near Westminster.

Died lately, at Leeds, in Yorkshire, one Mary Denton, who lived in the alms-houses there: her employment used to be to carry out meat for the butchers, for which she received one half-penny a turn: after her death there were found, sewed up in her cloaths, one hundred Queen Anne's guineas.

At Tregony, in Cornwall, Mr. Richardson, aged 102.

In Cornwall, Mr. George Williams, aged 109.

In Essex-Street, White-Friars, Mrs. Jackson, aged upwards of 100.

At Rainford, in Lancashire, Joshua Bibby, in the 105th year of his age.

FEBRUARY.

2d. The following noble Lords have solemnly declared and pledged themselves to the public, that they will persevere in availing themselves, as far as in them lies, of every right, and every power, with which the constitution has armed them for the good of the whole, in order to obtain full relief for the injured electors of Great Britain, and full security, for the future, against the late most dangerous usurpation upon the rights of the people; which, by sapping the fundamental principles of this government, threatens its total dissolution.

Dukes
Richmond
Manchester
Devonshire
Northumberland
Bolton.

Marquis
Rockingham.

Earls
Thanet
Aylesford
Suffolk and Berkshire
Huntingdon
Chatham
Coventry
Radnor
Scarborough
Stamford
Temple
Dartmouth
Berkeley
Effingham
Stafford
Albemarle
Fitzwilliam
Abingdon
Tankerville.

Viscount
Torrington.

Bishops
John Bangor
Fred. Exon.

Barons
Lyttelton
Grosvenor
Abergavenny
Audley
Wycombe
Camden
Chedworth
Craven
Archer
Romney
Trevor
Sondes
Boyle
King
Fortescue
Monson
Ponsonby
Milton
Hyde
                47
Teller,
Earl of Bucks 1
—
48
Last

CHRONICLE.

Last week two transports arrived at Spithead from Petersburg, with near 700 Russian soldiers on board. We expect three more transports daily from the above place with 800 or 900 men more. We hear the Russians are to be encamped on the South-Sea common. There are in Hasler's hospital upwards of 400 sick.

3d. A great riot happened this day at Chirk, in Denbighshire, to oppose the execution of the militia act in that county. Near 300 countrymen, armed with clubs and pitchforks, assembled at the meeting of the Justices, and drove away the constables, who were about to deliver in their lists; and after insulting the gentlemen present, and breaking the windows of the house where they met, dispersed without farther damage.

7th. The Supporters of the Bill of Rights met at the London Tavern, when Serjeant Glynn, the chairman, acquainted the society, that a remittance of 1500l. had been paid into the hands of Sir Thomas Hankey and Co. bankers in Fenchurch-street, for the use of the society, by order of the assembly of South Carolina, who had voted that sum.

Her Grace the Dutchess of Northumberland resigned her office as one of the ladies of the bedchamber to the Queen. And the same day her place was supplied by the Countess of Holderness.

This morning the parish church of Fordingbridge, Hants, was much damaged by a tornado, which entirely stripped the lead off the north side of the roof of the middle aisle, from the tower even to the west door,: the gust of wind was so furious, that the sheets of lead, weighing in the whole upwards of two tons, were many of them rent like paper, and all carried away with great velocity entirely over the said roof, and, falling on the opposite side, carried with it several yards of the parapet wall.

One of the patriotic sheriffs declared in a great assembly, that he should refuse to pay the land-tax in a county that was not represented; and it is said he will certainly try the consequences of abiding by the resolution.

9th. A most splendid entertainment was given at the Mansion-house, by the Right Hon. the Lord Mayor, at which a numerous and brilliant assembly of the first quality in the kingdom were present. The ball in the evening was opened by the Duke of Devonshire and the Lady Mayoress. The dancing continued till twelve, when a very grand supper was served up in the Egyptian Hall, with a fine desert, and a curious piece of confectionary. After supper, part of the company went into the ballroom, and continued dancing till near five o'clock on Saturday morning; at which time the whole company departed, highly satisfied with the elegancy of the entertainment, the order and regularity with which it was conducted, and the polite behaviour of the Lord Mayor and Lady Mayoress. There were present the Duke and Dutchess of Portland, the Duke and Dutchess of Richmond, the Duke and Dutchess of Bolton, the Duke and Dutchess of Queensbury, the Duke and Dutchess of Manchester, the Duke and Dutchess of Northumberland, Earl Temple, Earl of Suffolk, Lord Camden, Lord Lyttelton, General Paoli, the Russian ambassador, Lord George

ANNUAL REGISTER, 1770.

George Sackville, and many other noblemen; also Mr. Justice Willes, Sir George Savile, Edmund Burke, Esq. and several other members of the House of Commons, and their ladies. The following aldermen were also present: Sir Charles Asgill, Sir William Stephenson, Sir Robert Kite, Samuel Turner, Esq. Brass Crosby, Esq. Thomas Halifax, Esq. James Townsend, Esq. and his lady, John Sawbridge, Esq. and his lady, and a great number of merchants with their ladies. It is thought there never was so numerous and brilliant a company at the Mansion-house before.

12th. On Thursday evening a remarkable cause was tried before Sir J. Eardly Wilmot, in the Court of Common Pleas at Guildhall, where a travelling dealer in silks was plaintiff, and a riding custom-house officer, who lives at Dartford, in Kent, was defendant. The action was brought for the defendant (ex officio) stopping the plaintiff on the Greenwich road, as he was coming to London, and taking his horse, saddle, bridle, a pair of bags, containing 12 pieces of handkerchiefs, and a large parcel, containing 27 pieces of silk; all which the officer took along with him to Dartford before he examined, and sent the poor man to town on foot. On examination, the goods appeared to have been manufactured in Spitalfields. On the trial it was proved that the officer had used the plaintiff very ill, and had threatened to blow his brains out.—After a full hearing on both sides, the jury brought in a verdict for the plaintiff, with full value for all his silks, horse, saddle, &c. and 23l. for the assault; in all 180l. with full costs of suit.

There was the fullest House of Commons that has been known. No less than 451 members were present. By a list in the Court Calendar, 192 hold places under the government; and it is affirmed upon the best authority, that the number of public offices is now double what it was in 1740.

14th. Five of the eleven capital convicts were this day executed at Tyburn; the other six were reprieved.

After the execution a great disturbance happened, in consequence of a hearse being placed near the gallows, in order to receive the body of Dunk, the soldier, which some of his comrades imagining was sent there by the surgeons, they knocked down the undertaker, and, after beating his men, drove off with the body along the New Road, attended by a prodigious concourse of people, till they came to the end of Gray's-Inn-lane, where they buried the corpse, after first breaking its legs and arms, and throwing a large quantity of unslacked lime into the coffin and the grave.

On Wednesday last came on, at Westminster, a cause wherein a maid servant was plaintiff, and her mistress defendant: the action was brought for her mistress ill-treating her; when, after a trial of three hours, the jury brought in a verdict of 50l. damages.

Last week, at a Guild holden at Berwick, before the worshipful John Burn, Esq. Mayor, it was ordered, that the freedom of that corporation should immediately be presented to the present Lord Mayor of the city of London, and to Sir Joseph Mawbey, Bart.

Colonel Wedderburn, brother of Counsellor Wedderburn, is appointed

CHRONICLE.

pointed commander in chief of the Hon. the East-India Company's forces at Bengal.

At a committee for building Black Friars bridge, on casting up the receipts of the toll for the last quarter, it amounted to the sum of 4000l. per ann. And as it is highly probable that it will be very considerably increased on the passage being completed, there is a fair prospect that in a few years the whole debt on the bridge, which is about 47,000l. will be discharged, and the passage made free.

16th. His Majesty went to the House of Peers, and gave the royal assent to the following bills:

The bill for granting an aid to his Majesty, by a land-tax to be raised in Great Britain, for the service of the present year.

The bill to continue the duties on malt, mum, cider, and perry, for the service of the present year.

The bill to punish mutiny and desertion, and for the better payment of the army and their quarters.

The bill for regulating his Majesty's marine forces when on shore.

The bill to indemnify persons, acting by order of council, for preventing the spreading of the contagious distemper amongst the horned cattle.

The bill to enable Lord George Sackville, and his issue male, to take and use the surname of Germain, pursuant to the will of Lady Elizabeth Germain, deceased.

And also to several naturalization bills.

The unfortunate man who was murdered by his wife on Thursday last, in Pierpole-lane, had his skull fractured by her in three places, with a board on which he cut out his work. He was a clog strapmaker, and had lived very unhappily with the woman for some time: she often threatened to murder him, and on the night the horrid act was committed, abused him in a violent manner. It is supposed she killed him in his sleep, as the neighbours heard no noise after eleven o'clock, and she waked two of them about four o'clock, with a complaint that her poor husband was dying; on which they went to his assistance, and, finding him a most shocking spectacle, immediately charged her with the fact, which, after some time, she confessed.

18th. On Thursday night five men went on board the Mary and Isabella West Indiaman, Capt. Pearson, in the river, and were detected stealing tobacco, &c. The crew attacked them, struck one of the thieves with a handspike on the head, and killed him on the spot; another, in jumping to the boat, fell into the Thames, and was drowned; the other three tumbled the wounded man into the boat, but, finding him dead, threw him over; they then rowed for the stairs at Tower Wharf, where they attempted to land, but the centinel being called to, he fired at them, which obliged them to row across, and land on the Borough side, from whence they made their escape. The dead body of the fellow, who was killed with the handspike, was soon after taken up and landed on Tower Wharf: he appears to be between 70 and 80 years of age, and had on a sailor's jacket.

On Thursday the money collected at Liverpool for the relief of of the unhappy sufferers by the late dreadful fire at Antigua, amounting to 346l. 2s. 6d. was shipped on board the Favourite, Capt. Kevish, bound for the above island.

On Friday an indictment, which had been removed by *certiorari* into the Court of King's Bench, came on to be heard before Justice Aston. The cause of action was a nuisance of a new complexion. A person in the occupation of his trade, which is that of a feather-bed maker, was indicted for disturbing and annoying his neighbours in beating the feathers in the street within the parish of St. Mary-le-bone. Several witnesses were examined, and it appeared plainly to the court that this trade, and many others similar to it, ought not to be exercised within the streets of this metropolis, and that they are nuisances, if so occupied.

A most alarming thunder-storm happened at St. Keven, in Cornwall, during the time of divine service. The lightning shivered the steeple, and threw it upon the body of the church: the whole congregation was struck with astonishment: many had their cloaths singed by the fierceness of the lightning, and some their watches melted.

19th. A number of journeymen hat-dyers assembled in Southwark, and took one of their brother journeymen into custody, whom they charged with working over hours without any more pay, and for taking under price. They obliged him to mount an ass, and ride through all the parts of the Borough where hatters are employed, and also many streets in the city: a label was carried upon a pole before him, denoting his offence; and a number of boys attended with shovels, playing the rough music. At all shops they came to in their way of business, they obliged the men to strike, in order to have their wages raised.

In a great political society, the question relative to the expulsion and incapacity of a certain popular gentleman was finally determined. The numbers on the last division were 237 to 159, majority 78; so that the expulsion and the incapacity of that gentleman to be elected during the present p———t are now declared to be legal and constitutional.

The House of Lords have refused the petition of Mungo Campbell, now prisoner in the Tolbooth of Edinburgh, for the murder of Lord Eglington, praying for a writ of appeal with regard to the court by which he should be tried.

21st. Yesterday came on in the Court of Common Pleas, Westminster, a remarkable trial, when an ensign in the army was plaintiff, and a colonel was defendant: the action was brought for false imprisonment in Pensacola, for giving his opinion in a court-martial agreeable to his conscience: when after several learned arguments on both sides, a verdict was given for the plaintiff with 300l. damages.

23d. Matthew Kennedy and Patrick Kennedy, who. with Michael M'Mahon and John Evans, were indicted for the wilful murder of John Bigby, a watchman, on Westminster-bridge: after a trial of eight hours, the two unhappy brothers

thers were convicted, and received judgment to be executed on Monday, and afterwards diffected.

Several experienced ferjeants of the marines at Portfmouth have for fome time paft been employed by Admiral Elpbinfton in teaching the Ruffian foldiers on board the fleet the Englifh marine exercife, and manœuvres of fmall arms, hand-grenadoes, &c. aloft and in the tops; a difcipline with which they were heretofore totally unacquainted.

24th. This morning a remarkable caufe came on in the Court of King's-bench, Guildhall, before Lord Chief Juftice Wilmot; wherein Mr. Duval, a builder, near Mary-le-bone, was plaintiff, and Mr. Clough, mafter of the Swan alehoufe, in Salifbury-court, Fleet-ftreet, defendant. The plaintiff, in June laft, loft a bank-note of 100l. in Fleet-ftreet, and by properly tracing it, difcovered that the defendant had changed it at the Bank for a note of 60l. and the reft in cafh; and upon the plaintiff's applying to the defendant for his property, he refufed to reftore it, alledging that a perfon had dined at his houfe, whofe bill came to half a crown, and having no cafh for payment, offered him the bank-note, which he ran with to the Bank to get changed, and when he came back the man was gone. On the trial it appeared the bank-note had been found by two lads, who ftick bills about the city, &c., and they carried it to the defendant, who gave them a guinea each; but foon after, underftanding the value of the note, they threatened the defendant, till they got eighty pounds from him at different times. Every circumftance appeared fo clear on the whole, that the defendant was caft in full damages and coft.

New York, Dec. 18. At a meeting of the General Affembly here, Mr. Speaker laid before the Houfe a printed paper, which was delivered to him by the Mayor of this city, directed *to the betrayed Inhabitants of New York*, containing many reflections upon the conduct of the Affembly, and exciting the inhabitants to convene, and inflaming them to oppofe the proceedings of the Houfe: upon confidering this paper, the Affembly the next day voted it a falfe, feditious, and infamous libel, and offered a reward of one hundred pounds to any perfon who fhould difcover the author; and likewife fifty pounds for difcovering the writer of a hand-bill, which contained many fcandalous reflections on the conduct, honour, and dignity of the Houfe.

Bofton, Jan. 9. On Thurfday laft, his Honour the Lieutenant-Governor was pleafed to iffue a proclamation farther to prorogue the general court, which was to have met here on the 10th inftant, to Wednefday the 14th day of March next, in confequence of his Majefty's exprefs command received by the laft packet arrived at New York.

26th. This day came on the trial of Mungo Campbell before the Court of Jufticiary at Edinburgh, for the murder of Lord Eglington, when the libel being found relevant, the prifoner was found guilty.

This day a refpite came to Newgate, during his Majefty's pleafure,

for

for Matthew Kennedy, and Patrick Kennedy; who were to have been executed this morning.

28th. A motion was made in the House of Peers for increasing the navy, on account of the preparations carrying on by the neighbouring powers; but it passed in the negative by a great majority. It has since been confidently reported, that the court of Madrid has now actually in readiness three powerful fleets, one already in the West-Indies, with 4,000 regular troops at New Orleans; the other two ready to act as occasion requires. And it is likewise certain, that the French have a considerable force in the islands of Bourbon, ready to support any attempt they may resolve upon in the East Indies.

A great number of officers and subalterns presented a petition to his Majesty, praying an augmentation of their pay, and were graciously received.

The right of election of a minister to the living of Clerkenwell was this day adjudged by the Barons of the Exchequer to be in the inhabitants paying scot and lot.

This day came on the trial of Sir Francis Bernard, Bart. at the Cockpit, Whitehall. The articles preferred against him were, in the name of the General Assembly of the province of which he was lately Governor; but as that Assembly has never been suffered to sit since, they could not be supported, and the Governor was honourably cleared.

This day Mungo Campbell put an end to his life, by hanging himself in the Tolbooth at Edinburgh.

The sessions ended at the Old-Bailey. At this session seven prisoners, including the two for murder, received judgment of death. Thirty-nine were ordered to be transported for seven years, four were branded in the hand, six privately whipped, and sixteen delivered upon proclamation.

They write from Jamaica of a shocking murder lately committed in that island. The wife and overseer of Mr. Watts, a planter, having conspired together, entered the husband's bed-chamber in December last, while he was asleep, and the wife having attempted to cut his throat with a bill, her attempt failed, but the overseer finished him at two blows. They afterwards cloathed him, and carried him into the woods, where he was found the next day, brought home, and buried; and it being given out that he had been murdered by robbers, the widow cloathed herself in mourning, and made the most sorrowful lamentation. The overseer, however, in going to Kingston, lost his pocket-book, in which were some memorandums that led to a discovery; and there being some negroes privy to the murder, he was committed to prison, tried, and executed, and the widow is soon to share the same fate.

A very remarkable phænomenon is related in an article from Poland, where, in a shower of rain that happened at Stolpe, about the latter end of December, many living insects fell with it, some of them never seen before in that neighbourhood.

The French papers speak of a remarkable claim made by a saddler at Paris upon the title and arms of the famous Count d'Estaing, who in the late war was a prisoner

in

in England, and went from his parole, and afterwards commanded a squadron in the West Indies. This saddler it seems had been bred up at the Foundling Hospital; to the governors of which the old Count his father directed a letter before his death, the contents of which authenticated the birth and legitimacy of a child particularly described under their care; with this addition, that the mother was of a mean family; that he, the Count, had married her in his youth; had this child by her, but had afterwards prevailed on her to relinquish her connections; that he had since married a lady of family and fortune; and that it was necessary, in order to conceal his first marriage, to commit the child by the first privately to the care of the public; that upon the evidence of this letter a suit had been commenced; and that it was in litigation in one of their courts of law.

Extract of a Letter from Geneva, dated February 16.

Yesterday, at three, a very dangerous sedition broke out in this city. The design of the persons concerned in it was to murder the council, and afterwards the burgesses, and then to make themselves masters of the city. In half an hour more all had been lost. Two or three hundred had already begun to fire, but did no other mischief than slightly wounding a few. The alarm was then given, and the general beat. The garrison were in a moment under arms, and four of the seditious laid dead on the spot. Their main body, which exceeded two thousand, all active, bold persons, was at Fouro. We expect to-morrow six hundred men from Nyon, which, it is hoped, will put a final stop to this unhappy affair.

Married lately, Mr. Josiah Whitaker, aged 94, to Miss Sally Berrybridge, of Peckham, aged 16: Mr. Whitaker is possessed of a fortune of 50,000l.

Died, at Hollingbury, in Essex, Mr. William Salmon, aged 84; he had married ten wives, the last of whom survives.

At Leigh, near Liverpool, Elkin Brandwood, aged 102.

In New-street, St. Giles, John M'Donald, aged 108.

At Great Bavington, in Northumberland, Eleanor Lawson, widow of John Lawson, aged 105.

MARCH.

1st. This day came on at Doctors' Commons the so much talked-of cause between Lord and Lady Grosvenor, for the *admissibility* of a libel, which by the lady's council was admitted, and thereby an end was put to all farther explanations. An order was at the same time minuted, that letters, written messages, and other informations, relative to the affairs of Lord and Lady Grosvenor, should on no account be communicated by copies or otherwise, to any person except the immediate agents, previous to the determination of the cause in litigation.

A memorial was presented from the Livery of London to the Court of Common Council, desiring the concur-

concurrence of that court in a request to the Lord Mayor to assemble a Common Hall.

In a field adjoining to Kew, two gentlemen, encouraged by the Society of Arts and Sciences, have erected a building for the hatching of various eggs after the Ægyptian manner: their first attempt did not succeed, which they attributed to the dampness of the building. They have often succeeded in small quantities by the heat of dung: but this invention is intended to produce some millions annually.

5th. The Merchants trading to America attended the House of Commons, the motion for the repeal of the acts of the revenue affecting the Colonies being that day taken into consideration: the duties on glass, red lead, painters' colours, paper, &c. are to be remitted, but that of tea continued.

The four members for the city of London, the two Sheriffs, the city Remembrancer, Sir Henry Banks, and Mr. Deputy Ellis, went to the House of Commons, with a petition against the bill for levying a farther duty upon carriages, &c.

Extract of a Letter from Edinburgh.

A curious question arose with regard to the disposal of the body of Mungo Campbell. His sentence was to be hanged on the 11th of April, and his body thereafter to be given to Dr. Monro for dissection. Now as he had effectually prevented the first part of the sentence, how could that part of it consequent to the 11th of April take place? It was argued, that his having committed suicide was a sufficient cause for his body being at the disposal of the magistrates of Edinburgh, and sent to Surgeons-hall; but as we have no coroner in Scotland, the suicide could not be ascertained. The result is, his relations are allowed to inter his body.

6th. This day there was a very numerous Common Hall of the Livery of London, pursuant to a precept issued for that purpose.

Letters from Paris, of the 26th of last month, inform us, that a council of state has been held, which authorises the Duke de Choiseul, the prime minister and secretary of state, to assure the foreign courts by letter, that all the engagements and contracts made by the King with foreigners shall be faithfully acquitted by M. Magon de Balue, who will be provided with the necessary funds for this purpose.

7th. At a meeting of a great number of the electors of Westminster, at the Standard Tavern, in Leicester-fields, it was moved to follow the example of London, by presenting a petition to his Majesty; and a committee of twelve was appointed to draw it up.

Some villains attempted to break into the house of Mrs. Goldthorp, in Northumberland-street, in the Strand; but the family being alarmed, Mrs. Goldthorp herself had the courage to fire at the rogues, wounded one, who was afterwards secured by the watchman, but the rest made their escape. House-breaking in London was never known to be so frequent, seldom a night passing but some house or other is entered and robbed. The gang, as is said, consists fists of a numerous set of desperate young fellows, among whom are many smiths, joiners, carpenters, cabinet-makers, and builders, against whom no locks or bars can be a security.

One William Matthias was executed, pursuant to his sentence, at Lincoln assizes, for poisoning Francis, William, and Elizabeth Cook, and Elizabeth Emerson, an infant, by mixing arsenic with their butter.

This morning, between ten and eleven o'clock, a most dreadful fire broke out at Sturtly, half a mile from Bugden, in Huntingdonshire. In less than an hour three capital farm-houses, with their out-houses, stacks of corn, &c. were entirely consumed. The fire was raging at the same time in distant parts of the place There was a great want of water, and no fire-engine nearer than St. Neot's (four miles); and before it could arrive, the whole of that beautiful village, with most of the granaries, stacks, barns, &c. were reduced to ashes. This dreadful fire was occasioned by the carelessness of a servant girl heating an oven.

Yesterday all the ships bills put up at the New England Coffee-house for several parts of North America, were taken down and burnt.

The Talbot East Indiaman, Sir Charles Hudson, now clearing at Blackwall, was so distressed for fresh provisions in her passage home, as to be obliged to kill every thing eatable on board; among other things, a beautiful male and female buffaloe, from Madagascar, which Sir Charles intended as a present for Mr. Ashby, a Northamptonshire gentleman.

9th. This day died at his house in Great Portland-street, William Guthrie, Esq. a gentleman well known for his numerous literary productions.

11th. About three in the morning, the Chester mail was robbed between London and Islington, by a single highwayman, who has since been detected in negociating a bill, the payment of which had been stopped on the first news of the mail being robbed. He is a single man, had just taken a grocer's shop, and was soon to have been married.

Her Majesty dropped one of her ear-rings at court, and though the most diligent search was instantly made for it, the search proved fruitless: a foreign gentleman of distinction was seen to stoop, but it was, he said, to pick up his sleeve-button.

Friday morning a dreadful fire broke out in the hospital of Bethlehem, and burnt so furiously, that the firemen were obliged to break through the roof to release the unhappy people in the upper part of the house.

Exeter, March 8. Last Monday evening, between the hours of eight and nine, the grand mail, from London, was stopped near the five-mile-stone, between Honiton and Exeter, and robbed of the Ottery bag, containing letters, and about 3s. 6d. in money, by two footpads, one of whom presented a pistol to the boy's breast, while the other took away the bag. They were both tall men, one of whom wore a light-coloured frock, and the other a short jacket of a lightish colour. They likewise took from the boy two shillings and his hat.

The

14th. The Lord Mayor of London, properly attended, waited upon his Majesty, with an address, remonstrance, and petition.

It was debated, whether the exportation of wheat should be permitted; but rejected by a great majority.

16th. This day his Majesty went to the House of Peers, and gave the royal assent to the following bills:

The bill to continue an act for allowing the free exportation of tallow, hogs' lard, and grease, for a farther limited time.

A bill for better regulating and employing the poor in the parish of St. Paul Shadwell.

The bill for better regulating the navigation of the river Trent, from Wilden Ferry, in the county of Derby, to Gainsborough, in Lincolnshire.

And also to several road, inclosure, and naturalization bills.

The following state of Mr. Wilkes's affairs was published by the society for supporting the Bill of Rights:

London Tavern, March 13, 1770.

Supporters of the Bill of Rights.

William Tooke, Esq. in the chair.

An account of Mr. Wilkes's affairs having been this day laid before the society, it appeared that (since the establishment thereof on February 20, 1769) there have been paid by the voluntary subscriptions of this society,

	l.	s.	d.
To Mr. Wilkes, for his support	1000	0	0
To ditto, for his first fine	500	0	0
To the expences of his three last elections for Middlesex	1704	19	10
To compromise 1434 l. 15s. 8d. of his debts	4198	13	2
	7403	13	0
Debts of Mr. Wilkes remaining to be compromised	5445	16	2
And a second fine to be paid of	500	0	0
	5945	16	2

No money has hitherto been applied by this society to any other purpose whatever.

The cash now remaining in the treasurer's hands is 776 l. 6s. 2d.

N. B. 7149 l. 6s. 2d. of Mr. Wilkes's debts appear to have been incurred by his having been security for other persons.

19th. On Wednesday morning last, about one o'clock, some desperate persons broke into Aylesbury gaol (which they effected by forcing a passage through the roof), and released Berry and Turner, two prisoners capitally convicted at the last assize there.

Two *Resolutions* were passed upon the presentation of the city address: The first, That the declaring the present —— to be illegal, and that its acts are not valid, is unwarrantable, and manifestly tends to disturb the peace of the kingdom. The second, That to convey such unwarrantable doctrines under the specious pretence of a petition, is a gross and manifest abuse of the undoubted right of the subject to petition the crown.

Extract of a letter from Portsmouth.

We have an account spread about here, from on board his Majesty's

CHRONICLE.

jesty's sloop Merlin, concerning the death of the late Captain O'Hara, that he was not murdered by the Moors, as was reported, but that he died a natural death. The account is as follows:—When he arrived at the place, the Captain sailed up the river in a tender provided for that purpose, with swivel guns and small arms, and anchored within 200 or 300 yards of the shore; that Captain O'Hara, and five or six of his people, went on shore in the tender's small boat, leaving orders with the people on board to be in readiness with their guns and small arms, to fire in case he was attacked by the natives, which was to be made known to them by the firing of a pistol as a signal for their fire. As soon as the Captain landed, he was received civilly by the Moors. He told them he was come by order of the King, his master, to find that place, and likewise to fix the British flag (an English jack which he brought with him from his own sloop for that purpose) on an old ruined fort which they had: he did not by that intend the least harm. They did not seem to relish his fixing the colours on that fort, and made a little bustle about it; however, they seemed pacified, and asked the Captain, if the King, his master, had sent them any presents? He replied in the affirmative; and that, if some of them would go on board the tender, he would shew them the presents: on which a multitude of them crowded to the beach in order to launch their boats, or canoes, that were out of the water, to get on board, which the commanding officer on board the tender observing, and thinking that they were coming to seize the tender, and not seeing the Captain amongst them, immediately gave them all his fire of swivels and small-arms, which killed near twenty of the natives: then he slipt or cut his cable, and made off. The Moors on this directly attacked the Captain and his people, and wounded him slightly before he delivered up his sword. The Captain and his people were then made prisoners, and carried up the country. The Moors were satisfied when they found the Captain was not to blame. The poor Captain was seized with a fever in a few days, and for want of proper care, and with grief and disappointment, he died in less than a week. Had he survived, he would have been taken to Senegal, as his people were on a journey of upwards of 500 miles, and there ransomed. It is said the officer in the tender heard a pistol fired as a signal; others contradict it. Be it as it will, some fatal mistake was the cause of this poor gentleman's destruction.

This day the Right Hon. the Lord Mayor gave a most splendid entertainment at the Mansion-house to a very numerous though a select number of persons of both houses of parliament. The Egyptian-hall was illuminated in the most elegant manner, with new chandeliers, and other illuminations, which surpassed all description.

Amongst other loyal and patriotic toasts, the following, after silence for each was proclaimed by sound of trumpet, were drank, and

22d.

Vol. XIII.

and the pieces of music performed with the utmost elegance and approbation.

May true religion and virtue ever flourish and abound.

Health and long life to our sovereign Lord the King.

Coronation Anthem by Mr. Handel.

Health and long life to our gracious Queen, and all the Royal Family.

May happiness and glory be the portion of his Majesty, his family, and people.

Prosperity to the city of London.

Grand Martial Piece by Mr. Rush.

May justice and wisdom govern all the public councils.

May the fundamental liberties of England be ever revered and defended.

May the noble assertors and protectors of English liberty be had in perpetual honour.

Full Piece by Mr. Rush.

May the violators of the right of election and petition against grievances be confounded.

May the wicked be taken from before the King, that his throne may be established in righteousness.

Overture by Mr. Handel.

May corruption cease to be the measure of government.

May the spirit of the constitution prevail over secret and undue influence.

May perpetual union, social liberty, and universal justice, prevail, and render happy the whole British empire.

May the commerce of this city and kingdom, with the colonies, flourish for ever.

Full Piece by Mr. Rush.

While the truly noble company were at dinner, they were serenaded by the most excellent band of music which could be procured in this kingdom, and which was conducted by Mr. Rush. In a word, it was universally allowed to exceed any thing of the kind ever given by a private gentleman in this kingdom.

The ball was opened about ten o'clock, by the Duke of Devonshire and the Lady Mayoress; the dancing continued till half past four in the morning; and before five the whole company left the Mansion-house, greatly pleased with the grandeur and elegancy of the entertainment, as well as the order and regularity with which it was conducted. The company was so numerous, that the three long tables in the Egyptian-hall were not sufficient to accommodate them all. It is said that 600 dishes were served up.

List of the Company.

Dukes of Richmond, Bolton, Devonshire, Portland, Manchester, Northumberland.

Marquisses of Rockingham, Granby.

Earls of Piercy, Huntingdon, Suffolk, Berkley, Abingdon, Plymouth, Scarborough, Albemarle, Coventry, Tankerville, Effingham, Fitzwilliam, Temple, Belborough, Shelburne, Corke, Donnegal, Verney, Ludlow, Fife.

Lords Robert Sutton, George Cavendish, Frederick Cavendish, John Cavendish, Abergavenny, Craven,

Craven, King, Monfon, Fortefcue, Hyde, Lyttelton, Camden, Archer, Germaine.

Vifcounts Hereford, Torrington, Wenman, Downe.

Knights, John Delaval, John Molefworth, George Saville, George Colebrook, Jofeph Mawbey, George Younge, Thomas Frankland, Edward Winnington, Charles Sanders, Robert Clayton, Francis Vincent, William Codrington, Edward Aftley, William Meredith, Piercy Brett, Mat. Ridley, Cecil Wray.

Meſſieurs Anderfon, Adams, Anderfon, Aubrey, Allen, Baker, Barrow, Bailey, Bethel, Brickdale, Barre Colonel, Burke, Bynge, Cavendiſh, Calvert, Calcraft, Chomley, Collcraft, Cornwall, Coventry, Damer, Dawkins, Dempſter, Dowdefwell, Dunning, Fitzmaurice, Fletcher, Frankland, Fuller, Graves, Grey, Garth, Goddard, Gregory, Groves, Grenville Thomas, Grenville Henry, Glynn Serjeant, Hampden, Hamilton, Howard, Hope, Hobart, Hunt, Huſſey, Jenins Col. Keppel Admiral, Keppel General, Laſcelles, Laſcelles Daniel, St. Leger, Col. Luther, Mackworth, Martin, Mauger, Milles, Norris, Parker, Pennant, Popham, Pownall, Gov. Pulteney, Roll, Ruſhout, Seymour, Scrope, Scawen, Sawbridge Sheriff, Scudamore, Standert, Sturt, Tempeſt, Townſend Sheriff, Townſend Thomas, Taylor, Trecothick Alderman, Turner, Walſh, Walſingham, Wedderburn, Weſt, Whateley, Beauclerk, Bertie, Buller, jun. H. Crab Bolton, Clarke, Crosby, Damer, fen. Hanbury, General Irwin, Keck, Leman, Montague, Murray, Muſgrave, Alexander Popham, Capt. Phipps, Plumer, George Paulet, Pratt, Skipwith, Thoroton, Turner, Richard Whitworth.

Several perfons had their windows broken at night by the mob for not illuminating their houſes, particularly thoſe of Mr. Barclay, oppoſite Bow Church, in Cheapſide, were very much demoliſhed, ſo that it was neceſſary to take out the remains of the faſh-frames from ſix windows. Mr. Barclay, when his houſe was attacked, ſent out two of his ſervants to go amongſt the mob, and to fix upon any perſons they ſaw throwing ſtones againſt his windows, and not to leave them until they got intelligence where they might be found: in conſequence of theſe orders two perſons were this day taken before the Lord Mayor, and a propoſal was made to pay the damage; but Mr. Barclay refuſed to accept the offer, ſaying that he came for juſtice on the offenders, and not for the damage he had received; on which they were both ſent to the Compter.

Her Grace the Dutcheſs of Northumberland, in croſſing the channel from Dover to Calais, very narrowly eſcaped being drowned. By the violence of the waves, the cords which laſhed her chaiſe to the veſſel were burſt, and, had it not immediately been diſcovered, the next returning ſea would have carried her Grace overboard. She was on her journey to the court of Vienna, to be preſent at the nuptials of the Arch-dutcheſs with the Dauphin of France; but being driven back, and with the utmoſt hazard landed near Folkſtone, her Grace's deſign has been fruſtrated.

[G] 2 . The

The two Kennedys, who were condemned the laſt ſeſſions for the murder of Bigby, the watchman, have received the King's pardon, on condition of being tranſported for life.

The perſon who robbed the Cheſter mail laſt week in the City-road was taken into cuſtody on Wedneſday, on his firſt attempt to put off a ſmall bill on Meſſrs. Boldero and Co. facing the Manſion-houſe.

The above man was carried before the magiſtrates in Bow-ſtreet, when the poſt-boy, Daniel Wheeler, ſwearing to his perſon, he was committed to Newgate. It is ſaid he had juſt taken a houſe in Biſhopſgate ſtreet, in order to carry on the buſineſs of a grocer, and had laid in a quantity of goods in that way; and was on the point of being married to a tradeſman's daughter in that neighbourhood. On ſearching the priſoner's houſe laſt night, bills of exchange to the value of 300l. and a great number of letters taken out of the mail, were found. He pretended that a perſon had given him the bills, &c. to diſpoſe of, but could not tell his name.

23d. A joint addreſs of the Lords and Commons in parliament aſſembled, relative to the city remonſtrance, was this day preſented to his Majeſty, expreſſing the deepeſt concern on ſeeing the exerciſe of the ſubjects' undoubted right of petitioning the throne ſo groſsly perverted, by being applied to the purpoſe not of preſerving, but of overturning the conſtitution, and of propagating doctrines, which, if generally adopted, muſt be fatal to the peace of the kingdom, and tend to the ſubverſion of all lawful authority. At the ſame time aſperſing and calumniating one of the branches of the legiſlature, and expreſsly denying the legality of the preſent parliament, and the validity of its proceedings.

At a court of aſſiſtants of the Goldſmiths' Company, the following reſolutions were agreed to:

The Right Hon. the Lord Mayor having iſſued precepts for ſummoning the livery of this city to meet at Guildhall, on Tueſday the 6th inſt. to conſider of a farther application for redreſs of grievances, at which meeting a moſt indecent remonſtrance was ordered to be preſented to his Majeſty;

Reſolved and ordered, That for the future the wardens of this company do not ſummon the livery thereof to attend at any meeting in the Guildhall, (except for the purpoſe of elections) without the expreſs approbation or conſent of this court.

26th. There was a general court of the Eaſt India Company, at their houſe, in Leaden-hall-ſtreet, as by adjournment, for the determination, by ballot, of the following queſtion:

That the dividend on the capital ſtock of this company, for the half year, commencing at Chriſtmas laſt, and ending at Midſummer next, be at ſix per cent.

The balloting began at eleven o'clock in the forenoon, and continued till ſix in the evening, when an hour being taken up, as uſual, by the ſcrutineers, in adjuſting the numbers, at ſeven o'clock the poll was declared as follows:

For

For the question — 139
Against the question — 1

Majority ———— 138
The dividend thus declared, the court adjourned.

From the Frontiers of Italy, Feb. 16. The Emperor, in his late journey to Italy, had a long conversation at Forli with the Count Nicholas Papini, who did not, at that time, know his Imperial Majesty. Being afterwards informed of the honour which he had had, he wrote to the Emperor, and has received the following answer:

I shall always reflect with pleasure, my dear Papini, on the interview which I had with you in passing through Forli, and the good counsel which you was pleased to give me on that occasion. The freedom and candour with which you talked to me will not permit me to doubt the sincerity of the sentiments expressed in your letter to me of the first of December, and of all the happy passages therein announced. These sentiments you avowed to me at a time when you took me for a private man, and had no suspicion of that train of lofty dignity to which it has pleased the Divine Providence to raise me. The encomiums lavished on us, and all the things said to us, are unhappily addressed much more to our rank than to our person. Preserve for me this affection, my dear Papini; and be persuaded, that I shall be sorely grieved if you do not, in me, esteem the man! a title superior to all others that can be given me! and that Joseph prefers being beloved to all those outward protestations, and all those homages, which are continually bestowed on the Emperor. Believe, then, that the same sentiments will ever animate me. I pray God to keep you in his holy protection.

At Vienna, this first day of January, 1770. (Signed) JOSEPH.

Rome, Feb. 14. A courier arrived last night from Lisbon, with the news of the death of the new Cardinal de Mendonza.

28th. Was held a meeting of the electors of Westminster, when a remonstrance was unanimously agreed to, and in less than half an hour presented to his Majesty by Sir Robert Bernard, Mr. Connell, Mr. Charles Martyn, and the Rev. Dr. Wilson. His Majesty received, and immediately gave it to one of the lords in waiting, without speaking a word. The multitude on their return met with the S—r of the H—e of C— in his state coach, whom they grossly insulted with groans and hissings, but offered no violence to his person or carriage.

At a court of assistants of the Weavers' Company, like resolutions were passed with those already mentioned.

The assizes ended on the crown side at Hereford, when nine prisoners were tried for the murder of William Powell, Esq. six of whom received sentence of death, and were ordered for execution, and their bodies to be dissected; but two were afterwards ordered to be hung in chains near the place where the murder was committed, and three were acquitted. The names of those left for execution were William Spiggot, David Lewellin, Charles David Morgan, William Morris, William Walter Evan, and David Morgan. This trial

trial lasted from seven in the morning till eight at night.

Leghorn, Feb. 22. The Russian men of war, the Three Primates of 74 guns and 700 men, and the Providence of 48 guns and 450 men, arrived here.

The 17th inst. we had the most dreadful storm that has been since the year 1752 in these parts; all the vessels which were in the road were obliged to cut their cables, and run aground against the Tower of Morzocco. Among them is the Russian frigate the Postillion, who lost her rudder, and was much damaged: they despair of getting her afloat again. Most of the roofs of the houses were blown off, and the chimnies thrown down. The sea was so high, that the Pier was entirely covered; the Flotas were driven even on the Terrace before the old Fort. In short, many ships have been wrecked on this coast as well as on that of Sicily.

Paris, March 10. The comedians at Bourdeaux have been committed to prison by the Parliament there, for advertising the representation of a piece, called the Honest Criminal.

29th. This day his Majesty went to the House of Peers, and gave the royal assent to the following bills, viz.

The bill for raising 1,800,000l. by loans on Exchequer bills, for the service of the present year.

The bill for allowing the exportation of malt for a limited time.

The bill for applying the sum granted for the pay and cloathing of his Majesty's militia forces for this year.

And also to several road, inclosure, naturalization, and other bills.

30th. At a court of assistants of the Grocers' Company, held at their Hall, the following resolutions were agreed to:

The Right Honourable the Lord Mayor having issued precepts for summoning the livery of this city to meet at Guildhall on Tuesday the 6th instant, to consider of farther application for redress of grievances, which gave existence to a paper, entitled, The humble address, remonstrance, and petition, of the Lord Mayor, aldermen, and livery of this city, which was ordered, and afterwards presented to his Majesty;

Resolved, That this court entirely disapproves of the said paper, being fully persuaded that his Majesty's people, as well as his parliament, will reject with disdain every insidious suggestion of those ill-designing men, who are, in reality, undermining the public liberty, under the specious pretence of zeal for its preservation, and therefore look upon it as indecent, and highly disrespectful to his Majesty's person and dignity, injurious to the supreme authority of parliament assembled, and unwarrantable, as it tends to subvert the happy constitution of this kingdom.

Resolved and ordered, That for the future no warden of this company do summon the livery hereof to attend at any meeting in the Guildhall of this city (except for the purpose of elections) without the express order of this court.

The professor of anatomy finished his course of lectures this season at the Royal Academy, through throughout which he shewed great address in adapting them particularly to the arts of design, and for that purpose had one of the models of the Academy present, to shew at one view the appearance of the muscles with and without the skin, and the different forms they assume when put in action. Among other general observations, he discoursed on the different proportions of different ages, and the propriety and fitness of every part to answer the end proposed; and gave it as his opinion, that the idea of beauty was subsequent, and not attended to in the formation of the human figure.

A very numerous body of Middlesex freeholders met at the assembly-room, Mile-end, where a remonstrance was read by Mr. Sheriff Sawbridge, and only one hand was held up against it.

This morning, at two o'clock, a melancholy fire broke out at Wilton, in Wiltshire, which consumed six or seven dwelling-houses, besides several work-shops and out-houses. The wind, which had been northerly for a month before, suddenly shifted to the south-west, or a great part of the town must have been destroyed. This is the second fire which has happened there in the space of a few months.

A few days ago, a servant belonging to Mr. Hervie, of Brounlie, in Scotland, digging in a field adjoining to his master's house, discovered an earthen pot, with a cover of the same, about a foot from the surface of the ground, containing a considerable quantity of old Scots and English silver coins of the reigns of David, Robert, and Edward; they are mostly well preserved, and very legible: the inscriptions on many of them are *Civitas London*, *Civitas Cant*. *Civitas Aberden*. What is remarkable, there has been an old tradition current among the country people there, that a considerable treasure in pots lies concealed in that neighbourhood, and a former discovery in the same parish seems to justify the conjecture.

Letters from Leghorn declare, that a Russian frigate had arrived at Malta with the Marquis de Cavalcabo, who presented the Grand Master with a letter from the Empress of Russia, in which she requested, that all her vessels might be admitted into the ports of that Order, and that the Maltese squadron would join her fleet; but that the council had resolved only to admit three or four Russian vessels into their ports at a time, and by no means to make themselves parties in the present dispute between her 'Imperial Majesty and the Porte.

On the 14th of March, a new eruption of Mount Vesuvius broke out within an hundred yards of the crater, on the side of Pompeii, from whence issued a lava of about two miles in length, and 2,700 paces in breadth; at the same time that two vollies of stones, some not less than a ton weight, were thrown out of the crater to a very considerable height. The lava has not yet reached the cultivated parts of the mount.

A court martial was held in Portsmouth harbour, for the trial of the lieutenant who commanded the tender that waited for Capt. O'Hara, when that unfortunate gentleman went on shore on the coast

coast of Africa; when, after a trial of six hours, he was acquitted.

Married lately, Mr. Humphreys, a farmer, at Beckingham in Kent, to Miss Parrier, of the same place, with a fortune of 10,000l.

Died, Mrs. Gordon, a maiden lady, who has left a considerable sum to build an hospital for indigent old maids.

At Canterbury, the Rev. Mr. Monins Eaton, Rector of Ringwould, and Vicar of Charlton, near Dover: he has left a fortune of 30,000l. which devolves to his brother, a lieutenant in the army, and his sister, a maiden lady.

Fra. Mortis, aged 108, at Newcastle.

James Kearney, in Ireland, aged 115. He lately had a daughter married, aged 15.

APRIL.

1st. A fire broke out at Williamstead, within three miles of Bedford, occasioned by a chimney taking fire, which communicated the flames to the roof; and notwithstanding all possible assistance was had, a whole row of houses, twenty-six in number, were entirely consumed.

Last Tuesday came on at Chelmsford assizes, before Mr. Baron Smythe, two causes against Rawlings, Lycett, Ward, Kew, and Jones, Custom-house officers, for forcing themselves into the house of a lady in the parish of Eastham, ransacking the same, assaulting the lady in her own dwelling, as well as her visitors, and other enormities, because there was no prohibited booty for them; when two verdicts were found against the brutal, illegal searchers, with considerable damages and costs of suits in both actions.

Was committed to Guildford gaol, by the Rev. Dr. Burdett, a Russian soldier, on suspicion of committing a murder on the body of a woman at whose house he lodged, at Esher, in Surry, by cutting her throat. The woman was not more than twenty years of age, and was murdered in her bed, her young child, about two months old, lying by her.

On Friday the plough for making trenches for drains, brought out of Suffolk, and invented by one Makings, a poor farmer, was tried at Upton, near Stratford, on the grounds belonging to Mr. Pearce, before a Committee of the Society of Arts, &c. It cut, in the space of thirty-four minutes, a complete trench of about eighteen inches deep, two inches and a half broad at the bottom, and of the length of six hundred and sixty feet; executed in a manner that cannot be effected by the spade, even with any degree of labour. The force used for this performance was that of six horses, managed by two men, and without any greater strain than would have permitted them to have done a full day's work. It is computed, that, by this means, trenches for close drains may be cut at three farthings a rod, or considerably less, where the work of men and horses are cheap.

Extract of a letter from Portsmouth, April 2.

Yesterday the Russian Admiral's ship of eighty-four guns sailed out of the harbour, and saluted the English

English Admiral. Most of the foreign ministers, except the French, sailed out to Spithead in this ship, with several ladies and English officers, and were highly pleased. By the alterations Admiral Elphinston has made in the ship, she is looked upon to be equal to any ship of her rate in England.

5th. This day the King was pleased to invest his Royal Highness Prince William Henry, his Majesty's third son, with the ensigns of the most antient and most noble Order of the Thistle.

His Royal Highness being presented to the Sovereign by the two Senior Knights, and kneeling down, the Herald drew the sword, and (kneeling) delivered it to the Sovereign, who thereupon knighted his Royal Highness; then the Prince, having kissed his Majesty's hand, rose up; which done, Green Rod (having received the green ribbon, with the symbol of the Order hanging to it) presented the same (kneeling) to the Sovereign, upon a velvet cushion, who put the ribbon over the Prince's left shoulder, and then, kneeling down, he again kissed his Majesty's hand; which done, the Prince rose up, and, making a low reverence, withdrew.

Extract of a Letter from Paris, March 19.

Yesterday the court again sent an express to Holland, charged with bills of exchange to the value of 2,000,000 of livres, destined to fulfil the engagements contracted by the Sieur de Balue, the King's banker. These different remittances amount, it is believed, to about 8,000,000 of livres.

Letters from Detroit (by Monday's New York mail) inform us, that several boats with goods had been seventy days in crossing Lake Erie; in which time the distress of the people was so great, that they had been obliged to keep two human bodies, which they found unburied upon the shore, in order to collect and kill the ravens and eagles that came to feed on them, for their subsistence. Many other boats have been frozen up within forty miles of Detroit; and several traders' small boats, with goods, had been lost.

Cadiz, March 9. By letters from Mexico, we have an account of the deaths of the Abbe d'Auteroche, and one of the two officers of the Spanish marine, who had sailed with that gentleman to the island of California. They fell sick, with every one who accompanied them, on the 4th of June, the very day after they had made their observation of the Transit of Venus over the Sun. This observation, according to the same letters, was made with all possible advantage, the day being extremely fine, and the air remarkably serene. We learn, moreover, that the Sieur Paly, the famous geographer, who was among those who fell sick, happily arrived on the 14th of October at Port St. Blaise, in the White Sea, with all those who had the good fortune to escape the epidemic disease with which they were visited. Much is expected from the success of the observation, which was the grand object of the voyage of these astronomers.

6th. Came on at Kingston, before Mr. Justice Blackstone, the famous cause between the Right Hon. George Onslow, and the Rev. Mr.

ANNUAL REGISTER, 1770.

Mr. Horne, for two letters published the 14th and 28th of July last. The action was brought against Mr. Horne for 10,000l. damages. The trial lasted about an hour and a half, when Mr. Onslow was non-suited. It is supposed the expence to Mr. Onslow will amount to at least 1,500l.

The Durham, Cumberland, and Northumberland petitions for redress of grievances, were presented to his Majesty at St. James's, and received, but no answer was returned: they were given to the lords in waiting.

7th. The Synagogue of the Jews, in order to shew the detestation in which the body of them hold such practices of their wicked brethren, have advertised a reward for a detection of all such as are guilty of receiving stolen goods.

Last week, as Mr. Harding's men were plowing in his grounds at Tottenham, the plough struck rather lower than common in the earth, and turned up a large quantity of broad pieces of gold of James I. and Charles I. quite fresh, as if just coined: some men dug afterwards with a pitchfork, and threw up at one stroke 18 of the above pieces, also a horn with some silver at the bottom; the whole amounting to upwards of 70l. value.

9th. The Middlesex petition, remonstrance, and address, was presented to his Majesty at St. James's by Messrs. Sawbridge and Townsend, Sheriffs for the county, which was received, and given to a lord in waiting, but no answer returned.

The petition from the county of Kent was also presented to his Majesty by John Calcraft, Esq. member for Rochester, and some other gentlemen.

A general meeting of the East India Company was held at Paris, when the directors gave an account of their proceedings, by which the impossibility of compounding their debts and continuing their trade appeared, and it was proposed to put their whole effects into the hands of the King.

This day, about one o'clock, Stephen Gregory, a Russian, was executed at Esher, in Surry, amidst a great number of spectators, for the murder of Mrs. Herne. He was attended at the place of execution by the Russian Ambassador's chaplain, to whom he confessed the murder, and died very penitent. He had been a lodger in the house, and was suspected by Mrs. Herne of intending to rob them, which she informed her husband of, who turned him out of his house. It is supposed he committed the murder out of revenge. He attempted to conceal himself in the house the night before, as the man and his wife were from home, but was prevented by some neighbours who had charge of it in their absence. The morning the shocking affair happened, Mr. Herne left his wife in bed about a quarter after six to go to Lord Clive's garden to work; he left the door of his house unlocked, which was observed by the villain, who immediately went up to her chamber, and cut her throat in a most dreadful manner, so as nearly to sever her head from her body; then laid her on the floor, covered her with the bed-cloaths, left the young child naked in bed, rifled the drawers, and made his escape. The poor woman not being up so soon as ufual, her next door neighbour, between nine and ten o'clock, went to know the reafon, and found Mrs. Herne as before-mentioned, and the poor infant crying in bed. The Ruffian being obferved to come out of the houfe that morning, feveral went immediately in purfuit of him. He was taken at Godalming, committed to Guildford gaol, and from thence conveyed to Kingfton, where he was tried on Saturday, and hanged on Monday oppofite the houfe where he committed the fact. He was about twenty-two years of age, and a ftout well-made man. Five filver table fpoons were found upon him, which Mr. Herne made oath were his property.

12th. Yefterday the report was made to his Majefty of the malefactors under fentence of death in Newgate, when Jofeph Jarvis and Benjamin Milifent, for a burglary in the houfe of Mr. Evans, and Matthew Kennedy, for the murder of the watchman on Weftminfter-bridge, were ordered for execution.

Jofeph Nicholas, William Warraker, Richard Carter, and Patrick Kennedy, are refpited.

This day his Majefty went to the Houfe of Peers, and gave the royal affent to the following bills, viz.

The bill to continue an act for punifhing mutiny and defertion in the American colonies.

The bill for repealing part of an act for granting certain duties in the Britifh colonies in America.

The bill to rectify miftakes in the names of the commiffioners appointed to execute the land-tax act.

The bill to regulate the trials of contefted elections, or returns of members to ferve in parliament.

The bill for the better prefervation of the game in that part of Great Britain called England.

The bill to prevent the killing and deftroying of dogs.

The bill for building a workhoufe for the liberty of Saffronhill, Hatton-garden, and Ely-rents, in the parifh of St. Andrew, Holborn.

The bill for lighting, paving, and cleaning the town of Marybone, &c. and for regulating weights and meafures therein.

The bill to amend an act for making a navigable cut or canal from the Trent, at or near Wildenferry, in Derbyfhire, to the river Merfey, &c.

The bill to continue the terms and powers granted for keeping in repair the harbour of Minehead, in Somerfetfhire.

The bill to continue the duties granted for repairing the harbour and quay of Watchett, in the faid county.

And alfo to feveral road, inclofure, and naturalization bills.

This morning Capt. Bowen, of Killy-Own, who was concerned with Williams and others in the murder of Mr. Powell, of Glanereth, near Landovery, was apprehended at the Cock eating-houfe behind the Royal Exchange, by Meff. Williams and Price, two Welch gentlemen, who knew him. He was carried before the Right Hon. the Lord Mayor, who committed him to the Poultry Compter; and he is to be re-examined by his Lordfhip on Tuefday morning next. He was difcovered by a young man at Lambeth, of whom Bowen had enjoined

enjoined secrecy. The young fellow accordingly took no notice that he had seen him, till his master observed a note that was sent him by Bowen to meet him at ten o'clock in the morning at the Cock eating-house; in consequence of which, two of Sir John Fielding's men were sent for, who waited a considerable time, and then went away: however, the above gentlemen being afterwards informed by this young man when Bowen came, secured him. He is brother to Mrs. Powell, and has been at Lambeth ever since his escape from Wales.

Matthew Kennedy, who was to have been executed on Thursday next, has obtained his Majesty's pardon, on condition of being transported for life.

Madame Louisa, the King of France's youngest daughter, who is in her 33d year, having for some time entertained the project of becoming a Carmelite, retired to the monastery of the Carmelites of St. Dennis, after having obtained the King her father's permission for that purpose.

An order from the Crown Office, directed to the Marshal of the King's Bench prison, was delivered to the bench of justices for Surry, at their rotation-office, St. Margaret's-hill, empowering the said Marshal to discharge John Wilkes, Esq. he giving bond, as security for good behaviour for seven years, himself in 1000l. and two sureties, viz. Edward Burke, of St. Clement's Danes, vintner, and Matthias Hamberg, of St. Bride's, tailor, in 500l. each, agreeable to the sentence passed upon him.

This day a common hall was held at Guildhall, by virtue of a precept from the Lord Mayor, to receive the report of his Majesty's answer to the address, remonstrance, and petition of the Lord Mayor, aldermen, and livery of this city; as likewise to hear the resolutions and addresses of the Houses of Lords and Commons thereupon, and to take into consideration the late proceedings of the companies of goldsmiths, weavers, and grocers, respecting the same, as well as their resolution not to obey the orders of the Lord Mayor for summoning the livery of the respective companies to attend at such common halls.

The last committee of the livery was appointed to take into consideration what would be the proper mode of proceeding against the three aforesaid companies, and to report their opinion to the common council.

After which the thanks of the livery were returned to the Lord Mayor, aldermen, and common council, who carried up the remonstrance: and the same was ordered to be printed, signed by the town-clerk, in all the public papers.

The Good Intent, Nailor, from Guernsey, for Newcastle, ran aground near Robin Hood's Bay, and is lost. The master and one man were drowned; three others got on shore on the mast, which broke away by the deck; and one of them perished in the snow before any assistance could be had. The other two were near sharing the same fate, but fortunately a countryman discovered them from the hills by the sea, and came to their relief.

A second incendiary letter was received by the Dean of Westminster, her, threatening, as in a former letter, to put their design against his life into execution, as he has not yet made a passage through the wall in Dean-yard, which is not in his power to do, the said wall and ground not being his property.

14th. On the report of the committee who made trial of Making's drain plough, the Society of Arts, &c. agreed to the giving him fifty guineas for his invention, and a farther sum of ten guineas on his delivering a complete plough of that kind, with proper carriages, to the Society, for the use of the public.

The Lord Mayor gave a very grand entertainment in the Egyptian-hall, to more than 300 noblemen and gentlemen of the first distinction.

About ten in the evening, two gentlemen in a post-chaise, coming over Blackheath, were stopped by a single man on foot, dressed in a carter's frock. One of the gentlemen, a military officer, told the fellow, in a peremptory manner, that he would not be robbed, and desired him to desist; but the villain presenting a pistol, and threatening violence, the gentleman shot him dead on the spot.

The same gentlemen had not rode above three miles farther, on their way to town, when they were attacked again by a highwayman, well mounted, near the Red House. The gentleman who killed the footpad shot directly through the blind of the chaise, and is supposed to have wounded him, as the horse upon which he rode sprung into a ditch by the road side, and was afterwards found without his rider on the road adjoining to Kent-street turnpike that leads to Rotherhithe, and a great deal of blood was traced near the ditch where the horse had plunged.

As Lord Sandys was returning to town from his son's seat in Hertfordshire, he was overturned in his post-chaise coming down Highgate-hill. At first, it was thought he was not much hurt, but afterwards, it appeared, he received a contusion in his head that cost him his life.

About noon, the report 15th. of a pistol, fired somewhere in or about the King's palace at St. James's, alarmed the officers upon guard. The soldiers were interrogated, and their pieces examined, but no discovery could be made from what quarter it came.

The purser of the Hampshire East Indiaman, Capt. Sime, came to the India House, with an account of the above ship being safe arrived in the channel from Bengal. She has made her voyage in the shortest space of time that has been known; notwithstanding which, she has been very sickly, and lost many of her men. Scarce an officer on board escaped the sickness, except the captain and chief mate.

The Lord Holland East Indiaman, Capt. Nairne, in going round from Bengal to Madrass, was totally lost off the Eastern-braces. The chief mate and fifteen of the crew were unfortunately drowned.

The sum of 400,000l. per ann. which the East India Company annually pays to the government, is appropriated towards making good the supplies of the present year.

The sum of 9,650l. is granted for the support of the Foundling Hospital for the present year 1770.

The

17th. The committee of the supporters of the Bill of Rights settled all Mr. Wilkes's debts, and about six o'clock in the evening that gentleman was discharged from the King's-bench prison, and immediately set out in a post-chaise, accompanied by his daughter, for the country-house of Mr. Reynolds, his attorney, in Kent.

It has been remarked with astonishment, that there never was perhaps so general and voluntary illuminations and rejoicings on any occasion as on the event of Mr. Wilkes's release; not in London only, but in every part of England: and, to the praise of the lower order of patriots, no disorders have been complained of any where.

This morning Capt. Marmaduke Bowen was re-examined before the Right Hon. the Lord Mayor, when he confessed that one Mr. O—— had carried Williams in an open boat to France. He was remanded back to the Poultry Compter. His Lordship first ordered him to be sent to Newgate; but the prisoner seeming to be greatly affected with the thoughts of being committed to that prison, he was by his Lordship (on the intercession of Mr. Jones of Castle-yard, who acts for the prosecutor, and of Mr. Rice Williams, sen. who apprehended him) remanded to his former place of confinement. His cash being entirely exhausted, Mess. Williams and others contributed for his present support.

18th. Yesterday a woman, late of Elliot's-court in the Old-Bailey, paper-bag-maker, was tried at the sessions at Guildhall, for almost starving to death and cruelly beating her apprentice girl. It appeared on the trial, that the poor girl must have perished for want of the common necessaries of life, had not some of the neighbours thrown eatables to her out of a window, when she was tied to a post in the yard; that when she was at liberty to go out, she had often been seen to pick up and devour with great eagerness potatoe peelings, and such things as were thrown out for the dogs. The prisoner was sentenced to suffer six months imprisonment in Newgate, to pay a fine of 1s. and give security for her good behaviour for two years. The girl was put out by the parish of Pancras.

19th. The following is the bill of fare at the entertainment given by Sir Watkin Williams Wynn, at Wynnstay, on his coming of age.

30 Bullocks
1 Ditto roasted whole
50 Hogs
50 Calves
80 Sheep
18 Lambs
70 Pies
51 Guinea fowls
37 Turkeys
12 Turkey poults
84 Capons
25 Pie fowls
300 Chickens
360 Fowls
96 Ducklings
48 Rabbits
15 Snipes
1 Leveret
5 Bucks
421 Pounds of salmon
30 Brace of tench
40 Brace of carp
36 Pike
60 Dozen of trout

108 Flour.

108 Flounders
109 Lobsters
96 Crabs
10 Quarts of shrimps
200 Crawfish
60 Barrels of pickled oysters
1 Hogshead of rock oysters
20 Quarts of oysters for sauce
166 Hams
100 Tongues
125 Plum puddings
108 Apple pies
104 Pork pies
30 Beef pies
34 Rice puddings
7 Venison pies
60 Raised pies
80 Tarts
30 Pieces of cut pastry
24 Pound cakes
60 Savoy cakes
30 Sweetmeat cakes
12 Backs of bacon
144 Ice creams
18,000 Eggs
150 Gallons of milk
60 Quarts of cream
30 Bushels of potatoes
6,000 Asparagus
200 French beans
3 Dishes of green pease
12 Cucumbers
70 Hogsheads of ale
120 Dozen of wine

Brandy, rum, and shrub Rock-work shapes, landscapes, in jellies, blanchmange, &c. A great quantity of small pastry One large cask of ale, which held twenty-six hogsheads.

It is thought that there were at least 15,000 people at dinner in Sir Watkin's park all at the same time.

LENT CIRCUIT.

At Maidstone assizes, four were capitally convicted, two of whom were reprieved before the judge left the town.

At Chelmsford assizes, eleven were capitally convicted.

At Aylesbury assizes, five were capitally convicted, three of whom were reprieved.

At Bedford assizes, one was capitally convicted.

At the assizes at Cambridge, two were capitally convicted: a person for an attempt to commit a rape upon a child, was sentenced to suffer a year's imprisonment, and to the payment of a fine.

At Huntingdon assizes, three were capitally convicted.

At Oakham assizes, a private man belonging to the Lincolnshire militia received sentence of death for horse-stealing, but was afterwards reprieved.

At Nottingham assizes, James Wardley was condemned for horse-stealing, but reprieved before the judge left the town.

At Thetford assizes, one was capitally convicted, but reprieved.

At Northampton assizes, William Craddock and Anthony Harwood received sentence of death, for cruelly wounding and robbing Mr. William Walker the younger, of Kingsthorne.

At the assizes at York, eleven were capitally convicted; of whom William Varley and James Oldfield, for diminishing the gold coin, were found guilty of high treason. John Shirtcliff, game-keeper to Saville Finch, of Thriberg, Esq. charged with shooting William Brown, after a trial of above seven hours, was acquitted.

At Lancaster assizes, three were capitally convicted. James Donovan, for wilfully setting fire to the gaol in Liverpool, is to receive his sentence next assizes.

A re-

A remarkable cause came on at this assize, wherein the corporation of Liverpool were plaintiffs, and the proprietors of the copperworks, contiguous to that town, were defendants; when, after examining 35 witnesses in behalf of the plaintiffs, who proved beyond a doubt that the noxious effluvia of the said works were pernicious to health, injurious to the herbage, and a nuisance to the neighbourhood, it was agreed, that the calcining part should be immediately discontinued, and the proprietors be allowed two years to remove the works to a more remote situation.

At Shrewsbury assizes, two were capitally convicted. Sarah Evans, for attempting to murder her master, is to be imprisoned for three years, and find securities for her good behaviour for seven years.

At the assizes at Stafford, David Slack, for forging a draft of 20l. on Mess. Butler and Sons, of Birmingham, and procuring a forged indorsement on the same, was capitally convicted.

At Warwick assizes, four were capitally convicted.

At Hereford assizes, nine prisoners were tried for the murder of William Powell, Esq. six of whom received sentence of death, and were ordered for execution on Friday last, and their bodies to be dissected; but two were afterwards ordered to be hung in chains near the place were the murder was committed, and three were acquitted: the names of those left for execution were, William Spiggot, David Lewellin, Charles David Morgan, William Morris, William Walter Evan, and David Morgan. This trial lasted from seven in the morning till eight at night.

At the above assize, William Corbyn for sheep-stealing, John Webb for horse-stealing, and Charles Burgess for stealing 34l. 17s. were also capitally convicted.

At Monmouth assizes, two were capitally convicted for sheep-stealing; but were reprieved for transportation.

At Worcester assizes, three were capitally convicted, one of whom was reprieved; and four were ordered to be transported for seven years.

At Gloucester assizes, eight were capitally convicted, among whom was Sarah Pulham, for setting fire to the barn and ricks of Richard Cook.

At Salisbury assizes, John Franklin, for robbing the mail on the road between Marlborough and Chippenham; and Joseph Lamb, for stealing a mare at Sherborne, were capitally convicted.

At Winchester assizes, four were capitally convicted.

They write from Dublin, that their export of linen is less by 7,000,014 yards than it was the year before; in 1768, it was 18,490,195; in 1769, 17,790,705.

Extract of a Letter from Portsmouth, April 13.

Arrived and sailed the Colhourn, Oliver, for St. Kitt's. Sailed the Northumberland East Indiaman, and just now Admiral Elphinston and all his squadron have weighed from Spithead, but whether he will bring to at St. Hellen's or not is uncertain, as the wind is fair: his squadron consists of four ships of the

CHRONICLE.

the line, two frigates, one hospital-ship, and five transports.

Paris, April 6. The Pope has just published a bull, by which his Holiness has granted an universal jubilee, upon occasion of his exaltation to the see. It is to commence the 9th of this month, and finish on the 22d.

The following extraordinary Account is received from Italy.

Mr. Campani, an eminent Italian physician, has sent advice to Mr. Moreali, a famous practitioner at Modena, of the following extraordinary fact, which is properly authenticated.——" The wife of a tanner, living at a village called Palatapapoli, aged 25 years, being in the seventh month of her pregnancy, on the 11th of January last, heard distinctly the cries of the child she bore in her womb; the husband and several other persons also heard it the same day; and soon after, when she was at church at vespers, the child cried so audibly, and so strongly imitated the voice of a new-born infant, that the whole congregation concluded it was a child brought to be baptized. Mr. Campani adds, he has visited the poor woman several times, who is greatly concerned at this novelty, and daily falls away. We are impatient here to know the event of this singular miracle of nature."

21ft. The following order came out to the brigade of guards. Parole, Hounslow.

B. O. His Majesty has signified to the field officer in waiting, that he has been acquainted that Serjeant Bacon of the regiment, and Serjeant Park the Coldstream regiment; liam Powell, William Hart, J Potter, and Joseph Collins, vate soldiers in the first regir of foot-guards, were more or concerned in the rescue of M General Gansell, in Septen last: the King hopes, and is ling to believe, they did not kn the Major-General was arrest and only thought they were d vering an officer in distress: ho ever, his Majesty commands t they should be severely reprimar ed for acting in this business they have done; and strictly ord for the future, that no comm sioned officer or soldier do presur to interfere with bailiffs, or arres on any account or pretence wh soever, the crime being of a ve atrocious nature; and if any a found guilty of disobeying this c der, they will be most severe punished. This order to be re immediately at the head of eve company in the brigade of guard that no man may plead ignoran for the future.

The incessant rains that su ceeded a prodigious fall of sno upon the Pyrenean mountains, swelled the rivers in the south France, that the floods bore dow houses, mills, men, and cattle, ar laid waste a whole tract of countr of a vast extent. The deplorab situation of those who escaped th flood is not to be expressed.

The new bridge at Knutsfor near Leominster, fell down after was keyed in.

At the sale of Mr. Lemon's cı rious collection of birds, a gol pheasant was sold for 20 guinea and a peacock pheasant for 40 guineas.

Extract of a Letter from Mr. Boulton, late Surgeon of the Delight, dated Little Cape Mount, Dec. 10, 1769, to his Owner at Liverpool.

"On Sunday last, about three in the morning, we were all (who lay in the cabin) alarmed with a most horrid noise of the negroes, which was succeeded by several shrieks from Mr. Howard and several of the people upon deck. Surprized at such an uncommon uproar, I strove to awake Capt. Millroy, but, before I could make him sensible of what had happened, I received a stroke over my shoulders with a billet of wood, as also a cut with a cutlass on the back part of my neck.

"The cries of Mr. Howard, who was murdered under the windlass, as also those of several of the people whom the villains were butchering on the maindeck, had thrown me into such a state of stupidity, that I did not in the least feel the wounds I had received. Having by accident got hold of a pistol, which, to my mortification, I found not loaded, I cleared my way till I got upon deck; but how shall I paint the scene that there was acting! Gilbert Bagly, a promising young man, was laid upon deck crying for mercy, having had his arms and legs cut off by these butchers. Poor Millroy stabbed one in the side, and cut another in the forehead, before he was overcome.

"I saw none left but myself, the cook, and one boy, which were all in the maintop together; and about an hour after two others appeared, one of which was caught, and cut in pieces, and the other got into the top. I broke open the chests in the maintop to look for knives, bottles, &c.

"In the maintop I found two knives, two quart bottles, one half gallon ditto, which I gave (one knife excepted) to the people with me; and, going down the maintopmast stay, I got into the foretop, where I got another knife. As I was returning up the stay, I was discovered by the slaves, who strove all in their power to kill, by throwing billets of wood, and cut me; however, I was not much daunted after I got into the maintop, as I knew we were then able to defend ourselves against any of their weapons, except muskets, which I was in hopes they would not easily come at. But a woman who lay in the cabin soon put them in a method how to come at every thing that might compleat or forward their design. As they had cut both their cables some time before, I found we drove very fast towards the Apollo, which vessel I hailed several times, and was at last heard. But I had no sooner hailed, than the unmerciful butchers fired two muskets at me, which so terrified one of the people in the top, that he went down, thinking, by assisting in making sail, &c. they would spare his life: but he was much deceived; no sooner had he got down the shrouds, but his skull was split with the broad-axe, and his body thrown overboard.

"Captain Fisher gave us chace, and about eight o'clock came within gun-shot of us, and having fired a great gun into the vessel, the wretches were so incensed at me for

CHRONICLE.

for hailing, that they fired 17 muskets into the top, wounded a small boy, but did no other damage. Finding they could not get their muskets to bear upon us, a resolute dog attempted coming up the shrouds with a pistol and cutlass to dispatch us; but with a quart bottle I struck him over the head, which so stunned him, that he fell overboard.

"They engaged Capt. Fisher four hours, and killed one of his people; nor would they, I believe, have given up so soon, had not a barrel of powder blown up, and set the vessel on fire fore and aft. I immediately saw their confusion, hailed Capt. Fisher from the mast-head to board her, and went down myself upon deck, followed by the cook and a small boy, which were all that were left alive on board in the insurrection. As soon as Capt. Fisher boarded her, we set to work in putting out the fire, as most of the cloth in the vessel was in a blaze. The total loss I cannot well ascertain, but am sorry to observe it is very great, having nine white men killed, with at least double that number of slaves."

24th. The Lord Mayor, attended by the Aldermen Ladbroke, Stephenson, Turner, Trecothick, and Townshend, went in procession to Guildhall, in order to swear in John Wilkes, Esq. Alderman of Farringdon Without, when the motion for that purpose was carried without a division. Afterwards he took precedence from the time of his election, which was before Mess. Alderman Rossiter, Bird, and the two Sheriffs.

By the last accounts from Boston, in New England, it appears, that on the 5th of March a terrible engagement happened between the soldiery and the town's people, wherein four persons were killed on the spot, and several dangerously wounded.

Monday morning early a fire broke out at a house the bottom of Wych-street, behind St. Clement's, which entirely consumed the same, with a chandler's shop, and a glass-cutter's, and greatly damaged the inside of the house of Mr. Manning, breeches-maker. It burnt backwards, and much damaged the Angel-inn. St. Clement's Church was opened for the reception of the goods of the sufferers; and a party of the guards was sent for from the Savoy to prevent their being plundered.

Copy of the Question referred to Council by the Aldermen, on Mr. Wilkes's Election for the Ward of Farringdon Without.

Is Mr. Wilkes's said election to the office of Alderman a valid one? And is he, by law, entitled to be admitted by the said Court of Aldermen, by virtue of or in pursuance, of the said election?

ANSWER.

We are of opinion, that the judgments pronounced against Mr. Wilkes did not render him, by law, incapable of being elected an Alderman of the city of London; and that, upon such election, he may be admitted into the office by the Court of Aldermen; but we think it doubtful whether that court is compellable to admit him.

April 17, 1769.
Wm. De Grey,   J. Glynn,
Ch. Yorke,   Rd. Leigh.
J. Dunning.

Sir FLETCHER NORTON's *Answer to the above Question.*

I am of opinion, that Mr. Wilkes's election into the office of Alderman is not a valid election; and that he is not, by law, entitled to be admitted by the Court of Aldermen, by virtue of or in pursuance of the said election; and I think the crimes of which Mr. Wilkes has been convicted are of such a nature, as affords a legal justification to the Court of Aldermen for refusing to admit him; or, had Mr. Wilkes been in possession of the office, there would be cause of a motion. Besides, his present incapacity to attend the duty of the office furnishes another objection against admitting him; and if the Court of Aldermen wish to have this great constitutional question most satisfactorily decided, it may be done, without loss of time, and at no great expence, by putting Mr. Wilkes to bring his Writ of Mandamus to be admitted, and then returning the special matter, upon which the judgment of the Court of King's-bench may be obtained; and if either party should be dissatisfied with the determination of that Court, the cause may be carried by Writ of Error into the House of Lords.

Lincoln's Inn,
April 21, 1770. F. NORTON.

26th. At the masquerade at the Opera-House, given by the club at Arthur's, there were more than 1,200 of the principal nobility, foreign ministers, and persons of eminence, present. The illuminations were in the same style with those in the masquerade given by the King of Denmark, but much improved.

A bill of indictment was found at Hick's Hall against the author of the *Whisperer*, and warrants were issued for the apprehending him.

The sessions at the Old Bailey, which began on Wednesday, ended for Middlesex, when thirty convicts received sentence of death, among whom were four girls, the eldest not seventeen, for a robbery on the highway. At this sessions a greater number of prisoners were to be tried than ever was known, there being no less than 338 upon the Calendar, including those of London as well as Middlesex, and those under sentence at former sessions. As soon as a sentence was passed, the widow of Bigby, who was murdered upon Westminster-bridge, lodged an appeal against the two Kennedys, who at a former sessions were found guilty of the murder, but had been respited by his Majesty's clemency, and one of them [Matthew] actually on board in order to be transported for life. Patrick was brought to the bar, and a detainer lodged against him, and on Monday a warrant was issued for bringing back Matthew.

The society of Agriculture for the East Riding of Yorkshire chose Sir Digby Legard, Bart. their president.

27th. This morning, a little before two o'clock, a fire broke out in the lower part of the house of Messrs. Fry and Webb, paper-stainers, on Holborn-hill, near the end of Shoe-lane, which was consumed, with the furniture and stock in trade: Mr. Webb, Mrs. Fry's mother, an apprentice, and a maid-servant, perished in the flames; Mr. and Mrs. Fry, and their child, escaped by a back-way. The house of Mr. Bridgewater, grocer,

grocer, was also consumed, with the furniture and stock in trade.

From the LONDON GAZETTE.
An order of the House of Commons.
Jovis, 26 Die Aprilis, 1770.

Ordered. That Mr. Speaker do forthwith give notice, that the sum of one million five hundred thousand pounds capital stock of annuities, after the rate of three pounds ten shillings *per centum*, established by an act made in the 29th year of the reign of his late Majesty King George the Second, intituled An act for granting to his Majesty the sum of two millions, to be raised by way of annuities and a lottery, and charged on the Sinking Fund, redeemable by parliament, and for extending to Ireland the laws made in this kingdom against private and unlawful lotteries, will be redeemed and paid off on the 12th day of February next, after discharging the interest then payable in respect of the same, agreeable to the clauses and powers of redemption contained in the said act.

Which order, thus signified and published by me, is to be sufficient notice of the re-payment of one million five hundred thousand pounds, for which the said annuities were established, and of the redemption of the annuities as are attending the same,

FR. NORTON, Speaker.

30th. On April 18, was brought to his Majesty's warehouse at Weymouth, by Mr. John Bishop, and two other officers, 133 bags of tea, containing in quantity about 1,564lb. part of the cargo of the Hector cutter, Capt. Harvey.—On th night of the 25th, Mr. Bishop, having reason to believe that more goods would be run by the same vessel, ordered his boat to be manned, and went out to make his observations, when he discovered the cutter standing at a distance, waiting, as was supposed, for the return of the boat out of which the first cargo was seized. Mr. Bishop then made towards her, but never returned, being run down, it is thought, by the smugglers; by which act of cruelty, Mr. Bishop and his boat's crew, consisting of five stout men, all perished in the sea. One only has yet been taken up, about a mile from the place where the first seizure was made.

This day at noon came on, at St. Paul's, Covent Garden, the election of a representative in parliament for the city and liberty of Westminster, in the room of the Hon. Edwin Sandys, now Lord Sandys, when Sir Robert Bernard was elected without opposition. The voters were so determined that Sir Robert Bernard should not spend a shilling on his election, that they would not suffer him even to pay for the chocolate made use of in the vestry.

A lottery bill passed the House of Commons upon an entire new plan, very advantageous to the public. There are 50,000 tickets, valued at 14l. each, but intrinsically worth only 10l. each. And in order to induce the stock-holders of 4 per cent. bank annuities to subscribe their stock into the 3 per cents. consolidated, every subscriber of 100l. capital stock is to have two lottery tickets, on the payment of 20l. which two tickets, it is supposed, will sell for 30l. before the drawing of the lottery begins. The tickets that remain unsubscribed

scribed for in this manner are to be sold at the rate of 14l. each, and those who subscribe are to have the option of the purchase, in proportion to their respective subscription.

Vienna, April 21. On Thursday last, at six of the clock in the evening, the court assembled in the church of the Augustins, passing through the gallery which leads to it from the palace. This gallery was illuminated from one end to the other with wax-lights in glass sconces, ornamented with flowers: on each side of it were two lines of grenadiers; and the vestibule, at the top of the stairs leading to the Augustins, was decorated with large lustres and sconces, fastened by cords formed into festoons of flowers.

Near the high altar, on the gospel-side, was a canopy, under which were two chairs of state for their Imperial Majesties: at a small distance from this canopy, and in the same line, were other state-chairs for the royal family: an alcove, with two state-chairs, was erected in the front of the altar for the Archduke Ferdinand, the Proxy for the Dauphin, to espouse the Archdutchess in his name.

When their Majesties were seated under the canopy, the Archduke Ferdinand and the Archdutchess took the places appropriated for them in the front of the altar, which was magnificently adorned. After the benediction of the nuptial rings by M. Visconti, the Pope's Nuncio, assisted by several bishops and mitred abbots, and by the clergy of the Court, their Royal Highnesses advanced to the altar, and that prelate gave them the nuptial benediction with the usual ceremonies.

After this ceremony the Dauphiness admitted the ladies to an audience, and to kiss her hand: then followed a public supper, during which the music of the chapel performed several Italian airs, and different pieces of music.

Died. Lately, at her hut at Norwood, Bridget, the Queen of the Gipseys, who died worth above 1,000l.

At Fontainebleau, one Perrette Chaalon, in the 106th year of her age.

At Montauban, M. Jean Froment, widow of the Sieur Sourdez, of Figeac, aged 103 years.

MAY.

A motion was made in the House of Peers by the Earl of Chatham, for bringing in a bill declaring the resolutions of the House of Commons with regard to the expulsion of Mr. Wilkes to be illegal and arbitrary; but, after a long debate, the same was rejected by a majority of 46, there being 89 against it to 43 in favour of it; among the latter two bishops only: Dr. Ewer, bishop of Bangor, and Dr. Keppel, Bishop of Exeter. 1st.

The Lord Bishop of Chester presented Christ's Hospital with a benefaction of 200l. on which the thanks of the court were ordered to be given, and a staff to be sent to his Lordship.

The Pelham cutter, in the service of his Majesty's customs, stationed at Beaumaris, being at anchor at Port Usby's Bay, on the coast

coast of Wales, was piratically attacked by two large smuggling cutters, and a large wherry, the crew of which fired upon the officers on board, drove the men on shore for the preservation of their lives, boarded the Pelham, and plundered her, and drove her ashore among the rocks.

Letters from Bourdeaux bring an account of a terrible accident that happened there on Sunday the 8th of April, by the rising of the waters of the Garronne. That river was full of chalops and small vessels, laden with the goods and moveables of poor people. A large tree, borne down by the violence of the current, broke the cable of an old hulk, which set adrift five or six ships, and these drew along with them a hundred of those small craft, which were all driven towards the sea. The sight was dreadful. The crews of many of these vessels happened to be ashore; those who were on board could do nothing but pray to God to have mercy upon them. Most of the small craft perished with all those on board; three or four of the ships were entirely sunk, and every one of the rest were either run aground, or shared the fate of those that perished. The whole loss is estimated at six millions of livres.

3d. About 10 o'clock at night, a young man was mortally wounded, in his way home from Sadler's Wells: he was set upon by two young villains, whom he resisted; but a third starting up with a blunderbuss, discharged it full at his body, which tore him in such a manner that his bowels came out, after which they made their escape without robbing him. He lingered a few days, and then died. The murderers have since been taken.

A dreadful fire broke out in the little town of Eldgason, about two miles from Hanover, by which 120 houses were reduced to ashes.

By virtue of a warrant under the seal of Great Britain, directed to and received by John Toke, Esq. at Rochester, High Sheriff for the county of Kent, proper officers were dispatched to the transport ship then in the Downs, to take into custody, by attachment, the body of Matthew Kennedy, to answer to the appeal of Ann Bigby, widow, touching the murder of her husband; in consequence of which, the said Matthew Kennedy was safely lodged in Maidstone gaol. When a motion for the above warrant was moved for at the Old Bailey, the Recorder of London told the council who made it, that he had no power to stop him, nor even to hold him, if he had been present, unless a bill had been found in consequence of the appeal. To which the Lord Mayor made a spirited answer, and told him, that he would take it upon himself, and would sign the warrant; which he did, and dispatched it immediately: his Lordship also ordered Mr. Akerman to detain Patrick Kennedy; and assured the whole court, that no murderer should ever escape justice while he lived, and was able to bring him to it; and that he himself would be answerable for every bad consequence which might arise from the supposed illegal method of bringing Kennedy from the ship to take his trial at the next sessions.

[*H*] 4 By

By letters from Cadiz we learn, that the Spanish galleon, called Adventure, which has been a long time expected from Peru, is at length arrived in that harbour, after a dangerous voyage of eight months. She was entangled in vast quantities of ice near Cape Horn, and the crew during a whole month expected to perish every instant. They were at one part of that period thrown upon a floating bank of ice, and carried in that extraordinary situation between seven and eight leagues. After various perils, they had the good fortune to get into Rio Janeiro. The little hopes there were of the return of this vessel occasioned her to be insured at 10 per cent.

5th. A motion was made in the House of Lords, for presenting an address to his Majesty, that he would be graciously pleased to inform the House who the person was that advised his Majesty to give orders for proroguing the Irish parliament, when that step was taken; but it was rejected.

Two prizes were contended for by the Masters of Arts, at the University of Glasgow; the first for the encouragement of elocution; the other for the advancement of physic. The first was determined in favour of William Cruickshank; the second in favour of Mr. Archibald Arthur.

The Duke of Richmond had lately a narrow escape for his life. It seems his Grace hath long had a wolf at Goodwood, which was bred up tame; but breaking his chain one day, nature took place, and he marched off into the country; but being followed by several men, was brought back, and placed as before. His Grace afterwards going alone to view him, the creature flew at him, and catched hold of his waistcoat upon the belly; but that giving way, his Grace was retreating, when the beast again catched hold of the skirt of his coat; but fortunately his Grace after a long struggle escaped, leaving part of his coat behind him. The beast was immediately shot.

A letter received at Brest from the Guinea coast informs, that a French slaving ship, Captain Grandier, having been surprised by an insurrection of the negroes, who murdered most of the crew, the joiner, finding no possibility to escape the like fate, had set fire to the powder-room, and blew the vessel up with two hundred and seventy-four slaves on board.

A few days ago a servant man that lived with Mr. Holmes, a brickmaker at Woolwich, told his master that he had something very heavy on his mind: his master asked him what it was? when he told him, that he had formerly been a smuggler, and about six months ago had murdered a dragoon, and desired that he might be carried before a magistrate; he accordingly was carried before Justice Russel, where he made an ample confession of the whole, and was committed to Maidstone gaol.

10th. They write from Harwich, that on Tuesday night, as Mr. Day, wheelwright, at Ramsay, with his wife, sister, journeyman, apprentice, and a girl about fourteen, were returning from our fair in an open boat near the shore, the boy went up the mast to make the sail clear, which overset the boat, and the wife

wife was carried away by the tide, and drowned. The husband and apprentice went in search of her, and plunged about the ooze till they found a small boat, in which from fatigue and cold they lay and expired. The sister was brought off the mud about seven the next morning, and died soon after; but the girl and journeyman, who were found at the same time, are likely to recover.

The following remarkable catastrophe happened to a married couple in the city, who were buried a few days ago:—The wife was betwixt twenty and thirty, and the husband eight or ten years older. They went to bed in good health, and in the morning, the wife waking, found her husband dead and cold, from whence it might be concluded that he had expired five or six hours before. She appeared to bear the loss with moderate concern and fortitude, till the corpse was carried out of the house to be buried; at which time she burst into a violent flood of tears, which were succeeded by fits: when her fits went off, her reason appeared to have left her, and in a great degree her senses, as she seemed insensible of every thing that passed; and in this state she continued two days, and then died.

11th. The report was made to his Majesty of the malefactors under sentence of death in Newgate, when thirteen were ordered for execution, and seventeen respited.

Was held by Sir Robert Ladbroke, a general court of electors of the Hon. Artillery Company, when the long-contested dispute respecting the legality of the serjeants voting at the said court was absolutely and finally determined their favour.

A gentleman in town has laid before a learned body a new invented method of hatching chickens, and rearing them quicker for the spit than ever was before discovered; for which that respectable society has honoured him with a gold medal. The process is as follows:— The chickens are to be taken away from the hen the night after hatched, and are to be replaced with eggs, on which the hen will continue to sit, for a second and a third brood. When first taken from the hen, they are to be fed with eggs, boiled hard and chopped fine, mixed with bread, as larks and other birds are fed, for a fortnight; after which give them oatmeal and treacle, so mixed that it will crumble, of which the chickens are so fond, and with which they thrive so fast, that at two months end they will be as large as full-grown fowls.

15th. The King and Dauphin of France had the first interview with the young Dauphiness. They met at the bridge of Berne, in the forest of Compiegne, and their first salutation was very tender and affecting.

14th. A court of common council was held, to consider of an address, petition, and remonstrance to his Majesty, upon his Majesty's answer to the address, petition, and remonstrance of the common hall, and of the resolutions and address of both houses of parliament thereupon; when a motion was made, that the part respecting the answer given by his Majesty should be left out; but on a division, seven aldermen, and

105 commoners, were for retaining the part respecting his Majesty's answer, and eight aldermen, and fifty-seven commoners, were for rejecting the part respecting his Majesty's answer, and for confining it to the Middlesex election only.

Then a motion was made, that a committee be appointed, and that they do immediately withdraw, and prepare an humble petition, address, and remonstrance, respecting the Middlesex election, and the answer given by his Majesty to the livery address, &c. And the following committee was appointed, viz.

Aldermen:—Trecothick, Stephenson, Crosby, Townshend, Sawbridge, Wilkes.

Commoners:—George Bellas, Esq. Mr. Beardmore, Samuel Freeman, Esq. Deputy Judd, Deputy Sainsbury, Mr. Sharp, Mr. Anderson, Mr. Bishop, Mr. Burford, Mr. William Wilson, Mr. Plomer, Mr. Shove.

They withdrew, and prepared the address, &c. accordingly, and presented it to the court. On a division, for the address, &c. seven aldermen, and 91 commoners: against it, six aldermen, and 40 commoners.

The Earl of Chatham made a motion in the House of Lords for an address to the King, to desire he would dissolve this present parliament. He stated the public discontent in England, Ireland, and America; affirmed that the people had no confidence in the present House of Commons; and shewed, from the situation of public affairs, the great necessity of having a parliament in, whom the people can place a proper confidence. Arguments, however, were in vain: the question was called for, and carried in the negative.

Naples, April 24. The Duke of Dorset arrived here on Thursday last; and his courier, a Piedmontese, having had some words with the master of the ferry-boat, who demanded more than his due, at the passage of the Garigliano, and these words having produced blows, the ferryman deliberately fetched a gun, which he presented at the courier, who was then in the boat with his master: on this the courier jumped out of the boat, and screened himself behind some peasants who were standing by; but the ferryman still taking his aim at the courier, the latter ran up to him, who shot him dead upon the spot. His Sicilian Majesty, being informed of this transaction, immediately issued his orders for apprehending the ferryman; but it is most probable that he is fled into the Roman state.

This morning, between three and four o'clock, a 16th. fire broke out at the house of Mr. Pool, in Palsgrave-head Court, without Temple-bar, which consumed the same, with all the furniture. The family were obliged to jump out of the windows to save their lives, three of whom were much hurt. The house of Mr. Williams, surgeon, and all his furniture; that of Mr. Withaw, tailor, his furniture, and a large quantity of gentlemen's cloaths, &c. to a considerable value, were burnt; a watchmaker's house was likewise consumed, and part of Mr. Twining's tea warehouse is burnt down: not one house in the court on either side escaped the fury of the flames, but most of them are greatly damaged. Several persons

sons who forced their way in to view the fire were near being buried under the ruins of one of the houses which fell down. It is said, that a gentlewoman was so much burnt, that she died soon after.

The livery of the worshipful Company of Goldsmiths met at the Half-Moon Tavern, in Cheapside, and unanimously resolved, that the warden of their company could not be justified for disobedience to the Lord Mayor's precept; and they declared their readiness to testify their obedience to their chief magistrate on all occasions, particularly on that of a late common hall.

The thirteen convicts ordered for execution were conveyed to Tyburn in five carts, and executed according to their sentence: most of them were boys; the eldest not above twenty-two: some of them were greatly affected, others so hardened, that they ridiculed the punishment of death, and laughed at their companions for being afraid of it.

The ceremony of the nuptials of the Dauphin and Dauphiness was performed at the chapel royal at Versailles, by the Archbishop of Rheims. After supper, the King having conducted their Highnesses to their apartment, and the benediction of the bed having been made by the Archbishop, the King delivered the shirt to the Dauphin; and the Dutchess of Chartres performed the same office to the Dauphiness.

The following was the compliment paid by the Count de Noailles, Plenipotentiary Commissary from the King of France, when he received the Dauphiness from the hands of his Excellency the Prince de Stahrenberg, Plenipotentiary from the Empress Queen.—" The honourable commission which the King my Master has been pleased to entrust me with, enhances the measure of gratitude which I owe for favours received from him. I want no other felicity but to be able to represent faithfully to your Highness the sentiments of his Majesty, and his ardent desire to see you partake of his tenderness with the rest of his Royal Family. The whole nation, whose interpreter I am, sighs for the happy moment which is to announce to two great empires the perpetuity of their happiness, by securing to two of the most antient families of the universe the bands which unite them. What ought we not to hope for from a Princess, brought up in virtue by an august mother, the glory of her sex, and mother of kings! Formed by such great examples, the Dauphiness will find in the happiness she enjoys the pledge of that which she will procure to France."

19th. This day his Majesty went to the House of Peers, and gave the royal assent to the following bills, viz.

The bill for granting to his Majesty a sum out of the sinking fund, and for applying certain monies therein mentioned for the service of the present year.

The bill for redeeming the capital or joint stock of annuities, after the rate of 3l. 10s. per cent. established in the 29th year of the reign of his late Majesty.

The bill for establishing a lottery, and for other purposes.

The bill to continue an act for encouraging the making of indigo in the British plantations in America.

The bill to appropriate a fund for granting to his Majesty additional duties on certain foreign linens imported, and for establishing a fund for encouraging of the raising and dressing hemp and flax.

The bill to continue an act for granting a bounty on British and Irish linens exported.

The bill for registering the prices at which corn is sold in the several counties in Great Britain.

The bill to explain and amend the several acts for providing a public reward for discovering the longitude at sea.

The bill to prevent delays of justice by reason of privilege of parliament.

The bill for better regulating the persons employed in the service of the East India Company.

The bill for the relief of the coal-heavers working in the river Thames; and to enable them to make provision for themselves, their widows, and orphans.

The bill for compleating the navigation of the river Swale, from its junction with the Ure to Merton-bridge, in Yorkshire.

The bill for making a navigable canal from Leeds to the sea bank, near the North Ladies' walk, by Liverpool.

The bill for extending the like liberty to the exportation of rice from East and West Florida to the southward of Cape Finisterre, in Europe, as is granted to Carolina and Georgia.

And also to some other public and private bills.

After which his Majesty made a most gracious speech from the throne, and the Lord Speaker, by his Majesty's command, prorogued the parliament to the 19th of July next.

22d. This morning, between eight and nine o'clock, the Queen was happily delivered of a Princess. Her Royal Highness the Princess Dowager of Wales, his Grace the Archbishop of Canterbury, several lords of his Majesty's most honourable privy-council, and the ladies of her Majesty's bed-chamber, were present.

23d. One Grieves, a pawn-broker, taken up a few days ago, on suspicion of setting fire to his own house, the bottom of Wych-street, at the back of St. Clement's Church, with intent to defraud the insurance office, was re-examined before Sir John Fielding, when it appeared that he had insured his effects on the 30th of April last for 2,300l.; that he had begun a new book, containing an account of the pledges taken on the next day; that the number and value of the pawns entered from that day to the time of the late accident amounted to five times more than during the like number of days in any preceding month; that he had altered the value of many of the pledges entered in a former book: for example, he had charged a gown 10l. 9s. the ticket pinned upon which mentioned it to be only 1l. 9s.; another gown 10l. 6s. marked upon the ticket 1l. 6s.; a pair of stone buckles, ticket marked 10s. 6d. entered in the book 10l. 10s.; with a variety of other articles of a similar nature, all tending to prove his intention of defrauding the

the office. The list of the pawns from May 1 to last week appeared to be written all at one time.—In several places of the old book he had very evidently inserted articles.

The fire broke out in a stable adjoining to the back-yard of his house, about two o'clock on Monday morning last, when he was seen to be up by a washer-woman in the house. Some time after the fire in the stable was extinguished, the alarm was given that his house was on fire. Upon searching, one Woodward, a fireman, perceived, by peeping through the keyhole, a parcel of cloaths on fire in a room, the door of which was locked, up three pair of stairs, fronting the street, quite at a distance from the stable. The bed in another room up two pair of stairs backwards was found also on fire, though the windows, and every other part of the room, were not even discoloured by smoke: and some cloaths in the shop upon the ground floor, the door of which was locked, were also seen to be burning at the same time.

From these circumstances, there appeared such strong suspicions of his guilt, that he was committed to Newgate to take his trial at the ensuing sessions. Some pawnbrokers, who had been employed to value his goods, declare them to be not worth more than 700l. and that they cannot find many articles entered in the book.

25th. This morning, about 11 o'clock, Matthew Kennedy was brought to the bar of the Court of King's-bench, when, after reading the writ of Habeas Corpus, and the declaration of appeal, by a motion from Counsellor Wallace, he was turned over to the Sheriff, and is to appear next term, when the merits of the appeal will be fully debated; and in the mean time he is committed to the King's-bench prison. He was in double chains in a blue coat, with a handkerchief about his neck, and looked greatly dejected: he was only in court about ten minutes, when the court was extremely full. The declaration of appeal was against the two brothers, Patrick and Matthew, both laid to be in the custody of the same officer, whereas the one is in the custody of the Sheriff of Middlesex, and the other in the Sheriff of Kent; a circumstance which one perhaps may avail himself of. The widow was present, accompanied by the waterman's boy, one of the principal evidences upon the former trial, who declared in open court, that he was offered 100l. to keep out of the way. Lord Spencer, Lord Palmerston, George Selwyn, Esq. and several persons of distinction, friends to the unhappy prisoners, were likewise present.

A court of common council was held at Guildhall, when an address to his Majesty, on the birth of the young Princess, was agreed to. His Majesty has appointed next Wednesday for the reception of it.

The principal merchants concerned in the American trade sent down counter orders to the manufacturing counties to postpone the commissions for American exportation, on account of the parliament being prorogued, without full redress having been obtained for the grievances complained of from that continent.

This

27th. This night, between ten and eleven o'clock, as Mr. Venables, a wholesale carcass-butcher, in Whitechapel-market, and Mr. Rogers, cabinet-maker, in Houndsditch, were returning from the Blue-Anchor alehouse, at Stepney, they were attacked in Redman's Grove by three footpads, who demanded their money; and on their making resistance, the villains fired at them, shot Mr. Venables under the jaw-bone, and the ball went through the lower part of his head. Mr. Rogers was shot in the forehead just above his eye: they both expired immediately. The unfortunate deceased persons staying after their friends to have another bowl of punch, occasioned their meeting with the fatal accident.

Paris, May 18. The presents of jewels made by the King and the Royal Family to the Dauphiness upon her marriage are valued at three millions of livres, upwards of 130,000l. sterling.

The six companies of merchants of this city celebrated the marriage of the Dauphin with a benevolence that does honour to that body. The 17th they visited the prisons, and delivered such as had been confined for debts contracted for necessary provisions.

28th. William De Grey, Esq. his Majesty's Attorney-general, moved the Court of King's-bench for the discharge of Mr. Bingley: the Court refused to do it; but the Attorney-general, as law-officer to the crown, insisted upon it, as Mr. Bingley had suffered two years imprisonment, which was sufficient for any offence he may have been guilty of. He was set at liberty accordingly.

A very remarkable act was lately solemnized at Newstadt, in the Queen of Hungary's dominions. The bones of the great Emperor Maximilian I. were again interred, after a second absolution. The occasion was as follows: The Empress Queen, having ordered the imperial palace of that city to be fitted up for the use of the Theresian Military Academy just established there, and the church thereto belonging to be repaired and beautified, and new altars to be added, on the 21st of February, when the workmen were employed in taking down the great altar, a coffin was discovered under the masonry, very much decayed. Upon consulting the antient archives, it was found, that the body of Maximilian I. had been deposited in the church dedicated to St. George, the church in question; upon which the farther operations were suspended till after her Imperial Majesty's permission to open the coffin should be obtained: to do this, in order to confirm the truth of the antient record, her Majesty was graciously pleased to give her consent; and accordingly, on the 11th of March, the mouldered coffin was examined, and the sacred relics of that glorious prince were actually found. Her Imperial Majesty being certified of the fact, ordered a leaden coffin to be prepared, and inclosed in a coffin of wood, for the reception of those precious relics, in order that they might again be deposited in the same place, now under the great altar, with the usual ceremonies. Upon a nice examination of the body, before its second interment, it appeared to have been first covered with quick-lime, and then

CHRONICLE

to have been wrapt in white linen, over which it seemed to have been cloathed in a vest of white damask, with a mantle of scarlet velvet embroidered. It is remarkable, that not only the different vestments were still discernible, but also their different colours. On his breast was fixed a leaden plate, on which was engraven a Latin inscription.

29th. A placart was this day published by order of the States General, prohibiting, for six weeks, all commerce by land and water between the inhabitants of the Republic and the subjects of the Elector Palatine, the foundation of which was owing to some contraband proceedings on both sides; in consequence of which, much altercation has ensued. Sugars belonging to the Palatines have been detained at Rotterdam, and in return some boats have been stopped belonging to the Dutch upon the Lower Rhine. The affair is become serious, and if not speedily accommodated may possibly be productive of a rupture.

30th. On account of the Queen's safe delivery, a little before one, the Lord Mayor, the Aldermen, the Sheriffs, and Common Council, set out from Guildhall with the address.

In going, after the Lord Mayor, Sir Robert Ladbroke, Mr. Alderman Alsop, and Sir William Stephenson, had passed through Temple Bar, the gates were suddenly shut against Mr. Alderman Harley (who was next in the procession) by a mob, few in number, who directly began to pelt him with stones and dirt, and pulled him out of his chariot, opposite to the door of the Sun Tavern, into which he was forced to take, to preserve his life. After continuing here some time, he went away in a hackney coach, with a gentleman who had accompanied him, but not without being followed and insulted by part of the mob that at first beset him.

As soon as the Lord Mayor heard the gates were shut, he sent Mr. Gates, the City Marshal, back, who opened them without any obstruction, and the whole procession (Mr. Harley excepted) arrived at St. James's about ten minutes before two, the time appointed for their reception.

After the Lord Mayor had waited in the anti-chamber at St. James's a considerable time, the Lord Chamberlain came out with a paper in his hand, and read to the following effect: "As your Lordship thought fit to speak to his Majesty after his answer to the late remonstrance, I am to acquaint your Lordship, as it was unusual, his Majesty desires that nothing of this kind may happen for the future." The Lord Mayor then desired the paper might be delivered to him. The Lord Chamberlain said he acted officially, and had it not in orders to deliver the paper. The Lord Mayor then desired a copy: to which the Lord Chamberlain replied, he would acquaint his Majesty, and take his directions; but he did not return until the order was brought for the whole court to attend with the address.

Sir Robert Ladbroke complained to the Lord Mayor, that stones were thrown at his coach. The Lord Mayor called Mr. Gates, the City Marshal, face to face with the Father of the city, and asked him, if that was so, who contradicted Sir Robert? He then said, dirt was thrown.

thrown. The Lord Mayor anfwered, there was no dirt in the ftreet. Sir Robert then faid, that the mob fpit in at the windows of his coach.

In the Prefence Chamber, Mr. Rigby attacked the Lord Mayor, telling him he had promifed in parliament to be anfwerable for the peace of the city, and that he was informed by Sir Robert Ladbroke that there had been a great riot in the city, which his Lordfhip had taken no care to quell.

The Lord Mayor immediately replied, that he fhould be ready to anfwer for his conduct at all times, in all places, and on every proper occafion.

Mr. Sheriff Townfhend ftanding by the Lord Mayor, told him, Mr. Rigby fays there has been a great tumult in the city. Mr. Rigby replied, Sir Robert Ladbroke fays fo. Mr. Townfhend afked him, if Sir Robert Ladbroke was not a magiftrate? And why he had not appeafed the tumult, if there was one? Mr. Rigby faid, the magiftrates had been mobbed. Mr. Townfend replied, taking the whole together, in his opinion, the people had been mobbed by the magiftrates, and not the magiftrates by the people. *For the addrefs, and his Majefty's anfwer, fee the State Papers.*

31ft. This day the Lord Mayor, attended by the two Sheriffs, and fome other of the worfhipful Court of Aldermen, proceeded in ftate to the Old Bailey, where his Lordfhip laid the firft ftone of a new gaol, intended inftead of the prefent very inconvenient one of Newgate. His Lordfhip, after laying the above ftone, made a prefent of twenty guineas to the workmen, and then proceeded to the feffions-houfe to try the prifoners.

Edinburgh, April 25. Yefterday came on before the High Court of Jufticiary here, the trial of William Harris, alias Harries, concerned in the forging and iffuing out falfe notes of the Thiftle Bank of Glafgow. Upon the pannel's coming into court, his behaviour indicated fome degree of infanity; upon which his lawyer, Mr. Bofwell, fuggefted that he was not a proper object of punifhment. That objection, however, being overruled, about two o'clock the jury for the trial of forgery, &c. were chofen, and the proof taken before the court of feffion was read to them. They inclofed about feven; and this day at ten returned their verdict, unanimoufly finding him guilty; upon which he was fentenced to be hanged in the Grafs-Market, upon the 30th of May next. The above William Harries, before his being found out, had iffued 452 forged notes; and, when apprehended, there were found no lefs than 9,677, all for 20s. each. The laft were, according to an order of court, committed this afternoon to the flames, and burnt.

The Pynfent caufe, now depending in the Court of Chancery, and which has been heard three fucceeding Saturdays in this Eafter term, is founded on the doubtful right of the late Sir William Pynfent to bequeath his real eftates to the Earl of Chatham; the Rev. Sir Robert Pynfent, now Rector of Killymore, in the kingdom of Ireland, contending that the teftator had no right to make fuch bequeft to the prejudice of him the heir at law. On this iffue is joined:

feveral

several learned arguments have been urged on both sides, and the matter still depending is of 24,000l. value.

The grandest fire-works that have ever been known were this evening exhibited in the square of Lewis XV. at Paris, in honour of the Dauphin's marriage; but the fatal catastrophe that marked this exhibition will long be remembered with horror and regret. It appears that the plan of the fire-works was so vast, that it exceeded the powers of the engineer to regulate all its parts, and to restrain its effects; and some of the apparatus having exceeded his intention, or playing off untimely, threw sheets of fire upon the people. The dreadful consequences that ensued from this alarm might in a great measure be imputed to the inattention of the magistrates. In the first place, there was no scaffold erected for the convenience of the spectators; and in the next, the communications between the Place de Louis and the Boulevards, which consist of three streets, were in a manner blocked up: that on the left hand, the Ruë la Bonne Morue, being narrow, was rendered impassable by the coaches; that on the right, called Ruë St. Florentin, in which the Count St. Florentin, Secretary of State, has his residence, and in whose department the care of this metropolis is, and by whose order the fire-works were exhibited, for the conveniency of himself and friends, his Excellency would not permit the populace to pass; and this being the principal thoroughfare from the Place de Louis, where the fire-works were exhibited, to the Boulevards, there was only the middle street free for the foot-passengers. The astonishing multitude that had crowded to see the fire-works being seized with a panic, upon finding a hurry and confusion, for which the greater part of them were unable to account, endeavoured to escape through this narrow street, which they soon jammed up in such a manner as to make it impassable. The confusion increased to such a degree, that one trampled over another, till the people lay one upon another in heaps; those who were undermost stabbed those who lay above them, in order to disengage themselves. The pickpockets and robbers availed themselves of the confusion; and many ladies had their ear-rings torn out of their ears. A scaffold, erected near the palace of Bourbon, broke down with the over-weight of the spectators, who all fell into the river. There have been already taken up above a hundred drowned at St. Cloud, but many bodies have been driven beyond that place. The carnage was dreadful. It is computed that not less than 3,000 are either killed, wounded, or rendered cripples during the remainder of their days.

The humanity of the new-married pair on this melancholy occasion cannot be sufficiently applauded. The Dauphin, in the first transports of his grief, gave all the money allotted for his month's expences towards the relief of the sufferers; and in this act of generosity he was followed by the Dauphiness, whose mind was so deeply impressed with the relation of what had happened, that it was with difficulty she could be kept from fainting. His Majesty was

was also greatly affected, and issued orders, that no expence might be spared to succour and assist the miserable. In short, such a scene of real distress never before presented itself, and it is thought it will be a means of utterly abolishing that kind of entertainment for the future.

The number of the dead, so far as the bodies that were drowned have been recovered, appears by the latest and best accounts to have been in all 712. Among which were four monks, two abbés, and twenty-two persons of condition. It does not appear that there are any English among the number.

His Most Christian Majesty has ordered 100,000 livres to be expended towards the relief of the unfortunate persons who were hurt, or have lost their relations in the confusion on the night of the city fire-works. The Dauphiness and the Mesdames have also contributed.

At Grozette, in Italy, there has been discovered, at the depth of 8 feet, an antient furnace, about which were found some antique medals, but most of them so effaced with rust, that it was with difficulty the time of building the furnace could be made out. Upon the reverse of one of these medals, which appears to be of the Emperor Florio, the words *Victor Orbis* may plainly be read. This Emperor is not mentioned in the supplement published by Muratori and Vallemont; but in the line of Emperors recited by others, we find him in the second century of the vulgar æra, about which time this furnace seems to have been constructed. There is another medal of the Emperor Germanicus, but it is impossible to ascertain to which of the Emperors of that name it belongs. About the same depth, but in another place, there have likewise been discovered some fragments of baked earth, among which are several lachrymatory vases that were antiently placed by the coffins of the dead, and even some remains of the sepulchres in which these lachrymatories are supposed to have been deposited. Of the same earth some urns were found, about two feet high, one foot in circumference about the middle, and between six and seven in the neck; but what was most remarkable, these urns were not made flat at bottom, but ended in a point, which were stuck in the ground, in order to make them stand upright. Within these urns were found small bones, almost reduced to powder, from whence it should seem that they were formed for the preservation of some fragments of the dead.

York, May 22. There is now living in the parish of Wigan, in Lancashire, one Fairbrother, aged 138 years. The youngest of his four sons is now 104 years old, and the father still follows the trade of a cooper.

Died. Lately, Chauncy Townsend, Esq. member for Wigtown, in Scotland (being the first Englishman that ever represented any place in Scotland).

Mrs. Gordon, a maiden lady, supposed to have died worth upwards of 50,000l. great part of which she has left to charitable uses; among the rest, one thousand pounds for erecting an hospital for the relief of indigent old maids.

At Bath, in the 103d year of her age, Sarah Deson, of that city. At

CHRONICLE. [115

At Wooburn, in Bedfordshire, John Storey, aged 105 years, formerly gardener to his Grace the Duke of Bedford; from whose bounty he has enjoyed an annual pension of 20l. for upwards of 20 years last past.

JUNE.

1st. The committee of the court of common council, appointed to present the Earl of Chatham with the thanks of that court for his patriotic conduct in parliament, waited on his Lordship this day accordingly.

At the annual meeting of the charitable society for the relief of the widows and orphans of clergymen, held at Canterbury, 225l. 15s. was ordered to be distributed amongst 12 widows, and 22 orphans.

By a private letter from France we learn, that the third day after her marriage, the Dauphiness went to pay a visit to her aunt, the Princess Louisa, who has retired into the Carmelite nunnery at St. Dennis. That religious order is prodigiously severe, and the novitiate remarkably so. When the Dauphiness was received by the Princess, she was conducted to her cell by an old nun, and no other attendant, except Madame Sophia, the King of France's second daughter. The Princess Louisa opened the door of the cell herself. She appeared in the habit of a novice of the order, in a flannel shift and wooden shoes without stockings. She never touches either milk or butter, and flesh meat but twice a week; and during the last quarter of her noviciate she will not taste it at all. Her Royal Highness's bed is a mattress on the floor, with a single coverlid. She sleeps but five hours in the four and twenty, and will not take off her cloaths when she lies down, refusing any indulgence on account of her rank. She presented the Dauphiness with a small crucifix of gold, set with diamonds, which belonged to the Queen her mother, and was the only thing of value she had left herself. She had a crucifix made of box-wood, which she immediately hung on her breast instead of it.

The sessions ended at the Old Bailey. At this sessions 2d. 83 prisoners were tried, 13 received sentence of death, 3 to be transported for 14 years, 24 for 7 years, 2 were branded, and 4 whipped.

This morning, a little after nine, came on in the Court of King's-bench, Westminster Hall, before the Right Hon. the Lord Mansfield, the trial of Mr. Almon, by information, for *selling* the letter of Junius to the King in the London Museum. A little before twelve the jury went out, and staid upwards of two hours, when they returned, and put a question to the court, whether the master could be deemed guilty of publishing what had been only sold by his servant, and that without his knowledge? The judge answered, that in his opinion he was, as every master is answerable for the acts of his servant. The jury thereupon immediately brought him in guilty, and his sentence now remains in the breast of the court. But a new trial is moved for, and expected.

[*I*] 2 *Extract*

Extract of a letter from Portsmouth.

This day arrived the Tamer sloop of war, and the Florida store-ship, from Port Egmont, in Falkland Island, near the Streights of Magellan. By these ships we learn, that two Spanish frigates of 36 guns each came to Port Egmont, and, in the name of his Catholic Majesty, required our people to quit the island. The Spaniards have transported troops from Buenos Ayres, and have left a garrison on that part of the island lately settled by the French.

John Stretcher, a German, who had absconded with 185l. of his master's money, which he was entrusted to receive at the bank, was overtaken by Mr. Johnson, of Austin Friars, one of the partners in the loss, at Boulogne, and by the readiness of the magistrates of that city he was secured. On the first surprize of being taken, he delivered up the whole money, except the little he had expended; and Mr. Johnson, pleased with his repentance, gave him ten guineas to bear his expences to his own country.

4th. Charles Stevens, Henry Holyoak, and Henry Hughes, were executed at Tyburn, pursuant to their sentence, for the murder of Mr. Shaw, and afterwards carried to Surgeons-hall for dissection: the two latter declared that Stevens had brought them into a bad course of life.

6th. Was tried before Lord Chief Justice Wilmot, at Guildhall, a cause in which the assignee of a bankrupt was plaintiff. The plaintiff's case consisted in a charge against the defendant, for having encouraged the bankrupt to purchase goods on credit (under false pretences) of a linen-draper, to the amount of 500l. and upwards, in order to raise money thereon to answer his present exigencies, which goods it appeared the bankrupt sold to the defendant at the same price, though he only received half the money; for which the defendant forced the bankrupt to give him a receipt in full; but, notwithstanding these receipts, the jury found a verdict for the plaintiff to the amount of the short payments, viz. 258l.

8th. This morning, about half past six o'clock, her Royal Highness the Princess Dowager of Wales set out with a grand retinue, from Carlton-house, Pall-mall, for Dover, in order to embark for Germany. She was accompanied by the Duke of Gloucester, and attended by Lord Boston, chamberlain of the household, Lady Howe, one of the ladies of her bed-chamber, Miss Reynolds, and Miss Heinken, dressing-woman to her Royal Highness. It was thirty-four years, the latter end of April last, since her Royal Highness first landed in England in 1736.

Came on before Lord Mansfield in the Court of King's-bench, at Guildhall, a trial on an action brought against a stone-mason for putting bond timber, contrary to act of parliament, into a public house he lately built in this city; when the jury gave a verdict for the plaintiffs, with 40l. damages and costs of suit.

A very important cause came on to be tried in the Court of Common Pleas, at Guildhall, before Lord Chief Justice Wilmot, wherein Mr. Reynolds, of Lime-street,
Under

Under Sheriff of the county of Middlesex, was plaintiff, and a brewer at Stepney was defendant. This action, which concerned every attorney in this kingdom, was brought against the defendant, for illegally, and in an outrageous manner (assisted by ten or twelve men armed with great clubs, hired on purpose), rushing into a room in the King's-head-tavern in Fenchurch-street, where a cause was then on arbitration between one Capt. Smith, a client of Mr. Reynolds's, and Mr. T———, the defendant's partner, and taking and carrying away Mr. Reynolds's bag, which contained his client's papers. The fact was clearly proved; and the judge having summed up the evidence with great impartiality, and told the jury, in an excellent charge, that it was a matter of very great importance; that it did not concern only Mr. Reynolds, but every gentleman in the law in this kingdom; that it was of a most serious nature, and that no gentleman would be safe in entrusting an attorney with any papers, if such daring acts of violence were committed; that he could give the method which the defendant had taken in seizing the bag no other term than stealing, and that the jury should give such damages as might deter persons from doing such flagrant acts of violence for the future. They withdrew for about two minutes, and brought in a verdict for the plaintiff in 100l. damages, besides costs of suit.

13th. This morning, at nine o'clock, came on in the Court of King's-bench, at Guildhall, before Lord Mansfield, the trial of Henry Sampson Woodfall, the original printer of Junius's Letter, in the Public Advertiser of the 19th of December last.

The Attorney-general addressed the jury with a speech on the importance of juries; but confined them to the *bare fact* of the defendant publishing a paper which he called a libel; and then made an apology for bringing on Mr. Almon's trial for *selling only*, before the original printer's, and promised to prosecute all the printers and publishers of this celebrated paper.

Lord Mansfield, in his charge to the jury, said, they had nothing to do with the *intention*, nor with the other words in the information, such as *malicious, seditious*, &c. which he affirmed were all words of course; just as it is said in an indictment for murder, *that the person did, &c. at the instigation of the devil*. Then he remarked, as upon Mr. Almon's trial, that there were but two propositions for the consideration of the jury; one was, the *fact* of publishing the paper; the other, whether a *proper construction* was put, in the information, upon the *several* blanks in the paper in the information; and as to the contents of the paper, whether they were *true* or *false*, he said it was wholly immaterial.

At ten minutes before twelve the jury withdrew, and returned about nine, finding Mr. Woodfall guilty of *printing and publishing only*. The court had broke up about 4 o'clock, so that the jury, by order of Lord Mansfield, attended his Lordship with their verdict, at his house in Bloomsbury-square.

This day the address, petition, and remonstrance from the freeholders of the county of Surry was

pre-

presented to his Majesty at St. James's by Sir Francis Vincent, Bart. one of the representatives of that county in parliament, attended by the Hon. Peter King, Sir Robert Clayton, Sir Joseph Mawbey, Bart. and Benjamin Hayes, Esq.

Three children of a poor cottager in Ireland having eaten of the herb daho, or water-parsnep, two of them died, and the other was with difficulty saved.

A plowman near Bigglefwade, in Bedfordshire, threw up a pot of gold coins, supposed of Edward VI. one of them measured exactly one inch, one quarter, and one eighth in diameter: the representation on one side is a man in armour, in a ship, holding a sword in his right hand, and on his left arm a shield with four compartments of three lions and three fleur-de-lis. On the other side a large cross equally divided, the legend hardly to be made out. They are of pure gold, of seventeen shillings value.

The judgment of the governor and council of Calcutta was reversed by his Majesty's council here, on an appeal from William Bolts, Esq. for removing him from the council there without a sufficient cause.

14th. A comet was discovered by M. Messier, at Paris, about eleven in the evening. It was situated between the head and the bow of Sagittarius, in the milky way, and was scarcely visible with a two-foot telescope. The light of the nucleus was vivid and white. On the night between the 15th and 16th of June, the right ascension of the comet was 272 deg. 57 min. 37 sec. and its declination 15 deg. 55 min. 24 sec. south. On the night between the 20th and 21st, its right ascension was 273 deg. 21 min. 2 sec. By these observations, the motion of the comet in five days is found to be no more than 23 min. one half right ascension, and 1 deg. 25 min. 20 sec. declination. Its motion follows the order of the signs, rising towards the equator; and it passes the meridian about midnight. This comet increases in light, and may become considerable.

15th. Being the first day of term, the two Kennedys were brought before Lord Mansfield, in order to take their trial for murder a second time, on the appeal of the widow Bigby; but it appeared that the plaintiff had pleaded over on the appeal, but not on the bill, which must be done before the court can bring them to trial. This omission made it necessary for the prisoners to be sent back to the King's-bench till the necessary forms are gone through, so that the hearing is put off *fine die*.

About 12 o'clock at noon, a most terrible fire broke out at Foulsham, a market town in Norfolk, occasioned (as supposed) by a person throwing some hot wood-ashes on a dunghill adjoining to an old thatched stable. The weather being dry and windy, 14 houses were entirely consumed; the church, chancel, and steeple, were demolished, leaving only the bare walls standing. The flames raged so fierce and rapid, that many of the poor sufferers lost their all, to their inconceivable distress. The damage cannot yet be computed, but is supposed to amount to some thousands of pounds,

pounds, exclusive of the church. Sir Edward Astley's and Mr. Milles's engines came just time enough to stop the fire at Mr. Quarles's, or the whole town it is thought must have suffered, being mostly thatched buildings.

The governors of the city of London Lying-in hospital held their anniversary meeting, and collected 877l. 18s. 3d. towards the support of that charity.

16th. Was opened the fine monument at the west end of Westminster-abbey, to the memory of the late Richard Tyrrell, Esq. Rear-admiral of the White. The device seems to be taken from that expression in the burial service, *and the sea shall render up her dead.* The Admiral is represented rising into the clouds from the sea, surrounded with angels, one of whom is sounding the last trump, while a second reaches out his hand to assist him in his flight. The under part represents the sea with rocks, and a view of the Buckingham man of war. The figure of Hope is greatly admired; but the critics in sculpture say the whole is too crowded to be easily distinguished but by the eye of an artist.

17th. This evening her Royal Highness the young Princess was christened in the great Council-chamber by his Grace the Archbishop of Canterbury: her Royal Highness was named Elizabeth. The sponsors were, the hereditary Prince of Hesse-Cassel, represented by the Earl of Hertford, Lord Chamberlain of his Majesty's household; the Princess Royal of Sweden, represented by the Countess of Holderness, and the Princess of Nassau-Weilburg, represented by the Countess Dowager of Effingham.

At five o'clock this morning, died the Right Hon. William Beckford, Lord Mayor of the city of London. If his Lordship's character could want any additional lustre, it would receive it from the manner of his death; for notwithstanding his having a heavy cold on him (which he acquired at Fonthill the day before), so attentive was he to discharge the important duty committed to his trust, as chief magistrate of this city, that he travelled a hundred miles in one day, which increased his cold to a rheumatic fever, and thereby terminated the life of a man whose character will ever be held in the most honourable and grateful remembrance.

The late Lord Mayor has made the following disposition of his estate: he has bequeathed a legacy of 5,000l. to each of his natural children, except the eldest son, who was married to a lady of fortune in Jamaica; and to him he left only 1,000l. unless his wife should die before she came of age; and, in that case, 5,000l. in common with the rest: but as the will was made some time ago, and she is now of age, that 4,000l. lapses.

The greatest part of his fortune, real and personal, except some other inconsiderable legacies, he has left to his legitimate son; and in case of his death, to his eldest natural son; and in default of heirs of his body, to his other natural sons in succession, according to seniority.

The lady of the late Lord Mayor having a settlement on her marriage of 1,000l. a year, there is no provision made for her in the will of her husband.

Was finally determined by the Lords Commissioners in Chancery, the

the long depending cause between the Earl of Chatham, as representative of the late Sir William Pynsent, Bart. and —— Daw, Esq. when the decree obtained by his Lordship was reversed in favour of Mr. Daw. The sum contended for, with costs of suit, &c. will amount to between 14 and 15,000l.

22d. A remarkable cause came on this day, upon an action between a gentleman and Miss Jones, on a bond granted by the former to the latter for three thousand pounds. Several bonds had been granted and cancelled, but that of January 1769 was the bone of contention. Lord Bolingbroke gave evidence to the deed, as he himself had been a subscribing witness thereto. Lord Mansfield very properly observed, that if Miss Jones had been a common p——e, he would instantly have set aside the bond as void and null; but as it was granted for value, and that she lived with the gentleman at the time, giving her company to none other, the point of law was on her side, and the bond fell to be sustained; and so the jury, without going out of court, decided in her favour, with costs of suit, and other damages.

Was held, at the Guildhall of this city, a common hall for the election of a Lord Mayor for the remainder of this year, in the room of William Beckford, Esq. The Recorder made a very handsome speech in praise of the late Lord Mayor, which was received by the livery with much merited applause. He then opened shortly the lamented occasion of calling that 'common hall.' The names of the several aldermen who have served the office of sheriff were then put in nomination. The majority of hands was greatly for the two Aldermen Trecothick and Crosby, and was so declared by the Sheriffs; but a poll was demanded in favour of Sir Henry Bankes, which was accordingly granted, and ordered to open at two o'clock.

25th. Yesterday being Midsummer day, a common hall was held at Guildhall, London, for the election of sheriffs and other city officers.

The several aldermen below the chair, who had not served the office of sheriff, were put in nomination; as were likewise the gentlemen who had been drank to by the Lord Mayor. But Messrs. Baker and Martyn, who were nominated by the livery, had a great shew of hands, and were accordingly returned and declared duly elected with the greatest applause.

This day Sir William Henry Ashurst, Knt. was called to the degree of serjeant at law at the bar of the Court of Common Pleas, Westminster, with the usual ceremony, and afterwards took his seat as puisne judge of the King's-bench, in the room of Judge Blackstone, who took his place as puisne judge of the Common Pleas, in the room of Sir Joseph Yates, deceased.

Early this morning two highwaymen attempting to rob a stage-coach at Mims Wash, the guard fired at them, shot one dead, and shattered the arm of the other, whom they apprehended, and brought to town. Upon the report of the surgeon, before Sir John Fielding, that the man's life was in danger, he was carried to the Middlesex Hospital, where his arm was cut off. He confessed his name was Thomas Watson, and his companion's William Ward; that they were both postillions, and had robbed ever since January last.

Copenhagen, June 16. The noblemen and ladies who were appointed to attend Queen Sophia Magdalena's funeral, assembled in her Majesty's mourning apartments, at seven o'clock in the evening, on the 13th of June, from whence they went in procession to the chapel royal, where they were received by two marshals. Here two sermons, the one in the Danish, the other in the German language, were preached, and a solemn music was performed on the occasion. This part of the ceremony being ended, the coffin was carried out of the chapel by twelve colonels and officers of the marine, who were stationed round it during the service, and put into the hearse at the great palace gate, through which the procession began in the following manner: 1. A squadron of horse guards. 2. A herald on horseback. 3. The noblemen in coaches, according to their ranks, each having four servants bearing torches. 4. Twelve royal pages, with their governor on horseback. 5. The counsellors of justice. 6. The gentilshommes de chambre, and the gentilshommes de cour, all on horseback, each of them preceded by two servants on foot, bearing torches. 7. The liv-vogn, or state coach, of the late Queen, preceded by twelve lackies; and on each side of it a heyduk. 8. The royal hearse drawn by horses covered with black, adorned with escutcheons, and led by captains of the marine. Those who had carried the coffin out of the chapel attended the hearse on horseback. 9. The major-generals, counsellors of conferences, rear-admirals, and counsellors of state, attended on horseback. 10. The royal mourning coaches (before each of which went eight lackies of the royal livery with torches) and a squadron of horseguards closed the procession.

27th. This day Mr. Almon, who some time before had been found guilty by a special jury for publishing Junius's Letter addressed to the King, was admitted to shew cause before the judges of the Court of King's-bench for a new trial; but the arguments produced by his counsel not being judged satisfactory, the court unanimously dismissed the cause, and thereby confirmed the verdict.

A comet was discovered by Mr. Dunn, 33 min. after eleven in the evening. Its distance from the brightest star in the Harp was 41 deg. 10 min. and from the brightest star in the Eagle 22 deg. 10 min. refraction included; from which its place is determined between the right hand of Serpentarius and the Equator; is nearly S. at midn. with about $35\frac{1}{2}$ deg. merid. alt. and nearly opposite to the sun. It has no tail, but a silver-coloured nucleus, and a coma of about half a degree in diameter; that part of the coma next the sun being most illuminated. Dr. Bevis observed the same comet early in the morning.

At a grand levee held at St. James's, his Serene Highness Prince Ernest of Mecklenburgh-Strelitz, brother to her Majesty, was present for the first time since his arrival in England, which was on June 23.

The

The first stone of the new office for the New-River Company was laid by Mr. Holford, governor. The current coin of the kingdom was laid underneath the stone, and the following inscription engraved upon it:

First stone laid by Peter Holford, Esq. Governor.
Sir George Colebrooke, Bart. Deputy Governor.
Henry Berners, Esq. Treasurer.
June xxviii. M.DCC.LXX.
Robert Milne, Architect.

The site of this building is that of the play-house where Shakespeare acted.

Extract of a Letter from Mr. John Hill, of Hull, giving an Account of the Loss of the Betsey, Capt. Watson, from Virginia to Charles Town, South Carolina.

On the 16th of May, having left Cape Henry but three days, as we were standing to the southward, the wind came from the north to northwest, and blew extremely hard, which occasioned a great swell: before preparations could be made, our vessel was laid upon her beam-ends. In about five minutes we lost six hands off the decks, when our mizen-mast was cut away, but to no purpose: our main-mast was then cut by the board, and our fore-mast going at the same time, which we lashed together, our ship then sinking, obliged us to swim to the mast, where we lay floating seven and thirty hours, when we were taken up by an European ship bound for Glasgow. Our captain was lost, after breaking five of his ribs, occasioned by the force of the tiller standing at the helm. A young lady and her father, of the name of Hinght, were also lost, who expired in each other's arms; and also the aforesaid six hands. Our number saved was thirteen. Our ship and cargo belonged to Nathan Alben Smith, of Virginia, who is the greatest sufferer by the unhappy event.

29th. This day the poll for the Lord Mayor of the city of London, for the remainder of the mayoralty, ended at Guildhall; when the numbers were, for Alderman Trecothick 1,601; Crosby 1,434; Bankes 437; whereupon the return of the two former being made to the Court of Aldermen for their choice, the election was declared for Alderman Trecothick. He was therefore immediately invested with the gold chain.

The annual medals given by Lord Bruce to the students of Winchester-college were adjudged this year to the following gentlemen; the gold one, for the best copy of Latin verses, to Thomas Henry Lowth, Esq. the Bishop of Oxford's son; and the silver ones, for elocution, to Edward Sandford, and Francis Paul Stratford, Esqrs.

A tragical affair happened during the course of the present month at Lyons, in France: a young couple having conceived a violent passion for each other, and not being able to obtain their parents consent to marry, formed the extravagant resolution of constituting a kind of chapel, and setting up an altar before which they were reciprocally to swear eternal fidelity to each other, and then to shoot themselves through the head; all which they executed. It is added, that they had carried their romantic notion so far, as to purchase a dagger, to accomplish their purpose

pose of killing themselves, if the pistols had failed of that effect. The lad was the son of a fencing master, and the girl the daughter of a wealthy inn-keeper.

Letters from Venice declare, that the republic have done every thing in their power to convince the Turks of their being determined to maintain a strict neutrality. A corps of troops has been sent to Cephalonia, in order to seize the effects of Count Metaxa, and some others who entered on board the Russian fleet. The principal magistrate of this state at Corfu has confiscated the goods of Capt. Palicachia, who had armed a merchant ship he commanded, and joined the Imperial fleet. A reward of 200 ducats has been offered for the apprehending him.

The news from the Morea, during the course of the present month, has been favourable to the Russians and insurgents who have joined them. The Turks being reinforced, are said to have fallen upon them with great fury, to have retaken Patresso, and to have slaughtered without mercy all the Greeks and Russians who fell into their hands. The English Consul with his son and family escaped almost miraculously. The bloody rage that incenses the Turks and Christians against each other is productive of the most savage cruelties, and excites even to the ripping up of women and children.

They write from Paris, that the pleasing behaviour and extraordinary affability of the Dauphiness gain her universal admiration. With the King's permission she dispenses with several points of ceremony, inviting her brothers, and sisters, and her aunts, to sup with her as often as she pleases; and her Royal Highness goes to see them with the same freedom. She rides out with a master of the horse, and walks about unattended with servants, with that freedom which is suitable to her lively disposition, and at the same time conducive to her health.

Extract of a Letter from Paris.

The precedency given at the Ball Paré on the 19th ult. to Mademoiselle de Lorraine, who danced immediately after the Princes of the Blood, having given offence to many of the principal nobility, the King, in order to remove the pique they had taken on that account, wrote the following circular letter to them.

"The Ambassador from the Emperor and Empress Queen asked of me, on the part of his Master and Mistress, that I would be pleased to confer some mark of distinction on Mademoiselle de Lorraine on the present occasion of the marriage of the Dauphin my grandson with the Archdutchess. The dancing at the ball being the only thing that could not be deemed as a precedent for the future, the choice of the dancers being entirely dependant on my will, without regard or precedency, rank or dignity (except the Princes and Princesses of the Blood, who cannot be ranked with any other French family), and being unwilling to change or make innovations on what has been the practice and custom of my court, I think that the principal nobility of my kingdom will not depart from the fidelity, submission, attachment, and

and even friendship, which they have always shewn to myself as well as to my predecessors, nor act so as to displease me in any respect, and more especially on the present occasion, when I am desirous to testify my gratitude to the Empress Queen for the present she has made to me, which I hope, as well as you, will compleat the happiness of the remainder of my life."

The King finding that the above did not quite reconcile the alarms of the nobility, has been pleased to declare, that a lady of quality shall be the first who dances after the Princes and Princesses of the Blood, at the ball which shall be given on account of the marriage of his Royal Highness the Count de Provence. In consequence of this declaration, the Dukes have met to draw up an address of thanks to his Majesty.

The following copy of a letter, from M. de Voltaire to the Marshal Duke de Richlieu is handed about.

"I wish, my Lord, to have the pleasure of giving you my blessing before I die. The expression may be new to you, but it is nevertheless true. I have the honour to be a Capuchin: our general at Rome has just sent me my patent, in which I am styled spiritual brother, and temporal father Capuchin. Send me word which of your deceased mistresses you would wish to get out of purgatory, and I swear by my beard she shall not be there 24 hours longer. As in consequence of my new vocation I must give up the good things of this world, I have resigned to my relations what is due to me of the estate of the late Princess de Guise, and from that of Monsieur votre Intendant. They will apply to you for your directions in these affairs, which they will esteem a favour. I sincerely give you my blessing, and am, &c.

"An unworthy Capuchin."

Died. Lately, the Rev. H. Gibert, Rector of Rolton, in Lincolnshire, upwards of 50 years. He was a French protestant, and left his country for his religion.

Mr. Benj. Lee, of Saffron-hill, apothecary, aged 90.

Mr. Thomas Bernard, tallow-chandler, worth 100,000l.

Ann Hatfield, aged 105, at Tinsley, Yorkshire.

James Hatfield, aged 105, who is said to have saved his life by hearing St. Paul's clock strike 13 at Windsor.

John Haynes, aged 105, at Wooton-Basset, Wilts.

Ralph Nied, near Chester, aged 107: he had buried six wives.

JULY.

4th. This morning were executed at Tyburn, pursuant to their sentence, James Attaway and Richard Bailey, for stealing a quantity of plate in the house of Thomas Le Merr, Esq. in Bedford-row: Daniel Pfluyer, for a burglary in the house of Robert Walker, in Little Carter-lane: Francis Lutterell, for stealing wearing apparel, the property of Thomas Jackson, in the house of William Shepherd, in Bell-yard, Temple-bar; and John Read, alias Miller, for returning from transportation.

The

The robbery for which Attaway and Bailey suffered was one of the most artful and daring that has been known. About nine in the evening, Mr. Le Merr, the prosecutor, being in the country, they, with an accomplice not yet taken, knocked at the door of his house, and when it was opened, Bailey delivered a letter to the footman, which he said was for his master; but before the man could read the direction, they burst in at the door, shut it, and one of the villains stabbed him in the belly with a dagger; then took a cord which they had provided, tied his hands behind him, robbed him of his watch, and dragged him down stairs into the kitchen, where they undid his hands, and made him light a candle: this done, they tied his hands behind him a second time, bringing the rope first round his neck, then across his face, and in such a manner, that it went through his mouth, and confined it open, making the ends of the rope fast behind. Thus bound, they dragged him back into a dark place, and there bolted him in. In a few minutes one of them returned to see if he was fast, and being told, as well as the man could speak, that he was fast enough, they then burst open the pantry, where the plate was, and packed it up. In the mean time, the man had gnawed the rope in two with his teeth, and got his hands loose. " I then thought, (says the man in his evidence before the court) that if I could get a brick out at the top, I might get up into the area, and not stay bleeding there while they were robbing my master's house. I burst open the door, and listened in the passage, to see whether they heard me, thinking, if they did, I was a dead man. There is a skylight: I got hold of a leaden pipe, and got up, and burst the window with my head. In trying to get through, I stuck half in and half out, and could neither get one way nor the other, for about three or four minutes, with the rope about me. At last I got out, and into the stable, and from thence into the coach-house, and out of that into the yard; then I called for help as fast as possible. I went out of the back stable-yard to a public house, and immediately five or six men came."

This day there was a very full court of common council held at Guildhall, when a motion was made, that a statue might be erected of the late Right Hon. William Beckford, Esq. Lord Mayor, with an inscription containing the words which his Lordship spoke to his Majesty at St. James's, on presenting the city remonstrance; and a committee of six aldermen and twelve commoners is appointed to carry the same into immediate execution; and are empowered to draw on the chamber for any sum not exceeding 1,000l. towards defraying the expence of the same.

The new Imperial Ambassador had an audience of his Majesty, in order to deliver his credentials.

This day came on in the Court of King's-bench, Westminster, before the Right Hon. the Lord Mansfield, the great cause between Lord G—— and his Royal Highness the D— of C————. The damages were laid at 100,000l. and a great number of witnesses examined, which examination ended about two

two o'clock, when Mr. Dunning, counsel for his R—— H——, the defendant, recapitulated most of the material parts of the evidence, and observed thereupon, that though the intimacy of the accused parties had been sufficiently proved not only by the witnesses, but also by a variety of letters that passed between them, which were read in court, yet he asserted that the plaintiff had not brought any proof of the criminal act for which the action was laid.

At seven o'clock in the evening the Right Hon. Lord Mansfield gave his charge to the jury, when they withdrew, and his Lordship adjourned the court to his house in Bloomsbury-square: exactly at ten the jury left the hall, and proceeded to his Lordship's house, where they gave a verdict for the plaintiff, with ten thousand pounds damages.

At a general convention of the estates and legislature of the Isle of Mann, being the first High Court of Tynwald that has been holden there under the auspices of his present Majesty, since the regalities of Mann and the Isles have been annexed to the crown of Great Britain, the bishop and clergy of the diocese presented an address to his Excellency John Wood, Esq. the Governor, in which they congratulated his Excellency on the royal favour of being commissioned by his Majesty to the vicegerency of that island, and express their joy at seeing their antient, supreme, constitutional, and so much wished for court of Tynwald restored to its former or rather superior lustre and importance; and conclude with earnest supplications that his Majesty may never want so faithful a representative, the church so sincere a friend, or that island so acceptable a governor.

The Governor concludes his answer in a happy imitation of Shakespeare.

Your applause, my Lord, reflects a virtue on myself, and makes me proud indeed!

To the archdeacon and clergy he said, To deserve your esteem has ever been my peculiar study; to preserve it shall be my constant care. The same wise Providence which has inspired your goodness, will, I doubt not, teach me, as far as I am able, to encourage and reward its labours.

A large sum of money, being part of the produce of crown lands on the island of Grenada, was received at the treasury.

A young woodcock was taken in a nest near Preslie Car, and was shewn at Newcastle as a great curiosity. The old ones were seen, but escaped. In Borlace's account of Cornwall there is a print of a young woodcock found some years ago in that county.

The Duke of Orleans's Answer to the Chancellor of France at the Bed of Justice, held at Versailles the 27th of June, 1770, when his Majesty caused his Letters Patent to be registered.

' Even though not bound by
' the article of parliament to which
' I consented yesterday, I could not
' in conscience deliver my opinion
' in a place where voices are not
' free, upon Letters Patent, not less
' contrary to the laws and maxims
' of the kingdom than to the ho-
' nour of the country.'

The

The King then said to the Duke of Orleans, 'In case my parliament should assemble princes of the blood and peers, I forbid you to be present at the palace, and charge you to tell this to the other princes of the blood.'

ANSWER.

'SIRE,
'The other princes of the blood are here. This order will better become your mouth than mine; besides, I beseech you to excuse me.'

The King then turned towards the other princes of the blood, and said to them.

'Gentlemen, you hear.'

On which the Prince de Conti replied,

'Yes, Sire, we hear something very contrary to the rights of the peerage, and of very little advantage to Monf. le Duke D'Aiguillon.'

11th. Came on the election of a member to serve in parliament for the city of London, in the room of the late Right Hon. William Beckford, Esq. deceased, when Richard Oliver, Esq. was chosen without opposition. It is hoped the late examples of the cities of London and Westminster, in chusing their members without expence, will be followed by all the corporations throughout England, and then all complaints will cease.

Letters arrived this day with the news of the loss of his Majesty's sloop the Jamaica; Capt. Talbot, off the Coleradoes; the officers and men all saved, and brought to England by the Renown, lately arrived at Portsmouth.

Letters from Grenoble declare, that on the 15th inst. the lieutenant of the police there, in examining a native of Piedmont, who was charged with stealing a gold-watch from a merchant, was suddenly assaulted by the villain, who stabbed him in three places with a knife: on the clerk seizing the fellow behind, he received a stab from the latter in the stomach, of which he died. The desperado, seeing no prospect of escape, then stabbed himself in four places, and expired instantly. His body the next day was, by order of the parliament, drawn on a hurdle, and treated w' every mark of indignity.

They write from Boston, in Lincolnshire, that a few days ago a murder was committed by a private dragoon, in Bland's regiment, quartered there, on the body of a country man from Friskney:— The parties appeared very sociable, and had spent a great part of the day and night together at a public house: towards morning the deceased went to bed in the soldier's room, where the latter soon followed, and immediately on his entrance into the chamber drew a bayonet, and stabbed his companion in a most inhuman manner in several parts of his body; then with the club-end beat him very cruelly on the head, and, supposing him dead, left him weltering in his blood on the floor.— He then attempted the landlady's room (it is feared for the same purpose), which resisted his strongest efforts; but the noise he made alarmed the family, who soon discovered the murder, and had him properly secured: he was soon after

after conveyed to Lincoln-castle, guarded by constables, and two of the military; when enquiries were made, what could induce him to so great an act of cruelty, the only answer he would return was, *He thirsted for blood, and if in his power would have more.*—The poor unhappy victim survived but a few hours. The coroners returned their verdict, wilful murder, and his corpse was conveyed to the grave, attended by a distressed widow and several children.

13th. A new statute to regulate the academical habits was passed in the convocation at Oxford, by which the disputes that have lately agitated that seat of learning are finally terminated. These disputes were not of so trifling a nature as they have been represented to be; the point in question was not so much whether this or that rank or degree of academics should be distinguished by this or that peculiar gown or cap, as whether the statutes of the university should be dispensed with at the will and pleasure of any particular head of a college; or even by the authority of the heads of the houses in general, independently of the convocation, in which the legislative power resided: this statute has therefore placed the whole of this matter upon a proper footing.

Letters from Tunis, May 31, say, "On the 25th instant all the Greeks in this c.ty, both ecclesiastics and merchants, and their servants, amounting to about 150 in number, were arrested by order of the Bey; at the same time their effects were seized and put in the warehouses, and all their ready money, amounting to the value of about 25,000 Venetian sequins, was carried to the palace. The whole amount of their goods and money is computed at 800,000 piasters.

Tuesday last came on to be heard at the sittings in Westminster-hall, before the Right Hon. Lord Mansfield, a cause wherein Mr. Stock, an attorney at law in the city of Gloucester, was plaintiff, and Gabriel Harris, Esq. post-master of that city, defendant: the action was brought against the defendant for detaining a letter received at the post-office there directed to the plaintiff, and not delivering the same to the plantiff, at his place of abode in the said city; and the event will determine, whether the post-master is not obliged to deliver all letters received at his office to the inhabitants to whom the said are directed, at their places of abode, without any further composition or payment than the legal rate of postage. The jury gave a special verdict for the plaintiff, which will be argued before the Court of King's-bench in Michaelmas term.

18th. The sessions at the Old Bailey, which began on the preceding Wednesday, ended; at which seven persons, three of them for murder, received sentence of death. It was the largest sessions that has been known, and many very remarkable trials were heard, particularly that of Grieves, for setting his house on fire; and of the three murderers, two of them were for the murder of Messrs. Venables and Rogers, by shooting them dead on the highway; and the third, a watchman, for the murder of a woman with whom he cohabited, by stabbing her to the heart. Grieves was acquitted about two
this

this morning, for want of positive proof, though circumstances were strong against him.

Came on before Lord Mansfield and a special jury, at Guildhall, London, the trial of Mr. Miller, for republishing Junius's Letter in the London Evening Post: only seven of the special jury attended, so that five talesmen were allowed to be taken out of the box. The jury inclosed about eleven; and at seven they waited upon Lord Mansfield, at his house, with their verdict, not guilty.

The same day the trial of Mr. Baldwin came on before the same judge, and a special jury, at the same place: only seven of this jury likewise appeared, and therefore five were taken out of the box. They inclosed about three, and waited upon Lord Mansfield about five, with their verdict, not guilty.

His Majesty has been pleased to direct that the island of Dominica should be erected into a government, separate from and independent of the general government of the southern Caribbee islands, of which it before made a part; and to appoint Sir William Young, Bart. Governor thereof.

19th. Peter Conoway and Michael Richardson, for the murder of Mr. Venables and Mr. Rogers, were executed at Tyburn, pursuant to their sentence. They were convicted on the evidence of one Jackson, an accomplice, who swore, that the day before the murder was committed, they bought a brace of old pistols in George street; that they loaded them with bits of the handles of pewter spoons; that they stopped the deceased with intent to rob them, but, being stout men, they knocked Richardson, and Fox (not yet taken), down twice; that fearing to be overpowered, Richardson shot Venables, and Conoway shot Rogers at the same time. Conoway at first refused to plead, but being taken down, and shewn the apparatus for pressing him to death, if he refused, he relented, and after condemnation he seemed much moved, and blessed the judges for their kindness to him. They were both brought back from the place of execution to Surgeons'-hall, where their chairs were put on, and afterwards were hung upon a gibbet at Mile-end, near the place where the murder was committed.

John Purcell, the watchman, for the murder of the woman with whom he cohabited, was executed at the same time, and was brought to Surgeons'-hall, in order to be dissected. He was an old soldier, and enjoyed a petition for his former services. He denied the intention of murder, and said, that having been out with the deceased a drinking, they came home together late; that a dog they kept being troublesome, he in his passion flung a knife at him, which unfortunately took place in the deceased's heart. He never attempted to fly from justice, but told the neighbours what had happened; yet there was no reason to doubt of his guilt.

A cause came on lately to be tried in the Court of Common Pleas, at Guildhall, wherein a passenger in the P—— stage-coach was plaintiff, and the master of the said stage-coach was defendant. The charge was, that the passengers refusing to dine at an hedge-alehouse on the road, one

Vol. XII. [K] of

of the coachman's favourite houses, they went to another house at Epsom, and sent the coachman word whither they were gone, which house the coachman was obliged to pass, and accordingly did full drive, and left the passengers to return to London as they might. After applying to the master of the stage in vain, the plaintiff brought this action, wherein the jury found a verdict for the plaintiff, and 20l. damages.

20th. The post-boy carrying the Chichester mail had it privately stolen from him between Newington and Clapton, by cutting the straps which tied it to the cart, while the boy was asleep: it has since been found in a ditch, with most of the letters opened, and some of the bags carried off.

Was determined before the Lords Commissioners of the Great Seal, in Lincoln's-Inn Hall, the cause between the proprietors of Covent-Garden theatre. The bill was brought by the plaintiffs Messrs. Harris, Dagge, and Leake, against Mr. Colman and Mrs. Powell, the defendants praying that certain articles of agreement, dated May 14, 1767, under which Mr. Colman had assumed the management of the theatre, might be set aside; and that Mr. Colman might be restrained from acting in any manner in the business of the theatre, independent of the participation and concurrence of the plaintiffs, or that some proper person, or persons, might be appointed for managing the theatre, and for receiving the profits; and that an account might be taken of the profits from the 9th of September, 1768, and that the share belonging to the complainant, Mr. Harris, might be paid to him, and the remainder of the money in hand, arising, or to arise, from the theatre, might be paid into court, subject to farther order, and that the defendants might make satisfaction to the plaintiffs for their shares of all damages arising from the misconduct of the defendants since the 9th of Sept. 1768.

After a full hearing of five days, in the course of which the several points were most ably argued by the counsel on both sides, the court dismissed the bill as to every part of the above prayer, except what related to the article of damage, in regard to which the court was pleased to retain the bill, and reserve costs for a twelvemonth, with liberty to the plaintiffs, in the mean time, to bring their action at law for any damages pretended to have arisen to the theatre by any act of Mr. Colman, done after the disapprobation of the plaintiffs, in writing expressed, between the 9th of Sept. 1768, and the time of their filing the bill, which was in February 1769.

An account was received at the General Post-Office, that 23d. on Sunday the 3d of June, about 15 minutes after seven in the evening, they felt, at Cape Nicola Mole, four violent shocks of an earthquake: the most severe lasted two minutes and a half, accompanied with a noise much like the echo that is heard from the hills after the firing of cannon, but the town fortunately received no damage: and by a French sloop of war that arrived there three days after from Port au Prince on the same island, they received the melancholy account of the total demolition of that city, not one house left

left standing, and above 500 persons buried in the ruins; the severe shock there lasted four hours; that the towns of Petit Gouave, and Leogane, equally suffered; but that few of the inhabitants perished. The plains of Leogane, Cul de Sac, Port au Prince, and Petit Gouave, have not escaped, all their sugar-works being totally destroyed, and a small town, called La Croix de Bouguft, with the greatest part of its inhabitants, is swallowed up. St. Mark's, Port de Paix, the Cape, and Fort Dauphin, only felt the shock as they did at the Mole.

Was heard in the Court of Chancery, the cause which has been some years depending between Mr. Millar, late a bookseller in London, and Mr. Taylor, bookseller at Berwick, for vending a pirated edition of Mr. Thomson's Seasons; when the Lords Commissioners of the Great Seal were pleased to decree, that Mr. Taylor should account to Mr. Millar's executors for all that he had sold, and farther to decree a perpetual injunction against Mr. Taylor. Thus the question about literary property is finally closed, which is a matter of great concern to many of the booksellers in London, who have given large sums of money to authors for their writings; and the booksellers in town and country will do well to take warning, that they offend not by selling any pirated editions of books.

26th. A proposal made by the Lords of the Treasury to the City-Members, for the exchange of the Fleet-prison for ground in St. George's Fields, to erect a new gaol, was reported to a court of common council. The Lords of the Treasury proposed to exchange the site of the prison (not an acre and a half) together with the old materials (not worth one thousand pounds) for four acres and a quarter of ground at the circus in St. George's Fields, and five thousand pounds; and expect that the city will pull down the Fleet-market, and rebuild the same in the place of the prison, that the whole extent of the present market may become a street.

To the exchanging four acres of ground for an acre and a half, there was no opposition in common council; but it was said, that the most advantageous spot to erect houses for trade ought not to be chosen for a prison: it was judged, that four acres and a quarter in the best part of St. George's Fields was equal to one acre and a quarter in the situation of the Fleet, which is for the most part, and must for ever remain, back-ground. If so, to demand five thousand pounds is unreasonable; much more to expect that the city should pull down and rebuild a market, which to do, and to pave, would cost at least thirty thousand pounds.

That it had never been fully considered, whether the site of the prison would admit being made a market equally convenient with the present, and therefore that could not at once be admitted, though the proposal had been advantageous.

That if ever an exchange of ground took place, the removal of the market was not to be stipulated or expected. The proposal was therefore rejected; and a question proposed, that their Lordships be acquainted by the City Remembrancer, that this court cannot

[K] 2 agree

agree to their proposal; but that to accommodate the public they are ready to treat for an exchange of lands for the purpose of building a new prison in St. George's Fields, without being subject to any obligation to remove the Fleet-market from where it now stands. It was carried in the affirmative.

27th. This morning, about four o'clock, a fire was discovered at the upper end of the Laying-house, in the dock-yard, Portsmouth, which burning with great fury, soon afterwards communicated itself to the new hemp-house, the carpenters shops, and to the little mast-house, all which buildings are entirely consumed, with the greatest part of the stores which they contained, consisting of about two or three hundred tons of hemp, a great quantity of pitch, tar, sails, rigging, and masts, with all the timber, &c. which lay near the said buildings. We have not as yet been able to know the loss of lives on this dreadful occasion, but some have been lost, and many limbs broken. Mr. Eddowes's house-keeper died of the fright. The fire broke out in five different parts not contiguous to each other: several persons are in hold on suspicion of wilfully setting it on fire. These are consumed, besides the buildings, as many ropes, sails, masts, &c. as would have equipped 80 sail of men of war. [The loss sustained by this dreadful fire was at first estimated at half a million; but by a calculation since made at Portsmouth, and transmitted to the Lords of the Admiralty, it amounts only to the sum of 149,880l.]

Yesterday was held a court of common council at the Guildhall of this city, when a great variety of business was dispatched. The orphan bill was read twice, and the London workhouse bill passed. After the King's answer to the late address of the city to his Majesty on the birth of a Princess had been read, it was moved that the answer should be entered in the city books; on which Mr. Alderman Wilkes said, that, "if the entering the King's answer among the city records meant any thing more than the bare recording that historical fact, that on such a day his Majesty gave such an answer to the city's address; if it implied the slightest degree of approbation, he would oppose the motion; for he thought the answer contained a cruel and unjust suspicion of the loyalty of the city of London; that it was exceedingly ill-timed and uncourtly to affront the citizens at the instant of their coming, in the warmth of their hearts, to congratulate their Sovereign on the increase of the royal family; but that, however, he should never ascribe so obnoxious a measure to the King, but to those ministers who sought our ruin, who had planned the scheme for the shedding of innocent blood in St. George's Fields, and from the first moment of their power had constantly and sedulously endeavoured to create dissensions between the King and his people, and particularly the loyal inhabitants of this great capital, to serve their own private, abandoned, and wicked purposes." The answer of his Majesty was entered with only the date of the year and the day of the month.

The two following motions passed in the court of common council: "That the conduct of the Recorder

order of this city be taken into consideration at the next court of common council, and that the Lord Mayor be desired to order notice of it to be inserted in the summonses.

"That the oath taken by the Recorder on his admission into office be forthwith printed, and sent to every member of this court."

28th. Orders were sent to the several royal dock-yards to double the guards, and to admit no strangers for the future without a strict examination. One strong circumstance seems to confirm the opinion that the dock-yard at Portsmouth was wilfully set on fire, and that is, the men on board the Custom-house cutter perceiving a smoke in the dock-yard, observed it through a spying-glass, by which they could plainly discern it to issue from four different places at once, and took it to be a ship a-breaming. This was about three in the morning, two hours before it was discovered by the centinels on duty.

The Countess of Grammont was banished the court of Versailles, on account of some improper behaviour to the Countess of Barré, the King's mistress, at the play.

An insurrection of the populace at Cherbourg, in France, on account of the dearness of bread, alarmed the magistracy, who called in the military to suppress it, by which some lives were lost. At Rheims they plundered a magazine, and killed some monks who opposed them.

Advice was received of one of the most dreadful hurricanes happening in North Carolina, on the 28th of June last, that ever was known at that season of the year. Many ships were lost in the harbour, the wharfs ruined by the billows that broke against them with astonishing violence, and Charles Town providentially escaped by the lowness of the tide. The damage received is computed at 10,000l.

In the Mearnes of Scotland, a stone has been lately dug up with this inscription, R. IM. L. which probably means Roman Imperii Limes. As this is supposed to have been deposited in order to mark the limits of Cæsar's conquests in Britain, the doubt, says a writer in the public papers, whether that conqueror extended the Roman arms to the Grampian hills is now solved. To this it has been objected, that not Cæsar, but Agricola, extended the Roman conquests to the Grampian hills.

Edinburgh, July 23. Yesterday the court of sessions determined the great cause of the peerage of the antient and noble family of Caithness. The competition was between William Sinclair, of Rattler, Esq. and James Sinclair, in Reiss. The latter not being proved of lawful blood, the court affirmed the verdict of the jury on a former trial, in favour of Mr. Sinclair, of Rattler.

There is now living at Kettlewell, near Skipton, in Yorkshire, one Isaac Truman, an old soldier, aged 117 years, who enjoys his sight, and every other faculty, in as great perfection as he did at 30. He was sergeant in the first year of the reign of Queen Anne, has been in several campaigns abroad, and always behaved in a manner becoming a brave soldier. His whole time has been devoted to fishing ever since he left the regiment in which he served.

They write from Koningsberg, that one Schiel, a labourer, near 108 years of age, was taken with the small-pox last April, from which he is not only recovered, but now enjoys a perfect good state of health.

Died. Lately, the Rev. Dr. Tew, Rector of Boldon, near Newcastle. Among other charities, he has given 500l. to the Society for propagating the Gospel; 500l. to Christ's Hospital, where he had the rudiments of his education; and 200l. to the Sons of the Clergy.

Miss Symmonds, at Kensington. Her father died the week before, and left her 30,000l.

Mr. Jefferies, a farmer at Uxbridge, aged 104.

John Sparkes, of Brixham, aged 105. He was carried to the grave by eight men and women, all grand-children, the eldest of whom was forty years of age, and none of them married.

Mr. Jonas Berry, in the Grange, Southwark, aged 112. He was saddler to Queen Anne.

Robert Rossling, Esq. aged 95, the oldest inhabitant in Dorset.

At Wenesborg, in Sweden, a peasant named Svenson, aged 104 years. A year before his death he recovered his sight, which he had lost twelve years before.

At Abo, one Grellson, a peasant of that place, aged 112 years.

AUGUST.

1st. This morning were executed at Tyburn, pursuant to their sentence, William Donaldson, for a burglary in the house of Alderman Harley, in Aldersgate-street; William Sleight, otherwise Hotham, for a like crime in the house of Mrs. Parker, at Islington; and John Stretton, for robbing the mail. This last stopped the post-boy just as he was going out of town, and told him he only wanted a letter that was going to a young woman in the country; that they refused to let him have it at the office; and that he would take it out, and return the bag to his master in a hackney coach. As the night was dark, the post-boy could not swear positively to his person; but several bills being found in his custody that were proved to be taken out of the mail, left no room to doubt that he was the man who robbed it.

A poor labourer's wife at Gravesend was delivered of a monster that resembled a toad. It had an extraordinary large head, but no features or lineament of a face, except one eye, nor the appearance of any sex that could be distinguished. In the place of legs and arms were stumps, or rather flaps. The reason assigned for this production is, that the mother, in her pregnancy, being at work in a hop-ground, a toad jumped into her lap, and frightened her exceedingly.

This day came on at the assizes at Guildford, before the Right Hon. Lord Mansfield, the cause between the Right Hon. George Onslow, and the Rev. Mr. Horne. The jury, after staying out an hour and a half, brought in a verdict for Mr. Onslow with 400l. damages, which Mr. Onslow has ordered his attorney to pay into the hands of the Rev. Dr. Hallifax, treasurer of the

the fund for the relief of clergymen's widows and orphans in the county of Surry.

2d. At the assizes at Guildford, John Taylor, sergeant in the first, or Royal Scots regiment of foot, was tried for the murder of Mr. Smith, master of the Wheatsheaf-Inn, near Westminster-bridge; when James Edwards, a coachman to the deceased, swore particularly to the prisoner's drawing his sword, and making a plunge at the deceased; and it was also proved that the wound he then received was the cause of his death. Other witnesses confirmed the evidence of Edwards; adding, that when the prisoner had given the stab, he said, there d——n you, and ran away. It was proved likewise that the deceased had collared the sergeant, and was endeavouring to turn him out of the house, being very quarrelsome and abusive. It appeared that aggravating expressions against the Scots had provoked the sergeant, and that he was in a violent rage. The jury at first brought in their verdict *Guilty*; but the judge being of opinion the sentence was too severe, desired the jury to reconsider the matter, and then they returned their verdict *Special*. Immediately upon this, Mr. Jasper Smith, a near relation of the deceased, asked a counsellor present, whether he might be permitted to propose a question? The judge immediately enquired the person's name, and desired him to walk forward, which he did. After making a handsome apology, he said, he hoped there was no harm in speaking; to which his Lordship answered, No. Mr. Smith then observed, that he was much surprized at this transaction, and asked, whether it was usual after a jury had brought in a solemn verdict to have it cancelled? That he always understood, that after a verdict was brought in by a jury, it was decisive and final: and farther said, " If this is to be the case, I think juries to be entirely useless and unnecessary." His Lordship made no reply.

The Lords Commissioners of the Admiralty, by an advertisement in the London Gazette, promise a reward of 1,000l. for the discovery of any of the persons concerned in setting the buildings in Portsmouth-dock on fire, to be paid upon conviction.

The following is an estimate of the surprizing large vessels lately fixed up in Dickinson's brewhouse at Wapping: A copper which weighs eight tons, and boils at one time 200 barrels and 31 gallons; two casks which hold 304 barrels each; two mash-tubs which hold 60 qrs. of malt each, and boil 100 quarters per day; a cask called the Old Hen, which holds 150 barrels; seventeen casks called the Seventeen Chickens, which hold each 70 barrels. The great copper is filled by pumps in six minutes and three seconds; and the cocks, which are made to take off occasionally, weigh fifteen hundred, one quarter, and five pounds.

7th. The post-boy from Newcastle was robbed upon Gadshead Common of the mail from thence, containing two bags, ticketed Newcastle, and Newcastle and York, with the letters for London and intermediate places.

On Saturday last his Majesty sent a gentleman to Mr. Akerman, Keeper of Newgate, to pay the sum of one hundred pounds, which was levied by the House of Lords on Mr. Edmunds (late publisher of the Middlesex Journal, in which was inserted the Lords' Protest). The dues to the Black Rod are ordered not to be paid.

A remarkable trial came on at the assizes at ———, before Baron Adams, and a special jury, brought by a miller against his rector, on the statute of Hen. VIII. which inflicts a penalty of 10l. a month for non-residence; when a verdict was given for the miller with costs of suit. The non-residence was proved for ten months, the penalty for which is 100l.

Mr. Dennis Connel was committed to gaol at Lisbon in an arbitrary manner, in violation of the privileges granted to the British nation by the most solemn treaties, for refusing to sign a claim made by brokers for brokerage on sales at which they were not employed, with a design to lay the whole British commerce in that country under contribution.

The Pope held a secret consistory at Rome, in which he announced to the learned college, in an elegant speech, the reconciliation between the Holy See and the King of Portugal.

Nancy, July 30. A violent tempest, followed by a heavy rain, which continued 24 hours, has made terrible devastation in this province. At Plomberies in particular it was attended with the most lamentable consequences. The little river which runs through that town became a torrent, and, in a quarter of an hour, the water rose ten feet: seventeen houses were thrown down, and the baths filled with the ruins; and many persons perished in the water, or by the fall of the houses. The intendant of the province is gone thither to give the directions necessary on such a calamity.

Paris, July 30. Letters from St. Domingo confirm the melancholy account of the calamity which happened there on the 3d of last month. It is said the earthquake extended thirty-five leagues; the sea rose a league and a half up into the island; a river is choaked up, and in manner almost lost; four towns almost destroyed; and the sugar-works demolished. Fortunately it happened between seven and eight o'clock in the evening, when most of the inhabitants were out of their houses; but the number of white persons lost is above four hundred. The fortunes of several great families in this country must have suffered by it.

The young Prince of Prussia was christened at Potsdam, 8th, by the name of Frederick-William. The sponsors were the Emperor, Prince Ferdinand of Prussia, the Prince of Deux-Ponts, the Empress of Russia, and the Princess of Orange. That a popish Prince should be at the head of this list, and that of two protestant Sovereigns, nearly related, neither of them should be invited, is not easily accounted for.

To form some opinion of the mighty loss which the French nation has sustained by the late dreadful calamity in Hispaniola, we shall give our readers the following estimate, which has been handed about, and said to be a true account of the produce of that part of the island in their possession, generally known by the name of St. Domingo.

Sugar,

CHRONICLE. [137

	l.	s.	d.
Sugar, 2-3ds brown, 160,000 hhds. 10 cwt. each, at 15l. sterling per hogshead	2,400,000	0	0
Coffee, 5,000,000 lb. at 4d. per pound	83,333	6	8
Cotton, 8,000 bags, 300lb. each, at 15l. per bag	120,000	0	0
Tanned leather, 20,000 hides, at 20s. each hide	20,000	0	0
Indigo, 2,000,000 lb. at 3s. per pound	150,000	0	0
	2,773,333	6	8

9th. Their Majesties came from Richmond to St. James's, when the Prince of Hesse Darmstadt, with his family, appeared at court, and received particular marks of their Majesties' attention. Her Majesty made the young Princess a present of a rich diamond and pearl necklace, in a manner no less noble and generous than genteel. After shewing the jewels to the Princess, her Majesty asked if she might put them about her Highness's neck; which honour being politely accepted, after adjusting the collar, her Majesty declared they became her much, and hoped she would wear them as a token of her remembrance and regard. The Prince, with his family, who appeared incognito, took leave of their Majesties, and a few days after set out for Paris.

A quarrel happened between a man and his wife in Bermondsey-street, Southwark, when the woman snatched up a red-hot poker, and ran it in the man's eye: the husband in his agony threw a knife at his wife, and killed her on the spot. The Jury brought in their verdict accidental death.

During the violence of a thunder storm at Brighthelmstone, the sea flowed at one motion fifty feet. The oldest man living never remembered the like.

11th. A ship of very antient construction was discovered, and weighed up near Newcastle, the keel of which is upwards of 70 feet: her planks over-lap one another, and she appears to be Spanish built, and is supposed to be one of the ships sunk at the Spanish invasion.

Was determined at the assizes at York, before Mr. Justice Aston, and a special jury, the great lead-mine cause, being an issue directed by the Court of Chancery, wherein Mr. Thomas Smith, of Gray's Inn, was plaintiff, and the Earl of Pomfret defendant; when, after a full hearing, the jury having previously to the trial viewed the place in question, and it appeared plainly to have been an antient inclosure (bought above thirty years ago, and enjoyed as such by Mr. Smith), the jury found a verdict for the plaintiff. The above is the lead-mine in Swaledale, said to produce an immense sum, and mentioned lately to have been discovered in Lord Pomfret's estate.

The counsel for the plaintiff were Mr. Wedderburn, Mr. Wallace, Sergeant Aspinal, Mr. Johnson, and Mr. Eden; and for Lord Pomfret, Mr. Dunning (who went on purpose, and had 300 guineas), Messrs. Lee, Walker, Dawson, Davenport, and Chator.

15th. In

15th. In consequence of the verdict given in favour of Mr. Smith at York assizes, Lord Pomfret is said to have addressed the tenants of the manors of Healaugh Old Land and Healaugh New Land, at the Market-cross, Richmond in Yorkshire; in which among other things his Lordship said, 'That the jury assumed to themselves a legislative power, and had given to Mr. Smith, as his private property, the Hall Moor, which time immemorial had been their right of inheritance; that he doubted not bringing to shame the authors and abettors of those wicked proceedings;' and therefore encouraged them to assert their claim speedily, as the right of common-age all over England depended upon their success.

Last night, between eleven and twelve o'clock, a terrible fire broke out behind Mrs. Crawley's iron manufactory, at Greenwich, which consumed upwards of sixty houses: it is thought to have been maliciously done, with intention to destroy the King's warehouses at that place, which, by the shifting of the wind, were luckily preserved.

17th. A busto of his Danish Majesty, carved at Copenhagen, and sent by him as a present to the University of Oxford, was brought to the Queen's palace for their Majesties' inspection, who came to town about noon, and viewed it.

The 36th part of the King's moiety of the New River waterworks was sold by public auction at Garraway's coffee-house for the sum of 6,700l.

19th. Early this morning, the post boy carrying the Chester mail from London was robbed on Finchley Common by a single highwayman, who carried off two bags, ticketed *Colesbill* and *Irish*. It is said the letters in these bags would take a man a week to open and examine; but the Coleshill bag was found unopened, and the Irish bag with only some bundles wanting.

Last week was found, two feet deep in a piece of ground, called Friars-gardens, in the city of York, belonging to Mr. Telford, where the workmen were digging, some part of the foundation of a temple of Roman brick-work, so firmly cemented, that it resisted the stroke of a pick. This fragment was the sedgment of a circle, and a little below was taken up a flat grit-stone three feet long, two feet broad, and about eight inches thick, with the following inscription:

DEO SANCTO
SERAPI
TEMPLUM ASO
LO FECIT
CL. HIERONYMY
ANUS LEG
LEG VI VICIT;

with some Roman coins of Vespasian and others, but much defaced.

The Society of Arts have voted a silver medal to Mr. Jaffert, a farmer in the Isle of Thanet, for his account of the culture of the new kind of winter's food for cattle, called *the turnip-rooted cabbage*. This plant kept growing to the end of the spring. His produce from it, including both herb and root, was in proportion to 45 tons an acre. This is the proper time of sowing the seed, in order to be planted out early in the spring, and the spring following these plants will be at their full growth.

There

There has been lately discovered in the county of Caermarthen the foundation of an antient temple, with an altar entire, on one side of which appears a cornucopia, and on the other an augural staff. By the inscription it appears to have been dedicated to Fortune.

A cause was tried between the Rev. Mr. Hawkins, of Whitchurch Canonicorum, plaintiff, and the parishioners defendants. The action was brought against the defendants for refusing to pay a shilling tythe on every hogshead of cider, instead of 4d. for every orchard; when the jury, which was special, gave their verdict in favour of the defendants.

Extract of a Letter from Workington, in Cumberland, dated the 13th inst.

'A dreadful accident has happened at Sir James Lowther's colliery, at Seaton, near this town. Some foul air was suspected to be in the pit, and the men not being permitted to go down, but letting down a candle in a lanthorn, it set fire to the foul air, which went off with so loud an explosion, that it is said it was heard at Cockermouth, which is six miles distant. This explosion blew up one man quite over the gin-case, tree and all, and another in the waggon way, who were both killed: a third was so hurt that he died this morning. Sir James's principal steward is much scorched, and an under steward much hurt: a gentleman, who was a spectator, lost the sight of one eye; several others, whose curiosity led them to the spot, have suffered greatly.'

SUMMER CIRCUIT.

At Maidstone assizes, three were capitally convicted, but were all reprieved.

At Guildford assizes, five were capitally convicted, one of whom was reprieved.

At the assizes for Suffolk, at Bury St. Edmund's, two were capitally convicted.

At Lincoln assizes, the dragoon, for the barbarous murder committed on a countryman at Boston, was capitally convicted.

At York assizes, two were capitally convicted, one of whom was reprieved.

At the assizes at Durham, Robert Hazlit was tried on two indictments; one for robbing a lady, and the other for robbing the Newcastle mail, on both which indictments he was found guilty; but having returned all the bills and notes taken out of the mail, and having also made a frank confession where the mail was hid, so that every thing had been recovered, he has received a short reprieve, that his friends may have time to intercede in his behalf. He is a young man, and was clerk to Mr. Bamford, in London, and was upon a tour to see his friends in Yorkshire, when he committed the robberies of which he has been convicted.

At the Norfolk assizes, James Frith, for entering his mistress's bed-chamber in the night, and stealing thereout a trunk with 140l. in it, was tried and found guilty of the theft, but acquitted of the burglary. He is to be transported for seven years.

At

At Chelmsford assizes, a cause was tried before Mr. Baron Smythe, wherein Mr. Dines, of Althorn, was plaintiff, and an inhabitant of Margaret Rooting, defendant.— The plaintiff had engaged to marry the defendant's daughter Sarah, at the repeated instances of her father, on his promising a portion of 500l. to be paid on the day of marriage. In consequence of this promise, the plaintiff married the said Sarah on the 6th of August, 1766; and, previous to the marriage, the defendant promised to make his daughter worth 1,000l. or as much as the plaintiff's father should give to him. Soon after the marriage, the plaintiff's father put his son into the possession of two farms, and gave him stock upon the same worth at least 1,000l. notwithstanding which the defendant refused to fulfil his promises. On the 5th of April, 1768, the defendant being at the plaintiff's house, in company with divers other persons, and observing a child walking about the room, said, "he wished he could see some of the plaintiff's children." The latter answered, that "He was surprized he should be glad to see any of his, or to see his house filled with children, when he had not made good any one of his promises, or given any thing towards bringing up a family." The defendant replied, "he would be d——d if he did not give him 500l. on the birth of his first child, whether a boy or girl, and would stand godfather to the child;" and being asked to give a note or some other security for the fulfilling of his promise, he desired the plaintiff to write a note, which he accordingly did, and read it to the defendant, who likewise read it himself, and signed it in the presence of four witnesses, who subscribed their names to it. The defendant added, "I'll be d——d if I don't stand to this, if I never stand to any thing else as long as I live." On the 7th of July, 1769, the plaintiff's wife was delivered of a son; but the defendant refused either to stand godfather to the child, or to pay the said sum of 500l. It was alledged in his defence, that he was not sober when he signed the note; but the contrary being fully proved, the jury gave a verdict for the plaintiff for 500l.

At Stafford assizes, two were capitally convicted, but were both reprieved.

At Warwick assizes, three were capitally convicted.

At Shrewsbury assizes, 31 prisoners were tried, six of whom were capitally convicted.

At the assizes at Carlisle, two were capitally convicted, but were reprieved, and ordered for transportation.

At the assizes at Buckingham, Joseph Dobbs was tried for breaking open the stables of James Bailey, Esq. of Langleybroom, and cutting the sinews of a horse's leg in such a manner, that he bled to death. He was found guilty, and sentenced to be hanged; but at the intercession of the prosecutor he was reprieved for transportation.

At Winchester assizes, two were capitally convicted.

At Salisbury assizes, three were capitally convicted, but were reprieved for transportation.

At this assizes a remarkable trial came on, wherein a farmer was plaintiff,

CHRONICLE. [141

plaintiff, and his carter defendant. The action was brought against the defendant for debauching the plaintiff's daughter, a girl of fifteen, and having got a child by her, *per quod servitium amisit*. The jury found a verdict for the plaintiff with 100l. damages.

At the assizes at Dorchester, only one prisoner was capitally convicted, a man 70 years of age, for horse-stealing; but before the judge left the town he was ordered for transportation, which he at first refused, but afterward accepted of the clement offer.

Robert Bartlett, for the murder of his brother, was brought in manslaughter, and burnt in the hand.

At the assizes for the county of Devon, Mary Quarram, aged upwards of 64, for the murder of her grandson, an infant about a year and a quarter old, by drowning him, received sentence of death, but was respited; John Haggot, John Batting, and John Willon, for robbing John Royal, near Plymouth, of a silver watch, 2s. &c. James Matthews, for robbing John Cookfley on the highway of a silver watch, &c. and William Hallet, for housebreaking, received sentence of death; but are all reprieved.

A cause came on to be tried at these assizes, in which an attorney of Plymouth was plaintiff, and Stephen Drew, of the same place, Esq; defendant. Upon the trial it appeared, that the attorney had first given Mr. Drew the lie, and on his refusing to ask pardon, or give satisfaction, the defendant had spit in his face, and trod upon his toe. The jury brought in a verdict for the plaintiff with one halfpenny damages.

At the assizes for the county of Somerset, at Bridgewater, three persons were condemned, viz. George Shepherd, for feloniously carrying away upwards of 1,000l. in money, and several medals, &c. the property of Messrs. Harris at Taunton; John Moor, for stealing two oxen; and James Morgan, for stealing a linen handkerchief. Shepherd was left for execution, but Moor and Morgan were reprieved for seven years transportation. John Tidball, charged with breaking into the Custom-house at Minehead, was acquitted.

At Hereford assizes, two were capitally convicted, but were both reprieved.

Capt. Marmaduke Bowen, Lewis Bowen his son, and John Williams, the murderer, were brought to the bar, and severally arraigned; the first as an accessary before the fact, the two others as accessaries after the fact, in the murder of Mr. Powell; when a motion was made to put off their trials to the next assizes, which was agreed to.

At Monmouth assizes, one was capitally convicted, but afterwards reprieved.

Florence, July 31. We hear from Montemignaio, that a hermit, who died lately there, aged 77, after having led a solitary and exemplary life in his hermitage during 42 years, a few moments before his death, declared to his confessor, that he was Count Cæsar Solari, of Turin; that having lived in the married state five years, he had a son; and that afterwards he quitted his estate at Villanouva,

and

and turned anchorite. The papers found in his retirement confirmed his confession; and, in consequence, he was interred in a manner suitable to his birth.

Rome, July 28. We are assured that the Emperor of Japan died lately in his capital, aged 92 years. He did not marry till 75 with a woman of common rank, by whom he had a son, now 15 years of age.

Leeds, August 21. The account of the inhabitants of New York having agreed to the importation of goods from England was received here by our American merchants with great pleasure; since which great quantities of cloth have been sent down to Hull, in order to be shipped for the above place.

Edinburgh, August 18. At the late quarterly meeting of the proprietors of the Forth and Clyde navigation, held here, the new line of direction of the great canal, from Inch-belly-bridge westward, proposed by Mr. M'Kell, and approved of by Mr. Smeaton, engineers, was unanimously agreed to: by this new course the canal will be brought to within two miles northwest of Glasgow.

23d. A woman meanly dressed found her way up the backstairs to the Queen's private apartments, and entered the room where her Majesty was sitting with the Dutchess of Ancaster. The woman took a survey of the room with great composure, her Majesty and the Dutchess being too much frightened at first to interrupt her: at length the Dutchess had the presence of mind to ring the bell, which brought up the page in waiting, who with difficulty turned the intruder down stairs.

24th. This morning the post-boy carrying the Chester mail was robbed at the foot of Highgate Hill by a single highwayman, who took out of the cart a small mail, containing twelve bags. 200l. reward are offered for the discovery of the robber.

His Majesty has been pleased to grant his free pardon to Thomas Phillips the elder, and Thomas Phillips the younger, and William Phillips, George Phillips, Thomas Knight, and Richard Hide, who were convicted at a session of the High Court of Admiralty for plundering divers Dutch vessels on the high seas, off the coast of Sussex.

Some workmen employed to clean a large vault in Arlington-street discovered a spring of water; and one of the men putting down a lighted candle to take a fuller view of it, the foul air took fire, and it was with difficulty extinguished.

In the garden of Mr. Burrowes, of Stepney, has been dug up a large iron pot full of silver Commonwealth money, which it is thought will fetch a large sum.

25th. A bank note of 100l. has been sent from Newcastle to the secretary of the society of the Bill of Rights, for the service of Mr. Wilkes.

An express arrived at St. James's with an account of her Royal Highness the Princess of Brunswick being safely delivered of a Prince the 18th inst.

This morning their Majesties honoured the regiment of artillery with their presence in the warren of Woolwich. His Majesty came purposely to see some experiments tried.

CHRONICLE.

tried. Their Majesties were first taken to the royal elaboratory, attended by Col. Desaguliers, and went through the different rooms there, where all kinds of military stores were preparing, which took them up about an hour. They then proceeded to the water-side, where several shot were fired from an iron gun, by means of a lock being fixed to the vent. A sea service thirteen inch mortar was next fired three or four times, entirely filled with pound shot, which had a very good effect. Their Majesties next saw a heavy twelve pounder brass gun filled twenty-three times with shot in a minute, spunging between each fire, and loading with the greatest safety, which surprized every spectator, having far surpassed any quick firing ever yet practised.—The method is entirely new, and supposed to be the invention of Col. Desaguliers. Previous to their Majesties coming to the warren, they stopped on Woolwich Common, where they saw several shells fired from mortars and howitzers.

29th. This morning early the boy carrying the Chester mail was attacked near Brown's Wells, on Finchley Common, by three footpads; but the bags of letters being in one of the new-invented carriages, they could not get at them, and ordered the boy to unlock it; but he telling them he had no key, they damned him, and bade him drive on.

The case, that was some time ago published in the London papers, said to be the case of Capt. Preston, is like to prove of very bad consequence to that unfortunate gentleman. On its arrival at Boston, a committee of the town was ordered to wait upon the tain, to know if he was the He acknowledged he had up his case, but that it had through different hands, an been altered at different and, finally, that the publica the papers was variant fron which he sent home as his Being interrogated as to par parts of it, he declined ans that question, and said, 'T alterations were made by p who, he believed, might serving him, though he feare might have a contrary effec that his discriminating parts, were his own, from those had been altered by others, displease his friends at a time he might stand in need of t sential service.'

Died. Lately, in the East Lieut. Armstrong, in the East Company's service. He was dead with lightning, as he under a tamarind tree, w horse's bridle under his arm steel-hilted broad-sword is s to have attracted the lightn which he was killed. His was killed with the same flas

Mr. Muzere, aged 90, years an eminent piece broke never trusted any money out terest, but put it into an iro in which was found, at his about 9,000l.

At Peckham, in the 105 of his age, Mr. Ramsay, f a pawnbroker in the Mint.

At Whitchurch, in Shr in the 107th year of her a Jane Hammond.

One Patrick Blewet, age in the north of Ireland. H was known to be a week the time, and retained his and understanding to the last. He was gardener to a family for eight generations past.

At Reigate, in Surry, one Mary Gold, aged 111 years, who had her eye-sight, and was hearty till within an hour of her death.

At his house in Berwick-street, Soho, John Vickers, Esq. aged 95, who bore a commission under King William, and greatly distinguished himself at the battle of the Boyne.

Mary Johan, of Arlon, in Luxembourgh, relict of Louis de Villeneuve, Knight of St. Louis, and Lieutenant-Colonel of the regiment of Nice, killed in 1734 at the siege of Philipsburg, died at Thionville the 6th of June last, aged 108 years. She retained her memory and senses to the last, and had never seen any physicians in her life.

SEPTEMBER.

1st. Charles Saing, a paper-maker at Galston, in Scotland, has invented an engine for cutting rags, which will cut more in one day than eight men can do in the same time.

Mr. Rainsforth, High Constable of Westminster, attended by Mr. Flanagan his assistant, were obstructed in the execution of their office by a corporal and centinel in the first troop of horse-grenadier-guards, who, instead of assisting the civil power, confined the officiating officers in the guard-room. In this confinement they continued all night, the sergeant refusing to disturb the commanding officer till his usual hour of rising in the morning. Upon complaint being made to Sir John Fielding, the corporal and centinel were sent for and examined, and both committed to Tothill-fields Bridewell.

Lochgilhead, near Inverary, Aug. 21. This afternoon the following melancholy accident happened at this place:

As the packet yatt was carrying on board passengers to go from this to Greenock, she was run foul of by the packet, and overset: of 14 people who were on board, seven only could be saved.

On Friday morning one of the powder-mills, at Oore, near Feversham, belonging to Mr. Gruebar, was blown up: one man and a horse were killed, and two other men were very much hurt. One of the workmen, with amazing courage, went into an adjoining magazine, and rolled out a barrel of gunpowder; after which, the whole quantity, consisting of 30 barrels, were saved, and the terrible consequences prevented.

Last Friday a Custom-house officer was brought before the Magistrates, at the Rotation-office, on St. Margaret's-hill, for firing a loaded pistol at a young man, who refused to let him take away his bundle; without he would produce his authority for so doing, or go with him into a neighbouring house, and have his bundle searched. There being no contraband goods in it, the Magistrates obliged the officer to find sureties for his appearance, and the young man to prosecute at the next assizes. The same officer, about two months since, stopped a young woman, as she was going from service to her mother, and took out of her bundle an old silk handkerchief,

that

that was marked, and had been washed many times.

2d. It were greatly to be wished that stage coaches were put under some regulation as to the number of persons and quantity of luggage carried by them. Thirty-four persons were in and about the Hertford coach this day, which broke down by one of the braces giving way. One of the outside passengers (a fellmonger in the Borough) was killed upon the spot, a woman had both her legs broke, another had one leg broke; and very few of the number, either within or without, but were severely bruised.

7th. The Dolly, Peter Maddock, from the island of Tobago, consigned to Mr. John Blackburn, arrived at Cowes, laden with sugar.—This is the first vessel that ever cleared out for Europe with produce from that island. It is well assured that this island will, in a few years, make as much or rather exceed any of our Leeward islands in its produce: the land has been proved, by what it has yielded, to be of the best quality for sugar, which must render the island equal in value to any other of its neighbourhood: the negroes thrive extremely well, the planters are healthy, and, what adds to their happiness, is a spirit of concord and unanimity, that animates them in every part of their conduct.

Yesterday being the anniversary of Shakespeare's jubilee, the same was celebrated at Stratford-upon-Avon with uncommon festivity.

The court went into mourning for his Serene Highness Prince Clement Francis of Bavaria, for six days.

Vol. XIII.

Hugh Pallifer, Esq. Comptroller of the Navy, attended by the Surveyor-general, and several other officers of distinction, went down to Deptford, and very attentively surveyed the Dock-yard there, and concerted proper measures for preventing a like disaster to that which happened at Portsmouth, there being great reason to apprehend that foreign incendiaries are still watching opportunities to compleat their design.

Naples, August 14. There was another earthquake at Messina on the 22d ult. which has done considerable damage.

The Duke of Chablais, 10th. youngest son to the King of Sardinia, accompanied by several Sardinian noblemen, went on board his Britannic Majesty's ship Alarm, anchored in the bay of Villa Franca, and were received by Captain Jarvis with all possible marks of honour and respect. His Royal Highness shewed the greatest curiosity to be informed of the use of every thing he saw. He desired the chain-pumps to be worked, and a gun to be exercised, and between the several motions made the most pertinent remarks. Having satisfied his curiosity, his satisfaction was confirmed by the magnificent presents he made on that occasion. To the captain he gave a rich diamond ring, enclosed in a large gold snuff-box; to the two lieutenants a gold box each; to the lieutenant of marines, who mounted the guard, the midshipman who steered his Royal Highness, and the four who assisted him up and down the ship's side, a gold watch each, one of which was a Paris repeater, and another set with sparks, and a large sum of money

[L.] to

to the ship's company. His Royal Highness stayed about two hours; and was saluted on his going aboard and coming ashore with one-and-twenty guns.

12th. The committee appointed to superintend the direction of the statue for the late Lord Mayor, received drawings from seventeen artists without names, when two only met with approbation, which were claimed by Mr. John Macre, and Mr. Agostez Carlini.

The Sheriff and Justices of Bamffshire met at Portsoy (Scotland), and made a dividend of 799l. 12s. 2d. (issued from the treasury upon the first certificate,) to the proprietors of the cattle which had been slaughtered, in order to prevent the spreading of the contagious distemper then raging among them.

Came on to be tried before John Hawkins, Esq. and the rest of the magistrates at Hick's-hall, two indictments, wherein the Governors of the Foundling-hospital were the prosecutors, and Robert Berry and Elizabeth his wife were the defendants, for violently assaulting Sarah Powel (a foundling), their apprentice; when, after a full hearing of counsel on both sides, the jury, without going out of court, brought in the defendants guilty; and thereupon the chairman was pleased to pronounce sentence, that the wife should be imprisoned nine months, and the husband six.

14th. Thomas Robinson, corporal, and David Deane, the centinel, lately committed to Tothill-fields Bridewell, for imprisoning the High Constable of Westminster, were bailed by some officers in the army.

The same day the sergeant, tried for neglect of duty, in not calling the commanding officer during the imprisonment of Samuel Rainsforth, Esq. High Constable of Westminster, was broke by order of the Court Martial.

17th. The new cut out of the river Lee was opened at Limehouse into the Thames, when many barges and boats immediately passed up to try if it was navigable, and it proved to answer extremely well.

The Bench of Justices of the county of Middlesex, it is said, have come to a resolution to oblige all public places of entertainment to take down the organs, which are kept for the amusement of their customers.

The remains of the Right Hon. Lady Viscountess Townshend, Lady of his Excellency the Lord Lieutenant, were carried to Sir John's Quay, attended by the Right Hon. the Lord Mayor, and the two Sheriffs, in their carriages, the regiment of horse on Dublin duty, the officers, kettle-drummers, and trumpeters of which, with the battle-axe guards, &c. had scarfs, hatbands, and black gloves, the kettle-drums had a black crape over them, and the trumpets were muffled; the gentlemen domestics of his Excellency's household, all in deep mourning, walked in procession: the body was put on board the Southern, for Parkgate, from whence it is to be taken to the burial place of that noble family, and deposited. Minute guns were fired from the time the procession began till eleven o'clock, and the ships in the harbour half hoisted their banners in token of mourning, and continued so all day.

19th. The sessions ended at the Old Bailey, when sentence was passed on nine capital convicts, two of whom were women; 39 were ordered to be transported for seven years, two for fourteen years, three branded, and two whipped. One hundred and thirty prisoners have been tried this sessions.

A tender sailing down the river full of impressed men was suddenly stopped by the captives, who found means to open one of the hatches, and immediately issued upon deck; where, forming in a body, they overpowered the officers and crew, and made themselves masters of the vessel without much violence or any bloodshed. The victors ran the tender ashore at Grays, in Essex, to the number of 110, from whence they marched into the country, and divided into two bodies, one towards Rumford, the other to Bow. The catastrophe was only some of the officers landing at Gravesend with black eyes.

The following is an authentic copy of a letter sent on Monday night from the Admiralty to the Master of Lloyd's coffee-house, Lombard-street.

" The Favourite sloop of war being arrived off the Motherbank from Falkland Islands, brings an account, that a Spanish man of war and five frigates, with artillery and land forces on board, had dispossessed his Majesty of the settlement of Fort Egmont. I am commanded by the Lords Commissioners of the Admiralty to give you this information, that the merchants and others who are any ways interested therein may be fully acquainted therewith.

Signed ―――."
Admiralty Office,
Sept. 24, 1770.

The following is said to be an exact account of the ships sent by the Spaniards from Buenos Ayres to take possession of Falkland Islands, viz. one frigate of 30 guns, 190 seamen, and 100 soldiers. Three frigates of 28 guns, 803 seamen, and 840 soldiers. One frigate of 20 guns, 110 seamen, and 84 soldiers. All the papers and journals kept on board the Favourite sloop of war from Falkland Islands have been ordered up from Portsmouth for the inspection of the Lords Commissioners of the Admiralty; and the above sloop is ordered into dock, and her crew on board the guardship.

Press-warrants were sent to Portsmouth, and next morning the press-gangs went on board the merchant ships, and stripped them of all the hands they thought useful, before it was known in the town. They secured the impressed men in a tender, came on shore, and in the public houses and in the streets picked up many good sailors.

John Simpson was convicted by the magistrates at the Rotation-office, in Litchfield-street, in the sum of 20l. for stealing a spaniel dog belonging to Mr. Roberts, which he had killed and skinned: the skin being found upon him, and he not being able to pay the penalty inflicted, was committed to Clerkenwell Bridewell for six months.

A cart upon a new construction was brought to the General Post Office for carrying the mails. It is lined with thin plates of iron, yet it runs much lighter than any cart that has yet been brought to the office; and which, from its ingenious

nious contrivance for the security of the several bags of letters, has gained the approbation of the Post-Masters.

Extract of a letter from Neustadt, Sept. 24.

"Yesterday noon the King of Prussia arrived here, and alighted from his coach before he came to the head quarters, where his Imperial Majesty waited to receive him. The inhabitants of this city were extremely affected at the meeting of these two great Monarchs, insomuch that when they went together to the quarters allotted for the King of Prussia, most of the people kneeled down as they passed along. In the evening there was an opera. The grand manœuvres will begin this day.

Naples, Aug. 21. Two hundred soldiers of this garrison had formed a design to plunder the principal houses of this city, while the nobility were partaking of the diversions that were given in the evening of the Queen's birth-day; but the plot was happily discovered time enough to prevent the execution of it. There has been a fresh eruption this week from Mount Vesuvius, which has done a great deal of damage, and destroyed all the vineyards in the neighbourhood of Tour du Grec.

25th. At a Court of Aldermen held at Guildhall (at which were present the Lord Mayor, Sir William Stephenson, Sir Robert Kite, Messrs. Crosby, Peers, Nash, Halifax, Shakespear, Kennett, Plumbe, Kirkman, Townshend, Rossiter and Oliver) the Lord Mayor reported to the court that he had received a letter from the Lords of the Admiralty, desiring his Lordship to back the press-warrants for the city of London; which letter his Lordship read, as likewise an answer thereto sent by the Lord Mayor, signifying that it had never been usual for the Lord Mayor to sign such warrants, unless applied to by the Privy-council.

The Lord Mayor then read a letter from Mr. Recorder to his Lordship, desiring his Lordship to inform the court of Mr. Recorder's indisposition, and to request leave of absence for a month: that the court did consent to give Mr. Recorder leave of absence for a month from their court, but that they could not dispense with his attendance on the other court; and that it was therefore the unanimous opinion of the Court of Aldermen, that Mr. Recorder should address a letter to the Court of Common Council for a similar leave of absence.

At a Quarterly General Meeting of the Proprietors of East India stock, at their house in Leadenhall-street, Sir George Colebrooke, Bart. declared the half-yearly dividend at six per cent.

27th. A common council was holden at Guildhall, when the Lord Mayor opened the court with a speech, in which he informed them that the matters which he understood to be intended for their consideration at that time were about the disposal of the place of City Marshal, and the conduct of the Recorder: that since the Recorder was present, he hoped they would proceed first on his business. After some spirited debates, in the course of which the Recorder entered into an elaborate defence of his refusal

refusal to attend the delivery of the remonstrance of that court to his Majesty, Mr. Alderman Wilkes moved, "That it is the opinion of this court, that the Recorder, by refusing to attend the Lord Mayor, Aldermen, and Commons of this city, with their humble address, remonstrance, and petition, to his Majesty, acted contrary to his oath, and the duty of his office."

This motion being seconded, the question was put, and declared to be carried in the affirmative; but Mr. Paterson demanded a division. In the division there appeared to be six aldermen and 88 commoners, besides the two tellers, for the affirmative; and six aldermen and five commoners for the negative. Whereupon his Lordship declared the question to be resolved in the affirmative.

A motion for adjournment of this business being put, the question was resolved in the affirmative.

The City Remembrancer acquainted them, that the Lords of the Treasury had resolved to rebuild the Fleet Prison on the place where it now is.

Warrants were issued out to the constables of Westminster to impress seamen, &c.

Two powder-mills on Hounflow Heath blew up, by which accident one man was killed.

This day fifty boys, cloathed by Sir John Fielding, and properly equipped for the service, passed through the city, in order to be entered on board his Majesty's ships.

The crew of the Berwick, Capt. Moore, bound to London from St. Vincent's, were lately taken up by the Mars, Capt. Holland, bound to Liverpool. They were all ready to perish, the Berwick having foundered at sea four days before, and the whole crew, consisting of thirteen men, and one woman passenger, being crowded into an open boat, without provisions or shelter.

Extract of a Letter from Gravesend, September 24, 1770.

This afternoon a melancholy affair happened at this place, which, in all likelihood, will be attended with much noise: the officers of the Lynx man of war went on board the Duke of Richmond East Indiaman, in order to press the men; when they came on board, the commanding officer was told by the chief mate of the Indiaman, that the seamen had seized the arm-chest, and were determined not to be pressed. On this, at high water, the man of war dropped along-side of the Duke of Richmond: the chief mate hailed the man of war, and told the captain the seamen were armed and determined to resist, and that he could not be answerable for the consequences, if they persisted in pressing the people; however, the man of war laid the India ship along-side, and a scuffle ensued, in which one man on board the India ship was killed, and several dangerously wounded: notwithstanding this, they would not suffer the man of war's people to enter the ship; on which these last thought it adviseable to sheer off, and the India ship's people are now come on shore.

[150] ANNUAL REGISTER, 1770.

29th. This day a common hall was held at Guildhall, for the election of a Lord Mayor for the year ensuing; when all the aldermen below the chair, who had served the office of sheriff, were severally put in nomination. The shew of hands was greatly in favour of Brass Crosby, and James Townshend, Esqrs. and they were therefore returned to the court of aldermen, who made choice of Mr. Crosby, as being the senior, and he was immediately declared duly elected.

A motion was made by Mr. Lovel, that the thanks of the livery should be given to the two late patriotic Sheriffs, Townshend and Sawbridge, for their upright and impartial conduct in the discharge of their office, which was carried in the affirmative, and ordered to be entered in the records. The thanks of the hall were also given to the committee of the livery.

Worms, Sept. 17. The Count de Leriange Heidesheim has been lately seized in his castle at Heidelheim, by a party of 150 men belonging to the Palatine troops, by order of the Emperor. He has been declared incapable of governing his country.

Bologna, Aug. 28. A false bull, under the name of Clement XIV. has been handed about here, containing the suppression of the Jesuits. We have not yet been able to find out where it was printed.

Rome, Sept. 1. On the 24th ult. at night, the galley-slaves at Civita Vecchia, being 1,400 in number, found means to get off their chains, and were actually employed in digging a hole under the wall of the town, which they designed to plunder, and then to put to sea. The commanding officer immediately assembled a sufficient number of troops, who fired upon them with muskets and grenades, and the artillery of the fortress, by which means they were soon subdued. Eight of them were killed, and 22 dangerously wounded: the rest submitted to be conducted back to the place of their confinement.

Married. Lately, at Arborfield, in Berkshire, John Street, Gent. aged 87, to Miss Anne Marshall, of that place, a young lady in the 23d year of her age.

Died. At Walton, Philip Car, aged upwards of 100.

At Wells, Mr. Mills, aged 100 years and five days.

In the south of France, Thomas Milne, Esq. aged 111.

OCTOBER.

1st. The Magistrates and Society of Merchants in Bristol, in order to promote the public service, voted a premium of 20s. to every sailor that shall enter voluntarily with Captain Fanshawe, besides the bounty of 30s. allowed by government. This encourages the sailors to offer themselves freely, and the disagreeable service of impressing is avoided.

Letters from Corsica take notice, that there are still a great number of the natives that have not yet submitted to the French government: that executions are frequent of such of them as are taken; and that a priest who had concealed himself, having embarked with three of his kinsmen on board a felucca at San Peregrino, was pursued,

CHRONICLE. [151]

saed, and, not being able to escape, threw himself into the sea with all his treasure hung round his neck, and was drowned. His poor kinsmen, not having courage to follow the example of the holy father, were taken, and conducted prisoners to Bastia.

The freedom of King's Lynn, in Norfolk, was presented to John Wilkes, Esq. for his constitutional, spirited, and uniform conduct, in support of the liberties of this country.

2d. The common crier of the city read at the Royal Exchange his Majesty's proclamation, offering to such seamen who shall voluntarily enter into his service a bounty of thirty shillings.

From the LONDON GAZETTE.
Whitehall, October 2. By letters received from Jamaica, it appears, that the late earthquake, which happened in Hispaniola, was felt all over that island, but no considerable damage happened at any other place than at Port au Prince; but there its effects were terrible; 450 people lost their lives; the fortification on the island or key going in, is totally destroyed, and, except a few houses, the whole town lies in ruins. The governor and inhabitants, who are reduced to live in tents, are exerting themselves in building of wooden houses, having learned, from fatal experience, that buildings constructed with other materials are exceedingly dangerous, in a country where frequent earthquakes happen.

Yesterday the Commissioners for victualling his Majesty's navy contracted with Mr. Mellish for 2,000 oxen, at 23s. 9d. per hundred weight, to be killed between the present time and the 31st of December, at the Victualling-office, Tower-hill.

A root of the true rhubarb, which weighed 35lb. was taken up in the garden of the Lord Chief Baron, at Dean, in Scotland. The seeds of this plant were brought from China by Dr. Mounsey.

4th. At the general quarterly meeting of the Guardians of the Asylum for Female Orphans, the Hon. and Rt. Rev. the Bishop of Hereford was unanimously elected Vice-President of that charity, in the room of Sir Thos. Hankey, deceased.

The first stone of the new bridge at Exeter was laid by Joseph Dixon, Esq.

Dublin, Sept. 29. The Neptune, Broomhall, deeply laden with fish, from the banks of Newfoundland, foundered on the 12th of August, being the second day after putting to sea. She was bound to the west of England; had 33 servants on board, seven of whom were drowned; the others, with the captain and ship's company, were taken up by a French banker, who used them with great humanity for 19 days, when they met with a large cat, from Whitby, in the north of England, who received them on board, and landed them at Burlington, on the 17th inst. Of the unfortunate people who were drowned, it is said there were three English, two Irish, one Scotchman, and a black boy, about 15 years of age.

By letters from Leghorn we learn, that the destruction of the Turkish fleet was occasioned by the activity of Capt. Greig, Lieutenant Terrington, and Lieutenant Dugdale, three Englishmen, who com-

[L] 4

commanded the fire ships. When the latter had steered his vessel in the night close to a Turkish man of war of 84 guns, his design was discovered, which threw his crew of Russian sailors into such a consternation, that they immediately abandoned him, and rowed off in the boat: notwithstanding which, he bravely hooked the grapnel-iron into the rigging of the enemy, and then jumped into the sea, from whence he was luckily taken up, and soon after conveyed on board the Russian Admiral, who loaded him with caresses, advanced him to a command, and promised to recommend him for his gallant behaviour to the Empress.

They write from Boston, in New England, that the Assembly of that province had met at Cambridge the end of July, according to their adjournment, and after sitting about eight days, without doing any business, they refusing to act, as an Assembly, at any place out of Boston, they were prorogued to the 5th of September, then to meet.

Gloucester, Oct. 1. A few days ago a fisherman, who was fishing for salmon in the Severn, near the Old Passage, entangled in his net a large seal or sea-dog, which with difficulty he drew out of the water upon the sands, and some other men coming to his assistance, they took it alive. The animal, which the man has brought here to shew, is larger than a bull-dog, which it resembles very much about the head, only it has no ears. Its skin is covered with short hair, dark on the back, and spotted on the belly: its fore-feet or fins are about six inches long, with five claws upon each. The body runs taper to the tail, near which the hinder feet are placed, which are broad and webbed. It is kept in a large piece of water, in which it moves with great nimbleness.

8th. The Professor of Architecture read his first lecture in the Royal Academy, wherein he introduced the History of Architecture, and the sciences depending on it; the origin of houses, and of the Grecian and Roman orders; and concluded with general instructions on the study and practice of architecture.

Was read in full convocation, a letter from the Right Hon. the Earl of Litchfield, Chancellor of the University of Oxford, intimating, that it would be for the honour and advantage of the University to continue the Rev. Dr. Wetherell Vice-Chancellor for another year, and desiring the concurrence of convocation for that purpose, which was unanimously assented to.

Account of the Loss of his Majesty's Ship Swift, on the Coast of Patagonia; extracted from a Letter from a Gentleman who was on Board, to his Friend in London.

We sailed from Port Egmont on a cruize the 7th of March last, and had a violent gale of wind for some days, which drove us over to the coast of Patagonia. As we were sickly, and wanted refreshments, we resolved to go into Port Desire, finding ourselves within a few leagues of it: on attempting to work in, we struck on a rock, where we beat for an hour and a half before we were able to get the ship off. We then (the wind just at that time coming to the eastward) ran up the river: when we we got about half a mile up, we struck on another rock, and, as it was at this time ebb tide, our united efforts to get her off proved ineffectual: she hung upon this rock by the fore-feet, her stern being amazingly depressed, about three hours; she then slipt off, overset, and sunk in eight fathom water. This happened at six in the evening: some got on the rock, others swam for the shore, and some for the boats; so that we were all saved, with great difficulty, except three men. The hardships we met with afterwards can be better conceived than described, having nothing to lay upon in that tempestuous climate except a few sails, which were accidentally saved; and no other shelter than rocks and stones, for there is not a tree or bush in the whole country. We lived upon sea-lions, and sometimes sea-fowl, when we could get them, for we liked them rather better than the former, notwithstanding they were extremely fishy: we had nothing to drink but dirty brackish water, except when Providence was so kind as to send a shower of rain, at which time every one drank heartily out of the cavities of the rocks, but could not lay by a store of it, for want of vessels to keep it in.

Two days after the loss of the ship, our master and six men sailed in the cutter for Port Egmont, in order, if possible, to bring the Favourite to our relief. This was, perhaps, the most dangerous undertaking that ever was known; however, they succeeded, and returned to us with the Favourite about a month afterwards: every one, except four or five, had lost all hopes, and given her up a fortnight before she appeared in sight, and we were beginning to prepare for a march to Buenos Ayres; but, by what we have since learned, it would have been impossible for any of us to have got there; for the distance, as we could not have gone in a straight line, on account of the large rivers that are in the way, is near 2,000 miles; not to mention the want of provisions and water, the laying on the cold ground without any covering, and the dangers we had to dread from the native savages, which we have since been informed are very numerous for several hundred leagues to the southward to Buenos Ayres. —We saw no inhabitants during our stay at Port Desire, nor were we able to kill any guanacoes, although they were very plenty, but extremely shy. Capt. Farmer, and Mr. Thomson, our surgeon, went in a small boat about 50 leagues up the river, in hopes of making some discoveries, and getting some guanacoes, but were obliged to return on the fifth day, as they could get nothing to eat or drink. In short, it is the most barren, desolate country, I suppose, in the world.

10th. This morning, the five convicts under sentence of death in Newgate were executed at Tyburn, namely, Mary-Ann Ryan, Joseph Josephs, and James Simpson, for robbing William Wright on the highway, in Whitechapel; Henry Dixon, for burglary, and stealing goods in the house of James Wood, in Norman-street, in St. Luke's parish; and Charles M'Donald, for robbing John Tomlin on the highway of a silver watch. Mary-Ann Ryan was

was dressed in white with black trimmings, and her coffin on the cope of the cart, together with M'Donald on the right, and Dixon on her left hand, went in the first cart; and Josephs (being a Jew, was attended by one of that persuasion, who read to him in the Hebrew), together with Simpson, who seemed very ill, in the other cart. The last sessions, which proved fatal to Ryan, was the third in succession in which she had been tried at the Old Bailey for capital offences.

The first stone of the intended City of London Lying-in hospital, at the corner of the City-road, in Old-street, was laid by the Right Hon. Barlow Trecothick, Lord Mayor, and President of the said hospital, accompanied by John Paterson, Esq. one of the Vice-Presidents, and Treasurer, and a great number of the Governors, amidst the loud and repeated acclamations of a vast concourse of people assembled on the occasion.—After the ceremony, the building committee and officers, together with Mr. Mylne, the architect, and the contractors for the building, were elegantly and politely entertained at dinner by his Lordship at the Mansion-house.

They write from Parma, that there was lately erected in that city, by order of the Infant Duke, a white marble monument in the form of an antient altar, dedicated to Friendship. It is raised as a token to perpetuate the double alliance which at present subsists between his Royal Highness and the Emperor. The period that gave birth to this event, together with a Latin inscription composed by Father Paccindi, is engraved thereon.

Extract of a Letter from Rome, Sept. 10.

Two murderers were executed here last Saturday in the square Del Popolo, where it is computed upwards of 40,000 people were assembled; and just at the instant that the last of the criminals was going to be dispatched, the Abbé Merli, who had given him absolution, retiring too far backward, fell from the scaffold, and received a mortal wound on the head. This occasioned a great bustle, and the people pressed so eagerly to the spot to see the priest, that the Sbirri were not able to make any head against them, but were obliged themselves to retire. The confusion then became general, and great numbers had their arms and legs broke, and were otherwise terribly maimed.

Coyde, a tea-broker, charged with forging a warrant for the delivery of three chests of tea at the India House, was brought to be examined before a Court of Directors at the India House; and while they were debating, actually effected his escape, although three constables were placed to guard him. He is supposed to have got out of the court-room, through the door which leads to the Secretary's parlour, and gone unobserved from one room to another till he came into the street.

At a court of common council held this day, after very warm debates, a question was moved, that James Eyre, Esq. the present Recorder, be no more advised with, retained, or employed, in any of the affairs of this corporation, he being deemed by this court unworthy of their future trust or confidence.

12th.

fidence. The same was declared to be carried in the affirmative. For the question, six aldermen, and ninety-eight commoners, besides two tellers; against the question, seven aldermen, and forty-nine commoners, besides two tellers.

It was then moved by Mr. Judd, That, in all cases relative to the affairs of this city, where it may be necessary to have the advice, opinion, or assistance, of any counsel learned in the law, John Glynn, Esq. Serjeant at Law, shall for the future, on all occasions, be advised with, retained, and employed; which was carried in the affirmative. Mr. Beardmore moved, That the freedom of this city be presented to John Dunning, Esq. for having, when Solicitor-general to his Majesty, defended in parliament, on the soundest principles of law and the constitution, the rights of the subject to petition and remonstrate; which was carried without a debate or division.

Extract of a Letter from Dublin, Sept. 11.

"About ten days ago, one Shirdin, a farmer at Turvey-hill, near Rush, came to this city to receive 50l. and having a daughter married here to a chairman, he went with the farmer to receive the money: on seeing it paid, he demanded his wife's fortune, which the farmer refused till his death; on which the chairman swore he would be up with him, and they then parted, when the farmer went home without the least molestation: but the son-in-law hiring ten ruffians, they attacked the farmer's house in the night, and cut the throats of the old man, his wife, son, and daughter, from ear to ear. His grandson being at a neighbour's house, happening to come home the instant after this shocking deed was committed, he heard something was wrong, and took to his heels, when the ruffians overtook and killed him, as they supposed, and threw him into a potatoe rig; but he was found alive next morning, and, giving some account of them, three of these wretches were taken, and committed to the gaol of this city."

Dublin, Oct. 2. Joseph Daw, now in Newgate for the murder of the unfortunate people at Turvey, has made an ample confession of the fact, in which he acknowledges himself to be the only person concerned in the said murder: in consequence of which, John Ryan and John Farrel, now in custody on the former testimony of the said Daw, are to be enlarged. Joseph Daw acknowledges that he perpetrated the murder thus: he called the old man, his son, and grandson, one by one, to the back of their dwelling; then stabbed each of them with a pitchfork, and afterwards cut their throats. The old woman he strangled in her bed.

At a court of common council held this day, the 19th. Lord Mayor acquainted the court, that he called them to proceed on the adjourned business of the last court; but as the report of the committee to consider of the embankment at Durham-yard was part of the business, he thought proper to inform them, that he had held a court of conservancy, and that five bills of indictment had

had been found against different persons for encroachments on the river.

The report of the aforesaid committee was then read: a motion was made by Alderman Crosby to agree with the committee in their report. After a debate of near three hours, he withdrew his motion, and made another, that the report be printed, and a copy sent to each member of the court; which was carried in the affirmative.

Another motion was made, that the evidence the said committee have had be likewise printed, by way of appendix, and sent with the foregoing; which was likewise carried in the affirmative.

Another motion was made by the Lord Mayor elect, that a committee be appointed to join the committee of the livery, to have the opinion of counsel concerning their memorial presented at a former court.

Another motion was made, that the memorial be now read, and it was read accordingly.

Mr. Potter desired the Lord Mayor to ask the memorialists, for what purposes they thought themselves appointed a committee of the livery? But Mr. Alderman Townshend moved, that they might withdraw, which they accordingly did, without being asked the question.

After much debate, the first question being withdrawn, Mr. Wilson made a motion, that a committee be appointed of the members of that court only, to consider of the allegations contained in the memorial, and to have such advice therein as they shall think proper, and report to that court their opinion thereon; which was carried in the affirmative, and a committee was accordingly appointed of six aldermen and twelve commoners, viz. Aldermen Crosby, Stevenson, Townshend, Sawbridge, Wilkes, and Oliver.— Commoners, Holker, Judd, Townshend, Sharp, Hurford, Beardmore, Bollas, Bishop, Stavely, Gofs, and Nicholson.

A motion was made, that they be impowered to draw on the Chamberlain for a sum not exceeding 500l. which was agreed to.

The petition of the livery of the company of Goldsmiths was read, and a motion being made that it be referred to the former committee, the same was agreed to, and ordered, that they have such advice thereon as they shall think proper, and report their opinion to that court.

This morning, about two o'clock, an express arrived at the Duke of Rutland's, at Knightsbridge, with the melancholy news of the death of the Right Hon. the Marquis of Granby, who died at Scarborough on Thursday evening, at six o'clock, of the gout in his stomach.—His Lordship finding himself much out of order in his stomach and bowels, sent for Dr. Daltrey, from York, who, with Dr. Mouffey, who attended his Lordship before, were well convinced he had strong symptoms of the gout, and accordingly advised the Marquis to put his feet and legs into hot water, at the same time administering the highest cordials to drive it into the extremities, which soon had the desired effect; that immediately after his feet swelled, looked inflamed, and had all the appearance of the disorder being settled there, when his Lordship retired to another room, where he was immediately

20th.

diately seized with a fainting fit, and expired without a groan, in the presence of his physicians.

Orders are sent to the Lords Lieutenants of the different counties to issue out their warrants to the Constables and Headboroughs in their respective districts, to impress men, for the more expeditious manning the Royal Navy, that shall appear to have no visible way of living.

They write from Parma, that the late Cardinal Borini, Bishop of Pavia, had, for the encouragement of population, directed by his will the sum of twelve hundred crowns to be annually divided among twenty-four young women as marriage portions.

On Thursday the Lieutenant of a pressgang was brought before the Lord Mayor, and severely reprimanded by his Lordship for impressing men in the city without being attended by a constable.

At a general assembly held at the Tholsel of Dublin, "*Resolved*, That it would be a very salutary and constitutional proceeding, in the corporation of the city of Dublin, to present a petition to the King, expressive, in the most grateful terms, of that zeal and loyalty which warm the breasts of his Majesty's faithful citizens of Dublin; and at the same time, in the most humble and dutiful manner, to present to the throne the many grievances sustained by this kingdom in general, and city in particular, by the late prorogations of parliament."

27th. Between eleven and twelve last night, their Royal Highnesses the Princess Dowager of Wales, and the Duke of Gloucester, landed at Dover, from Germany; and after taking some refreshment, they set out for London, and arrived at Carleton House this morning about ten o'clock, in perfect health. His Majesty being previously informed of their arrival, came to town from Richmond, and after staying some time to congratulate them on their safe arrival, returned to Richmond. Their Royal Highnesses set out from hence on their tour to Germany on the 8th of June last.

John Shine, a journeyman barber, impressed as a seaman, by virtue of a warrant from the Lords of the Admiralty, and backed by the Lord Mayor, was brought before John Wilkes, Esq. the sitting Alderman at Guildhall; when the Alderman adjudged the impressing illegal, and ordered Shine to be discharged.

The Lords of the Admiralty having written to several noblemen and gentlemen for their assistance in providing hands for manning his Majesty's fleet, and among others to his Grace the Duke of Northumberland, Lord-lieutenant and Custos Rotulorum for the county of Middlesex, that nobleman has written to Sir John Fielding upon the subject, the contents of which his worship communicated to the other Justices of the Peace, who met at Guildhall Westminster; after which the Bench took the matter into consideration, and resolved to put in force every legal method to forward the above necessary business.

On Tuesday the Commissioners for paving, &c. the city, fined a bricklayer the sum of 5l. for taking up the pavement, and making a cellar-window, in Thames-street, without leave of the said Commissioners.

The

The report of the committee appointed to inspect the embankment at Durham-yard, delivered to the court of common council on Friday last, sets forth, that the buildings erected by Messr. Adams project into the river 28 feet, and that their farther encroachments, by earth and rubbish, project into the river 175 feet in depth, and 397 feet in length:

That Mr. Paine's buildings project at the east end 18 feet, at the west end 9 feet; in length from west to east 83 feet six inches; and that Mr. Paine's farther encroachment by rubbish, &c. projects into the river 108 feet in depth, and about 461 feet in length:

That the encroachment by Mr. Kitchiner is 52 feet at the west end, and 40 feet at the east end, and about 104 in length:

That these encroachments are "prejudicial to the public, and hurtful to the navigation:" and that the representations and memorial of the committee of watermen's and lightermen's company, of the chief owners of coal craft, and of the corn lightermen, contain allegations against the said encroachments, which the committee find by evidence to be fully verified and established.

Warrants were yesterday issued out at the Admiralty, signed by Sir Edward Hawke, and sent to the constables of the different parishes within twenty miles of London, ordering them to impress able-bodied men for his Majesty's sea service. They are to be paid 20s. for each man, and sixpence a mile for bringing them up, not exceeding 20 miles, and to deliver them at the rendezvous in Mark-lane.

Orders are given for several small sloops and armed cutters to cruise in the channel, and on the Scotch coast, to prevent any ships putting into our ports suspected of being infected.

His Royal Highness the Duke of Gloucester, in his tour through Germany, dined the 16th ult. with the Emperor, but was taken ill the same evening.

The curious in astronomy, by letting the sun's image through a telescope on white paper, may now see several solar spots, appearing larger than Venus did at the transit.

29th. The sessions at the Old Bailey, which begun on Wednesday, ended, when eight prisoners capitally convicted received sentence of death, viz. Charles Burton, for a burglary; Bartholomew Langley, for the detestable crime of bestiality with a she-ass, in a hovel near Knightsbridge; John Barton, for horse-stealing; Joseph Knight, Thomas Bird, and William Payne, for robbing the house of Mrs. Jeredare of a large quantity of silver plate; William Williams for a highway robbery; and William Brent for a burglary in the house of Lewis Cartier, in Spur-street, Leicester-fields, and stealing a pair of diamond ear-rings of great value, several bank notes of the value of 1,500l. 240 guineas, and six Portugal pieces, valued 10l. 16s. the property of Edward Jordan, Esq. At this sessions thirty were ordered to be transported for seven years; one was branded in the hand, who was a hackney-coachman, for manslaughter; four were ordered

ordered to be privately whipped, one publicly whipped, and thirteen were discharged upon proclamation.

Amongst others who were acquitted at this last sessions, was a school-master, who was indicted for killing one of his scholars, a young gentleman, son to a late general, who being very inattentive to instruction, his master, after repeated admonitions, intending to give him a small box on the ear, the unfortunate youth standing near the fire, and shrinking from the correction, most unhappily struck the side of his head against a corner, or moulding, in the chimney-piece, which beat in a piece of the skull, and the extravasated blood issuing from the contusion pressing the brain, he died early the next morning. The master had a most excellent character for his ability, tenderness, and care, of his scholars, and particularly to this youth.

Extract of a letter from Charles Town, Aug. 24, 1770.

Our Assembly has been sitting since the 14th inst. The Lower House has come to several resolutions concerning the council, which they have communicated to them, and to which a reply is preparing. The bone of contention is the 1,500l. sterling voted the Bill of Rights People. The Lieutenant-governor has communicated to the Assembly a Royal instruction, conceived in very strong terms, respecting the said 1,500l. and suggesting some new modes in passing money-bills, on which the Commons House hath addressed his Honour for copies of his letters to the King's Ministers on that affair, which have been refused. We have agreed to stop all commercial intercourse with New York, on account of that province breaking the non-importation agreement, which we strictly adhere to.

Admiral Knowles has obtained permission to enter into the Czarina's service. He is to rank First Admiral of the Czarina's fleet, and have a seat in her Council. His pension is ten thousand rubles (2,250l.) a year, and a 1,000l. sterling annually to be paid to his lady and family, with the benefit of survivorship. A compliment of five hundred guineas is to be made for present pocket expences, and he is to be received, in his journey, at her Majesty's expence, at his arrival on the edge of the Russian dominions. Upon quitting the Czarina's service, he has a promise of being reinstated in his present rank.

The secretary of the society of agriculture of Leon hath drawn up a memorial, wherein he proves, that the great number of useless dogs in the kingdom annually consume of aliments proper for the human species to the amount of sixteen millions, which would furnish subsistence for upwards of 300,000 men.

A most horrible attempt has been made at Cortona, in Italy. All the monks of the convents of the Serviles were poisoned by something put in their victuals, but they were preserved from death by the speediness with which remedies were brought. They are making all possible search to find out those who were culpable of this enormous crime.

This morning, about ten, a prodigious number of people crowded

crowded into Westminster-hall, which continued to fill till noon, when Mr. Wilkes came into the hall, attended by Mr. Sawbridge; and having received several huzzas, he ascended the stairs, and after informing the company of the intent of their present meeting, he began to read a paper of instructions to their members, the purport of which was, That as petitions, addresses, and remonstrances, to the throne, for a redress of grievances hitherto unprecedented, had been of late despised, and, by the advice of evil counsellors, dismissed from the throne; therefore, that their representatives be instructed to move for an impeachment of Henry North, commonly called Lord North, as not only the contriver and schemer, but even the carrier into execution, of these cruel and unconstitutional machinations.

Mr. Sawbridge opposed the instructions, for this reason, "That Lord North, having places and pensions at his disposal, was at the head of a set of people, against whom the nation had evident reason to complain; that in the House of Lords he had the Bishops and Scots Peers; and all the placemen in the House of Commons on his side; that if his conduct was brought into question in either or both Houses, he would be acquitted, and they precluded from any complaint hereafter." He therefore moved for a remonstrance, and the question being put, it was carried in the affirmative. A committee went out to draw it up, and returned with it in half an hour, the heads of which were as follow:

1. That a bill be brought in and passed for establishing triennial parliaments.

2. That his M———y would remove from his presence and councils all his ministers and secretaries of state, particularly Lord M. and not admit a Scotsman into the administration.

3. That a law be made that the electors of Great Britain be empowered to chuse any representatives they think proper, without regard to any sentence whatsoever.

4. That no general warrants be ever issued, even in case of manning a fleet, or recruiting the army.

5. That a law be made for appealing to a superior court, and bringing in an additional witness to convict a man, even after he has been acquitted by a jury, or from some favourable circumstances has obtained the royal mercy.

It was then agreed, that it should be presented by Sir Robert Bernard, not, as Mr. Sawbridge politely observed, out of any disrespect to Lord Percy, whom they could not help thinking a worthy representative and a friend to liberty, but because that nobleman was out of the kingdom.

Married. At Camberwell church, Mr. William Barton, aged 82, late of the George and Vulture Tavern, Cornhill, to Miss Smith, of Orchard-row, Camberwell, aged 25.

Died. Lately, aged 101, Mr. Joseph Davis, many years ago in the African trade.

NOVEMBER.

A woman in the Old Bailey received the following letter from her husband, who was gone to his garden near Islington: 1st.

"Dear

"Dear wife, before this reaches you, I shall be no more. The weight of my misfortunes, which I have brought upon myself by my criminal intercourse with Mrs. D. I am not able to bear any longer, and am therefore determined to quit a life that for some years has been but of little use to you or my children. Farewell, for ever. From him who once was an indulgent husband."—As soon as she received the above letter, she hasted with a friend to endeavour to divert him from his purpose, but, to her grief, found him hanging in his own summer-house, quite dead.

The collector of the customs at Irvine, in Scotland, ordered all the smuggling vessels about the point of Froon to be seized and secured, lest they should be a means of importing the plague. This was effected without the least opposition.

4th. Being the birth-day of our glorious deliverer, King William, the equestrian statue of his late Royal Highness William Duke of Cumberland was opened for the inspection of the public, in the centre of Cavendish Square. The inscription is as follows: "William, Duke of Cumberland, born April 15, 1721; died 31st of October, 1766. This equestrian statue was erected by Lieutenant-general William Strode, in gratitude for his private kindness, in honour to his public virtues, Nov. 5, Anno Domini 1770."

5th. This morning Michael Thomas, a black, and Ann Brandley, a white, were married at St. Olave's, Southwark; but while the ceremony was performing, a press-gang interrupted the minister in the celebration of his office: upon which a contest arose, and the clergyman received a blow on the breast; but a constable being called immediately, the lieutenant was secured, and carried before a magistrate; but after proper submission, was, by the generosity of the minister, released without farther prosecution. The poor black, with his bride, made his escape in the fray.

6th. The two Kennedys were brought to the bar of the Court of King's-bench, in order to plead to the appeal lodged against them by the widow Bigby; but the matter being made up before-hand, she did not appear, and suffered a non-suit. An evening paper says, that when she went to receive the money (350l.), she wept bitterly, and at first refused to touch the money that was to be the price of her husband's blood; but being told that nobody else could receive it for her, she held up her apron, and bid the attorney, who was to pay it, sweep it into her lap.

7th. The Westminster remonstrance was presented to his Majesty at St. James's by Sir Robert Barnard, one of the members for that city, which was received, but no answer returned. It was signed, "By-order of the general meeting, JOHN WILKES, Chairman."

8th. At a Court of Aldermen held at Guildhall, Brass Crosby, Esq. the Lord Mayor elect, was sworn into that office for the year ensuing. Upon this occasion Mr. Trecothick addressed himself to the hall, to explain the motives of his conduct during his mayoralty: he observed, that many ill-natured reflections had been thrown out against him for backing press-warrants

warrants in the city, in which, he remarked, he was juſtified by the precedents of all the former Lord Mayors; that, at a time when the whole nation was alarmed with the enemy's great preparations for war, he ſhould have thought himſelf inexcuſable, as Chief Magiſtrate, if he had thrown any obſtruction in the way which might have retarded the manning of our fleet; that though he had his doubts with reſpect to the legality of preſs-warrants, yet, as an individual, though in ſo high a ſtation, he thought it too weighty a matter for him ſingly to determine upon, and the more particularly as the parliament was ſo near upon meeting, under whoſe conſideration only ſuch buſineſs could with propriety come. Mr. Trecothick ſaid farther, that he deſpiſed the low and illiberal means that had been made uſe of to prejudice him in the minds of the public; and as he had, in every reſpect, executed the buſineſs of Chief Magiſtrate to the beſt of his judgment and abilities, his conſcience was perfectly eaſy, and he did not doubt but he ſhould meet with the approbation of all his impartial fellow-citizens. His ſpeech was received with applauſe.

9th. A letter from Portſmouth of this day's date alarmed the whole city of London: it imported, that at Spithead there was an outward-bound Dutch Eaſt Indiaman, which had on board 286 men, of whom upwards of 90 were ſick of an epidemical fever; and that two cuſtom-houſe officers, who were put on board her, were already dead. As the plague is now ſo general in many parts of Europe, every body dreaded that moſt fatal diſtemper; but it has ſince appeared that the fever on board this ſhip, though infectious, was not peſtilential, but only a kind of gaol fever, owing to foul air, to remedy which, Dr. Hales's ventilator has been ſucceſsfully applied.

Mr. Serg. Glynn moved in the Court of Common Pleas for a rule to ſhew cauſe why the verdict againſt Mr. Horne ſhould not be ſet aſide; when, after a full hearing, the court granted the rule.—On this occaſion the right of petitioning was aſſerted and proved: if, then, the right of petitioning is the right of the ſubject, it muſt follow that the freedom of debate is the right of the ſubject alſo, otherwiſe the right of petitioning would be nugatory. If the evil conduct of miniſters, for inſtance, is the grievance againſt which the ſubject has cauſe to complain, how can that evil conduct be juſtified, if it is not fully proved? and how can this be proved, if it is not fully and freely debated? Freedom of debate muſt therefore be incloſed in the right of petitioning, as the law gives every thing neceſſary to the enjoyment of a right when it gives the right to be enjoyed.

13th. This day his Majeſty went in the uſual ſtate to the Houſe of Peers, and opened the ſeſſion with a moſt gracious ſpeech from the throne.

15th. The infectious fever on board the Dutch outward-bound Indiaman at Portſmouth is ſo far abated, that the captain intends ſailing the firſt fair wind. No perſon has taken the infection from any of the crew on board, except the two cuſtom-houſe officers already mentioned.

A motion was this day made at a court of common council held at at Guildhall, that an humble address, remonstrance, and petition, be presented to his Majesty, touching the violated right of election, and praying for a dissolution of parliament; which was declared in the affirmative; and a committee was appointed to prepare and bring it in, which was done accordingly, approved, and ordered to be presented.

A motion was then made, that the thanks of the court be given to Barlow Trecothick, Esq. the late Lord Mayor, for his upright conduct during his mayoralty, by the strict attendance to the administration of justice, his constant endeavours for preserving the peace and harmony of the city, and for preventing every encroachment on the just rights and liberties of his fellow-citizens, which was agreed to unanimously.

A letter from Mr. Sergeant Glynn to the Lord Mayor was read, expressing his acknowledgment of the honour they had conferred upon him in the resolution of the 12th of October last; which was ordered to be entered in the journal of the court.

London Gazette, Saturday 17.

Bounties offered by the undermentioned cities and towns to encourage seamen to enter voluntarily into his Majesty's service.

City of London. Forty shillings to every able seaman to enter voluntarily into his Majesty's service.

City of Bristol. Twenty shillings to every able seaman, and fifteen shillings to every ordinary seaman.

Town of Montrose. Two guineas to every able, and one guinea to every ordinary seaman.

City of Edinburgh. The same as Montrose.

Town of Aberdeen. One guinea to every able seaman, and fifteen shillings to every landman.

Town of Lynn. One guinea to every able seaman.

N. B. These bounties are over and above the bounties granted by government.

The greatest part of the spacious old church at Tedbury, in Gloucestershire, being, as is supposed, undermined by the floods, tumbled down, and the organ, pulpit, reading-desk, and most of the pews, were all crushed to pieces by the falling in of the roof.

This morning, about twenty minutes after two, 17th. a fire broke out at the coach-office, the bottom of Surry-street, in the Strand, which entirely consumed the same, together with the house of —— Neale, Esq. above it, and on the other side, the house of Mr. Comyns, the quaker, who planned the taking of Senegal. The flames raged with great fury, and it was with much difficulty Mr. Crosby, head clerk of the coach-office, and three young women, his daughters, saved their lives by getting along the gutter on the roof into the garret of Robert Smith, Esq. whose house, having a strong party-wall, happily put a stop to the farther spreading of the conflagration. Mrs. Comyns, mother of Mr. Comyns, being old, was carried out on a feather-bed.

Mr. Stephens, author of the pamphlet against the illegality of imprisonment for debt, was, by a bench rule, called up before Lord Mansfield, and the rest of the judges of the King's-bench, where he spoke for above half an hour on the subject of his pamphlet and his case, quoted Magna Charta, and several acts of parlia-

parliament with great readiness, and insisted on his releasement, which he urged was no more than his right, and the right of every subject in Great Britain. Lord Mansfield heard him very attentively the whole time, and when he had concluded, said, 'it was not in his power to comply with his request;' and remanded him back to prison. Mr. Stephens then asked, Whether that was his Lordship's final opinion? And being answered in the affirmative, 'he desired his Lordship to take care whether the prisoners would not right themselves.' Accordingly, when the account of his ill-success arrived at the prison, those confined there immediately arose, secured the turnkeys, and seven of them, who were in upon writs of *ad satisfaciendum*, made their escape. The marshal then sent directly to the Tower for a party of the guards, by which the rest were secured.

20th. His Majesty has been pleased to give 1000l. towards the relief and assistance of the Protestant Dissenting Ministers, settled in Nova Scotia, in North America; and likewise 500l. towards building a church in the Savoy for the use of reformed German Protestants.

Lord Mansfield gave the opinion of the Court of King's-bench in the case of the King against Woodfall, the purport of which was as follows: That Mr. Woodfall, being charged in the information with printing and publishing Junius's Letter to the King, if the word *only* had not been inserted in the verdict, the court would have ordered it to be entered up as legal; but as the addition of that word seemed to imply a reservation as well as a difference of opinion in the jury, they were of opinion there was sufficient ground for a new trial; which was accordingly awarded.

21st. This day, at one o'clock, Brass Crosby, Esq. Lord Mayor of this city, attended by Aldermen Trecothick, Stephenson, Townshend, and Oliver, the two Sheriffs, and about an hundred of the common council, proceeded from Guildhall to St. James's, to present to his Majesty the city remonstrance. They arrived about two o'clock, and were introduced to his Majesty by the lords in waiting, when the remonstrance was read by Sir James Hodges, Town-clerk (the Recorder not attending).

To which his Majesty was pleased to return the following answer:

"As I have seen no reason to alter the opinion expressed in my answer to your address upon this subject, I cannot comply with the prayer of your petition."

The waters by the late rains were so much out at Henley, in Oxfordshire, that there was no road over the bridge observable but by ropes as directions; the Henley, Abingdon, and Oxford coaches, were obliged to have eight horses to draw them. A brick wall, which stands near the Thames, was carried away by the current; and on Sunday a bay horse, with a saddle and bridle on, swam out of the Thames without a rider, who is unknown. The waters were so much out at Staines, that the express was hindered for some time: part of the bridge at Wallingford, Berks, is carried away by the great flux of waters; a waggon and a

coach

coach were overset at Maidenhead-bridge: guides are placed on the roads; and there is no navigation on the Thames, in that part of the country.

23d. A rule was granted in the Court of King's-bench, on a motion made by Mr. Moreton, and seconded by the counsellors Wallace and Dunning, for an information against seven of the ringleaders concerned in breaking out of the King's-bench last Monday, and are now confined in the county gaol.

26th. Came on at the Court of Common Pleas, before Lord C. J. Wilmot, and the rest of the judges of that court, a motion to set aside the verdict in the case of the Rt. Hon. G. Onslow against Mr. Horne.—Sergeant Whitaker, counsel for Mr. Onslow, opened the pleadings by observing, that though no immediate damages could be proved by Mr. Onslow, in consequence of the words spoken, yet the reflections made use of by Mr. Horne, aspersive of his character, must sensibly affect him as a gentleman, and therefore he hoped the verdict would be confirmed. He was seconded by Serg. Leigh, who pleaded how tender the law was of the character and good name of even the subordinate classes of men, how much more of those in the higher ranks of life; and concluded with asking, what greater imputation could be thrown on the character of a gentleman than by representing him as a man ready to promise, but regardless of keeping his word? He, therefore, was clear in his opinion, that the verdict ought to be confirmed.

Serg. Glynn, after considering the words spoken, proceeded to shew the nature of the meeting at which they were spoken,—a legal meeting of the electors of a county, for constitutional purposes, where freedom of debate and freedom of investigation were essentially necessary, and where, if the characters of representatives were not to be canvassed, the very purpose of the meeting must wholly be defeated. He concluded with averring, that no precedent could be produced in any of our law-books where words spoken against a representative, merely affecting his character in that capacity, were deemed actionable. In this he was supported by Serg. Johnson, who quoted a number of precedents to the contrary. Upon the whole, the court was of opinion, that the matter was of too much weight to be hastily determined, and that it was too late in the term to give judgment and, therefore, ordered that it lie over till next term.

28th. His Excellency the Count de Guigne, the new French Ambassador, notified his arrival to the Secretaries of State; but has not yet delivered his credentials.

Mr. Almon, the Bookseller, received sentence for selling, in a monthly pamphlet, Junius's Letter to the K——; to pay a fine of ten marks, and to find sureties for his good behaviour for two years, himself to be bound in 400l. and his sureties in 200l. each. Mr. Justice Aston pronounced the sentence; Lord M————d having left the court before the pleadings were ended.

Forty

Forty thousand seamen were voted for the service of the ensuing year. The expence, it is said, will amount to two millions sterling.

Insurances upon outward-bound ships arose from four to ten per cent.

At a general court at Christ's Hospital, a donation from Mrs. Webb of 200l. was received; and another of the like sum from Thomas Calverly, Esq.

29th. This day his Majesty went, with the usual state, to the House of Peers, and gave the royal assent to the bill for prohibiting, for a farther limited time, the exportation of corn, grain, meal, malt, flour, bread, biscuit, and starch; and to such other bills as were ready.

Notice was given at the Castle of Dublin, that it was his Majesty's pleasure that all officers belonging to the army should forthwith repair to their respective regiments, except such as were employed on necessary services.

At the anniversary meeting of the Royal Society held in Crane-court, the annual gold medal of that society was given to Mr. William Hewson, for his curious papers on the lymphatic system in animals.

They write from Manchester, that as the ship Mars was going out of Liverpool, for Jamaica, attended by several gentlemen, clerks, women, and pilots, to the amount of 22 persons, the pilot-boat, meeting with a strong easterly wind, and losing her stays, was driven upon Hoyle's Bank, where she struck: most of the people immediately took to the punt, but she sinking in the breakers, and it being an ebb-tide, was driven on the bank again. When she was relieved, eleven men got into her, to fetch the people on shore from the pilot boat; but the tide being against them, eight of the men died at the oar with the fatigue: the pilot-boat was beaten to pieces, and all the persons on board perished (among whom was the owner of the ship), except two pilots and a clerk: one of the pilot's sons being quite spent with rowing, came to his father, laid his head on his knee, and instantly expired.

The Sieur Ranzonet, watchmaker at Nancy, in Lorrain, has made a watch of the common pocket-size, in which he has fixed an instrument of his own invention, which plays an air *en duo*. All the parts of this little piece of mechanism are distributed with such art, as not in the least to affect the movement of the watch. It is also so nicely constructed, as not to be affected either by heat or cold, dryness or moisture.

The King of Denmark, looking on the liberty of the press as one of the most efficacious means to forward the progress of the sciences, has published a rescript, dated at the Castle of Hirscholm, the 14th of September, in which he exempts from every kind of censure all books which shall be printed in his dominions.

The plague continues to make cruel ravages in Constantinople. Not less than 1000 persons fall victims daily to this dreadful scourge. Poverty and famine are said to fill up the measure of their calamities, and render their condition horrible.

A Greek

A Greek lady having lately complained to the Tornagi Bachi, that a Turk had killed her husband, the Bachi told her, that he feared the people would oppose the punishment of the murderer. The woman wept bitterly. The judge, to appease her, said, "I have hit upon a method of consoling you: embrace the religion of our great Prophet, and I will force the murderer of your husband to marry you."

The Empress of Russia has published an ordonnance, commanding all who profess the Jewish religion to depart her dominions in a limited time. The reason assigned is, that these people hold a correspondence with their enemies.

They write from Oran, a fortress on the coast of Barbary belonging to the Spaniards, that one of their powder magazines was lately set on fire there by lightning, by the blowing up of which seventy persons perished.

Florence, Nov. 6. The excessive rains have occasioned so great a swell of the Tiber, that it has overflowed its banks, and done great damage at Rome and the adjacent country.

Berlin, Nov. 6. We learn from Cosel, in the Upper Silesia, that a lady with several domestics, who came there a few days ago from Poland, all died suddenly the night after their arrival: this accident at first caused great consternation amongst the inhabitants, who thought those persons died of the plague; but their fears soon subsided, when it appeared that they had been poisoned by eating champignons.

Extract of a Letter from Dublin, November 26.

"On the 7th inst. we had a violent storm on this coast, when great damage was done amongst the shipping. The following particulars are come to hand: the Endeavour, of Whitehaven, Mackmerry, lost, and all hands. The Harlequin, Johnson, of ditto, lost, and all hands. The Primrose, Steel, of Warkington, lost, and all hands. A Brig, Messenger, of Maryport, lost, the crew saved, except the master and one hand. A Brig, Biscoe, of ditto, lost, all hands saved. A Brig, Musgrave, of ditto, lost, all hands saved. A Brig, Simpson; the Good Intent, Thompson; a Sloop, Jackson; and the Pretty Jenny, Perkins, are all supposed to have foundered at sea, no account having been heard of them."

The accounts that have been received, during the course of the present month, of the melancholy effects of the floods in several parts of the kingdom, exceed any thing of the kind that has happened in the memory of man. The cities and towns situated on the banks of the Severn have suffered very great distress; those on the Trent have suffered still more; the great Bedford level is now under water; houses, mills, bridges, on almost every brook, have been borne down: but the most affecting scene of all happened at Coventry, where the waters in the middle of the night came rolling into the lowermost street of the town, and almost instantastantaneously rose to an alarming height. The poor there fill the houses from top to bottom: those who occupied the lower apartments perished immediately; some who dwelt on the first floors ascended higher, and saved their lives; but those who attempted to escape by wading, perished by the inundation. More than seventy persons have been taken up drowned in that city only, and accounts have been received of many more in other places.

Died. On the first of October, the Rev. George Whitefield, at Newbury-port, New England. The following anecdote reported of him is truly characteristic.— In the early part of his life, he was preaching in the open fields, when a drummer happened to be present, who was determined to interrupt his pious business, and rudely beat his drum in a violent manner, in order to drown the preacher's voice. Mr. Whitefield spoke very loud, but was not so powerful as the instrument; he therefore called out to the drummer in these words:—"Friend, you and I serve the two greatest Masters existing, but in different callings: you may beat up for volunteers for King George; I for the Lord Jesus Christ. In God's name, then, don't let us interrupt each other: the world is wide enough for us both, and we may get recruits in abundance." This speech had such an effect, that the drummer went away in great good humour, and left the preacher in full possession of the field.

Mrs. Gray, aged 121, at Northfleet; she was born deaf and dumb.

DECEMBER.

His Royal Highness Prince Edward and Princess Augusta Sophia were inoculated for the small-pox by Pennel and Cæsar Hawkins, Esqrs. 3d.

A cause came on to be heard before the Lords Commissioners Smythe and Bathurst, wherein Mr. Macklin, late of Covent-garden theatre, was plaintiff, and two booksellers were defendants. It appeared that the defendants were the publishers of a monthly production, and had hired a person to take down the first act of a farce called Love A-la-mode, written by the plaintiff; they then inserted it in their magazine, 4,500 of which were printed, and 3,500 sold: the plaintiff therefore prayed, that the defendants might account for the profits, and might be restrained by the court from selling any more of the said books. After hearing counsel on both sides, the court granted Mr. Macklin a perpetual injunction.

In consequence of a petition of several merchants of London, trading from Hamburgh and Bremen, setting forth, that there doth not appear to be the least symptom of an epidemical distemper within several hundred miles of either of those places; that the linens imported by the petitioners are all manufactured in different parts of Germany, where there are not the least signs of any infection; and praying, that all ships from Hamburgh and Bremen, that have no rags or cotton-wool on board, be not obliged to perform quarantine; his Majesty, being

being defirous to remove all re-
ftraints upon trade, fo far as may
be confiftent with the fafety of his
fubjects, is pleafed to order that
the quarantine at prefent fubfifting
upon all fhips and veffels coming
from Hamburgh and Bremen be
taken off, provided that they have
no rags or cotton-wool on board,
and that the mafter, &c. of fuch
fhip do firft make oath before the
cuftom-houfe officers or chief magiftrate, on their arrival at the
place they are bound to, that they
did not touch at any place from
whence quarantine is required to
be performed, nor had communication with any fhip or veffel fubject thereto during the voyage;
and that the crew are all in
health.

This day all the rendezvous-
lieutenants attended the Lord
Mayor (as being in office fince the
laft), in order to have their warrants new backed for preffing,
when the fame was refufed; he
adding, That the city bounty was
intended to prevent fuch violences.

A farmer near Swinehead, in
Lincolnfhire, having a fmall field
of high ground which the late
flood did not reach, but appeared
as a little ifland in the midft of a
large lake, a quantity of fheep
took refuge thereon, which the
farmer fearing would be ftarved to
death, employed men with boats
to fetch them away, and among
them picked up above twenty
brace of hares, which had herded
with them.

4th. This day John Barton,
Thos. Knight, Thos. Bird,
William Brent (this laft for fteal-
ing Bank notes, &c. to the value
of 2,900l. from Lady Mayo), and
Bartholomew Langley, for beftiality,
were all executed at Tyburn.
During their execution a large
fcaffold fell down, by which fome
were killed, and many hurt.—
Payne was capitally convicted fome
time ago for abufing Mary Brand,
a little girl under eight years of
age, but received the King's pardon. Langley denied the fact for
which he fuffered with the. facra-
ment in his mouth.

The lieutenants in the prefs
fervice waited on the Lord Mayor
of this city with a meffage from
the Admiralty, defiring his Lordfhip to back the prefs-warrants,
which his Lordfhip refufed.

Came on at Doctors' Com- 6th.
mons, the admiffibility of Lady Grofvenor's recriminate allegations, charging his Lordfhip with
acts of adultery with feveral different women fome time before her
Ladyfhip was charged with the
like crime by his Lordfhip, when
part of the allegations were rejected and part admitted.

The feffions ended at the 8th.
Old Bailey, when five capital
convicts received fentence of death;
John Clarke and John Jofeph De-
foe, for robbing Alexander Fordyce, Efq. of a gold watch, on
the highway; Thomas Meekins,
for affaulting Sufannah Mafemore
on the highway, ravifhing and
robbing her; Mark Marks, a Jew,
for robbing Jofhua Crowden in
Duke's Place; and Thomas Hand,
a Cowkeeper, for wilfully and ma-
lidoufly firing a piftol at Jofeph
Holloway (executor to the pri-
fone's brother), one of the balls of
which entered above his wrift, and
came out near the elbow.

At this feffions 60 prifoners
were tried, one received fentence
to be tranfported for 14 years;
14 to

14 to be transported for seven years; 16 to be whipped, and two fined and imprisoned.

A resolution has passed, that 378,752l. shall be granted for the ordinary supply of the navy for 1771.

A resolution has also passed, to grant 423,747l. for defraying the charge of buildings and rebuildings, and repairs of ships, for 1771.

10th. A trial came on in the Court of King's-bench, wherein a clergyman in Cambridgeshire was plaintiff, and a corn merchant, his neighbour, defendant. The action was brought for the seduction of the plaintiff's daughter; when the jury, that was special, gave 1,200l. damages.

Whitehall, Dec. 8. The Halifax schooner, Capt. Glassford, is arrived from Boston, and brings advice, that the trial of Captain Preston, on the indictment preferred against him in consequence of what happened on occasion of the riot in that town on the 5th of March last, came on in the superior court of judicature and court of assize and general gaol delivery, on Wednesday the 24th of October, and continued till the 30th, when he was fully acquitted.

Friday was tried in the Court of King's-bench, the great cause between Daniel M'Kercher, Esq. plaintiff, and Francis Heylon Peacock, Esq. defendant, concerning a will, wherein was devised about 50,000l. a year to the former by the wife of the said Peacock; and after a long hearing the jury brought in a verdict for the defendant.

The council for the Royal Academy in Pall-Mall gave ten gold and silver medals (being the first impressions from their new dies), executed by Mr. Pingo, from a design of Mr. Cipriani, to the undermentioned artists, whose performances were adjudged worthy of premiums last year. Inscribed round the edge of each is the following:

GOLD MEDALS.

To Mr. James Gandon, for the best design in architecture, 1769.

To Mr. Mauritius Lowe, for the best historical picture, 1769.

To Mr. John Bacon, for the best model of a bas-relief, 1769.

SILVER MEDALS.

To Mr. Matthew Liart, for a drawing of an academy figure, 1769.

To Mr. John Graffi, for ditto.

To Mr. John Kitchingman, for ditto.

To Mr. Joseph Strutt, for ditto.

To Mr. Thomas Hardwicke, for a drawing of architecture, 1769.

To Mr. P. M. Van Gilder, for a model of an academy figure, 1769.

To Mr. John Flaxman, jun. for a model of ditto.

13th. At a court of common council a motion was made, that the thanks of the court be given to the Rt. Hon. the Lord Mayor and committee, for their diligence in prosecuting the intentions of the court to procure seamen for his Majesty's service; by which means the former disagreeable method of impressing seamen has become unnecessary, &c. which was unanimously agreed to. It appeared by the committee's account, that 482 men were entered,

tered, and received the city's bounty.

An article having appeared in the public papers, setting forth, "that the two young Princes at present under inoculation are kept in a large room without a fire, and no curtains to the bed they lie on," Dr. Wintringham, under whose care they are, has thought fit to contradict the same; first, as an absolute falsehood; and, secondly, as it might be the occasion of carrying into practice what would be attended with pernicious consequences.

16th. This day the following bills received the royal assent by virtue of a commission from his Majesty, viz.

The bill to continue the duties on malt, mum, cider, and perry.

The bill for the better supply of mariners and seamen to serve in his Majesty's ships of war, and vessels, and on board merchant ships, and other trading vessels.

The bill to amend an act, for the general quiet of the subjects against all pretences of concealment.

And to such other bills as were ready.

The following account is received of the loss of the ship Grocer, Capt. John Beatson, master, bound from Leith to London: she struck upon the Spurn rocks, near the mouth of the Humber, on the Yorkshire coast, on the 27th of November, and went to pieces that night. It appeared that there were 14 persons in all saved; viz. the captain, his son, and nephew, with four others, in the boat, and the mate with six others drove on shore by the wreck; and that 19 persons in all perished.

By accounts from Liverpool, we learn that on the 6th inst. a most violent storm of wind from the South-West set in with the tide, and kept increasing until about high water, when it shifted to the North-West, doing on that day, and the two days following, incredible damage to the ships both in and out of the docks. A sloop from Scotland, with refined sugar, being driven among the flats and small craft, was bulged and sunk. At noon tide the water rose over the quay, opposite the custom-house, and washed away upwards of 2,000 deal planks, besides great quantities of balks. Several casks of butter and tallow were driven on shore near Formby, with the Cork mark upon them; and as two vessels are expected from Cork, it is feared that at least one of them is lost. Several coasters to Preston, Lancaster, and Carlisle, are lost, and three pilot-boats are missing. The Whale, Ashburn, from Liverpool for Carlisle, drove ashore near Formby land-mark: the people are all saved, but the cargo is entirely lost.

By the storm of wind which began last night, and continued to blow with great violence this morning, incredible damage has been done to the shipping all along the sea coast, particularly at Yarmouth, where sixteen sail were driven upon the sands, and every soul on board perished.

19th.

This morning, about a quarter before one, a whole range of the east battlement of Westminster-hall gave way, the binding and cement being thoroughly decayed. The stones fell upon Oliver's Coffee-house, broke through the ceiling, though of lead, and through the

corner

corner of the porch or gallery over the hall gate, but no lives were lost. The stones of which this antient and noble pile is built were brought from Caen, in Normandy, and are something between limestone and freestone, of a sandy texture, and, by age, a yellowish cast.

The company of Grocers have ordered 200l. to be distributed among their poor members by way of Christmas relief; also have given 100l. to the Marine Society for fitting out poor and deserted boys for the King's ships; besides a donation of 20l. to ten poor clergymen's widows.

The trial of Mr. Robinson, for publishing one of Junius's Letters, came on at Guildhall. Whilst the judge was giving his charge, one of the jury started up, and cried out, "You need not say any more, for I am determined to acquit him;" on which the Attorney-general moved to have that man removed from the jury; but this was objected to by Sergeant Glynn; on which the trial was put off till next term.

Thiel, Dec. 5. The Rhine and the Waal have risen to an uncommon height for some days past, and this day we received the melancholy account that the Rhine Dyke, between Opheusden and Lakemond, was broken through last Sunday; by which all Betuve, Thielward, Curen, Cuilenberg, Beest, Renay, Acquoy, Asperen, and Heukelom, with all the country between the Waal, the Rhine, and the Leek, to the Deisdyk and Gorcum, are laid under the water. Thus all the inhabitants are again in the utmost misery, this being the same country that was over-flowed in a former winter by the Dykes breaking near the little town of Heussen.

Extract of a Letter from Edinburgh, Dec. 16th.

"I am extremely sorry to inform you of the loss of the Belfast Trader, which happened on Tuesday night the 11th inst. In turning the point of Girvin in a violent gale of wind, she was driven against the rocks near that place, beat to pieces, and every soul perished: she was laden with linens, butter, hides, &c. and had several passengers on board. The Earl of Cassills immediately repaired to the spot, with some servants and dependants, erected a tent on the shore, gave orders that such dead bodies as were cast on shore should be taken due care of, decently interred, and the money or effects found upon them to be preserved for their friends."

An embargo was laid by 20th. his Excellency the Lord Lieutenant of Ireland on all shipping, laden with Irish provisions, in the ports of that kingdom, except to Great Britain and the dominions thereunto belonging. By this measure both Spain and France will be very much distressed to victual their respective fleets.

This day the following bills 22d. received the royal assent, by a commission from his Majesty, viz.

The bill for granting an aid to his Majesty by a land tax, to be raised in Great Britain for the service of the year 1771.

The bill for punishing mutiny and desertion, and for the better payment of the army and their quarters.

The

The bill for the better regulation of his Majesty's marine forces when on shore.

The bill to continue an act for allowing the free importation of salted provisions from Ireland, and from the American colonies, for a farther limited time.

The bill for shutting up certain foot-paths in Kentish-town, and opening others in their room.

And to several private bills.

A few days since, as a young man was washing himself in his father's kitchen near the Tower, a woman who lived in the house came to him with a child in her arms, desiring him to kiss it: he replied, that he would kiss no bastard; upon which she threatened to turn him out of doors, as she had done his sister: words arising, he ran up stairs, fetched a loaded pistol, with which he wounded her in the throat, and she died yesterday. The young man immediately surrendered himself to Justice Pell, and was committed to the Tower gaol.

25th. Notwithstanding it being Christmas-day, there was a great Board of Admiralty held.

Their Royal Highnesses Prince Edward and the Princess Augusta-Sophia, who were lately under inoculation for the small-pox, are now so well recovered as to be able to go abroad.

Mr. Arnod, watch-maker, in St. James's street, presented to his Majesty a small repeating watch in a ring, the cylinder of which he made of an oriental ruby. Its diameter is the 54th part of an inch, its length the 47th, and its weight the 200th part of a grain.

Mr. Cunningham, a merchant in Belfast, in Ireland, having caused a man to be apprehended who had committed waste on the estate of the Earl of Donnegal, more than 1,000 armed ruffians assembled next day, set fire to his house, and burnt it to the ground, with all the valuable furniture; the whole damage sustained amounted to 8,000l. On leaving the town they took several merchants as hostages for the release of the prisoner, whom it was thought proper to set at large in order to regain the hostages. As soon as that was obtained, a party of the military went in pursuit of them, but with what success is not yet publicly known.

A very melancholy accident happened to a poor family at Horncastle, in Lincolnshire, by burning charcoal in an iron pot to dry a new plaistered chamber, in which lay a man and his wife, and three children. The wife being taken ill in the night, the husband got up to call some neighbours to her assistance: two women came directly, who with the man, his wife, and the three children, were all suffocated by the fumes. A caution this against sleeping in rooms with burning charcoal.

The general increase of agriculture in the several provinces of France, for the last six years, is worthy of attention, and may one day or other affect the general œconomy of this nation more than the advantages they can ever obtain over us by a war. It appears by exact accounts delivered in to government, that the wastes inclosed and cultivated within the short term of five years (without including the present year) amount to 360,000 arpents, or 400,000 English acres nearly. At the
lowest

lowest estimation, these wastes that were before barren have produced 900,000 quarters of grain; and that the lands before in tillage, by the great improvements that have been lately made in their culture, have equalled the above in their additional increase. Upon calculation it has been found, that 1,800,000 quarters of corn will supply 1,500,000 people with bread a whole year, or the whole French nation one month.—If peace should continue, and the spirit of agriculture increase, France will become the common granary of Europe for corn.

Dr. Rotheram, in a Philosophical Enquiry into the Nature and Properties of Water, lately published, says, "One effect of snow, which I can assure my readers of, is, that a certain quantity of it, taken up fresh from the ground, and mixed in a flour pudding, will supply the place of eggs, and make it equally light: the quantity allotted is two table spoonsful instead of one egg; and if this proportion be much exceeded, the pudding will not adhere together, but will fall to pieces in boiling. I assert this from the experience of my own family; and any one who chuses to try it will find it to be a fact."

A letter from Mr. Edmonstone, who was one of the passengers saved out of the ship Grocer, says, that it is supposed the sand bank at the mouth of the Humber, on which the ship struck, was thrown up by the rapidity of the stream and the meeting of the tide, during the late great floods in that river, as ships went into the Humber some months ago without meeting with any obstructions. This is mentioned as a caution to seamen.

The answer returned to such mercantile bodies as have applied for the protection of their trade, is, that their requests shall be granted, if a war be declared before the time they require it; and this regards the applications of the India Company and Carolina merchants, as well as other bodies of capital traders.

Lord Bute is at Venice, and has lately sent to England three boxes of human and other bones, which may be counted a curiosity, and come from a place in Istria, which his Lordship calls, in a letter of his, The Catacombs of the World. It is certain that in an island opposite Dalmatia there were found, after digging through the surface about four feet, such a quantity of human bones, going a prodigious depth, and running under the sea, probably to the opposite shore, as is astonishing and wholly unaccountable. The bones are not all human, but mixed with those of other animals; nor can they be a *lusus naturæ*, having all the properties of bones, except that of stinking when put in the fire, which they may have lost through the prodigious time they must have been deposited.

27th. Sir Charles Knowles, lately appointed Chief President of the Admiralty to the Empress of Russia, set out with his family for Petersburgh, by the way of Calais, to take on him that office.

30th. This night there was a very hot press on the river Thames; they paid no regard to protections, but stripped every vessel of all their hands that were useful. They boarded the Glatton East Indiaman; but the crew made a stout a stout defence, got on shore, and came into London about twelve o'clock. It is computed that on the river, and on shore, they took upwards of 700.

This day arrived in town from Boston, in New England, Capt. Preston, who was tried there lately on account of some lives being lost in a riot between the town and the soldiery, but was honourably acquitted.

A fresh eruption of Mount Vesuvius has lately alarmed the adjacent country, but serves to amuse the curious. The aperture is not above a foot in diameter. The river of liquid fire runs down the side of the mountain at a great rate, not less than five miles in an hour; but as this stream is not more than twelve or fourteen feet at the broadest parts, and spreads itself over former lavas as soon as it reaches the great valley that lies between Vesuvius and the mountain of Somma, it is hoped it will not reach the fertile and inhabited parts, unless it should increase greatly. The mouth of the volcano smokes much, but neither casts up stones, nor makes any noise, so that one may walk upon the banks of this extraordinary river with the greatest safety.

Letters received by the general post this day are full of the damage done by the dreadful storm on the coasts of this kingdom. Near twenty sail of the colliers laden for London were wrecked off Yarmouth, and many of the crews perished. One of the government armed vessels, with 123 men on board, suffered in the same manner. From every quarter the like melancholy accounts of wrecks and dead bodies filling the shores arrive daily. There has not been so general a destruction among the shipping on our coasts in the memory of man.

Letters from Mahon advise, that two chests, one containing the gospel, most curiously bound, with golden covers, and a very curious set of Communion-plate, all richly embossed; and the other containing equally magnificent vestments for the priests of the Greek church at Mahon, has been sent as a present by the Empress of Russia, which were received by them the third of October, the coronation-day of the Empress.

Rome, Dec. 19. Cardinal Colarina, Vicar to the Pope, has published a placard, by which all women, of what degree soever, are forbid to appear in the churches with their faces uncovered.

Hague, Dec. 21. On Wednesday last, being the day appointed for christening the new-born daughter of their Serene and Royal Highnesses the Prince and Princess of Orange, that ceremony was performed with the greatest solemnity, in the great church of this town. —The young Princess was named Frederica-Louisa-Wilhelmina, and had the honour to have the King of Great Britain, the King of Prussia, and their Mightinesses, among her sponsors. The Prince of Orange entertained the States-General, &c. in a splendid manner at dinner, after the ceremony was over, at the palace called the Old Court.

Yesterday, and this day, deputations from the States-General, and the different provinces and towns, have had the honour to
wait

wait upon the Princess of Orange, and accompanied their compliments of congratulation with the free gift of their constituents to the new-born Princess; which amount to upwards of 35,000 florins yearly for her life.

It appears by the abstracts of the accounts laid by the Black-friars-bridge committee before the Court of Aldermen, that the sum of 166,217l. 3s. 10¼d. paid to the several artificers, in the bridge account, includes the sum of 5,830l. for arching and filling up Fleet-ditch, and making the way from Fleet-street to the upper ground in the parish of Christ Church, Surry; 5,000l. for piling the foundation of the several piers; 400l. for the three privies at the ends; and 2,167l. for making, altering, and repairing the temporary bridge, which being deducted, the nett expence of the building the bridge is 152,840l. 3s. 10½d. and was completed by Mr. Mylne in ten years and three quarters from the time of his being employed by the city for that purpose, for which his salary for himself, as surveyor, architect, engineer, measurer, and his clerks, amount to 3,762l. 10s.

It appears also by the said abstract, that the repairs of London-bridge amounted to 80,060l. for which the architects and surveyor had five per cent. on the artificers bills, and one per cent. of the purchases.

Westminster-bridge cost 218,810l. and was eleven years and nine months in building, for which the parliament granted for building and procuring the several conveniencies requisite thereto, from the year 1737 to 1749 inclusive, the sum of 389,500l. and the persons employed in the characters of architect, engineers, surveyor, and comptroller to the bridge and avenues, received the sum of 10,731l. 10s. exclusive of gratuities to the inventors of centers, and of the several engines and machines used in the said work; all which business we find Mr. Mylne has done for 3,762l. 10s.

There has been according to the above abstract, on the 22d of last January, 70,000 load of rubbish laid on the marsh grounds on the Surry side of Black-friars-bridge, towards making the new roads from thence by the Magdalen-hospital to the turnpike, in order to give it a solidity before gravelling.

By the said abstract it also appears, that the tolls received by the temporary bridge paid the expence of paying the interest-money to the Watermen's Company, for the Sunday ferry, and the charge of erecting, altering, and watching it, and added to the building fund the sum of 1,757l.

Died. Lately, in Scotland, in the 102d year of his age, John Dennis, a labouring man. He was in the militia at the battle of Killicranky; followed his ordinary employment till within 14 days of his death; and retained his senses to the last.

At Massiac, in Auvergne, John Amouroux, in the 117th year of his age. He enjoyed a pension from the King for these five years past, on account of his great age.

At a village near Cardigan, in South Wales, one Joseph Mackey, carpenter, aged 106.

A gene-

CHRONICLE. [177

A general Bill of all the Christenings and Burials, from December 12, 1769, to December 11, 1770.

Christened	Buried
Males 8761	Males 11210
Females 8348	Females 11224
17109	22434

Increased in the burials this year 587.
Increased in christenings 395.

Died under two years of age 7994
Between	2 and	5	2127
	5 and	10	926
	10 and	20	875
	20 and	30	1789
	30 and	40	2178
	40 and	50	1992
	50 and	60	1603
	60 and	70	1468
	70 and	80	1026
	80 and	90	397
	90 and	100	56
	100		0
	100 and	102	1
	100 and	103	1
	100 and	107	1

At Paris, Births 19549. Deaths 18719. Marriages 4775. Foundlings received in the hospitals, 6918. Increased in the births this year 104. Increased in the deaths 292.

City and suburbs of York, christened 517. Marriages 173. Burials 429. Increased in christenings 57. Decreased in burials 32.

In the course of last year 3890 ships have been cleared from Newcastle, of which 3520 were coastwise, and 370 only for foreign countries, being 58 less than were cleared out last year.

Vol. XIII.

The Gross Produce of the Duty on Hops for one year, ending the 5th of January, 1771.

	l.	s.	d.
Barum	43	9	2
Bath	0	6	6
Bedford	48	16	0
Bucks	19	9	4
Cambridge	64	15	5
Canterbury	27650	4	2
Cornwall	121	8	5
Derby	406	11	0
Doncaster	15	4	4
Dorset	14	6	2
Essex	2781	19	8
Exon	15	10	3
Gloucester	23	10	5
Grantham	43	11	0
Hants	8324	12	11
Hereford	7065	2	4
Hertford	55	12	8
Lincoln	1798	7	4
Lynn	22	7	3
Manchester	75	13	10
Northampton	2	6	5
Norwich	22	16	2
Oxon	0	8	11
Reading	1221	7	11
Rochester	28243	12	8
Sarum	129	15	8
Salop	9	2	0
Sheffield	704	18	8
Suffolk	1191	10	0
Surry	138	17	11
Sussex	13687	2	8
Taunton	6	13	0
Tiverton	4	11	4
Wales. { East	0	15	4
Middle	19	9	0
West	4	7	3
Wolverhampton	4340	14	10
Worcester	2811	14	4
Total	101,131	2	8

[N] BIRTHS

ANNUAL REGISTER, 1770.

BIRTHS for the year 1770.

Jan. 2. Lady of Lord Viscount Gage, of a child still-born.
7. Lady Susan Burgersh, of a daughter.
11. Lady of Lord Viscount Bellasyse, of a daughter.
Dean of Worcester's Lady, of a son.
23. Lady of Lord Viscount Weymouth, of a son.
29. Right Hon. Lady Hope, of a daughter.
Feb. 1. Dutchess of Gordon, of a son and heir.
Lady of Sir Sampson Gideon, Bart. of a daughter.
11. Lady of the Hon. George Hobart, of a daughter.
The Lady of Sir John Gresham, of a daughter.
24. Countess of Ossory, of a daughter.
Lady of Lord Fortescue, of a daughter.
Mar. 6. Lady of the Right Hon. Lord Archibald Hamilton, of a son.
Lady of Sir James Lake, of a daughter.
22. Right Hon. Lady Arundel, of a daughter.
Lady of Sir William Wake, of a daughter.
Dutchess of Grafton, of a son.
Countess Dowager of Dumfries, of a son.
May 3. Princess of Wurtemburgh, of a Prince.
Lady of the Right Hon. Lord Milbourn, of a son.

May 7. Lady Mountstewart, of a son.
Countess of Fingal, of a son.
21. Lady of Sir Thomas Champneys, Bart. of a son.
22. Between eight and nine o'clock, the Queen was happily delivered of a Princess, at her Majesty's palace, St. James's-park.
June 9. Lady of Sir William Maxwell, of a son.
Lady of Sir William Stapleton, of a son.
July 1. Her Grace the Dutchess of Portland, of a son.
19. Lady of Sir Thomas Egerton, Bart. of a daughter.
Aug. 3. Princess Royal of Prussia, of a Prince.
18. Her Royal Highness the Princess of Brunswick, of a Prince.
Her Grace the Dutchess of Manchester, of a daughter.
Countess of Drogheda, of a son.
Sept. 1. Lady of Lord Craven, of a son.
11. Countess of Thanet, of a son.
Countess of Dalhousie, of a son.
22. Countess of Cork, of a son.
Lady of Sir John Trevelion, of a son.
Lady of the Hon. and Rev. Mr. Byron, of a son.
Lady of Sir Robert Bewick, of a son.

Sept.

Sept. 22. Lady of Sir James Ibbetson, of a daughter.
Oct. 5. Lady of Sir Henry Hunlock, Bart. of a daughter.
10. Her Grace the Dutchess of Buccleugh, of a daughter.
Countess of Ancram, of a daughter.
Nov. 1. Countess of Lauderdale, of a daughter.
9. Lady of the Right Hon. Lord Viscount Powerscourt, of a daughter.
Lady of Sir Fitzgerald Aylmer, Bart. of a son.
Lady of the Right Hon. Lord Blany, of a son.
22. Dutchess of Parma, of a son.
Lady Viscountess Sudley, of a daughter.
Dec. 3. Lady of Sir Peter Rivers Gray, Bart. of a son.
7. Lady Germaine, of a son.
17. Countess of Dunmore, of a son.
20. Her Grace the Dutchess of Marlborough, of a son.
Her Royal Highness the Princess of Orange, of a Princess.
21. Lady of Prince Gallitzin, the Russian Ambassador at the Hague, of a son.
29. Lady of Sir Sampson Gideon, Bart. of a son.

MARRIAGES, 1770.

Jan. 9. Isaac Spooner, Esq. to the eldest daughter of Sir Henry Gough, Bart.
Hon. and Rev. Mr. Henry Beauclerk, to Miss Drummond.
Feb. 15. Edwin Lascelles, Esq. to Lady Flemming.
William Leslie Hamilton, Esq. to Lady Isabella Erskine, sister to the Earl of Buchan.
24. Captain Fitzgerald, to the sister of the Right Hon. Thomas Connolly.
Mar. 5. Henry Lord Borthwick, to Miss Drummond.
7. Sir Charles Stile, Bart. of Wateringbury, Kent. to the Hon. Miss Wingfield, daughter to Lord Powerscourt.
9. Thomas Hogg, jun. of Newliston, Esq. to a daughter of Lord Lauderdale.
13. At Edinburgh, Sir William Murray, of Auchtertire, Bart. to Lady Augusta Mackenzie, daughter of Lord Cromartie.
19. Hon. and Rev. John Harley, Alderman of Hereford, and brother to the Earl of Oxford, to Miss Vaughan, of South Wales, with a fortune of 3,000l. a year.
20. Sir David Dalrymple, Bart. to Miss Ferguson.

March

Mar. 22. The Earl of Carlisle, to the second daughter of Earl Gower.

26. The Right Hon. the Earl of Jersey, to Miss Fanny Twisden.

— Sir Gilbert Heathcote, Bart. to Miss Hudson.

April 2. David Gavin, Esq. of Langtown in Scotland, to Lady Maitland, eldest daughter of the Earl of Lauderdale.

14. The Hon. Thomas Willoughby, brother to Lord Middleton, to Miss Chadwick.

— The Hon. Thomas Erskine, to Miss Moore.

20. The Right Hon. the Earl of Albemarle, to Miss Miller.

23. The Earl of Exeter, to Miss Anna Maria Cheatham, of Sodorhall, Yorkshire.

—— Churchill, Esq. to Lady Louisa Greville, youngest daughter to the Earl of Warwick.

May 19. The Dauphin of France, to the Arch-dutchess Antoinetta, of Austria.

21. Charles Deering, Esq. to Miss Farnaby, sister to Sir Charles Farnaby.

23. Sir Archibald Grant, Bart. to Mrs. Millar, Pall-mall.

24. Bennet Langton, Esq. of Langton, in Lincolnshire, to the Countess of Rothes.

June 1. Sir George Cooke, Bart. to Miss Middleton, sister to Sir William Middleton.

June 2. Col. Clements, to Miss Webb, only daughter to General Webb.

7. Sir John Wrottesley, Bart. to the Hon. Miss Courtenay, one of the Maids of Honour.

9. Alderman Trecothick, to Miss Meredith, sister to Sir William Meredith.

20. The Hon. and Rev. Dr. Shute Barrington, Lord Bishop of Llandaff, to Miss Guise, niece to the late General Guise.

26. Alexander Fordyce, Esq. Banker, to Lady Margaret Lindsay, second daughter to the Earl of Balcarras.

July 11. Earl Fitzwilliam, to Lady Charlotte Ponsonby, daughter to the Earl of Besborough.

Aug. 7. Right Hon. Lord Milsington, to Miss Lascelles.

30. Rev. Mr. Bowles, to Miss Hales, sister to Sir Tho. Pym Hales, Bart.

Sept. 17. At Calais, Monsieur de Prades de la Valette, Captain in the regiment of Piedmont, in garrison at Calais, to Miss Harriot Edgcumbe, daughter to Lady Fenoulhet, and niece to George Lord Edgcumbe.

24. The Right Hon. the Earl of Buckinghamshire, to Miss Connolly, daughter of Lady Anne Connolly.

Sept.

Sept. 24. John Bateman, Esq. to the Countess of Ross.
25. Sir Robert Goodyere, to Miss Pits.
Oct. 13. At New York, Sir William Draper, Knight of the Bath, to Miss Susanna de Lancey, daughter of the Right Hon. Oliver de Lancey.
16. Sir Brownlow Cust, Bart. to Miss Drury.
Charles Nelson Cole, Esq. of the Inner-Temple, to Miss Abdy, sister to Sir Anthony Abdy, Bart. of Albys, Essex.
Right Hon. the Earl of Eglington, to a daughter of Lord Glencairn.
26. Lord Digby, to Miss Polly Knowler, of Canterbury.
Nov. 5. Major General John Scott, to Lady Mary Hay, eldest daughter to the Earl of Errol.
At Dublin, John Hamilton, Esq. representative in Parliament for the borough of Strabane, to the Hon. Miss Hamilton, daughter of Lord Viscount Boyne.
General M'Kay, to Miss Car, with 30,000l.
Captain Bathurst, of the Royal Regiment of Horse Guards blue, to Miss Ashby, of Derby, with 20,000l.
Thomas Ackland, Esq. to Lady Mary, daughter to the Earl of Ilchester.

Principal PROMOTIONS for the year 1770, from the London Gazette, &c.

Jan. 17. Right Hon. Charles Yorke, Esq. to be Keeper of the Great Seal, a Privy Counsellor, and likewise Lord High Chancellor of Great Britain, and he accordingly took his place at the Board.
18. Right Honble. Charles Yorke, Esq. Lord High Chancellor, the dignity of a Baron of Great Britain, with remainder to his heirs male, by the name, style, and title, of Lord Morden, Baron of Morden, in the County of Cambridge.
19. Duke of Somerset, a Privy Counsellor.
22. Sir Sidney Stafford Smythe, Knight, one of the Barons of his Majesty's Court of Exchequer, the Honourable Henry Bathurst, Esq. one of the Justices of his Majesty's Court of Common Pleas, and Sir Richard Aston, Knight, one of the Justices of his Majesty's Court of King's-bench, Lords Commissioners for the Custody of the Great Seal, in the room of Lord Morden, deceased: — Lord Mansfield, by a Commission under the Great Seal, to supply the place of Lord Chancellor, or Lord Keeper, in the House of Peers.
23. Right Hon. Sir Fletcher Norton, Speaker of the House of Commons.
28. Lord North, First Lord Commissioner of the Treasury, in the room of the Duke of Grafton, resigned.
29. Earl of Bristol, Groom of the Stole, and First Lord of the Bed-Chamber. — Peter Chester,

Chester, Esq. Captain-general and Governor in Chief of West Florida.

Feb. 2. Right Hon. Welbore Ellis, one of the Vice Treasurers of Ireland, in the room of the Right Hon. James Grenville, resigned.

6. Charles Townshend, Esq. one of the Lords of the Treasury.

— 9. The Earl of Hallifax, Lord Privy Seal, in the room of the Earl of Bristol.

13. Hon. Thomas Robinson, Esq. Vice Chamberlain to the Queen, in the room of Lord Villers, now Earl of Jersey.—Right Hon. Sir Edward Hawke, Knight of the Bath, John Buller, Esq. the Right Hon. Henry Viscount Palmerston, of the kingdom of Ireland, Charles Spencer, Esq. commonly called Lord Charles Spencer, the Right Hon. Wilmot Viscount Lisburne, of the kingdom of Ireland, and Francis Holburne, and Charles James Fox, Esqrs. Lords Commissioners of the Admiralty.

19. Right Honble. Thomas Robinson, Esq. Vice Chamberlain to her Majesty, a Privy Counsellor.—James Sampson, Consul-general at Tetuan.—George Pitt, Esq. Ambassador Extraordinary and Plenipotentiary to his Catholic Majesty.—Alexander Munro, Esq. Consul at Madrid.

Mar. 9. Major Gorham, Lieutenant-governor of Placentia, in the room of Otho Hamilton, Esq. deceased.——William Faulkener, Esq. to be Fort-adjutant of Fort Augustus, in Scotland, in the room of Richard Trought, Gent. deceased.

Mar. 19. Major-general Clavering, Governor of Landguard Fort, in the room of the late Lieutenant-general Robert Arminger.—William Stewart, Esq. Lieutenant-governor of the island of Tobago.—Israel Wilkes, Esq. brother to John Wilkes, Esq. Consul at Aleppo, in Syria. —Colonel James Cunningham, Governor of the island of St. John's, Newfoundland.—Edward Thurlow, Esq. Solicitor-general, in the room of Mr. Dunning. —John Nicholson, Esq. Solicitor to the Stamp-office, in the room of Mr. Cruwys, deceased.—Thomas Davison, Esq. to be Collector-general of his Majesty's customs for the island of Jamaica.

April 10. The Earl of Drogheda, Master-general of the Ordnance in the kingdom of Ireland.

16. Soame Jenyns, Edward Elliott, John Roberts, William Fitzherbert, Robert Spencer, (commonly called Lord Robert Spencer) George Greville, (commonly called Lord Greville) and William Northey, Esqrs. Commissioners for Trade and Plantations.

30. His Royal Highness Major-general William Duke of Gloucester, Colonel of the first regiment of foot guards, in the room of Field-marshal John Earl Ligonier, deceased.—Lieut. Gen. John Earl of Loudon, Colonel of the third regiment of foot guards, in the room of the Duke of Gloucester.—Major-general John Parflow, Colonel of the 30th regiment of foot, in the room of the Earl of Loudon.——GENERALS: Sir John Mordaunt; the Hon. James Cholmondeley; Peregrine Lascelles; Lord John Murray; John Earl of Loudon; William Earl of Panmure; William Marquis of Lothian; William Earl of

of Harrington; Hugh Warburton.—LIEUTENANT-GENERALS: William Skinner; the Hon. Robert Monckton; John Henry Baſtide; Edward Sandford; Theodore Dury; John Parker; John Lambton; the Hon. Charles Colvill; John Parſlow; William Browne; the Hon. Thomas Gage; George Viſcount Townſhend; Lord Frederick Cavendiſh; John Earl de la War; Charles Duke of Richmond; Henry Earl of Pembroke; John Severn; Sir John Sebright, Bart.; Henry Whitley; John Clavering; the Hon. George Cary; George Gray; James Adolphus Oughton; James Duke of Leinſter; his Royal Highneſs William Duke of Glouceſter.—MAJOR-GENERALS; Mariſco Frederick; William Earl of Glencairn; William Deane; John Thomas; Robert Dalrymple; Horne Elphinſtone; William Evelyn; John Salter; Thomas Earle; Richard Worge; James Johnſton; Hon. Philip Sherrard; the Hon. George Lane Parker; James Giſborne; Charles Earl of Drogheda; Nevill Tatton; Francis Grant; Richard Bendiſhe; the Hon. Alexander Mackay; William Auguſtus Pitt; John Scott.

May 4. John Bourke, Eſq. Arthur Viſcount Dungannon, Hugh Valence Jones, Eſq. Bellingham Boyle, Eſq. Right Hon. John Beresford, and Sir William Oſborne, Bart. to be Chief Commiſſioners of the Revenue and Exciſe, and Chief Commiſſioners and Governors of all and every other part of his Majeſty's revenues in the kingdom of Ireland.—The Right Hon. George Rice, Eſq. Treaſurer of his Majeſty's Chamber, a Privy Counſellor.—Juſtice Bathurſt took place in the Court of Common Pleas, in the room of Sir Edward Clive, Knight, reſigned.—Juſtice Gould, in the room of Juſtice Bathurſt.—And Sir Joſeph Yates, from the Court of King's-bench, as junior judge in the ſaid court.—And in the Court of King's-bench, Juſtice Aſton took place in the room of Sir Joſeph Yates.—Judge Willes, in the room of Juſtice Aſton.—And William Blackſtone, Eſq. Solicitor to her Majeſty, junior judge of the ſaid court, and a Knight.

May 7. Lord Miltown, Sir William Oſborne, Sir Archibald Acheſon, Sir Arthur Brooke, Mr. James Forteſcue, Mr. Henry King, Mr. Ralph Howard, Mr. Silver Oliver, and Mr. Edward Cary, Privy Counſellors of the kingdom of Ireland.

19. The Right Hon. Catharine Counteſs of Egmont, (ſecond wife of John now Earl of Egmont in Ireland, Baron Lovel and Holland in Great Britain, and ſiſter to Spencer Compton, now Earl of Northampton) the dignity of a Baroneſs of the kingdom of Ireland, by the title of Lady Arden, Baroneſs Arden of Lohort Caſtle, in the county of Cork, to hold the ſaid dignity unto her the ſaid Counteſs of Egmont, and the dignity of a Baron of the ſaid kingdom of Ireland to the heirs male of her body lawfully begotten, by the title of Lord Arden, Baron Arden of Lohort Caſtle, in the ſaid county of Cork.—The Right Hon. William Henry Forteſcue, Eſq. and the heirs male of his body, the dignity of a Baron of the ſaid kingdom, by the title of Baron Clermont of Clermont, in the county of Lowth.—Thomas Dawſon,

Dawſon, Eſq. and the heirs male of his body, the dignity of a Baron of the ſaid kingdom, by the title of Baron Dartrey of Dawſon's Grove, in the county of Monaghan.—William Henry Dawſon, Eſq. and the heirs male of his body, the dignity of a Baron of the ſaid kingdom, by the title of Baron Dawſon of Dawſon Court, in the Queen's county.—Bernard Ward, Eſq. and the heirs male of his body, the dignity of a Baron of the ſaid kingdom, by the title of Baron Bangor of Caſtle Ward, in the county of Downe.—And Sir Peniſtone Lamb, Bart, and the heirs male of his body, the dignity of a Baron of the ſaid kingdom, by the title of Lord Melbourne, Baron of Kilmore, in the county of Cavan.—Colonel John Burgoyne, Comptroller of Cheſter, in the room of Edward Herbert, Eſq. deceaſed.—William Bromhill, Eſq. Patent Cuſtomer of the Ports of Southampton and Portſmouth.—William Senhouſe, Eſq. Surveyor-general of the cuſtoms in Barbadoes, and all the Leeward Iſlands, in the room of the Hon. Thomas Gibbs, Eſq. deceaſed.—Dr. Spencer Madan, a Prebend in the cathedral of Peterborough.

June 20. William Aſhurſt, Eſq. a Knight, and one of the Judges of the Court of King's-bench.

July 14. Sir William Young, Bart. Governor of the iſland of Dominica.—General James Cholmondeley, Governor of the Garriſon of Cheſter, in the room of the Earl of Cholmondeley, deceaſed.—Major David Home, Lieutenant-governor of the ſaid garriſon, in the room of General Cholmondeley.

July 24. The Right Hon. Hans Stanley, Eſq. Vice-Admiral of the Iſle of Wight.

Auguſt. Hugh Palliſer, Eſq. Comptroller of the Navy.—George Mackenzie, Eſq. Commander in Chief of his Majeſty's ſhips and veſſels on the Jamaica ſtation, in the room of Commodore Foreſt.—William Fraſier, Eſq. Under Secretary to Lord Weymouth, Gazette Writer, in the room of Edward Weſton, Eſq. deceaſed.—The Right Hon. L. C. J. Paterſon, a Privy Counſellor of Ireland.—John M'Kenzie, Eſq. of Devine, Deputy Keeper of his Majeſty's Signet in Scotland, in the room of the late Alexander M'Millan, Eſq. deceaſed.

Oct. 5. William Fawcet, Eſq. Lieutenant-governor of Pendennis Caſtle, in the room of Richard Bowles, Eſq. deceaſed.—Hon. John Forbes, and Francis Holborn, Eſq. Admirals of the White.

18. Sir Thomas Frankland, Bart. his Grace the Duke of Bolton, Sir Charles Hardy, Knt. Right Hon. George Earl of Northeſk, Right Hon. Sir Charles Saunders, Knight of the Bath, Admirals of the Blue.—Thomas Pye, Eſq. Sir Samuel Corniſh, Bart. Francis Geary, Eſq. Vice-Admirals of the Red.—Sir George Bridges Rodney, Bart. Sir William Burnaby, Baronet, James Young, Eſq. Vice-Admirals of the White.—Sir Piercy Brett, Knight, Sir John Moore, Knight of the Bath, Sir James Douglas, Knt. Sir John Bentley, Knt. Vice-Admirals of the Blue.—Right Hon. George Lord Edgcumbe, Samuel Graves, Eſq. William Parry, Eſq. Hon. Auguſtus Keppel, Rear-Admirals of the

the Red.—John Amherst, Esq. his Royal Highness Henry Frederick Duke of Cumberland, Sir Peter Denis, Bart. Matthew Buckle, Esq. Rear-Admirals of the White.—Robert Man, Esq. Richard Spry, Esq. Robert Harland, Esq. Right Hon. Richard Lord Visc. Howe, Rear-Admirals of the Blue.

Oct. 24. Sir George Bridges Rodney and Sir William Burnaby, Barts. to be Vice-Admirals of the Red.—Sir Piercy Brett, Knt. Sir John Moore, Bart. and Knt. of the Bath, Sir James Douglas and Sir John Bentley, Knts. to be Vice-Admirals of the White.—The Right Hon. George Lord Edgcumbe, Samuel Graves and William Parry, Esqrs. the Hon. Augustus Keppel, John Amherst, Esq. and his Royal Highness Henry Frederick Duke of Cumberland, to be Vice-Admirals of the Blue.—Sir Peter Denis, Bart. Matthew Buckle and Robert Man, Esqrs. to be Rear-Admirals of the Red.—Richard Spry, Esq. to be Rear-Admiral of the White.—And the following gentlemen were appointed flag officers, viz.—Robert Hughes, Esq. to be Rear-Admiral of the Red. —Clark Gayton, John Barker, and Lucius O'Brien, Esqrs. to be Rear-Admirals of the White.—John Montagu, Thomas Craven, and James Sayer, Esqrs. to be Rear-Admirals of the Blue; and to rank as such with officers of the same flag, according to their seniority as Captains.—General Conway, Colonel of the Royal Regiment of Horse Guards Blue, in the room of the Marquis of Granby, deceased.

25. Sir Jeffery Amherst, Knt. of the Bath, Lieutenant-general of his Majesty's Forces, Governor of the Island of Guernsey, the Castle of Cornet, and all other islands, forts, and appurtenances, thereunto belonging.—Thomas Hutchinson, Esq. Capt. General, and Governor in Chief of his Majesty's Province of the Massachuset's Bay, in New England.—Andrew Oliver, Esq. Lieutenant-governor; and Thomas Flucker, Esq. Secretary of his Majesty's said province of the Massachuset's Bay.—William Stewart, Esq. Lieutenant-governor of his Majesty's Island of Dominica.—William Young, Esq. Lieutenant-governor of his Majesty's Island of Tobago.

Oct. 27. The Hon. and Rev. Brownlow North, D. L. and one of his Majesty's Chaplains in Ordinary, the place of Dean of the metropolitical Church of Canterbury, void by the death of Dr. John Potter.—Rev. Benjamin Kennicott, D.D. the place of a Canon of the cathedral Church of Christ, in the University of Oxford.—Hon. and Rev. James Cornwallis, Clerk, M.A. the place of a Prebendary of the collegiate Church of St. Peter Westminster, void by the resignation of Dr. Kennicott.—Rev. Dr. Lumner, Vice-chancellor of the University of Cambridge.

Dec. 8. Earl of Dunmore, Governor of New York, to be Lieutenant and Governor-general of Virginia, in the room of Lord Bottetourt, deceased.—Wm. Tryon, Esq. Governor of North Carolina, to be Governor in New York, in the room of the Earl of Dunmore. —And Henry Martin, Esq. Governor of North Carolina.—Rt. Hon. Earl Cornwallis, to be Constable of the Tower of London, in the room of John Lord Berkeley, of Stratton, resigned.

Dec.

Dec. 19. Earl of Rochford, Secretary of State for the Southern department, in the room of Lord Weymouth, resigned.—Earl of Sandwich, principal Secretary of State for the Northern department.—Right Hon. Frederick Thynne, Esq. a Privy Counsellor, and joint Post-Master General with Lord Despenser.

DEATHS, 1770.

Jan. 2. At Dalhousie Castle, the Right Hon. Lady Jean Ramsay, aunt to the Earl of Dalhousie.

9. Rt. Hon. Nath. Booth, Lord Delamer, and Bart. He is succeeded in the title of Baronet by the Rev. Mr. Booth, of St. John's Square.

Miss Stapylton, only surviving child of the late Sir Miles Stapylton, Bart.

At his Dutchy, Nicholas Leopold, Prince of Salm-Salm, Duke of Hoogstraton, &c.

20. Rt. Hon. Charles Yorke, Esq. Lord High Chancellor of Great Britain. He had but newly accepted the important office of Chancellor, which, upon the dismission of Lord Camden, was pressed upon him by his Majesty; and while the patent for his peerage was making out, under the title of Baron Morden, he suddenly departed this life, as supposed by the rupture of a vessel inwardly. It is reported, upon good authority, that he accepted the seals in obedience to the will of his Sovereign, without any reversionary conditions whatever.

22. Rt. Hon. Sir John Cust, Bt. late Speaker of the House of Commons. He had been member for Grantham in Lincolnshire in five parliaments. The great fatigue of this honourable employment is supposed to have hastened his death.

Jan. 23. Sir Wm. Baker, Knt. Alderman of Bassishaw Ward.

25. Sir Andrew Estcourt, Queen's Square.

His Excellency Count Cobenzil, the acting Minister under Prince Charles of Lorrain, for the Austrian Netherlands: he resided at Brussels about twenty years, and was universally esteemed as one of the greatest statesmen of the age.

Rt. Hon. Nicholas Count Taaffe, aged 92. He is succeeded in honours and estate by his son Francis, now colonel commandant of a regiment in the Imperial service.

Feb. 7. Right Hon. Sir Robert Deane, in Ireland.

12. Sir Peter Leicester, Bart. at Tabley, in Cheshire.

13. Hon. Mrs. Villers Clara Hannam, Lady of John Hannam, Esq. and sister to the Earl of Chatham.

17. Sir William Morden Harbord, Bart. at Gunston, in Norfolk.

Sir Tyrrel Hewit, Bart. in Bedfordshire.

24. Right Hon. Earl of Harborough, Lord Sherrard, and Baron Leitrim, in Ireland.

Lady Cope, relict of Sir John Cope.

Capt. Middleton, F. R. S. who for his curious observations in the discovery of the N. W. passage, in 1740, received a medal.

Dr. Lamy, Professor of Ecclesiastical History in the University of Florence.

March 4. Sir Wm. Robinson, Bart. uncle to the Earl of Stamford.

6. Hon. Wm. Molesworth, at Bath.

Hon.

Hon. Lady Humble, sister to the Earl of Darlington.

March 7. Sir Thomas Stanhope, a Colonel in the Marines.

9. At his house in Spring Gardens, in the 93d year of his age, the Hon. and Rev. Henry Moore, D. D. Rector of Malpas and Wimslow, in the county of Chester, third son of the late Right Hon. Henry Earl of Drogheda.

10. In Wardour-street, Soho, Lady Dunboyne, Lady of Lord Dunboyne, who is now in Ireland.

12. Sir Richard Mill, Bart.

14. In Great Wild-street, Lincoln's-inn-fields, —— Stanhope, Esq. next heir to the Earl of Chesterfield.

16. Hon. Lady Amelia West, daughter of Earl Delawar.

18. The Hon. Col. Butler, aged 95, a near relation to the late Duke of Ormond.

Lieut. Gen. Rob. Armiger, Gov. of Languard Fort, aged 68. He married a young lady over night, and died next morning.

In Grosvenor-square, Lady Diana Duncomb.

Charles Mac Carthy More, lineally descended from the Kings of Ireland.

Baron Capellis, lately in the Tyroleze, aged 104, is said to have left a wife in the seventh month of her pregnancy, having had seven children by her before.

21. Sir John Dryden, Bart. in Northamptonshire.

25. At Paris, Robert Dillen, Esq. titular Earl of Roscommon in Ireland, Baron of Weir Kilkenny, colonel of a regiment of foot, and a marshal in the armies of France.

At Chaillot, near Paris, Lady Mary Janssen, widow of Charles Calvert, Baron Baltimore.

April 3. Rt. Hon. Lord Visc. Chetwynd, Master of the Mint, and member for Stafford. His title and estate devolve upon his son Wm. Chetwynd, now at Brussels.

11. Rt. Hon. Lady Eliz. Gordon, aunt to the Earl of Aboyne.

Of a consumption, Lord Mounthermer, son of his Grace the Duke of Montagu.

12. At Virginia, Sir Thomas Adams, Bart. Commander of his Majesty's frigate the Boston, lately appointed to that station.

The Hereditary Prince William Louis Charles de Nassau Weilbourg, in the 9th year of his age.

18. The Princess of Diesback, at Fribourg, Switzerland, aged 104.

The Cardinal Prince Bishop of Spire.

Dennis de Berdt, Esq. Agent for New York and Massachuset's Bay.

21. Rt. Hon. Samuel Lord Sandys. He was created a peer Dec. 20, 1743. He married Letitia, eldest daughter and coheir of Sir Thomas Ripping, Bart. by whom he had seven sons and three daughters. He is succeeded in his title and estate by his eldest son, the Hon. Edwin Sandys, member in the present parliament for Westminster.

Sir Lister Holte, Bart. at Aston Hall, near Birmingham.

Hon. Master Spencer, son of Lord Charles Spencer.

24. The Abbe Nollet, Professor of Experimental Philosophy in the Royal College of Paris.

28. Right Hon. John Ligonier, Earl Ligonier, Baron of Ripley, Visc. Ligonier of Clonmel in Ireland, Field-marshal of his Majesty's forces, and Colonel of the 1st reg. of foot guards, Knight of the Bath, and F. R. S. His Lordship served in

in all the wars of Queen Anne under the Duke of Marlborough, and in every succeeding war, with a bravery and conduct that deservedly raised him to the chief posts in his profession.

May 1. Rt. Hon. Lord George James Montague, youngest son to his Grace the Duke of Manchester.

9. Prince Charles, the reigning Landgrave of Hesse Philipsthal, in the 88th year of his age.

Sir William St. Quintin of Harpham, Yorkshire, Bart. His title and estate devolve to his son William.

15. Lady of Sir William Innes, Bart. at Ipswich.

18. Claud. Wm. Testu, Marquis de Balincourt, First Marshal of France, Knight of the King's orders, Governor of the town and citadel of Strasbourg, &c. in the 91st year of his age.

21. Rt. Hon. Alexander Lord Colville.

Lately, Thomas Shewell, Esq. who has left the following charities by will: to the charity-school for girls at Hadley, in Middlesex, 20l.—To the charity school for girls of the parish of St. Luke, Old-street, 20l.—To the incorporated society in Dublin, for promoting English protestant schools in Ireland, 500l.—To the Small Pox Hospital in Coldbath-fields, 500l.—To St. Bartholomew's Hospital, 1,500l.—To the Hospital for Lunatics, commonly called St. Luke's Hospital, 1,000l.—To Christ's Hospital, 1,000l.

22. Lord James Murray, the Duke of Athol's second son.

25. At Geannies, in Rossshire, by a fall from his horse, Sir Alex. Mackenzie, of Gerlock, Bart.

Lady Emilia Chichester, youngest daughter of the Earl of Donnegal.

Miss Turnour, sister to Lord Winterton.

Lady Lambert, relict of Sir Daniel Lambert.

May 27. Queen Sophia Magdalena, Dowager of Christian VI. and grandmother to the present King of Denmark, at the palace of Christianbourg, in the 70th year of her age.

June 2. Hon. and Rev. Mr. Howe, brother to Lord Chedworth.

7. Sir Joseph Yates, Knt. one of the honestest Judges that ever filled the bench.

Mrs. Gunning, housekeeper of Somerset-house, and mother to the present Dutchess of Hamilton.

10. Right Hon. George Earl of Cholmondeley, Viscount Malpas. He is succeeded by his grandson, just come of age.

18. Sir James Cotter, Baronet, in Ireland.

21. Right Hon. William Beckford, Esq. Lord Mayor of London.

Francis Ernest, Count Salma Ruffercheid, Bishop of Tournay, aged 75.

Hon. Arthur Trevor, Esq. only son of Lord Viscount Dungannon, member for Hilsborough.

Hon. Miss Dormer, niece to the Earl of Shrewsbury.

July 3. Lady of the Right Hon. Lord William Beauclerk, brother to the Duke of St. Alban's.

Sir Thomas Hankey, Knight, the great Banker.

5. Sir David Cunningham, of Corsehill, Scotland.

Lady Pesball, mother of Sir John Pesball.

14. Relict of Sir John Wray, Bart.

18. In Ireland, the lady of Robert

Robert Stewart, Esq. and daughter to the Earl of Hertford.

July 19. The Hon. Mr. Liddell, brother to Lord Ravensworth.

24. Rt. Hon. Lord Charles William Cavendish Bentinck, son to the Duke of Portland.

The famous old man of the North, Christian Jacob Drakenberg, lately died at Aarhuus, in the 146th year of his age. He was born at Stravanger in Norway, in the year 1624, and lived single till the age of 113 years, when he married a widow of 60 years of age. During the latter part of his life he was frequently visited by persons of the highest rank, who were curious to see and converse with him.

It is said there is a print of this old man in England curiously engraved.

Aug. 6. Duke Clement of Bavaria, first cousin and presumptive heir to the Elector. He has left no issue by his Dutchess, sister to the Elector Palatine. His income was very considerable.

18. Rt. Hon. Lady Bulkeley, mother to the present Lord Bulkeley, and lady to Col. Sir Hugh Williams, Bart. member for Beaumaris, at Barnhill, North Wales.

Sir Thomas Wallace, Bart. of Cragie, in Scotland.

In France, the Rt. Hon. John Lord Nairn.

Sir Robert Clarke, Baronet, of Frockenham, in Norfolk.

John Lord Baron Bellew, of Duleek, Ireland.

Sep. 12. Lady Drummond, sister to James late Duke of Perth.

Rt. Hon. William Annesley, Viscount Glerawley, and Baron Annesley of Castle-William, in the county of Down, Ireland.

Lady Monnoux, at Wooton, Bedfordshire.

Hon. Mrs. Elizabeth Hume Campbell.

At Millbank, Westminster, the Hon. Mrs. Crofs, relict of the late Sir John Crofs, Bart.

Sep. 14. In Ireland, the Rt. Hon. Lady Viscountess Townsend: she was the only surviving child of James, the fifth Earl of Northampton, and Baroness Ferrers, of Chartley, in right of her mother. She married Viscount Townsend, the present Lord Lieutenant of Ireland, in December 1751, and by his Lordship has had seven children, five of whom are living, viz. four sons and a daughter.

26. Lady of Sir Edward Hales, Bart. of Silterton, Canterbury.

30. Rt. Hon. Sir Thomas Robinson, Lord Grantham, Knt. of the Bath, one of the Privy Council, and F. R. S.

Oct. 1. Sir Richard Lyttleton, Knt. of the Bath, at Chelsea.

4. Rt. Hon. Lady Euphemia Stuart, sister to the Earl of Moray. Edinburgh.

Most Noble George Marquis of Tweedale, Earl of Gifford, Viscount Walden and Peebles, and Baron Yester, in the 13th year of his age.

10. Rt. Hon. Lady Jane Nimmon, sister to the Earl of Marchmont.

14. Lady Hankey, relict of Sir Joseph Hankey, Bart. at Bath.

Hon. Mrs. Rooke, aged 70, relict of Geo. Rooke, Esq. son of the famous Admiral, and sister to Lord Viscount Dudley.

Oct. 11. At Belvoir Castle, to the irreparable loss of his country, and the inexpressible grief of all

true

true Englishmen, the Most Noble the Marquis of Granby, eldest son to his Grace the Duke of Rutland, by Bridget (only daughter and heiress to Robert Sutton, Lord Lexington), who was married to the Duke of Rutland, August 27, 1717. The Marquis was born January 2, 1720-21, and was elected for Grantham in three Parliaments; and in those of 1754, 1761, and 1768, for Cambridgeshire, and is the 24th in paternal descent from Sir Robert de Manners, the patriarch of his family.

In the rebellion in 1745 his Lordship raised a regiment of foot for his Majesty's service; and March 4, 1755, was promoted to the rank of Major-general of his Majesty's Forces.

In May 1758, his Lordship was appointed Colonel of the Royal Regiment of Horse Guards, and promoted to the rank of Lieutenant-general on February 5, 1759. The 25th of August following, he was constituted Commander in Chief of all his Majesty's forces then serving in Germany in his Majesty's army under Prince Ferdinand of Brunswick. In which command he not only shared the fatigues and danger of the troops under his command, but, when the British forces were but in very indifferent quarters (not owing to any defect in his conduct), he procured provisions and necessaries for the private soldiers at his own expence, his table being at the same time open to the officers.

On September 15, 1759, he was appointed Lieutenant-general of the Ordnance; and Prince Ferdinand being elected a Knight of the Garter, his Lordship was nominated first plenipotentiary for investing his Serene Highness with the ensigns of the order, which he performed in October following, with all the magnificence that a camp would admit of, and entertained the new knight and his retinue with a sumptuous dinner.

His Lordship was declared a Privy-Counsellor on May 2, 1760; and, resigning the office of Lieutenant-general of the Ordnance, was, on May 14, 1763, constituted Master-general of that department.

On February 21, 1764, he was declared Lord Lieutenant and Custos Rotulorum of Derbyshire.

His Lordship married, September 3, 1750, the Lady Frances Seymour, eldest daughter of Charles Duke of Somerset by his second wife, the Lady Charlotte Finch; and by her, who died January 25, 1760, he had John Lord Roos, born August 27, 1751, and died June 3, 1760; Charles, now Marquis of Granby, born March 15, 1754; Lady Frances, born March 24, 1753; Lady Catherine, born March 28, 1755, and died January 4, 1757; Lord Robert, born February 6, 1758; and Lady Caroline, who died an infant.

Oct. 19. Lady Turner, mother of the present Sir Ed. Turner, Bart.

Rt. Hon. Lady Herbert, aunt to the Earl of Portsmouth.

Rt. Hon. Lady Anstruther, at Baleaskie House, Fifeshire.

Sir David Murray, Bart. at Leghorn.

23. Hon. Arthur Barry, in Dublin.

The Hon. Mrs. Mary Colvil, sister to the late Lord Colvil.

28. Rt. Hon. David Lord Oliphant.

30. Sir Samuel Cornish, Bart. a brave

brave and experienced Admiral; remarkable for his fervices, as well in the late as in former wars.

At Poole, Sir Peter Thompfon, Knight.

Nov. 6. The Rev. Sir Afhurft Allen, Bart.

Marquis de Feuente, Minifter Plenipotentiary from the King of Spain to the States of Holland.

Baron Munckhaufen, Prime Minifter to the Electorate of Hanover.

9. In the 77th year of his age, his Grace John Duke of Argyll, great mafter of the houfehold in Scotland, one of the fixteen peers of Scotland, general of his Majefty's forces, colonel of the royal regiment of grey dragoons, governor of Limerick, knight of the thiftle, and one of his Majefty's moft honourable privy council. In 1761 he fucceeded his coufin Archibald, third Duke of Argyll, in titles and eftate. By his Lady, a fifter of the late Sir Henry Belanden, he has left three fons and one daughter, viz. John (now Duke of Argyll), married to the Dutchefs of Hamilton; Lord Frederick, married to the Countefs Dowager of Ferrers; Lord William, Gov. of Nova Scotia, married to Mifs Iffards, of Charles Town, S. Carolina; and the Right Hon. the Countefs of Aylefbury, Lady of Gen. Conway, and mother to her Grace the Dutchefs of Richmond.

Right Rev. Dr. James Leflie, Bifhop of Limerick, Ardfert, and Aghadoe. He was promoted to thofe fees in 1755, on the death of Dr. Burfcough.

His Excellency Lord Bottetourt, Lieut. and Gov. General of Virginia, greatly lamented by the whole colony.

Alexander Thompfon, Efq. of New York; by whofe indefatigable pains the non-importation agreement was abolifhed, and commerce with the mother-country revived.

Rt. Hon. Countefs of Harborough, at Bath.

Nov. 13. Rt. Hon. Geo. Grenville, member for Buckingham, and one of his Majefty's moft honourable Privy Council. He was born in 1712, and in 1749 he married the daughter of Sir William Wyndham, Bart. and fifter to the late Earl of Egremont, by whom he had two fons and three daughters. When his body was opened, the blood veffels in the head were nearly empty; the rib bones on one fide rotten, and two on the other fide the fame.

At Paris, the celebrated Henry Francis Ledran, Surgeon General of the French King's armies.

23. The Rt. Rev. Dr. Mathias Mawfon, Lord Bifhop of Ely. His Lordfhip was the oldeft confecrated bifhop in England and Ireland, being a bifhop in the year 1738, on the death of Dr. Harris, Bifhop of Llandaff, from which fee he was in 1740 tranflated to that of Chichefter on the death of Dr. Hare, and in 1754 promoted to Ely on the death of Bifhop Gooch. His Lordfhip has left to Corpus Chrifti College, of which he was formerly mafter, 6000l. for founding fcholarfhips and exhibitions; and 3000l. for rebuilding the College.

Hon. Mafter Byng, only fon of Rt. Hon. Lord Vifcount Torrington.

The Princefs Wilhelmina-Maria, Landgravine of Heffe-Hombourg, aged 93.

Dec. 4. At his houfe in Pallmall, the Rt. Hon. John Percival Earl of Egmont, in Ireland, May 7, 1762:

1762: his Lordship was called to the House of Peers by the title of Lord Lovel and Holland of Enmore, Somersetshire. He is succeeded in title and estate by his eldest son the Rt. Hon. John James Visc. Percival, col. of a company in the foot guards.

Dec. 12. At her house in Hill-street, Mrs. Levercey grandmother to Lord Viscount Molyneux.

16. Sir Thos. Frederick, Bart. The title descends to John Frederick, of Burwood, Surry, and his estate to his two daughters.

27. Rt. Hon. Lady Mary Whitbread, Bedwell Park.

The Rt. Hon. Matthew Ducie Moreton, Lord Ducie of Moreton, in Staffordshire, and Lord Ducie of Tortworth, in Gloucestershire, who succeeded his father, May 2, 1735, and was created Lord Ducie of Tortworth, with remainder in failure of issue to Thomas Reynolds, Esq. his nephew, and his heirs; and in the failure of his issue, to his brother Francis Reynolds, Esq. April 23, 1763. Sir Robert Ducie, one of his Lordship's ancestors, was Lord Mayor of London in the reign of Charles the First, and though he lent his Majesty 80,000l. which was lost by the King's being driven from London, he died, however, worth 400,000l. His Lordship is succeeded in his title and estates by his sister's son, Major Reynolds, eldest son of Francis Reynolds, Esq. the present member for Lancaster.

APPENDIX

APPENDIX to the CHRONICLE.

Two PROTESTS of the HOUSE of LORDS.

Veneris, 2do Die Februarii, 1770.

THE order of the day was read for taking into consideration the State of the Nation, and for the Lords to be summoned. It was moved, That the House should be put into a Committee thereupon. Accordingly,

The House was adjourned during pleasure, and put into a Committee. After some time The House was resumed.

Then it was moved to resolve, That the House of Commons, in the exercise of its judicature in matters of election, is bound to judge according to the law of the land, and the known and established law and custom of parliament, which is part thereof.

Which being objected to, and a question stated thereupon, after long debate,

The previous question was put, Whether the said question shall be now put.

It was resolved in the affirmative. Contents 96, not Contents 47.

Dissentient,

1. Because the resolution was in our judgment highly necessary to lay the foundation of a proceeding in this House, which might tend to quiet the minds of the people, by doing them justice at a time when the decision of the other House, which appears to us inconsistent with the principles of the constitution, and irreconcileable to the law of the land, has spread so universal an alarm, and produced so general a discontent throughout the kingdom.

2. Because, although we do not deny, that the determination on the right to a seat in the House of Commons is competent to the jurisdiction of that House alone; yet when to this it is added, that whatever they, in the exercise of that jurisdiction, think fit to declare to be law, is therefore to be so considered, because their lies no appeal, we conceive ourselves called upon to give that proposition the strongest negative; for, if admitted, the law of the land, by which all courts of judicature, without exception, are equally bound to proceed, is at once overturned and resolved into the will and pleasure of a majority of one House of Parliament, who, in assuming it, assumes a power to over-rule at pleasure the fundamental right of election, which the antient constitution has placed in other hands—those of their constituents. And if ever this pretended power should come to be exercised to the full extent of the principle, that House will be no longer the representative of the people, but a separate body, altogether independent

ent of them, self-existing, and self-elected.

3. Because, when we are told that expulsion implies incapacity, and the proof insisted upon is, that the people have acquiesced in this principle by not re-electing persons who have been expelled, we equally deny the position as false, and reject the proof offered as in no way supporting the position to which it is applied. We are sure the doctrine is not to be found in any statute or law book, nor in the journals of the House of Commons; neither is it consonant with any just or known analogy of law. And as not re-electing would at most but infer a supposition of the electors' approbation of the grounds of the expulsion and by no means their acquiescence in the conclusion of an implied incapacity, so, were there not one instance of a re-election after expulsion but Mr. Woolaston's, That alone demonstrates, that neither did the constituents admit, nor did the House of Commons maintain, incapacity to be the consequence of expulsion. Even the case of Mr. Walpole shews, by the first re election, the sense of the people, that expulsion did not infer incapacity; and that precedent, too, which is the only one of a declaration of incapacity, produced as it was under the influence of party violence in the latter days of Queen Anne, in so far as it relates to the introduction of a candidate having a minority of votes, decides expressly against the proceedings of the House of Commons in the late Middlesex election.

4. Because, as the constitution has been once already destroyed by the assumption and exercise of the very power which is now claimed, a day may come, when freedom of speech may be criminal in that House, and every member, who shall have virtue enough to withstand the usurpations of the times, and assert the rights of the people, will, for that offence, be expelled by a factious and corrupt majority, and by that expulsion rendered incapable of serving the public; in which case the electors will find themselves reduced to the miserable alternative of giving up altogether their right of election, or of chusing only such as are enemies of their country, and will be passive at least, if not active, in subverting the constitution.

5. Because, although it has been objected in the debate, that it is unusual and irregular in either House of Parliament to examine into the judicial proceedings of the other, whose decisions, as they cannot be drawn into question by appeal, are, it is said, to be submitted to without examination of the principles of them elsewhere; we conceive the argument goes directly to revive and establish the exploded doctrine of passive obedience and non-resistance, which, as applied to the acts of any branch of the supreme power, we hold to be equally dangerous; and though it is generally true, that neither House ought lightly and wantonly to interpose even an opinion upon matters which the constitution has entrusted to the jurisdiction of the other, we conceive it to be no less true, that where, under colour of a judicial proceeding, either House arrogates to itself the powers of the whole legislature, and *makes* the law, which it professes to *declare*, the other not only may but ought to assert its own rights, and those of the

the people; that this House has done so in former instances, particularly in the famous case of Ashby and White, in which the first resolution of the Lords declares, "that neither House of Parliament has any power, by any vote or declaration, to create to themselves any new privilege that is not warranted by the known laws and customs of parliament." We ought to interfere at this time the rather, as our silence on so important and alarming an occasion might be interpreted into an approbation of the measure, and be the means of losing that confidence with the people, which is so essential to the public welfare, that this House, the hereditary guardians of their rights, should at all times endeavour to maintain.

6. Because, upon the whole, we deem the power which the House of Commons have assumed to themselves, of creating an incapacity unknown to the law, and thereby depriving in effect all the electors of Great Britain of their invaluable rights of free election, confirmed to them by so many solemn statutes, *a flagrant usurpation*, as highly repugnant to every essential principle of the constitution as the claim of ship-money by King Charles I. or that of the suspending and dispensing power by King James II.; this being, indeed, in our opinion, a suspending and dispensing power, *despotically assumed and exercised by the House of Commons, against the antient and fundamental liberties of the kingdom*.

Then it was moved to resolve, That any resolution of the House, directly or indirectly impeaching a judgment of the House of Commons in a matter where their jurisdiction is competent, final, and conclusive, would be a violation of the constitutional right of the Commons, tends to make a breach between the two Houses of Parliament, and leads to a general confusion.

Dissentient,

1. Because we apprehend that the rights and powers of the Peerage are not given for our own particular advantage, but merely as a constitutional trust, to be held and exercised for the benefit of the people, and for the preservation of their laws and liberties; and we should hold ourselves betrayers of that trust, unworthy of our high rank in the kingdom, and of our seats in this House, if we considered any one legal right of the subject, much less the first and most important of all their rights, as a matter indifferent and foreign to the Peers of this kingdom.

2. Because, by this resolution, it is declared to the world, that if the House of Commons should change the whole law of election; should transfer the rights of the freeholders to copyholders and leaseholders for years, or totally extinguish those rights by an arbitrary declaration; should alter the constitution of cities and boroughs, with regard to their elections; should reverse not only all the franchises of suffrage which the people hold under the common law, but also trample upon the sanctions of so many acts of parliament, made for declaring and securing the rights of election; that, even in such a critical emergency of the constitution, the people are to despair of any relief whatsoever from any mode of, direct or indirect, interference of this House.

3. Because, by this resolution, the House not only refuses to stand by the people, in case they should suffer

suffer the most grievous injuries from their representatives, but it abdicates its antient and unquestioned province and duty of the hereditary Council to the Crown rendering itself unable to gives its advice in a point in which, of all others, the King may stand in the greatest need of the wisdom and authority of the Peers; a point, such as the present, in which numbers of the constituents have, in a manner agreeable to law, carried up their complaints to the throne against their representatives.

4. Because, by the said resolution, we do a most material injury to the House of Commons itself. The resolution, by the studied latitude of the words, *directly or indirectly to censure*, puts it out of the power of the Lords to offer, either in the present or in any future unfortunate difference between them and their constituents, even in the way of friendly conference, our amicable and healing mediation; the want of which may be a means of letting such difference run to extremities fatal to the House of Commons itself, to the constitution, and to the nation.

5. Because we consider ourselves also, as an House of Parliament, to be most materially interested that the people should be legally and constitutionally represented; for as the House of Commons makes an essential part of parliament, if that House should come to be chosen in a manner not agreeable to the laws and constitution of the kingdom, the authority of parliament itself must suffer extremely, if not totally perish: the Peers can no more, in their legislative capacity, do any valid act, *without a legal House of Commons*, than without a legal prince upon the throne.

6. Because, by this resolution, the constitutional controul has been given up, which this House, as appears by antient and recent precedents, have constantly claimed and exercised, and for the purpose of which the legislature has been divided into separate branches. We are far from denying such a reciprocity of controul in the other House, even in matters within our separate and final jurisdiction; neither arrogating to ourselves, or acknowledging in others, any power distinct from or above the law of the land. But *we cannot behold, without the utmost shame and indignation, this House making a voluntary surrender of its most undoubted, legal, necessary, and sacred rights*; not only omitting, but refusing to examine, precedents; not previously desiring a conference with the other House, to discover whether they were inclined to admit in this House a correspondent immunity from interposition on their part in matters within the particular jurisdiction of the Peers. These proceedings are as derogatory from the dignity of the House as they are contrary to its duty and its interest. They cannot fail of lowering this House in the opinion of mankind, who will not believe that the Peers can have any attention to the welfare of the people, *when they have shewn so little regard to their own honour*. This resolution must tend to forward *that plan*, which, with great uneasiness, we have seen, for a long time, *systematically carried on for lowering all the constitutional powers of the kingdom, rendering the House of Commons odious, and the House of Peers contemptible.*

7. Because the impropriety of this resolution was infinitely aggravated

gravated by the sudden and surreptitious method by which it was brought into and carried through this House. That a resolution new in matter, wide in extent, weighty in importance, involved in law and parliamentary precedents, should be moved at midnight, after the House was spent with the fatigue of a former debate; that an adjournment of only two days, to enable the Lords to consult the journals on this important point, should be refused; and that an immediate division should be pressed, are circumstances which strongly mark the opinion of the movers upon the merit of their own proposition. Such a proceeding appears to us altogether unparliamentary and *unjust*, as it must, in every instance where it is practised, preclude all possibility of debate; and when, by this means, all argument and fair discussion is suppressed, the deliberations of this House will degenerate into silent votes.

We think ourselves, therefore, as Peers, and as Englishmen and Freemen, (names as dear to us as any titles whatsoever) indispensably obliged to protest against a resolution utterly subversive of the authority and dignity of this House, equally injurious to the collective body of the people, to their representatives, and to the Crown, to which we owe our advice upon every public emergency; a resolution, in law unconstitutional; in precedent, not only unauthorised but contradicted; in tendency, ruinous; in the time and manner of obtaining it, unfair and surreptitious. And *we here solemnly declare and pledge ourselves to the Public, that we will persevere in availing ourselves, as far as in us lies, of every right and every power, with which the constitution has armed us for the good of the whole, in order to obtain full relief for the injured electors of Great Britain, and full security, for the future, against this most dangerous usurpation upon the rights of the people; which, by sapping the fundamental principles of this government, threatens its total dissolution.*

E. Temple,	L. Fortescue,
L. Audley,	D. Bolton,
L. Craven,	L. Wycombe, E.
L. Camden,	of Shelburne,
D. Portland,	L. King,
D. Richmond,	D. Manchester,
E. Radnor,	L. Chedworth,
E. Thanet,	L. Ponsonby, E.
L. Lyttelton,	of Besborough,
E. Suffolk,	E. Chatham,
E. Aylesford,	L. Hyde,
E. Fitzwilliam,	L. Monson,
L. Trevor,	E. Albemarle,
M. Rockingham,	E. Scarborough,
E. Berkeley,	E. Huntingdon,
E. Coventry,	L. Abergavenny,
E. Stamford,	L. Boyle, E. of
B. Bangor,	Corke,
B. Exeter,	E. Buckingham-
V. Torrington,	shire,
E. Tankerville,	L. Milton,
E. Effingham,	D. Northumber-
L. Archer,	land.

5 Dukes, 18 Earls, —— 41

N. B. The same Lords signed the two Protests, with the exception of the Earls of Suffolk and Buckinghamshire, who signed only the first.

Die Martis, 1° *Maii,* 1770.

THE order of the day being read for the Lords to be summoned,

The Earl of Chatham presented to the House a bill entituled,

" A Bill for reversing the Adjudications of the House of Commons, whereby John Wilkes, Esq. has been adjudged incapable of being elected

elected a member to serve in this present parliament, and the freeholders of the county of Middlesex have been deprived of one of their legal representatives."

Whereas the capacity of being elected a representative of the commons in parliament is (under known limitations of law) an original inherent right of the subject; and forasmuch as to deprive the subject of this high franchise birthright, otherwise than by a judgement according to the law of the land, and the constant established usage of parliament conformable thereto, and part thereof, is directly contrary to the fundamental laws and freedom of this realm, and in particular to the act, " Declaring the Rights and Liberties of the Subject, and settling the Succession of the Crown, at the ever-memorable Period of the Revolution, when free election of members of parliament was expressly vindicated and secured:

And whereas John Wilkes, Esq. having been duly elected and returned a knight of the shire to serve in this present parliament for the county of Middlesex, was, on the 17th of February, 1769, without being heard, adjudged incapable of being elected a member to serve in this present parliament, by a resolution of the House of Commons, as follows:

" Resolved, That John Wilkes, Esq. having been in this session of parliament expelled this House, was and is incapable of being elected a member to serve in this present parliament."

And whereas on the same day the said House of Commons farther resolved as follows: " That the late election of a knight of the shire to serve in this present parliament for the county of Middlesex is a void election:"

And whereas the said John Wilkes, Esq. having been again duly elected and returned a knight of the shire to serve in this present parliament for the county of Middlesex, the said House of Commons did, on the 17th of March, 1769, resolve in the words following, " That the election and return of John Wilkes, Esq. who hath been by this House adjudged incapable of being elected a member to serve in this present parliament, are null and void:"

And whereas the said John Wilkes, Esq. having been again duly elected and returned a knight of the shire to serve in this present parliament for the county of Middlesex aforesaid, and having on the original poll books eleven hundred and forty-three votes in his favour, against two hundred and ninety-six, in favour of Henry Lawes Luttrell, Esq. the House of Commons did, on the 15th of April, 1769, without a hearing of parties, and in manifest violation of the indubitable right of the freeholders of the county of Middlesex to chuse their own representative in parliament, resolve as follows:

" That Henry Lawes Luttrell, Esq. ought to have been returned a knight of the shire to serve in this present parliament for the county of Middlesex, and thereupon ordered the said return to be amended accordingly:"

And whereas, by another resolution of the 8th of May, 1769, the said H. of C. did, upon hearing the matter of the petition of the freeholders of the county of Middlesex, as far as the same related to the election of Henry Lawes Luttrell, Esq. farther resolve as follows:
" That

"That Henry Lawes Luttrell, Esq. is duly elected a knight of the shire to serve in this present parliament for the county of Middlesex:"

And, forasmuch as all the resolutions aforesaid, cutting off the subject from his indubitable birthright by a vote of one House of Parliament, exercising discretionary power, and legislative authority, under colour of a jurisdiction in elections, are most arbitrary, illegal, and dangerous:

Be it therefore declared and enacted, by the King's most excellent Majesty, by and with the advice and consent of the Lords spiritual and temporal, and Commons, in this present parliament assembled, and by authority of the same, "That all the adjudications contained in the abovementioned several resolutions are arbitrary and illegal, and the same are and shall be hereby reversed, annulled, and made void, to all intents and purposes whatsoever."

After the first reading of the said bill, it was moved, That the said bill be read the second time on Thursday next. Which being objected to, after a long debate, the question was put thereupon. It was resolved in the negative by 89 to 43.

Then it was moved, That the said bill be rejected. The question was put thereupon, and it was resolved in the affirmative.

Dissentient,

Because the foundations of this bill being so fully laid in the reasons contained in two protests entered upon the journals of this House on the 2d day of February last, We think it indispensably necessary to protest against the rejection of the same, to the intent that it may be delivered down to posterity, that this great constitutional and effectual method of remedying an unexampled grievance hath not been less unattempted by us; and that, to our own times, we may stand as men determined to persevere in renewing, on every occasion, our utmost endeavours to obtain that redress for the violated rights of the subject, and for the injured electors of Great Britain, which, in the present moment, an over-ruling fatality hath prevented from taking effect; thereby refusing reparation and comfort to an oppressed and afflicted people.

Chatham, Portland, Plymouth, Rockingham, Abingdon, Boyle, Grofvenor, Stanhope, Ponsonby, Suffolk, Richmond, Radnor, Archer, Fitzwilliam, Temple, Torrington, Rutland, John Bangor, Wycombe, Fortescue, Huntingdon, Tankerville, Abergavenny, King, Ferrers, Lyttelton, Bolton, Camden, Coventry, Buckinghamshire, Scarborough, Northumberland, Manchester.

To the King's Most Excellent Majesty.

The humble Address, Remonstrance, and Petition, of the Lord Mayor, Aldermen, and Livery of the City of London, in Common Hall assembled.

(*Presented at St. James's, on Wednesday, the 14th of March, 1770.*)

"May it please your Majesty,

"WE have already, in our petition, dutifully represented to your Majesty the chief injuries we have sustained: we are unwilling

unwilling to believe that your Majesty can slight the desires of your people, or be regardless of their affection, and deaf to their complaints. Yet their complaints remain unanswered, their injuries are confirmed; and the only judge removeable at the pleasure of the crown has been dismissed from his high office for defending in parliament the laws and the constitution.

"We therefore venture once more to address ourselves to your Majesty, as to the father of your people; as to him who must be both able and willing to redress our grievances; and we repeat our application with the greater propriety, because we see the instruments of our wrongs, who have carried into execution the measures of which we complain, more particularly distinguished by your Majesty's royal bounty and favour.

"Under the same secret and malign influence, which, through each successive administration, has defeated every good, and suggested every bad, intention, the majority of the House of Commons have deprived your people of their dearest rights.

"They have done a deed more ruinous in its consequences than the levying of ship-money by Charles the First, or the dispensing power assumed by James the Second. A deed, which must vitiate all the future proceedings of this parliament: for the acts of the legislature itself can no more be valid without a legal House of Commons than without a legal prince upon the throne.

"Representatives of the people are essential to the making of laws; and there is a time when it is morally demonstrable that men cease to be representatives. That time is now arrived. The present House of Commons do not represent the people.

"We owe to your Majesty an obedience, under the restriction of the laws, for the calling and duration of parliaments; and your Majesty owes to us, that our representation, free from the force of arms or corruption, should be preserved to us in parliament. It was for this we successfully struggled under James the Second; for this we seated and have faithfully supported your Majesty's family on the throne. The people have been invariably uniform in their object, though the different mode of attack has called for a different defence.

"Under James the Second they complained that the sitting of parliament was interrupted, because it was not corruptly subservient to his designs: We complain now, that the sitting of this parliament is not interrupted, because it is corruptly subservient to the designs of your Majesty's ministers. Had the parliament under James the Second been as submissive to his commands as the parliament is at this day to the dictates of a minister, instead of clamours for its meeting, the nation would have rung, as now, with outcries for its dissolution.

"The forms of the constitution, like those of religion, were not established for the form's sake; but for the substance. And we call God and men to witness, that, as we do not owe our liberty to those nice and subtle distinctions which places, pensions, and lucrative employments, have invented, so neither will we be deprived of it by them;

them; but as it was gained by the stern virtue of our ancestors, by the virtue of their descendants it shall be preserved.

"Since, therefore, the misdeeds of your Majesty's ministers in violating the freedom of election, and depraving the noble constitution of parliaments, are notorious, as well as subversive of the fundamental laws and liberties of this realm; and since your Majesty, both in honour and justice, is obliged inviolably to preserve them, according to the oath made to God and your subjects at your coronation; we, your Majesty's remonstrants, assure ourselves, that your Majesty will restore the constitutional government and quiet of your people by dissolving this parliament, and removing those evil ministers for ever from your councils.
Signed by order,
James Hodges, Town Clerk."

To which Address, Remonstrance, and Petition, his Majesty was pleased to return the following Answer.

"I shall always be ready to receive the requests and to listen to the complaints of my subjects; but it gives me great concern to find that any of them should have been so far misled, as to offer me an Address and Remonstrance, the contents of which I cannot but consider as disrespectful to me, injurious to my parliament, and irreconcileable to the principles of the constitution.

"I have ever made the law of the land the rule of my conduct, esteeming it my chief glory to reign over a free people. With this view I have always been careful as well to execute faithfully the trust reposed in me, as to avoid even the appearance of invading any of those powers which the constitution has placed in other hands. It is only by persevering in such a conduct that I can either discharge my own duty, or secure to my subjects the free enjoyment of those rights which my family were called to defend: and while I act upon these principles, I shall have a right to expect, and I am confident I shall continue to receive, the steady and affectionate support of my people."

To the King's Most Excellent Majesty.

The humble Address, Remonstrance, and Petition, of the Lord Mayor, Aldermen, and Common Council of the City of London.

(*Presented on Wednesday, May 23d.*)

May it please your Majesty,

WHEN your Majesty's most faithful subjects, the citizens of London, whose loyalty and affection have been so often and so effectually proved and experienced by the illustrious house of Brunswick, are labouring under the weight of that displeasure which your Majesty has been advised to lay upon them, in the answer given from the throne to their late humble application, we feel ourselves constrained with all humility to approach the Royal Father of his people.

Conscious, Sire, of the purest sentiments of veneration which they entertain for your Majesty's person, we are deeply concerned that what the law allows, and the constitution teaches, hath been miscon-

misconstrued by ministers, instruments of that influence which shakes the realm, into disrespect to your Majesty.

Perplexed and astonished as we are by the awful *sentence of censure* lately passed upon this city in your Majesty's answer from the throne, we cannot, without surrendering all that is dear to Englishmen, forbear most humbly to supplicate, that your Majesty will deign to grant a more favourable interpretation to this dutiful though *persevering claim* of our *invaded birth-rights*; nothing doubting that the benignity of your Majesty's nature will, to our unspeakable comfort, at length break through all the secret and visible *machinations* to which the city of London owes its late *severe repulse*) and that your kingly justice, and fatherly tenderness, will disclaim the malignant and pernicious *advice* which suggested the answer we deplore: *an advice of the most dangerous tendency*; inasmuch as thereby the exercise of the clearest rights of the subject, namely, to petition the King for redress of grievances, to complain of the violation of the freedom of election, and to pray for a dissolution of parliament, to point out mal-practices in administration, and to urge the removal of evil ministers, hath, under the generality of one *compendious word*, been indiscriminately checked with reprimand; and your Majesty's afflicted citizens of London have heard, from the throne itself, that the *contents* of their humble Address, Remonstrance, and Petition, laying their *complaints* and *injuries* at the feet of their Sovereign, as *father of his people*, able and *willing* to *redress their grievances*, cannot but be considered by your Majesty " as disrespectful to yourself, injurious to your parliament, and irreconcileable to the principles of the constitution."

Your Majesty cannot disapprove, that *we here* assert the clearest principles of the constitution, against the insidious attempts of evil counsellors to *perplex*, *confound*, and *shake* them. We are determined to abide by those rights and liberties which our forefathers bravely vindicated at the ever-memorable Revolution, and which their *sons will* ever resolutely defend. We therefore now renew, at the foot of the throne, our claim to the *indispensable right* of the subject,—— a *full*, *free*, and *unmutilated* parliament, *legally chosen in all its members*;—a right which THIS House of Parliament have manifestly violated, depriving, at their *will* and *pleasure*, the county of Middlesex of one of its legal representatives, and *arbitrarily nominating*, as a knight of the shire, a person not elected by a majority of the *freeholders*. As the only constitutional means of reparation now left for the injured electors of Great Britain, we implore, with most urgent supplications, the *dissolution* of this present parliament, the removal of evil ministers, and the total extinction of that fatal influence which has caused such national discontent.

In the mean time, Sire, we offer our constant prayers to Heaven, that your Majesty may reign, as Kings only can reign, *in* and *by* the hearts of a loyal, dutiful, and *free* people.

His

His Majesty's Answer.

'I should have been wanting to the public as well as to myself if I had not expressed my dissatisfaction at the late address.

'My sentiments on that subject continue the same; and I should ill deserve to be considered as the father of my people, if I could suffer myself to be prevailed upon to make such an use of my prerogative as I cannot but think inconsistent with the interest and dangerous to the constitution of the kingdom.'

After his Majesty had been pleased to make the foregoing answer, the Lord Mayor requested leave to reply, which being granted, his Lordship addressed him in the following words:

"Most gracious Sovereign,

"WILL your Majesty be pleased so far to condescend, as to permit the Mayor of your loyal city of London to declare in your Royal presence, on behalf of his fellow-citizens, how much the bare apprehension of your Majesty's displeasure would, at all times, affect their minds: the declaration of that displeasure has already filled them with inexpressible anxiety, and with the deepest affliction.

"Permit me, Sire, to assure your Majesty, that your Majesty has not in all your dominions any subjects more faithful, more dutiful, or more affectionate to your Majesty's person and family, or more ready to sacrifice their lives and fortunes in the maintenance of the true honour and dignity of your crown.

"We do, therefore, with the greatest humility and submission, most earnestly supplicate your Majesty, that you will not dismiss us from your presence without expressing a more favourable opinion of your faithful citizens, and without some comfort, without some prospect, at least, of redress.

"Permit me, Sire, farther to observe, that whoever has already dared, or shall hereafter endeavour by false insinuations and suggestions, to alienate your Majesty's affections from your loyal subjects in general, and from the city of London in particular, and to withdraw your confidence to and regard for your people, *is an enemy to your Majesty's person and family, a violator of the public peace, and a betrayer of our happy constitution as it was established at the glorious and necessary Revolution.*"——

The Lord Mayor waited near a minute for a reply, but none was given.

To the Right Honourable the Lords Commissioners of the Admiralty.

London, Oct. 26.

My Lords,

I AM under the necessity of representing to your Lordships, that a measure very injurious to the inhabitants of this city, as well as derogatory of the authority of its laws and of its magistracy, hath lately been taken, under the sanction of your Lordships' authority—I mean, that of granting to citizens, carrying on the several branches of business, protections from the Admiralty for the men employed by them, provided they are not seamen; to obtain which protections,

protections, the citizens are at the trouble of resorting to the Admiralty Office, at much loss of time, and are besides obliged to pay a *guinea* for each protection.

I am sure that no such idea can be entertained by your Lordships, as that any protection, besides that of the laws, is necessary to secure persons employed in the manufactures and commerce of this city. I beg leave, therefore, to submit to your Lordships, that this mode of protection be desisted from; and whether it may not tend to the more quiet and effectual carrying on the public service, if the naval officers employed to impress men be enjoined by your Lordships to pay due regard to certificates, attested by the magistrates of the city, in favour of persons (not seamen) employed by the inhabitants in their respective business, and described in the manner required by your Lordships' protections. I have the honour to be, with great respect,

My Lords,
Your Lordships' most obedient humble servant,
BARLOW TRECOTHICK,
Mayor.

To the Right Honourable the Lord Mayor of the City of London.

Admiralty Office, Oct. 26.

WE have received your Lordship's letter of this day's date, representing that a measure very injurious to the inhabitants of this city, as well as derogatory of the authority of its laws and of its magistracy, hath lately been taken under the sanction of our authority, viz. That of granting to citizens, carrying on the several branches of business, protections from this office, for the persons employed by them, and submitting, whether this mode of protection may not be desisted from, and whether it may not tend to the more quiet and effectual carrying on the public service, if the naval officers employed therein be enjoined by us to pay due regard to certificates attested by the Magistrates of the city, in favour of persons (not seamen) employed by the inhabitants, and described in the manner required by our protections.

We are to acquaint your Lordship, that application being made to us for protections for persons under the description above-mentioned, they were at first refused, and those who solicited them told, they were unnecessary, the officers employed on the service of raising men being restrained from impressing landmen; but several persons in great branches of business repeating their solicitations, and asserting that their men, from the apprehensions of being impressed, could not be prevailed upon to follow their work, we did therefore, in order to remove such apprehensions, which, however groundless, might prove prejudicial to them in their business, at length comply with their request; but, in regard to your Lordship's representation, we shall for the future desist from granting any such protections.

We are farther to observe to your Lordship, that the warrants issued by us to the officers employed in procuring men for his Majesty's fleet do not authorize them to impress any but seamen, seafaring men, and persons whose occupations

APPENDIX to the CHRONICLE. [205

cupations and callings are to work in vessels and boats upon rivers; and that the instructions accompanying those warrants expressly restrain them from impressing any landman: and we assure your Lordship, that in case any officer shall presume to exceed the powers granted him by such warrants, or disobey the orders conveyed to him by such instructions, he shall be exemplarily punished, and the parties injured have reasonable redress. Under these circumstances, therefore, it seems unnecessary for us to give such officers particular instructions with respect to the certificates your Lordship proposes; and, indeed, we apprehend such certificates would in their nature be a mode of protection which we are not authorized to give any sanction to.

We are, my Lord, your Lordship's most humble servants,

E. HAWKE,
C. SPENCER,
C. J. FOX.

(A copy.)

Copy of the Letter transmitted yesterday by the Lords of the Admiralty to the Right Hon. the Lord Mayor.

Admiralty Office, 20 Nov. 1770.

My Lord,

THE city remembrancer having attended Sir Edward Hawke, with a copy of the resolution of a common council, held the 15th inst. at Guildhall, offering a bounty for the encouraging seamen to enter into his Majesty's sea-service; and signified the request of the said court, that Sir Edward Hawke would, at a proper opportunity, lay the same before his Majesty, as an humble testimony of their zeal and affection for his most sacred person and government; and Sir Edward being prevented by illness from attending the King therewith, he transmitted a copy of it to Lord Weymouth, one of the principal Secretaries of State, for his Majesty's information; and his Lordship having this day acquainted us, that he took the earliest opportunity of laying the said resolution before the King, and that his Majesty was pleased to express great satisfaction upon receiving this mark of zeal and affection for his person and government; we signify the same to your Lordship; and are, my Lord,

Your Lordship's
Most humble servants,

Rt. Hon. Brass Crosby, Esq. Lord Mayor of London.

J. BULLER,
PALMERSTONE,
C. SPENCER,
LISBURN,
F. HOLBURNE.

Wednesday, Nov. 21, 1770.

To the KING's Most Excellent Majesty.

The humble Address, Remonstrance, and Petition, of the Lord Mayor, Aldermen, and Commons of the City of London, in Common Council assembled.

Most gracious Sovereign,

WE, the Lord Mayor, Aldermen, and Commons of the city of London, in common-council assembled, most humbly beg leave to approach your Majesty, and most dutifully to lay again at the foot of the throne our aggravated grievances and earnest supplications: although, through prevalence of evil counsellors, our

just

just complaints have hitherto met with repulfe and reprimand, neverthelefs we will not forego the laft confolation of the unhappy hope that our fufferings will at length find an end from the innate goodnefs of your Majefty; the gracious effects of which have, to our unfpeakable grief, been intercepted from your injured people by a fatal confpiracy of malevolent influence around the throne.

We, therefore, again implore your Majefty in this fad crifis, with hearts big with forrow, and warm with affection, not to be induced by falfe fuggeftions, contrary to the benignity of your Royal nature, to fhut up your paternal compaffion and juftice againft the prayers of unhappy fubjects, claiming, as we now again prefume to do, with equal humility and freeborn plainnefs, our indifputable birth-rights, freedom of election, and right of petitioning.

We have feen the known law of the land, the fure guardian of right, trodden down; and, by the influence of daring minifters, arbitrary difcretion, the law of tyrants, fet up to overthrow the choice of the electors, and nominate to a feat in parliament a perfon not chofen by the people.

Your Majefty's throne is founded on the free exercife of this great election:—to preferve it inviolate, is true loyalty; to undermine and deftroy it, is the moft compendious treafon againft the whole conftitution.

Deign then, Sire, amidft the complicated dangers which furround us, to reftore fatisfaction and harmony to your faithful fubjects, by removing from your Majefty's prefence all evil counfellors, and by recurring to the recent fenfe of your people taken in a new parliament.

By fuch an exertion alone of your own Royal wifdom and virtue the various wounds of the conftitution can be effectually healed; and, by reprefentatives freely chofen, and acting independently, the falutary awe of parliament cannot fail to fecure to us that facred bulwark of Englifh liberty, the trial by jury, againft the dangerous defigns of thofe who have dared openly to attempt to mutilate its powers and to deftroy its efficacy.

So will diffatisfaction, and national weaknefs, change at once into public confidence, order, ftrength, and dignity; and this boafted conftitution of England, fo late the envy of nations, no longer be held forth to the derifion of Europe, electors not fuffered to elect, juries forbid to judge of the whole matter in iffue before them, and dutiful petitioners, remonftrating the moft flagrant grievances, branded by the minifters who opprefs them, as feditious infractors of that conftitution which we religioufly revere, and, together with your Majefty's facred perfon, will unceafingly defend againft all enemies and betrayers.

His Majefty's Anfwer.

"As I have no reafon to alter the opinion expreffed in my anfwer to your laft addrefs upon this fubject, I cannot comply with the prayer of your petition."

Account of the Proceedings at the County Meeting at York, in a Letter from a Gentleman prefent.

"THOUGH I live very diftant from York, yet, as a friend to liberty and the conftitution, I went

went to the county meeting advertised for the 25th inst. About noon Sir George Armitage was requested to take the chair. After expressing his sense of the honour conferred on him, and giving assurance of the exertion of his abilities in the business for which they were assembled, he told them he would first read their late petition, and then give an account of its reception, which was nothing more than that the King received it with a smile.

"Sir G. Saville then rose up, and gave a very brief account of what had been done in the House, tending to remedy the grievances so long complained of, but said nothing to countenance a remonstrance.

"Sir George Armitage (without taking the sense of the freeholders concerning a remonstrance) begged leave to read a paper, containing thanks to their worthy representatives for their conduct in parliament the last session.

"The next speaker at this meeting was Charles Turner, Esq. He did not in the least disapprove what Sir George Armitage had proposed, but thought if this was all they intended by calling the freeholders together,—if they took no notice of the contempt of their dutiful and loyal petition to the throne, most of the freeholders would be greatly disappointed; that they should be the laugh of the ministry; that they should be thought to forsake the cause in which they had embarked; and therefore proposed a conditional remonstrance, in support of which he was very warm, and spoke to the satisfaction of some, who, before, had not the most friendly opinion of him.

"It was then agreed, that the letter of thanks should be first voted;—and then the sense of the freeholders taken concerning a remonstrance. The letter of thanks was assented to without one dissenting voice.

"Mr. Turner had proposed a committee, with whom was to be trusted the whole affair: this was the next subject of consideration. Sir George Armitage then proclaimed aloud, ' all who are for ' the committee hold up their hand; ' all who are against the committee ' hold up their hand likewise.' This causing some confusion, a division was agreed upon, and those who were not freeholders were requested to leave the room for a few minutes. —Against the committee a great majority.

"Lord John Cavendish was, I think, the next speaker: he recommended lenient and gentle measures, as the most probable method of having all their complaints redressed, when his Majesty perceived they did not oppose the measures of government for the sake of opposition, but in defence of their own privileges, when violated and infringed.

"After some trifling altercation, it was next proposed by (if I am not mistaken) Sir Cecil Wray, that the sense of the freeholders should be taken concerning a remonstrance; when it was observed by Lord J. Cavendish, that, in the letter already assented to, they had expresly declared they forbore to reiterate their complaint before the throne, and that they now were, in direct contradiction to themselves, going to reiterate: Accordingly all was quashed, and Sir George Armitage left the chair."

The

The following is the Letter of Thanks to the Knights of the Shire above alluded to.

To Sir George Saville, Bart. and Edwin Lascelles, Esq.

"York, Sept. 25, 1770.

"Gentlemen,

"WE, the freeholders of the county of York assembled here, desire to express our sentiments to you on the present dangerous situation of affairs.

"In presenting a petition to the throne, we acted from the strongest conviction that it was our duty to represent to his Majesty how severely we thought the rights of all the electors of Great Britain struck at by that resolution which nominated a representative to a county, in opposition to the votes of a majority of the freeholders.

"We had reason to hope, that an application so full of affectionate loyalty to our Sovereign, and presented in a mode so agreeable to the principles of the constitution, would have met with a favourable reception. But we neither can nor will impute its failure to any other cause than the arts and management of those, who have no other means of justifying their own misconduct to their Sovereign than by misrepresenting the desires and affections of a loyal people.

"Hopeless of success from a reiterated petition whilst the same influence prevails, we forbear to make a farther application to the throne; being confident that the former will remain an authentic testimony of our unalterable sentiments, which, by every justifiable method, we are determined to support; and we doubt not, that, by a steady perseverance in these principles, the electors of Great Britain must finally obtain redress of their violated rights.

"Your conduct, gentlemen, hath justly merited the thanks of your constituents; and we have the satisfaction to declare, that we entirely approve all that you have done and said in support of their liberties.—By the explicit, manly, and determined part you have taken, during the last session of parliament, the sentiments of those whose interest is entrusted to your care have been most faithfully expressed.

"It is not, therefore, to admonish or instruct, but to point you out as examples to animate and encourage others, that we now express our sense of the firmness and vigilance of your conduct in these times of new and dangerous doctrines, when not only redress for the violation of the right of election hath not been obtained, but every attempt to secure that right from future violations hath been evaded.

"It is become but too evident, that neither the most sacred rights of the people, nor the honour of the crown, have been objects of their care whose stations render them more peculiarly responsible for a strict attention to both.

"The public welfare, then, demands that those who are chosen to guard its interest should employ their utmost attention to enquire into the causes of that general dissatisfaction which prevails in the minds of a free, a generous, and a loyal people; and, should there be found any just objects of national resentment, we trust, that neither ministerial power shall be able

APPENDIX to the CHRONICLE.

able to defeat, nor retirement from power elude the effect of that enquiry.

"That the minds of his Majesty's subjects may be united in a dutiful submission to legal authority, and a steady resistance to illegal power, and that the rights of the people may be secured by the virtue and prudence of their representatives, the natural guardians of those rights, is the fervent wish of every friend of the constitution: and you may be assured, that, in pursuit of those objects, you will always be supported by the freeholders of the county of York.

By order of the meeting,
GEO. ARMITAGE, *Chairman.*"

To the Freeholders of the County of York, assembled September 25, at York.

"Gentlemen,

"HAVING had the honour of receiving, by the hands of Sir George Armitage, a communication of your sentiments, I beg leave in the first place to return you my grateful acknowledgment for such parts of it as regard myself.

"I have always thought myself fortunate in the opportunities I have had of knowing from time to time the sentiments of my constituents; and it has been my particular happiness to meet on those occasions with their approbation. I could, indeed, no longer serve them with satisfaction to my own mind, than I had reason to believe that my opinions coincided with their's, at least in essential and fundamental points.

"The importance of the subject, the impression it has made on my mind, and the variety of matter contained in the paper transmitted to me, oblige me to extend my answer beyond the length that is usual or necessary in mere returns of compliment, or in answers on more ordinary occasions.

"It is impossible for me not to lament with you, that any unhappy interposition of interested men between a gracious sovereign and his people should make it eligible to forbear a second application:· hoping and trusting at the same time that your confidence is well founded, I do hold it to be impossible, while one grain of purity or vigour remains in the constitution, that principles and doctrines directly subversive of it can take root and flourish, nay, that they can even exist with any continuance. I am tempted so far to go beyond the limit of what is more essentially a necessary part of my answer, as to express the satisfaction it affords me to observe, that while you decline a measure, which to many might naturally seem more directly tending to redress, you have taken effectual care plainly to draw the line, and strongly to mark the distinction (that distinction so essential in *Questions of Right*) between forbearance and acquiescence.

"I accept with a pride, which I will acknowledge and avow every where, the testimony you bear to the little I can have done in the prosecution of my duty; and I wish you to be assured, that I will persevere not only in asserting, but in maintaining, to the utmost of my power, those principles you have approved,---the principles of the constitution; and more especially that first right, the right of election, under which alone my office exists,

exists, and without which even the two characters in which we are now conversing, the represented and the representative, are mere illusory fictions.

"I desire likewise to assure you, that I will omit no opportunity of fulfilling that particular duty which the present occasion has called upon you to remind me of; I mean the searching out the causes of public dissatisfaction, and the objects of a just public resentment; trusting to your candour, if the success does not answer to the warm expectations of many honest men, and the ardent wishes of all. You have more than once over-rated my abilities to serve you: I wish I had not reason to fear that in this instance you experience a striking example of it.

"It is my first duty to join in your wish, that due order and submission, as well as a resolute adherence to the rights of freemen, may prevail. It is the most perfect self-interest and the highest ambition to join with you in the other, that I may be in any degree the fortunate instrument in preserving those rights.

"I beg leave to subscribe myself, Gentlemen,
Your much obliged, and
faithful humble servant,
GEORGE SAVILLE."

To the Freeholders assembled at York, on the 25th of September, 1770.

Gentlemen,

"IT is scarce possible for words to express the lively sense of gratitude I feel for the very favourable opinion you are pleased to entertain of my public conduct.

"It has always been my greatest ambition to gain the approbation of gentlemen of your characters. If I have been so fortunate as to succeed, I must think I am more indebted to your partial opinions than to any real or substantial merit of my own.

"I know it would be vain and impertinent to expect any future favours from you, was I ever to betray the trust you have condescended to honour me with.

"I flatter myself, whilst I preserve my independency, and am not actuated with views of ambition, avarice, and lust of power, you will have no cause to withdraw your usual indulgence from me.

"I have ever considered the very unfortunate decision of the rights of the freeholders of Middlesex as highly detrimental to those of all the electors of Great Britain; therefore shall steadily persevere to contribute all in my power to obtain redress of those violated rights.

"I most heartily concur with you, gentlemen, in all your constitutional wishes. My greatest ambition is, to render myself worthy of your choice, which I know can only be effected by supporting the fundamental principles of our constitution, and the undoubted birth-right of our fellow subjects. When you find me deficient in those grand points, I desire to enjoy no longer the honourable station of being one of your representatives; but, until that event happens, the only favour I now ask of you, is, to give me credit for my unshaken loyalty to our most gracious Sovereign, my esteem and regard for the interest of our fellow subjects, and my implicit veneration for our most excellent constitution.

"I have

APPENDIX to the CHRONICLE.

"I have the honour to be, with the most sincere esteem and regard, Gentlemen,

Your most obliged, and most faithful humble servant,

"EDWIN LASCELLES.

"*Gouldesborough, Sept.* 28."

The unhappy Riot at Boston *has been so variously represented, and is in itself of so interesting a Nature, that we think it necessary to lay the different Accounts of it before our Readers.*

"*Boston, March* 12.

"ON the evening of Monday, being the 5th current, several soldiers of the 29th regiment were seen parading the streets with their drawn cutlasses and bayonets, abusing and wounding numbers of the inhabitants.

"A few minutes after nine o'clock, four youths, named Edward Archibald, William Merchant, Francis Archibald, and John Leech, jun. came down Cornhill together, and, separating at Dr. Loring's corner, the two former, in passing a narrow alley, where a soldier was brandishing a broad sword, of an uncommon size, against the walls, out of which he struck fire plentifully, and a person of a mean countenance, armed with a large cudgel, by him, Edward Archibald bade Mr. Merchant take care of the sword; on which the soldier turned round, struck Archibald on the arm, and then pushed at Merchant.—Merchant then struck the soldier with a short stick, and the other person ran to the barrack, and brought with him two soldiers, one armed with a pair of tongs, the other with a shovel: he with the tongs pursued Archibald back through the alley, collared and laid him over the head with the tongs. The noise brought people together, and John Hicks, a young lad, coming up, knocked the soldier down, but let him get up again; and more lads gathering, drove them back to the barrack, where the boys stood some time as it were to keep them in. In less than a minute ten or twelve soldiers came out with drawn cutlasses, clubs, and bayonets, and set upon the unarmed boys, who, finding the inequality of their equipment, dispersed. On hearing the noise, one Samuel Atwood came up to see what was the matter, and met the soldiers aforesaid rushing down the alley, and asked them if they intended to murder people? They answered, Yes, by G—d, root and branch! With that one of them struck Mr. Atwood with a club, which was repeated by another, and, being unarmed, he turned to go off, and received a wound on the left shoulder, which reached the bone. Retreating a few steps, Mr. Atwood met two officers, and said, Gentlemen, what is the matter? They answered, You'll see by and by. Immediately after, these heroes appeared in the square, asking where were the boogers? where were the cowards? Thirty or forty persons, mostly lads, being by this means gathered in King-street, Capt. Preston, with a party of men with charged bayonets, came from the main-guard, and, taking their stations by the custom-house, began to push and drive the people off, pricking some, and threatening others; on which the people grew clamorous, and, it is said, threw snow-balls. On this the Captain commanded his men to fire; and more snow-balls coming, he again said, d—n you, fire, be the consequence what it will—

[P] 2

One

One soldier then fired, and a townsman with a cudgel struck him over the hands with such force that he dropped his firelock, and, rushing forward, aimed a blow at the Captain's head, which grazed his hat, and fell pretty heavy upon his arm: however, the soldiers continued the fire, successively, till seven or eight, or, as some say, eleven guns were discharged.

"By this fatal manœuvre several were laid dead on the spot, and some lay struggling for life; but what shewed a degree of cruelty unknown to British troops, at least since the House of Hanover has directed their operations, was an attempt to fire upon, or stab with their bayonets, the persons who undertook to remove the slain and wounded! At length,

"Mr. Benjamin Leigh, of the Delph Manufactory, came up, and, after some conversation with Capt. Preston relative to his conduct, advised him to draw off his men; with which he complied.

"The dead are, Mr. Samuel Gray, killed on the spot, the ball entering his head, and beating off a large portion of his skull.

"A mulatto man, named Crispus Attucks, born in Framingham, who was here in order to go for North Carolina, also killed instantly; two balls entering his breast, one of them in special goring the right lobe of the lungs, and a great part of the liver, most horribly.

"Mr. James Caldwell, mate of Capt. Morton's vessel, in like manner killed by two balls entering his back.

"Mr. Samuel Maverick, a promising youth of seventeen years of age, son of the widow Maverick, mortally wounded; a ball went through his belly, and was cut out at his back: he died the next morning.

"A lad, named Christopher Monk, about seventeen years of age, apprentice to Mr. Walker, shipwright, wounded: a ball entered his back about four inches above the left kidney, near the spine, and was cut out of the breast on the same side: apprehended he will die.

"A lad, named John Clark, about seventeen years of age, whose parents live at Medford, wounded: a ball entered just below his groin, and came out at his hip, on the opposite side: apprehended he will die.

"Mr. Edward Payne, of this town, merchant, standing at his entry-door, received a ball in his arm, which shattered some of the bones.

"Mr. John Green, tailor, coming up Leverett's-lane, received a ball just under his hip, and lodged in the under part of his thigh, which was extracted.

"Mr. Robert Paterson, a seafaring man, wounded: a ball went through his right arm, and he suffered great loss of blood.

"Mr. Patrick Carr, about 30 years of age, who worked with Mr. Field, leather breeches maker, in Queen-street, wounded: a ball entered near his hip, and went out at his side.

"A lad, named David Parker, an apprentice to Mr. Eddy, the wheelwright, wounded: a ball entered his thigh.

"The people were immediately alarmed with the report of this horrid massacre, the bells were set a ringing, and great numbers soon assembled

assembled at the place where this tragical scene had been acted: their feelings may be better conceived than expressed; and while some were taking care of the dead and wounded, the rest were in consultation what to do in those dreadful circumstances. But so little intimidated were they, notwithstanding their being within a few yards of the main-guard, and seeing the 29th regiment under arms, and drawn up in King-street, that they kept their station, and appeared, as an officer of rank expressed it, ready to run upon the very muzzles of their muskets. The Lieut. Governor soon came into the Townhouse, and there met some of his Majesty's council, and a number of civil magistrates: a considerable body of the people immediately entered the council-chamber, and expressed themselves to his Honour with a freedom and warmth becoming the occasion. He used his utmost endeavours to pacify them, requesting that they would let the matter subside for the night, and promising to do all in his power that justice should be done, and the law have its course. Men of influence and weight with the people were not wanting on their part to procure their compliance, by representing the horrible consequence of a promiscuous and rash engagement in the night. The inhabitants attended to these suggestions, and the regiment under arms being ordered to their barracks, they separated, and returned to their dwellings by one o'clock. At three o'clock Captain Preston was committed to prison, as were the soldiers who fired a few hours after him.

"Tuesday morning presented a most shocking scene, the blood of our fellow-citizens running like water through King-street and the Merchants' Exchange, the principal spot of the military parade for above 18 months past. Our blood might also be tracked up to the head of Long-lane, and through divers other streets and passages.

"At eleven o'clock the inhabitants met at Faneuil-hall, and after some animated speeches they chose a committee of fifteen respectable gentlemen to wait upon the Lieut. Governor in council, to request of him to issue his orders for the immediate removal of the troops.

The Message was in these words.

"That it is the unanimous opinion of this meeting, that the inhabitants and soldiery can no longer live together in safety; that nothing can rationally be expected to restore the peace of the town, and prevent farther blood and carnage, but the immediate removal of the troops; and that we therefore most fervently pray his Honour that his power and influence may be exerted for their instant removal."

His Honour's Reply.

"Gentlemen,

"I am extremely sorry for the unhappy differences between the inhabitants and troops, and especially for the action of the last evening, and I have exerted myself upon that occasion, that a due enquiry may be made, and that the law may have its course. I have in council consulted with the commanding officers of the two regiments who are in the town. They have their orders from the General at New York. It is not in my power to countermand those orders. The council have desired that the two regiments may be removed to the Castle. From the particular concern which the 29th regiment has had in your differences, Colonel Dalrymple, who is the commanding officer of the troops, has fignified that that regiment shall, without delay, be placed in the barracks at the Castle, until he can send to the General, and receive his farther orders concerning both the regiments; and that the mainguard shall be removed, and the 14th regiment so disposed and laid under such restraint, that all occasion of future disturbances may be prevented."

The foregoing Reply having been read and fully considered—the question was put, Whether the report be satisfactory? Passed in the negative, only one dissentient out of upwards of 4000 voters.

"It was then moved, that John Hancock, Esq. Mr. Samuel Adams, Mr. William Molineux, William Philips, Esq. Dr. Joseph Warren, Joshua Henshaw, Esq. and Samuel Pemberton, Esq. be a Committee to wait on his Honour the Lieutenant-governor, and inform him, that the reply made to the vote of the inhabitants is by no means satisfactory; and that nothing less will satisfy than a total and immediate removal of all the troops."

"The Committee having waited upon the Lieutenant-governor, his Honour laid before the Board a vote of the town of Boston, passed this afternoon, and then addressed the Board as follows:

"*Gentlemen of the Council*,

"I lay before you a vote of the town of Boston, which I have just now received from them, and I now ask your advice, what you judge necessary to be done upon it."

"The Council thereupon expressed themselves to be *unanimously* of opinion, 'that it was absolutely necessary for his Majesty's service, the good order of the town, and the peace of the province, that the troops should be immediately removed out of the town of Boston;' with which opinion Colonel Dalrymple gave his word of honour that he would acquiesce."

Upon the above report, the inhabitants expressed the highest satisfaction; and after measures were taken for the security of the town, the meeting was dissolved.

A most solemn procession was made through Boston at the funeral of the four murdered youths. On this occasion all the shops were shut up, all the bells in the town were ordered to toll, as were those in the neighbouring towns, and the bodies that moved from different quarters of the town met at the fatal place of action, and were carried together through the main streets, followed by the greatest concourse of people ever known, all testifying the most sensible grief, to a vault provided for them in the middle of the great burying ground.

From the time of this fatal tragedy, a military guard of town militia has been constantly kept in the Town-house and Town-prison, at which some of the most respectable citizens have done duty as common soldiers.

In consequence of this affair, the inhabitants of Roxburg petitioned the Lieutenant-governor Hutchinson to remove the troops from Boston; and received for answer, *That he had no authority to order the King's troops from any place where*

APPENDIX to the CHRONICLE.

where they are posted by his Majesty's order; at the same time he acquainted them with what had been done, with the concurrence of the commanding officer.

Case of Captain Thomas Preston, of the 29th Regiment.

IT is matter of too great notoriety to need any proofs, that the arrival of his Majesty's troops in Boston was extremely obnoxious to its inhabitants. They have ever used all means in their power to weaken the regiments, and to bring them into contempt, by promoting and aiding desertions, and with impunity, even where there has been the clearest evidence of the fact, and by grosly and falsely propagating untruths concerning them. On the arrival of the 64th and 65th, their ardour seemingly began to abate; it being too expensive to buy off many, and attempts of that kind rendered too dangerous from the numbers. But the same spirit revived immediately on its being known that those regiments were ordered for Hallifax, and hath ever since their departure been breaking out with greater violence. After their embarkation, one of their Justices, thoroughly acquainted with the people and their intentions, on the trial of the 14th regiment, openly and publicly, in the hearing of great numbers of people, and from the seat of justice, declared, " that the soldiers must now take care of themselves, *nor trust too much to their arms,* for they were but a handful; that the inhabitants carried weapons, concealed under their clothes, and would destroy them in a moment, if they pleased." This, considering the malicious temper of the people, was an alarming circumstance to the soldiery. Since which several disputes have happened between the town's people and soldiers of both regiments, the former being encouraged thereto by the countenance of even some of the Magistrates, and by the protection of all the party against Government. In general, such disputes have been kept too secret from the officers. On the 2d instant, two of the 29th going through one Gray's ropewalk, the rope-makers insultingly asked them if they would empty a vault. This unfortunately had the desired effect by provoking the soldiers, and from words they went to blows. Both parties suffered in this affray, and finally the soldiers retired to their quarters. The officers, on the first knowledge of this transaction, took every precaution in their power to prevent any ill consequences. Notwithstanding which, single quarrels could not be prevented; the inhabitants constantly provoking and abusing the soldiery. The insolence as well as utter hatred of the inhabitants to the troops increased daily; insomuch, that Monday and Tuesday, the 5th and 6th instant, were privately agreed on for a general engagement; in consequence of which several of the militia came from the country, armed, to join their friends, menacing to destroy any who should oppose them. This plan has since been discovered.

On Monday night, about eight o'clock, two soldiers were attacked and beat. But the party of the town's people, in order to carry matters to the utmost length, broke into two meeting-houses, and rang the

the alarm-bells, which I supposed was for fire, as usual, but was soon undeceived. About nine some of the guard came to, and informed me, the town inhabitants were assembling to attack the troops, and that the bells were ringing as the signal for that purpose, and not for fire, and the beacon intended to be fired to bring in the distant people of the country. This, as I was Captain of the day, occasioned my repairing immediately to the main-guard. In my way there I saw the people in great commotion, and heard them use the most cruel and horrid threats against the troops. In a few minutes after I reached the guard, about an hundred people passed it, and went towards the Custom-house, where the King's money is lodged. They immediately surrounded the centinel posted there, and with clubs and other weapons threatened to execute their vengeance on him. I was soon informed by a town's man, their intention was to carry off the soldier from his post, and probably murder him. On which I desired him to return for farther intelligence; and he soon came back, and assured me he heard the mob declare they would murder him. This I feared might be a prelude to their plundering the King's chest. I immediately sent a non-commissioned officer and twelve men to protect both the centinel and the King's money, and very soon followed myself to prevent (if possible) all disorder; fearing left the officer and soldiery by the insults and provocations of the rioters should be thrown off their guard, and commit some rash act. They soon rushed through the people, and, by charging their bayonets in a half circle, kept them at a little distance. Nay, so far was I from intending the death of any person, that I suffered the troops to go to the spot where the unhappy affair took place, without any loading in their pieces, nor did I ever give orders for loading them. This remiss conduct in me, perhaps, merits censure; yet it is evidence, resulting from the nature of things, which is the best and surest that can be offered, that my attention was not to act offensively, but the contrary part, and that not without compulsion. The mob still increased, and were more outrageous, striking their clubs or bludgeons one against another, and calling out, ' Come on, you rascals, you ' bloody backs, you lobster scoun- ' rels; fire if you dare, G—damn ' you, fire, and be damn'd: we know ' you dare not;' and much more such language was used. At this time I was between the soldiers and the mob, parleying with and endeavouring all in my power to persuade them to retire peaceably; but to no purpose. They advanced to the points of the bayonets, struck some of them, and even the muzzles of the pieces, and seemed to be endeavouring to close with the soldiers. On which some well behaved persons asked me if the guns were charged? I replied, yes, They then asked me if I intended to order the men to fire? I answered no, by no means; observing to them, that I was advanced before the muzzles of the men's pieces, and must fall a sacrifice if they fired; that the soldiers were upon the half-cock and charged bayonets, and my giving the word fire, on those circumstances, would prove me no officer. While I was thus speaking,

one

one of the soldiers, having received a severe blow with a stick, stepped a little on one side, and instantly fired; on which turning to, and asking him why he fired without orders, I was struck with a club on my arm, which for some time deprived me of the use of it; which blow, had it been placed on my head, most probably would have destroyed me. On this a general attack was made on the men by a great number of heavy clubs, and snow-balls being thrown at them, by which all our lives were in imminent danger; some persons at the same time from behind calling out, 'Damn your bloods, why do not you fire?' Instantly three or four of the soldiers fired, one after another, and directly after three more in the same confusion and hurry.

The mob then ran away, except three unhappy men who instantly expired, in which number was Mr. Gray, at whose rope-walk the prior quarrel took place: one more is since dead, three others are dangerously and four slightly wounded. The whole of this melancholy affair was transacted in almost twenty minutes. On my asking the soldiers why they fired without orders, they said they heard the word 'Fire,' and supposed it came from me. This might be the case, as many of the mob called out, 'Fire, fire:' but I assured the men that I gave no such order, that my words were, 'Don't fire, stop your firing.' In short, it was scarcely possible for the soldiers to know who said fire, or don't fire, or stop your firing. On the people's assembling again to take away the dead bodies, the soldiers, supposing them coming to attack them, were making ready to fire again, which I prevented by striking up their firelocks with my hand. Immediately after a town's man came and told me, that 4,000 or 5,000 people were assembled in the next street, and had sworn to take my life, with every man's with me; on which I judged it unsafe to remain there any longer, and therefore sent the party and sentry to the main-guard, and when they arrived there, telling them off into street firings, divided and planted them at each end of the street to secure their rear, momently expecting an attack, as there was a constant cry of the inhabitants, 'To arms, to arms—turn out with your guns,' and the town drums beating to arms. I ordered my drum to beat to arms, and being soon after joined by the different companies of the 29th regiment, I formed them as the guard into street firings. The 14th regiment also got under arms, but remained at their barracks. I immediately sent a sergeant with a party to Colonel Dalrymple, the commanding officer, to acquaint him with every particular. Several officers going to join their regiment were knocked down by the mob, one very much wounded, and his sword taken from him. The Lieutenant-governor and Colonel Carr were soon after met at the head of the 29th regiment, and agreed that the regiment should retire to their barracks, and the people to their houses; but I kept the piquet to strengthen the guard. It was with great difficulty that the Lieutenant-governor prevailed on the people to be quiet, and retire: at last they all went off, excepting about a hundred.

A coun-

A council was immediately called, on the breaking up of which three justices met, and issued a warrant to apprehend me and eight soldiers. On hearing of this procedure, I instantly went to the sheriff, and surrendered myself, though for the space of four hours I had it in my power to have made my escape, which I most undoubtedly should have attempted, and could easily have executed, had I been the least conscious of any guilt. On the examination before the justices, two witnesses swore that I gave the men orders to fire: the one testified he was within two feet of me; the other, that I swore at the men for not firing at the first word. Others swore they heard me use the word, fire; but whether do or do not fire, they could not say; others, that they heard the word fire, but could not say it came from me. The next day they got five or six more to swear I gave the word to fire. So bitter and inveterate are many of the malecontents here, that they are industriously using every method to fish out evidence to prove it was a concerted scheme to murder the inhabitants. Others are infusing the utmost malice and revenge into the minds of the people, who are to be my jurors, by false publications, votes of towns, and all other artifices. That so, from a settled rancour against the officers and troops in general, the suddenness of my trial after the affair, while the people's minds are all greatly inflamed, I am, though perfectly innocent, under most unhappy circumstances, having nothing in reason to expect but the loss of life in a very ignominious manner, without the interposition of his Majesty's justice and goodness.

An Account of the Trial of Captain Preston, at Boston, in New England.

THE trial began on Wednesday, the 24th of October, and was continued from day to day, Sunday excepted, till Tuesday the 30th. The witnesses who were examined on both sides amounted to about 50. The lawyers for the crown were Mr. Barne and Mr. Samuel Quincy; for the prisoner, Mr. Auchmuty and Mr. John Adams. Each of them spoke three hours at least. About Monday noon the judges began their charge. Judge Trowbridge, who spoke first, entered largely into the contradictory accounts given by the witnesses, and declared, that it did not appear to him that the prisoner gave orders to fire; but if the jury should think otherwise, and find it proved that he did give such orders, the question then would naturally be, What crime is he guilty of? They surely could not call it murder.—Here he explained the crime of murder in a very distinct manner, and gave it as his opinion, that by law the prisoner was not guilty of murder; observing, that the King had a right to send his troops here; that the commanding officer of these troops had a right to place a centinel at the Custom-house; that the centinel placed there on the night of the 5th of March was in the King's peace; that he durst not quit his post; that, if he was insulted or attacked, the captain of the guard had a right to protect him; that the prisoner and his party who came there for that purpose were in the King's peace; that while they were at the Custom-house, for the purpose

pose of protecting the centinel, it was plainly proved that they had been assaulted by a great number of people; that the people assembled there were not in the King's peace, but were by law considered as a riotous mob, as they attacked the prisoner and his party with pieces of ice, sticks, and clubs; and that even one of the witnesses against him confessed he was armed with a Highland broadsword; that the rioters had knocked down one of the soldiers of the party, laid hold of several of their muskets; and that, before the soldiers fired, the cry was, Knock them down! Kill them! Kill them! That all this was sworn to by the witnesses, and, if the jury believed them, the prisoner could not be found guilty of murder. He then proceeded to explain what the law considered as manslaughter, and observed, as before, that if they give credit to the witnesses, who testified the assaults made on the prisoner and his party, they could not find him guilty of manslaughter; and concluded with saying, that if he was guilty of any offence, it could only be excusable homicide; that this was only founded on the supposition of the prisoner's having given orders to fire, for if this was not proved, they must acquit him.

Judge Oliver, who spoke next, began with representing, in a very nervous and pathetic manner, the insults and outrages which he, and the court through him, had received on a former occasion (meaning the trial of Richardson), for giving his opinion on a point of law; that, notwithstanding, he was resolved to do his duty to his God, his King, and his country; that he despised both insults and threats, and that he would not forego a moment's peace of conscience for the applause of millions. He agreed in sentiment with the former judge, that the prisoner was not guilty.

Judge Cushing spoke next, and agreed entirely with the other two, with regard to the prisoner's case.

Judge Lyndex concluded. He spoke a considerable time, and was of the same opinion with the other judges. Towards the close of his speech he said, "Happy I am to find, that, after such strict examination, the conduct of the prisoner appears in so fair a light; yet I feel myself, at the same time, deeply affected, that this affair turns out so much to the disgrace of every person concerned against him, and so much to the shame of the town in general." The jury returned their verdict, *Not Guilty*. He was immediately discharged, and is now in the Castle. Great numbers attended during the whole trial, which was carried on with a solemn decency.

Account of the Trial of Mungo Campbell, *for the Murder of* Alexander, *Earl of* Eglingtoun.

THE account of the prisoner, of the fact for which he was tried, and the law by which he was condemned to die for murder, are in substance as follow:

Mungo Campbell was born at Ayre, in Scotland, in the year 1712, being in the 58th year of his age when the dispute happened in which Lord Eglingtoun was killed. He was one of 24 children, and his father was Provost of Ayre, a man much respected as a merchant and

and a magistrate, and descended from the noble families of Marchmont, Loudon, and Argyle. Having, however, a large family, and sustaining many considerable losses, he died, in indifferent circumstances, and his children were dispersed among the relations and friends of the family. Mungo, who at his father's death was an infant, was taken by his godfather, who, dying soon afterwards, left him about 1000 merks*, and recommended him to a relation, who educated him with his own children, till he was about 18 years old.

As he had not money enough to go into trade, or to support him in a course of study for any of the learned professions, he enlisted in the Scots Greys, a regiment which was commanded by a namesake and relation, from whom he hoped preferment. He served in this corps 12 years, and was, among other engagements, at the battle of Dettingen, yet he obtained no preferment; he was once offered a quarter-master's place, worth about 300l. if he would advance 100l.; but not being able to procure such a sum, he soon after obtained his discharge, which is dated 1744.

In 1745, he returned into Scotland, where he found his countrymen in arms against each other: he accompanied his chief and kinsman, Lord Loudon, in the Highlands; and, after their return, his Lordship procured him a commission as officer of the excise, with a recommendation to station him in Ayreshire, that he might be among his relations and friends in his native spot.

'Upon this duty he entered in 1746, four-and-twenty years ago, and was at length finally stationed at Saltcoats, where he would have chosen rather to continue than to have been raised to a higher office, which would have carried him from his native spot. Being known and esteemed by the neighbouring gentry, he had licences from Lord Loudon, and many others, to hunt upon their grounds, with authority to preserve the game, and prosecute poachers. He had, however, no such licence from Lord Eglingtoun. Of these licences he did not avail himself often, being, especially of late time, infirm, having a disorder in his breast, and a lameness from a broken leg: he used now and then to kill a little game as presents for his friends, but never sold a bird in his life, nor was ever considered as a common fowler or poacher. In the year 1766 he sold his pointer, and never afterwards had a dog; but he kept his gun, which was necessary, as the smugglers, whom it was his duty to detect, always went armed; and with his gun he sometimes shot sparrows, and sometimes gulls, as he passed along the shore. Lord Eglingtoun, who was very strict in preserving the game, prohibited all persons from fishing in the waters of Garnock by public advertisement; and Campbell, to avoid all possibility of offending his Lordship in this particular, gave away his fishing rod, which was very curious and valuable, to an acquaintance

---

* About 55l. 12s. sterling.

acquaintance of his Lordship's, Mr. Lietch, of Glasgow.

It happened, however, that Campbell one day last spring being out in search of smuggled goods, with some others, saw a hare start out of a bush at the side of the highway on Lord Eglingtoun's grounds, which, he says, partly from surprize, and possibly from the instigation of those with him, he shot, having before shot two gulls in the course of their walk.

Lord Eglingtoun, who was then at Park House, very near the spot, heard the gun, and dispatched a servant to enquire about it. Campbell related the fact, as it is related here; but Lord Eglingtoun not being satisfied, sent the servant back with one Bartleymore, another servant, and required Campbell to come to him.

He accordingly returned with them to his Lordship, who used many harsh expressions; but Campbell asking his pardon, and promising never more to offend, they parted, as he says, without any demand being made of his gun, Lord Eglingtoun knowing that he was no poacher.

There are, however, two credible witnesses, lieutenants in the army, who swear, that, being in company with Campbell at Saltcoats, and talking about game, Campbell said that he had been severely challenged by Lord Eglingtoun for shooting a hare, and that his Lordship had threatened to take his gun from him, but had not persisted in the demand; that he had then told his Lordship he would rather die than part with his gun; adding, with an oath, that if Lord Eglingtoun had persisted to take his gun from him, he would have shot him.

If the testimony of these witnesses is true, Campbell's assertion, that Lord Eglingtoun never would have demanded his gun but for the instigation of Bartleymore, is false.

Bartleymore, however, appears to have been much more criminal than any trespass to shoot game could make Campbell. This fellow, a favourite servant of Lord Eglingtoun's, abusing his Lord's confidence, employed his horses and his cart to smuggle goods. On the 8th of last July, Campbell, in consequence of previous information, detected him driving off 80 gallons of rum with a cart and horse of Lord Eglingtoun's. Campbell and his assistants seized the rum; but the horse and cart appearing to be my Lord's property, were not taken, nor condemned with the rest. It may easily be supposed that this event produced much enmity between Campbell and Bartleymore, especially on the side of Bartleymore, who did the wrong. What influence it had on the fatal affair of the 24th of October the reader must judge.

On the morning of that day, about ten o'clock, Campbell, in company with one Brown, a tidewaiter, set out from Saltcoats, principally, as he says, with a view to examine several places that were the known haunts of smugglers, but at the same time to amuse themselves by shooting: for both these purposes they proposed to walk from Saltcoats to Montfod Bank, by a common road that led through Lord Eglingtoun's grounds, and return by another along the sea-shore. They had no dog, neither had Brown a gun; they proposed only to look for a woodcock on Montfod Bank, which was not game, and therefore Campbell had no need of Dr. Hunter's licence, which, however, was in his pocket.

When they arrived at Montfod, about three miles distant from Saltcoats, they searched the wood for a cock, but found none; and then passed from Montfod over the Burn, into Lord Eglingtoun's grounds, and walked along the shore within the sea-mark, looking for a shot of plover.

In the mean time, Lord Eglingtoun set out from his house in a coach, attended by one Wilson, called a *Wright*, who was employed in some of his Lordship's works, John Millikin, John Hazel, John Cooper, and James Hutcheson, servants, on horseback; they stopped some time at Park House, to the N. W. of Saltcoats, where they were joined by Bartleymore, and proposed to go on to Ardrossan and Fairly. When they got about half a mile from Park House, in their way to Fairly, one of the servants having discovered Campbell and Brown, told Lord Eglingtoun that he observed more shooters, having seen some that day before. Wilson endeavoured to divert his Lordship from taking notice of them, as they had a pretty long ride before them; but he asked who they were, and being told by Bartleymore that one of them was Campbell, he came out of the coach, and, mounting a horse which was led by one of his servants, without whip, stick, or weapon of any kind, he rode towards the persons he saw, who were retired from the ground where they had been first discovered towards the sea-sands: when he came within about ten yards of them, he said, "Mr. Campbell, I did not expect to have found you so soon hunting upon my grounds, after your promise when you shot the hare;" at the same time demanding his gun. Campbell refused to deliver it; upon which Lord Eglingtoun gave his horse a kick, having no spurs on, to get nearer to him. Campbell retreated, and desired his Lordship to keep off, pointing his gun towards him, not raising it to his shoulder, but having his hand upon the lock. Lord Eglingtoun then stopped his horse, and said, smiling, "Are you going to shoot me?" to which the other answered, "I will, if you do not keep off." Lord Eglingtoun then dismounted, and said, that if he had his gun he could shoot pretty well, too; and immediately called to John Hazel, who was near him, "John, bring me my gun." Hazel accordingly went back to the coach in which the gun lay, and giving it to Millikin, another servant, ordered him to carry it as fast as possible to my Lord. Millikin took the gun; but it being his office to take care of the arms, and carry the ammunition, he knew it was not charged: he primed it, however, endeavouring to charge it as he went along.

In the mean time Lord Eglingtoun advanced some steps towards Campbell, leading his horse in his hand, and many times desired him to deliver up his gun, which he as often refused. Lord Eglingtoun then dropped the bridle, which Wilson, being at hand, took up, and continued to advance towards Campbell, who still retired, sometimes

APPENDIX to the CHRONICLE.

times backward and sometimes sideways, but always pointing his gun towards Lord Eglingtoun. While his Lordship was thus advancing, or dodging, Campbell said, "I beg your pardon, my Lord;"—to which my Lord replied, "Well, then, deliver me your gun." Campbell said again, "I beg pardon, my Lord; I will deliver my gun to no man: keep off, or by God I will shoot you." After some farther altercation, which was not heard by any of the bystanders, Bartleymore came up and said, "For God's sake, Mr. Campbell, deliver up your gun to my Lord;" to which Campbell replied he would not, for that he had a right to carry a gun. Lord Eglingtoun said, "You may have a right to carry a gun, but not upon my lands without my liberty." Campbell replied, "I ask your pardon," and still continuing to retreat, with the gun pointed to Lord Eglingtoun, and his thumb upon the cock, he struck his foot against a stone, and fell backward, and by the force of the fall the gun flew up, and, passing the perpendicular, pointed backwards. Lord Eglingtoun, seeing him lie on his back, stopped a little, and then moved his left foot, as if intending to pass by Campbell's feet; upon which he raised himself upon his elbow, pointed the gun at Lord Eglingtoun, and fired it into the left side of his body, not being more than three yards distant.

At this time Millikin was got within about twenty yards with Lord Eglingtoun's gun; but Lord Eglingtoun having received the shot, laid his hand upon the wound, walked a few paces, and said he was gone. Millikin rushed forwards, attacked Campbell, who had recovered his legs, and endeavoured to secure him. Campbell stood upon his defence, and would have wrested the gun from Millikin, if Bartleymore had not run to his assistance: in the struggle they gave Campbell several severe blows, upon which Lord Eglingtoun called out "Don't use him ill." When he was secured, one of the attendants carried him up to my Lord, who was lying upon the ground; and my Lord, looking at him, said, "Campbell, I would not have shot you:" to which the unhappy wretch made no reply.

Lord Eglingtoun was borne to his coach, and in that carried back to his house. Campbell, having his hands tied behind him, was carried prisoner to Saltcoats: upon his way thither he was asked what his gun was charged with? to which he replied, "It did not signify, as he had got as much as would do for him, if he was all the earls in Scotland." He was farther asked if he was not sorry for what he had done? to which he replied, "No; for I would yield my gun to no man: if it was to do, I would do it again; for I would rather part with my life than my gun."

The witnesses all seemed to agree, that during the altercation both my Lord and Campbell appeared to be angry. Brown, the tidewaiter, who was with Campbell, ran away almost as soon as Lord Eglingtoun came up.

About nine o'clock in the evening of the same day, Lord Eglingtoun was visited by a surgeon: when he entered the room, his Lordship, who was in bed, said, "I am glad to see you; but you can be of no use to me now: it is all over." Upon searching the wound, the shot appeared to have entered the left side, and torn the bowels, in the passage to the right, in a dreadful manner: some part had entered the liver, and the belly was full of extravasated blood: his Lordship died a little after twelve o'clock.

It was urged in defence of the prisoner upon the trial, 1st, "That the gun went off by accident. 2dly, That, supposing it to have been fired with an intention to kill, the act was *justifiable*, being done upon just provocation, and in defence of property and life. And, 3dly, Supposing the fact not justifiable, it could not be murder, the homicide being sudden, and during an affray, and not from malice."

It was answered, first, that there was indubitable evidence of Campbell's declaring an *intention* to kill the Earl, if he persisted in the attempt to seize his gun: 2dly, That the fact, if *intentional*, was not justifiable for these reasons: 1st, There was no provocation, nothing but words being pretended, and words not being esteemed provocation in law. 2dly, The Earl had a right to seize the prisoner's gun; for by act 13, parl. 1707, it is expresly enacted, "that no common fowler shall presume to hunt on any grounds without a warrant from the proprietor, under the penalty, among others, of *forfeiting* dogs, *guns*, and nets, to the apprehender or discoverer; from which it follows, that the apprehender has a right to seize dogs, *guns*, and nets. Nor is this new in law, for all statutes against smuggling authorize the officers of the revenue to begin with seizing the goods, leaving it afterwards to be tried whether they have been justly seized or not. 3dly, It is of no moment whether the prisoner was or was not on the Earl's ground when the gun was demanded: he had been upon the Earl's ground immediately before, under the Earl's observation; and as it must be presumed that as he was there with an intention to kill game, if he had found any, the Earl had the same right to seize his gun as if he had got up with him before he left the grounds; so that the act not being justifiable, was, under these circumstances, murder.

He was sentenced to be hanged on the 11th day of April then next, and to have his body given to Dr. Monro, professor of anatomy, to be dissected; but on the 28th of February, the day after sentence was passed upon him, he hanged himself, by fastening a handkerchief to the end of a form which he set upright for that purpose.

Genuine Copy of a Letter sent by a Committee of the Supporters of the Bill of Rights to the Honourable the Commons House of Assembly of South Carolina, in Answer to the Letter from the Assembly of South Carolina, concerning a Subscription to the Society of Fifteen Hundred Pounds sterling.

To the Hon. Commons House of Assembly of South Carolina.

"Gentlemen,

WE are directed by the Society, Supporters of the Bill of Rights, to transmit to you their

their thanks for the very honourable testimony you have at once given of your own sentiments, and of your approbation of their conduct.

'The same spirit of union and mutual assistance which dictated your vote in our favour animates this Society. We shall ever consider the rights of all our fellow-subjects throughout the British empire, in England, Scotland, Ireland, and America, as stones of one arch, on which the happiness and security of the whole are founded. Such would have been our principle of action, if the system of despotism which has been adopted had been more artfully conducted; and we should as readily have associated in the defence of your rights as our own, had they been separately attacked.

'But Providence has mercifully allotted to depraved hearts weak understandings: the attack has been made by the same men, at the same time, on both together, and will serve only to draw us closer in one great band of mutual friendship and support.

'Whilst the Norman troops of the first William kept the English in subjection, his English soldiers were employed to secure the obedience of the Normans. This management has been too often repeated now to succeed.

'There was a time when Scotland, though then a separate and divided nation, could avoid the snare, and refused, even under their own Stuarts, to enslave their antient enemies. The chains which England and Scotland disdained to forge for each other, England and America shall never consent to furnish.

'Property is the natural right of mankind; the connection between taxation and representation is its necessary consequence. This connection is now broken, and taxes are attempted to be levied, both in England and America, by men who are not their respective representatives. Our cause is one—our enemies are the same. We trust our constancy and conduct will not differ. Demands which are made without authority should be heard without obedience.

'In this, and in every other constitutional struggle on either side of the Atlantic, we wish to be united with you, and are as ready to give as to receive assistance.

'We desire you, gentlemen, to be persuaded, that, under all our domestic grievances and apprehensions, the freedom of America is our particular attention; and these your public act and solemn engagement afford us a pleasing presage, and confirm our hopes, that, when luxury, misrule, and corruption, shall at length, in spite of all resistance, have destroyed this noble constitution here, our posterity will not, like your gallant ancestors, be driven to an inhospitable shore, but will find a welcome refuge, where they may still enjoy the rights of Englishmen amongst their fellow-subjects, the descendants and brothers of Englishmen,

We are, gentlemen,
  With the greatest respect,
    Your most obedient servants
      and affectionate fellow-
  Signed   subjects,
JOHN GLYNN,   Chairman.
RICHARD OLIVER, } Treasurers.
JOHN TREVANION,
ROBERT BERNARD,
JOSEPH MAWBEY, } Committee.'
JAMES TOWNSEND,
JOHN SAWBRIDGE,

Abstract

Abstract of an Act to regulate the Trials of controverted Elections, or Returns of Members to serve in Parliament.

AS the present mode of decision upon petitions complaining of undue elections or returns of members to serve in parliament frequently obstructs public business, occasions much expence, trouble, and delay to the parties, is defective, for want of those sanctions and solemnities which are established by law in other trials, and is attended with many other inconveniencies, for remedy thereof, it is hereby enacted, that, after the present session, on complaint of undue election or return, a precise time is to be fixed for considering thereof. The Speaker is to give notice thereof, and order attendance; but not within 14 days after appointment of the Committee of Privileges. The House may alter the time on like notice and order. The Sergeant at Arms, before the reading of the orders of the day, is to require the attendance of the members, and at his return the House is to be counted, which for want of a hundred members is to adjourn, till a hundred be present. In presence of a hundred, the petitioners, with their counsel, agents, &c. are to be ordered to the bar; and then the names of all the members of the House are to be put into six boxes or glasses; to be drawn alternately, and read by the Speaker, till forty-nine be drawn. Voting members at the election, or complainants, are to be set aside. All above sixty years old are excused, or those who have served on a select committee in the same session, unless the number who have not served be insufficient. Members excused shall not be deemed to have served; and, members verifying other excuses, their allegations are to be entered; and if the House resolve that they are unable to serve, they are to be excused; instead of whom, others are to be drawn to complete the number forty-nine. Petitioners may name one, and sitting members another, who may for like causes be set aside, or excused, and others named. The door of the House, that, during this business of chusing by lot, was kept locked, is then to be opened, and the House may proceed on other business. Lists of the forty-nine are to be then given to the petitioners, their counsel, agents, &c. who, with the Clerk, are to withdraw, and to strike off one alternately, till the number be reduced to thirteen. The Clerk, with in one hour, is to deliver a list of them; and they, with the nominees, shall be sworn a select committee, and the House is to order them to meet in twenty-four hours. On the parties withdrawing, as aforesaid, the House shall continue sitting; and the fifty-one members, so chosen and nominated, shall not depart the House till the time for the meeting of the said select committee shall be fixed. Petitioners, &c. declaring that any member drawn is intended for a nominee, and the member consenting thereto, he is to serve as such, and another is to be drawn to supply his place; but, on neglect of nomination, deficiencies are to be supplied by lot, leaving always fifteen as a select committee. Previous to taking any such petition into consideration, the Clerk is to put the

APPENDIX to the CHRONICLE. [227

the names of the members drawn into a box or parcel, and attest the same; and the Speaker is to seal the same, and attest the making up thereof in his presence. The names of members undrawn may be read by the Clerk. The Chairman is to be elected out of the members chosen by lot; and, in case of equality in election, the member first drawn to have a casting voice. Such select committee is impowered to send for persons, papers, and records; to examine witnesses, and determine finally. The House thereupon is to confirm, or alter, the return; or issue a new writ for a new election. The select committee is not to adjourn for more than twenty-four hours, without leave; and, if the House be then sitting, business is to be stayed, and motion made for farther adjournment. Sunday or Christmas day intervening are not to be deemed included. A select committee-man is not to absent himself without leave, nor the committee to sit, till all who have not leave be met. On failure of meeting within one hour, a farther adjournment is to be made, and reported with the cause thereof. The Chairman, at next meeting, is to report the absentees, who are directed to attend next fitting; and censured or punished at discretion, unless unavoidable absence be proved. If thirteen do not attend, the committee is to adjourn; and if less for three days, then it is to be dissolved, and another chosen; and past proceedings are to be void. The resolutions of the committee, other than the determination of complaint, may be reported, and the House may make such order thereon as to them shall seem proper. Persons disobeying summons, or prevaricating, are to be reported to the Chairman. When the committee chuse to deliberate, the room is to be cleared. Questions are to be determined by a majority, the Chairman to have a casting vote, and no determination to take place unless thirteen be present; nor any member to vote who has not attended every sitting. The oath taken in the House is to be administered by the Clerk, and those before the select committee by the Clerk. The penalties on perjury are extended thereto. This act is to continue in force seven years, and till the end of the session of parliament next after the expiration of the said seven years, and no longer.

Abstract of an Act for the better Preservation of the Game within that part of Great Britain called England.

THE game having of late been much destroyed at improper seasons, in that part of Great Britain called England: For remedying thereof, it is hereby enacted, that if, after June 24, 1770, any person or persons shall wilfully, upon any pretence whatsoever, take, kill, or destroy, any hare, pheasant, partridge, moor game, heath game, or grouse, in the night, between one hour after sun-setting and one hour before sun-rising; or use any gun, dog, snare, net, or other engine, for taking, killing, or destroying, any hare, pheasant, &c. in the night, as aforesaid; and shall be convicted thereof

thereof upon the oath or oaths of one or more credible witness or witnesses, before any one or more justice or justices of the peace for any county, riding, division, or place; every such person shall, for the first offence, be imprisoned not less than three months; and, for other offence, not less than six months; and for each to be publicly whipped. Offenders on Sunday, using any gun or engine for destroying game, on conviction are to forfeit 20l. to be levied by distress with charges, and to be applied to the informer and the poor: for want of such distress, the offender is to be committed for any time not exceeding six calendar months, nor less than three. Persons aggrieved may appeal to the quarter-sessions, giving fourteen days notice to persons complained against. The justices are to hear, determine, and award costs; and their determination is to be final, and not to be removed by certiorari.

Abstract of an Act for preventing the Stealing of Dogs.

THE practice of stealing dogs having of late years greatly increased: For remedy thereof, it is hereby enacted, that from and after the first of May, 1770, if any person shall steal any dog or dogs, of any kind or sort whatsoever, from the owner or owners thereof, or from any person or persons entrusted by the owner or owners thereof with such dog or dogs; or shall sell, buy, receive, harbour, detain, or keep, any dog or dogs, of any kind or sort whatsoever, knowing the same to have been stolen, every such person, upon being convicted thereof upon the oath of one or more credible witness or witnesses, or by his or her own confession, before any two or more justices of the peace for any county, riding, division, or place, shall for the first offence forfeit not less than 20l. and charges of conviction; or, till the penalty and charges are paid, be committed to gaol, for any time not exceeding twelve calendar months, nor less than six, or until the penalty and charges shall be paid. A person guilty of a subsequent offence is to forfeit not less than 30l. and charges, to be paid to the informer and the poor; and on non-payment to be imprisoned 12 months, and publicly whipped. Justices are to grant warrants to search for dogs stolen or their skins; and the persons in whose custody the dogs or their skins are found are liable to like penalties. Persons aggrieved may appeal to the quarter-sessions. Fourteen days notice of appeal are to be given. Justices are to hear, determine, and award costs; and their determination is to be final, and not to be removed by certiorari.

An Abstract of the Act for registering the Prices at which Corn is sold in the several Counties of Great Britain, and the Quantity exported and imported.

IT has by some fatality happened, that the preambles to acts of parliament, which were formerly of great use in explaining the reasons for passing them, have of late been very much shortened, or wholly omitted: the preamble to this act only suggests, that a register of the

the prices at which corn is sold in the several counties of Great Britain will be of public and general advantage: for which reason the justices of the peace for each county in Great Britain are required, at their quarter-sessions next after Sept. 29, annually to direct returns to be made weekly of the prices of wheat, rye, barley, oats, and beans, from so many market-towns within their respective counties as they shall think proper, not being less than two, nor more than six; and to appoint a proper person to send the same to a person to be appointed to receive them; and in case such person shall die, neglect his duty, or become incapable of performing it, any two justices acting for the county may appoint another till the next quarter-sessions, at which the justices may either confirm such appointment, or chuse another.

By this act, the meal weighers of the city of London are to take an account of the prices at the markets within the said city, and return the average weekly to the person appointed to receive the same.

The justices for each county shall cause also a standard Winchester bushel of eight gallons to be kept at every market-town from whence such returns shall be made; and such returns shall be the average prices by the customary measure of each respective market, and also by that Winchester bushel.

By this act the Lord High Treasurer is empowered to appoint a fit person to receive the returns at the treasury, and to enter them fairly in a book kept for that purpose; and all exports and imports of grain from and into Great Britain, with the bounties paid and received thereon, to be transmitted annually to the same person, and registered in proper books by the person appointed to receive the returns of the prices from the several counties.

No salary is allotted by this act to the person to be appointed at the treasury. It is to continue in force for seven years.

Abstract of an Act to prevent Delays of Justice by reason of Privilege of Parliament.

IT is hereby enacted, that from the 24th of June next, any person may, at any time, commence and prosecute any action or suit, in any court of record, or court of equity, or of admiralty, and in all causes matrimonial and testamentary, in any court having cognizance of causes matrimonial and testamentary, against any peer or lord of parliament of Great Britain, or against any of the knights, citizens, and burgesses, and the commissioners for shires and burghs of the House of Commons of Great Britain, or against their menial or other servants, or any other person entitled to the privilege of parliament of Great Britain; and no such action, suit, or any other process or proceeding thereupon, shall at any time be impeached, stayed, or delayed, by or under colour or pretence of any privilege of parliament.

It is nevertheless provided, that nothing in this act shall extend to subject the person of any of the members of the House of Commons to be arrested or imprisoned upon any such suit or proceedings; but, whether by neglect or design, nothing

thing is said about the imprisonment of the Lords. By this act, however, obedience may be enforced to any rule of his Majesty's courts, against any person entitled to privilege of parliament, by distress infinite; and the issues arising from such distress may be sold from time to time for payment of the plaintiff's costs.

Extraordinary Conduct of the Regulators in the Back Settlements of North Carolina.

From the New York Gazette.

Newbern, North Carolina, Oct. 5.

ON Wednesday last a special messenger arrived in town from Granville County, to his Excellency the Governor, with the melancholy account of a violent insurrection, or rather rebellion, having broke out in Orange County, among a set of men who call themselves Regulators, and who for some years past have given infinite disturbance to the civil government of this province, but now have sapped its whole foundation, and brought its courts of justice to their own controul.

These people have for a long time opposed paying all manner of taxes, have entertained the vilest opinion of the gentlemen of the law, and often threatened them with their vengeance. Accordingly, as the Hon. Judge Henderson and several gentlemen of the law were returning from Salisbury circuit to Hillsborough, to hold the court there, they were way laid by a number of them with their rifles; but happily having notice of their hellish design, by taking a contrary rout, eluded their bloody plot. They still gave out their threats of meeting them at Hillsborough, and wreaking their vengeance on them there.

These menaces were treated with contempt, or rather as the violent ravings of a factious and discontented mob, than any settled and fixed resolutions of men of property to commit so daring an insult to the laws of the country, and accordingly the court was opened, and proceeded to business: but on Monday, the second day of the court, a very large number of those people, headed by men of considerable property, appeared in Hillsborough, armed with clubs, whips loaded at the end with lead or iron, and many other offensive weapons, and at once beset the court-house. The first object of their revenge was Mr. John Williams, a gentleman of the law, who they assaulted as he was entering the court: him they cruelly abused with many and violent blows with their loaded whips on the head, and different parts of his body, until he by great good fortune made his escape, and took shelter in a neighbouring store. They then entered the court-house, and immediately fixed their attention on Colonel Fanning as the next object of their merciless cruelty: he for safety had retired to the Judge's seat, as the highest part of the court-house, from which he might make the greatest defence against these blood-thirsty and cruel savages: but vain were all his efforts, for, after behaving with the most heroic courage, he fell a sacrifice to numbers.

They seized him by the heels, dragged him down the steps, his head striking very violently on every step, carried him to the door, and

and, forcing him out, dragged him on the ground over stones and brickbats, struck him with their whips and clubs, kicked him, and spit and spurned at him, and treated him with every possible mark of contempt and cruelty; till, at length, by a violent effort of strength and activity, he rescued himself from their merciless claws, and took shelter in a house. The vultures pursued him there, and gave him a stroke that will probably destroy one of his eyes. In this piteous and grievously maimed condition they left him for a while, retreated to the court house, knocked down and very cruelly treated the deputy clerk of the crown, ascended the bench, shook their whips over Judge Henderson, told him his turn was next, ordered him to pursue business, but in the manner they should prescribe, which was, that no lawyers should enter the court-house, no juries but what they should pack, and order new trials in cases where some of them had been cast for their malepractices. They then seized Mr. Hooper, a gentleman of the law, dragged and paraded him through the streets, and treated him with every mark of contempt and insult.

This closed the first day. But the second day presented a scene, if possible, more tragic: immediately on their discovering that the judge had made his escape from their fury, and refused to submit to the dictate of lawless and desperate men, they marched in a body to Colonel Fanning's house, and, on a signal given by their ringleaders, entered the same, destroyed every piece of furniture in it, ripped open his beds, broke and threw in the streets, every piece of china and glass ware in the house, scattered all his papers and books in the winds, seized all his plate, cash, and proclamation money; entered his cellar, and, gorging their stomachs with his liquors, stove and threw in the streets the remainder. Being now drunk with rage, liquor, and lawless fury, they took his wearing cloaths, stuck them on a pole, paraded them in triumph through the streets, and, to close the scene, pulled down and laid his house in ruins; Hunter and Butler, two of their chiefs, stripping in buff, and beginning the heroic deed.

They then went to a large handsome church bell, that Colonel Fanning at the expence of 60 or 70l. had made a present to the church of Hillsborough, and split it to pieces, and were at the point of pulling down the church; but their leaders, thinking it would betray their religious principles, restrained them. Their revenge being not yet satiated on this unhappy gentleman, they again pursued him, again cruelly beat him, and at length with dogs hunted him out of town, and, with a cruelty more savage than blood-hounds, stoned him as he fled.

When they had fully glutted their revenge on the lawyers, and particularly Colonel Fanning, to shew their opinion of courts of justice, they took from his chains a negroe that had been executed some time, and placed him at the lawyer's bar, and filled the judge's seat with human excrement, in derision and contempt of the characters that filled those respectable places.

The Lord Mayor's Queries, in respect to the Legality of Press Warrants.

COPY.

QUERY 1. May the Lords of the Admiralty of themselves, by virtue of their commission, or under the direction of the Privy Council, legally issue warrants for the impressing of seamen?

Q. 2. If yea, is the warrant annexed in point of form legal?

Q. 3. Is the Lord Mayor compellable to back such warrants: if he is, what may be the consequence of a refusal?

"The power of the crown to compel persons pursuing the employment and occupation of seamen to serve the public in times of danger and necessity, which has its foundation in that universal principle of the laws of all countries, that all private interest must give way to the public safety, appears to us to be well established by antient and long continued usage, frequently recognized; and in many instances regulated by the legislature, and noticed at least without censure by courts of justice; and we see no objection to this power being exercised by the Lords of the Admiralty under the authority of his Majesty's orders in council.

"The form of the warrant, as well as the manner in which such warrants have been usually executed, appear to us to be liable to many considerable objections; but the nature of those objections leads us to think it the more expedient that the authority of a civil magistrate should interpose in the execution of them to check and controul the abuses to which they are liable; and, therefore, although we do not think that the Lord Mayor is compellable to back the warrants, or liable to any punishment in case of his refusal, we think it right to submit it to his Lordship's consideration, whether it will not be more conducive to the preservation of the peace of the city, and the protection of the subject from oppression, if he conforms in this instance to what we understand to have been the practice of most of his predecessors upon the like occasion."

AL. WEDDERBURN,
J. GLYNN,
J. DUNNING.

Nov. 22, 1770.

To the KING's Most Excellent Majesty.

The humble Address of the Lord Mayor, Sheriffs, Commons, and Citizens of the city of Dublin, in Common Council assembled.

Most gracious Sovereign,

WE, your Majesty's most dutiful, loyal, and affectionate subjects, the Lord Mayor, Sheriffs, Commons, and Citizens of your faithful city of Dublin, in common council assembled, beg leave humbly to approach your Majesty with the most sincere assurance of our steady attachment to your Majesty's illustrious person and family, and our ardent wishes that your reign over us may be long, and as transcendently distinguished as your virtues.

Emboldened by our experience of that attention which your Majesty affords to every part of your subjects,

subjects, permit us, most gracious Sir, to represent, at the foot of your throne, that for some defects in the present laws relative to corn, flour, and other necessaries of life, in the laws affecting the police of this city, and from the expiration of several temporary statutes, a situation in which we most humbly conceive we can only be relieved by the meeting of parliament, your faithful subjects of this metropolis experience many and great difficulties, and apprehend yet greater.

Pardon, most gracious Sovereign, that we presume farther to submit to your parental goodness, that certain public works necessary to the commerce of this city, which were begun and promoted by national bounty, must be indebted to the said bounty for their completion; and that your subjects of this metropolis, who, by large importations of the manufactures of Great Britain, have provided for their domestic consumption, which in every alternate year increases in proportion to the number assembled for national business, do already feel a decay of their trade and credit, even from a temporary decrease of inhabitants.

Grateful for the many blessings derived to us from your Majesty's parental affection, and conscious that relieving the wants of your people succeeds to the knowledge of them, we presume to intrude our cares upon your Majesty's more weighty concerns; and humbly beseech your Majesty to take these our circumstances into your Royal consideration, and to grant us such relief as your Majesty in your Royal wisdom shall think fit.

In testimony whereof we have caused the common seal of the said city to be hereunto affixed, this twenty-ninth day of October, in the year of our Lord one thousand seven hundred and seventy.

SUPPLIES granted by Parliament, for the Year 1770.

JANUARY 25, 1770.

1. THAT a number of land forces, including one thousand five hundred and twenty-two invalids, amounting to seventeen thousand six hundred and sixty-six effective men, commission and non-commission officers included, be employed for the year 1770.

2. For defraying the charge of this number of effective men, for guards, garrisons, and other of his Majesty's land forces, in Great Britain, Jersey, and Guernsey, for the year 1770.................... 624,992 0 2

3. For maintaining his Majesty's forces and garrisons in the plantations and Africa, including those in garrison at Minorca and Gibraltar, and for provisions for the forces in North America, Nova Scotia, Newfoundland, Gibraltar, the ceded islands, and Africa, for the year 1770.................. 383,248 1 11¼

4. For defraying the charge of the difference of pay between the British and Irish establishment of five battalions and four companies of foot, serving in the Isle of Man, at Gibraltar, Minorca, and the ceded islands, for the year 1770................. 4,533 12 8

5. For the pay of the general and general staff-officers in Great Britain, for the year 1770...... 12,203 18 6½

6. For defraying the charge of full pay, for 365 days, for the year 1770, to officers reduced, with the tenth company of several battalions reduced from ten to nine companies, and who remained on half pay at the 24th day of December, 1765............... 4,513 16 8

7. For the paying of pensions to the widows of such reduced officers of his Majesty's land forces and marines as died upon the establishment of half pay in Great Britain, and were married to them before the 25th day of December, 1716, for the year 1770.. 664 0 0

8. Upon account of the reduced officers of his Majesty's land forces and marines, for the year 1770... 123,233 2 6

9. For defraying the charge for allowances to the several officers and private gentlemen of the two troops of horse-guards reduced, and to the superan-

APPENDIX to the CHRONICLE. [235

nuated gentlemen of the four troops of horse-guards, for the year 1770............................... 1,289 1 3
10. For the charge of the office of ordnance, for land service, for the year 1770................. 166,984 11 5
11. For defraying the expence of services performed by the office of ordnance, for land service, and not provided for by parliament in 1769............. 40,933 10 8

1,362,595 15 10

FEBRUARY 2.

That 16,000 men be employed for the sea service, for the year 1770, including 4,287 marines. And That a sum, not exceeding 4l. per man per month, be allowed for maintaining the said 16,000 men, for 13 months, including ordnance for sea service....... 832,000 0 0

FEBRUARY 6.

1. For the ordinary of the navy, including half pay to sea and marine officers, for the year 1770..... 406,380 13 11
2. Towards the buildings, and rebuildings, and repairs of ships of war in his Majesty's yards, and other extra works, over and above what are proposed to be done upon the heads of wear and tear and ordinary, for the year 1770........................ 283,687 0 0

FEBRUARY 15.

1. Towards defraying the extraordinary expences of his Majesty's land forces, and other services, incurred to the 20th day of December, 1769, and not provided for by parliament....................... 235,264 10 9¼
2. Upon account, towards defraying the charge of out-pensioners of Chelsea-hospital, for the year 1770 112,423 4 7

1,869,755 9 3¼

FEBRUARY 22.

1. Upon account, for defraying the expences of the civil establishment of his Majesty's colony of West Florida, and other incidental expences attending the same, from the 24th of June, 1769, to the 24th of June, 1770........................... 4,800 0 0
2. Upon account, for defraying the expences of the civil establishment of his Majesty's colony of East Florida, and other incidental expences attending the same, from the 24th of June, 1769, to the 24th of June, 1770............................ 4,750 0 0
3. Upon account, for defraying the charges of the civil establishment of his Majesty's colony of Georgia, and other incidental expences attending the same, from the 24th of June, 1769, to the 24th of June, 1770................................ 3,086 0 0

4. Upon

4. Upon account, for maintaining and supporting the civil establishment of his Majesty's colony of Nova Scotia, for the year 1770............... 4,239 0 3

5. Upon account, for defraying the expences attending general surveys of his Majesty's dominions in North America, for the year 1770........... 1,885 4 0

18,760 4 5

6. That provision be made for the pay and cloathing of the militia, and for their subsistence during the time they shall be absent from home, on account of the annual exercise, for the year 1770.

March 12.

1. On account, for defraying the charges of the civil government of Senegambia, for the year 1770.. 5,550 0 0

2. For paying off and discharging the exchequer bills made out by virtue of an act, passed in the last session of parliament, entitled, 'An act for raising a certain sum of money by loans, or exchequer-bills, for the service of the year 1769,' and charged upon the first aids to be granted in this session of parliament.. 1,800,000 0 0

March 13.

To be employed in maintaining and supporting the British forts and settlements on the coast of Africa, under the direction of the committee of a company of merchants trading to Africa................... 13,000 0 0

March 19.

To enable his Majesty to assist the inhabitants of the island of Barbadoes in defraying the expence of cleansing the channel, repairing the mole, and rendering the harbour there more safe and commodious 5,000 0 0

1,823,550 0 0

March 29.

1. To make good to his Majesty the like sum, which has been issued by his Majesty's orders, in pursuance of the addresses of this House............ 13,100 0 0

2. Towards enabling the trustees of the British Museum to carry on the execution of the trust reposed in them by parliament......................... 2,000 0 0

3. Towards carrying on and completing an additional building, for a more commodious passage to the House of Commons, from St. Margaret's-lane, and Old Palace-yard......................... 2,000 0 0

APPENDIX to the CHRONICLE.

April 10.

Upon account, to enable his Majesty to discharge the debts owing upon the forfeited estates in Scotland; and also for paying and discharging the prices agreed to be paid to the Lords superiors, for the purchase of the superiorities of, and likewise for their claims of property to, certain specified estates which were forfeited in that kingdom.................. 72,000 0 0

To replace to the sinking fund the like sum paid out of the same, to make good the deficiency on the 5th day of July, 1769, of the fund established for paying annuities, in respect of five millions borrowed, by virtue of an act of the 31st George II. towards the supply granted for the service of the year 1758 .... 46,463 12 8

To make good the deficiency of the grants for the year 1769.................................... 55,011 7 5½

190,575 0 1¾

April 12.

1. To discharge such unsatisfied claims and demands for expences incurred during the late war in Germany as appear to be due to the Landgrave of Hesse Cassel, by the reports of the commissioners appointed by his Majesty for examining and stating such claims and demands..................... 45,565 12 0

2. To be advanced to the governor and company of the merchants of England, trading to the Levant seas, to be applied in assisting the said company in carrying on that trade....................... 5,000 0 0

3. Upon account, to enable the Foundling-hospital to maintain and educate such children as were received into the said hospital on or before the 25th day of March, 1760, from the 31st of December, 1769, exclusive, to the 31st day of December, 1770, inclusive; and that the said sum be issued and paid for the use of the said hospital, without fee or reward, or any deduction whatsoever.............. 9,650 0 0

4. For enabling the said hospital to put out apprentice the said children, so as the said hospital do not give with one child more than 7l............ 3,500 0 0

63,715 12 0

April 26.

1. That the sum of one million five hundred thousand pounds capital stock of annuities, after the rate

of three pounds ten shillings per centum, established by an act made in the 29th year of the reign of his late Majesty King George the Second, entitled, 'An act for granting to his Majesty the sum of two millions, to be raised by way of annuities and a lottery, and charged on the sinking fund, redeemable by parliament, and for extending to Ireland the laws made in this kingdom against private and unlawful lotteries,' be redeemed and paid off on the 12th day of February next, after discharging the interest then payable in respect of the same.

2. To enable his Majesty to redeem and pay off the said capital stock of annuities.................. 1,500,000 0 0

3. To pay the benefit prizes in the present lottery, charged upon the supplies of the current year....... 500,000 0 0

MAY 3.

1. Upon account of the expences of the new roads of communication, and building bridges, in the Highlands of North Britain, in the year 1770...... 6,998 10 2

2. Towards paying off and discharging the debt of the navy................................. 100,000 0 0

MAY 8.

1. To enable his Majesty to make compensation to Francis Dalby, of London, merchant, for the damages which the said Francis Dalby hath suffered by the stoppage and loss of his ship, called the Britannia, at Mahon, by order of the late Admiral Mathews, and by the use, employment, and detainer, of his ship called the Francis, by order of the commanders of his Majesty's fleets........... 6,195 8 11

2. To enable his Majesty to make good the like sum, which has been paid to several persons in the county of Southampton, as a compensation, and in full satisfaction of their losses and expences, incurred pursuant to several orders of council, for preventing the spreading of the infectious distemper among the horned cattle....................... 796 7 6

2,113,990 6 7

MAY 11.

1. To be advanced to John Hatsell, Esq. Clerk of this House, towards defraying the expence of printing the journal of this House, from the end of the last session of parliament to the end of this present session, with a proper index thereto.............. 600 0 0

2. To be advanced to such person or persons as the Speaker of this House shall authorize to receive

APPENDIX to the CHRONICLE. [239.

the same, towards farther defraying the expence of making a general index to the journals of this House — 500 0 0

MAY 16.

Towards defraying the expence of printing one thousand two hundred and fifty copies of such parliamentary and other records as his Majesty shall think fit.................................. 6,000 0 0

Sum total of the supplies granted this session....... 7,455,042 8 3

Ways and Means for raising the above Supply granted to his Majesty, agreed to on the following Days, viz.

JANUARY 29, 1770.

THAT the duties upon malt, mum, cider, and perry, be continued from the 23d of June 1770, to the 24th of June, 1771, and charged upon all malt which shall be made, and all mum which shall be made or imported, and all cider and perry which shall be made for sale within the kingdom of Great Britain, 700,000l.

FEBRUARY 8.

That the sum of 3s. in the pound, and no more, be raised, within the space of one year, from the 25th day of March, 1770, upon lands, tenements, hereditaments, pensions, offices, and personal estates, in that part of Great Britain called England, Wales, and the town of Berwick upon Tweed; and that a proportionable cess, according to the ninth article of the treaty of union, be laid upon that part of Great Britain called Scotland, 1,528,568l. 11s. 11¼d.

MARCH 3.

That the charge of the pay and cloathing of the militia, in that part of Great Britain called England, for one year, beginning the 25th day of March, 1770, be defrayed out of the monies arising by the land tax granted for the service of the year 1770.

13. That, towards raising the supply granted to his Majesty, the sum of 1,800,000l. be raised, by loans, or exchequer-bills, to be charged upon the first aids to be granted in the next session of parliament; and such exchequer-bills, if not discharged, with interest thereupon, on or before the 5th day of April, 1771, to be exchanged and received in payment, in such manner as exchequer-bills have usually been exchanged and received in payment.

29. That, towards raising the supply granted to his Majesty, there be issued and applied the sum of 299,375l. 6s. 0¼d. remaining in the exchequer, on the 5th day of January, 1770, for the disposition of parliament, of the monies which had then arisen of the surplusses, excesses, or overplus monies, and other revenues, composing the fund commonly called the sinking fund.

APRIL 9.

That the sum of 400,000l. which, by an act made in the last session of parliament, entitled, ' An act for carrying into execution certain proposals made by the East India Company for the payment of the annual sum of 400,000l.

for

for a limited time, in respect to the territorial acquisition and revenues lately obtained in the East Indies,' is directed ;to be paid, within the present year, into the receipt of his Majesty's exchequer, by the said company, be applied towards making good the supply granted to his Majesty.

April 12.

1. That the bounties granted on the British and Irish linens exported, by an act made in the 29th year of the reign of his late Majesty, be continued.

2. That the duties on the importation of foreign raw linen yarn made of flax, which are taken off by the said act, be farther discontinued.

3. That a bounty be allowed on the exportation of British chequed and striped linens. And,

4. That the sum of fifteen thousand pounds, granted by an act passed in the seventh year of his present Majesty's reign, entitled, ' An act for granting to his Majesty additional duties on certain foreign linens imported into this kingdom, and for establishing a fund for the encouraging of the raising and dressing of hemp and flax,' be appropriated.—A bill or bills were ordered to be brought in upon the said resolutions.

5. That, towards making good the supply granted to his Majesty, there be applied the sum of seven hundred and seventy-three thousand two hundred and forty pounds sixteen shillings and one halfpenny; being the surplus of the produce of the sinking fund, for the quarter ended the 5th day of April, 1770, remaining in the exchequer, for the disposition of parliament.

6. That, towards making good the supply granted to his Majesty, there be applied the sum of thirteen thousand five hundred and ninety-six pounds five shillings and tenpence halfpenny, remaining in the receipt of the exchequer, on the 5th day of April, 1770, for the disposition of parliament, over and above the surplus of the sinking fund then remaining for the same purpose.

20. That the sum of one million five hundred thousand pounds, capital stock of annuities, after the rate of three pounds ten shillings per centum, established by an act made in the 29th year of the reign of his late Majesty King George the Second, entitled, ' An act for granting to his Majesty the sum of two millions, to be raised by way of annuities and a lottery, and charged on the sinking fund, redeemable by parliament, and for extending to Ireland the laws made in this kingdom against private and unlawful lotteries,' will be redeemed and paid off on the 12th day of February next, after discharging the interest then payable in respect of the same, agreeable to the clauses and powers of redemption contained in the said act.

That any person or persons, bodies politic and corporate, who being possessed of, or entitled to, annuities after the rate of four pounds per centum, which were consolidated by an act of the second of his present Majesty, shall, on or before the seventh day of May next, in books to be opened at the Bank of England for that purpose, subscribe their names, or signify their consent to accept, in lieu thereof, annuities after the rate

APPENDIX to the CHRONICLE.

rate of three pounds per centum, to commence from the 5th day of January, 1770, and to be added to, and make one joint stock with, certain annuities consolidated by the act of the 25th of George the Second, and several subsequent acts of parliament, shall, for every one hundred pounds of capital stock so subscribed, until the several sums subscribed shall amount together to two millions five hundred thousand pounds, be entitled to receive two tickets in a lottery, to consist of fifty thousand tickets, at the rate of fourteen pounds each; and that every such subscriber, in consideration of such subscription, shall have a receipt from the cashiers of the Bank of England for four pounds, in part for the said fourteen pounds for each ticket to which such subscriber shall be entitled; and shall pay, for and in respect of every such ticket, the sum of one pound, on or before the 15th day of June next; the farther sum of two pounds, on or before the 20th day of July next; the farther sum of three pounds, on or before the 21st day of August next; and the farther sum of four pounds, on or before the 25th day of September next: that, upon such payments being completed, tickets shall be delivered, as soon as the same can be prepared, to the persons holding and possessed of the receipts herein before directed to be given by the cashiers of the Bank of England to the several subscribers, as aforesaid; the sum of five hundred thousand pounds shall be distributed into prizes, for the benefit of the proprietors of the fortunate tickets in the said lottery; which prizes shall be paid at the Bank of England, in money, to such proprietors, upon demand, on the first day of March, 1771, or as soon after as certificates can be prepared, without any deduction whatsoever; and that every person possessed of, and holding, such receipts, as aforesaid, who shall pay in the whole of the money to be paid on each ticket, on or before the 17th day of August next, shall be allowed an interest, by way of discount, after the rate of three pounds per centum per annum on the sums so completing his payments, respectively, to be computed from the day of completing the same to the 25th day of September next.

That in case the full and entire sum of two millions five hundred thousand pounds, in the said four pounds per centum annuities, shall not have been subscribed on or before the 7th day of May next, and that, in consequence thereof, any number of tickets, in the said lottery, shall remain unsubscribed for; any person or persons shall be at liberty to contribute for the purchase of such remaining tickets, at the rate of fourteen pounds for each ticket, in the manner herein after mentioned; that is to say, every such contributor or contributors to make a deposit of four pounds, for and in respect of such ticket, on or before the 10th day of May next, as a security for making good his or their future payments; the farther sum of one pound on or before the 15th day of June next; the farther sum of two pounds, on or before the 20th day of July next; the farther sum of three pounds, on or before the 21st day of August next; and the farther sum of four pounds, on or before the 25th day of September next; tickets to be delivered, as soon as the same can be prepared,

Vol. XIII. [R]

to such contributor or contributors, upon his or their completing their payments; and that every contributor who shall pay in the whole of the money to be paid on each ticket, on or before the 17th day of August next, shall be allowed an interest, by way of discount, after the rate of three pounds per centum per annum, on the sums so completing his payments respectively, to be computed from the day of completing the same to the 20th day of September next. And,

That all the monies that shall be received by the cashiers of the Bank, for or on account of the whole of the said fifty thousand tickets, shall be paid into the receipt of his Majesty's exchequer, to be applied, from time to time, to such services as shall then have been voted by this House, and not otherwise; and that the sum of five hundred thousand pounds, herein before directed to be distributed into prizes, for the benefit of the proprietors of the fortunate tickets in the said lottery, shall be charged upon the aids and supplies granted in this session of parliament, for the service of the year 1770.

MAY 3.

1. That, towards raising the supply granted to his Majesty, there be issued and applied the sum of one million seven hundred thousand pounds, out of such monies as shall or may arise of the surplusses, excesses, or overplus monies, and other revenues composing the sinking fund.

2. That the sum of fifty-five thousand four hundred and ninety-five pounds fifteen shillings eight-pence farthing, remaining in the office of the Paymaster-general of his Majesty's forces, subject to the disposition of parliament, be applied towards making good the supply granted to his Majesty, towards defraying the extraordinary expences of his Majesty's land forces, and other services incurred, to the 26th day of December, 1769, and not provided for by parliament.

3. That a sum not exceeding twenty thousand pounds, out of such monies as shall be paid into the receipt of the exchequer after the 4th day of April, 1770, and on or before the 5th day of April, 1771, of the produce of all or any of the duties and revenues, which, by any act or acts of parliament, have been directed to be reserved for the disposition of parliament, towards defraying the necessary expences of defending, protecting, and securing the British colonies and plantations in America, be applied towards making good such part of the supply as hath been granted to his Majesty, for maintaining his Majesty's forces and garrisons in the plantations, and for provisions for the forces in North America, Nova Scotia, Newfoundland, and the ceded islands, for the year 1770. And,

4. That such of the monies as shall be paid into the receipt of the exchequer, after the 4th day of April, 1770, and on or before the 5th day of April, 1771, of the produce of the duties charged by an act of parliament, made in the 5th year of his present Majesty's reign, upon the importation and exportation of gum-seneca and gum-arabic, be applied towards making good the supply granted to his Majesty.

5. That the duties now payable upon the importation into this kingdom

APPENDIX to the CHRONICLE.

kingdom of baſt or ſtraw, chip, cane, and horſe-hair hats and bonnets, and upon certain materials for making the ſame, do ceaſe, determine, and be no longer paid.

That, in lieu of all former rates and duties, all baſt or ſtraw, chip, cane, and horſe-hair hats and bonnets, which, from and after the 24th day of June, 1770, ſhall be imported into this kingdom, ſhall be rated to, and pay, the old ſubſidy, granted by the act of tonnage and poundage, made in the twelfth year of the reign of King Charles the Second, according to the rates and values of twelve ſhillings and ſix-pence for every dozen, each hat or bonnet not exceeding twenty-two inches in diameter; and one pound five ſhillings for every dozen of ſuch hats or bonnets as ſhall exceed twenty-two inches in diameter each.

That, in lieu of all former rates and duties, all platting, or other manufactures of baſt or ſtraw, chip, cane, or horſe-hair, to be uſed in, or proper for making of, hats or bonnets, which, from and after the ſaid 24th day of June, 1770, ſhall be imported into this kingdom, ſhall be rated to and pay the ſaid old ſubſidy, according to the rate and value of ſix ſhillings and eight-pence for every pound weight avoirdupois.

That the full amount of the ſeveral duties, now payable for every twenty ſhillings of the value of the ſaid goods reſpectively, be raiſed and collected, according to the ſaid reſpective rates before-mentioned. And,

That a ſum not exceeding three thouſand nine hundred forty-eight pounds three ſhillings and ſeven-pence, being the final balance of the account of Thomas Earl of Kinnoull, formerly Paymaſter-general of his Majeſty's forces, ſubject to the diſpoſition of parliament, be applied towards making good the ſupply granted to his Majeſty, towards defraying the extraordinary expences of his Majeſty's land forces, and other ſervices, incurred to the 26th day of December, 1769, and not provided for by parliament.

Theſe were the reſolutions of the Committee of Ways and Means, which were agreed to by the Houſe; and the ſums thereby provided for, ſo far as they can at preſent be aſcertained, ſtand as follow:

	l.	*s.*	*d.*
By the reſolution of January 29	700000	0	0
By that of February 8	1528568	11	11¼
By that of March 13	1800000	0	0
By that of March 29	299375	6	6¼
By that of April 9	400000	0	0
By the fifth of April 12	773240	16	0¼
By the ſixth of ditto	13596	5	10¼
By that of April 26	500000	0	0
By the firſt of May 3	1700000	0	0
By the ſecond of ditto	55495	15	8¼
By the third of ditto	20000	0	0
By the laſt of May 8	3948	3	7
Sum total of ſuch proviſions as can be aſcertained	7794224	19	8¼
Exceſs of the proviſions	344182	11	5¼

STATE

STATE PAPERS.

His Majesty's most gracious Speech to both Houses of Parliament, on Tuesday the 9th of January, 1770.

My Lords and Gentlemen,

IT is with much concern that I find myself obliged to open this session of parliament with acquainting you, that the distemper among the horned cattle has lately broke out in this kingdom, notwithstanding every precaution that could be used for preventing the infection from foreign parts. Upon the first notice of its actual appearance, my next attention was to endeavour to stop, if possible, its farther progress; and, as the success of those endeavours must, in all probability, have been entirely defeated by any the least degree of delay in the application of them, I thought it absolutely necessary, with the advice of my privy council, to give immediate directions for every step to be taken that appeared most capable of checking the instant danger of the spreading of the infection, until I could have an opportunity of consulting my parliament upon some more permanent measures for securing us against so great a calamity: and to your immediate and serious consideration I earnestly recommend this very important subject.

I have given my parliament repeated assurances, that it has always been my fixed purpose to preserve the general tranquillity; maintaining at the same time the dignity and honour of my crown, together with the just rights and interests of my people. The uncommon burthens, which my subjects have borne so cheerfully, in order to bring the late war to a happy conclusion, must be an additional motive to make me vigilant to prevent the present disturbances in Europe from extending to any part where the security, honour, or interest of this nation may make it necessary for my crown to become a party. The assurances which I receive from the other great powers afford me reason to believe that my endeavours will continue to be successful. I shall still make the general interest of Europe the object of my attention: and while I steadily support my own rights, I shall be equally careful not to acknowledge the claims of any other powers, contrary to the limitations of the late treaties of peace,

It is needless for me to recommend to the serious attention of my parliament the state of my government in America. I have endeavoured, on my part, by every means, to bring back my subjects there to their duty, and to a due sense of lawful authority. It gives me much concern to inform you, that the success of my endeavours has not answered my expectations; and that, in some of my colonies, many

many persons have embarked in measures highly unwarrantable, and calculated to destroy the commercial connection between them and the mother country.

Gentlemen of the House of Commons,

I have ordered the proper estimates for the service of the current year to be laid before you. I am persuaded that your affection for my person and government, and your zeal for the public good, will induce you to grant such supplies as are necessary; and you may be assured, that, on my part, they shall be managed with the strictest œconomy.

My Lords and Gentlemen,

As the welfare and prosperity of my people have always been the object of my wishes and the rule of my actions, so I am persuaded, from my experience of your conduct, that you will be governed in your proceedings by the same principles. My ready concurrence and support in every measure that may serve to promote those ends, you may always depend upon. On you it will be now, more than ever, incumbent most carefully to avoid all heats and animosities amongst yourselves, and to cultivate that spirit of harmony which becomes those who have but one common object in their view, and which may be most likely to give authority and efficacy to the result of your deliberations. Such a conduct on your part will, above all things, contribute to maintain, in their proper lustre, the strength, the reputation, and the prosperity of this country; to strengthen the attachment of my subjects to that excellent constitution of government from which they derive such distinguished advantages; and to cause the firm reliance and confidence which I have in the wisdom of my parliament, as well as in their zeal for the true interest of my people, to be justified and approved both at home and abroad.

The humble Address of the Right Honourable the Lords Spiritual and Temporal, in Parliament assembled, January 9, 1770.

Most gracious Sovereign,

WE, your Majesty's most dutiful and loyal subjects, the Lords Spiritual and Temporal, in parliament assembled, return your Majesty our humble thanks for your most gracious speech from the throne.

We beg leave to assure your Majesty, that it is with the greatest concern we have understood that the distemper among the horned cattle has lately broke out in this kingdom. We desire to express our gratitude for your Majesty's paternal care and attention to the welfare of your people, in the steps which it has pleased your Majesty to take, with the advice of your privy council, to check the instant danger of the spreading of the distemper, upon the first notice of its appearance; and to assure your Majesty, that we will immediately enter into the most serious consideration of this very important object, and will exert our utmost endeavours in taking such effectual measures as may secure us against so great a calamity.

We return your Majesty our thanks for the repeated assurances your Majesty has been pleased to give us of your fixed purpose to preserve the peace; maintaining, at the same time, the dignity of your crown, and the interests of your people. We have a dutiful sense of your Majesty's provident attention to prevent the necessity of involving your subjects in fresh difficulties, after the great burthens to which they so cheerfully submitted, in order to bring the late war to a happy conclusion; and we have great satisfaction in finding that the assurances given to your Majesty by the other great powers of Europe afford reason to believe, that, without prejudice either to the honour of your crown, the rights of your people, or the general interests of Europe, it may still be in your Majesty's power to continue to your subjects the farther enjoyment of the blessings of peace.

We assure your Majesty, that we will take into our most serious consideration the state of your government in America. We beg leave to express our utmost concern, that the success of your Majesty's endeavours to bring back your subjects there to a due sense of lawful authority have not answered your Majesty's expectations. We shall be ready to give every assistance in our power, for rendering effectual these your Majesty's gracious intentions, and for discountenancing those unwarrantable measures practised in some of your Majesty's colonies, which appear calculated to destroy the commercial connection between them and the mother country.

We think it our duty to assure your Majesty, that we are thoroughly sensible that the welfare of your people has ever been the object of your wishes, and the rule of all your actions; and that we will endeavour to deserve the favourable opinion, which your Majesty is graciously pleased to express, of our being governed by the same principles. That we have a perfect reliance on your Majesty's promised support in such measures as may serve to promote those ends. That, as it is peculiarly incumbent upon us at present to avoid heats and animosities among ourselves, so we shall endeavour to cultivate that harmony which is so necessary to the common cause, and which alone can render our deliberations respectable and effectual; being fully persuaded, that such a conduct, on our part, must greatly contribute to the happiness and prosperity of this country, and to establish a due sense of the very distinguished advantages of our happy constitution, as well as a firm attachment to it; and must justify, both at home and abroad, your Majesty's gracious confidence in the wisdom of your parliament, and in their zeal for the true interests of your people.

His Majesty's most gracious Answer.

My Lords,

I thank you for this affectionate and loyal address. Your resolution to enter immediately into the consideration of such measures as may best secure us against the spreading of the distemper among the horned cattle, affords me great satisfaction.

I have

I have strong reliance on your determination to give me every assistance in your power to support my government in America.

Your assurances of duty and loyalty towards me, and your resolution to cultivate harmony among yourselves, give me very sincere pleasure.

The humble Address of the House of Commons to the King.

Most gracious Sovereign,

WE, your Majesty's most dutiful and loyal subjects, the Commons of Great Britain, in parliament assembled, beg leave to return your Majesty our humble thanks for your most gracious speech from the throne.

We cannot but look upon it as a very serious misfortune, that, notwithstanding every precaution which could be used for preventing the communication of the infectious disorder among the horned cattle from foreign parts, that most alarming distemper appears to have again broke out in some parts of the kingdom: at the same time, we are truly sensible of your Majesty's paternal care and vigilance for the security of your people, in having given the earliest directions for every measure to be pursued that might be most likely to give an immediate check to the first spreading of the infection; and we will not fail to take this most important matter into our immediate consideration, and to make such provisions as shall appear best calculated to carry into effectual and complete execution your Majesty's salutary intentions; and thereby, as far as by human means can be accomplished, to guard against the danger of so great a calamity becoming general.

Your faithful Commons have too just a sense of the blessings of peace, and feel with your Majesty too tender a concern for the ease of their fellow-subjects, not to rejoice at the prospect which the assurances given by the other great powers of Europe afford to your Majesty, that the present disturbances will not extend to any part where the security, honour, or interest of this nation may make it necessary for your Majesty to become a party. We have the fullest confidence that your Majesty will never be unmindful of those important objects; and we observe, with great satisfaction, your Majesty's wise attention to the general interests of Europe, in your determination not to acknowledge any claims of any of the other powers of Europe, contrary to the limitations of the late treaties of peace.

We sincerely lament that your Majesty's endeavours to bring back your subjects in America to a just sense of their duty have hitherto proved so little successful. The state of your Majesty's government there does undoubtedly well deserve the serious attention of parliament: and no endeavours shall be wanting on our part to make effectual provisions against the unwarrantable measures carried on in some of your Majesty's colonies, which are so irreconcileable to every principle of commercial subserviency to the interest of the mother country that ought to prevail in colonies, and which, by attempting to subject the highest legal authority to the controul of indivi-

individuals, tend to subvert the foundation of all government.

Your Majesty may be assured, that we will with the utmost cheerfulness and dispatch grant the necessary supplies for the service of the current year.

We acknowledge, with the warmest gratitude, that the welfare of these kingdoms has been the constant object of your Majesty's wishes, and the unvaried rule of your actions. Permit us, Sir, at the same time, to offer to your Majesty our most dutiful thanks for the favourable opinion which your Majesty is pleased to entertain of the conduct of your parliament; and to assure your Majesty, that we will steadily persevere in such principles as are most agreeable to the true spirit of this free constitution, and invariably pursue such measures as are most conducive to the real happiness of the people.

Earnestly desirous of justifying, to all the world your Majesty's gracious declaration of your confidence in us, we will make it our study to avoid all heats and animosities, and to cultivate that harmony amongst ourselves, which, we are truly sensible, is at this time peculiarly necessary to give weight to our deliberations, to establish the prosperity, and to maintain in its true lustre the reputation of this country.

And while we on our part are faithfully executing the trust reposed in us, by endeavouring to the utmost of our power to promote these good ends, we trust that all who live under this happy constitution will be convinced how indispensably it is their duty to pay that obedience to the laws, and just reverence to lawful authority, by which alone their own rights can be preserved, and the distinguished blessings which they enjoy above all other nations be rendered secure and permanent.

The humble Address of the Right Honourable the Lords Spiritual and Temporal, and Commons, in Parliament assembled, presented March 23, to his Majesty.

Most gracious Sovereign,

WE, your Majesty's most dutiful subjects, the Lords Spiritual and Temporal, and Commons of Great Britain, in Parliament assembled, having taken into consideration the Address lately presented to your Majesty, under the title of, ' The ' humble Address, Remonstrance, ' and Petition of the Lord Mayor, ' Aldermen, and Livery of the ' City of London, in Common ' Hall assembled,' together with the answer which your Majesty was pleased to make to the same, think ourselves indispensably obliged, upon this occasion, to express to your Majesty the extreme concern and indignation which we feel at finding that an application has been made to your Majesty in terms so little corresponding with that grateful and affectionate respect which your Majesty is so justly entitled to from all your subjects; at the same time aspersing and calumniating one of the branches of the legislature, and expressly denying the legality of the present parliament, and the validity of its proceedings.

To present petitions to the throne has at all times been the undoubted right of the subjects of this

this realm. The free enjoyment of that right was one of the many blessings restored by the revolution, and continued to us, in its fullest extent, under the Princes of your Majesty's illustrious house. And, as we are duly sensible of its value and importance, it is with the deepest concern that we now see the exercise of it so grossly perverted, by being applied to the purpose not of preserving, but of overturning the constitution; and of propagating doctrines, which, if generally adopted, must be fatal to the peace of the kingdom, and which tend to the subversion of all lawful authority.

Your Majesty, we acknowledge with gratitude, has ever shewn the most tender regard to the rights of your people, not only in the exercise of your own power, but in your care to preserve from every degree of infringement or violation the powers entrusted to others. And we beg leave to return your Majesty our unfeigned thanks for the fresh proof you have given of your determination to persevere in your adherence to the principles of the constitution.

Permit us also to assure your Majesty, that it is with the highest satisfaction we see your Majesty expressing so just a confidence in your people. In whatever unjustifiable excesses some few misguided persons may, in this instance, have been seduced to join, your Majesty's subjects in general are too sensible of what they owe both to your Majesty and your illustrious family ever to be capable of approaching your Majesty with any other sentiments than those of the most entire respect and affection; and they understand too well their own true interests to wish to loosen the bands of obedience to the laws, and of due subordination to lawful authority. We are therefore fully persuaded that your Majesty's people, as well as your parliament, will reject with disdain every insidious suggestion of those ill-designing men, who are in reality undermining the public liberty under the specious pretence of zeal for its preservation; and that your Majesty's attention to maintain the liberties of your subjects inviolate, which you esteem your chief glory, will, upon every occasion, prove the sure means of strength to your Majesty, and secure to you that zealous and effectual support, which none but a free people can bestow.

His Majesty's Answer.

My Lords and Gentlemen,

I return you my thanks for this very loyal and dutiful address. It is with great satisfaction that I receive from my parliament so grateful an acknowledgment of my tender regard for the rights of my subjects. Be assured that I shall continue to adhere to the true principles of our excellent constitution; from which I cannot deviate without justly forfeiting the affections of a free people.

By the KING.

A PROCLAMATION,

For encouraging Seamen to enter themselves on board his Majesty's Ships of War.

GEORGE R.

WHEREAS it is our royal intention to give all due encouragement to all such seamen who

who shall voluntarily enter themselves in our service; we have thought fit, by and with the advice of our Privy Council, to publish this our Royal Proclamation. And we hereby promise and declare, that all such able seamen, not above the age of fifty, nor under the age of twenty years, fit for our service, who shall, on or before the 21st day of October next, voluntarily enter themselves to serve in our Royal Navy, either with the captains or lieutenants of our ships, or the chief officers on board such tenders, as shall be employed for raising men for the service of our navy, shall receive, as our royal bounty, the sum of thirty shillings each man; and all such ordinary seamen fit for our service, who shall so enter themselves as aforesaid, shall receive the sum of twenty shillings each man, as our royal bounty: such respective sums to be paid them by the respective clerks of the checque, residing at the ports or places where the ships into which they shall be entered shall be, immediately after the third muster of such seamen.—And we do declare, that the qualifications of the seamen so entering themselves as aforesaid shall be certified by the captain, master, and boatswain of the ship or vessel where they shall enter. And for prevention of any abuses by any persons leaving the vessels to which they shall belong, and entering themselves on board any other our ships or vessels, in order to obtain the said bounty-money, we do hereby declare and command, that such seamen belonging to any of our ships, or vessels, as shall absent themselves from any of the said ships or vessels to which they shall belong, and shall enter themselves on board any other of our said ships or vessels in order to obtain the said bounty, shall not only lose the wages due to them in the ships or vessels they shall leave, but also be severely punished, according to their demerits.

Given at our court at St. James's, the 22d day of September, 1770, and in the tenth year of our reign.

GOD save the KING.

His Majesty's most gracious Speech to both Houses of Parliament, on Saturday, the 19th of May, 1770.

My Lords and Gentlemen,

THE season of the year, and the dispatch you have given to the public business, make it proper for me to put an end to this session of parliament.

The temper with which you have conducted all your proceedings has given me great satisfaction, and I promise myself the happiest effects from the firmness, as well as the moderation, which you have manifested in the very critical circumstances which have attended your late deliberations.

With respect to foreign affairs, I have nothing material to communicate to you. I will continue my endeavours to appease, if possible, the troubles which still prevail in some parts of Europe, or at least to prevent them from spreading farther. In all events it shall be my first and constant care to watch over the interests, and to preserve undiminished the rights of my people.

Gentle-

Gentlemen of the House of Commons,

I return you my thanks for the supplies you have so cheerfully granted for the service of the current year, as well as for your attention to make use of every opportunity of reducing the national debt. The provision you have been able to make in this session for discharging so considerable a sum, without laying any farther burthen on my subjects, cannot but be highly advantageous to public credit.

My Lords and Gentlemen,

I most earnestly recommend to you to exert, in your respective counties, the same zeal and prudence that you have shewn in parliament for promoting the peace and welfare of the kingdom: nothing can be so favourable to the wishes of those who look with jealousy on the strength and prosperity of this country, as the prevalence of animosities and dissentions amongst ourselves: let it, therefore, be your care to discountenance every attempt to infuse groundless suspicions and discontent into the minds of your fellow-subjects; make them sensible of my constant attention to promote their happiness; and convince them, that nothing can so effectually secure their liberties as the maintenance of every part of our excellent constitution, in its due force and authority.

To the KING's Most Excellent Majesty.

The humble Address of the Lord Mayor, Aldermen, and Commons, of the City of London, in Common Council assembled, on Wednesday May 30, 1770.

"Most gracious Sovereign,

"WE wait upon your Majesty with our sincere congratulations on the happy delivery of our most gracious Queen, and on the birth of another Princess; and to assure your Majesty, that there are not in all your dominions any subjects more faithful, more dutiful, and more affectionate to your Majesty's person and family, or more ready to sacrifice their lives and fortunes in the maintenance of the true honour and dignity of your crown.

"Long may your Majesty reign the true guardian of the liberties of this free country, and be the instrument, in the hands of Providence, of transmitting to our posterity these invaluable rights and privileges, which are the birth-right of the subjects of this kingdom."

To which the King gave the following gracious answer.

"I receive with great satisfaction your congratulations on the happy delivery of the Queen and the birth of a Princess; and I return you my hearty thanks for the duty and affection to my person and family, and the zeal for the true honour and dignity of my crown, which you express upon this occasion.

"The city of London, entertaining these loyal sentiments, may be always assured of my protection."—They all had the honour of kissing his Majesty's hand.

His

His Majesty's most gracious Speech to both Houses of Parliament, on Tuesday the 13th Day of November, 1770.

My Lords and Gentlemen,

WHEN I last met you in parliament, I renewed to you the assurances which I had before given you, that it was my fixed purpose to preserve the general tranquillity, maintaining, at the same time, the honour of my crown, together with the just rights and interests of my people; and it was with much satisfaction that I indulged the hope of being still able to continue to my subjects the enjoyment of peace with honour and security. Since that time, those very considerations, which I then promised you that I would never sacrifice even to the desires of peace, have laid me under an indispensable necessity of preparing for a different situation.

By an act of the Governor of Buenos Ayres in seizing by force one of my possessions, the honour of my crown, and the security of my people's rights, were become deeply affected. Under these circumstances, I did not fail to make an immediate demand from the court of Spain of such satisfaction as I had a right to expect for the injury I had received. I directed also the necessary preparations to be made, without loss of time, for enabling me to do myself justice in case my requisition to the court of Spain should fail of procuring it for me. And these preparations, you may be assured, I shall not think it expedient to discontinue, until I shall have received proper reparation for the injury, as well as satisfactory proof that other powers are equally sincere with myself in the resolution to preserve the general tranquillity of Europe. In the mean time, I have called you together thus early, in order that I may be able to receive from you such advice and assistance, as, in the farther progress of this very important business, may happen to become requisite.

With respect to the state of my colonies in North America, although I have the satisfaction to acquaint you that the people in most of them have begun to depart from those combinations which were calculated to distress the commerce of this kingdom, yet, in some parts of the colony of the Massachusett's Bay, very unwarrantable practices are still carried on, and my good subjects oppressed by the same lawless violence which has too long prevailed in that province.

I hope, and trust, that the precautions which have already been used for securing this country against the visitation of that fatal calamity which has of late appeared in some of the distant parts of Europe, will, with the blessing of God, prove successful. But if, from any alteration of circumstances, it should at any time be found that farther provisions will be wanted, I cannot doubt of your ready concurrence for so salutary a purpose.

Gentlemen of the House of Commons,

I will order the proper estimates for the service of the ensuing year to be laid before you. They must unavoidably, in our present situation, exceed the usual amount. Every unnecessary expence my concern for the ease of my good subjects

subjects will ever make me careful to avoid: but I should neither consult their interest, nor their inclination, if I were to decline any expence which the public security, or the maintenance of the national honour, does at any time require.

My Lords and Gentlemen,

I am sensible how little I need say to you, at this time, to prevail upon you to unite in whatever may best promote the true interest of your country. In all your deliberations upon points of a domestic nature, let the extension of our commerce, the improvement of the revenue, and the maintenance of order and good government, be always in your view. With respect to foreign measures, there will, I am persuaded, be no other contest among you, than who shall appear most forward in the support of the common cause, in upholding the reputation and promoting the prosperity of the kingdom. For the attainment of these ends, you shall ever find me ready to exert myself to the uttermost. I have no interest, I can have none, distinct from that of my people.

The humble Address of the Right Honourable the Lords Spiritual and Temporal, in Parliament assembled, November 13, 1770.

Most gracious Sovereign,

WE, your Majesty's most dutiful and loyal subjects, the Lords Spiritual and Temporal, in parliament assembled, return your Majesty our humble thanks for your most gracious speech from the throne.

We beg leave to offer your Majesty our very sincere congratulations on the safe and happy delivery of the Queen, and the birth of a Princess; and to assure your Majesty of our unfeigned joy at the increase of your domestic happiness; and that we consider every addition to your illustrious house, from which these kingdoms have received the most important benefits, as a farther security to our religious and civil liberties.

We are too sensible of the blessing of peace not to feel the greatest concern at any event which threatens to interrupt its continuance, and defeat your Majesty's wise and gracious purpose to maintain it. But, grateful as we are for this proof of your Majesty's paternal regard to the repose and happiness of your people, we owe your Majesty no less thanks for your anxious vigilance over the honour of your crown, and the interests of your people.

We return your Majesty our most thankful acknowledgments, as well for the immediate demand, which your Majesty has been pleased to make from the court of Spain, of satisfaction for the injury received, as for the instant preparations that your Majesty made to do yourself justice in case your requisition should fail of procuring it. And we are exceedingly happy to be assured, that your Majesty will think it expedient to continue prepared to assert the honour of your crown, and the security of the rights of your people, upon an event so deeply affecting both, until the injury shall be properly repaired, and satisfactory proof be given of the
sincere

sincere resolution of other powers to preserve the general tranquillity of Europe. We, on our part, beg leave to assure your Majesty, that we will not fail to make the utmost efforts in our power to maintain objects so justly dear to us as the dignity of your Majesty's crown, and the security of the national right.

We are very happy to be informed, that the people in most of your Majesty's colonies in North America are departing from those combinations which were calculated to distress the commerce of this kingdom; and we hope soon to see an entire end of those unwarrantable practices which have so long oppressed your Majesty's subjects in one of those provinces.

We are highly sensible of your Majesty's goodness and care in taking such precautions to secure this country against the visitation of that fatal calamity which has of late appeared in some of the distant parts of Europe: and we shall always be ready to concur in any measures that shall be found necessary to the support of your Majesty's endeavours for so salutary a purpose.

We have the most grateful sense of your Majesty's favourable opinion of our constant endeavours to promote the true interest of this country. We will, in all our deliberations upon points of a domestic nature, exert ourselves for the extension of our commerce, the improvement of the revenue, and the maintenance of order and government: and we flatter ourselves, that your Majesty will not be disappointed in the gracious expectations you have formed of our zeal in the support of your Majesty's crown, and the reputation and prosperity of your kingdoms.

His Majesty's most gracious Answer.

My Lords,

It gives me great satisfaction to find that you entertain so just a sense of the importance of peace, while that desirable object can be maintained consistently with the honour of my crown and the rights of my people. You may depend upon my best endeavours to preserve that inestimable blessing, so long as it is compatible with objects still more essential to the happiness and prosperity of my kingdoms.

The affectionate part you take in the happy delivery of the Queen and the increase of my family gives me much pleasure.

The humble Address of the House of Commons to the King.

Most gracious Sovereign,

WE, your Majesty's most dutiful and loyal subjects, the Commons of Great Britain, in parliament assembled, return your Majesty our humble thanks for your most gracious speech from the throne.

We beg leave to offer to your Majesty our congratulations on the happy delivery of her Majesty, and on the birth of another Princess; esteeming every increase of your Majesty's royal family an additional security for the continuance of that happiness which we have already experienced under its auspicious government.

Among

Among the many proofs we have received of your Majesty's constant attention to the welfare and prosperity of your people, your Majesty's earnest desire to continue to us the blessings of peace could not fail to inspire us with sentiments of gratitude and affection: but we could have reaped little real satisfaction from the enjoyment of those blessings, had we not at the same time been able to place the justest confidence in your Majesty, that you would never be induced, by a mistaken tenderness for the present ease of your people, to sacrifice their more essential and more lasting interests. These we cannot but consider as having been dangerously struck at by the violence lately committed by a Spanish governor upon one of your Majesty's possessions. Under these circumstances, your Majesty's determination to make an immediate demand from the court of Spain of such satisfaction as you had a right to expect, and at the same time to direct the necessary preparations to be made, without delay, for enabling your Majesty to do yourself justice, in case your requisition to the court of Spain should fail to procure it, demands our most hearty acknowledgments; and we rejoice to find that your Majesty will not discontinue these preparations until you shall have received a proper reparation for the injury, as well as satisfactory proof that other powers are equally sincere with your Majesty in the resolution to preserve the general tranquillity. In the prosecution of this your Majesty's purpose, your Majesty will not be disappointed in your expectation of receiving from your faithful Commons every degree of support which in the progress of this very important business will become requisite: with this view, we shall enter without delay into the consideration of the supplies for the ensuing year; and whatever extraordinary expences the public service shall require, we will cheerfully provide for, in such manner as may be least burthensome to your Majesty's subjects.

In considering the state of your Majesty's colonies in North America, we will neglect no means of securing the commercial interests of this kingdom, or of providing for the protection of your Majesty's good subjects there from every degree of violence and oppression.

We return your Majesty our unfeigned thanks for the timely precautions you have used for guarding against the introduction of that fatal contagion which has of late appeared in some of the distant parts of Europe. And while, with your Majesty, we place our ultimate reliance upon the Divine Providence for our preservation from so great a calamity, we shall consider it as our indispensable duty to make use of every reasonable precaution which human foresight can suggest to us.

We assure your Majesty, that we will apply ourselves with all due diligence to the dispatch of the public business; in which we will not fail steadily to pursue those great ends recommended to us by your Majesty in your speech from the throne, as well as by your royal example. And if any hopes should have been conceived, or it may have been any where surmised, that among your Majesty's people there were any such differences subsisting as could in the least degree

gree abate the ardour of their affectionate attachment for your Majesty, or prevent their joining, as one man, in seconding your Majesty's views for maintaining unsullied the lustre of your crown, and preserving undiminished the rights of your people, we doubt not, by our proceedings, to convince the world how false and injurious are all such surmises; and to make it manifest, that, whenever we are called upon in the cause of our King and country, there will be but one heart and one voice among your faithful Commons.

CHARACTERS.

Of the Russians; *from the Account of a Journey into* Siberia, *made by Order of the King of* France. *By* M. L'Abbé Chappe D'Auteroche, *of the* Royal Academy of Sciences *at* Paris.

AS soon as the sovereign is on the throne, he is supposed to have no more relations, and no one dares to claim any connection with the Royal Family. A foreign courtier, having found that the Countess of Woronzof was related to the Empress Elizabeth, went immediately and complimented her with the news, which he thought was a discovery of political importance: the Empress turned pale, and told him he was mistaken.

It was forbidden, on pain of death, to keep any coin stamped with the image of the young Iwan. The people dared not play with roubles, which bear the impression of the sovereign. One cannot pass before the palace, facing the Emperor's apartments, without pulling off one's hat, or letting down the glass, if one is in a carriage; otherwise one is exposed to insults from the soldiers. Any person who should write the name of the Empress in small characters upon a letter, would be liable to be severely punished for it.

These trifling circumstances are mentioned merely to give an idea of the extent of the absolute power of Russian monarchs.

The nobility dare not come near the throne without fear and trembling. They are banished into Siberia for the slightest political intrigue, and, their possessions being confiscated, one whole family thus falls a victim to the artful insinuations of the courtier. When I was at St. Petersburgh, I was one day on a visit at the house of a stranger, who was in office: being desirous of information, I asked whether the prince Iwan was living or not? It was immediately whispered in my ear, that in Russia no one spoke of that prince. We were, however, no more than three Frenchmen in the room, which was upwards of thirty feet square. On the eve of the death of the Empress Elizabeth, no one dared to enquire concerning her health; and when she was dead, although it was universally known, yet every body was afraid to speak of it.

The mutual distrust in which people live in Russia, and the total silence of the nation upon every thing which may have the least relation either to the government or to the sovereign, arises chiefly from the privilege every Russian has, without distinction, of crying out in public, *Slowo Dielo*; that is to say, I declare you guilty of high

high treason both in words and actions. All the bystanders are then obliged to assist in taking up the person accused. A father arrests his son, and the son his father, and nature suffers in silence. The accused and the accuser are both conveyed immediately to prison, and afterwards to St. Petersburgh, where they are tried by the secret court of chancery.

This tribunal, composed of a few ministers chosen by the sovereign, leaves the lives and fortunes of all families at their mercy. This jurisdiction is of so odious a nature, that a subject, who shall even be indifferent to these agents of tyranny, is often found guilty, although the accuser should not be able to bring convincing proofs of the crime; and this happens chiefly when the impeacher answers for the guilt of the person accused with his own shoulders; that is to say, submits to receive the punishment of the knout. If he bears this without recanting, the person accused is found guilty, condemned to death, and part of his estate forfeited to the accuser. If some very extraordinary circumstances indicate the innocence of the person accused, the impeacher is then punished a second time. He is also punished, but only once, when, not having demanded the trial of the knout, he is found incapable of proving the guilt of the man whom he impeaches.

This jurisdiction has been established merely that tyranny might enjoy the privilege of sacrificing all such persons as have become the object of despotic jealousy. It was therefore necessary that the crime of the false accuser should not be punished with death; and the punishment of the knout was always made milder in his favour.

The nobility, thus bowed under the yoke of the most dreadful slavery, do not fail to retaliate upon the people: the people are slaves to them, to the sovereign, or to the waywodes who represent him.

Two kinds of slaves are distinguished in Russia among the people; some belong to the sovereign, others to the nobility. The first only pay tribute to the Empress, the others both to the sovereign and to their lord. The nobles estimate their riches by the number of farmers which belong to them. The slaves of the crown pay into the royal treasury the sum of one hundred and ten copecs, or four shillings and seven-pence of English money, and the others pay two shillings and eleven-pence to the crown. The lords impose what tax they please upon their slaves, and sometimes seize upon the small fortune they may have acquired by their abilities. If these slaves, by cultivating the land, and by industry, do not get enough to pay the lord, he allows them to hire themselves to merchants, strangers, or other persons, who have no slaves. For this purpose, he gives them a passport only for a few years. The slave is obliged to remit his wages annually to his lord, who gives him up what he thinks proper out of them.

The lords sell their slaves as cattle is sold in other parts of the world. They chuse out from among them the number of servants they want, and treat them with great inhumanity. They are not allowed a civil power of life and death over their servants any more than

than over their other flaves; but as they have the privilege of punishing them with the *padogi*, they have them chaftized in fuch a manner, that they may be faid, in fact, to have acquired the right of putting them to death.

In weighty offences, a lord, according to law, ought to bring his flave to be tried at the ordinary courts of juftice. In 1761, the fenate publifhed an edict, whereby all the lords were allowed to fend any flaves they were difpleafed with to work in the mines; but the lords prefer, and will ever do fo, chaftizing them at home, and keeping them to themfelves.

The nobility of Ruffia never enter into the priefthood; fo that there is no intermediate ftate in the ecclefiaftical body, which is made up entirely of the common people, or the children of the priefts, who are often the moft diffolute; fo that the ignorance and depravity of the Ruffian clergy are the natural confequences of their not having received any principles of education. Their power was dangerous only in the times of the primitive church, as they were then a better conftituted body; and that the whole nation was inflamed with zeal, which is no where to be found at prefent, but among the lower clafs of people.

The common people are bigotted, even to fanaticifm, in favour of the Greek religion: this extravagance increafes the farther we get from the capital; but thefe very people are fo little acquainted with their religion, that they are perfuaded they fulfil all its duties by complying with fome external ceremonies, and efpecially by keeping the Lent fafts with the greateft ftrictnefs. In other refpects, they give themfelves up to debauchery and to every kind of vice. Morality is lefs to be met with among the Ruffians than among the Pagans their neighbours. The opinions of the Ruffians with regard to Chriftianity are fo extraordinary, that it fhould feem as if that religion, fo well adapted in itfelf for the happinefs and good order of fociety, had only ferved to make this people more wicked. A murderer being taken and condemned, and being afked in the courfe of his trial whether he had kept the Lent fafts, appeared as much furprized as the moft upright man would have been, if his honefty had been called in queftion. He immediately anfwered with warmth, that he was incapable of neglecting the duties of his religion. Yet this very man was at the head of a fet of ruffians, and, whenever they feized upon any travellers, he readily gave up all the booty to his companions, if they did but deliver him thefe unhappy victims alive. He firft undreffed them, and tied them naked to a tree, without any regard to their fex; he then opened their breaft near the heart, and drank their blood. He declared, that he took great pleafure in feeing the dreadful contortions and convulfions of thefe wretched people. This fact, though it may feem fcarcely credible, was told me by fome Ruffians.

Such examples are rarely to be met with in Ruffia; and I have mentioned this only to fhew, that, in this country, lefs attention has been given to form the manners of the people by religion than to oblige them to obferve certain ceremonies,

monies, which do not always improve the morals of mankind.

The men in Siberia are tall, stout, and well made, as they are almost all over Russia: they are excessively fond of women and drinking. As they are slaves to a despotic prince, they exert the same absolute authority over their slaves or inferiors with still greater severity.

The women are in general handsome at Tobolsky: their skin is exceedingly fair, and their countenance agreeable: their eyes are black, languishing, and down-cast; for they never dare look a man full in the face: they wear no caps, but use coloured handkerchiefs, which they interweave so curiously among their hair, generally black and unpowdered, that this kind of head-dress gives them a very bewitching look. They all use paint, young girls as well as married women: and this custom prevails even among the servant maids, and some of the common people.

The women are commonly well-made till the age of eighteen or twenty; but their legs as well as their feet are always large. Nature in this respect seems to have had in view the bulk they usually acquire, which seems to want very firm supporters.

The baths they use twice a week contribute chiefly to spoil their shapes: they cause such a relaxation in all the parts of the body, that the beauty of the women is quite gone before they are thirty years of age.

Their dress at present is very much like that which is in use throughout Europe. The men's dress is exactly the same at Tobolsky, and all over Russia. Some merchants, the noblemen's stewards, and the common men, are almost the only persons who have kept to the old dress, as well as to the custom of wearing the beard. I saw only a few gentlemen at Tobolsky, who had been disgraced, still conforming to these old customs, which they certainly had lately taken up again. The dress of the women at Tobolsky (I except the head-dress) differs from that used in Europe only in our peculiar fashions, with which they are unacquainted: they generally wear a loose gown like a domino. On public days, their gowns are much like the robes formerly worn in France. This dress came from St. Petersburgh to Tobolsky.

The men, as well as the women, are generally richly dressed: they get their stuffs and silks from Mosco, and sometimes from China; but at Tobolsky, as throughout Russia, both the sexes are very uncleanly, notwithstanding the baths they use twice a week. The women change their linen but seldom; and are unacquainted with that variety of undress to which the Europeans are accustomed, and which is often more bewitching than the richest ornaments; so that there are few opportunities of being present at the toilet of the Russian women.

In the houses of people of the first rank at Tobolsky, as in most other parts of Russia, there is but one bed for the husband and wife, and sometimes one for the children: all other persons in the house lie promiscuously upon benches or upon mats, which they spread on the

the ground, in the different apartments*. There are no curtains to the beds; and instead of a bolster, the husband and wife have each of them seven or eight pillows, one less than the other, raised up in form of two pyramids. This bed is generally the principal piece of furniture. Sometimes there are at Tobolsky, in bedrooms, some wooden chairs, a large stove, and a small table.

In the whole city of Tobolsky, there was not a single house that had any carpeting in it: some beams placed one upon another, but made smoother than common, some benches, and a few wooden chairs, made up all the furniture of their apartments.

At Tobolsky men are very jealous of their wives, as they are throughout the greater part of Russia: beyond the city of Mosco, however, they are seldom in company with them; spending most of the day in drinking, and generally coming home drunk. The women seldom go out; they live wholly sequestered from society, given up to laziness and indolence, which are the causes of the depravity of their manners.

That kind of delicate love which proceeds from sensibility, and against which the severest virtue cannot always guard itself, is here totally unknown.

Here a lover never has the satisfaction of seeing the confusion and disorder of his mistress, endeavouring, but unable, to conceal her tenderness. Such situations are never met with in Siberia, nor in the greatest part of Russia, where the polished manners of the rest of Europe have not yet prevailed. In these barbarous regions, men tyrannize over their wives, whom they consider and treat as their slaves, requiring of them the most servile offices: in their matrimonial engagements they are obliged to bring them a handful of rods, in great ceremony, and to pull off their boots, as a token of the superiority of the husband, and the subjection of the wife. Availing themselves more than any where else of their superior power, they have established the most unjust laws, which neither the beauty nor delicacy of the sex have yet been able to abolish or soften. We are not therefore to be surprized, that that delicacy of sentiment which characterizes the people of more civilized nations is so rarely to be met with here. If such women are worth the attempt, boldness is often sufficient to insure success; but opportunities of this kind seldom occur, as women are scarce ever seen but when their husbands are present; and if the least attention is shewn them on these occasions, it is very probably one may not see them a second time.

I saw some foreigners at Tobolsky, who had been there ever since the beginning of the last war: unacquainted with the customs of the country, they often experienced disagreeable consequences

---

* In 1663, the people of quality used to lie upon boards or benches, on which a skin or other covering was spread: there was no furniture in the houses; and very few tables were covered with a cloth at meals.—*M. de Voltaire, Histoire de la Russie,* tom. i. page 20.

from the idea that women were to be treated with the same politeness and attention here as in the rest of Europe. They afterwards became more cautious, being convinced of the necessity of taking no notice of the ladies before their husbands; and, joining in with the convivial pleasures of the latter, soon found means of being admitted to greater familiarities with their wives in private. Thus the depravity of the sex in Russia is owing to the tyranny of the men.

The women are captivated merely by sensual pleasures, often giving themselves up to their slaves; among which they take care to chuse such as are most healthy and robust.

The manners of this people will never be improved while the women are kept in a state of slavery, and do not partake of the pleasures of society. Although the men are remarkably severe to their wives, yet are they very indulgent to their daughters. They think that married women should be entirely taken up with their husbands, but that greater liberty may be allowed to the unmarried, thereby to give them opportunities of getting husbands: they very soon avail themselves of this freedom, without the consent of their parents, or the sanction of the church. At twelve or thirteen years they are frequently no strangers to the other sex; but such is the inconsistency of this people, that they expect their daughters should still be virtuous, while they allow them such liberty as ought ever to be regulated by a good education: they also pretend to determine, with an absolute certainty, whether their daughters are still virgins; this is done by a jury of skilful women, who determine this matter by entering into the strictest examination, which, in other countries, would be considered as very indecent.

On the day appointed for the marriage ceremony, after the parties have been joined by a priest, as in our church, the lady's parents give an elegant supper, at which the husband's family is present, some friends, and a magician, who comes with an intent to counteract the witchcraft which might be practised by other magicians, to prevent the consummation of the marriage. The newmarried couple, attended by a godfather and a godmother, are conducted with the greatest ceremony into the nuptial chamber before supper.

The magician walks first, the godfather follows conducting the bride; the bridegroom gives his hand to the godmother, and the bridesman his to the husband's nearest female relation, who is one of the jury, which is generally composed of three or four women. During this procession to the nuptial apartment, every thing is got ready for the feast in the room where the company stays, who wait only the return of the married couple to begin their mirth; being thoroughly persuaded, that the decision of the jury will be favourable to the bride.

The marriage chamber contains in general nothing but a bed, which is usually very neat, and without curtains; the images given by the godfather and godmother to the married couple; a few chairs, and a table, with bottles of of brandy, and glasses, near which an old matron is placed.

The procession having reached the marriage chamber, the matron offers the bride a waiter, on which are glasses filled with brandy and other liquors: the bride then presents them to the magician first, and afterwards to the whole company round; the magician prepares his magic art; the bride is then undressed, and left with a small petticoat and an under-waistcoat only, both of them made on purpose for this day, which is consecrated to voluptuousness. The bridegroom is also undressed, and a nightgown thrown over him: the bride then kisses all the company round, offers them again a glass of brandy; and when every body has drank a second time, they retire into an antichamber, leaving the married couple alone with the matron, who assists at the ceremony; in which she is the more interested, as she receives a reward if the lady is acknowledged to be a virgin; whereas she is obliged, if the contrary happens, to drink out of a broken glass, in the midst of the company, which is considered as a mark of ignominy.

After consummation, the jury of women is called in, who strip the bride quite naked, in order to decide whether she was a virgin.

[We shall here pass by the proofs that are given to the company upon this occasion in confirmation of the lady's chastity.]

When all the company is perfectly satisfied, the lady dances for a few minutes with her husband, and every body sits quickly down to the table, where most of the men commonly get drunk.

There were several marriages while I stayed at Tobolsky; but I could never get any admission to any of the feasts: one lady in particular, otherwise a very amiable woman, was always against it; saying, she was afraid I should think their ceremony ridiculous, and give an account of it to the public. In my way from Tobolsky back again to St. Petersburgh, I was invited to a wedding, and appointed bridesman, so that I had then an opportunity of seeing the whole transaction.

European manners have gained very little ground in Russia, because they are not conformable to the despotism of the government: they have nevertheless introduced luxury, and brought on a communication between Russians and foreigners, which has only contributed to make the Russians more unhappy, by giving them an opportunity of comparing their state of slavery with that of a free people.

As I have seen the Russians at the distance of eight hundred leagues from court, I have been enabled to acquire a competent knowledge of this people.

Upon the whole, there is very little society in Russia, especially beyond Mosco: neither is it possible there should be much, under a government where no man enjoys that civil liberty, by which the safety of the citizen, in other countries, is secured. A mutual fear prevails among individuals; from hence arises mistrust, disguise, and deceit. Friendship, that sentiment which contributes to the happiness of our lives, has never been known in Russia: it supposes a sensibility which makes an absolute union of the two friends, and

and effusions of the heart, which divide their pleasures and pains reciprocally. As the men have but little respect for the women beyond Mosco, they are not attended to in company, although company is nothing without them. They are almost always confined to their houses, where they pass their tedious days among their slaves, without authority and without employment: they do not even enjoy the satisfaction of reading, for most of them know not how to read. The men are as ignorant as the women. They visit now and then with great ceremony: the governors and chief magistrates give grand dinners several times in a year. Relations also meet now and then, to keep the feast of their family saint; but they seldom admit any person at these feasts who is not one of the family. At the great entertainments, both men and women are invited together, but they neither sit at the same table, nor in the same room. The mistress of the house does not appear in the men's apartments till they are just sitting down to dinner: she brings in with her a large waiter covered with glasses full of brandy, which she presents, in a very submissive manner, to all the guests, who do not even look at her: the glasses are returned to her, and she withdraws immediately.

There are always a great number of people at these feasts, to which persons of all stations are invited. Officers, clergy, magistrates, and merchants, are all placed at the same table; but with this difference, that rank is more strictly attended to than in any German court. Military men are placed according to their several ranks, and persons of other professions are disposed in the same manner: no regard is paid to birth.

All the dishes are served up at once. Their soup is made by cutting the meat into small pieces in the broth. They have some ragouts, which nobody who is not used to can eat of. The table is generally covered with several pyramids of roast meat; most of them composed of different kinds of game, the rest of butchers' meat. Chinese sweetmeats are served up at the same time, and some made of the fruits of the country.

Their manner of sitting at table, and their customs, seem to be very similar to those which prevail in some districts of Germany; but they have adopted only the ridiculous parts of them, which they have even rendered still more ridiculous. A profound silence is observed during dinner, which is interrupted only at times by the healths that are drank.

As soon as they sit down to table, each man pours into his glass some of the made-wine I have mentioned before; and then all rise to drink each other's health. Each guest is drank to by his christian and surname; and a drop of wine is swallowed to each person's health.

I have been at some of these dinners, where there were more than sixty people all drinking to each other at the same time. Their attitudes, and the confusion of different sounds, had a very singular effect. Peter, not being able to make James hear him, was stretching himself over the table, and bawling out as loud as he could;

at

at the same instant he was interrupted by Francis, who was bowing to him, or by a knock of the head from Philip, who was turning about from right to left without perceiving the posture Peter was in. Philip's turn came next: as he was lifting his glass to his mouth, his neighbour gave him a jog of the elbow, and, spilling part of his wine, interrupted him at the most interesting moment. Such scenes as these, varied in different ways, were repeated almost at every part of the table; and the pleasantry of them was enhanced by observing the impatience of some of the people. As to myself, I could never find an opportunity of drinking any one's health; but kept my head in constant motion, to the right and left, and forwards. It is reckoned a qualification to catch the opportunity so seasonably as to drink to every person's health, without descending from one's dignity, or meeting with any accident.

The first health being over, every body sits down, and is at liberty to eat for a few moments. Glass tumblers of a cylindrical form, six inches high, and four wide, are placed in different parts of the table. Every guest within reach of one of these tumblers takes it up, and drinks out of it: it would be thought very unpolite, if he was to take a glass in order to avoid drinking out of the same tumbler as his neighbour. This custom is not only disagreeable, but at the same time very dangerous, on account of the scurvy, which is extremely frequent in Russia.

When the company has ate for a few minutes, the Emperor's health goes round. This toast is given in a different manner. A large glass bottle, to which there is also a glass top, is placed on the table before the person of the highest rank. This person rises from his seat, as well as his right hand neighbour, to whom he gives the head of the bottle, and, pouring some wine into the cup, gives out the Emperor's health, bowing to the whole company. As soon as he has drank, he gives the bottle to his neighbour, who passes the top to the person sitting next to him. All the company drink the Emperor's health in the same manner, while a band of musicians is employed in singing songs adapted to the ceremony.

The healths of the princes and princesses of the Royal Family are then drank in the same order, and eating goes on for a little time longer.

The healths of all the guests are then carried round, with another glass bottle, which is not so beautiful as the first, and is covered with a crust of bread.

This toast goes round nearly in the same way as the former, except that, when the lid of the bottle is given to one's neighbour, it is usual at the same time to tell him the christian and surname of the person whose health is going round; and this must be repeated, making a bow to him: this custom is very troublesome to strangers, as the Russians have generally three or four christian names. This ceremony is carried on with the utmost gravity, and one must be very exact in the whole detail, which extends all round the table. However desirous I was of being exact, yet I was always puzzled when the toast came to me. I used to forget the

the number of faints named to me, most of which were never inrolled in our lift. I was, however, very much mortified at this. Besides, I had usually for my neighbour a Russian, who was a very strict observer of rules: he had acquired by his exactness a right of presiding over the police of the table, and was very much out of temper whenever any one was deficient in this point. This gentleman was so obliging as to set me right frequently; but on one occasion he was as much puzzled as myself, when two crusts of bread were presented to me from each side, one of which had fell several times, contrary to order, into the plates and into the bottle. Not knowing whom I was to answer, nor what I was to do with these two crusts, I referred the whole affair to him, and sat down. He was informed, that, the company consisting of sixty guests, a second bottle had been called for, to hasten the ceremony; but he decided, that it was better to be detained two hours longer at table than to neglect any of the usual forms.

At last, the company rose from table, and went into another room. I imagined, at first, that the dinner was over, and that we were now to drink coffee; but was much surprized at the sight of a table covered with Chinese sweetmeats. Four servants waited for the company, with bottles of mead, beer, and different liquors made with brandy. Others brought in waiters with glasses. The company then set in for drinking again; and from this time ceremony was at an end. The Russians, though accustomed to this manner of living, seldom bear the quantity of liquors drank after dinner, which are not only very strong, but the drinking is also incessantly continued till the evening. If the company chuses to take a walk, the bottles and glasses are carried along with them; and this is looked upon as doing the honours completely.

Some travellers assert, that the women as well as the men give themselves up to all the excesses of drinking; but I have always seen the contrary. The women, after dinner, remain in the same room, growing tired of one another; for it is impossible it should be otherwise, where thirty women meet together without one man.

There is no other kind of social amusement in use throughout the whole nation, from Mosco to Tobolsky: they dance sometimes, but that is very rare, except at weddings.

It is about fifty years since the women at Mosco and St. Petersburgh have shaken off the yoke of slavery to which they were subjected by their husbands. Before that time, they lived and were treated in the same way as in other parts of Russia. If the manners have not been much bettered from this change, it is owing to their excessive depravity before it took place. Throughout Russia, in general, a man has much to answer for, if he is but agreeable.

Mosco appeared to me preferable, in many respects, to St. Petersburgh. The city of Mosco not being more than two hundred short leagues distant from St. Petersburgh, the governors are too near the sovereign to be tyrannical; and the inhabitants far enough from the seat of government not to be afraid

CHARACTERS.

afraid of a scaffold for slight indiscretions of society*. Pleasure is sought after at Mosco, while the inhabitants can hardly venture to speak of it at St. Petersburgh.

The common people in Russia, having no ideas of liberty, are much less unhappy than the nobles. Besides, they have but few wishes, and consequently their wants are less: they are unacquainted with either industry or commerce, especially beyond Mosco. The Russian, having no property of his own, is usually indifferent to every thing which might better his fortune. Even the nobles, who are constantly in fear of banishment, and of having their estates confiscated, are not so much employed in improving them as they are in expedients to raise a speedy supply of ready money to gratify their present inclinations.

The Russian country people live upon very indifferent kind of food; and, therefore, readily giving way to laziness in their stoves, they pass their lives in the debaucheries of women and brandy, which liquor, however, they are not always able to procure. If we were to judge of them merely from the languid life they lead, it might be imagined, that they have but few ideas; on the contrary, they are artful, cunning, and greater rogues than in any other nation. They are also remarkably dexterous at thieving. They are not endowed with that courage which some philosophers have ascribed to the northern nations: the Russian peasants are, on the contrary, pusillanimous and cowardly to an incredible degree.

There are no principles of morality among them: they are more afraid of neglecting the Lent fasts than of murdering a fellow-creature, especially if he is a foreigner; for they do not reckon foreigners among the number of their brethren.

The Russian and the Polish slave seem to differ from each other in every respect: the Russian neglects agriculture; is generally immoral, crafty, and subtle. On the contrary, the Polish slave takes a pleasure in cultivating the land: he is moral and stupid. These contrarieties seem to me sufficiently accounted for from the different constitution of the two nations, exclusive of other causes, which may possibly have contributed to establish them.

The slave in Poland is in possession of lands which are his own property; it is natural, therefore, he should delight in improving them, since by that he is enabled to satisfy all his wants, and to enjoy the comforts of life, without having recourse to criminal actions. He is moreover subject to a set of free nobles, who may venture, in every instance, to be virtuous with impunity. If he is stupid, it is because he is enslaved. The Russian slave not having one inch of ground at his own disposal, agri-

* M. de Montesquieu observes, in the 12th chapter of his 12th book, wherein he treats of indiscreet words, that in the manifesto published by the late Czarina against the Olgoroufki family, in 1740, one of those princes is sentenced to death for having used some indecent expressions about the Czarina's person: another for having misinterpreted her wise regulations for the good of the empire, and for having offended her sacred person by words not sufficiently respectful.

culture

culture is indifferent to him: he is willing to enjoy himself, and is fond of drinking brandy; but as he can seldom get it without theft, or trespassing against the laws, the fear of punishment makes him cautious and subtle.

Slavery has set aside all the rights of nature among the Russians: the human species is in Russia a commercial article, sometimes sold at a very low price. Children are often forced from their mothers' arms to be sold to persons given up to debauchery. The joy which other people conceive on the birth of their legitimate children is here unknown. This event, on the contrary, is a sorrowful one to a young woman, who knows that her child may be taken away from her at the instant that he is playing on her knee: she suckles him, and takes a great deal of trouble in bringing him up: he grows, and the time draws near when she is in continual apprehension of losing him. She never can flatter herself that in this beloved child she shall find support and a friend in her old age. If, when somewhat farther advanced in life, the child perceives the tears starting from his mother in consequence of these dreadful reflections, he asks her the reason, presses her cheeks between his little hands, soothes her with kisses, and at length mixes his tears with her's.

The meanest animals enjoy the happiness caused by the birth of their young. Man, in Russia, is the only being who cannot partake of it. This depravity stifles all principles of humanity, and all kind of sentiment. Going, on my return from Tobolsky, to St. Petersburgh, into a house where I was to lodge, I found a father chained to a post in the middle of his family: by his cries, and the little regard his children paid to him, I imagined he was mad: but this was by no means the case. In Russia, people who are sent to raise recruits go through all the villages; and pitch upon the men proper for the service, as butchers, in all other parts, go into the stable to mark the sheep. This man's son had been selected for the service, and had made his escape without the father's knowledge: the father was made a prisoner in his own house; his children were his gaolers, and he was in daily expectation of receiving his sentence. I was so much shocked with this account, and with the scene I beheld, that I was forced to seek another lodging immediately.

This practice has made the Russians cruel and inhuman: they are animals whom their masters think they must crush with a rod of iron, while they continue under the yoke[*].

The Russian nobility, having cruel and wicked slaves constantly before their eyes, have acquired a severity which is not natural to them: as they crouch before their sovereign, to their superiors, and to all those from whom they have any

---

[*] The common people in Russia are at present so corrupt, that they must be kept in a state of rigid servitude while they continue enslaved: but any man, who allows himself to reflect, will easily conceive, that, with proper care, they might be restored to liberty, without having any thing to fear from some inconveniencies which may be thought to follow at first. While they are slaves, they will ever be vicious.

thing

thing to expect, they exercise the greater rigor over all persons subject to their authority, or who have not the power to resist them.

The common people in Russia having nothing to contest with the sovereign, one might reasonably expect to find happiness among this class. In all other parts of the world, the country people get together on holidays: the fathers meet at a public house, oftentimes resting from their labours under the shade of a tree, and indulging in a cheerful glass; they discourse about increasing their stock, and sometimes their conversation turns upon politics, while a wretched fidler, sitting on a cask, makes their children exquisitely happy.

Such pleasures are unknown in Russia: the common people dance now and then, chiefly on certain days of the Carnival, when they are entirely given up to debauchery and drunkenness; so that one can scarce venture to travel at such a time, for fear of being ill treated by the mob. The peasants in Russia generally stay in their stoves on holidays, standing at the door without taking any exercise: laziness is the greatest pleasure they have, next to women and drinking. If a Russian peasant has got a little money, he goes to the public house by himself, spends it, and gets drunk in a few minutes: he is then no longer in fear of his fortune being taken from him.

[We shall conclude this article with the account our author gives of the progress which the arts and sciences have hitherto made in Russia.]

Peter I. ascended the throne of Russia in 1689; and immediately framed the design of enlightening his nation, sunk in ignorance for more than seven hundred years past. He undertook a journey into Europe, that he might become acquainted with the arts and sciences, and with every circumstance which could possibly tend to complete the designs he had formed. In the course of his journey, nothing escaped his notice: he visited the learned; he sought out the artist in his manufactory; made himself master of the art; and being thereby enabled to judge of the abilities of the artists, engaged them in his service, whenever he found them to excel.

All the sovereign powers interested themselves warmly in promoting the schemes of this great man; numbers of learned men and artists of all kinds, from the several parts of Europe, set out for Russia. Peter I. on his return into his own dominions, raised public buildings consecrated to the arts and sciences. Establishments, which in Europe were formed by degrees, arose in Russia all at once: the nobility laid aside their beards, as well as their antient manner of dress: the women, before confined wholly to their houses, now made their appearance in public meetings, unknown in Russia till this period. The court became brilliant. Peter I. seemed to have formed a new nation, though he had made no alteration in the political constitution of the government: the nation remained in a state of slavery, which he still made more severe. He forced all the nobility, without distinction, to serve in the army. A number of young slaves were chosen out from among the people, and fixed in the academies and schools: of these,

some

some were destined to literature, others designed for the arts and sciences, without any regard to their particular talents or inclination. Peter himself visited the academies and the manufactories, and often took the plane and the chisel in his own hands; but snatched the pencil from the hands of a young artist, who was painting Armida in the arms of Rinaldo, and ordered him to be flogged.

The successors of Peter I. pursued the same plan: the Academy of Sciences, however, gained a reputation. Bernouilli, Delisle, Herman, and Euler, kept up the credit they had acquired in other countries: the arts shone forth with some kind of splendor; but the Academy lost its repute, and the arts sensibly decreased as the great men first invited into Russia either died or left the country. The sovereigns still continued to supply their subjects with able masters, and to encourage and protect men of abilities; but, notwithstanding these advantages, not one Russian has appeared in the course of more than sixty years whose name deserves to be recorded in the history of the arts and sciences.

Men of abilities, invited into Russia from foreign parts, appear mostly to be discouraged, and not to persevere in their studies with the same earnestness as they did in their own country. In the year 1761, several foreigners of the first rank in the republic of letters belonged to the Academy of St. Petersburgh; among these may be mentioned M. Epiney, Leman, Braun, Tauber, Stelin, and Muler, formerly secretary to the Academy, and at present director of a school at Mosco, as I was informed at my return into France. The late Mr. Lomanosew, a Russian, was a man of genius, and would have made a considerable figure in any other academy. Mr. Rumouski, as yet too young a man to have acquired any great degree of reputation, is possessed of great natural abilities, and a thirst after knowledge, very uncommon among the Russians.

Notwithstanding this number of learned men, it should seem as if genius in most of them was weakened as soon as they came into Russia, so that the academies and schools seem to derive their chief credit from the names only of the learned which are in Russia. The annals of the sciences furnish incontestible proofs of this assertion; and any man who has not examined these, may be convinced of this truth, by consulting thousands of travellers, who have resided at St. Petersburgh and at Mosco.

This state of the arts and sciences in Russia implies a defect, the cause of which must be sought for either in a want of genius peculiar to the nation, or in the nature of the government, and the climate. A philosopher*, whose name will be held in veneration by the latest posterity, speaking of the difference of men with respect to climate, represents the people of the North as having coarser organs, and being animated with fluids of a grosser kind, better adapted to produce large robust bodies than men of genius; but this philosopher would have us

* Montesquieu, liv. xiv. chap. II.

consider

CHARACTERS.

consider them, at the same time, as a very brave, simple, unreserved, unsuspecting people, without policy or craft, having few vices, and several virtues, a great deal of sincerity and honesty, and whose dispositions are not very amorous. When I travelled in Russia, I every where met with a people very different from what I expected to find from the ideas of this celebrated philosopher. It must be allowed, however, that, in what he has said on this subject, he has considered the people of the North independently of their government; which has so far altered the nature of man in Russia, by subduing even those faculties which are least under the controul of the authority of the sovereign, that it is extremely difficult to ascertain the distinguishing character of the nation; and it is for this reason that I have hitherto confined myself to the relation of facts upon this point.

The spirit of invention is as uncommon among the Russians as genius; but they have a peculiar turn for imitation. In Russia, locksmiths, masons, carpenters, &c. are formed as a soldier is in other countries. Each regiment has, in its own corps, all the necessary artists; and is not obliged to have recourse to manufacturers, as is the custom every where else. They determine by the stature what employment a man is most fit for. They give a soldier a lock for a pattern, with orders to make others like it, and he does it with the greatest dexterity; but the original must be perfect, otherwise he would copy it with all its defects, however easy it might be to correct them. The same may be observed with regard to artists and workmen of all kinds.

This particular talent of the Russians is so remarkable, that one may see it prevail in the nation, immediately on coming into Russia. One may easily perceive, that the Russians possess it in so eminent a degree, that they might have been formed into a very different people from what they are at present.

I have observed that the Russians were naturally cheerful, that they have the true spirit of society, and that they delight in it: these circumstances are evident in the Russians who travel into foreign countries. Why, then, is a Russian, at least in some respects, so different from what he might be? The nature of education, and of the government, will furnish the solution of this problem.

In a good government, the education of children should be directed to virtue, the love of our country, and the happiness of society. Such an education is intimately connected with the political system of a good government; but it supposes that the interest of the sovereign should be the same as that of the nation. The regularity and harmony of a good administration consist in the relations and exact combinations of these two interests: this constitutes the power of the sovereign, and the happiness of the people. Hence arises that love of our country, which induces every citizen to consider the good of the nation as his own: public gratitude inspires and keeps up the love of fame, brings forth great men, and insures them the veneration of posterity.

The love of fame and of our country is unknown in Russia: despotism debases the mind, damps the genius, and stifles every kind

of

of sentiment. In Russia no person dares venture to think: the soul is so much debased, that its faculties are destroyed. Fear is almost the only passion by which the whole nation is actuated.

I have seen in their schools a young mathematician studying Euclid with a piece of wood fastened to his neck, and masters commanding abilities as an army is taught to exercise.

I was told by a famous foreign artist, who had the direction of one of these schools, that he once found among his pupils one of a superior genius. Desirous of pushing a young man forward who might do him honour, he took great care in instructing him: he was well pleased to observe the daily improvements of his pupil; but in a little time the young man stopped short. The artist, having tried to encourage him by all kinds of mild proceedings, asked him at last, in a very friendly manner, Why he had taken a dislike to his business? I am, answered the young man, slave to M***; when he finds that I am a proficient, he will oblige me to work in his own house, where I shall meet with such ill treatment, that I had much rather live in the same manner as my companions.

I have known several persons who were persuaded that the Russians were incapable of making any considerable improvements in any thing. I think this opinion is entirely groundless; such facts as I have been relating of this young slave have given rise to this mistake. These facts, on the contrary, imply at least a great share of judgment.

The government has attempted to rectify some of these inconveniencies, by ordering that all persons who should distinguish themselves at the schools should no longer be slaves to their lords, but should belong to the state. In this case, the lords will either avoid sending their slaves to the schools, or will find some means of keeping them to themselves, so that they must still remain in a state of slavery.

I could mention a number of facts of the same kind as the former, of which I have been witness; but I shall pass them over, to avoid giving offence to some persons at present in Russia. The fatal effects of despotism are extended over all the arts, all the manufactures, and are conveyed into all the workshops. The artists are chained down to their work. This I have seen frequently, especially at Mosco; and it is with such workmen that the Russians imagine they can imitate the manufactories of Lyons.

Some Account of the Tartars of Kasan, under the government of Russia. From the same.

AT length I came to Birna, a village inhabited by Tartars; many of whom came out to meet me, at the distance of a werst from the village, expressing, by signs, their great desire to serve me. It was evident, from the candour and tranquillity observable in their countenances, that these professions were sincere; so that I followed them without any apprehensions. They placed themselves before my carriage, and conducted me to the house of the chief person in the village,

village, who was held in great estimation among them: his merit and his virtues had entitled him to rule over them, without the form of an election. They had prepared a kind of dinner for me, consisting of honey, butter, and a few vegetables. Their houses are as neat as those of the Siberians are dirty. In other respects they live nearly after the same manner, except that they are Mahometans.

Their dress has some resemblance to that of the Russians. The Tartars wear a woollen jacket, which they bind with their girdle; over this they have a full long robe hanging loose and flowing. They always have boots on. Their heads are shaved, except on one spot at the back part, which they cover with a small piece of leather. They wear a cap edged with fur. They are tall, strong, and well made; and their dress is perfectly becoming. Notwithstanding the mildness of their countenances, they have still the appearance of a warlike and independent people; and have indeed preserved their former privileges. In war-time, they furnish the Russians with a certain number of troops, which are kept in pay by the latter.

The dress of the Tartar women differs but little from that of the men; it is shorter, and they wear the girdle above the robe. Their head-dress is a cap, sometimes made in form of a sugar-loaf, and covered with copecs and glass beads: a large piece of cloth fastened to the back part of the cap, and hanging down below the waist, is ornamented in the same manner. They wear boots, and might be taken for men at first sight, if not distinguished by their head-dress. They share most of their husbands' labours, by whom they are very mildly treated, and there is not the least superiority on either side. The married women seemed to enjoy a perfect freedom; the girls on the contrary are much confined; but notwithstanding the watchfulness of fathers and mothers, they contrive to slip away upon some occasions, which they make the most of. In Siberia, the married women are confined, and the girls left more at liberty, which they also do not fail to take advantage of, as we have before observed, so that in all these countries the girls seem to be very troublesome.

The dress of the Russians differs from that of the Tartars, inasmuch as the first wear a kind of waistcoat instead of a tunic, and that they often leave their shirts hanging out of their breeches. Over the waistcoat they wear a kind of jacket with a girdle. They have no boots, but wrap up their legs in cloth, which they fasten from the bottom with a cord. Their shoes are commonly made of the bark of trees. All the common people of Russia have kept their beards, and they all wear caps. The dress of the Tartars is in every respect preferable to that of the Russian men: the first is elegant, but the latter scanty. The same cannot be said of the dress of the women. That of the Tartar women is generally more rich, but not always so pleasing. The Russian women, when at home, wear above their shifts a tunic, which reaches down to their heels, and is buttoned at the fore-part. When they go out of doors, they put on a gown over this,

Vol. XIII. C

this, and sometimes a mantle. Their head-dress is more like a hat than any thing else, and is usually ornamented with copecs and glass beads. The girls dress in the same manner, excepting only that they have never any caps on, and that they only bind their heads with a kind of riband.

When I left Birna, the Tartars doubled my number of horses, on account of the mountains we were to cross, without making any difference in the price; neither would they accept of any consideration for the entertainment they had given me.

[Those Tartars whom our author has described live in a very remote and desolate country: he gives the following account of those that inhabit the capital city of Cazan, and the cultivated country in its neighbourhood.]

I arrived at Cazan the first of October; where a Tartar prince was the governor, who received me very graciously: he had ordered an apartment to be got ready for me; but M. Weroffchin, a Russian, whom I had the honour of seeing at St. Petersburgh, had been so kind as to give me a lodging at his house, to which I was conducted.

The next day I waited upon the governor; after a few compliments had passed, which I did not understand, we seated ourselves round a table covered with a beautiful carpet, on which were placed four large pipes, and a china bowl full of Chinese tobacco: I smoked for a few minutes. After this some *liqueurs* of the country were served up, with sweetmeats, fruits, and a water melon; which last fruit is so exceedingly delicious here, that I ate nothing else. Melons are in great plenty at Cazan, and never do any hurt, how much soever one may eat of them. I found this fruit so much better than any I had ever met with of the kind any where else, that I brought away some of the seeds; but they did not answer in France.

A great many of the inhabitants of Cazan are Tartars, who are so far from being persecuted there, that, on the contrary, they are treated with the utmost consideration; so that they are firmly attached to their sovereign. They have preserved the innocence of their manners, their probity, and their truth, and are most of them possessed of small fortunes. Their dress is much richer than that of the other Tartars I have already spoken of: the dress of the women is even different in some respects, chiefly with regard to their head; for I never saw any caps there in form of a sugar-loaf. Their head-dress is very similar to that of the Russians, except that they have jewels and pearls intermixed with their hair. They also make ornaments of the same kind, some of which they put upon the sleeves of their gowns; others are fastened round the neck, and hang down upon the breast.

An Account of the following singular People, from the same Writer, will, we doubt not, be agreeable to our Readers.

Of the WOTIAKS.

SOWIOLAVA is a hamlet inhabited by the Wotiaks. I resolved to spend part of a day with these people, on account of their singular appearance and dress. Some authors have reckoned them among the Tartars, but I could not observe the least analogy between the two nations. The Wotiak men and women, in general, are no more than four feet a few inches high, and are of a very weak and delicate constitution. The dress of the men is the same as that of the Russians; but the dress of the women has not the least resemblance to those I have seen in Siberia. They wear a shift of coarse linen, slit at the bottom like a man's shirt, and hemmed at this opening with thread or worsted of different colours. There is also a little ornament of a triangular figure wrought on the right side of the shift. Their gown is woollen, and bears a great resemblance to the habit of the Jesuits in college: the sleeve of the upper gown are slit in the middle, to give passage to the arms; and the lower part of the sleeve generally hangs down. This gown, which reaches down to the legs, is fastened at the forepart merely by a girdle, curiously wrought. They wear also coarse cloth stockings. and sandals, the same as the Russians. Their headdress is very remarkable: they first wrap up their heads with a towel, over which they fasten, with two strings, a kind of helmet, made of the bark of a tree, and ornamented at the fore-part with a piece of cloth and with copecs. This helmet is afterwards covered with a handkerchief, wrought with thread or worsted of various colours, and edged with a fringe. This head dress is above one foot high. Their hair is divided into two tresses, which fall down upon the breast with a necklace, such as the Tartars wear. One of my attendants, being desirous of examining this necklace, opened one of these women's shifts in such a manner as to uncover all her breast; at which she was so far from being displeased, although it was done in public, that she laughed at his curiosity.

M. Strahlemberg thinks these people some of the most antient in Siberia. They have professed Christianity for several years past, but are so ignorant, that they have not the least idea of this religion. The Russians sent them priests, and some troops, to convert them. I found a Russian missionary at Sowiolava who was deputed to instruct and baptize them. Although he was unacquainted with their language, he nevertheless made Christians of them; so tha[t] they still adhere to all the superstitious parts of their religion.

As I was desirous of purchasing one of the women's dresses, one was brought me, which they sold me for about a guinea. As soon as the people of the village were acquainted with this circumstance, they got together, and claimed the dress back again; for they looked upon this as a sacrilegious bargain, the punishment of which would fall on the village, because they are obliged, by the articles of their religion, to bury the women with their cloaths on. The woman from whom I had bought the dress was called upon to answer the charge brought against her: she owned she had sold it; but alledged in her defence, that it belonged to her late mother, who lived at the time

time they were made Christians, when the Empress had forbidden them to bury the dead with their cloaths on. The woman was acquitted; but the Wotiaks were still inclined to make me return the dress; which I should not have been able to keep, without the assistance of the soldiers, who were put in a posture of defence.

The Wotiak women are generally very ugly, and more slovenly than any other people of the North, except the Samoyedes, according to the account I received of them from Russians who have travelled in that province. The Samoyedes never wear any shift: their dress is made of the skin of the rein deer, in form of a bag. Their stockings are of the same skin, and they sometimes wear sandals, according to the Russian fashion. A Russian, who has travelled among the Samoyedes, made me a present of one of these dresses.

Some Account of the Life, Misfortunes, and Character, of the celebrated Favourite, Prince Menzikoff; *taken from General* Manstein's *Historical, Political, and Military Memoirs of* Russia.

CATHERINE, whose ascent to the throne was owing to the affection of Peter I. died on the 16th of May, 1727; and Peter II. as lawful heir of this vast empire, succeeded in course. This Prince was born in 1715, from the marriage of the Czarewitz with the Princess of Wolfenbuttel. He was but eleven years and an half old at his accession to the crown; upon which consideration, Catherine had, in the second article of her will, ordered that he should be under the tuition of a regency, constituted of the Princesses her daughters, Anne and Elizabeth, of the Duke of Holstein, husband of the Princess Anne, of the Prince of Holstein, Bishop of Lubeck, contracted to marry the Princess Elizabeth, and of the members of the council of state, which at that time consisted of six persons, until he had accomplished the age of sixteen. The council of state was composed of the following members: the Prince Menzikoff, the High-admiral Apraxin, the High-chancellor Count Golowskin, the Vice-chancellor Count Osterman, the actual Privy-counsellors Prince Demetrius, Michelowitz Gallitzin, and Basilius Loukitz Dolgorucki.

This regency never assembled in a body but one single time, which was on the day that the Empress Catherine died, when nothing was done but to ratify the will, which was broke into two hours after; for it was therein expressly ordered, that all affairs should be decided by a plurality of votes. This by no means suited Prince Menzikoff, who meant to be sole arbiter and master of affairs, insomuch that the others were only to obey his orders.

It was easy for him to succeed in this design, no one daring to oppose whatever he resolved without risking his ruin. He had immediately, on the death of Peter I. got the whole power into his hands; and, in order to maintain himself in it, he had disposed the Empress Catherine to accept of one of his daughters for spouse to the Emperor. She had made an article of this

this in her will, and Menzikoff, to prevent any one's access to the Emperor without his leave, made him be lodged in his own palace from the very day of the decease of the Empress; and this while the Duke of Holstein and his ministers were amusing themselves with exultations on the noble stroke they thought they had struck, in making the regency be given them by the will of Catherine, for it was in this light they considered this arrangement. The Dutchess being at the head of affairs, and having the presidency in the council, they imagined they should have all the votes of it at their disposal; but Menzikoff, more alert and dexterous than they, had taken early care to the contrary.

It is in Russia a custom, at every change of reign or of ministry, to set free some prisoners of state. Peter II. not to be wanting in such a point, gave order for the enlargement of his grandmother, the Empress Eudoxia Feodorowna Lapouchin, whom Peter I. had divorced, and confined to a convent in 1696: he ordered her a court proportioned to her rank, and invited her to Petersburgh. But this Princess, having too great an aversion against this town, and not finding the ministry pliable enough to give her any share in the government, resolved to remain at Moscow, where she lived in retirement.

The family of the Lapouchins, near relations to that Empress, were also recalled from the exile in which they had been for several years.

These acts of grace had been carried against the inclination of Menzikoff, at the suggestion of some of the members of the high council, who had found means to soften the young monarch in favour of his grandmother, and of her near relations, and had persuaded him to insist on their release from imprisonment.

Though all this was not very pleasing to Menzikoff, he durst not however openly oppose it, but endeavoured to beset the Emperor, to the exclusion of every one that was not of his creatures; not enjoying a moment's rest, in the fear of having ill offices done him, being sensible that the whole nation detested him.

Some of the great had already, in the precedent reign, entered into a combination against him, and wanted the Empress to remove him from her councils. Those nobles, who had projected this, had been employed by Peter I. in the affair of the Czarewitz, and were afraid of the revenge of Peter II. in case of his coming to the throne, for the ill treatment which his father had received. They tried then to persuade Catherine to send the young Prince to foreign countries to pursue his studies; having resolved, that if the Empress should chance to demise while he was absent, to give him the exclusion, and raise the Dutchess of Holstein to the throne.

For this they had taken their time, while Menzikoff was in Courland, to settle every thing; and for fear that he should disconcert their designs on his return, they had undertaken to give the Empress bad impressions of him, in which they had so far succeeded,

that

that her Majesty had actually signed an order for putting him under an arrest, before he should re-enter Petersburgh.

By singular good-luck for Menzikoff, the Count of Bassewitz, first minister of the Duke of Holstein, had taken it into his head to support this favourite, and easily persuaded his master to it, who entreated of the Empress her forgiveness of him, and obtained it. Menzikoff being returned to the court, was made acquainted with the sinister designs of his enemies against him. He caused a strict research to be made of them, and all the partizans of the house of Holstein were taken up, and severely punished. Menzikoff's own brother-in-law, a Portugueze, called De Vyeira, and the General Pisarew, underwent the knout; their estates were confiscated, and themselves sent into Siberia. An actual Privy-counsellor, Tolstoy, as well as his son, the General Butterlin, and some others, were also banished to Siberia: the Count Alexander Narifkin, and the General Ouschakow, were respectively confined to their estates.

It was said, that the Count de Bassewitz, who, by an over-confidence in Prince Menzikoff, had communicated to him the overtures made him by some of the great men of the court, touching their partial dispositions in favour of the Dutchess of Holstein, had furnished Menzikoff with the occasion, of which he instantly availed himself, of breaking all their measures. The others, who still remained attached to the court of Holstein, were extremely intimidated at this; and conceived, at the same time, not only a great distrust, but a great contempt for Bassewitz.

But Prince Menzikoff was not satisfied with their being punished at that time, and was determined to preserve the memory of it to all Russia, so as to prevent any temptation to hurt him for the future. Accordingly the council of state issued a proclamation, by which solemn warning was given against any such dangerous confederacies, under the penalty of being punished with great rigour.

The edict was signed the 6th of June, and on the same day were celebrated the espousals of the young Emperor with the daughter of Prince Menzikoff. Her father then imagined himself on the pinnacle of earthly felicity. There remained for him the execution of but one project more to set him above all danger. He wanted to marry his son to the Grand Dutchess, Natalia, sister to the Emperor; in virtue of which, he was to transmit the throne of Russia to his posterity. The plan was not ill imagined; but it failed of execution. In the mean while, he got himself declared generalissimo by sea and land.

The Duke and Dutchess of Holstein were now the only personages that gave umbrage to Menzikoff, who was afraid lest the Dutchess should form a new party, that might oppose his vast designs. He at the same time imagined, that, after their quitting the field to him, no one would dare to stir. On a sudden, then, he ceased to keep any measures with them: so that, throwing in their way every kind of difficulty and disgust, he constrained them, at length, to
leave

leave Ruſſia. Their departure, however, did not leſſen the number of his enemies: the truth is, that he had drawn upon himſelf the univerſal hatred of the nation.

He had taken the precaution to place in attendance about the Emperor none but his own creatures, and ſuch as owed their fortune to him; but as he had directly counteracted and ſhocked all the antient families, and as, among thoſe whom he could not well debar of acceſs to the Emperor, there were ſome who ſaw with pain their relations in exile, they ſeized an occaſion of making the young Prince remark, that Menzikoff was exerciſing a perfect deſpotiſm, which he was hoping ſtill more to confirm, by the conſummation of the Emperor's marriage with his daughter; that, in ſhort, to judge of him by his ambition, he might take it into his head to attempt aſcending the throne. They at the ſame time earneſtly entreated the Emperor to keep their ſecret, which he promiſed; and actually did diſſemble, till he found a fair occaſion for venting his reſentment: Menzikoff ſoon furniſhed it, by a ſtroke of terrible giddineſs or imprudence.

The company of maſons had, I do not juſtly now remember on what occaſion, made a free gift to the Emperor of nine thouſand ducats. This Prince, having a mind to give his ſiſter the pleaſure of this preſent, ſent her that ſum by one of his gentlemen; who, being met by Menzikoff, was aſked by him, where he was going with that money? The gentleman told him. The other replied, "The "Emperor is as yet too young to "know how to diſpoſe of money: "carry it to my apartments; I "will take an opportunity to "ſpeak to him of it." The gentleman, who knew how dangerous it was to oppoſe the will of Menzikoff, did not fail of obeying him. The next day, the Princeſs, ſiſter to the Emperor, came to pay him a viſit, according to cuſtom. She was no ſooner in the room, than he aſked her, if the preſent he had ſent her was not worth a compliment of thanks. The Princeſs naturally anſwering that ſhe had received nothing, the Emperor flew into a great paſſion. The gentleman was called, and being aſked by him what he had done with the money given him to carry to the Princeſs, was obliged, in his own defence, to ſay that Menzikoff had taken it from him. But this only the more irritated the Emperor, who ordered Menzikoff to be ſent for, and, when he came, demanded of him, in a great rage, how he came to have the boldneſs to hinder his gentleman from executing his orders? The Prince, who was not uſed to hear the Emperor ſpeak to him in that tone, was perfectly thunderſtruck. He anſwered, however, that it was very well known that the ſtate was in want of money; that the treaſury was exhauſted; and that he had propoſed that very day to preſent a project of the manner in which that ſum might be more uſefully employed. He added, "If, however, your Majeſty com- "mands it, I will not only cauſe "to be returned the nine thouſand "ducats, but advance you a "million of rubles out of my own "purſe."

The Emperor was not pacified with this answer; but, stamping with his foot, said, "I will make you know that I am Emperor, and that I will be obeyed." Then, turning his back upon him, left him. Menzikoff followed him, and, at length, with much intreaty, appeased him for that time; but this calm did not last long.

A few days afterwards, Menzikoff fell dangerously ill. This gave his enemies time to make sure of his ruin. The Princes Dolgorucki, and especially the Knez Iwan, whose great favour was beginning at that time, prevailed so as entirely to alienate from him the mind of their master. Menzikoff was not ignorant of these cabals against him, nor of the decline of his credit; but he hoped soon to recover his former degree of favour, and to over-awe the Emperor by that tone of authority which he had used to take towards him.

As soon, then, as Menzikoff was recovered, he committed a fresh fault, in going to his country-house at *Oranjenbaum*, which was about two miles from Peterhoff, where the court had removed during his illness. He had built a chapel at Oranjenbaum, which he wanted to have consecrated. The Emperor and all his court were invited to assist at the ceremony. But his enemies, who had too much cause to dread his revenge, in case of his reconciliation with the Emperor, persuaded this Prince to excuse himself on the day of the ceremony, under pretence of an indisposition. He followed their advice; and yet, for all that, Menzikoff did not apprehend that this betokened his entire disgrace. He had even the imprudence, during the festival, to seat himself on a kind of throne which had been placed for his Majesty. His enemies did not fail of making the most of this circumstance, which contributed to determine his fall.

The same evening Menzikoff repaired to Peterhoff, where he did not find the Emperor, who had been carried a hunting. He addressed himself to the Count Osterman, with whom he had a conversation full of acrimony, and even accompanied with high words. He remained that day and the next at Peterhoff; but the Emperor not returning, and all the countenances being frozen to him, he took the resolution of going to Petersburgh: probably he thought he should be more formidable in the midst of the court. In fact, being arrived at the capital, far from acting the disgraced courtier, he employed the whole morning in going the round of the colleges, and giving orders every where. He regulated particularly the reception intended for the Emperor in his palace, where he imagined he would continue to lodge; but towards noon, the General Soltikow came, with an order to remove from his palace the Emperor's furniture, and carry it to the imperial summer palace. This was a thunder stroke to him, at which he lost all presence of mind; but what shocked him most was, the sending back the goods and furniture of his son, who, in quality of High-chamberlain, was to lodge officially near the Emperor. In this confusion of head he fell into another fault, that of sending into quarters the regiment of of Ingermanland, which, for his safety, he had ordered to encamp on the island of Wasili Ostrow*, at a small distance from his palace. This regiment, of which he had been colonel from the first of its being raised, was entirely devoted to him; and it is certain that it had impressed his enemies with a great awe of him.

In the evening, the Emperor returned to Petersburgh, and the General Soltikow was once more employed on a message to Menzikoff, by which he announced to him an order of arrest. His wife and children repaired immediately to the summer palace, to throw themselves at the feet of the Emperor, but were refused admittance. Mean while, Menzikoff was made to believe that he would be only deprived of, his offices; that he would nevertheless have all his fortune left him, and that he would be permitted to pass the remainder of his days at Oranjenburgh, a pretty town on the frontiers of the Ukraine, which he had built, and even a little fortified. In fact, the free disposal of his goods and fortune was left to him, while he remained at Petersburgh; and when he went out of it, his train had not in the least the air of a minister in disgrace. He was accompanied by his whole family, and by a great number of domestics; and, in the manner he was treated on the first days of his journey, it did not appear that there was any intention to do him more hurt. But, on his arrival at Tweer, a town situate on the road between Moscow and Petersburgh, he there found an order for all his effects to be sealed up, and nothing more to be left him than bare necessaries. His guard was doubled, and he was more narrowly watched during the rest of his journey. Scarce was he arrived at Oranjenburgh, when there were sent to him whole reams of complaints made against him for grievances. These were instantly followed by commissaries who proceeded to his trial. He was condemned to pass the rest of his life at Berosowa, situate on the most distant frontiers of Siberia. His wife, grown blind with weeping, died by the way: the rest of his family followed him into exile. He bore his misfortunes with more firmness than one would have imagined in him; and from being full of gross humours, with a bad habit of body, he recovered health and plumpness. There were allowed him ten rubles a day; a sum which not only sufficed him for his wants, but he saved enough out of it to build a church, at which he himself worked hatchet in hand. He died in November 1729, of a repletion of blood; because, as it was said, there was not one person to be found at Berosowa who knew how to open a vein.

The general opinion on the origin of Menzikoff is, that his father was a peasant, who had placed

---

* *Wasili Ostrow* is an island which makes part of the town of Petersburgh; the palace of Menzikoff stood there. Peter I. had made him a present of the whole island, but resumed it some time afterwards, in the intention that the whole town of Petersburgh should be built there; which however was not executed.

him,

him, at Moscow, with a pastry-cook, and that he carried about little pies, singing along the streets; that the Emperor Peter I. having stopped to speak to him, he had pleased him with the wit and liveliness of his repartees. Upon this he put him servant to Monsieur Le Fort; thence he took him about his own person, and by degrees made his fortune.

Others again say, that his father was an officer in the service of the Czar, Alexis Michaëlowitz; and that, as it is not extraordinary to see gentlemen serve in the stables of the Czar, Menzikoff had also been employed in them, in quality of one of the head grooms: that Peter, having often spoke to him, had taken notice of the wit and shrewdness of his answers, insomuch that he took him out of the stables, and placed him as a more immediate attendant on himself; when, observing great talents in him, he had, in a few years, raised him to the first posts in the empire.

I have always thought the first of these opinions the nearest to the truth; for it is certain that he was of an obscure birth, and that he began with being a common servant; after which the Emperor placed him as a private soldier in the first company of regular troops, which he raised under the appellation *Preprovojdenie*[*]. Peter I. having thence taken him about his person, gave him his entire confidence, in such a manner, that, on many occasions, Menzikoff governed Russia with the same despotism as his master. His credit had, however, been greatly diminished during the last years of the reign of Peter I. and it is believed, that, if that Emperor had lived some months longer, there would have been great changes at court, and in the ministry.

By the following character, any one may decide which preponderated, the good or bad qualities of Prince Menzikoff.

He was strongly attached to his master, and to the maxims of Peter I. for civilizing the Russian nation; affable and polite towards strangers; that is to say, with such as did not pretend to have more wit than himself; neither did he misbehave to those of the Russians who shewed submission to him. He treated all who were his inferiors with gentleness, never forgetting a service done him. Brave withal, he gave, on occasions of the greatest dangers, incontestible proofs of the necessary personal courage. Wherever he had once taken a friendship, he continued a zealous friend.

On the other hand, he was possessed with a boundless ambition; he could not endure a superior or an equal, and less yet one that he could suspect of pretending to surpass him in understanding. His avarice was insatiable. He was an implacable enemy. He did not want for natural wit; but, having had no education, his manners were rather coarse. His avarice had led him into several disagreeable explanations with Peter I. who had sometimes condemned him to pay arbitrary fines: notwithstanding which, there was found, on his imprisonment, the

---

[*] *Preprovojdenie*, for amusement.

value

value of three millions of rubles, in jewels, in plate, and ready money.

He had a son and two daughters: she who had been betrothed to the Emperor died, before her father, in exile; the other was married, under the reign of the Empress Anne, with the General Gustavus Biron, brother to the Duke of Courland, and died in the beginning of the year 1737. The son is major in the guards. So long as his father was in favour and prosperity, all the world allowed him a great deal of wit, though he was but a child: since the disgrace and death of his father, there are few persons in the whole empire of Russia that have less than he.

Menzikoff, who, from the lowest condition, had been raised to the highest stations of life, would have finished his career with honour, if he had not been so infatuated with ambition as to seek to place his posterity on the throne of Russia. It is the same rock against which all the favourites that followed him have struck, and sunk like him.

Some Account of Count Biron, *late Duke of* Courland; *from the same.*

BIRON, who had served many years in quality of gentleman of the chamber, while the Empress was Dutchess of Courland, was declared Count, and had the blue riband, and withal the place of High-chamberlain, vacant by the exile of Prince Iwan Dolgorucki.

Now, as this same Biron has long acted so very great a part at the court of Petersburgh, it may not be improper to give the reader some knowledge of him.

His grandfather, whose proper name was *Bieren*, was head groom of the stables to the Duke James III. of Courland; and, as he attended him every where, found means to acquire his favour, insomuch that, by way of gratuity, he gave him a farm in free gift. This *Bieren* had two sons, of which one, entering into the service of Poland, began with carrying a musket, and got to be promoted to the rank of general.

The other, father of the Biron of whom I have been just speaking, remained in the service of Courland, and followed the Duke Alexander, the youngest of the Duke's sons, when he went to Hungary, in 1686. The Prince was wounded before Buda, and died of his wounds. Bieren, who had followed him, in quality of his groom of the horse, with the title besides of lieutenant, brought back his equipages to Courland, where they gave him the employ of a master huntsman; so that what with that, and the small inheritance of his father, he was in tolerably easy circumstances.

He had three sons; the eldest of them, Charles, began by serving in Russia, where he was advanced to the rank of an officer, and was taken prisoner by the Swedes, in an action with the Russians. Having found means to escape out of confinement, he went to Poland, took on the service, and had risen to the rank of lieutenant-colonel. He afterwards returned to the service of Russia, where, in a very few years, he got to be a general officer.

officer. He was the most brutal of all men; and was maimed and marked with the number of wounds which he had received in various scrapes, into which his drunkenness and quarrelsomeness had brought him. At length, in Russia, every one was come to dread him, and to avoid having any thing to say to him, since his brother was become the favourite, and omnipotent in the government.

The second son was Erneftus John, who rose to the dignity of Duke of Courland.

The third son, Guftavus, was also a general officer in the Ruffian service. He had begun with serving in Poland. The Empress Anne being seated on the throne, sent for him, and appointed him major of a new-raised regiment of guards. As he was brother to the favourite, he could easily obtain promotion. He was a very honest man, but without education, and of no understanding.

I return to the second brother: He had been for some time at the academy of Koningsberg in Pruffia, when he was obliged to leave it, to avoid being arrested for some bad affairs he had had in Courland. Finding that he could not subsist without service, he went in 1714 to Peterfburgh, and solicited a gentleman's place at the court of the Princess, spouse to the Czarewitz. It was then thought an impertinent presumption that one of so low a birth should pretend to such a post. He was not only rejected with contempt, but advised to make the best of his way instantly out of Peterfburgh. At his return to Mittau, he made an acquaintance with Beftucheff, father of the high-chancellor, who was then master of the household at the court of the Dutchess of Courland. Soon he got into her good graces, and had a place of gentleman of the chamber. He was scarce settled in it, before he fell to work at the ruin of his benefactor; in which he succeeded so well, that the Dutchess not only forbid him her court, but persecuted him as much as she could, and sent De Korf expressly to Mofcow, to carry on a suit against him.

This Bieren, as to his person, was very handsome, and soon got deep into the favour of the Dutchess, who took such delight in his company, that she made him her confidant.

The nobility of Courland conceived a great jealousy against this new favourite; some carried it such a length, that they laid out for occafions to pick quarrels with him. As then he stood in need of a support among the nobility, he sought the alliance of some antient family. He met with several refusals; at length he prevailed over Mademoiselle de Treiden, maid of honour to the Dutchess, and married her, even before he had got the consent of her friends. By this marriage he hoped to gain admission into the body of the nobility: he solicited it, and was harshly refused.

The ministry of Ruffia did not more like him than the nobility of Courland. The scurvy trick he had played Beftucheff had set the whole world against him, so that he was detefted and despised at Moscow. This went to such a pitch, that when, a little while before

before the death of Peter II. De Korf solicited an augmentation of pension for the Dutchess, the ministers of the council of state declared to him frankly, and without any mincing of the matter, that every thing should be done for her Highness, but that they would not have Bieren dispose of it. On the Emperor's demise, Anne being elected Empress, one of the proposals made to her by the deputies at Mittau was, that she should leave her favourite behind her there. She consented, but he presently followed her. After she had declared herself absolute sovereign, she made him her chamberlain, and, on the day of her coronation, he was raised to the honours above-mentioned.

The Duke Ferdinand of Courland, and last of the house of Kettler, being dead, he managed so successfully, by his arts and cabals, that he was elected duke, and consequently became the sovereign of a country, of which the nobility had, but a few years before, refused to admit him into their body.

When he began to advance himself in the career of fortune, he took the name and arms of the dukes of *Biron* in France. This man it is who, during the whole life of the Empress Anne, and some weeks after her death, reigned with perfect despotism over the vast empire of Russia. He had no sort of learning, nor yet any education, except what he took of himself. He had not that kind of wit as gives the power of pleasing in society or conversation; but he was not, however, destitute of a certain degree of natural good sense, though there are some that aver the contrary. It is not without reason that the proverb might be applied to him, "that affairs form men;" for, before his arrival in Russia, he had not, perhaps, so much as heard of the name of politics; whereas, after having resided there some years, he knew perfectly well all that related to that empire. The two first years he made as if he meddled with nothing, but at length he took a taste for business, and governed every thing.

He loved to excess pomp and magnificence, and had especially a great fancy for horses. The minister of the Emperor, Count Ostein, who detested him, used to say, "When the Count Biron talks of horses, he speaks like a man; but when he speaks of men, or to men, he speaks as a horse would do."

His temper was none of the best: he was haughty and ambitious beyond all bounds; abrupt, and even brutal; avaricious, an implacable enemy, and cruel in his punishments. He took a great deal of pains to learn to dissemble, but could never attain any degree of perfection in it comparable to that of Count Osterman, who was master of the art.

Of the Cossacks; *and the singular Customs of the* Zaporavian *Republic.*

THERE are several kinds of the Cossacks; the most known are those of the Don, the Zaporavian Cossacks, and those of the Ukraine. They inhabit

the

the *Ukraine*, which is also called *Mala Russia*, or *Little Russia*, and is unquestionably one of the finest countries in Europe: one half of it belongs to the Emperor of Russia, the other to Poland. The Borysthenes or Dnieper divides this country into two parts, forming at the same time their respective frontiers.

These Cossacks were once a free nation, descending from the same race as the Polanders; but, as to their religion, they follow the Greek church. When these people were united, they could bring a hundred and fifty thousand men into the field. They were long under the protection of the republic of Poland, and did it great service in its wars against the Turks; but, the Polanders attempting to treat them like slaves, they revolted about an hundred years ago, under the conduct of the Hettman Chelmninski, who put himself under the protection of the Turks. Some years after the death of Chelmninski, the successor, Doroschonko, gave himself and country up to Russia. This brought on a war, which terminated in the destruction of the town of Czigrin; at that time the capital of the Ukraine. This happened in the year 1764.

For the first years ensuing they preserved all their privileges, and were governed by a prince of their own chusing among themselves. But the Hettman Mazeppa having taken the part of Charles XII. King of Sweden, Peter I. reduced this restless people to a condition of inability of striving to shake off their yoke.

At present they have no longer any privileges, and are looked upon in the light of a conquered province. Their last Hettman, Apostel, dying in 1734, they were not left at liberty to chuse another; and are actually now governed by a Russian regency, which resides at Glouchow[*]. They can absolutely bring two-and-twenty thousand men into the field. They served in the Russian armies during the last wars against the Turks, without having been good for any thing but to augment the number of their troops. It is not without reason believed that their pristine valour is totally extinct. In the last campaign they scarce did any other service than that of bringing waggons of provision to the army.

The Zaporavian Cossacks inhabit the islands of the Borysthenes, and a small tract of country on the side of Crimea, beyond the cataracts. They are a collection of all nations, mostly however of Polanders, of Russians, and of the Ukraine Cossacks. They were, formerly, sometimes under the protection of the Turks or Tartars of Crimea, sometimes under that of Russia. If I am not mistaken, it was since the year 1734 that they resumed their submission to Russia, having precedently been attached to the Turks since the time of Charles XII.th's recourse to Bender.

Their general, or chief of their republic, has the appellation of Roschowy Hettman. They chuse

---

[*] These Memoirs were already written, when the Empress Elizabeth restored to the inhabitants of the Ukraine a great part of their antient privileges. She gave them at the same time the liberty of chusing a new Hettman: the choice fell on Kirila Rasoumouski, brother of her Majesty's favourite; and in 1751 he went to the Ukraine to take possession of that regency.

him among themfelves, and, for fo long a time as pleafes them, they pay him a blind obedience; but the moment they are difcontented with him, they depofe him, without farther ceremony, and chufe another in his place.

It is, however, requifite, fince their fubmiffion to Ruffia, that fuch their election fhould be always confirmed by the regency of Glouchow; nor is it at all improbable that the principal motive for their changing fo often their Rofchowy is, that it is cuftomary for the court to make, on this occafion, a prefent of feven thoufand rubles to the new Rofchowy, who commonly fhares them among the principal Coffacks, to attach them to him; but very often they do not let him keep his poft above a few months, when he is degraded, and becomes again only a private Coffack: many of them have even been maffacred, without any other reafon but the having incurred the difpleafure of the multitude.

In time of war the court pays them penfions, and furnifhes them provifions for the campaign.

They have but one fecretary, or rather writer, who dares fend or receive letters: if any other was to hold any the leaft correfpondence, he would be put to death without mercy, were it even the Rofchowy himfelf. But, in cafe of any letter coming, it is carried to the fecretary, who reads it in prefence of the Elders.

The number of troops they can bring into the field is not fixed. In the laft war againft the Turks, eight thoufand of their horfe ferved in the Ruffian armies; but on a ftretch, with their beft efforts, they could raife twelve or fifteen thoufand.

Their cuftoms are fingular. No Zaporavian Coffack is allowed to be married within the precincts of their territory. If he is married, his wife muft live in fome neighbouring country, where he reforts to her from time to time; and even this intercourfe muft be without the knowledge of the Elders; but every one may quit this fociety when it no longer pleafes him, and that without acquainting any one. Another may come and have his name inrolled, without any other ceremony than that of declaring that he will conform to their cuftoms, and fubmit to their laws. It is for this reafon that they can never precifely afcertain the number of their forces. They are divided into different chambers or comradefhips; and all who are prefent in their capital are obliged to dine and fup in their public halls or refectories.

They do not even fuffer women to remain at any ftranger's that fhould come among them, and bring any of that fex with them. While the Ruffians were at war againft the Turks, the Zaporavians had received in their capital a garrifon of regular troops, which is nothing more than a retrenched village, called Setz. The Lieutenant-colonel Glebow, who commanded thofe troops, being unapprifed of their cuftom, had fent for his wife to come to him. No fooner was fhe arrived, than that all the Coffacks, having affembled for the purpofe, furrounded this commanding officer's houfe, and demanded what women there were in it to be delivered to them, that
they

they might each have their share. Monf. Glebow had a good deal of difficulty to appease them, nor could effect it without sacrificing to them some casks of brandy. He was, however, obliged to send away his lady, for fear of a fresh revolt.

Their manner of punishing is as singular as their manner of living. They are great thieves and robbers; but if any one should offer to steal any the least thing from his comrade, he is tied to a post in the openest public place of the town: a bottle of brandy, a loaf of bread, and a number of stout sticks, are set by his side, when every one that passes has a right to give him as many blows as he pleases, after which he may give the wretch the refreshment of a drop of brandy, and a morsel of bread. The sufferer, at the discretion of the judges, remains thus tied to the post a whole night and day, and often five times twenty-four hours. After which, if he has the good luck to survive the blows, he is received anew into the society.

The whole republic is merely made up of thieves and vagabonds, who subsist of nothing but rapine, both in peace and war. The Haidamacks, who infest Poland, are no other than these Zaporavian Cossacks. The court of Russia cannot hinder their continual excursions; nay, is even obliged to keep measures with them, for fear of their changing sides.

The Cossacks of the Don inhabit that tract which is between the river Don, the same as the antient Tanais, and the Donwitz, or Little Don. They have a very good country, several pretty towns, and large villages. Their capital is called Czerkaskoi. They are originally, by descent, all Russian peasants, to whom the yoke of their masters having proved unsufferable, they, little by little, took refuge in this country, where they formed a commonwealth. In process of time they voluntarily put themselves under the protection of the Russian empire, by which they are treated with great gentleness and moderation. They are excellent soldiers, and can bring as far as fifteen thousand men into the field. The Russians draw great service from them against the Turks, and Tartars of Cuban. Their general, or chief of their republic, is styled Voïskowoy Attaman: he is chosen by themselves from among the principal officers of their nation, but he must be confirmed by the court.

Of the Antient Scandinavians; from M. Mallet's Northern Antiquities.

I HAVE already hinted, that the antient Scandinavians breathed nothing but war, which was at once with them the source of honour, riches and safety. Their education, laws, prejudices, morality, and religion, all concurred to make that their ruling passion and only object. From their most tender age they applied themselves to learn the military art; they hardened their bodies, and accustomed themselves to cold, fatigue, and hunger. They exercised themselves in running in the chase, in swimming across the greatest rivers, and in handling their arms. The very sports of childhood itself, and of early youth, were directed all towards this end: dangers

gers were always intermingled with their play; for it consisted in taking frightful leaps, in climbing up the steepest rock, in fighting naked with offensive weapons, in wrestling with the utmost fury: it was, therefore, common to see them at the age of fifteen years already grown robust men, and able to make themselves feared in combat. It was also at this age that their young men became their own masters, which they did by receiving a sword, a buckler, and a lance. This ceremony was performed in some public meeting. One of the principal persons of the assembly armed the youth in public. "This," we are told by Tacitus, "was his *Toga Virilis*, his entrance upon dignities: before this, he made only part of a family; now he became a member of the state." After this he was obliged to provide for his own subsistence, and was either now to live by hunting, or by joining in some incursion against an enemy. Particular care was taken to prevent these young soldiers from enjoying too early an acquaintance with the opposite sex, till their limbs had acquired all the vigour of which they were capable. Indeed, they could have no hope to be acceptable to the women but in proportion to the courage and address they had shewn in war and in their military exercise. Accordingly we see, in an antient song preserved by Bartholin, a King of Norway extremely surprized, that, as he could perform eight different exercises, his mistress should presume to reject his suit. I shall frequently have occasion to produce new instances of this manner of thinking among their women: it is sufficient at present to observe, that they were not likely to soften their children by too much delicacy or indulgence. These tender creatures were generally born in the midst of camps and armies. Their eyes, from the moment they were first opened, saw nothing but military spectacles, arms, effusion of blood, and combats either real or in sport: thus, as they grew up from their infancy, their souls were early disposed to imbibe the cruel prejudices of their fathers.

Their laws, for the most part (like those of the antient Lacedemonians), seemed to know no other virtues than those of a military nature, and no other crimes but cowardice. They inflicted the greatest penalties on such as fled the first in battle. The laws of the antient Danes, according to Saxo, excluded them from society, and declared them infamous. Among the Germans this was sometimes carried so far as to suffocate cowards in mud; after which they covered them over with hurdles: to shew, says Tacitus, that though the punishment of crimes should be public, there are certain degrees of cowardice and infamy which ought to be buried in eternal silence. The most flattering distinctions were reserved for such as had performed some signal exploit; and the laws themselves distributed men into different ranks, according to their different degrees of courage. Froto, King of Denmark, had ordained, according to Saxo, that whoever solicited an eminent post in the army ought upon all occasions to attack one enemy; to

Vol. XIII.　　　　D　　　　face

face two; to retire only one step back from three; and not to make an actual retreat till assaulted by four. Hence was formed that prejudice so deeply rooted among these people, that there was no other way to acquire glory but by the profession of arms, and a fanatic valour: a prejudice, the force of which displayed itself, without obstruction, at a time when luxury was unknown; when that desire, so natural and so active among men, of drawing upon themselves the attention of their equals, had but one single object and support; and when their country and their fellow-citizens had no other treasure but the fame of their exploits, and the terror thereby excited in their neighbours.

The rules of justice, far from checking these prejudices, had been themselves warped and adapted to their bias. It is no exaggeration to say, that all the 'Gothic and' Celtic nations entertained opinions on this subject quite opposite to the theory of our times. They looked upon war as a real act of justice, and esteemed force an incontestable title over the weak; a visible mark that God had intended to subject them to the strong. They had no doubt but the intentions of this divinity had been to establish the same dependance among men which there is among animals; and, setting out from the principle of the inequality of men, as our modern civilians do from that of their equality, they inferred thence that the weak had no right to what they could not defend. This maxim, which formed the basis of the law of nations among the antient inhabitants of Europe, being dictated by their most darling passion, we cannot wonder that they should so steadily act up to it in practice. And which, after all, is worst;—to act and think as they did, or like the moderns, with better principles, to act as ill? As to the antient nations, we attribute nothing to them here but what is justified by a thousand facts. They adopted the above maxim in all its rigour, and gave the name of Divine Judgment not only to the JUDICIARY COMBAT, but to conflicts and battles of all sorts; victory being, in their opinion, the only certain mark by which Providence enables us to distinguish those whom it has appointed to command others. "Va-" lour," says a German warrior in Tacitus, "is the only proper " goods of men. The Gods range " themselves on the side of the " strongest*."

Lastly; Religion, by annexing eternal happiness to the military virtues, had given the last degree of activity to the ardour and propensity these people had for war. There were no fatigues, no dangers, nor torments, capable of damping a passion so well countenanced, and the desire of meriting so great a reward. We have seen what motives this religion offered to its votaries; and we cannot fail to recal them in reading some instances of that courage which distinguished the antient Scandinavians, and of their contempt of death itself, which I shall produce from the most authentic chronicles of Iceland.

History informs us, that HAROLD, surnamed BLAATAND, or

* Tacit. Hist. lib. IV. c. 17. Pelloutier Hist. des Celtes, tom. I. p. 415.

BLUE

CHARACTERS.

BLUE TOOTH (a King of Denmark, who reigned in the middle of the tenth century), had founded on the coasts of Pomerania, which he had subdued, a city named Julin, or Jomsburg, where he sent a colony of young Danes, and bestowed the government on a celebrated warrior named Palnatoko. This new Lycurgus had made of that city a second Sparta, and every thing was directed to this single end, to form complete soldiers. The author who has left us the history of this colony assures us, that "it was forbidden there so much "as to mention the name of Fear, "even in the most imminent dan- "gers*." No citizen of Jomsburg was to yield to any number, however great, but to fight intrepidly without flying, even from a very superior force. The fight of present and inevitable death would have been no excuse with them for making any the least complaint, or for shewing the slightest apprehension: and this legislator really appears to have eradicated from the minds of most of the youths bred up under him all traces of that sentiment, so natural and so universal, which makes men think on their destruction with horror. Nothing can shew this better than a single fact in their history, which deserves to have a place here for its singularity. Some of them having made an irruption into the territories of a powerful Norwegian Lord, named Haquin, were overcome, in spite of the obstinacy of their resistance; and the most distinguished among them being made prisoners, were, according to the custom of those times, condemned to death. The news of this, far from afflicting them, was, on the contrary, received with joy. The first who was led to punishment was content to say, without changing countenance, and without expressing the least sign of fear, "Why should not the same happen to me as did to my father? "He died, and so must I." A warrior, named Thorchill, who was to cut off the head of the second, having asked him what he felt at the sight of death, he answered, "that he remembered too "well the laws of Jomsburg to "utter any words that denoted "fear." The third, in reply to the same question, said, "he re- "joiced to die with glory, and "that he preferred such a death "to an infamous life like that of "Thorchill's." The fourth made an answer much longer, and more extraordinary. "I suffer with a "good heart; and the present "hour is to me very agreeable. I "only beg of you," added he, addressing himself to Thorchill, "to be very quick in cutting off "my head; for it is a question "often debated by us at Jomsburg, "whether one retains any sense "after being beheaded. I will, "therefore, grasp this knife in my "hand. If after my head is cut "off I strike it towards you, it "will shew I have not lost all "sense: if I let it drop, it will "be a proof of the contrary. "Make haste, therefore, and de- "cide the dispute."----"Thor- "chill," adds the historian, "cut "off his head in a most expeditious "manner; but the knife, as might "be expected, dropped from his

---

* See Jomswikings Saga, in Bartholin, de Dauja Contempt. Mort. lib. I. c. 5.

"hand."

"hand." The fifth shewed the same tranquillity, and died rallying and jeering his enemies. The sixth begged of Thorchill that he might not be led to punishment like a sheep*:, "Strike the blow in my face," said he, "I will sit still without shrinking; and take notice whether I once wink my eyes, or betray one sign of fear in my countenance; for we inhabitants of Jomsburg are used to exercise ourselves in trials of this sort, so as to meet the stroke of death without once moving." He kept his promise before all the spectators, and received the blow without betraying the least sign of fear, or so much as winking his eyes†. "The seventh," says the historian, "was a very beautiful young man, in the flower of his age. His long fair hair, as fine as silk, floated in curls and ringlets on his shoulders. Thorchill asked him, What he thought of death? I receive it willingly," said he, "since I have fulfilled the greatest duty of life, and have seen all those put to death whom I would not survive. I only beg of you one favour;—not to let my hair be touched by a slave, or stained with my blood‡."

This constancy in the last moments was not, however, the peculiar effect of the laws and education of the Jomsburgians. The other Danes have often given the same proofs of intrepidity; or, rather, this was the general character of all the inhabitants of Scandinavia. It was with them an instance of shameful pusillanimity to utter upon such occasions the least groan, or to change countenance, but especially to shed tears. "The Danes," says Adam of Bremen §, "are remarkable for this, that, if they have committed any crime, they had rather suffer death than blows. There is no other punishment for them but either the axe, or servitude. As for groans, complaints, and other bemoanings of that kind, in which we find relief, they are so detested by the Danes, that they think it mean to weep for their sins, or for the death of their dearest relations." But if a private soldier looked upon tears as peculiar to weakness or slavery, their great warriors, the chiefs, all who aspired to fame and glory, carried the contempt of death much farther. King Regner, who died singing the pleasure of receiving death in the field of battle, cries out at the end of a stanza, "The hours of my life are passed away; I shall die laughing∥:" and many passages in antient history plainly shew that this was not a poetical hyperbole. Saxo, speaking of a single combat, says, that one of the champions FELL, LAUGHED, AND DIED: an epitaph as short as energetic¶. An

* Barthol. lib. I. c. 5. p. 5¦. † Barthol. ibid.
‡ In Bartholin it is, *Id unicum a te peto, ne mancipia me ad mortem ducant, neq; quis te inferior capillum meum tangat*, &c. M. Mallet has omitted the circumstance of the hair in his second edition.
Bartholin gives the speech of the EIGHTH person, which, though spirited, being not so striking as the former, our author has omitted.
§ Adam Bremen de situ Daniæ, c. 213. ∥ Barthol. p. 4.
¶ Saxo Gram. lib. II. at side Rodvas's Biarka-Saga apud Barthol. lib. I. n. 1, p. 4.

officer

officer belonging to a King of Norway, celebrating in verse the death of his master, concludes his eulogium with these words: "It shall "hereafter be recorded in histories, "that King Halfer died laughing*." A warrior having been thrown upon his back in wrestling with his enemy, and the latter finding himself without his arms, the vanquished person promised to wait, without changing his posture, while he fetched a sword to kill him: and he faithfully kept his word. To die with his arms in his hand was the vow of every free man; and the pleasing idea they had of this kind of death would naturally lead them to dread such as proceeded from disease and old age. In the joy, therefore, which they testified at the approach of a violent death, they might frequently express no more than their real sentiments, though doubtless it was sometimes intermixed with ostentation. The general tenor of their conduct proves that they were most commonly sincere in this; and such as know the power which education, example, and prejudice, have over men, will find no difficulty in receiving the multitude of testimonies which antiquity hath left us of their extraordinary valour. "The philosophy of the Cimbri," says Valerius Maximus, "is "gay and courageous. They leap "for joy in a battle, that they are "going to quit life in so glorious "a manner: in sickness they la- "ment, for fear of a shameful and "miserable end†." Cicero remarks, that in proportion as men are intrepid in war, they are weak and impatient under bodily pains. "Happy in their mistake," says Duncan, "are the people who live "beneath the pole! Persuaded "that death is only a passage to "a long life, they are undisturbed "by the most grievous of all fears, "—that of dying. Hence they "eagerly run to arms, and their "minds are capable of meeting "death; hence they esteem it "cowardice to spare a life which "they shall so soon recover‡." The history of antient Scandinavia is full of passages expressive of this manner of thinking. The illustrious warriors, who found themselves wasting by some lingering illness, were not always content barely to accuse their fate: they often availed themselves of the few moments that were yet remaining to shake off life by a way more glorious. Some of them would be carried into a field of battle, that they might die in the engagement; others slew themselves; many procured this melancholy service to be performed them by their friends,

---

* Barthol. p. 6.   † Val. Max. lib. II. cap. 6, p. 11.   Cicero Tusc. Quæst. lib. II. cap. ult.

‡ As only a loose paraphrase of Lucan's words is given in the text, the reader will be glad to see the original here.

Orbe alio longæ, canitis si cognita, vitæ
Mors media est. Certe populi quos despicit Arctos
Felices errore suo! quos ille timorum
Maximus haud urget lethi metus; inde ruendi
In ferrum mens prona viris, animæque capaces
Mortis: et ignavum redituræ parcere vitæ.   Lib. I.

who considered this as a most sacred duty. "There is on a mountain in Iceland," says the author of an old Icelandic romance*, "a rock so high, that no animal can fall from the top and live. Here men betake themselves when they are afflicted and unhappy. From this place all our ancestors, even without waiting for sickness, have departed unto Odin. It is useless, therefore, to give up ourselves to groans and complaints, or to put our relations to needless expences, since we can easily follow the example of our fathers, who have all gone by the way of this rock." There was such another in Sweden, appropriated to the same use, which was figuratively called the HALL OF ODIN, because it was a kind of vestibule or entry to the palace of that god†. Lastly; if none of

---

* The old SAGA, or history here quoted, contains a mixture of truth and fiction, but shews us plainly what opinion was held of SUICIDE, and how commonly it was practised heretofore in the North.

Procopius attributes the same thing to the Heruli, a Gothic people. *Apud Herulos*, says he, *nec senibus, nec ægrotis fas erat vitam producere: et si quem senium occupasset, aut morbus, rogare is cogebatur propinquos, ut quamprimum hominum numero eum tollerunt.* Procop Goth. lib. II. c. 14.

Silius says of the antient inhabitants of Spain,——

Prodiga gens animæ, & properare facillima mortem;
Namque ubi transcendit florentes viribus annos,
Impatiens ævi spernit novisse senectam
Et fati modus in dextra est.

All these authorities, which it would be easy to multiply, prove that I attribute nothing to the northern nations which is not positively confirmed by historians, as well strangers as their own countrymen; and that one cannot reproach the antient Scandinavians with these barbarous prejudices, without condemning at the same time the ancestors of half the nations of Europe. Vid. Pelloutier, tom. II. lib. iii. c. 18.

† We have a particular description of this place by Sir William Temple, which it will be worth while to produce at large.

"I will not," he says, "trouble myself with more passages out of the Runic poems concerning this superstitious principle [of preferring a violent death, &c.], but will add a testimony of it, which was given me at Nimeguen by Count Oxenstern, the first of the Swedish ambassadors in that assembly. In discourse upon this subject, and in confirmation of this opinion having been general among the Goths of those countries, he told me there was still in Sweden a place which was a memorial of it, and was called ODIN'S HALL; that it was a great bay in the sea, encompassed on three sides with steep and ragged rocks; and that, in the time of the Gothic paganism, men that were either sick of diseases they esteemed mortal or incurable, or else grown invalid with age, and thereby past all military action, and fearing to die meanly and basely (as they esteemed it) in their beds, they usually caused themselves to be brought to the nearest part of these rocks, and from thence threw themselves down into the sea, hoping, by the boldness of such a violent death, to renew the pretence of admission into the Hall of Odin, which they had lost, by failing to die in combat, and with their arms."——Miscellanea, Part II. Essay 3, part 4.   T.

these

these reliefs were afforded, and especially when Christianity had banished these cruel practices, the heroes consoled themselves at least by putting on complete armour as soon as they found their end approaching; thus making (as it were) a solemn protest against the kind of death to which they were forced involuntarily to submit.--- After this, it will not be thought wonderful that the clients of a great lord, and all those who enlisted under a chief for some expedition, should make a vow not to survive their commander; or that this vow should always be performed in all its rigour*. Neither will it be surprizing that private soldiers should sometimes form among themselves a kind of society or confraternity, in which the several members engaged, at the expence of their own lives, to avenge the death of their associates, provided it were honourable and violent. All these dangers were, in their opinion, so many favourable and precious occasions of meriting glory and eternal happiness. Accordingly we never find any among these people guilty of cowardice, and the bare suspicion of that vice was always attended with universal contempt. A man who had lost his buckler, or who had received a wound behind, durst never more appear in public. In the history of England†, we see a famous Danish captain named Siward, who had sent his son to attack a province in Scotland, ask, with great coolness, those who brought the news of his death, Whether he had received his wounds behind or before? The messengers telling him he was wounded before, the father cries out, "Then I have only cause to rejoice; for any other death would have been unworthy of me and my son." A conqueror could not exercise a more terrible vengeance upon his captives than to condemn them to slavery. "There is," says Saxo, "in the heart of the Danes, an infurmountable aversion to servitude, which makes them esteem it the most dreadful of all conditions‡." The same historian describes to us a King of Denmark, named Frotho, taken in battle by a King his enemy, and obstinately refusing all offers of life which that Prince could make him. "To what end," says he, "should I reserve myself for so great a disgrace? What good can the remainder of my life afford me that can counterbalance the remembrance of my misfortunes, and the regret which my misery would cause me? And even if you should restore me my kingdom, if you should bring me back my sister, if you should repair all the loss of my treasure, would all this recover my honour? All these benefits would never replace me in my former state; but future ages would always say, FROTHO HATH BEEN TAKEN BY HIS ENEMY." In all combats (and the number of them is prodigious in the antient histories of the North) we always find both parties continually re-

---

* The same thing prevailed among divers Celtic nations: they called those who thus engaged themselves to their chiefs, *soldurii*.
† Brompton. Ubb. Jom. Chronic. p. 946.
‡ Saxo Gramm. lib. XII.

D 4 peating

peating the words glory, honour, and contempt of death; and by this means raising one another to that pitch of enthusiasm which produces extraordinary actions. A general never forgot to remind his troops of these motives when he was going to give battle; and not unfrequently they prevented him, and flew to the engagement of themselves, chanting songs of war, marching in cadence, and raising shouts of joy.

Of Rollo, the Conqueror of Normandy; from the same.

HAROLD Harfagre, having completed the conquest of Norway about the year 870, and being desirous of procuring that repose for such of his subjects as dwelt along the coasts, which they themselves would not grant to their neighbours, prohibited all pirates of Norway, under the severest penalties, from exercising any hostilities against their own country;[*] but, notwithstanding this prohibition, a Norwegian Duke[†], named ROLF, or ROLLO, sprung, as it is said, from the antient Kings of Norway, made a descent on the province of Viken, nor retired thence till laden with a great booty of cattle. Harold, who was in the neighbourhood, was enraged at Rollo to the last degree for thus daring to disobey him almost in his very presence, and instantly condemned him to perpetual banishment from Norway. In vain the mother of this unfortunate youth threw herself at the King's feet, imploring pardon for her son, and chanting, according to the custom of those times, these verses, which the chronicles have preserved to us:—" Is the very " name of our race become hate- " ful to you? You drive from his " country one of the greatest men " it has ever produced, the ho- " nour of the Norwegian nobi- " lity. Ah! why will you pro- " voke the wolf to devour the " flocks, who wander defenceless " through the woods? Fear, lest, " becoming outrageous, he should " one day occasion great misfor- " tunes." The King remained inflexible; and Rollo, perceiving that he was for ever cut off from all hopes of return to his own country, retired with his fleet among the islands of the Hebrides to the north-west of Scotland, whither the flower of the Norwegian nobility had fled for refuge ever since Harold had become master of the whole kingdom. He was there received with open arms by those warriors, who, eager for conquest and revenge, waited only for a chief to undertake some glorious enterprize. Rollo, setting himself at their head, and seeing his power formidable, sailed towards England, which had been long, as it were, a field open on all sides to the violences of the northern nations. But the great Alfred had, some years before, established such

[*] Torfæi Hist. Norveg. tom. XI. lib. 11. Ejusd. Dissertat. de Gaungo Rolfo, p. 60.
[†] Called, in their own language, JARL; a title of the same original and import as our Anglo-Saxon EARL. T.

order

order in his part of the island, that Rollo, after several fruitless attempts, despaired of forming there such a settlement as should make him amends for the loss of his own country. He pretended therefore to have had a supernatural dream, which promised him a glorious fortune in France, and which served at least to support the ardour of his followers. The weakness of the government in that kingdom, and the confusion in which it was involved, were still more persuasive reasons to assure them of success. Having therefore sailed up the Seine to Rouen, he immediately took that capital of the province, then called NEUSTRIA, and, making it his magazine of arms, he advanced up to Paris, to which he laid siege in form. The events of this war properly belong to the history of France; and all the world knows, that it at length ended in the entire cession of Neustria, which Charles the Simple was obliged to give up to Rollo and his Normans, in order to purchase a peace. Rollo received it in perpetuity to himself and his posterity, as a feudal dutchy dependant on the crown of France*. A description of the interview between Charles and this new Duke gives us a curious picture of the manners of these NORMANS (as they were called by foreigners); for the latter would not take the oath of fealty to his sovereign lord any other way than by placing his hands within those of the King; and absolutely refused to kiss his feet, as custom then required. It was with great difficulty he was prevailed on to let one of his warriors perform this ceremony in his stead; but the officer to whom Rollo deputed this service suddenly raised the King's foot so high, that he overturned him on his back; a piece of rudeness which was only laughed at. To such a degree were the Normans feared and Charles despised†.

Soon after, Rollo was persuaded to embrace Christianity, and he was baptized with much ceremony by the Archbishop of Rouen in the cathedral of that city. As soon as he saw himself in full possession of Normandy, he exhibited such virtues as rendered the province happy, and deserved to make his former outrages forgotten. Religious, wise, and liberal, this captain of pirates became, after Alfred, the greatest and most humane prince of his time. Far from treating Normandy as a conquered province, his whole attention was employed to re-establish it. This country was, by the frequent devastations of the Scandinavians, rendered so desert and uncultivated, that Rollo could not at first reside in it; but Charles was obliged to yield up Britanny to him for a while, till Normandy

---

* This famous treaty was concluded at S. Clair, A. D. 912, by which K. Charles agreed to give his daughter Gisele in marriage to Rollo, together with that part of Neustria since called Normandy, upon condition that he would do homage for it, and would embrace the Christian religion. (Vid. Abrege Chronologique de l'Hist. de France, par M. Henault.)

† Wilhelm. Gemmet. lib. II. c. 11.

was

was in a condition to furnish subsistence to its new masters. Nevertheless, the fertility of the soil seconding the industry of the people, it became, in a few years, one of the finest provinces of Europe. Thus it was that this Prince, afterwards known under the name of ROLLO or RAOUL I. secured, to his children this noble possession, which they, two hundred years afterwards, augmented by the conquest of England: as if it were destined that this island should at all times receive its sovereigns from among the northern nations. As to the French historians, they agree with the Icelandic chronicles in describing Rollo as a man of uncommon wisdom and capacity; generous, eloquent, indefatigable, intrepid, of a noble figure and majestic size. Many other Scandinavian princes and captains are drawn in the same colours. Such were Harold Harfagre, Olave Trygguefon, Magnus King of Norway, Canute the Great, &c. men born with truly heroic qualities, which they, alas! degraded by injustice and inhumanity, but who wanted only another age and another education to render them most accomplished persons.

[To illustrate the character of this Norman conqueror, we shall subjoin the following extract from Velley's account of him in his history of France.]

Such was the state of France when attacked by Rollo, one of the most illustrious chiefs of the Normans, and whom a thousand fine qualities both of mind and heart, with the gracefulness of his person, raised above the epithet of barbarian. Having been obliged to leave Denmark, he got together a numerous corps of adventurers, with whom he crossed over into England, where he gained two signal victories; then putting to sea again, makes a descent in Friesland, which he compelled to pay a tribute. Afterwards, sailing towards France, he seized on Rouen, and repaired its walls and towers, to serve him as place of arms; from whence he used to fally out, sometimes into England, sometimes into France. Here, irritated by his miscarriage at the siege at Chartres, his ravages and cruelties were such, that deputies came from all parts, petitioning the King to purchase peace at any rate. Rollo insisted on all that sea coast which he had so often ravaged, and there was no denying him. Thus that part of Neustria, which soon came to be called Normandy from the name of its usurpers, became a separate state dependant on the crown only by an empty form of homage; and Britanny, once a kingdom, sunk into an arrierefief.

The new Duke, after some instruction in our holy mysteries, was baptised in the cathedral of Rouen, now the capital of his dominions. It is observed on this occasion, that the Normans, though such enemies to the Christian name, never offered at compelling any one to renounce Christianity. The only blots in Duke Rollo or Robert's character were, that his consort Gisela, daughter to Charles IV. pined to death for his ill treatment of her; and his beheading two persons of note, whom the King had sent with a remonstrance against

against such ungenerous behaviour. As for his subjects, them he governed with the most exemplary wisdom and goodness; and so effectually suppressed all rapine and violence, that, under his government, a pair of gold bracelets hung on an oak during three years, without any one offering to touch them. It is well known, that, for a long time after his death, the bare calling out his name implied an order for the magistrates to hasten and quell some disturbance. This gave rise to the cry *haro* in Normandy; a word derived from *ha* and *raoul*, as calling out for that Prince's assistance. Such was the foundation of that renowned Norman colony, whose blood, mingled with that of the Franks, gave kings to England and Sicily.

Some Account of the Albigenses; *from* Velley's *new History of* France.

THE church had enjoyed a perfect tranquillity for near two centuries, when Aimery de Chartres, a doctor of the University of Paris, disseminated some very offensive dogmas. This visionary, who had more learning than was usual in his time, advanced, that paradise and hell were chimeras; that the pleasure of rectitude was all our heaven and all our hell, guilt and ignorance; that the love of the Holy Spirit had abolished that of Jesus Christ; that the soul of it was charity, and that its flame gave a sanction to adultery itself. The heresiarch, being cited to Rome, was obliged to retract; and, though grief and shame shortened his life, the evil ended not with him. A council, meeting at Paris, condemned to the stake all persons convicted of holding such maxims; sparing only the women, and some mean people, whose ignorance had been the more easily imposed on. Aimery's corpse was digged up, his bones burned, and his ashes hurled about in the air. A book was likewise committed to the flames, as the source from whence the doctor had drawn his impious subtilties:—this was *Aristotle's Metaphysics*, which the French at Constantinople had lately transmitted to their own country; and the reading, or copying, and even the keeping, of it in one's house was prohibited, under penalty of excommunication. Aimery's followers, terrified at such rigorous procedures, forsook house and relations, and went and incorporated themselves with the Albigenses.— That was the name given to all sectaries agreeing among themselves to contemn the authority of the church, to oppose the use of the sacraments, and set aside the antient discipline. Under this general appellation were comprehended the Arians, who denied the divinity of Christ; the Manichees, who held two principles, one good, the other evil; the Vaudois, or the Poor of Lion, whose only error at first was a veneration for inactive poverty, and a contempt of the clergy; the Petrobusians and Henricans, who rejected the sacraments, and all outward worship; the Apostolics, who boasted that they alone were Christ's true mystical body; the Politicians, who would not allow of any temporal dominion or jurisdiction

risdiction in ecclesiastics; the Poplicans, or Publicans, who execrated baptism, the eucharist, and marriage; the Patarians, whose characteristic doctrine was infamous; and the Catharians, who made profession of a singular purity. These were all called Albigenses, either from the council of Albi's anathematising their errors, or from that city and its environs being particularly infected with them.

The sketch of their doctrines and manners, as drawn by cotemporary authors, carries in it something so absurd and horrid, as almost to leave a suspicion of exaggeration. The Albigenses, say they, believed two Gods;—one benevolent, the author of the New Testament, who had two wives, Collant and Colibant, and was the father of several children; among others, of Christ and the devil; the other malevolent, sanguinary, and deceitful, the institutor of the old law, and who both persecuted the patriarchs whilst living, and had damned them all after their death. They likewise held two Christs: one all wickedness, born at Bethlehem, and crucified at Jerusalem, and who *had a concubine called Mary Magdalen, noted for having been caught in adultery;* the other all goodness, invisible, and who never dwelled in this world but spiritually, and then in the body of St. Paul. They said that the church of Rome was the great whore spoken of in the Revelations; they accounted the sacraments futilities, called marriage prostitution, the eucharist a chimera, the resurrection a ridiculous tale, and the worship of images detestable idolatry. They had several orders; as the *Perfect*, the *Believers*, all professing the highest purity, yet all immersed in the vilest sensualities, on this detestable principle, *That there is no sin below the girdle.*

The vehemence of the sectaries in propagating such tenets rouzed the church's zeal. Pope Innocent appointed two Bernardine monks to try these miscreants, with a power of excommunicating them; and, by the censures of the church, of compelling the lords and others to confiscate their substance of any kind, to drive them out of their lands, and, when refractory, to put them to death. This was the first foundation of the inquisition.

The croises soon increased to five hundred thousand men; and, the Count de Toulouse being then chief of the Albigenses, this multitude first fell on Beziers, his capital, which was carried at the first assault, and near seventy thousand souls murdered in cold blood, without regard to age or sex. It is said that the croises, previously to the assault, consulted the Abbot De Citeaux what they should do, as there was no distinguishing the catholics from the heretics. "Kill " all," answered the monk: "God " knows his own." So true it is, that no fire burns so fierce as that kindled at God's altar.

The Character of Constantine the Great; from the first Volume of Mr. Le Beau's History of the Lower Empire, lately published.

WHEN Constantius Chlorus was made Cæsar, in 292, and was sent into Gaul for the defence

defence of the West, Constantine was entering upon his nineteenth year. Dioclesian kept him near his person as a hostage, to assure himself of the fidelity of his father, and caused him to be treated at his court with the most flattering honours and distinctions. He took him into Egypt with him; and in the war against Achilles, Constantine, equally qualified to obey and to command, gained the esteem of the Emperor and the love of the troops by his bravery, his understanding, his generosity, and a strength of body that resisted every fatigue. It was probably in this expedition that he was made Tribune of the First Order.

His rising glory drew upon him every eye. At his return from Egypt the people ran out to meet him, and pressed with eagerness to obtain a sight of him:——every thing announced a Prince born for the empire. He marched at the right hand of Dioclesian:——his comeliness distinguished him from the rest. A noble haughtiness, and an air of strength and vigour, marked throughout his whole person, excited, at the first glance, a sentiment of fear. But this warlike aspect was softened by an agreeable serenity spread over his features. He had a heart great, liberal, and inclined to magnificence; full of courage, probity, and a love of justice, which moderated his natural ambition.——Without this counterpoise, there was nothing he would not have been capable of undertaking and executing. His temper was quick and ardent, without being precipitate; penetrating without mistrust, and without jealousy; prudent, and at the same time ready in determining. In short, to finish here his portrait, his visage was broad, and of a fresh colour, with but little hair and beard; his eyes large; his look piercing, but conciliating; his neck rather thick; and his nose aquiline: his constitution delicate, and rather unhealthy, but which he contrived to save by leading a sober and abstemious life, and by moderation in his pleasures.

He was chaste in his manners. His youth, entirely occupied with great and noble designs, was free from the follies incident to that age. He married young, and, as it should seem, about the time of his going into Egypt. The birth of Minervina, his first wife, is as unknown as that of Helena, and authors are not less divided about her rank. The issue of this alliance was a Prince called Crispus, eminent for his good qualities and his misfortunes. He was born about the year 300; and it was consequently in the East, where his father resided at that time, and not at Arles, as some authors have supposed.

Historians are not agreed in respect to Constantine's knowledge and taste for letters: some allow him only a slight tincture; others make him entirely ignorant; a few represent him as thoroughly versed in them. His panegyrist Eusebius very highly extols his knowledge and his eloquence, and gives rather an unfortunate proof of these great eulogiums by a very long and very tiresome speech, which he puts into the mouth of Constantine. It is true, that, after he was Emperor, he did even more for the sciences and literature

ture than they require of a great prince. Not satisfied with protecting them, with looking upon them as one of the greatest ornaments of his empire, and encouraging them by his bounty, he was fond of composing and even of pronouncing orations. But, besides that the taste for letters was not that of the court in which he had been brought up, and that none of the princes of that time, except Maximin, piqued themselves upon their knowledge, we see, by the little that remains of his writings, that he had scarcely more learning and eloquence than was necessary to gain the applauses of his courtiers, and to persuade himself that he was not destitute of those qualities.

I cannot believe, what some historians say, that Dioclesian, jealous of Constantine's merit, wished to destroy him. So black a design agrees better with the character of Galerius, to whom others attribute it. It appears, that, after the expedition into Egypt, Constantine attended the latter in several wars. His singular valour gave umbrage to this base and arrogant man: Galerius, determined to ruin him, immediately removed him from the rank of Cæsar, which was due to him by his merit, by his quality, as son of Constantius, by the esteem of the Emperors, and by the love of the people. He retained him, however, at his court, where the life of this young Prince was in greater danger than in the midst of battles.

Under the pretence of procuring him glory, Galerius exposed him to the greatest perils. In a war against the Sarmatians, when the two armies were in sight of each other, he commanded him to attack a chief, who, from his prodigious size, appeared the most formidable of all the barbarians. Constantine rushes straight upon the enemy, strikes him down, and, dragging him by the hair, brings him trembling to the feet of his general. Another time, he received orders to fling himself on horseback into a morass, behind which were posted the Sarmatians, and of which the depth was not known. He passes it, shews the way to the Roman troops, overthrows the enemy, and returns, after having gained a glorious victory. It is even said, that, the tyrant having obliged him to combat a furious lion, Constantine came off from this combat also, triumphing over that terrible animal, and the wicked designs of Galerius.

Constantius had several times demanded the return of his son, without being able to get him out of the hands of his colleague. At last, being upon the point of going into Great Britain to make war against the Picts, the bad state of his health made him fear the leaving him at his death to the mercy of an ambitious and bloody tyrant. He spoke in a firmer tone: the son, on his side, warmly solicited permission to rejoin his father; and Galerius, who dared not break openly with Constantius, consented, at last, to the departure of Constantine. He gave him in the evening the necessary warrant for post-horses, with express injunctions not to set off the next morning till he had received fresh orders from him. It was with regret that he suffered his prey to escape, and he only made use of this

this delay, that he still might find some pretence to stop him, or that he might have time to give notice to Severus to detain him, when he should pass through Italy. The next day Galerius affected to remain in bed till noon, and, having ordered Constantine to be called, was astonished to hear that he had set off in the beginning of the night. Trembling with rage, he orders him to be pursued and brought back; but the pursuit was become impossible: Constantine, flying with the utmost expedition, had had the precaution to cause all the post-horses that he left on his rout to be ham-stringed; and the fruitless rage of the tyrant only left him the regret of not having dared to perpetrate the last crime.

Constantine like lightning traversed Illyria, and the Alps, before Severus could have any news of him, and arrived at the port of Boulogne as the fleet was setting sail. The joy of Constantius at this unhoped-for encounter is not to be expressed: he receives into his arms the son whom so many dangers had rendered still dearer to him; and mixing together their tears, and every mark of their affection, they arrived in Great Britain, where Constantius, having conquered the Picts, fell sick, and died the 25th of July, in the year 306.

[We have beheld our hero with all the rays of the rising sun reflected upon him; let us now travel along with our author, and behold his picture in that sober light, where, divested of all glare, the parts appear in their true colours; when all mankind are the judges, and power can neither prevent censure, nor riches gain a plaudit.]

Constantine died the 22d of May, being Whitsunday, at noon, in the Consulate of Felicianus and Titian; having reigned thirty years, nine months, and twenty-seven days, and lived sixty-three years, two months, and twenty-five days.

As soon as he was dead, his guards shewed signs of the most poignant grief: they tore their clothes, they threw themselves upon the ground, and beat their heads. In the midst of their sobs and lamentable cries, they called him their master, their emperor, their father. The tribunes, the centurions, and the soldiers, who had so often been witnesses of his valour in the field, seemed desirous of following him even to the grave. This loss was more grievous to them than the most bloody defeat. The inhabitants of Nicomedia ran confusedly through the streets, mixing their groans and tears. It was a particular mourning in every family; every one, in weeping for his Prince, wept for his own private loss.

The body was carried to Constantinople in a golden coffin covered with purple. The soldiers in pensive silence preceded and followed the corpse. It was deposited adorned with the purple and diadem in the principal apartment of the palace, upon an elevated estrade, in the midst of a great number of flambeaux in golden candlesticks. The guards surrounded it night and day. The generals, counts, and great officers, came every day, as if he had been still living, to pay their duty at

stated

stated times, and saluted him with the bended knee. The senators and magistrates entered afterwards in their turn; and after them a crowd of people of every age and sex.

The whole empire lamented this great Prince. His conquests, his laws, the superb edifices with which he had adorned all the provinces, Constantinople itself, the whole of which was one magnificent monument erected to his glory, had gained him the general admiration: his liberality and love for his people had acquired him their affection. He was fond of the city of Rheims, and it is undoubtedly to him, and not to his son, that we ought to attribute the building of hot-baths there at his own expence: the pompous eulogium which the inscriptions of these baths bears can only be applicable to the father: he had discharged Tripoli in Africa, and Nice in Bithynia, from certain burthensome contributions to which the preceding Emperors had subjected these cities for more than a century. He had accepted the title of Strategus or Prætor of Athens, a dignity which since Gallicanus was become superior to that of Archon: he caused a large quantity of corn to be distributed there annually; and this donation was established for ever. Rome signalized itself beyond the other cities by the excess of her grief. She reproached herself with having occasioned this Prince many bitter afflictions, and with having forced him to prefer Byzantium: penetrated with regret, she accused herself as the guilty cause of the elevation of her modern rival. The baths and markets were shut up; the spectacles and all other public amusements were forbid; the general conversation was upon the loss which they had sustained. The people declared aloud that they would have no other Emperors than the children of Constantine. They demanded with importunity, that the corpse of their Emperor should be sent to them; and their grief augmented when they learned, that it remained at Constantinople. They paid honours to the picture of him, in which he was represented as seated in heaven. Idolatry, ever extravagant, placed him amongst the number of those gods which he had overthrown; and, by a ridiculous confusion, several of his medals bear the title of God with the Monagram of Christ. In the cabinets of antiquarians are preserved others, such as Eusebius describes: Constantine is there seen seated in a car drawn by four horses; he appears to be drawn up to heaven by a hand, which comes out of the clouds.

The church has paid him more real honours. Whilst the Pagans were making him a god, the Christians made him a saint. His festivals were celebrated in the East with that of Helena, and the service for him, which is very antient among the Greeks, attributes to him miracles and cures. At Constantinople a monastery was built under the name of St. Constantine. Extraordinary honours were paid to his tomb and to his statue, which were placed upon a column of porphyry. The fathers of the council of Chalcedon thought they did honour to Marcian, the most religious of princes, by saluting him with the name of the New Constantine. In the ninth century, at Rome, they still recited his

name

name at Mass with that of Theodosius the First, and of the rest of the most respected princes. In England there were several churches and altars dedicated to him. In Calabria there is the town of Saint Constantine, four miles from Mount Saint Leo. At Prague, in Bohemia, his memory was for a long time honoured, and some of his relics were preserved there. The invocations of Constantine and of Helena have extended even into Muscovy; and the modern Greeks commonly give him the title of *Equal to the Apostles.*

Constantine's failings will not suffer us to subscribe to so hyperbolical an eulogium. The frightful spectacles of so many captives devoured by wild beasts; the death of his son, who was innocent; that of his wife, whose too precipitate punishment bore the appearance of injustice, sufficiently evince that the blood of the barbarians still flowed in his veins; and that, if he was good and merciful in his character, he became cruel and unmerciful through passion. Perhaps he had sufficient cause to put to death the two Licinii; but posterity has a right to condemn princes who have not taken the trouble to justify themselves at their tribunal. He loved the church; it owes its liberty and splendor to him; but, easy to be seduced, he tormented it when he thought to serve it. Relying too much upon his own understanding, and reposing with too much credulity upon the good faith of wicked men who surrounded him, he delivered up to persecution prelates who, with greater reason, deserved to be compared to the apostles. The exile and deposition of the defenders of the faith of Nice, balance at least the glory of having assembled that famous council. Incapable himself of dissimulation, he too easily became the dupe of heretics and courtiers. Imitator of Titus Antoninus and Marcus Aurelius, he loved his people, and wished to be beloved by them; but this very fund of goodness, which made him cherish them, rendered them miserable: he spared even those who pillaged them; quick and ardent in prohibiting abuses, slow and backward in punishing them; covetous of glory, and perhaps rather too much in trifles. He is reproached with having been more addicted to raillery than becomes a great prince. As for the rest, he was chaste, pious, laborious, and indefatigable; a great general, successful in war, and deserving his success by his shining valour, and by the brightness of his genius; a protector of arts, and an encourager of them by his beneficence. If we compare him with Augustus, we shall find that he ruined idolatry by the same precautions, and the same address, which the other employed to destroy liberty. Like Augustus, he laid the foundation of a new empire; but less skilful, and less politic, he could not give it the same stability. He weakened the body of the state by adding to it, in some measure, a second head in the foundation of Constantinople; and, transporting the center of motion and strength too near the eastern extremity, he left without heat, and almost without life, the western parts, which soon became a prey to the barbarians.

The Pagans were too much his enemies to do him justice. Eutropius

tropius says, that, in the former part of his reign, he was equal to the most accomplished princes, and in the latter to the meanest. The younger Victor, who makes him to have reigned more than one-and-thirty years, pretends that in the first ten years he was a hero, in the twelve succeeding ones a robber, and in the ten last a spendthrift. It is easy to perceive, with respect to these two reproaches of Victor's, that the one relates to the riches which Constantine took from idolatry, and the other to those with which he loaded the church.

An Account of the Circoncelliones, *in* Africa; *from the same.*

OUR author, after giving an account of the Donatists, proceeds as follows:

A haughty, extravagant, fiery sect, was a subject thoroughly prepared for fanaticism; accordingly there rose among them (in what year is not precisely known, but during the life of Constantine) a species of madmen, who were called *Circoncelliones*, because they were continually rambling round the houses in the country. It is incredible what ravages and cruelties these vagabonds committed in Africa through a long series of years. They were illiterate, savage peasants, who understood only the Punic language. Intoxicated with a barbarous zeal, they renounced agriculture, professed continence, and assumed the title of Vindicators of Justice, and Protectors of the Opprest. To accomplish their mission, they enfranchised slaves, scoured the roads, forced masters to alight from their chariots, and run before their slaves, whom they obliged to mount in their place; and discharged debtors, killing the creditors if they refused to cancel their bonds. But the chief object of their cruelty was the Catholics, and especially those who had renounced Donatism. At first, they used no swords, because God had forbid the use of one to St. Peter; but they were armed with clubs, which they called the clubs of Israel; and which they handled in such a manner, as to break all the bones of a man without killing him on the spot; so that he languished a long time, and then died. When they took away a man's life at once, they looked upon it as a favour. They became less scrupulous afterwards, and made use of all sorts of arms. Their shout was, *Praise be to God:* these shouts in their mouths were a signal of slaughter more terrible than the roaring of a lion. They had invented an unheard-of punishment, which was to cover with lime, diluted with vinegar, the eyes of those unhappy wretches, whom they had crushed with blows, and covered with wounds, and to abandon them in that condition. Never was a stronger proof what horrors superstition can beget in minds destitute of knowledge and humanity. These brutes, who had made a vow of chastity, gave themselves up to wine, and all sorts of impurities; running about with women and young girls as drunk as themselves, whom they called sacred virgins, and who often carried proofs of their incontinence. Their chiefs took the name of *Chiefs of the Saints.* After having glutted

glutted themselves with blood, they turned their rage upon themselves, and sought death with the same fury with which they gave it to others. Some scrambled up to the top of rocks, and cast themselves down headlong in multitudes: others burned themselves, or threw themselves into the sea. Those who proposed to acquire the title of martyrs published it long before; upon which they were feasted, and fattened like oxen for sacrifice: after these preparations, they set out to be destroyed. Sometimes they gave money to those whom they met, and threatened to murder them if they did not make them martyrs. Theodoret gives an account of a stout, bold young man, who, meeting with a troop of these fanatics, consented to kill them, provided he might bind them first; and having by this means put it out of their power to defend themselves, whipped them as long as he was able, and left them tied in that manner. Their bishops pretended to blame them, but really made use of them to intimidate such as might be tempted to forsake their sect; they even honoured them as saints. They were not, however, able to govern these furious monsters; and more than once found themselves under a necessity of abandoning them, and even of imploring the assistance of the secular power against them. The Counts Ursacius and Taurinus were employed to quell them: they destroyed a great number of them, of whom the Donatists made so many martyrs. Ursacius, who was a good Catholic, and a religious man, having lost his life in an engagement with the barbarians, the Donatists did not fail to triumph in his death, as an effect of the vengeance of heaven. Africa was the theatre of these bloody scenes during the remainder of Constantine's life.

Character of Lewis XIII. *of France, from Lord* Herbert *of* Cherbury's *Memoirs.*

THIS being done, I presented to the King a letter of credence from the King my master; the King assured me of a reciprocal affection to the King my master, and of my particular welcome to his court: his words were never many, as being so extreme a stutterer, that he would sometimes hold his tongue out of his mouth a good while before he could speak so much as one word; he had besides a double row of teeth, and was observed seldom or never to spit or blow his nose, or to sweat much, though he were very laborious, and almost indefatigable in his exercises of hunting and hawking, to which he was much addicted; neither did it hinder him, though he was burst in his body, as we call it, or Herniosus; for he was noted in those sports, though oftentimes on foot, to tire not only his courtiers, but even his lackeys, being equally insensible, as was thought, either of heat or cold: his understanding and natural parts were as good as could be expected, in one that was brought up in so much ignorance, which was on purpose so done that he might be the longer governed; howbeit he acquired in time a great knowledge in affairs, as conversing for the most part with wise and active persons. He was noted to have two qualities incident

incident to all who were ignorantly brought up,...suspicion and dissimulation; for as ignorant persons walk so much in the dark, they cannot be exempt from fear of stumbling; and as they are likewise deprived of, or deficient in, those true principles by which they should govern both public and private actions in a wise, solid, and demonstrative way, they strive commonly to supply these imperfections with covert arts, which, though it may be sometimes excusable in necessitous persons, and be indeed frequent among those who negotiate in small matters, yet is condemnable in princes, who, proceeding upon foundations of reason and strength, ought not to submit themselves to such poor helps: howbeit I must observe, that neither his fears did take away his courage, when there was occasion to use it, nor his dissimulation extend itself to the doing of private mischiefs to his subjects, either of one or the other religion: his favourite was one Monsieur De Luynes, who, in his non-age gained much upon the King, by making hawks fly at all little birds in his gardens, and by making some of those little birds again catch butterflies; and had the King used him for no other purpose, he might have been tolerated; but as, when the King came to a riper age, the government of public affairs was drawn chiefly from his counsels, not a few errors were committed.

The queen-mother, princes, and nobles of that kingdom, repined that his advices to the King should be so prevalent, which also at last caused a civil war in that kingdom. How unfit this man was for the credit he had with the King may be argued by this: that when there was question made about some business in Bohemia, he demanded whether it was an inland country, or lay upon the sea?

A Short Character of the late Sir Joseph Yates.

THE late Sir Joseph Yates was one of those who, very early in life, attached himself to the study of the laws, not as the generality of students do, either from the appointment of parents, or the mere motives of drawing pecuniary resources from the profession, but from the more liberal principle of informing himself in a science, which only appeared important to him from being capable of defending the lives and properties of individuals. With this open and enlarged turn of mind, he pursued his enquiries with a perseverance and precision almost peculiar to himself, till the profession repaid him, by storing his mind with an universal knowledge of its laws, which very rarely falls to the lot of the greatest talents, or most diligent researches. His invincible modesty, however, repelled him the notice of the public for many years, till at last the repeated justness of his opinions, and forcibility of his pleadings, procured him a coif, from whence he was some time afterwards promoted to one of the judges of the King's-bench.

In this character he always conducted himself with a dignity and impartiality that reflected honour even on that respectable situation. The right of the subject and the dignity of the crown were never

occa-

occasionally explained by will or favouritism, but by the established language of the law; and a steady impartial observance of it formed the invariable rule of his conduct.

His charges to Juries were not the charges of an Asiatic Cadi delivering his own will, but the charges of a British judge in the land of liberty, and will be remembered for many years with pleasure by the lovers of freedom and oratory. In these he appeared more the guardian of the people than an officer of the crown; and hit that nice medium, as a distributor of justice, so strictly, that the offending party, whilst they felt the chastisement, could not refrain applauding the chastiser.

Though universal in his knowledge of the laws, his forte confessedly lay in common pleadings, with which he was the most minutely acquainted of any man of his time. Sensible that his talents drew him more strongly this way, he, on the late resignation of Judge Clive, solicited to change from the King's-bench to the Common-pleas, which he succeeded in, but which he did not long live to enjoy, thereby depriving the world of one of the greatest judges, of that court, England perhaps ever boasted of.

His character as a lawyer, though so particularly marked for knowledge and candour, was by no means diminished as a gentleman. His intimate knowledge of the arts and sciences, a fine taste of the belles lettres, joined to an uncommon philanthropy of temper, engaged him not only the esteem but the ardent admiration of his acquaintances; and, when he died, left a chasm in their friendships, which can only be filled up by a recollection of what he was.

Genuine Anecdotes of the Life of the late Peter Collinson, F. R. S.

THE ingenious author of this little piece justly observes, that to place before the public an example worthy of imitation is no inconsiderable service. The great and good Author of Nature has implanted a principle in every breast which necessarily approves of a conduct directed to the advantage of mankind. Of what we approve we are naturally emulous, and the tribute that is publicly paid to the memory of a worthy man may well be considered as a kind of reward offered for the encouragement of merit.

Mr. Peter Collinson was of an antient family in the North, and the great grandson of Peter Collinson, who lived on his paternal estate called Hugal-Hall, or Height of Hugal, near Windermere-lake, in the parish of Stavely, about ten miles from Kendal, in Westmoreland. What was his father's profession, or where he lived, does not appear.

He was born in the year 1693, and bred to trade as a wholesale dealer, in what is called man's mercery: a brother, whose name was James, seems also to have been bred to the same business, probably by their father.

Peter and James became partners, which was a fortunate circumstance for them both, because, living in great harmony, and their business not requiring their presence together, they had both leisure to attend their particular studies and pursuits,

pursuits, whether of pleasure or improvement.

Peter, while a youth, had discovered a strong attachment to natural history: insects, and their several metamorphoses, employed many of those hours, which, at his time of life, are generally spent upon other objects. Plants also engaged his attention, and he very early began to make dried specimens.

While he was yet a young man, his diligent curiosity, with respect to these objects, procured him the acquaintance of the most eminent naturalists of that time, particularly of Derham, Woodward, Dale, Lloyd, and Sir Hans Sloane. He contracted a friendship also with the late Sir Charles Wager, who enriched Sir Hans' collection, now constituting the British Museum, with many curiosities, which, being excited by Mr. Collinson, he picked up in the course of his many voyages, encouraging also the commanders under him, who were stationed in different parts of the globe, to procure whatever was rare and valuable in every branch of natural history, for the same kind and liberal purpose.

Among the vast variety of articles in that immense treasury of nature, there were very few with the history of which Mr. Collinson was not yet acquainted, his familiarity with Sir Hans being such that he visited him at all times, and continued to do so till his death.

Besides his acquaintance with natural history, his knowledge of the antiquities of his own country was very considerable. In December 1728, when he was about five-and-thirty years old, he was elected a Member of the Royal Society, and was a Member of the Society of Antiquarians from its first institution.

To the Royal Society he was one of the most diligent and useful members it had: he not only supplied many curious observations himself, but he promoted and preserved a most extensive correspondence with the learned and ingenious of all countries. The antiquarians he also furnished with many curious articles of intelligence and observation with respect to the particular objects of their enquiry, as well at home as abroad.

Wherever he was, or however seemingly engaged, nothing that deserved his notice at any time escaped him, and he minuted down every striking hint that occurred either in reading or conversation. With such hints, conversation perhaps furnished him still more than books; for there was scarce a man of learning and ingenuity, whatever was his profession, in England, that was not of his acquaintance: and of the foreigners who came hither, either for improvement or pleasure, those who were eminent for their knowledge of natural history, or proficiency in any art or science, were constantly recommended to his notice and friendship: among these were the celebrated Linnæus, with whom, during his residence in England, Mr. Collinson contracted an intimate friendship, which was reciprocally increased by a multitude of good offices, and continued without any diminution to the last.

These recommendations were the natural consequences of his extensive foreign correspondence, which he maintained with the greatest punctuality. He acquainted the learned and ingenious in diſtant parts of the globe with the diſcoveries and improvements that were made here in various branches of knowledge; and there is ſcarce any part of the world from which he did not receive informations of the ſame kind in return.

From this correſpondence of Peter Collinſon, his native country has, in many inſtances, derived great advantage and honour.

In the year 1730, a ſubſcription library was ſet on foot at Philadelphia, in America, to which Mr. Collinſon made ſeveral valuable preſents, and procured others from his friends.

To the directors of this library, among whom was Dr. Franklin, Mr. Collinſon tranſmitted the earlieſt account of every new European improvement in agriculture and the arts, and every philoſophical diſcovery. In 1745 he ſent over an account of ſome new experiments in electricity, which had then been made in Germany, with a glaſs tube, and ſome directions how it might be uſed ſo as to repeat them.

This was the firſt notice that Dr. Franklin had of that curious ſubject, which, encouraged by the friendly reception that Mr. Collinſon gave to his letters concerning it, he proſecuted with a ſucceſs that has made him eminent in every country in Europe, and procured to his own the honour of having firſt reduced phenomena to ſcience, with reſpect to this great natural agent, powerfully and perpetually operating, though hitherto ſcarce known to exiſt.

Perhaps, in ſome future period, the account which Mr. Collinſon procured of the management of ſheep in Spain, with reſpect to their migrations from the mountains to the plains, and back from the plains to the mountains, which he publiſhed in the year 1764, may not be conſidered among the leaſt of the benefits that have accrued from his extenſive and inquiſitive correſpondence.

When America is better peopled, the mountainous parts more habitable, the plains unloaded of their vaſt foreſts, and cultivated, the fineſt ſheep in the world may poſſibly cover the plains of Carolina, Georgia, and Eaſt and Weſt Florida, in the winter months, and retreat to the mountains as the ſummer heats increaſe and dry up the herbage. We are at preſent utter ſtrangers to this œconomy, which might, perhaps, be practiſed with advantage even in England; with this difference, that the hills ſhould be choſen for the reſidence of theſe animals in winter, proper ſhelter being made for them, and the wetter low lands reſerved for their paſture in ſummer.

So long ago as the year 1740, he was conſiderable among thoſe who were beſt acquainted with botany and natural hiſtory in England. His collection was very large; his ſpecimens were well choſen; he had a botanical garden at Mill-hill, near Endfield, which at that time contained many curious plants not to be found in any other, the number of which was continually increaſing till his death.

This collection and garden brought him acquainted with many perſons of rank and diſtinction in this kingdom, who were diſtinguiſhed by their taſte in planting and horticulture, or deſirous to

make

make rural improvements. With some of these he frequently spent a few days at their seats, commending and censuring what he approved and disapproved, in the designs they were carrying on, with an integrity and taste that did equal honour to the simplicity of his manners and the rectitude of his judgment. Frequent opportunities, during a long life, had furnished him with an extensive experience of the effects of different methods of cultivation, and of the particular soil and aspect which were best adapted to different plants and trees; how beauties might be best improved, and incurable defects hidden: by this knowledge he often prevented young planters from committing capital mistakes, rectified others into which they had been misled either by the ignorant or the designing, and prevailed upon many of his friends to adopt this rational amusement, and persevere in it, to the mutual advantage of themselves and their country. I never knew an instance, said, Mr. Collinson, in which the pursuit of such pleasures did not either find temperance and virtue, or make them.

He was the first that introduced the great variety of seeds and shrubs which are now the principal ornaments of every garden; and it is owing to his inquisitive industry that so many persons of the first distinction are now able to see, in their own domains, groves that have been transplanted from the Western continent, flourish with the same luxuriance as those which are indigenous to Britain.

As his mercantile business was transacted chiefly with North America, he interested himself in whatever might contribute to its advantage. He used to observe to the Virginians, that their present staple is tobacco; a plant of which the consumption depends wholly upon the caprice of custom and fashion, and he therefore frequently urged them to think of something more permanent, something necessary to the natural subsistence or enjoyment of life. He observed, that vines would thrive as well in their country as tobacco; but, said he, do not keep them close to the ground, as we are forced to do for want of a little more sun and heat: your summer-heats exceed, as much as our's fall short; allow your vines, therefore, longer stems; let them be trained to and supported by trees, and hide their fruit among the foliage, as they do in the warmer parts of Europe. On this occasion our author observes, that in most of our northern and southern colonies there is a great variety of native grapes growing wild in the woods, and twining among the trees and bushes for support: that several of these are capable of producing a rich good wine, as appears by experiment: and that, where the attempt has failed, the fault has been not in the fruit, but in the want either of skill or care in making the wine. I have myself, says he, tasted some very good wine from the wild uncultivated grape of America, which has been hastily made without experience, and sent over to England. It is reasonable, therefore, to conclude, that if proper care was taken to improve the grape by cultivation, and the wine by a diligent and skilful process in the making it,

America

America might become one of the most celebrated wine countries upon earth.

Mr. Collinson was also of opinion, that flax, hemp, and silk, might be cultivated in our American colonies with equal advantage to them and to us.

He was a remarkable instance, that he who is never idle need never be in a hurry! He was always doing something, and therefore he transacted all his domestic and mercantile affairs, and preserved his extensive and multifarious correspondence with a quiet regularity and silent dispatch that equally prevented embarrassment and delay. The blameless simplicity of his manners, and the careful œconomy of his time, kept his mind perpetually serene, and serenity is always easily improved into cheerfulness.

His stature was below the middle size, and his body was rather corpulent; his habit was plain, having been bred a quaker; his aspect kind and liberal, and his temper open and communicative. He was an œconomist, but his œconomy was by no means severe. He had a heart that sympathised with distress, and a hand that was always open to relieve it. As his pure and rational pleasures saved him from the fashionable follies which generally encroach far upon the night, he rose very early in the morning. When he was in London, he applied to the business of his counting-house; when in the country, he was almost continually employed in his garden, observing and assisting the progress of vegetation, which equally contributed to his pleasure and his health.

He was in the highest degree fond both of flowers and fruit. Of fruit he always made the principal part of his meal; and his house was never without flowers, from the early snowdrop to the autumnal cyclamen.

Notwithstanding his temperance, he was sometimes attacked by the gout: but in other respects he enjoyed perfect health, and great equality of spirits.

In the autumn of the year 1768, he went to visit Lord Petre, for whom he had a singular regard, at his house in Essex; and while he was there, he was seized with a total suppression of urine, which, baffling all the efforts of medicine, put an end to his life on the 11th day of August, just as he had arrived at the 75th year of his age.

Inclosed in his will was found a paper importing, "That he hoped "he should leave behind him a "good name, which he valued "more than riches; that he had "endeavoured not to live uselessly; "and that his constant aim "through life had been to be a "friend to mankind."

Without any pretensions to what is generally called learning, he knew more both of nature and of art than nine in ten of those who pride themselves in having it. His time had been spent not in learning the names of things in different languages, but in acquiring the knowledge of their nature and properties, their productions and use. Without public station, he was the means of national advantages: he had an influence that wealth cannot give, and will be honoured when titles are forgotten.

Memoirs

Memoirs of the Rev. Mr. George Whitefield.

THE confiderable figure which the late Mr. Whitefield for many years made in his ecclefiaftical capacity, ranking his death in the catalogue of memorable events, a curfory memoir of his life cannot fail of giving general fatisfaction; we have therefore from his own journal felected what we judge neceffary for the principal execution of the tafk, and fhall regulate our opinion of his general character by the beft accounts we can obtain from his cotemporaries.

I was born in Gloucefter, fays Mr. Whitefield, in the month of December, 1714, at the Bell Inn, and *can* truly fay I was froward from my mother's womb.—— I was fo brutifh as to hate inftruction, and ufed purpofely to fhun all opportunities of receiving it. I can date fome very early acts of uncleannefs. Lying, filthy talking, and foolifh jefting, I was much addicted to.—Sometimes I ufed to curfe, if not fwear.—Stealing from my mother I thought no theft at all, and ufed to make no fcruple of taking money out of her pocket before fhe was up.——I have frequently betrayed my truft, and have more than once fpent money I took in the houfe in buying fruits, tarts, &c. to fatisfy my fenfual appetite.——Numbers of fabbaths have I broken, and generally ufed to behave myfelf very irreverently in God's fanctuary.—— Much money have I fpent in plays, and in the common entertainments of the age.—Cards, and reading romances, were my heart's delight. Often have I joined with others in playing roguifh tricks, but was generally, if not always, *happily detected*.——For this I have often fince, and do now, blefs and praife God.

It would be endlefs to recount the fins and offences of my younger days——they are more in number than the hairs of my head.——My heart would fail me at the remembrance of them, was I not affured that my Redeemer liveth ever to make interceffion for me.—However the young man in the gofpel might boaft how he had kept the commandments from his youth, with fhame and confufion of face I confefs, that I have broken them all from my youth.——Whatever forefeen fitnefs for falvation others may talk of, and glory in, I difclaim any fuch thing.—If I trace myfelf from my cradle to my manhood, I can fee nothing in me but a fitnefs to be damned; and if the Almighty had not prevented me by his grace, and wrought moft powerfully upon my foul, quickening me by his free fpirit when dead in trefpaffes and fins, I had now either been fitting in darknefs, and in the fhadow of death or condemned, as the due reward of my crimes, to be for ever lifting up my eyes in torments.

But fuch was the free grace of God to me, that though corruption worked fo ftrongly in my foul, and produced fuch early and bitter fruits, yet I can recollect very early movings of the Bleffed Spirit upon my heart, fufficient to fatisfy me that God loved me with an everlafting love, and feparated me, me, even from my mother's womb, for the work for which he afterwards was pleased to call me.

I had early some convictions of sin; and once, I remember, when some persons (as they frequently did) made it their business to teaze me, I immediately retired to my room, and, kneeling down, with many tears, prayed over that psalm wherein David so often repeats these words:—*But in the name of the Lord I will destroy them.* I was always fond of being a clergyman, used frequently to imitate the ministers reading prayers, &c. Part of the money I used to steal from my parent I gave to the poor; and some books I privately took from others (for which I have since restored four-fold) I remember were books of devotion.

My mother was very careful of my education, and always kept me, in my tender years, from intermeddling in the least with the public business.

About the tenth year of my age, it pleased GOD to permit my mother to marry a second time. It proved what the world would call an unhappy match; but GOD overruled it for good.——

When I was about twelve, I was placed at a school called St. Mary de Crypt, in Gloucester, the last grammar-school I ever went to. Having a good elocution and memory, I was remarked for making speeches before the corporation at their annual visitation. But I cannot say I felt any drawings of GOD upon my soul for a year or two, saving that I laid out some of the money that was given me on one of the aforementioned occasions in buying Ken's Manual for Winchester scholars; a book that had much affected me when my brother used to read it in my mother's troubles, and which, for some time after I bought it, was of great benefit to my soul.

During the time of my being at school, I was very fond of reading plays, and have kept from school for days together, to prepare myself for acting them. My master, seeing how mine and my schoolfellows vein run, composed something of this kind for us himself, and caused me to dress myself in girl's cloaths, (which I had often done), to act a part before the corporation. The remembrance of this has often covered me with confusion of face, and I hope will do so, even to the end of my life.

Before I was fifteen, having, as I thought, made a sufficient progress in the classics, and, at the bottom, longing to be set at liberty from the confinement of a school, I one day told my mother, since her circumstances would not permit her to give me an university education, more learning, I thought, would spoil me for a tradesman; and, therefore, I judged it best not to learn Latin any longer. She at first refused to consent; but my corruptions soon got the better of her good nature.— Hereupon, for some time, I went to learn to write only: but my mother's circumstances being much on the decline, and being tractable that way, I from time to time began to assist her occasionally in the public house; till, at length, I put on my blue apron and my snuffers, washed mops, cleaned rooms, and, in one word, became a professed and common drawer.

Notwithstanding I was thus employed in a large inn, and had

sometimes

sometimes the care of the whole house upon my hands, yet I composed two or three sermons, and dedicated one of them in particular to my elder brother. One time I remember I was very much pressed to self-examination, and found myself very unwilling to look into my heart. Frequently I read the Bible when sitting up at night. Seeing the boys go by to school has often cut me to the heart. And a dear youth (now with GOD) would often come entreating me, when serving at the bar, to go to Oxford. My general answer was, *I wish I could.*

After I had continued about a year in this servile employment, my mother was obliged to leave the inn. My brother, who had been bred up for the business, married, whereupon all was made over to him; and I being accustomed to the house, it was judged best that I should continue there as an assistant. But it happened that my sister-in-law and I could by no means agree; and, therefore, after continuing a long while under a great burden of mind, I at length resolved (thinking that my absence would make all things easy) to go away. Accordingly, by the advice of my brother, and consent of my mother, I went to see my elder brother, then settled at Bristol.

Here GOD was pleased to give me great sensible devotion, and fill me with such unspeakable raptures, particularly once in Saint John's Church, that I was carried out beyond myself. I felt great hungerings and thirstings after the blessed sacrament, and wrote many letters to my mother, telling her I would never go into the public employment again. Thomas à Kempis was my great delight, and I was always impatient till the bell rung to call me to tread the courts of the Lord's house. But in the midst of these illuminations something secretly whispered, *This would not last.*

And, indeed, it so happened; for (oh, that I could write in tears of blood!) when I left Bristol (as I did in about two months), and returned to Gloucester, I changed my devotion with my place. Alas! all my fervour went off, and I had no inclination to go to church, or draw nigh unto GOD. However, I had so much religion left as to persist in my resolution not to live in the inn; and, therefore, my mother gave me leave, though she had but a little income, to have a bed upon the ground, and live at her house, till Providence should point out a place for me.

Having now, as I thought, nothing to do, it was a proper season for Satan to tempt me. Much of my time I spent in reading plays, and in sauntering from place to place. I was careful to adorn my body, but took little pains to deck and beautify my soul. Evil communications with my old schoolfellows soon corrupted my good manners. By seeing their evil practices, all sense of religion gradually wore off my mind; and I at length fell into a secret sin, the dismal effects of which I have felt and groaned under ever since.

Having lived thus for some considerable time, a young student, who was once my schoolfellow, and then a servitor of Pembroke College, Oxford, came to pay my mother a visit. Amongst other conversation, he told her how he had discharged

CHARACTERS.

discharged all college expences that quarter, and received a penny.—Upon that my mother immediately cried out, "This will do for my son."——Then, turning to me, she said, "Will you go to Oxford, George?" I replied, *With all my heart*. Whereupon, having the same friends that this young student had, my mother, without delay, waited on them. They promised their interest to get me a servitor's place in the same college. She then applied to my old master, who much approved of my coming to school again.

In about a week I went and entered myself, and spared no pains to get forward in my book. God was pleased to give me his blessing, and I learned much faster than I did before. But all this while I continued in sin; and at length got acquainted with such a set of debauched, abandoned, atheistical youths, that if God, by his free, unmerited, and especial grace, had not delivered me out of their hands, I should long since have sat in the scorner's chair.——By keeping company with them, my thoughts of religion grew more and more like their's. I went to public service only to make sport, and walk about. I took pleasure in their lewd conversation. I began to reason as they did, and was in a fair way of being as infamous as the worst of them.

But (oh, stupendous love!) God even here stopped me, when running on in a full career to hell; for just as I was upon the brink of ruin, he gave me such a distaste of their principles and practices, that I discovered them to my master, who soon put a stop to their proceedings.

Being thus delivered out of the snares of the devil, I began to be more and more serious, and felt the spirit of God at different times working powerfully and convincingly upon my soul. One day in particular, as I was coming down stairs, and overheard my friends speaking well of me, God so deeply convicted me of hypocrisy, that though I had formed frequent but ineffectual resolutions before, yet I had then power given me over my secret and darling sin. Notwithstanding, some time after being overtaken in liquor (as I have been twice or thrice in my lifetime), Satan gained his usual advantage over me again.—An experimental proof to my poor soul, how that wicked one makes use of intemperate men as machines to work them up to just what he pleases.

Thus far we have proceeded in Mr. Whitefield's own words; but the narrowness of our limits obliging us to practise brevity, we shall only add, that Mr. Whitefield, being admitted a servitor at Oxford, very soon distinguished himself by the austerities of his devotion, and acquired considerable eminence in some religious assemblies of that city; " lying whole days and weeks prostrate on the ground in silent or vocal prayer, leaving off the eating of fruits; chusing the worst sort of food, though his place furnished him with variety; thinking it unbecoming a penitent to have his hair powdered; wearing woollen gloves, a patched gown, and dirty shoes," to contract a habit of humility.

At the age of twenty-one the fame of Mr. Whitefield's piety recommended him so much to Dr. Benson,

Benson, the then Bishop of Gloucester, that he made him a voluntary offer of ordination, which Mr. Whitefield at last thought proper to accept, and, immediately after this regular admission into the ministry, applied himself to the most extraordinary, the most indefatigable duties of his character, preaching daily in prisons, fields, and open streets, wherever he thought there would be a likelihood of making proselytes; till having at length made himself universally known in England, he embarked for America, where the tenets of Methodism began to spread very fast under his friends, the Mr. Wesleys, and first determined upon the institution of the orphan-house at Georgia, which he afterwards effected.——At what time Mr. Whitefield married, or with whom, we are not able, nor is it perhaps material, to inform our readers.——Suffice it, that after a long course of peregrination, his fortune increased as his fame extended among his followers, and he erected two very extensive buildings for public worship, under the name of Tabernacles; one in Tottenham Court Road, and the other in Moorfields: here, with the help of some assistants, he continued for several years, attended by very crowded congregations, and quitting the kingdom only occasionally.—America, however, which always engaged much of his attention, was destined to close his eyes: and he died at Newbery, about forty miles from Boston in New England, on the 30th of last September. His disorder was a violent asthma, which in a few hours put a period to his life, in the 56th year of his age.

Besides the two tabernacles already mentioned, Mr. Whitefield, by being chaplain to the Countess Dowager of Huntingdon, was connected with two other religious meetings, one at Bath, and the other at Tunbridge, chiefly erected under that lady's patronage.—His influence among his followers was extensive; and so universally was he esteemed the principal teacher of the Methodists, that many characters have been given in the public prints to this effect.

As the worth of this truly pious and extraordinary person must be deeply impressed upon the hearts of every friend to true, genuine, and vital christianity, who hath profited by his unwearied labours, little need be said to convince them that their loss is irreparable.——In his public ministrations throughout different parts of Europe, and on sundry visits to British America, he hath, for above 30 years, astonished the world as a prodigy of eloquence; by which he was enabled to melt the hearts of the most obdurate and stubborn sinners.

In spite of a constitution of body originally delicate and tender, he continued to the last day of his life to preach with a frequency and fervour that seemed to exceed the natural strength of the most robust. Being called to the public exercise of his functions at an age when most young men are only beginning to qualify themselves for it, he had not time to make any considerable progress in the learned languages; but this defect was amply supplied by a lively, fertile, and penetrating genius, by the most unwearied zeal, and by a forcible and most persuasive delivery, which never failed of the desired effect

CHARACTERS.

effect upon his ever crowded and admiring audiences. And though in the pulpit he often found it necessary *by the terrors of the Lord to perfuade men,* he had nothing gloomy in his nature, being fingularly charitable, and tender-hearted; and in his private converfation cheerful, communicative, and entertaining. To the very meaneft he was always eafy of accefs, and ever as ready to liften to and relieve their bodily as their fpiritual neceffities, fhewing himfelf in every refpect a faithful fteward of the extenfive charities he drew from his numerous and compaffionate hearers. It ought alfo to be obferved, that he conftantly and moft pathetically enforced upon his audience every moral duty; particularly, induftry in their different callings, and obedience to their fuperiors; and in a moft efpecial manner loyalty to our amiable fovereign, never once endeavouring in thefe diftracted times to make a factious ufe of the great influence he held among his numerous adherents. He was the firft of thofe (fince known by the name of *Methodifts*) who endeavoured by the moft extraordinary efforts of preaching in different places, and even in the open fields, to roufe the lower clafs of the people from the laft degree of inattention and ignorance to a fenfe of religion, among whom he hath left an impreffion which cannot be foon effaced.—For this, and for his other labours, the name of George Whitefield will long be remembered with efteem and veneration not only by his perfonal acquaintance, by thofe who were awaked by his miniftry, but by all true chriftians of every denomination, whilft vital and practical religion hath a place in the Britifh dominions.

Such is the portrait drawn of Mr. Whitefield by the Methodifts: the enemies of that fect, however, particularly the very learned author of *The Enthufiafm of Methodifts and Papifts compared*, are fo far from admitting his pretenfions to an extraordinary portion of fanctity, that they pofitively pronounce him a moft profligate hypocrite: his piety they attribute to avarice; his zeal to pride; and his very humility to oftentation.—They tell us, that during life he was continually boafting of his poverty, yet at his death they talk of his being immenfely rich.—This is not all: his late progrefs to America is fet down to the groffeft account; an attachment to a woman, by whom he had a child while his wife was living; and it is even added, that this child was the firft infant ever entered into his orphan-houfe of Georgia. How far the character on either fide may be juft, we do not by any means pretend to affirm: the chief particulars of his hiftory we have extracted from his own writings; and, as we have given the moft flattering eulogium that has been publifhed by his friends, we cannot be deemed partial in mentioning the opinion of his enemies.

NATURAL

NATURAL HISTORY.

An extraordinary Case of three Pins swallowed by a Girl, and discharged at her Shoulder. In a Letter to Frank Nicholls, *M. D. F. R. S. from Dr.* Lysons, *of Gloucester.*

To Charles Morton, M. D. Sec. R. S.

[Read January 26, 1769.]

Epsom,
Nov. 25, 1768.

DEAR SIR,

INCLOSED I send you a most extraordinary case, which is transmitted to me by Dr. Lysons, a gentleman of great learning and credit, and physician to the Gloucester hospital. It seems to be exactly drawn, and the doctor's veracity may be depended on. I think it well worth preserving in the Memoirs of the Society; and believe that the Council will have the same opinion of it as,

SIR,
Your very humble servant,
Fran. Nicholls.

SIR,

UPON my mentioning the case of a girl who swallowed three pins, which were afterwards discharged at her shoulder, you thought it might be proper for the Philosophical Transactions, and desired me to send it you. I have drawn it from notes, taken during my attendance upon her, with as much accuracy as possible, and it is as follows.

Eleanor Kaylock, a robust, strong girl, aged twenty-two, was admitted a patient in the Gloucester infirmary, May 29, 1766, for a pain in her side proceeding from pins swallowed three quarters of a year before. The occasion of the accident was thus. Being employed in the business of a kitchen, as she was scumming the pot (her mouth being open, and three pins in it), she received a quantity of the vapours, which obliged her to swallow, and the pins at the same time passed into the *æsophagus*, where they remained for eight weeks, notwithstanding various methods were used for their removal; but they were at last forced down by the whalebone instrument used by surgeons for that purpose.

Whilst the pins were in her throat, the parts became inflamed, and swoln, which occasioned an hoarseness, attended with great pain, and difficulty of breathing: being also capable of receiving but very little nourishment, and that only liquids, she was reduced to so weak a state as not to be able to get out of her bed. After the

pins

pins were removed she could swallow solids, and recovered strength sufficient to go out again to service in her former employment. She was hired as an under-servant in a gentleman's kitchen, but was soon obliged to quit her place, and apply for relief; any extraordinary motion aggravating her complaints, and occasioning violent convulsions, from which she did not recover for eight or nine hours. When she came to the infirmary, she appeared full of flesh, of a ruddy complexion, and in perfect health, excepting the following complaints.

She had a pain in her right side, below the false ribs, which she first felt immediately upon the removal of the pins from the *œsophagus*, and it continued to the time of her admission at the hospital, but was most violent when she moved the trunk of her body forwards round towards the left, or lifted up her right arm. At her admission, and from the time of the removal of the pins, the hoarseness she was troubled with, soon after the pins first stuck in her throat, continued; she often spit up blood, and had a violent cough, by which, as well as by labour, or any excess of motion, the pain in her side being greatly aggravated, she was obliged to sit or fall down immediately, and could not recover herself, so as to be able to stand, in less than an hour. In these paroxysms she had always a pain in her head, was sick at stomach, and frequently brought up blood.

Whilst she was in the infirmary, the violence of the pain three times occasioned convulsion-fits, by which the *musculus rectus superior* of the right eye was so violently affected, that, notwithstanding the eye was open, yet the pupil was entirely covered by the eye-lid; and, after one of these fits, continued so for a fortnight. The left eye was also inverted in the same manner, but the constriction was removed in a week. When these spasmodic affections left her, she did not recover her eye-sight for some days; the optic nerve being probably oppressed; but the left eye always recovered sooner than the right, being never so strongly convulsed. None of the other muscles appeared to be affected, except in the paroxysms.

While the pins were in the *œsophagus*, the surgeon was utterly at a loss where to direct his instruments, as there was no certain indication where the pins were lodged. And the physician's practice could be only palliative, using bleeding, with anodyne and lubricating medicines, according as the various symptoms occasionally required. In this manner things went on to the beginning of August, when a small painful tumour, the size of a man's thumb, appeared upon the right shoulder, which disappeared in the compass of a week without coming to suppuration. Afterwards such another small tumour appeared upon the left shoulder, which increased, and, by the care of Mr. Crump, the attending surgeon, was brought to suppuration, and opened by him, August 20, when a large table spoonful of matter was discharged. Upon removing the dressings, the next day, a larger quantity of matter flowed out, and with it issued one of the pins. Mr. Crump then examined with his probe if he could find either of the others, but could not: however, the day following, the other two pins were also discharged at the same wound. These pins were all of the same length, each measuring five quarters of an inch. The wound at which these pins were discharged was upon the superior part of the scapula. After the girl had received her cure, and was discharged from the infirmary (which happened September the fourth), I compared her shoulder with Cowper's Anatomical Tables on the Muscles; and, as near as I can guess, the wound was upon the fleshy belly of the trapesius. And yet the pain in the patient's side attended her as long as the pins remained in the wound, but left her soon after they were discharged, as did also her cough, and spitting of blood. Being obliged to lead a sedentary life in the infirmary, and to keep herself as quiet as possible, her catamenia left her; but her spitting of blood could not be attributed to that defect, because she was very regular before her admission, and yet she had spit blood from the time the pins were removed from the œsophagus, which was some months before she came to the infirmary.

It would be matter of considerable satisfaction, could the exact course be ascertained which was taken by these pins, in their passage from the œsophagus to their exit at the left shoulder. From the cough and spitting of blood, one should suppose that the lungs were injured by them. From the pain under the false ribs, it may be imagined that the diaphragm was affected. And yet, from their being discharged at the shoulder, it may be presumed, that neither of these parts were ever wounded; but that the pins, being forced through the substance of the œsophagus into the muscles of the neck and shoulder, passed thence to the part whence they were discharged.

The first symptom observable upon the removal of these pins from the passage of the œsophagus was, that the patient immediately felt a pain in her right side, below the false ribs, which was most violent when she turned the trunk of her body forwards round towards the left, or lifted up her right arm. Now if the pins, being forced out of the œsophagus, penetrated the serrati, rhomboides, and trapesius muscles on the right side, this symptom must necessarily happen. For the serrati being muscles of respiration, and the serratus superior posticus, attached to the second, third, fourth, fifth, and sixth ribs; and the serratus inferior posticus being attached to the tenth, eleventh, and the extremity of the twelfth ribs, a pain in the side will be produced by the constant efforts of respiration. And the office of these muscles being to elevate the ribs, and draw down the arm, the pain in the side will be most sensibly felt whenever the right arm is lifted up; because then the extremities of these muscles, attached to the ribs, will be most tense. For although a wound may be given to a muscle in its most fleshy part, yet the irritation occasioned by it will exert itself most forcibly in that part where there is the greatest tension.

The rhomboides muscle lying upon the serratus superior, and the trapesius being incumbent upon it, and all closely connected by the cellular membrane, they must all be be in some degree affected by respiration. But the office of the rhomboides and trapesius muscles being to draw the arm downwards, and backwards, the pain in the side would be increased whenever the right arm and trunk of the body were turned forwards towards the left side.

Being thus, as we may suppose, arrived at the true cause of the pain in the side, the cough comes next under consideration. And this will be found to proceed from the same cause that the cough of a pleuretic person does; only with this difference, that in one the pleura and intercostal muscles are affected by an internal inflammation, by which respiration is disturbed; in the other, the malady arises from irritation caused by an extraneous body. The effects are the same in both: respiration being impeded, nature endeavours to relieve herself by a cough, which increases the irritation and inflammation of the parts obstructed; these again increase the violence of the cough; and thus, each being aggravated by the other, the lungs are often so violently agitated, that a blood vessel bursts, and thence blood is thrown up from the lungs, as was the case in the present instance.

Whoever considers the communication between the third pair of nerves, the intercostal the cardiac, and the recurrents, together with the other nerves dependant upon them, will easily perceive the cause of the violent spasm upon the eyes, the sickness at stomach, and the general convulsion, as being all primarily dependant upon the irritation given to the intercostal nerve on the right side. And it may be observed, that although both the motores oculorum were affected, yet the right eye was convulsed most violently.

From the symptoms attending this uncommon case, it is reasonable to conclude, that the three pins were all of them at the same time forced from the œsophagus into the serrati muscles on the right side, which immediately communicated an irritation or impulse to the intercostal nerve, from whence arose the pain in the side, and thence the sickness at stomach, and convulsions of the eyes and other parts. But whatever caused the pain in the right side, upon the removal of the pins from the œsophagus, that cause continued to act until all the three pins were discharged at the left shoulder; for so long did the pain in the right side continue.

The thickness of the two serrati, the rhomboides, and trapesius muscles, may be thought too great for pins five quarters of an inch long to penetrate all of them at the same time. But if it be observed, that one of the pins was discharged at a time when neither of the two others could be felt with the probe, it may be supposed, that one of the three passed into the rhomboides and trapesius, whilst the two others remained in the serrati, and there continued until the first was discharged at the trapesius; after which they took the same course, and were discharged at the same outlet.

Thus might we give a very probable account of this extraordinary case, had the pins been discharged at the right shoulder; but they were discharged at the left. By those who think that, the nerves communicating with one another, the cause and effect produced may be on opposite sides of the body, it may be said, that the pins might be forced from the œsophagus into the muscles of the left side, notwithstanding the pain was felt in the right. This will not be generally allowed. Neither can I perceive any reason why a tumour exactly resembling that from whence the pins were afterwards discharged, at the left shoulder should arise upon the right, and disperse without coming to suppuration.

Since I drew out the above account, I have seen a case nearly similar to it, recorded in the Philosophical Transactions, No. 461. A small needle being lodged in a woman's left arm, about six inches below the shoulder, passed thence to her right breast, whence it was extracted many months after it first entered the body. About a month after the accident, she felt a pain above the place where the needle run in, which extended up her shoulder. It lasted there three or four days, and then returned by fits. About seventeen weeks before the needle was extracted, she felt a pain at her stomach, was sick, and had reachings to vomit. These symptoms continued to afflict her (especially in the morning), until within two days of the needle being extracted, at which time she thought a pin had got into her right breast. This directed the surgeon to make an opening there, and he extracted the same needle that had entered at her arm from the part where the pricking pain was: after which she had never any return of pain in her breast, stomach, shoulder, or arm.

If, upon perusal of this case, you think it merits the attention of the curious, as corroborating the other, your recommendation of it to the Royal Society will be esteemed an honour to,

SIR,

Your most obliged,

humble servant,

Gloucester,
Sept. 1, 1768.   D. LYSONS.

A Letter from the Honourable William Hamilton, *his Majesty's Envoy Extraordinary at* Naples, *to* Matthew Maty, *M.D. F.R.S. containing some farther Particulars on Mount* Vesuvius, *and other Volcanoes in the Neighbourhood.*

[Read Feb. 2, 1769.]

Villa Angelica, near Mount
Vesuvius, Oct. 4, 1768.

SIR,

I HAVE but very lately received your last obliging letter of the 5th of July, with the volume of Philosophical Transactions.

I must beg of you to express my satisfaction at the notice the Royal Society have been pleased to take of my accounts of the two last eruptions of Mount Vesuvius. Since I have been at my villa here, I have enquired of the inhabitants of the mountain after what they had seen during the last eruption. In my letter to Lord Morton, I mentioned nothing but what came immediately under my own observation: but as all the peasants here agree in their account of the terrible thunder and lightning, which lasted almost the whole time of the eruption, upon the mountain only,

I think

I think it a circumſtance worth attending to. Beſides the lightning, which perfectly reſembled the common forked lightning, there were many meteors, like what are vulgarly called falling ſtars. A peaſant in my neighbourhood loſt eight hogs by the aſhes falling into the trough with their food: they grew giddy, and died within a few hours. The laſt day of the eruption, the aſhes, which fell abundantly upon the mountain, were as white almoſt as ſnow; and the old people here aſſure me, that it is a ſure ſymptom of the eruption being at an end. Theſe circumſtances, being well atteſted, I thought worth relating.

It would require many years cloſe application to give a proper and truly philoſophical account of the volcanos in the neighbourhood of Naples; but I am ſure ſuch a hiſtory might be given, ſupported by demonſtration, as would deſtroy every ſyſtem hitherto given upon this ſubject. We have here an opportunity of ſeeing volcanos in all their ſtates. I have been this ſummer in the iſland of Iſchia: it is about eighteen miles round, and its whole baſis is lava. The great mountain in it, near as high as Veſuvius, formerly called Epomeus, and now San Nicolo, I am convinced was thrown up by degrees; and I have no doubt in my own mind, but that the iſland itſelf roſe out of the ſea in the ſame manner as ſome of the Azores. I am of the ſame opinion with reſpect to Mount Veſuvius, and all the high grounds near Naples; as having not yet ſeen, in any one place, what can be called virgin earth. I had the pleaſure of ſeeing a well ſunk, a few days ago, near my villa, which is, as you know, at the foot of Veſuvius, and cloſe by the ſea-ſide. At 25 feet below the level of the ſea they came to a ſtratum of lava, and God knows how much deeper they might have ſtill found other lavas. The ſoil all round the mountain, which is ſo fertile, conſiſts of ſtratas of lavas, aſhes, pumice, and now and then a thin ſtratum of good earth, which good earth is produced by the ſurface mouldering, and the rotting of roots and plants, vines, &c. This is plainly to be ſeen at Pompeii, where they are now digging into the ruins of that antient city: the houſes are covered, about ten or fifteen feet, with pumice and fragments of lava, ſome of which weigh three pounds (which laſt circumſtance I mention to ſhew, that, in a great eruption, Veſuvius has thrown ſtones of this weight ſix miles, which is its diſtance from Pompeii, in a direct line): upon this ſtratum of pumice or rapilli, as they call them here, is a ſtratum of excellent mould, about two feet thick, on which grow large trees, and excellent grapes. We have then the Solfaterra, which was certainly a volcano, and has ceaſed emptying, for want of metallic particles, and over-abounding with ſulphur. You may trace its lavas into the ſea. We have the Lago d'Averno and the Lago d'Agnano, both of which were formerly volcanos; and Aſtroni, which ſtill retains its form more than any of theſe. Its crater is walled round, and his Sicilian Majeſty takes the diverſion of boar-hunting in this volcano; and neither his Majeſty, or any one of his court, ever dreamed of its former ſtate. We have ſeen that curious moun-

mountain, called Montagno Nuovo, near Puzzole, which rose, in one night, out of the Lucrine Lake: it is about 150 feet high, and three miles round. I do not think it more extraordinary, that Mount Vesuvius, in many ages, should rise above 2000 feet, when this mountain, as is well attested, rose in one night, no longer ago than the year 1538. I have a project, next spring, of passing some days at Puzzole, and of dissecting this mountain, taking its measures, and making drawings of its stratas; for, I perceive, it is composed of stratas, like Mount Vesuvius, but without lavas. As this mountain is so undoubtedly formed entirely from a plain, I should think my project may give light into the formation of many other mountains that are at present thought to have been original, and are certainly not so, if their strata correspond with those of the Montagno Nuovo. I should be glad to know whether you think this project of mine will be useful; and, if you do, the result of my observations may be the subject of another letter.

I cannot have a greater pleasure than to employ my leisure hours in what may be of some little use to mankind; and my lot has carried me into a country which affords an ample field for observation. Upon the whole, if I was to establish a system, it would be, that *mountains are produced by volcanos, and not volcanos by mountains.*

I fear I have tired you; but the subject of volcanos is so favourite a one with me, that it has led me on I know not how: I shall only add, that Vesuvius is quiet at present, though very hot at top, where there is a deposition of boiling sulphur. The lava that runs in the Fossa Grande during the last eruption, and is at least 200 feet thick, is not yet cool: a stick, put into its crevices, takes fire immediately. On the sides of the crevices are fine crystalline salts: as they are the pure salts, which exhale from the lava that has no communication with the interior of the mountain, they may perhaps indicate the composition of the lava. I have done. Let me only thank you for the kind offers and expressions in your letter, and for the care you have had in setting off my present to the Museum to the best advantage; of which I have been told from many quarters.

I am,
SIR,
Your most obedient,
humble servant,
W. HAMILTON.

Extract of a Letter from Mr. B. Gooch, Surgeon, of Shottisham, near Norwich, to Mr. Joseph Warner, F. R. S. and Surgeon to Guy's Hospital. Communicated to the Royal Society by Mr. Warner, November 16, 1769.

[Read Nov. 16, 1769]

Shottisham,
Sept. 9, 1769.

DEAR SIR,

ACCORDING to your desire, and my promise, I have sent you the wonderful cuticular glove, which I shewed you, when I had the pleasure of your company here. The history of the case, which, I believe, has no precedent, is taken from the gentleman's own relation

relation of it to me in writing, without varying his sense; and confirmed by Mr. Swallow, a surgeon of character at Watton, whose son, I know, was under your tuition. Mr. Swallow attended the patient many times in the fevers which produced these strange phænomena, with whom I took an opportunity of having a particular conversation relative to this matter, that I might be able to speak with the more authenticity. Mr. Swallow has now one of these gloves in his possession, the gentleman himself has another, and several he has given to the curious: yet some have been so sceptical as to doubt the matter of fact upon such evidence and authority. I wish you would get an accurate drawing of the glove; and I shall be glad to know, at your leisure, the sentiments of the learned, not forgetting your own, upon this extraordinary case.

I am, DEAR SIR,
Your sincere friend,
as well as obliged
humble servant,
B. GOOCH.

History of the CASE relating to the CUTICULAR GLOVE.

MR. William Wright, of Saham Tony, in the county of Norfolk, attorney at law, about fifty years of age, rather of a weak and lax constitution from his youth, was first seized about ten years ago with the following singular kind of fever. The physical gentlemen he at different times consulted were at a loss to know what name or character to distinguish it by. It has returned many times since: sometimes twice in a year, attended with the same symptoms and circumstances; but not to so great a degree since the year 1764 as before; and it has been generally observed to come on upon obstructed perspiration, in consequence of catching cold, to which he is very subject.

Besides the common febrile symptoms upon the invasion of this disease, his skin itches universally, more especially at the joints; and the itching is followed by many little red spots, with a small degree of swelling: soon after his fingers become very stiff, hard, and painful at their ends, and at the roots of his nails. In 24 hours, or thereabouts, the cuticle begins to separate from the cutis, and, in ten or twelve days, this separation is general from head to foot; when he has many times turned the cuticle off from the wrists to the fingers' ends, completely like gloves; and in the same manner also to the ends of his toes: after which his nails shoot gradually from their roots, at first attended with exquisite pain, which abates as the separation of the cuticle advances; and the nails are generally thrown off by new ones in about six months.

The cuticle rises in the palms of his hands, and soles of his feet, resembling blisters, but has no fluid under it; and when it comes off it leaves the subjacent skin very sensible for a few days. Sometimes, upon catching cold, before he has been quite free from feverish symptoms, he has had a second separation of the cuticle from the cutis; but then it is so thin as to appear only like scurf, which demonstrates the quick renewal of this part.

Of the different Quantities of Rain which appear to fall, at different Heights, over the same Spot of Ground. By William Heberden, M. D. F. R. S.

[Read December 7, 1769.]

A Comparison having been made between the quantity of rain which fell in two places in London, about a mile distant from one another, it was found, that the rain in one of them constantly exceeded that in the other, not only every month, but almost every time that it rained. The apparatus used in each of them was very exact, both being made by the same artist; and upon examining every probable cause, this unexpected variation did not appear to be owing to any mistake, but to the constant effect of some circumstance, which, not being supposed to be of any moment, had never been attended to. The rain-gage in one of these places was fixed so high as to rise above all the neighbouring chimnies; the other was considerably below them; and there appeared reason to believe, that the difference of the quantity of rain in these two places was owing to this difference in the placing of the vessel in which it was received. A funnel was therefore placed above the highest chimnies, and another upon the ground of the garden belonging to the same house, and there was found the same difference between these two, though placed so near one another, which there had been between them when placed at similar heights in different parts of the town. After this fact was sufficiently ascertained, it was thought proper to try, whether the difference would be greater at a much greater height; and a rain-gage was therefore placed upon the square part of the roof of Westminster Abbey, being at such a distance from the western towers as probably to be very little affected by them, and being much higher than any other neighbouring buildings. Here the quantity of rain was observed for a twelvemonth, the rain being measured at the end of every month, and care being taken that none should evaporate, by passing a very long tube of the funnel into a bottle through a cork, to which it was exactly fitted. The tube went down very near to the bottom of the bottle, and therefore the rain, which fell into it, would soon rise above the end of the tube, so that the water was no where open to the air except for the small space of the area of the tube; and by trial it was found, that there was no sensible evaporation through the tube thus fitted up.

The following table will shew the result of these observations.

NATURAL HISTORY.

From July the 7th, 1766, to July the 7th, 1767, there fell into a rain-gage fixed

	Below the top of a house.	Upon the top of a house.	Upon Westminster Abbey.
	inch.	inch.	inch.
1766 from the 7th of July to the end	3,591	3,210	2,311
August	0,558	0,479	} 0,508
September	0,421	0,344	
October	2,364	2,061	1,416
November	1,079	0,842	0,632
December	1,612	1,258	0,994
1767 January	2,071	1,455	1,035
February	2,864	2,494	1,335
March	1,807	1,303	0,587
April	1,437	1,213	0,994
May	2,432	1,745	1,142
June	1,977	1,426	} 1,145
from the 1st of July to the 7th	0,395	0,309	
	22,608	18,139	12,099

By this table it appears, that there fell below the top of a house above a fifth part more rain than what fell in the same space above the top of the same house; and that there fell upon Westminster Abbey not much above one-half of what was found to fall in the same space below the tops of the houses. This experiment has been repeated in other places with the same event. What may be the cause of this extraordinary difference has not yet been discovered; but it may be useful to give notice of it, in order to prevent that error which would frequently be committed in comparing the rain of two places without attending to this circumstance.

It is probable, that some hitherto unknown property of electricity is concerned in this phænomenon. This power has undoubtedly a great share in the descent of rain, which hardly ever happens, if the air and electrical apparatus be sufficiently dry, without manifest signs of electricity in the air. Hence it is, that in Lima, where there is no rain, they never have any lightning or thunder;[*] and that, as M. Tournefort was assured, it never rains in the Levant but in winter, and that this is the only season in which any thunder is heard.[†] If this appearance, therefore, could be accounted for, it would probably help us to some more satisfactory causes of the suspension of the clouds, and of the descent of rain.

[*] See the English translation of the voyage of Don George Juan and Don Antonio de Ulloa to South America, vol. II. book i. chap. 6. p. 69 and 79.
[†] Voyage du Levant, let. X. p. 429.

Experiments

Experiments to prove that the Luminousness of the Sea arises from the Putrefaction of its animal Substances. By John Canton, *M. A. and F. R. S.*

[Read Dec. 21, 1769.]

I SHALL not enter into the consideration of the several opinions of philosophers concerning the luminous appearance of the sea, as not one of them, that I know of, has been well supported; but I shall immediately relate a few experiments, which any person may very easily make, and which, I think, will be allowed to point out the true cause of that appearance, when compared with the descriptions given of it by those who have accurately observed it.

EXPERIMENT I.

Into a gallon of sea water in a pan about 14 inches in diameter, I put a small fresh whiting, June 14, 1768, in the evening; and took notice that neither the whiting, nor the water when agitated, gave any light. A Fahrenheit's thermometer in the cellar, where the pan was placed, stood at 54 degrees. The 15th, at night, that part of the fish which was even with the surface of the water was luminous, but the water itself was dark. I drew the end of a stick through the water, from one side of the pan to the other, and the water appeared luminous behind the stick all the way, but gave light only where it was disturbed. When all the water was stirred, the whole became luminous, and appeared like milk, giving a considerable degree of light to the sides of the pan that contained it; and continued to do so for some time after it was at rest. The water was most luminous when the fish had been in it about 28 hours, but would not give any light by being stirred, after it had been in it three days.

EXPERIMENT II.

I put a gallon of fresh water into one pan, and a gallon of sea water into another, and also into each pan a fresh herring of about three ounces. The next night the whole surface of the sea water was luminous without being stirred, but much more so when put in motion; and the upper part of the herring, which lay considerably below the surface of the water, was very bright. The fresh water was quite dark, as was also the fish that was in it. There were several very bright luminous spots on different parts of the surface of the sea water; and the whole, when viewed by the light of a candle, seemed covered with a greasy scum. The third night, the light of the sea water while at rest was very little, if at all, less than before; and when stirred, its light was so great, as to discover the time by a watch; and the fish in it appeared as a dark substance. After this, its light was evidently decreasing, but was not quite gone before the seventh night. The fresh water and fish in it were perfectly dark during the whole time. The thermometer was generally above 60.

EXPERIMENT III.

Into a gallon of fresh water I put common or sea salt, till I found by an hydrometer it was of the same specific gravity with the sea water. In another gallon of fresh water I dissolved two pounds of salt, and into each of these waters I put a small fresh herring. The next

next evening the whole surface of the artificial sea water was luminous without being stirred, but gave much more light when it was disturbed. It appeared exactly like the real sea water in the preceding experiment, and its light lasted about the same time, and went off in the same manner*. The other water, which was almost as salt as it could be made, never gave any light. The herring, which was taken out of it the seventh night, and washed from its salt, was found firm and sweet; but the other herring was very soft and putrid; much more so than that which had been kept as long in the fresh water of the last experiment. If a herring, in warm weather, be put into ten gallons of artificial sea water instead of one, the water will still become luminous, but its light will not be so strong.

N. B. The artificial sea water may be made, without the use of an hydrometer, by the proportion of four ounces avoirdupois of salt to seven pints of water, wine measure.

From the second and third experiments it is evident, that the quantity of salt contained in sea water hastens putrefaction; as the fish that had been kept in water of that degree of saltness was found to be much more putrid than that which had been kept the same time in fresh water. This unexpected property of sea salt was discovered by Sir John Pringle, in the year 1750, and published in the 46th volume of the Philosophical Transactions, with many very curious and useful experiments on substances resisting putrefaction; but the greatest quantity of salt there mentioned is less than what is found in sea water: it is probable, therefore, that if the sea were less salt, it would be more luminous. And here it may be worth remarking, that though the greatest summer heat is well known to promote putrefaction, yet 20 degrees more than that of the human blood seem to hinder it: for putting a very small piece of a luminous fish into a thin glass ball, I found that water of the heat of 118 degrees would destroy its luminousness in less than half a minute; which, on taking it out of the water, it would begin to recover in about ten seconds, but was never after so bright as before.

I shall now only add to these experiments the most circumstantial accounts I can find of the sea's luminous appearance. The Honourable Robert Boyle, in the third volume and 91st page of Doctor Birch's edition of his works, says,
" When I remember how many
" questions I have asked naviga-
" tors about the luminousness of
" the sea; and how in some places
" the sea is wont to shine in the
" night as far as the eye can
" reach; at other times and places,
" only when the waves dash against
" the vessel, or the oars strike and
" cleave the water; how some seas
" shine often, and others have not
" been observed to shine; how in
" some places the sea has been
" taken notice of to shine when
" such and such winds blow,

---

* Several river-fish, as the bleak, the dace, the carp, the tench, and the eel, were kept in artificial sea water to putrefy, without producing any light that I could perceive; but a piece of carp made the water very luminous, though the outside, or scaly part of it, did not shine at all.

" whereas

"whereas in other seas the observation holds not; and in the same tract of sea, within a narrow compass, one part of the water will be luminous, whilst the other shines not at all; when, I say, I remember how many of these old phænomena, belonging to those great masses of liquor, I have been told of by very credible eye-witnesses, I am tempted to suspect, that some cosmical law or custom of the terrestrial globe, or, at least, of the planetary vortex, may have a considerable agency in the production of these effects."

Father Bourzes has given a still more particular account of the luminous appearance of the sea; part of which I have extracted from the third edition of Jones's Abridgment of the Philosophical Transactions, Vol. V. Part ii. p. 213. "When the ship ran apace, we often observed a great light in the wake of the ship, or the water that is broken and divided by the ship in its passage. This light was not always equal: some days it was very little, others not at all; sometimes brighter, others fainter; sometimes it was very vivid, and at other times nothing was to be seen. As to its brightness, I could easily read by it, though I was nine or ten feet above it from the surface of the water; as I did particularly on the 12th of June, and the 10th of July, 1704. But I could read only the title of my book, which was in large letters. As to the extent of this light, sometimes all the wake appeared luminous to thirty or forty feet distant from the ship; but the light was very faint at any considerable distance. Some days one might easily distinguish in the wake such particles as were luminous from those that were not: at other times there was no difference. The wake seemed then like a river of milk, and was very pleasant to look on. At such times as we could distinguish the bright parts from the others, we observed that they were not all of the same figure. Some of them appeared like points of light; others almost as large as stars, as they appeared to the naked eye. We saw some that looked like globules of a line or two in diameter; and others like globes as big as one's head. It is not always that this light appears, though the sea be in great motion; nor does it always happen when the ship sails fastest; neither is it the simple beating of the waves against one another that produces this brightness, as far as I could perceive. But I have observed, that the beating of the waves against the shore has sometimes produced it in great plenty; and on the coast of Brazil the shore was one night so very bright, that it appeared as if it had been all on fire.

"The production of this light depends very much on the quality of the water: and, if I am not deceived, generally speaking, I may assert, other circumstances being equal, that the light is largest when the water is fattest, and fullest of foam; for in the main sea the water is not every where equally pure; and sometimes, if one dips linen
"into

NATURAL HISTORY.

"into the sea, it is clammy when it is drawn up again. And I have often observed, that when the wake of the ship was brightest, the water was more fat and glutinous; and linen moistened with it produced a great deal of light, if it were stirred or moved briskly. Besides, in sailing over some places of the sea, we find a matter or substance of different colours, sometimes red, sometimes yellow. In looking at it, one would think it was saw-dust: our sailors say it is the spawn or seed of whales. What it is, is not certain; but when we draw up water, in passing over these places, it is always viscous and glutinous. Our mariners also say, that there are a great many heaps or banks of this spawn in the north; and that sometimes in the night they appear all over of a bright light, without being put in motion by any vessel or fish passing by them.

"But, to confirm farther what I say, videlicet, that the water, the more glutinous it is, the more it is disposed to become luminous, I shall add one particular which I saw myself. One day we took in our ship a fish, which some thought was a boneta. The inside of the mouth of the fish appeared in the night like a burning coal; so that, without any other light, I could read by it the same characters that I read by the light in the wake of the ship. Its mouth being full of a viscous humour, we rubbed a piece of wood with it, which immediately became all over luminous; but, as soon as the moisture was dried up, the light was extinguished.

"I leave it to be examined whether all these particulars can be explained by the system of such as assert, that the principle of this light consists in the motion of a subtle matter, or globules, caused by a violent agitation of different kinds of salts."

Of a singular Disease, with which two Butchers of the Royal Hospital *of the Invalids were seized. From the History (just published) of the* Royal Academy *of Sciences at* Paris, *for the Year* 1766.

A VERY singular event has given room to a dissertation which M. Morand read to the Academy on that subject. The 7th of October, 1765, two butchers, of the Royal Academy of Invalids, killed each an ox for the provision of the house, and the meat was employed as usual for the officers and soldiers, without the least ailment attending on those who had eaten of it, roasted or boiled.

The next morning, however, one of the two butchers, aged 27 years, had his eye-lids swelled and a head-ach: the swelling got to his cheek; the head-ach increased, and a fever succeeded. In this state he was carried to the infirmary of the hospital: the disorder came to a considerable height, and bleeding procured him no other relief than a slight lessening of his head-ach. An emetic, which had been given him the fourth day, seemed to ease him a little. There arose on his eye-lids, and different parts of his face, blisters which threatened to be gangrenous. These accidents, notwithstanding, diminished; yet there was an eschar under the blisters that came with difficulty to a suppuration, and the patient was again vomited and purged. The 15th the eschar fell, and left open a considerable wound, which had the usual dressings; but, the 20th, the left thigh was attacked with a sharp pain; and the next day the like accident happened to the right leg, the bath having only increased the pain and swelling. Then recourse was had to ordinary cataplasms; the ailing parts came to a suppuration; both were opened, and yielded only a purulent matter like that of a simple phlegmon: the patient went out of the infirmary the 3d of January, having been there near three months.

The other butcher was not taken ill of the disease till two days after he had killed the ox; but he met with a worse treatment from it than his companion; for, besides the accidents that were common to both, the swelling of the face got to the neck, and afterwards to the bosom, and there formed a shining emphysema, which distended the skin in all parts like a drum, and threatened him with an entire suffocation. M. de Morand, having opened one of the blisters of the face, applied an actual cautery to it, in order to bring on a suppuration; and, having perceived a swelling in the thighs and legs, he applied blisters to them. These remedies, together with bleeding and vomiting, which were at first administered without much success, effected a cure, causing a great quantity of humours to flow. This man left the infirmary the 8th of December, upwards of three weeks before his comrade, who was not, in the main, so grievously affected.

So singular a disease, as well by its effects as cause, engaged M. Morand to make all possible inquiries in regard to it. The two oxen had been visited, according to the constant custom of the house, and no disease, nothing amiss, had been observed in them, only that they appeared somewhat fatigued. They were knocked down and bled as usual; their blood seemed nothing different from that of others, and neither of the butchers had an open wound whereby the blood might have penetrated into the interior parts of their body. No extraordinary smell, also, was observable at the opening of the oxen.

The undertaker of the butchery had been in the same office for the army in the last war, and he informed M. Morand, that they had often killed oxen which had been over-fatigued for the provision of the army, without any soldier or officer being thereby incommoded; but it often happened, and the butchers who had slain them had been attacked by the same disease as the invalid butchers, and that even some of them had died of it.

Hence it was not difficult to perceive what had happened to the oxen of the invalids: among the beasts that are drove to Paris, there are always some stragglers, which do not follow the rest without being much worried by dogs, or by the drivers; and it probably happens to them as to a jaded or over-ridden horse. It is well known, that a horse, in a foundered state, is in great danger of

losing

losing his life; and that those who bargain for horses have an action for having their money refunded by him who had jaded the horse.

It is therefore very possible, that the body of an ox killed in that state, being still hot, and perhaps his blood more so, may exhale a pernicious vapour, affecting those that touch the body, or receive the blood of the animal on their skin. But what can be the degree of malignity of these vapours, and why do they principally attack the cellular membrane? This is not easily explained. What is singular is, that the vapours of animals, labouring under the bovilla pestis, or murrain, does not in any wise affect those that open them, dead or dying. A surgeon-major had opened upwards of 200, in the mortality of 1712, without being in the least incommoded. It appears likewise, by several examples, that the flesh of these animals were eaten without any inconveniency: it is true, that one only example that happened in Dauphiny seems to insinuate the contrary; but it follows, however, from all M. Morand's observations, that the oxen killed as the invalids had been, probably, overdrove, and killed before they recovered from their lassitude; that butchers killing animals in that state run the risk of their lives, but that the flesh may be eaten with impunity, though it should be wholesomer if the animal had time to recruit himself of his fatigue.

The reading of the circumstances of this fact before the Academy caused M. du Hamel to recollect a like accident, that happened in his part of the country: among some oxen, driven from Limosin to Paris, one of the finest, weighing about 800 lb. was not able to follow the rest. By the advice of some graziers and butchers, who were of opinion he had been ailing, he was sold to a butcher of Pithiviers, who sent his journeyman to kill him in the stable of the inn where he was kept. During his operations, this person, having put his knife into his mouth for a few moments, was some hours after attacked with a swelling of his tongue, and a straightening of his chest, with a difficulty of breathing. There appeared black pustules over his whole body, and he died the fourth day of a general gangrene.

The inn-keeper having the palm of his hand pricked by a bone of the same ox, a livid tumour arose in the part; the arm fell into a sphacelus, and he died at the end of the 7th day: his wife having received some drops of blood on the back of her hand, the hand swelled, and she had some difficulty in getting cured: the servant-maid, having passed under the ox, soon after it was hung up, received some drops of blood on the cheek, which brought on the part a great inflammation, terminating in a black tumour. She was cured, but remained disfigured by it. In fine, the surgeon of the hospital at Pithiviers, by having opened one of these tumours, and put his lancet between his wig and forehead, his head swelled, and an erysipelas was formed, which he long continued ill of.

It is very certain, that the blood of this ox was very contagious; yet his flesh was sold to the best houses of Pithiviers and its environs,

rons, and none were in the least incommoded by the eating of it. It would, perhaps, be curious to know if the animals, which might have eaten of it raw, or drank the blood, had been affected. The resemblance of the two facts of Pithiviers and the invalids is sufficiently manifest: the cause of the first is not equivocal; and there is great reason to believe that it is the same which occasioned the second.

The Case of the Rev. Mr. Winder, who was cured by Lightning of a Paralytic Disorder.

THE Rev. Mr. Winder, whose case is the subject of this memoir, is Rector of Halsted, in Kent. His form is robust, rather athletic, inclining to corpulency; his countenance florid, his disposition cheerful, generally serene, somewhat jocular: and he was of a constitution so happy, that, at the age of fifty-four, he was a stranger to disease; and, which is very uncommon at such a period of life, almost totally unacquainted with the sensation of any considerable pain. But a reverse of this serenity of health was at hand.

For, June 3, 1761, whilst he was performing the duty of his office, it was observed by many of his congregation, though unperceived by himself, that his voice was altered, and that he did not articulate and pronounce his words with the usual facility. The following week, though still it escaped his notice, his friends remarked the extraordinary change and faltering in his speech; yet, when they mentioned it to him, he did not regard it as a matter of sufficient importance to deserve any serious attention. But the consequence proved otherwise; for July 1, at evening, whilst he was sitting with a few neighbours about him, cheerful as usual, he suddenly fell from his chair to the floor, by a stroke of the palsy. The paroxysm over, and when a little recovered, he found himself almost totally deprived of the faculty of speech, and his senses reduced to a very imperfect condition. He was, therefore, the day after the accident, carried to an eminent physician in London, who ordered him to take a tea-spoonful of the following mixture: R. Tinct. Cort. Peruv. Canel. alb. Sp. Lavend. ana ʒji. to apply blisters to the occiput, and to continue the temperate diet he had usually pursued. By carefully observing of which, he grew so much better, as in a few weeks after to be able, by the help of a cane, just to remove himself from place to place, for a very small distance. His tongue still continued faltering, hardly intelligible; his hands trembling much; his head vertiginous; and his intellectual faculties so much impaired, that his mind became subject to temporary wanderings, as if sympathising with the infirmities of the body.

In this condition he now spent one miserable year in pain and despondency, when he was advised, on the 8th day of June 1762, to have recourse to the Chalybeate waters of Tunbridge. To which he conformed, strictly and regularly persevering in the course for the space of six weeks; at the expiration of which term, he returned home,

home so considerably relieved, as to be then able to walk, by the help of a cane, nearly half a mile; his hand was become so steady, that he could again write his name in a legible manner, which he had not done before since his first attack. But he still perceived an universal infirmity in all the muscular parts of his frame, and an inaptitude, or inability in them to correspond with the dictates of his intention. He was still, at times, affected with violent palpitations of the heart, tremblings of his limbs, subsultus tendinum; besides which, he was frequently afflicted with vertigoes. But these temporary effects of his malady were but trivial inconveniencies in comparison to the great misery he suffered from a constant, very oppressive, heavy perception of pain fixed deep in his breast, which was always accompanied with that dejection of spirit, seldom to be removed from a state of anguish and trouble, when no farther hope of recovery remains. In this unhappy situation of very imperfect health, he continued for three weeks, after his leaving Tunbridge, despairing ever to receive a more complete cure; when, on the 24th of August, 1762, about ten o'clock at night, whilst he was asleep in bed, the atmosphere being thick, and the sky very cloudy, though none, or very little, rain fell, and scarce a breeze of air could be perceived, it began to thunder with great violence, accompanied by thick and frequent flashes of lightning at every explosion, which were so loud, that the patient was thereby startled suddenly from his sleep; and at the instant of waking he was surprized by the perception of a quick, strong shock, affecting him universally, as if he were thunderstruck; but so rapid, it was gone almost before he could think of it, leaving upon his mind, according to his own representation, the same idea as we recollect from having undergone a stroke of electricity, which may be better imagined than described. At the very same moment the chamber he lay in appeared filled with lightning, which instantaneously vanished, leaving behind it a remarkable phosphorous smell. And from that point of time he thought he found his natural parts more alert, and his feelings so greatly altered, that he fancied his cure to be accomplished; of which he was induced to persuade himself, from a sudden sensation, described by him to be as if some obstruction in his chest, or a great adhesion therein, had been suddenly removed, and his breast had then recovered its former full liberty or expansion: the oppression and confinement he had there before suffered seeming to be entirely gone. And he now enjoyed, in imagination at least, the agreeable opinion of repossessing perfect health. But how much greater was his joy, when he arose in the morning, and began to move about, on finding the fancy he had indulged during the night fully verified by the entire ease and complete health he then really enjoyed. His head was quite serene; his breast unladen of its wonted oppression, and eased of its habitual pain: he could move all his limbs with as much steadiness and agility as he used before his complaint: torpors, tremblings, and the long unhappy train of miseries which afflicted

afflicted him before, were now gone: the joy of health was, like the dawn of morning, renewed; and every paralytic symptom, with his despair of recovery, vanished like the preceding night! and he avers, that though the day before he was unable to walk more than half a mile, and that with great difficulty and pain, he could, the morning after the shock the lightning gave him, have walked with ease ten or twelve miles: so propitious was the event. And on the 20th of September, 1762, he was, and I believe still continues, in a perfect state of health. To establish and secure which blessing, so signally recovered, he was then returned to a course of the Tunbridge waters; where this account was delivered by himself of his disorder, and the cure.

It may not be improper here to observe, that as Mr. Winder is well known to be a gentleman of strict veracity, and sound, plain sense, we cannot suspect, therefore, either his head or his heart capable of deceiving us in this relation, which himself delivered, and which I was very careful to note down as circumstantially as possible, that it might be as satisfactory to all who may think it of so much importance as to be favoured with their attention.

Account of the Needles in the Isle of Wight. Extracted from Mr. Edwards's Natural History.

IN the beginning of June, 1761, I had the curiosity to visit the Isle of Wight, where I spent a week in seeing what was curious in that part of the island, and went off to sea several times under the stupendous rocks and cliffs called the Needles. Many strangers of our southern counties visit these parts yearly on the same account. When we enter some of our great cathedrals, their greatness and solemn gloominess strike us with a pleasing reverential kind of chilling horror; and when we view the magnificent palaces of sovereign princes, we are struck with beauty, harmony, and regularity, and a striking sense of the richness, power, art, and fine taste, that could form such terrestrial heavens; but, O! when I had launched a little way into the ocean, and taken a full view of this most amazing and stupendous work of nature, all the sensations produced by temples and palaces, the works of art, were like shadows compared with real substances. The stupendous greatness of the rocks strikes the beholder with chill, horror, and amazement, never felt before. While a stranger is near them, he fears that some protuberant masses of the rock will give way, and wreck his vessel, and drown the presumptuous spectator. It is necessary to keep a quarter of a mile's distance at least, to make any judgment of the height of the cliffs. In some places it is perpendicular; in others overhanging; in others there are rows of shelves or lodgments for the birds called the Puffins and Razor-birds, where they sit thick, in rows, though hardly distinct to be seen separately, but their motion discovers them. In certain places high in the cliff, as well as under water-mark, you see great chasms and deep caverns, that seem to enter far into the rock. Here and there are crystal streams and broken

broken rippling waters issuing forth pretty high in the rock. The strata of chalk, stone, flints, &c. divided in some parts on an almost plain surface for the depth of six hundred feet, the height of the rock, in many places, affords great entertainment to a curious and inquisitive mind. It is strange to see sheep and lambs feeding near the water's edge in the lower part of this cliff, and not easily conceivable how they get thither without being precipitated into the deep, but they have the power of treading surely in places inaccessible to man. Though the birds are not counted eatable, yet many of them are destroyed through wantonness. When a gun is discharged from sea under the rock, they fly off in such amazing numbers as to darken the sea under them. Great numbers are always seen fishing in the sea, others sitting in the cliffs, and many always passing and repassing over your boat. The fishermen make baits of their flesh to catch lobsters, crabs, &c. The ignorant on this part of the island suppose that these birds are found in no part of the world but at the Needles. The face of this stupendous rock extends about four miles, and very nearly, if not precisely, facing the south. The west point terminates in what is properly called the Needles, which are several vast rude obelisks, or pillars, separated by time and force of the sea from the main rock, and stand detached from each other, arising immediately out of the sea. These birds, they say, are seen here not much above two months in the year, and first appear in the beginning of May. The fishermen, who are always about these rocks, declare that these birds are seen three or four times in the winter, for a day or two each time, in as great numbers as at their breeding-time; and that they know when to expect them, which is after a little mild weather, when the sun lies warm on the cliff, and the sea beneath is pretty calm, to give them an opportunity to seek their food. The top of the cliff is barren, chalky, and stony, down which feed a great number of sheep: cormorants, shags, gulls, Cornish choughs, jackdaws, starlings, wild pigeons, and many sorts of small birds, breed annually on these rocks.

An Account of the Tailor Bird, with a Description of an Indian Forest; from Mr. Pennant's Indian *Zoology.*

HAD Providence left the feathered tribe unendowed with any particular instinct, the birds of the torrid zone would have built their nests in the same unguarded manner as those of Europe; but there the lesser species, having a certain prescience of the dangers that surround them, and of their own weakness, suspend their nests at the extreme branches of the trees: they are conscious of inhabiting a climate replete with enemies to them and their young; with snakes that twine up the bodies of the trees, and apes that are perpetually in search of prey; but, heaven-instructed, they elude the gliding of the one, and the activity of the other.

An Indian forest is a scene the most picturesque that can be imagined; the trees seem perfectly animated; the fantastic monkies give life to the stronger branches; and the weaker sprays wave over your head, charged with vocal and various plumed inhabitants. It is an error to say that nature hath denied melody to the birds of hot climates, and formed them only to please the eye with their gaudy plumage: Ceylon abounds with birds equal in song* to those of Europe; which warble among the leaves of trees, grotesque in their appearance, and often loaden with the most delicious and salubrious fruit. Birds of the richest colours cross the glades, and troops of peacocks complete the charms of the scene, spreading their plumes to a sun that has ample powers to do them justice. The landscape in many parts of India corresponds with the beauties of the animate creation: the mountains are lofty, steep, and broken, but cloathed with forests, enlivened with cataracts † of a grandeur and figure unknown to this part of the globe.

But to give a reverse of this enchanting prospect, which it is impossible to enjoy with a suitable tranquillity, you are harassed in one season with a burning heat, or in the other with deluges of rain: you are tormented with clouds of noxious insects: you dread the spring of the tiger, or the mortal bite of the naja.

The brute creation are more at enmity with one another than in other climates; and the birds are obliged to exert unusual artifice in placing their little brood out of the reach of an invader. Each aims at the same end, though by different means: some form their pensile nest in shape of a purse, deep and open at top; others with a hole in the side; and others still more cautious, with an entrance at the very bottom, forming their lodge near the summit ‡.

But the little species we describe seems to have greater diffidence than any of the others: it will not trust its nest even to the extremity of a slender twig, but makes one more advance to safety by fixing it to the leaf itself.

It picks up a dead leaf, and, surprising to relate, sews it to the side of a living one §, its slender bill being its needle, and its thread some fine fibres: the lining, feathers, gossamer, and down: its eggs are white, the colour of the bird light yellow, its length three inches, its weight only three-sixteenths of an ounce; so that the materials of the nest and its own size are not likely to draw down a habitation that depends on so slight a tenure.

The following account, from the same ingenious author, may contribute to give us some idea of the heat of that fervid climate. In treating of the black-capped pigeon, he says:

* That which the Portuguese call Dominiquin, is particularly fine.
† Those of the island of Celebes are distinguished for their magnificent scenery, as appears from the drawings in possession of Mr. Loten.
‡ This instinct prevails also among the birds on the banks of the Gambia, in Africa, which abounds with monkies and snakes: others (for the same end) make their nests in holes of the banks that overhang that vast river. Purchas. 11. p. 1576.
§ A nest of this bird is preserved in the British Museum.

This

This most elegant species is painted the size of life. It was found on the ground in the isle of Java, having dropped down dead in one of those hot days that are known only in the torrid zone, when the fowls of the air often perish, unable to respire; when lions, leopards, and wolves, immerge themselves up to their nostrils in the water to preserve themselves from the scorching sun*; and when even men themselves have been forced to ascend the highest tree, in order to draw in a more temperate air†.

Such a day occasioned the discovery of this species.

The fore part of the head, the cheeks, and beginning of the breast, were white: the hind part of the head black: the chin yellow.

The rest of the neck, the breast, upper part of the belly, the back, coverts, and secondary feathers of the wings, of a fine green: the quill feathers of a dark purple.

The lower belly and vent feathers of a fine yellow: the outside of the thighs green: the inside white: the lower side of the tail crimson: the legs red.

* Boone's Account of the Climate and Diseases of Senegal.
† Philosophical Transactions, 1767.

ANTIQUITIES.

The Thirty-second Fable of the Edda, *or the antient* Icelandic *Mythology; translated from the Original, by Mr.* Mallet.

Of the Twilight of the Gods.

GANGLER then enquired; What can you tell me concerning that day? Har replied; There are very many and very notable circumstances which I can impart to you. In the first place, will come the grand, 'the desolating' Winter; during which the snow will fall from the four corners of the world; the frost will be very severe; the tempest violent and dangerous; and the sun will withdraw his beams. Three such winters shall pass away, without being softened by one summer. Three others shall follow, during which war and discord will spread through the whole globe. Brothers, out of hatred, shall kill each other; no one shall spare either his parent, or his child, or his relations. See how it is described in the VOLUSPA:
" brothers becoming murderers,
" shall stain themselves with bro-
" thers' blood; kindred shall for-
" get the ties of consanguinity;
" life shall become a burthen;
adultery shall reign throughout the world. A barbarous age! an age of swords! an age of tempests! an age of wolves! The bucklers shall be broken in pieces; and these calamities shall succeed each other, till the world shall fall to ruin." Then will happen such things as may well be called prodigies. The Wolf FENRIS will devour the Sun: a severe loss will it be found by mankind. Another monster will carry off the Moon, and render her totally useless: the Stars shall fly away and vanish from the heavens *: the earth and the mountains shall be seen violently agitated; the trees torn up from the earth by the roots; the tottering hills to tumble headlong from their foundations; all the chains and irons of the prisoners to be broken and dashed in pieces. Then is the Wolf Fenris let loose; 'the sea rushes impetuously over the earth, because the Great Serpent, changed into a spectre, gains the shore. The ship *Naglefara* is set afloat: this vessel is constructed of the nails of dead men; for which reason great care should be taken not to die with unpared nails; for he who dies so, supplies materials towards the building of that vessel, which gods and men will wish

---

* Goranson has it, *Stellæ de cælo cadunt.* See other variations in his Latin Version, which seems, in some respects, more spirited than that of M. Mallet, here followed. T.

were

were finished as late as possible. The Giant *Rymer* is the pilot of this vessel, which the sea, breaking over its banks, wafts along with it. The Wolf Fenris, advancing, opens his enormous mouth; his lower jaw reaches to the earth, and his upper jaw to the heavens, and would reach still farther, were space itself found to admit of it. The burning fire flashes out from his eyes and nostrils. The Great Serpent vomits forth floods of poison, which overwhelm the air and the waters. This terrible monster places himself by the side of the Wolf. In this confusion the heaven shall cleave asunder; and by this breach the Genii of Fire enter on horseback. *Surtur* is at their head: before and behind him sparkles a bright glowing fire. His sword outshines the Sun itself. The army of these Genii, passing on horseback over the bridge of heaven, break it in pieces: thence they direct their course to a plain; where they are joined by the Wolf Fenris, and the Great Serpent. Thither also repair LOKE, and the Giant RYMER, and with them all the Giants of the Frost, who follow LOKE even to death. The Genii of Fire march first in battle array, forming a most brilliant squadron on this plain, which is an hundred degrees square on every side. During these prodigies, HEIMDEL, the door-keeper of the Gods, rises up: he violently sounds his clanging trumpet to awaken the Gods, who instantly assemble. Then ODIN repairs to the fountain of *Mimis*, to consult what he ought to do, he and his army. The great Ash Tree of *Ydrasil* is shaken; nor is any thing in heaven or earth exempt from fear and danger. The Gods are clad in armour: ODIN puts on his golden helmet, and his resplendent cuirass; he grasps his sword, and marches directly against the Wolf Fenris. He hath THOR at his side: but this God cannot assist him; for he himself fights with the Great Serpent. FREY encounters SURTUR, and terrible blows are exchanged on both sides till FREY is beat down; and he owes his defeat to his having formerly given his sword to his attendant *Skyrner*. That day also is let loose the dog named *Garmer*, who had hitherto been chained at the entrance of a cavern. He is a monster dreadful even to the Gods; he attacks TYR, and they kill each other. THOR beats down the Great Serpent to the earth, but, at the same time, recoiling back nine steps, he falls dead upon the spot, suffocated with floods of venom, which the Serpent vomits forth upon him. ODIN is devoured by the Wolf Fenris. At the same instant VIDAR advances, and, pressing down the monster's lower jaw with his foot, seizes the other with his hand, and thus tears and rends him till he dies. LOKE and HEIMDEL fight, and mutually kill each other. After that, SURTUR darts fire and flame over all the earth: the whole world is presently consumed. See how this is related in the VOLUSPA. " Heim-
" del lifts up his crooked trumpet,
" and sounds it aloud. Odin
" consults the head of Mimis:
" the great Ash, that ash sublime
" and fruitful, is violently shaken,
" and sends forth a groan. The
" Giant bursts his irons. What is
" doing among the Gods? What
" is doing among the Genii? The
" land

"land of the Giants is filled with uproar: the Deities collect and assemble together. The Dwarfs sigh and groan before the doors of their caverns. Oh! ye inhabitants of the mountains, can you say whether any thing will yet remain in existence? [The sun is darkened; the earth is overwhelmed in the sea; the shining stars fall from heaven; a vapour, mixed with fire, arises; a vehement heat prevails, even in heaven itself[*].]"

The Thirty-third Fable; or, The Sequel of the Conflagration of the World.

ON hearing the preceding relation, Gangler asks, What will remain after the world shall be consumed; and after Gods, and Heroes, and Men, shall perish? For I understand by you, adds he, that mankind were to exist for ever in another world. Thridi replies, After all these prodigies, there will succeed many new abodes, some of which will be agreeable, and others wretched: but the best mansion of all will be *Gimle* (or HEAVEN), where all kinds of liquors shall be quaffed in the Hall called *Brymer*, situated in the country of *Okolm*. That is also a most delightful palace, which is upon the mountains of *Inda*[†], and which is built of shining gold. In this palace good and just men shall abide. In *Nastrande* (i. e. the shore of the dead) there is a vast and direful structure, the portal of which faces the north. It is compiled of nothing but the carcasses of serpents, all whose heads are turned towards the inside of the building: there they vomit forth so much venom, that it forms a long river of poison: and in this float the perjured and the murderers; as is said in those verses of the VOLUSPA: "I know that there is in *Nastrande* an abode remote from the Sun, the gates of which look towards the north: there drops of poison rain through the windows. It is all built of the carcasses of serpents. There, in rapid rivers, swim the perjured, the assassins, and those who seek to seduce the wives of others. In another place, their condition is still worse; for a wolf, an all-devouring monster, perpetually torments the bodies who are sent in thither." Gangler resumes the discourse, and says, Which, then, are the Gods that shall survive? Shall they all perish, and will there no longer be a heaven nor an earth? Har replies, There will arise out of the sea another earth, most lovely and delightful: covered it will be with verdure and pleasant fields: there the grain shall spring forth and grow of itself, without cultivation. VIDAR and VALE shall also survive, because neither the flood nor the black conflagration shall do them any harm. They shall dwell in the plains of *Ida*, where was formerly the residence of the Gods. The sons of THOR, MODE, and MAGNE, repair thither: thither

---

[*] The passage in brackets is given from the Latin of Goranson, being omitted by M. Mallet. T.
[†] This and the preceding names are very different in the edition of Goranson. T.

come

ANTIQUITIES.

come BALDER and HODER, from the mansions of the dead. They sit down and converse together; they recal to mind the adversities they have formerly undergone. They afterwards find among the grass the golden Dice[*], which the Gods heretofore made use of. And here be it observed, that while the fire devoured all things, two persons of the human race, one male and the other female, named *Lif* and *Lifthrafer*, lay concealed under an hill. They feed on the dew, and propagate so abundantly, that the earth is soon peopled with a new race of mortals. What you will think still more wonderful is, that *Sunna* (the SUN), before it is devoured by the Wolf FENRIS, shall have brought forth a daughter as lovely and as resplendent as herself, and who shall go in the same track formerly trod by her mother: according as it is described in these verses: "The brilliant monarch of Fire[†] shall beget an only daughter, before the Wolf commits his devastation. This young virgin, after the death of the Gods, will pursue the same track as her parent."

Now, continues Har, If you have any new questions to ask me, I know not who can resolve you; because I have never heard of any one who can relate what will happen in the other ages of the world: I advise you therefore to remain satisfied with my relation, and to preserve it in your memory.

Upon this, Gangler heard a terrible noise all around him; he looked every way, but could discern nothing, except a vast extended plain. He set out, therefore, on his return back to his own kingdom; where he related all that he had seen and heard: and ever since that time, this relation hath been handed down among the people by oral tradition.

We shall add a few of our Author's remarks on these two curious Fables.

Had the EDDA had no other claim to our regard than as having preserved to us the opinions and doctrines of the 'antient northern nations[‡],' on that important subject, an existence after this life, it would have merited, even on that account, to have been preserved from oblivion. And really on this head it throws great light on history: whether we consider that branch of it which principally regards the ascertainment of facts, or that which devotes itself rather to trace the different revolutions of manners and opinions. Such

---

[*] Goranson renders it *Crepidas*, "Sandals." But M. Mallet's Version is countenanced by Bartholin. *Deauratia orbes aleatorij.* p. 597. T.

[†] There seems to be a defect or ambiguity in the Original here, which has occasioned a strange confusion of genders, both in the French of M. Mallet and the Latin Version of Goranson. The former has "LE ROI *brillant du feu engendrera une fille unique avant que d'etre englouti par le loup; cette fille suivra les traces de* SA MERE, *apres la mort des dieux.*" The latter, *Unicam filiam genuit rubicundissimus* ILLE REX *antiquam* EUM *Fenris devoraverit; qua cursura est, mortuit Diis, viam* MATERNAM. I have endeavoured to avoid this, by expressing the passage in more general terms. T

[‡] *Les Celtes.* French Orig.

as are only fond of the former species of history, will find in these concluding Fables the principles of that wild enthusiastic courage which animated the ravagers of the Roman empire, and conquerors of the greatest part of Europe. Such as interest themselves more in the latter, will see (not without pleasure and astonishment) a people, whom they were wont to consider as barbarous and uncultivated, employed in deep and sublime speculations; proceeding in them more conclusively; and coming, possibly, much nearer to the end than those celebrated nations who have arrogated to themselves an exclusive privilege to reason and knowledge.

I have before observed, that * the philosophers of the north* considered Nature as in a state of perpetual labour and warfare. Her strength was thus continually wasting away by little and little; and her approaching dissolution could not but become every day more and more perceptible. At last, a confusion of the seasons, with a long and preternatural winter, were to be the final marks of her decay. The moral world is to be no less disturbed and troubled than the natural. The voice of dying Nature will be no longer heard by man. Her sensations being weakened, and, as it were, totally extinct, shall leave the heart a prey to cruel and inhuman passions. Then will all the malevolent and hostile powers, whom the Gods have heretofore with much difficulty confined, burst their chains, and fill the universe with disorder and confusion. The host of Heroes from VALHALL shall in vain attempt to assist and support the Gods; for though the latter will destroy their enemies, they will nevertheless fall along with them: that is, in other words, in that great day all the inferior Divinities, whether good or bad, shall fall in one great conflict back again into the bosom of the Grand Divinity; from whom all things have proceeded, as it were emanations of his essence, and who will survive all things. After this the world becomes a prey to flames: which are, however, destined rather to purify than destroy it; since it afterwards makes its appearance again more lovely, more pleasant, more fruitful than before. Such, in a few words, is the doctrine of the EDDA, when divested of all those poetical and allegorical ornaments which are only accidental to it. One sees plainly enough, that the poem called VOLUSPA hath been the text, of which this Fable is the comment; since in reality the same ideas, but expressed with a superior pomp and strength, are found in that old poem. It may perhaps afford some pleasure to peruse the following extracts, given literally from the translation of Bartholin †.

" The Giant Rymer arrives
" from the east, carried in a cha-
" riot: the ocean swells; the
" Great Serpent rolls himself fu-
" riously in the waters, and lifteth
" up the sea. The eagle screams,

---

* Les Celtes. French.
† Vid. CAUSÆ Contemptæ a Danis Mortis, 4to. 1689. Lib. 11. cap. 14. p. 590. & seq. I have rather followed the Latin of Bartholin than the French Version of our Author. T.

" and

"and tears the dead bodies with his horrid beak. The veffel of the Gods is fet afloat.

"The veffel comes from the eaft: the hoft of Evil Genii‡ arrives by fea: Loke is their pilot and director. Their furious fquadron advances, efcorted by the Wolf Fenris: Loke appears with them §.

"The black prince of the Genii of Fire ‖ iffues forth from the fouth, furrounded with flames: the fwords of the Gods beam forth rays like the fun. The rocks are fhaken, and fall to pieces. The female Giants wander about 'weeping.' Men tread in crowds the paths of death. The heaven is fplit afunder.

"New grief for the Goddefs who defends Odin. For Odin advances to encounter Fenris; the fnow-white flayer of Bela*, againft the 'black' prince of the Genii of Fire†. Soon is the fpoufe of Frigga beaten down.

"Then runs Vidar, the illuftrious fon of Odin, to avenge the death of his father. He attacks the murderous monfter, that monfter born of a Giant; and with his fword he pierces him to the heart.

"The fun is darkened: the fea overwhelms the earth: the fhining ftars vanifh out of heaven: the fire furioufly rages: the ages draw to an end: the flame, afcending, licks the vault of heaven."

Many other pieces of poetry might be quoted, to fhew that the Scandinavians had their minds full of all thefe prophecies, and that they laid great ftrefs upon them.

[We fhall pafs by the analogy, which our Author takes pains to trace, between the Mythology of the Northern Nations and the doctrine taught by Zeno and the Stoics, and only give a few paffages, in which he fhews, from fome of the Grecian and Roman writers, fo far as they have entered into the fubject, that the religious opinions of the Celtes feemed in a great meafure to coincide with thofe of the Scandinavians.] He fays.

We are, it is true, but very moderately acquainted with what the Gauls, the Britons, or the Germans, thought on this head; but as the little we know of their opinions coincides very exactly with the EDDA, we may fafely fuppofe the fame conformity in the other particulars of which we are ignorant. Let thofe who doubt this, caft their eyes over the following paffages.

‡ *Muspelli Incolæ*. Bartholin.

§ A ftanza is here omitted, being part of what is quoted above in the 32d Fable, p. 176; as alfo one or two ftanzas below.   T.

‖ *Surtur*. Ifland. orig.

* Sc. FREY.   † Sc. SURTUR.

"Zamolxis

"Zamolxis (a celebrated Druid of the Getæ and Scythians) taught his contemporaries, that neither he nor they, nor the men who should be born hereafter, were to perish; but were on the contrary to repair, after quitting this life, to a place where they should enjoy full abundance and plenty of every thing that was good." Herod. L. 4. § 95.

"If we may believe you," (says Lucan to the Druids) "the souls of men do not descend into the abode of darkness and silence, nor yet into the gloomy empire of Pluto: you say that the same spirit animates the body in another world, and that death is the passage to a long life." Luc. Lib. 1. v. 454.

"The Gauls" (says Cæsar) "are particularly assiduous to prove that souls perish not." Cæf. Lib. 6. cap. 14.

Valerius Maximus, in a passage quoted above in my REMARKS on the 16th Fable, comes still nearer to the doctrine of the EDDA; for he tells us that the Celtes looked upon a quiet peaceable death as most wretched and dishonourable, and that they leaped for joy at the approach of a battle which would afford them opportunities of dying with their swords in their hands.

"Among the antient Irish," says Solinus, "when a woman is brought to bed of a son, she prays to the Gods to give him the grace to die in battle." This was to wish salvation to the child. (See Solin. c. 25. p. 252.)

These authorities may suffice: they do not indeed say all that the EDDA does; but that makes this work so much the more valuable.

The Runic Chapter, or the Magic of Odin.

THIS great conqueror and legislator of the northern nations, to enforce his laws, and inspire a dread and veneration for his person, pretended not only to an extraordinary knowledge superior to the rest of mankind, but to the most supernatural and wonderful powers; an imposition that has been as successfully as generally practised by the founders of states, in all the dark ages, and all the different parts of the world. As he attributed to himself the invention of letters, of which it is probable they had not the smallest idea in Scandinavia before his time, he profited of that ignorance; and though that noble art was in itself sufficiently wonderful to attract in the highest degree the veneration of the people towards the teacher of it, he made it still more awful, by causing it to be regarded as the art of magic, and by attributing to letters the power of making all nature subservient, and of working the greatest miracles. We see by the following little poem the extraordinary virtues which he attributes either to letters or poetry, or probably to a combination of both.

"Do you know (says he) how to engrave Runic characters? how to explain them? how to procure them? how to prove their virtue?" He then goes on to enumerate the wonders he could perform, either by means of these letters, or by the operations of poetry.

"I am possessed of songs: such as neither the spouse of a king, nor any son of man, can repeat.

"One

"One of them is called the HELP-
ER: it will help thee at thy need,
sickness, grief, and all adversities.

"I know a song, which the sons
of men ought to sing, if they
would become skilful physicians.

"I know a song, by which I
soften and inchant the arms of
my enemies, and render their
weapons of none effect.

"I know a song, which I need
only to sing when men have
loaded me with bonds; for the
moment I sing it, my chains fall
in pieces, and I walk forth at
liberty.

"I know a song, useful to all
mankind; for as soon as hatred
inflames the sons of men, the
moment I sing it they are appeased.

"I know a song of such virtue, that, were I caught in a
storm, I can hush the winds, and
render the air perfectly calm.

"When I see (says he) Magicians travelling through the air,
I disconcert them by a single
look, and force them to abandon
their enterprize." He had before spoken of these ærial travellers.

"If I see a man dead, and hanging aloft on a tree, I engrave
Runic characters so wonderful,
that the man immediately descends, and converses with me.

"If I will that a man should
neither fall in battle, nor perish
by the sword, I sprinkle him
over with water at the instant
of his birth.

"If I will, I can explain the
nature of all the different species of Men, of Genii, and of
Gods. None but the wise can
know all their differences.

"If I aspire to the love and the
favour of the chastest virgin, I
bend the mind of the snowy-
armed maiden, and make her
yield wholly to my desires.

"I know a secret, which I will
never lose: it is to render myself always beloved by my mistress.

"But I know one which I will
never impart to any female, except my own sister, or to her
whom I hold in my arms. Whatever is known only to one's self,
is always of very great value."

After this, the Author concludes
with exclamations on the beauty of
the things he has been describing.

"Now (says he) have I sung in
my august abode my sublime
verses; which are both necessary
to the sons of men, and useless
to the sons of men. Blessed be
he who hath sung them! Blessed
be he who hath understood
them! May they profit him
who hath retained them! Blessed
be they who have lent an ear
to them!"

*Extracts from the Ode of King Reg-
ner Lodbrog.*

THIS Ode was dictated by the
fanaticism of Glory, ani-
mated by that of Religion. Regner, who was a celebrated Warrior, Poet, and Pirate, reigned in
Denmark about the beginning of
the ninth century: after a long series of maritime expeditions into
the most distant countries, his fortune at length failed him in England. Taken prisoner in battle
by his adversary Ella, who was
king of a part of that island, he
perished by the bite of serpents,
—with

with which they had filled the dungeon he was confined in. He left behind him several sons, who revenged this horrible death, as Regner himself had foretold in the following verses. There is some reason, however, to conjecture that this prince did not compose more than one or two stanzas of this Poem, and that the rest were added, after his death, by the Bard, whose function it was, according to the custom of those times, to add to the funeral splendor, by singing verses to the praise of the deceased. Be that as it may, this Ode is found in several Icelandic Chronicles, and its versification, language, and style, leave us no room to doubt of its antiquity. Wormius has given us the text in Runic characters, accompanied with a Latin version, and large notes, in his Literatura Runica, Vid. p. 197. It is also met with in M. Biorner's collection. Out of the twenty-nine strophies, of which it consists, I have only chosen the following, as being what I thought the generality of my readers would peruse with most pleasure. I have not even always translated entire stanzas, but have sometimes reduced two stanzas into one, in order to spare the reader such passages as appeared to me uninteresting and obscure.

" We fought with swords, when, in my early youth, I went towards the east to prepare a bloody prey for the ravenous wolves: ' ample food for the yellow-footed eagle.' The whole ocean seemed as one wound: the ravens waded in the blood of the slain.

" We fought with swords, in the day of that great fight, wherein I sent the inhabitants of Helsing to the Hall of Odin. Thence our ships carried us to Isa*: there our steel-pointed lances, reeking with gore, divided the armour with a terrible clang: there our swords cleft the shields asunder.

" We fought with swords, that day wherein I saw ten thousand of my foes' rolling in the dust near a promontory of England. A dew of blood distilled from our swords. The arrows which flew in search of the helmets bellowed through the air. The pleasure of that day was equal to that of clasping a fair virgin in my arms†.

" We

* Or the Vistula.

† I cannot help thinking, that the Reader will censure our ingenious Author, as not having here exerted his usual good taste in selecting, when he finds he has omitted such stanzas as the following, particularly the two last.

" We fought with swords, in the Northumbrian land. A furious storm descended on the shields: many a lifeless body fell to the earth. It was about the time of the morning, when the foe was compelled to fly in the battle. There the sword sharply bit the polished helmet. The pleasure of that day was like kissing a young widow at the highest seat of the table."

." We fought with swords, in the Flemmings' land: the battle widely raged before King Freyr fell therein. The blue steel, all reeking with blood, fell at length

ANTIQUITIES.

"We fought with swords, that day when I made to struggle in the twilight of death that young chief so proud of his flowing locks*; he who spent his mornings among the young maidens; he who loved to converse with the handsome widows......... What is the happy portion of the brave, but to fall in the midst of a storm of arrows †? He who flies from wounds, drags a tedious miserable life: the dastard feels no heart in his bosom.

"We fought with swords: a young man should march early to the conflict of arms: man should attack man, or bravely resist him. In this hath always consisted the nobility of the warrior. He who aspires to the love of his mistress ought to be dauntless in the clash of swords.

"We fought with swords: but now I find for certain that men are drawn along by fate: there are few can evade the decrees of the Destinies. Could I have thought the conclusion of my life reserved for Ella, when, almost expiring, I shed torrents of blood? When I thrust forward my ships in the Scottish gulphs? When I gained such abundant spoil for the beasts of prey?

"We fought with swords: I am still full of joy, when I think that a banquet is preparing for me in the palace of the Gods. Soon, soon in the splendid abode of Odin, we shall drink BEER out of the skulls of our enemies. A brave man shrinks not at death. I shall utter no words expressive of fear as I enter the Hall of Odin.

"We fought with swords. Ah! if my sons knew the sufferings of their father; if they knew that poisonous vipers tore his entrails to pieces! with what ardour would they wish to wage cruel war! For I gave a mother to my children, from whom they inherit a valiant heart.

"We fought with swords: but now I touch upon my last moments. A serpent already gnaws

length upon the golden mail. Many a virgin bewailed the slaughter of that morning."

"We fought with swords; the spear resounded; the banners reflected the sunshine upon the coats of mail. I saw many a warrior fall in the morning: many an hero in the contention of arms. Here the sword reached betimes the heart of my son: it was Egill deprived Agnar of life. He was a youth who never knew what it was to fear."

"We fought with swords, in the isles of the South. There Herthiofe proved victorious: there died many of my valiant warriors. In the shower of arms, Rogvaldur fell: I lost my son. In the play of arms came the deadly spear: his lofty crest was dyed with gore. THE BIRDS OF PREY BEWAILED HIS FALL: THEY LOST HIM THAT PREPARED THEM BANQUETS."

Vid. Five Pieces of Run. Poet. p. 31, 32, 35, &c.   T.

* He means Harold, surnamed Harfagre, or Fairlocks, King of Norway.

† Literally, a hail-storm of darts. *Une grêle de traits.*

"my

" my heart. Soon shall my sons black their swords in the blood of Ella: their rage is in flame: those valiant youths will never rest till they have avenged their father.

" We fought with swords, in fifty and one battles under my floating banners. From my early youth I have learnt to dye the steel of my lance with blood, and thought I never could meet with a king more valiant than myself. But it is time to cease: Odin hath sent his Goddesses to conduct me to his palace. I am going to be placed on the highest seat, there to quaff goblets of BEER with the Gods. The hours of my life are rolled away. I will die laughing."

Some Account of the Arabic *Manuscripts at the Escurial, with a Translation of some curious Passages from* Casiri's *Digression on Arabic Poetry; taken from Mr. Baretti's Journey from* London *to* Genoa, *&c.*

YOU know that at the *Escurial* there is a vast library, in which, amongst thousands of valuable manuscripts in various languages, there is a large number of Arabic, of which the learned world has long wished for an account.

Several attempts have been made at different times to gratify that wish; but always in vain, until King Ferdinand, who was predecessor to his present Majesty, commanded Dr. *Michael Casiri*[†] to assume this undertaking.

This *Casiri*, a Syro-Maronite by birth, who has long been the King's librarian at the Escurial, has at last, after many years labour, published a volume (to be followed by several more), intituled, BIBLIOTHECA ARABICO-HISPANA ESCURIALENSIS, *sive librorum omnium MSS. quos Arabicè ab auctoribus magnam partem Arabo-Hispanis compositos Bibliotheca cœnobii Escurialensis complectitur. Recensio et explanatio opera et studio* MICHAELIS CASIRI, *Syro-Maronite, Presbyteri. S. Theologiæ Doctoris, &c.* TOMUS PRIOR.

This book, just come out of the press in this town, is a folio of about 550 pages, printed with the best types on the best paper; and the manuscripts noted down in it amount to the number[‡] of 1628, arranged under twelve heads; that is,

Grammatici.
Rhetorici.
Poetici.
Philologici et Miscellanei.
Lexicographi.
Philosophi.
Ethici et Politici.
Medici.
Ad Historiam Naturalem pertinentes.
Theologici.
Dogmatici, Scholastici, Morales, &c.
Christiani.

Many and very curious are the notices that *Casiri* gives us in his Bibliotheca, which he could ne-

---

[†] M. Clark calls him Syri.
[‡] They amount to 1630, though the last is marked 1628. Mere chance has made me observe, that the class of the POETICI begins by mistake with the number 268, when it ought to be marked 270, as the preceding class of the RHETORICI ends with the number 269, by another mistake marked 259.

ver have compiled, were he not a most stupendous master of the oriental tongues, and full-fraught with the most extensive erudition. But I am writing a letter, and not a volume; therefore I pass over a multitude of those notices, and will only skim over a few.

In the division entitled MEDICI there are several Arabic versions from the Greek of HIPPOCRATES, GALEN, and DIOSCORIDES, with several commentaries by the Arabic interpreters, besides a number of original works by several Arabic physicians, amongst which RASIS, who was a native of Persia; AVICENNA, the son of a Persian, but born at Bokhara in Arabia; BAITAR, a native of Malaga in Spain; and MAIMONIDES, of Jewish extraction, born at Cordova.

Still under this division, Dr. Casiri gives us (in his own Latin from the Arabic) the lives of the above seven personages, besides those of PLATO and ARISTOTLE, part of whose works, as it appears by this Bibliotheca, the Arabians had severally translated, as well as those of *Hippocrates, Galen,* and *Dioscorides.*

In the division entitled *Ad* HISTORIAM-NATURALEM *pertinentes,* under the account of the codex that has the number CMI, we have a catalogue of those Arabic authors who wrote on *husbandry.*

The division entitled THEOLOGICI, is chiefly made up with manuscripts of the Alcoran, and with commentaries upon it.

Only eleven codexes form the division that is entitled CHRISTIANI. The second of them is *a confutation of the Alcoran,* written both in Arabic and Latin, by a Roman Friar; and the last is a *Grammatica Trilinguis*; that is, of the *Arabic, Persian,* and *Turkish* tongues, with a version in Latin in every opposite page.

But the division that took most of my attention, is that which is entitled POETICI. The manuscripts numbered under this division amount to the number of *two hundred and twenty-one,* of which *thirty-one* are in folio, *one hundred and five* in quarto, and the remaining *eighty-five* in octavo. Yet you are not to think that the whole division contains nothing but poets. *Casiri* has brought under it both the writers of poetry and the writers upon poetry, especially critics and commentators. I am very angry this very moment with my fate, that did not direct me to the study of the Arabic language, that I might go to the Escurial to read those two hundred and twenty-one volumes, or understand at least the short specimens out of them, which the doctor has brought into his book. How the Roman Arcadians would stare to hear me expatiate, on my return, upon the merits of the sublime poets, Zohair, Abulol, Mahlab, Abdelmagid, or the immortal commentators *Alsaied, Khalil, Abdalla, Fadlalla,* and a hundred others!

Several specimens of Arabic poetry Dr. *Casiri* has turned into Latin prose; but acknowledging, upon a certain occasion, that in his literal version, they appear rather childish than otherwise, he adds these words by way of apology.

Hæc carmina, si sensum spectes, peracuta sunt; si verba, haud parum ingeniosa. Cæterum, ut in aliis contingit linguis, Arabici versus in alteram linguam conversi, non eam gratiam

gratiam ac dulcedinem servani, quam apud se et domi habent : nec mirum unus enim quisque sermo quandam elocutionis vim ac legem habet planè ab ea diversum, quæ in ceteris obtinet.

In English thus :

"These verses, with respect to the sentiment, are very acute, and the expression is ingenious. But it happens to Arabian poetry as to poetry in other languages, that it loses by translation its native grace and melody : nor is this to be wondered at, since every language has its own peculiar phraseology and force of expression different from those of other tongues."

To this remark, which must be obvious to any one who knows but two languages well, *Casiri* adds a digression of his own, which he intitles *Arabicæ Poeseos Specimen et Pretium.*

In this digression we are told, that the Arabs cultivated poetry with the greatest ardour; that the great people amongst them were most liberal to their great poets; that early in the morning of some stated days, the poets of Fez used to assemble at the house of the governor to recite verses in praise of Mahomet to a vast concourse of people; and that he whose verses were most applauded received a hundred golden ducats, a rich robe, a fine horse, and a pretty maiden. The rest of the poets had but fifty ducats a piece; that, in more remote ages, great skill in poetry intitled to nobility; that when any poet endowed with uncommon powers came to a town, the women belonging to this and that tribe would go to meet him with timbrels and other musical instruments in their hands, as they did when going to a nuptial feast; would treat him with a sumptuous dinner, and point him out to children as a pattern for imitation. The poet *Alaeldin* (adds *Casiri*) received once five thousand golden ducats *(nummi aurei)* from *Malek Aldhaer Bibar*, King of Egypt, for two distichs only, which (this I will add myself) would not in our days fetch five-pence from any monarch living. The distichs I will transcribe, that you may have a guess at their worth.

Moerore ne afficiaris. Quod deus decrevit, illud erit ; quodque inevitabili decreto statutum est, fiet.

At inter motum et quietem ex momento res componitur, et negotium hoc facile reddetur.

I suppose that, in the original Arabic, the two distichs are very fine; yet modern sovereigns know better the value of five thousand ducats than to bestow them upon distichs, be they ever so excellent.

Suffer me now to transcribe some paragraphs out of *Casiri*'s digression on Arabic poetry, as they contain several singularities which seem very curious.

Now the Arabs do not, like the Europeans, act either tragedies or comedies; nor does any author inform us that they have written such poems : we have, however, in our library one or two comedies written in Arabic. There is not in their poetry any intermixture of Grecian mythology ; for they hold in the utmost abhorrence the names as well as the worship of heathen deities. They have, however, fables of their own, adapted to their own genius and religion. They extol the virtues of heroes, and

and celebrate their atchievements under feigned perfonages. They inveigh againſt vice, and fatirize corruption of manners; and in this ſpecies of poetry they have had ſome writers who have eminently excelled.

Arabic poetry, therefore, like that in other languages, is confined to certain laws of metre, but thoſe of a peculiar kind, as will preſently appear. There are to be found in Arabic almoſt all thoſe kinds of poetry which we have received from the Greeks and the Latins; namely, idylliums, elegies, epigrams, odes, fatires, &c. all which, taken together, paſs under the general title of *Divan*; that is to ſay, *Academica*; with which title the writings of their poets are uſually inſcribed.

The Arabians call their poetry (that is, the metrical part of it) by the word *Scheer*; that is, *hair* (or *hair-ſkin*), and compare its ſtructure to the ſtructure of a tent made of goats' hair (or goat ſkin), and compacted with cords and ſtakes: for which reaſon a verſe is called *Bait (a houſe)*, as being a ſtructure of finiſhed metre, and, as it were, a complete building.

An Arabic verſe conſiſts of long and ſhort ſyllables, out of which they form four feet; the firſt of which is called the *light chord*, being made up of two ſyllables, one long, the other ſhort; or, as the Arabians expreſs it, a conſonant *moved*, and a conſonant *quieſcent*: the ſecond foot is called the *heavy (or grave) chord*, conſiſting of conſonants which are *moved* (that is, have a vowel annexed to them not *quieſcent*, but pronounced): the third foot is called the *conjoined ſtake* (proceeding ſmoothly and uninterruptedly), having its two firſt conſonants *moved*, and its laſt *quieſcent*: the fourth foot is called the *diſjoined ſtake*, in which a *quieſcent* letter ſtands between two others, each of which is moved (that is, pronounced with a vowel).

Of theſe feet the parts of their verſe are compoſed, the chords and the ſtakes following each other alternately, from the different combination of which their poems receive their different denominations. Metrical quantity, or meaſure, the Arabians denote by the following technical terms. MOSTAFELON, which denotes a ſeries of three feet; namely, a *light chord*, a *diſjoined ſtake*, and again a *light chord*: FAELATON, by which they underſtand likewiſe three feet; firſt a *light chord*, ſecondly a *conjoined ſtake*, and laſtly a *light chord*. FAULON, which denotes a combination of two feet only, the firſt of which is a *conjoined ſtake*, the other a *light chord*: MOTAFAILON, which denotes three feet; a *grave chord*, a *light chord*, and a *conjoined ſtake*: MOTAFAILATON, by which are underſtood three feet in a ſeries; namely, a *conjoined ſtake*, a *grave chord*, and a *light chord*.

The menſuration, therefore, and quantity of the Arabic verſe, conſiſt in nothing but in the determinate and alternate number of moveable and quieſcent conſonants: this is twofold, *Metrical* and *Rhythmical*. The former conſiſts of alternate feet only; the latter, beſides its regular number of feet, requires that each verſe terminate in ſyllables of the ſame ſound (that is, in rhyme). This is ſometimes alternate, as in epigrams, odes, &c. and ſometimes ſucceſſive; but only

only in such poems as consist of more than seven verses.

Each verse consists of two hemisticks, which taken together make up one intire verse. Either of the two hemisticks is called a *door* or *gate*; both put together, a *bivalve* or *double gate*, by a metaphor taken from a gateway, which is shut on each side by a *valve* or *folding door*.

The former part of the hemistick they call the * *access* (or approach); the latter the *proposition*; the last syllable of the latter hemistick, which gives the rhyme, they call the *pulsation* (or *knocking*).

From the different order and position of the chords and stakes arise fifteen kinds of verses, which are comprised in five *periods* or *circles*.

The first *circle*, which is styled VARIOUS (or *variegated*), comprehends three kinds of verses, the *long*, the *extended*, and the *expanded*; which consist of ten long syllables and four short ones, or of fourteen *moved*, and ten *quiescent*: where it must be observed, that these three kinds are distinguished from each other not on account of the greater or less quantity of their syllables, but merely on account of the letters either *moved* or *quiescent*, which accordingly are ranked in different degrees.

The second circle is styled the COMPOSITE, under which are contained two kinds of verses, the *perfect* and the *copious*. Each has fifteen letters that are *moved*, and six *quiescent*, placed in a different order: the measure of the first kind is MOTAFAALON repeated six times; the measure of the other is MOFAALATON, which likewise is six times successively repeated.

The third circle is called SIMILAR; to which belong three kinds of poems, the *ode* (or *song*), the *satyr*, and the idyllium (or shorter kind of poem), each of which contains twelve consonants that are *moved*, and eight *quiescent*.

The fourth circle is called the CONTRACTED; under which are comprised six pieces of verse; the *quick*, the † *ejaculatory* (or *impetuous*),

---

* As the Arabians dwelt in tents, we are not surprized at their taking their metaphors from objects about which they were so frequently employed, and applying them to what Milton calls the *building of verse*. The word rendered by Cafiri *Accessus*, is translated by Golius in his Arabic Lexicon *anterior pars pectoris, sive thorax*. It may very well, therefore, signify the *anterior part* or *porch of the tent*. The next word *propositio* is more obscurely expressed. The original is derived from a word signifying *to offer* or *present* any thing; and it is translated by Golius *palus tentorii*. As this *palus tentorii* was the vestibule or threshold of the tent, first presenting itself before you entered the interior part, hence I conceive it took its name, and afterwards became a technical term in metre. But the word *propositio* conveys no such idea, as far as I can see.

† The first three and the last of these six words convey in the original very nearly the same idea. They are words signifying the quick, impetuous, and abrupt motion of an animal, such as a horse leaping, or a stag bounding in its course. I think *impetuous* would be a better translation of *emissum* than *ejaculating*, and *abrupt* a better word than

ous), the *light*, the *similar*, the *concise*, and the *convulsed* (or *abrupt*), each of which consists of twelve letters that are *moved*, and nine *quiescent*.

The fifth circle is called the CONCORDANT, to which one kind of verse only belongs, styled the *conjoined*; this is made up of twelve consonants that are *moved*, and seven *quiescent*.

To these fifteen kinds of verses already enumerated, others add a sixteenth, which they call the *double rhymed Dhubait*, in which each hemistick ends with a rhyme. This is a great object of contention with the Arabian poets, and is what the Persians are much delighted with.

The Arabic poetry is not so scrupulously observant of these laws, but that their writers may be sometimes at liberty either to add or retrench a syllable or two; especially when either a weighty and pithy sentence, or an epiphonema, or a poignant and acute sentiment, seems to require it: and liberties of this kind often occur both in the Greek and Latin poets of the first repute.

The addition of one or more syllables in a verse the Arabians call by the word *Tarphil*, the Greek by the word *Prosthesis*; in this case the verse, when enlarged by one foot, changes the cosma *matafaaqlon* into that of *matafaalaton*: the abridging or dropping of syllables at the end is called by the Arabians *Athram*, by the Greeks *Apheresis*; and let this suffice concerning the Arabic poetry, as far as relates to my present purpose. He who is curious enough to desire farther information upon this article, may consult (among others who have treated this subject in Latin) *Father Philip Guadagnoli*, in a work published at Rome in Latin and Arabic in the year 1642, intitled *Institutions of the Arabic Language*. In this book Guadagnoli has rendered into Latin the whole system of Arabic metre, which *Dhialdin*, surnamed Alkhazragœus, by birth a Spaniard, the first of poets, has given us in most elegant verse: at the end of which treatise we are also presented with various specimens of Arabic poetry.

I hope this long quotation from Casiri's work will prove acceptable, as it gives an idea of Arabic prosody, which is a thing not easily got at in books. But is it not surprising, that a nation so fond of poetry as the Arabs seem to have been, and possessed once of large tracts of land in three parts of the world, should never think of having theatrical exhibitions, and neither write tragedies nor comedies? What difference between nations and nations!

Dress of the Ancient French, *from Velly's New History of* France.

SIGEBERT was buried in St. Medard's church, at Soissons, where his statue is still seen in long clothes with

An. 576.

---

than *convulsed*. They relate to the metre, and not to the subject matter of composition.

N. B. The Author of this book owes this and the foregoing note, as well as the greatest part of the English translation of this long passage, to the learned Mr. Wheeler, professor of poetry, at Oxford.

the mantle which the Romans called *chlamys*. This was the dress of Clovis's children, whether as more noble and majestic, or that they looked on the title of Augustus as hereditary in their family. However it be, long clothes were for several ages the dress of persons of distinction, with a border of sable, ermine, or miniver. Under Charles V. it was emblazoned with all the pieces of the coat of arms. At that time, neither ruffs, collars, nor bands, were known, being introduced by Henry II. Till his time, the neck of our kings was always quite bare, except Charles the *Wise*, who is every where represented with an ermine collar. The short dress, anciently worn only in the country and the camp, came to be the general fashion under Lewis XI. but was laid aside under Lewis XII. Francis I. revived it, with the improvement of slashes. The favourite dress of Henry II. and his children was a tight, close doublet, with trunk hose, and a cloak scarce reaching to the waist.

The dress of the French ladies, it may be supposed, had likewise its revolutions. They seem, for near nine hundred years, not to have been much taken up with ornaments. Nothing could require less time or nicety than their head-dress, and the disposition of their hair. Every part of their linen was quite plain, but at the same time extremely fine. Laces were long unknown. Their gowns, on the right side of which was embroidered their husband's coat of arms, and on the left that of their own family, were so close as to shew all the delicacy of their shape, and came up so high as to cover their whole breast, up to the neck. The habit of widows had very much of that of our nuns. It was not until Charles VI. that they began to expose their shoulders. The gallantry of Charles the VII.th's court brought in the use of bracelets, necklaces, and ear-rings.— Queen Anne de Bretagne despised those trinkets; and Catherine de Medicis made it her whole business to invent new. Caprice, vanity, luxury, and coquetry, have at length brought them to their present enormity.

Clause in the Salic Law; from the same.

AUTHARIS, King of Lombardy, induced Gariraldaldus, Duke of Bavaria, to shake off the Austrasian[*] yoke; and, to attach him the more firmly to his interest, asked his daughter Theodolinda in marriage. It is said that he himself went in disguise with his ambassadors. The princess, according to the custom of the people over whom she was soon to reign, presented the goblet to the envoys; Autharis, in returning it, squeezed her hand, a presumption which put her to the blush: she suspected it could be no other than the King of Lombardy himself, and she was confirmed in her surmise by the warmth with which this prince kissed the hand, which had the honour of touching her. This passage brings to mind

An. 590.

---

[*] Lorrain, which, with its dependencies, formed a considerable kingdom.

a curious article of the *Salic law* [*]. *He who squeezes the hand of a free woman, shall pay a fine of fifteen golden sols.*

Case of the unhappy Chundon; *from the same.*

An. 593. A WIFE of Gontran, King of Burgundy, in her last moments, requested of him to put two physicians to death, whose medicines she pretended had been fatal to her: he was so weak as to promise it, and had the cruelty to keep his word. The same King seeing one day a wild bull newly killed, he caused the ranger of the forest to be apprehended, who laid it on a chamberlain of the King's named Chundon, and he denied the fact. The King ordered the dispute to be decided by combat. The party accused, being aged and infirm, he put in his stead one of his nephews, who mortally wounded the accuser, but, going about to disarm him, killed himself with his adversary's poniard. The champion's death being considered as a conviction of the chamberlain, the monarch ordered him to be seized, and he was stoned on the spot. This was what those barbarous times called a regard to justice. It will appear matter of surprise, that, amidst all the elogiums for piety and devotion which Gregory de Tours bestows on Gontran, he should add, *that he had a concubine named Veneranda.* But the wonder vanishes on reflecting that concubinage, which however infamous it became afterwards, was then a legal union; and, if less solemn, was not less indissoluble than marriage. The civil law authorized it, when, by the Roman laws, the want of portion or birth in the woman prohibited her being married with persons of a certain rank. Now, though a concubine did not enjoy the same consideration in the family as a wife of equal condition, yet was it a name of honour very different from that of mistress; and her children, according to the antient custom of the Francs, were, with the father's approbation, not less qualified to inherit. The Western church, for several centuries, held this kind of alliance entirely lawful. The first council of Toledo expressly decides, *A man is to have but one wife or one concubine at his option.* St. Isidore, of Seville, the council of Rome under Eugene II. another held in the same city under Leo IV. speak to the same purpose. If these marriages came to be abolished, it was not on account of any intrinsic illegality, especially when the engagement was real and for ever, but on account of the numberless abuses arising from the want of the canonical solemnities. It was likewise for this reason that the Roman laws, though legitimating the issue by such union, excluded them from the right of succession.

Advantages which France *derived from the antient Monks; from the same.*

An. 750. AMONG other advantages accruing to the government from so many pious foundations, it is to the skill and industry of the recluses that

[*] Lex Salic. tit. 22.

France owes a great part of its present fertility. It had been frequently ravaged by the incursions of the barbarians: the eye every where met with wastes, forests, heaths, moors, and marshes, that bequeathing to the monks' estates of no produce, was thought but a very small matter; accordingly they had as much land given them as they could cultivate. These worthy solitaries, far from devoting themselves to God, with a view of living in idleness, grubbed up and cleared the land, drained, sowed, planted, and built, so that these dreary wastes soon became pleasant and fruitful tracts. So opulent were some abbies, that they could raise a little army; and on this account the abbots were afterwards summoned to the assemblies in the *March-Field*.

State of Trade in the 8th and 9th Centuries; from the same.

THERE was a settled trade between England and France, till Charlemain, offended at the presumption of Offa, King of the Mercians, prohibited all manner of dealing between the two nations; and it was not till two years after that it returned into its former channel. In these times, scarce any other trade was known than that carried on in markets or fairs; these were almost the only places for providing one's self with necessaries. Artificers and dealers lived apart dispersed in the country; the towns were chiefly inhabited by the clergy and some handicraftsmen, with few or no monks or nuns; the far greater part of the monasteries being either in the open countries or the neighbourhood of the cities. The nobility lived on their estates, or attended on the court. The poor people were so far under their lord's power, as not to quit the place of their birth without his leave; the villain was annexed to the estate, and the slave to the master's house or land. Such a dispersion was little promotive of trade, which loves large and policed communities; and it was to remedy this inconvenience that our kings established so many fairs. One of the most famous was that of St. Dennis, traders resorting to it not only from all parts of France, but from Friesland, Saxony, England, Spain, and Italy. We find, however, that, in more distant ages, trade was not absolutely confined to those markets alone, or to European foreigners. The city of Arles, under the first reigns of the Merovingians, was in great repute for its manufactures, its embroideries, and gold and silver inlaid works, and, like Narbonne and Marseilles, frequented by ships from the Levant and Africa; but this prosperity gradually sunk under the devastations of continual wars, the Asiatics and Africans no longer coming to our ports. Such however is the force of original and innate dispositions, that Narbonne, Arles, and Marseilles, still retain that commercial and naval genius which had made them the staples of the universe under the Carlovingians. They kept a certain number of ships trading to Constantinople, Genoa and Pisa, and Alexandria. Lewis the *Gracious* granted a charter to a body of merchants without any other acknowledgment or obligation than to come once a year, and account with his exchequer.

The

The French appear to have little bufied themfelves in trade under the two firft races of our kings, leaving it almoft entirely to foreigners. Spain furnifhed them with horfes and mules; Friefland, with party-coloured mantles, upper garments furred with marten, otter, and cat fkin; England, with grain, iron, tin, lead, leather, and hounds; the Eaft and Africa, with drugs, exquifite vines, and Egyptian paper, the only fort ufed in France till the eleventh century, and olive oil, which at that time was fo fcarce in our climates, that, at a council held at Aix la Chapelle, monks were permitted to ufe bacon oil. If foreigners imported only common goods to France, its exports were anfwerable, confifting ufually of potters' ware, brafery, wine, honey, madder, and falt.

Specimen of the Wit and Satire of the Middle Ages; from the fame.

An. 1252. ABOUT this time died one of thofe brave knights againft whom the moft malignant envy could not bring the leaft reproach: a poet who revered him compofed the panegyric on his virtues, which, on the other hand, was a fevere fatire on great perfonages, and, being a fketch both of the wit and of the princes of thofe times, it may not be unacceptable: here it follows in its literal plainnefs: " In this doleful lay I will lament Blacus, and well indeed may I lament his death. The moft cordial friend! the moft worthy lord!—with him all the virtues have taken their flight. This is fuch an afflictive ftroke, that I do not know any expedient for the vaft lofs, but to take that noble heart of his, and fhare it among thefe barons who have none, and they will have heart fufficient. The firft piece fhould be eaten by the Emperor of Rome, if he is for recovering thofe lands which the Milanefe have wrefted from him, in fpite of all his bulky Germans could do. We would likewife counfel the illuftrious King of France to partake of it, that he may retrieve Caftile, which he is fo fillily lofing; but fhould his good mother know it, be won't touch it; for all the world fees what a dutiful child he is, how very obedient to all fhe fays, never doing any thing that may difpleafe her. King of England, eat thou a lufty gob, for no heart haft thou; and then thou wilt be a hero, and regain thofe provinces which,—fy upon thy cowardice and negligence!—thou haft fhamefully fuffered to fall into the French hands. The King of Caftile fhould eat two fhares, having two kingdoms, and not capable fo much as to govern one; but when he is for eating, let him, too, get out of his mother's fight: fhould it come to her ears, fhe would give him a found warming. I would have the King of Arragon not to be fparing of this animating heart: he has two blots in his efcutcheon, one got at Marfeilles, and the other at Milan, and this is the only way to make all clean and bright again. The King of Navarre fhall not go without a good bit; for, by what I hear, he was better thought of when a Count, than now on the throne, to which he has been fo fortunately raifed. A fad thing indeed! when they whom God has exalted are

brought

brought low by their base want of courage. The Count de Toulouse, must think that he has no small need of t, if he is pleased to call to mind what he has been, and what he is now; and he should eat it with a good will, for his own heart is known to be such a poor thing, that it will never help him to recover his losses."

A Dissertation on Joduta, the Idol of Saxony, and of the Marche. By M. Kuster.

LOTHARIO, Duke of Saxony, being at war with the Emperor Henry V. gave him battle in the year 1115, near Gerbstadt, in the county of Mansfeldt, defeated him, and killed him 45,000 men. To perpetuate the memory of his victory, Lothario caused a statue to be erected in the figure of a man, in the habiliments of war, holding in his right hand a cestus, and having on his left arm a buckler, on which were the arms of Saxony, viz. a white horse on a red shield. This statue being a monument of his victory as owing to the Divine assistance, which was most probably expressed in Latin or Italian, the ignorant and superstitious vulgar took the Latin word *adjutorium*, or the Italian *ajuto*, for a proper name, and the statue for that of the saint whose name it was, and made of it St. *Joduta*, or *Jodutte*, and by corruption *Zedutte*, *Zeduck*, and *Geduette*. Among other virtues ascribed to it, is that of curing the tooth ach, by taking a little bit of the wood, and holding it in the mouth. This pretended saint is also held in veneration in many other parts of Germany; hence there is a vulgar proverb in Westphalia, *I'll beat you, till you invoke Jodutha*.

There was another statue of *Jodutha* near Writzen on the Oder, in the Middle Marche: travellers usually stopped to worship it, and to beg its assistance on account of the bad roads into which they were entering; in particular, the Saint was desired to take the horses under his protection, lest the drivers, through their brutality, or wanting to drive them too hard, should do them a mischief. Adam Spengler, inspector of Writzen, caused this statue, in the last century, to be thrown into the river, where it was swallowed up. Our author finds other traces of *Jodutha* at Marbourg, Bremen, &c. This Italian or Latin name, translated into German, was also given by way of imitation to other statues or images of Saints and Saintesses. Charlemagne built a church in Westphalia, in the year 783, to which he gave the name of *Sant Hulpe*, or *Holy* Assistance. In another church in Holstein was a chalice, on which our Saviour, fixed to the cross, had at his feet his mother and St. John, with this inscription, *St. Hulpe, pray for us*. In the same place was a wooden image, which the people of the place called *St. Hulpe*; and there was a hole in the wall, to which they gave the name of *Sant Hulpen Khms*, or *St. Hulpen's Niche*, in which probably there had been an image of the Virgin.

Anecdote of Shakespeare, never printed in his Works.

EDWARD Alleyn, the Garrick of Shakespeare's time, had been on the most friendly footing with our Poet, as well as Ben Jonson. They used frequently to spend their evenings together at the sign of the Globe, somewhere near Black Friars, where the Play-house then was. The world need not be told, that the convivial hours of such a triumvirate must be pleasing as well as profitable, and may truly be said to be such pleasures as might bear the reflections of the morning. In consequence of one of these meetings, the following letter was written by G. Peel, a Fellow of Christ Church College, Oxford, and a Dramatic Poet, who belonged to the club, to one Marle, an intimate of his.

" Friend Marle,

" I must desyre that my Syster hyr watche, and the Cookerie book you promysed, may be sente bye the man—I never longed for thy company more than last night: we were all very merrye at the Globe, when Ned Alleyn did not scruple to affyme pleasauntely to thy friende Will, that he had stolen his speeche about the qualityes of an Actor's excellencye in Hamlet bys Trajedye, from conversations manyfold whych had passed betweene them, and opinyons given by Alleyn touchinge the subjecte — Shakespeare did not take this talke in good sorte : but Jonson put an end to the strife with wittylye remarkinge, ' This affaire needeth no contentione ; you stole it from Ned, no doubte ; do not marvel. Have you not seen him act tymes, out of number ?'

Believe me most syncerilie,
Your's,
G. PEEL."

As Mr. Alleyn is a character at present little known in the theatrical world, though we need not subjoin any other testimony to his merits than the above compliment from such a judge as Ben Jonson, we shall, however, beg leave to add (by way of shewing it was no friendly partiality) the opinions of two gentlemen, whose established literary characters are too well known to doubt their complimenting at the expence of their genius and sincerity.

Dr. Fuller, in his Worthies, says, " that Alleyn made any part, especially a majestic one, become him." And Sir Richard Baker, who was a cotemporary of his, calls him and Burbage " the best actors of our time;" adding, " what plays were ever so pleasing, as when their parts had the greatest part."—And in his Chronicle we find him once more joining Alleyn with Burbage in the following encomium: " They were two such actors, as no age must ever look to see the like."

USEFUL

USEFUL PROJECTS.

A Letter from Mr. J. Moult to Dr. Percival of Manchester, *F. R. S. containing a new Manner of preparing Salep.*

[Read January 12, 1769.]

SIR,

AS the specimen of salep which I left you some time ago meets with your approbation, so far as to think it deserving to be laid before the Royal Society, I now send you my method of curing the common orchis roots of our own country, so as perfectly to resemble what comes to us from Turkey. And if the communication be of any public utility, I shall think myself sufficiently gratified for the trouble I have had in prosecuting the experiments necessary thereto.

The roots I have hitherto made use of are those of the *orchis morio mas foliis maculatis* of Parkinson, the *cynosorchis morio mas* of Gerard, and the *cynosorchis major, vulgo* dog-stones: though, from a specimen of the *orchis palmata major mas* of Gerard, which you have among the salep, that root likewise appears capable of being made to answer the same purposes as the others. The best time to gather the roots is when the seed is formed, and the stalk going to fall; for then the new bulb, of which the salep is made, is arrived to its full size, and may be known from the old one, whose strength is then spent by the preceding germination, by a white bud rising from the top of it, which is the germ of the plant of the succeeding year. This new root, being separated from the stalk, is to be washed in water, and a fine thin skin, that covers it, to be taken off with a small brush; or, by dipping in hot water, it will come off with a coarse linen cloth.

When a sufficient quantity of the roots is thus cleaned, they are to be spread on a thin plate, and set into an oven, heated to the degree of a bread oven, where they are to remain six, eight, or ten minutes; in which time they will have lost their milky whiteness, and have acquired a transparency like that of horn, but without being diminished in size. When they are arrived at this state, they may be removed to another room to dry and harden, which will be done in a few days; or they may be finished in a very slow heat, in a few hours. I have tried both ways with success.

The orchises abovementioned grow spontaneously in this part of the country, and throughout the whole kingdom. They flourish best in a dry, sandy, barren soil. As the method of curing this root is so easy, I hope it will encourage the cultivation of so nutritious a vegetable, so as to reduce it from its present high price, which confines it to people of fortune, to one so moderate as would bring it into common use, like other kinds of meal or flour; and so become a valuable addition to our present list of eatables, its quality of thickening water being to that of fine flour nearly as $2\frac{1}{4}$ to 1, with this difference, that the jelly of salep-powder is clear and transparent, whereas that of flour is turbid and white.

If this should find you in the same sentiments respecting it, I give you liberty to make use of it accordingly.

And am,

With all respect,

Your very humble servant,

Rochdale, Nov.
10, 1768.   J. MOULT.

[Received October 31, 1769.]

Some Account of an Oil, transmitted by Mr. George Brownrigg, *of North Carolina. By* William Watson, *M. D. R. S. S.*

[Read December 14, 1769.]

To the Royal Society.

GENTLEMEN,

THE application of natural productions to the benefit of mankind has always been an object of our excellent institution; and endeavours to extend the utility of substances already very obscurely known have always met from you a favourable reception.

It is with this view that I lay before you some pods of a vegetable, and the oil pressed from their contents. They were sent from Edenton, in North Carolina, by Mr. George Brownrigg, whose brother, Dr. Brownrigg, is a worthy member of our society; and are the produce of a plant well known, and much cultivated, in the southern colonies, and in our American sugar islands, where they are called ground nuts, or ground pease. They are originally, it is presumed, of the growth of Africa, and brought from thence by the negroes, who use them as food, both raw and roasted, and are very fond of them. They are therefore cultivated by them in the little parcels of land set apart for their use by their masters. By these means, this plant has extended itself not only to our warmer American settlements, but it is cultivated in Surinam, Brasil, and Peru.

The plant which produces these has been mentioned and described by the botanical writers of the later times. Ray, in his History of Plants, calls it *Arachis Hypogaios Americanus*. It is the *Arachidna quadrifolia villosa* of Plumier. Sir Hans Sloane, in his History of Jamaica, calls it *Arachidna Indiæ utriusque tetraphylla*. Piso and Marograac both mention it among the Brasilian plants, under the name of *Mundubi*. Linnæus has constituted a genus of this plant, of which only one species is as yet known, under Mr. Ray's generical name of *Arachis*.

This plant, together with a very few of the trifoliate tribe, has the property of burying its seeds under ground, which it does in the following manner: as soon as the plant

plant is in flower, its flower is bent towards the ground until it touches it. The pointal of the flower is then thrust into the ground to a sufficient depth, where it extends itself, and forms the seed-vessel and fruit, which is brought to maturity under ground, from whence it is dug up for use.

This plant, which is a native of warm climates, will not bear being cultivated to advantage in Great Britain, or in the northern colonies; but, according to Mr. Brownrigg, in southern climates its produce is prodigious; and what adds to its value is, that rich land is not necessary for its cultivation, as light sandy land, of small value, will produce vast crops of it. Besides what the negroes cultivate for their own use, some planters raise a considerable quantity of it for the feeding of swine and poultry, which are very fond of the ground pease; and, when they are permitted to eat freely of them, soon become fat.

Mr. Brownrigg, from whom, as I before mentioned, I received the oil, considers the expressing oil from the ground pease as a discovery of his own: it may, perhaps, at this time, be very little practised either in North Carolina, the place of his residence, or elsewhere. But certain it is, that this oil was expressed above fourscore years ago; as Sir Hans Sloane mentions it, in the first volume of his History of Jamaica; and says, that this oil is as good as that of almonds. It is probable, however, that small quantities only were expressed, and that even at that time the knowledge of it did not extend very far. Mr. Brownrigg, therefore, is highly praise-worthy in reviving the remembrance of procuring oil from these seeds. It is obtained by first bruising the seeds very well, and afterwards pressing them in canvass bags, as is usual in procuring oil from almonds or linseed.

To have the oil in the best manner, no heat should be used. The heating the cheeks of the press increases the quantity of the oil, but lessens its goodness, where it may be intended to be used as food, or as a medicine. For other purposes, the larger quantity of oil, obtained by heat, will answer equally well.

Neither the seeds nor oil are apt to become rancid by keeping; and as a proof of this, the oil before you, which was sent from Carolina in April last, and, without any particular care, has undergone the heats of last summer, is yet perfectly sweet and good. These seeds furnish a pure, clear, well-tasted oil; and, as far as appears to me, may be used for the same purposes, both in food and physic, as the oils of olives or almonds. It may be applied likewise to many, if not all, the œconomical purposes with the former of these.

But what greatly adds to the merit of what Mr. Brownrigg has informed us of, is, the low price at which this oil may be obtained. He says, that ten gallons of the pease, with the husks unshelled, will, without heat, yield one gallon of oil: if pressed with heat, they will afford a much larger quantity. The value of a bushel of these, in Carolina, does not exceed, as I have been informed, eight-pence, or thereabouts. These will furnish a gallon of oil; the labour and apparatus to procure which cannot cost much. This price will not amount to so much

as

as a fourth of what the best Florence oil of olives costs in England. This therefore ought to be considered as valuable information, as, on account of its cheapness, a larger portion of mankind than at present may be permitted to use oil with their food, from whom it is now withheld on account of its price.

Great quantities of olive oil are sent from Europe to America. New England alone, Mr. Brownrigg says, annually consumes twenty thousand gallons. The quantities used in his Majesty's other dominions in America must be prodigious. The oil from ground pease, of which any quantity desired may be raised, may and would supply this consumption of olive oil. It would likewise, I am persuaded, bear exportation to any of those places where the oil of olives is usually carried; and thereby become a valuable article of commerce.

After the oil has been expressed from the ground pease, they are yet excellent food for swine.

Presuming that a more intimate knowledge of the vegetable production before you than what we were lately possessed of would not be disagreeable to the Royal Society, I take the liberty of laying the present account before you; and am,

GENTLEMEN,

Your most obedient,

humble servant,

W. WATSON.

Improvements and Experiments in Agriculture; from Mr. Young's Six Months Tour.

Of POTATOES, *and the amazing Crops which they produce by a proper Culture.*

I SHALL first lay before you a general state of their culture and produce, and, if it gives rise to any average accounts, shall extract them accordingly.

At *Sandy* in *Bedfordshire*.
  Soil. A rich deep black sand.
  Rent, 3l. 10s.
  Seed and distance. Twenty bushels at one foot every way.
  Culture. Hoe them thrice.
  Product. 250 bushels, 20l. 16s.
  Expences, 12l. 18s. 6d.
  Profit, 7l. 17s. 6d.
About *Doncaster*.
  Soil. A fine light rich loose sand.
  Product. 250 bushels.
About *York*.
  Soil. Light. 12s per acre.
  Planted in two feet rows, and earthed up with hoe.
  Product. 60 bushels.
At *Cottingham*, near *Hull*.
  Soil. Rich loam and mixed clay, at 3l. per acre.
  Seed, &c. twenty bushels. Hoe several times.
  Product. 180 bushels.
About *Stillingfleet*.
  Soil. Sandy, at 14s.
  Seed, &c. Sixteen bushels, rows two feet, plants one foot: horse-hoe them two or three times, and hand-weed them.
  Product. 80 bushels.
Mr. *Turner*, at *Kirkleatham*.
  Soil. A light poor sand, at 8s.
  In rows three feet, plants
  one

one foot; horse-hoed once, and hand-hoed once; twice weeded.
Product. 588 bushels.

Mr. *Turner*, at *Kirkleatham*.
Soil. A rich black loam, well manured.
In beds four feet wide, three rows on each; alleys two feet; plants eighteen inches asunder.
Product. 166 bushels.

Mr. *Crow*, *Kiplin*.
Soil. Clay, at 12s. 6d.
Culture. Manures with long dung or haulm; plants in rows two feet asunder, plants nine inches; twelve bushels to the acre; four horse-hoeings, and well hand-hoed.
Product. 120 bushels. Feeds all sorts of cattle.

Mr. *Smelt*, at *The Leases*.
Soil. Gravel.
Culture. Manure, four loads of long dung; sets in rows fifteen inches, ten from set to set; fifteen bushels seed. Kept clean from weeds.
Product. 130 bushels.

Swinton moor-side farms.
Soils. Black moory land, at 4s. 6d.
Product. 120 bushels.

The Colliers' moor husbandry.
Soil. Black peat earth.
Culture. In rows two feet, sets one foot; thirteen bushels.
Product. 158 bushels.

Mr. *Dalton*, *Sleninford*.
Soil. Light loam on limestone, at 8s.
Culture. Rows, three feet; ten loads of dung. Horse and hand-hoed.
Product. 150 bushels.

Mr. *Scroope*, at *Danby*.
Soil. A sandy loam, at 12s. 6d.
Culture. Plants. one foot asunder, a handful of dung to each five loads; eight bushel sets; horse and hand-hoed.
Product. 216 bushels.

Near *Newcastle*.
Soil. Sandy, at 20s.
Culture. Twelve bushels of sets, at one foot square; hand-hoe twice, and hand-weed.
Product. 226 bushels.

At *Morpeth*.
Soil. A loamy clay, in general 12s. but planters give 5l.
Culture. Twenty-five loads, dung; dibbled one foot square, dig for them; twenty-three bushels; hand-hoe thrice.
Product. 350 bushels. Expences, 12l. 5s. 6d. Profit, 5l. 4s. 6d.

At *Alnwick*.
Soil. Gravelly loam, at 15s.
Culture. Dig and plough for them, and dung; nine bushels seed; twelve inches square.
Product. 150 bushels.

At *Belford*.
Soil. Strong loam, at 15s. 6d.
Culture. Fourteen inches square; six bushels; hand-hoe twice.
Product. 42 bushels.

About *Rothbury*.
Soil. Gravel, sand, and moory, at 10s. 6d.
Culture. Manure, and hand-hoe once or twice.
Product. 80 bushels.

At *Glenwelt*.
Soil. Sandy, &c. 12s. 6d.
Culture. Twelve loads long dung; twenty bushels in one foot square; hoe twice.
Product. 220 bushels.

South of *Carlisle*.
Soil. Light loam, at 15*s*.
Culture. Manure well, in rows eighteen inches, one foot plant to plant: horse-hoe.
Product. 300 bushels.

About *Penrith*.
Soil. Various, at 8*s*. 9*d*.
Culture. Manure with long dung; rows eighteen inches, one foot the plants; hand-hoe.
Product. 120 bushels.

Keswick.
Soil. Hazel-mould, sand, &c. at 25*s*.
Culture. Two sorts; in furrows eighteen inches by twelve. Manure well; horse-hoe, and weed. The other the lazy-bed, dung on grass, and earth out of trenches.
Product. In the first 300 bushels, which is more than the other.

From *Kendal* to *Burton*, about *Holme*.
Soil. Light loam on limestone, at 21*s*.
Culture. Lazy-bed, dung the grass well; eighteen bushels sets, seven inches square.
Product. 180 bushels.

At *Kabers*.
Soil. Light loam and sand, at 17*s*.
Culture. Plough for, dibble eight or ten inches square; weed them.
Product. 150 bushels.

About *Garstang*.
Soil. Light loam, at 17*s*.
Culture. Dig all the land nine inches deep; dibble in nine inches asunder; hand-weed.
Product. 380 bushels.

Around *Ormskirk*.
Soil. Light loam, at 15*s*.
Culture. Manure well, on both grass and arable; plough for them; sets nine inches square; hand-weed.
Product. 150 bushels.

About *Altringham*.
Soil. Sandy loam, at 20*s*.
Culture. Dig for them; manure well, dibble twenty-two bushels; hand-weed and hand-hoe.
Product. 700 bushels.

At *Knotsford*.
Soil. Sandy, at 16*s*.
Culture. Dig grass; twenty bushels, at one foot square, dibbled; hand-hoe and weed.
Product. 500 bushels.

Around *Stone*.
Soil. Sandy, at 16*s*.
Culture. Manure, grass well, and dig it in; hand-hoe.
Product. 450 bushels.

About *Shenstone*.
Soil. Sandy, at 15*s*.
Culture. Dung grass well, and dig in; dibble ten inches square; hand-hoe well.
Product. 400 bushels.

Near *Birmingham*.
Soil. Sandy, at 17*s*. 6*d*.
Culture. Dig up grass land, and dibble in sets.
Product. 550 bushels.

At *Bendsworth*.
Soil. Clay, and some light, at 21*s*.
Culture. Manure well with long dung; dibble in rows, one foot square.
Product. 350 bushels.

Kensington.
Soil. Sand and gravel, at 40*s*.
Culture. Dung well, and plough in rows, one foot, plants six inches: hoe twice, and weed.
Product. 15*l*. as they grow.

As there is a great variety in these products, I shall throw them into divisions according to the quantity, without any other rule; as it will then in general appear what soil and management are most adapted to them. First, all that produce five hundred bushels and upwards; second, such as yield from two to five hundred; and, third, those that yield under two hundred.

As these tables are of a greater length than our limits will admit, we shall only give the first of them.

Crops of 500 Bushels, &c.

Places.	Soil.	Sets.	Rows.	Culture.	Product.
Mr. *Turner*,	Sand, 8s.	—	3 feet by 1,	Horse and hand-hoed,	588
Ditto,	Black loam, worth 40s.	—	18 inches,	Dug for,	1166
Altringham,	Sandy loam, 20s.	22	—	Dig for them, manure, hand-hoe, and weed,	700
Knotsford,	Sand, 16s.	20	1 foot sq.	Dig grass, dibble, hand-hoe, and weed,	500
Birmingham,	Sand 17s. 6d.	—	—	Dig grass and dibble in sets,	500
Averages,	— 20s.	21	—	—	— 700

It is very evident from this table that rent is no more a guide to product than the wind; nor is any particular soil (except the sandy and light being generally the best) a mark whereby to point out the scale of produce. The distance of the rows, and the quantity of sets, as well as the material articles of manuring and cleaning, are none of them, separately taken, at all decisive in fixing the superiority. Thus much, however, may be observed, that the more considerable products are those that are in general very spiritedly cultivated: all in the first division, except one, are dug for, and likewise the best of those in the second: this seems as if digging for them was much superior to ploughing. The strong variations we otherwise observe must certainly be attributed to fertility of soil, richness of manuring, or a general excellent management: a circumstance greatly encouraging to all who are willing to cultivate this most useful vegetable; for there is great reason to suppose, that a vigorous conduct in raising potatoes will more than balance every other advantage.

It should be observed, that these roots

USEFUL PROJECTS.

roots are every where considered as an excellent fallow crop, greatly meliorating the soil, and preparing in every respect for wheat in particular, or for any other grain in a very superior manner. It is extremely evident from the preceding table that their culture is uncommonly profitable. In numerous places I was assured that they made infinitely more by potatoes than by any other crop. The prices of them are various, but, at 1*s*. 6*d*. a bushel, the average product amounts to above 28*l*. but 1*s*. 6*d*. is a low price: it is a great error in many parts of this kingdom, the not cultivating potatoes in large quantities.

No fallow crop is more advantageous to the soil, nor could there be a greater improvement in three-fourths of the counties of *England*, than introducing potatoes into the courses of their fields, as regularly upon soils proper for them, as turneps or any other vegetable.

The common objection to cultivating them in large quantities is the want of a market; but such a plea is an absolute piece of gothicism: the most advantageous use they can be applied to, where they bear an high price, most certainly is to sell them: but where the prices are low, or the market overstocked, this root should be applied to feeding and fattening cattle, in which the profit will be very great, both in the price paid for the crop and in the great improvement of the farm, by raising large quantities of manure; an object which ought always to be foremost with every farmer: tho intelligence received of Mr. *Crowe*, of this application of his crops at *Kiplin* to feeding all sorts of cattle and poultry, is particularly valuable: it is well known, in several places, that no food is better for rearing and fattening hogs, but I never before heard of feeding promiscuously all the flock in a farm-yard on them; but that gentleman's long experience proves it not only to be eligible, but extremely profitable.

If potatoes came in once every course of crops on light or rich soils, not very heavy, and were all applied to fatten numerous herds of swine, or to maintain oxen, cows, young cattle, &c. the improvement of the whole farm would be the certain consequence; for the fields in which they are cultivated are finely enriched by themselves, and their consequences in manuring would perform the same office to others.

From what I have remarked in the tour, I have reason to think digging a much superior method to ploughing, with the sets laid in the furrows. The latter way may be very proper in a very light rich sand; but in sandy or gravelly loams the digging is superior: if I was to recommend a practice, it should be the following, which, I think, from the preceding minutes, as well as my own experience, is excellent. Unite the ploughing and lazy-bed methods; first plough the land fine, in beds about five feet broad, then spread your dung: if the soil is very light, it should be well rotted and mixed together; but if the land is inclinable to stiffness, then long dung, old thatch, stubble, or any thing of that kind. Upon the manure lay the potatoe slices promiscuously, about a foot asunder; cover them three inches deep, with

earth

earth dug out of the furrows, a trench in each like a water furrow, about eighteen inches wide. When the potatoes are about four or five inches high, weed them, dig another spit in the trenches, and cover the beds and plants two inches deeper: this will stop the growth of most weeds; but if any arise, draw them out, but never hand-hoe unless the surface binds, which on proper soils it will not do. Vast crops may be had in this method, and the beds left in excellent order for a crop of any thing else.

Of Cabbages.

SINCE the publication of Mr. Baker's report, we have had no fresh intelligence concerning cabbages: there is not extant in print a single experiment upon the Great Scotch sort: it is with the utmost pleasure that I minuted in my journey all the intelligence I could gain concerning this vegetable. I was fortunate enough to meet with many gentlemen that had cultivated it for several years; some of them, from the curiosity of the object, had made accidental minutes of several circumstances of the culture, expences, produce, &c. These they favoured me with, and in other particulars gave me, accounts from their own memory, and that of their servants; but as I had not any regular registers of experiments in a series, I threw the intelligence I received into as clear and methodical an order as I was able. So far did very well for each minute; but as the circumstances of culture, product, and value, have great variations, it is here absolutely necessary to draw all these fugitive articles into one point of view; to compare the intelligence, and to draw the averages of every circumstance, that the culture and value of cabbages may be completely known. I shall make the extract in as few words as possible: the article begins with

Mr. *Middlemore*, at *Grantham*.
Sort. *Battersea*, turnep and *Scotch*.
Soil. A red sand.
Time of sowing. Beginning of *March*. Once pricked out, and planted at Midsummer.
Rows. Four feet asunder, from one foot to eighteen inches from plant to plant. 6000 per acre.
Culture. Weeded in dry weather.
Duration. To *April*.
Product. Turnep cabbage 5lb. or nineteen tons per acre; *Battersea* 11lb. or forty-two tons per acre; *Scotch* 14lb. or fifty-four tons. Used for fatting oxen and feeding sheep.
Expences. Pricking out and transplanting, 1s. per thousand.

Mr. *Lyster*, at *Bawtry*, the *Scotch* sort.
Soils. A very light sand.
Rent, 11s.
Time of sowing, &c. End of *Jan.* or beginning of *Feb.* Transplant the middle of *June.*
Rows. Four feet asunder, plants two feet. 6240 plants.
Culture. Horse-hoed thrice, and hand-hoed.
Duration. Begin to burst in *October;* all must be done by *Christmas.*
Product. Twenty-seven tons.
Feeding

Feeding cows both dry and milch, rearing young cattle, and feeding sheep. Will not go near so far as turneps.
Expences. Six men plant an acre a day.

Mr. *Wharton*, at *Doncaster*. The Great *Scotch*.
Soil. A light sand.
Rows. Three feet, plants two.
Culture. Hand-hoeing.
Duration. Late in spring, to turning into grass.
Product. Two acres completely fat three large beast.

Mr. *Tucker*, at *Rotherham*. The Great *Scotch*.
Soil. A light sandy loam, extremely rich.
Rent, 2*l*. 5*s*.
Preparation. Winter fallow; and ten loads rich rotten dung.
Time. Middle of *August*, and the spring. The first pricked out the middle of *October*; transplant the last week in *May*; the others not pricked out at all. The winter plants the largest.
Rows. Four feet; plants, two and two and a half. 5000 per acre.
Culture. Watered if dry; two horse-hoeings, and hand-hoeing.
Duration. End of *March*; some to beginning of *April*. Some want cutting before *Christmas*, the winter plants.
Product. One crop 30*lb*. another 10*lb*. average 20*lb*. or forty-four tons *per* acre.—— Two acres and a half, under 10*lb*. kept (with some straw) twelve cows the principal part of the winter. If milch cows are kept constantly on them, without other food, the butter is rank. Fat oxen; feed pigs.
Expences. A man plants two thousand in a day.
Profit. Very great. More than ten quarters of oats after them, and eight the second crop.

Mr. *Ellerker's*, at *Risby*. Large *Scotch*.
Soil. Loam on a chalkstone.
Rent, 9*s*. 3*d*.
Preparation. A winter fallow; manures, ten loads of farm-yard dung.
Time. Sows the end of *February*—pricks out once; plants the beginning of *June*.
Rows. Three feet; plants two.
Culture. Water in dry seasons. Horse-hoe once to thrice.
Duration. To the end of *April*.
Product. Fats two beast completely of thirty-six stone each (14*lb*.) Completely fats such, and finishes others of eighty stone: has sold oxen of 23*l*. from cabbages.
Expences. A man plants an acre in three days.
Profit. Exceedingly great.

Marquis of *Rockingham's Kentish* farm. Great *Scotch*.
Soil. A rich, deep, black loam.
Time. Sows the end of *February*; plants the middle of *June*.
Rows. Three feet, and plants three feet.
Culture. Water in dry weather.——From three to five horse-hoeings, besides hand-hoeing.
Product. Worth, for feeding any cattle, a half-penny each, the number of plants being 4840; that is, 10*l*. 1*s*. *per* acre. Fat oxen chiefly.

His Lordship's *Hertfordshire* farm, the

the fame as the preceding, except only hand-hoeing.

Mr. *Wilſon, Ayton, Scotch* ſort.
Time. Sows in *September*, plants in *May*.

Mr. *Turner*, at *Kirkleatham*. The average of twelve experiments.
Soil. Clay, loam, and rich ſandy loam.
Rent 15s.
Preparation. Winter fallowed; and ſome a whole year. Some crops limed.
Time. Sows the latter end of *February*, and in *March* for ſpring plants; and in *Auguſt* for winter ones. Tranſplants through the months of *May* and *June*.
Rows. Three to four feet, and plants two. Generally 5445 plants.
Culture. Horſe-hoed twice, and hand-hoed as often. Never waters.
Duration. To *Candlemas*.
Product. In general from twenty tons to fifty-eight; average thirty-nine. Fats and feeds oxen, cows, young cattle, and ſheep, infinitely better than any other food. The increaſe of one cow's milk from cabbages two quarts a day, but it taſted. The improvement of an ox of 80 ſtone (14lb.), fatting four months on cabbages, is on an average 5l. 10s. and in proportion *per* ton (the hay he eats deducted) is 8s. 6d. the value of the cabbages. Upon the whole, go much farther than turneps, and prepare much better for ſpring corn.
Quantity eat. An ox of eighty ſtone, 210lb. in twenty-four hours, beſides 7lb. of hay.
Expences. After a ſummer fallow, 3l. 15s. 6d. a winter ditto, 2l. 7s.—Expence of watering is 2s. 11d. planting 4s. 6d. hand-weeding 4s. 6d.
Anjou cabbages tried, but proved good for little.

Mr. *Crowe*, at *Kiplin*. The average of eight years. Great *Scotch*.
Soil. Clay.
Rent, 12s. 6d.
Preparation. Winter fallows and limes, a chaldron *per* acre.
Time. Sows in *Auguſt* for winter plants, pricks out at *Michaelmas*, and tranſplants in *March*: for ſpring plants (of which he has but few), ſows in *February*, tranſplants the end of *May*, or beginning of *June*.
Rows. Four feet, and plants two.
Culture. Horſe and hand-hoe, as requiſite; never waters.
Duration. Until *May-day*.
Product. In 1762, they weighed *per* cabbage 12lb. or, *per* acre. ——————— 29 *tons*.
1763, — 14lb. — 34
1764, — 12lb. — 29
1765, — 20lb. — 48
1766, — 18lb. — 43
1767, — 15lb. — 36
1768, — 11lb. — 27
Average 35 tons.
Uſed for all ſorts of cattle, and with univerſal ſucceſs.
Expences. At 10s. rent, the total 2l. 4s. 6d. Seed, 6d. Pricking out and tranſplanting, 5s. each. Hand-hoeing, 4s.

Mr.

USEFUL PROJECTS. 119

Mr. Swait, at *The Leafes.*
The average of five years.
Soil. Sandy, gravel.
Preparation. Winter fallow, and manure with seven loads of rotten dung.
Time. Sows the beginning of *March,* and transplants in *May.*
Rows. Four feet asunder, and two the plants.
Culture. Horse-hoes four times, and hand-hoes and weeds
Duration. Until the end of *March.*
Product.
In 1763, the cabbages weighed upon an average 7*lb.* or per acre — — 17 *tons.*
In 1764, — 8*lb.* — 19
In 1766, — 8*lb.* — 19
In 1767, — 8*lb.* — 19
In 1768, — 6*lb.* — 13
Average 18 tons.
Uses them for steers and sheep, but principally for cows, on account of the butter being incomparable, and given in great quantities, not more in height of summer: butter keeps a fortnight, but the cows must have no decayed leaves.

A gentleman near *Craik-hill.*
The Great *Scotch* fort.
Soil. Gravel.
Rent, 13*s.*
Average of four years 17*l.* 15*s.* 2*d.*
Uses them for oxen, cows, and sheep, with the utmost success. Two cows in *January,* one that had newly calved, and the other to calve at *Lady-Day,* produced in a week 17*lb.* 10 *oz.* of butter.

Mr. *Dalton,* at *Slewingford.*
Soil. Light loam on a lime-stone, very shallow.
Rent, 8*s.*
Preparation. Winter fallow, and a dunging.
Time. *Scotch,* transplanted the beginning of *June.* Turnep cabbage sown in spring, transplanted in *May.*
Rows. Four feet by twenty-two inches.
Culture. Horse and hand-hoeing.
Product. *Scotch,* 4*lb.* and 1*lb.*; average 2¼, or 6 tons. Turnep 5*lb.* 12 tons. The first given to cows, and made the butter absolutely stink, but attributed it to the decayed leaves not being taken off. The latter were given to sheep the middle of *April,* who were very fond of them.

Mr. *Scroop,* at *Danby.* The *Scotch.*
Soil. Clay, loam, and rich black land.
Rent, 4*s.* 6*d.* to 25*s.*; average 14*s.* 9*d.*
Preparation. Winter fallow, and upon all but the richest soils, manures with composts or lime.
Time. Sows early in the spring, and transplants the end of *May* or beginning of *June.*
Rows. Four feet, and two feet from plant to plant.
Culture. Never waters. Two horse and two hand-hoeings.
Duration. Till the end of *April* or beginning of *May.*
Product. Average value of seven years, at 5*s.* 9*d.* per ton, 9*l.* 16*s.*

                      Tons.
1765, - - - - 34
1766, - - - - 52

1766, - - - - - - 40
Ditto, - - - - - 23
Ditto, - - - - - 25
1767, - - - - - - 40
Ditto, - - - - - 25
Ditto, - - - - - 53
1768, - - - - - 35
Ditto, - - - - - 50
Ditto, - - - - - 30
Average 37 tons.

Oxen of 100 ftone, that have had the fummer's grafs, are finifhed, and without delay, never going back in flefh (the cafe oftentimes with turneps), and improving fafter than on any other food. All kinds of young cattle maintained through winter in full health and growth to great profit. Cows fed with them to more advantage fix to one than on any other food; the milk being in great quantity, perfectly fweet, and the butter excellent, but the precaution muft be obferved of picking off the decayed leaves. Fat fheep are carried forward in great perfection, better infinitely than on turneps. Lambs of ewes fed on them have always proved uncommonly fine and ftrong. Swine feed very freely on them, and are kept in very good condition without other food.

Quantity eat. An ox of an 100 ftone (14*lb.*) in twenty-four hours ate 168*lb.* and 7*lb.* of hay.

Expences. Average of feven years, 2*l.* 16*s.* 6*d.*

Profit, Ditto, 6*l.* 16*s.* 9*d.* part at 5*s.* 9*d. per* ton.

The turnep cabbage tried one year, the fame culture as *Scotch*, weight 8*lb.* Sheep ate them freely, but preferred the *Scotch*.

Mr. *Scroope*, at *Dalton*.
Soil. Some light loam on limeftone, and black moory land.
Culture. The management in every refpect the fame as at *Danby*.
Product. The weight of each crop not minuted, but in general it was from 15 to 34 tons *per* acre: average 24.

Earl of *Darlington*, at *Raby*. *Scotch*.
Soil. Strong gravel and loam.
Rent; 16*s.*
Preparation. Some on paring and burning; others only a winter fallow.
Time. Plants from the end of *May* to the end of *June*.
Rows. Three feet, plants two.
Culture. Horfe-hoed twice, hand ditto once.

Tons.
Product. 1766 — 14*lb.* ⎱ 45
  per cabbage,   ⎰
  1767 — ditto   45
  1768 — 10*lb.*   32
Average 40 tons.

Ufed conftantly for milch cows (the decayed leaves all taken off): the butter particularly excellent, and none keeps better.

Mr. *Dixon*, at *Belford*. *Scotch*.
Soil. Clayey loam.
Rent, 15*s.* 6*d.*
Preparation. Winter fallow, and a dunging.
Time. Sows in *Auguft*; tranfplants from middle of *March* to beginning of *April*.
Rows. Three feet, plants two.
Culture. Horfe and hand-boed.
Product. The weight of all the crops not minuted, but that that is, is 15*lb. per* cabbage, or *per* acre 48 tons. Ufes them

USEFUL PROJECTS.

them for milch cows; the butter very plentiful, and excellent; a lofs of cabbages, the lofs of the winter's butter.

Having thus brought all the intelligence concerning cabbages into one view, I muft, in the next place, draw it into such averages as the nature of the fubject requires.

In the firft place the general produce muft be difcovered, and reduced to value in money. The only method of doing this will be to difcover an average value per ton.

Average value per ton at *Kirkleatham*, by fatting oxen, 8s. 6d.
Ditto Mr. *Scroope*, — 5s. 9d.
Average, 7s. 1½d.

This muft be our guide for valuing thofe crops of *Stotch* cabbage whofe weight only is fpecified. They are as follow:

	Tons.
Mr. *Middlemore*	4
Mr. *Lyfter*,	27
Mr. *Tucker*,	44
Mr. *Turner*,	39
Mr. *Crowe*,	35
Mr. *Smelt*,	18*
Mr. *Scroope*,	37
Ditto at *Dalton*,	24
Earl of *Darlington*,	40
Mr. *Dixon*,	48

Average 36 tons, which at 7s. 1½d. is 12l. 16s. 6d. per acre.

In addition to this average, we muft infert others that were not difcovered by weight.

	£. s. d.
The Marquis of *Rockingham's* Kentifh farm,	10 1 0

	£. s. d.
Medium of the crops at *Craikhill*,	17 15 2

The general average of which three valuations is 13l. 10s. 10d. per acre.

It is here proper to remark, that this price muft undoubtedly be under the real mark: it is partly formed by a valuation of cabbages in fattening beafts at 7s. 1½d. per ton; but thofe who have been converfant in feeding cattle muft be fenfible that a value taken from one application only *may* be under the mark: that *it is* fo, muft ftrike every one who confiders, that turneps, and other articles of food, will fat an ox, though not fo well as cabbages; but turneps will not feed fheep through the months of *March* and *April*; and neither turneps nor hay will keep cows in plentiful as well as fweet milk all the winter; thefe two ufes are peculiar to cabbages, and fuch an application of them muft confequently make a greater return than a ufe in which other fpecies of food rival them.

Thofe who have been ufed to the enormous expence of wintering cattle on hay, will eafily believe that 7s. a ton for cabbages can by no means be an adequate price: the very propofition on comparifon with hay is ftriking. And as to the turneps, the comparifon is yet clearer. It before appeared, that the average value of turneps in the north of *England*, that is, the fame country the cabbages are all cultivated in, is 3l. 1s. 6d. per acre: now from the attentive manner in which I viewed as well as weighed

---

* It would be a great injuftice to include Mr. *Dalton's*: one pound average proves fufficiently that the foil, a fhallow furface on a limeftone, is *abfolutely* improper.

thofe

those at *Kiplin*, that fine and rich turnep soil, I was well convinced the average weight was not above five tons, which is better than 12s. per ton: now the superiority of cabbages to turneps is absolutely fixed by the preceding intelligence; those cultivators who think the contrary, bearing no proportion to their antagonists; consequently, cabbages are of much more value than 12s. per ton, or probably double the amount I have calculated them at; which circumstance must certainly convince every one, that cabbages are, in those calculations, much undervalued: and for the use of such as may be of this opinion, I shall add the value of the average crop at more estimation.

	£.	s.	d.
Thirty-six tons at 10s.	18	0	0
11s.	19	16	0
12s.	21	12	0
13s.	23	8	0
14s.	25	4	0

Had I been fortunate enough to have gained other clues to discover the value of cabbages, particularly in making butter for sale in winter, and spring feeding sheep and lambs, I have no doubt, but the average sum would have been very high in this scale, if not exceeded the utmost of it. But for want of other facts to calculate upon, I must make use of such as I possess.

In the next place I must compare the product with the rent of the land.

Mr. *Lyster*,	11s.	27 tons
Mr. *Tucker*,	45s.	44
Mr. *Turner*,	15s.	39
Mr *Crowe*,	12s. 6d.	35

		tons
Mr. *Scroope*,	14s. 9d.	37
Ditto,	4s.*	24
Earl of *Darlington*,	16s.	40
Mr. *Dixon*,	15s. 6d.	48
Average rent,	16s. 8d.	
At and under 15s. rent average,	} 11s. 5d.	32
Ditto about 15s.	25s. 6d.	44

It appears from hence, that cabbages depend very much on being planted in a rich soil; and this is precisely the opinion of most of the preceding cultivators, as well as perfectly consistent with reason; for the plant is a most vigorous one, roots very strong and deep, and consequently is very well calculated for improving proportionably to the fertility of the soil.

Forty-four tons at 7s. 1¼d. is	} 15 13 4
Thirty-two at ditto,	11 8 0
Superiority of the former,	} 4 5 4

This comparison shews the great profit of applying the best land of a farm to the culture of cabbages; and it proves at the same time the advantage of manuring and fallowing well. I apprehend there are few more beneficial ways of applying manure than to this culture. But to carry this comparison the farther, I shall next state the soils and product.

On clays and strong loams.

Mr. *Turner*,	-	-	39 tons
Mr. *Crowe*,	-	-	35
Mr. *Scroope*,	-	-	37
Earl of *Darlington*,	-	40
Mr. *Dixon*,	-	-	48

Average 39 tons.

On rich deep light loam.

Mr. *Tucker*,	-	-	44

* Never yielded any thing, but I call it 4s.

On other inferior soils.

Mr. *Middlemore* - 54 tons
Mr. *Lyster* - - - 27
Mr. *Smelt* - - - 18
Mr. *Scroope*, at *Dalton* 24
Average 30 tons.

The inferiority of the last to the two others shew how much the cabbages affect a rich soil; but, at the same time, the product on inferior soils proves clearly that this admirable vegetable thrives to vast profit on all sorts.

Of Carrots.

THIS excellent root is not so universally known as a food for cattle as it well deserves: the experiments I met with upon it are not numerous, but some of them are very valuable.

The Duke of *Bedford* finds them of great use for winter feeding large stocks of cattle and deer.
Soil. A sand.

Gardeners, at *Sandy*.
Soil. A rich deep fine sand, at 3*l.* 10*s.*
Culture. Sow at *Lady-day* on one spit digging; hoe very carefully three times; leave them from eight to ten inches asunder.
Product. Two hundred bushels per acre, at 2*s.*
Expences. Digging, 1*l.* Seed, 3*s.* Sowing, 6*d.* Raking, 4*s.* Hoeing, 1*l.* 5*s.* Digging up, 10*s.*

Parsneps these gardeners also cultivate in the same manner, but the crop never equal to that of carrots by fifty or sixty bushels.

Mr. *Lyster*, at *Bawtry*.
Soil. A very light sand.
Culture. No hoeing, but hand-weeding.
Produce. They are found to be of incomparable use in feeding hogs.

Duke of *Norfolk*, at *Workson*.
Soil. A light sand.
Culture. Hoes and weeds thoroughly.
Product. They answer incomparably.

Mr. *Hewett*, at *Bilham*.
Soil. A fine light hazel mould, a foot deep.
Culture. Sowed during four years, in drills one foot asunder, the middle of *April*; four pound and a half of seed per acre; horse-hoed thrice, and hand-weeded once. Left at the distance of six inches in the rows.
Product. Six hundred and forty bushels per acre, 32*l.* at 1*s.* per bushel. Beasts fatted on them and turneps, which evidently preferred the carrots so much, that it was soon difficult to make them eat the former at all. Six horses kept on them through the winter with oats: they performed their work as usual, and looked equally well. A lean hog was fatted on carrots in ten days time, eating nothing else, and the fat very fine, white, and firm, nor did it boil away in the dressing: he ate fourteen stone. Hogs in general feed on them with great eagerness.

Mr. *Turner*, at *Kirkleatham*.
Soil. A black rich sand, and a white poor one.
Culture. Six acres were sown in 1767, summer fallowed and sown broadcast the beginning of *April*, hand-weeded four times, and also hand-hoed; but

but the crop left within three or four inches of each other.

Product. The size in the black sand from six to eight inches long, but less than a man's wrist. In the white five inches long, and less than the other. Fed milch cows and hogs; the first very fond of them, and their milk received no ill taste from them. Several hogs of six stone (14*lb.*) were fatted on them. No pork could be finer. They fatted quick and exceedingly well. The carrots given raw.

Expence. Weeding, hoeing, and taking up, 2*l.* 10*s.* per acre.

Mr. *Scroope*, at *Danby*.
Soil. The rich fine black loam.
Culture. Drilled in single rows four feet asunder: horse-hoed thrice, but left thick in the rows.
Produce. Very fine; eighteen inches long, and eleven in circumference. Given to hogs, who fatted so well upon them, that a few pease finished them, and the fat was very fine and very firm.

Mr. *Wilkie*, of *Hetton*.
Soil. A light loam.
Culture. Sows the end of *March*; hoes them twice, to the distance of five inches.
Product. Grow to the size of a man's wrist, and twelve inches long. All cattle are very fond of them, particularly hogs.

These minutes clearly prove the great importance of the culture. The products, drawn into one view, are as follow: £. *s. d.*
Sandy gardeners, at 2*s.* per bushel, 200 } 20 0 0
Mr. *Hewett*, 640 bushels, at 1*s.* } 32 0 0
Ditto, at 2*s.* - - - 64 0 0

I think it fair to add the last valuation, as it is the actual one of the first inserted; nor do I think 2*s.* an extravagant price: the average is 38*l.* 13*s.* Rejecting the last price, it is 26*l.*

In the use of them several very important facts appear in the preceding intelligence. Mr. *Lyster's*, Mr. *Turner's*, Mr. *Hewett's*, Mr. *Scroope's*, and Mr. *Wilkie's* experiments all prove, that carrots raw are of incomparable use in both feeding and fattening hogs; the particular instances of fattening them quick and well are extremely valuable. It also appears from Mr. *Turner's* trials, that they are very fine food for milch cows, giving the butter no bad taste. Mr. *Hewett's* intelligence shews, that oxen fat to much advantage on them, and that they completely supply the place of oats to horses.

Of LUCERNE.

I SHALL review the experiments I minuted on several other vegetables besides cabbages, that are not commonly cultivated. Of these, lucerne claims the first attention.

Mr. *Bramstone*, at *Wooburn*.
Soil. Very loose, black, rich sand.
Culture. Broad cast; drilled at eighteen inches, and transplanted at two feet.
Product. The broad cast yields most at first; but it is apprehended that the drilled will exceed it, and that the transplanted will last longer than either.

Mr. *Middlemore*, at *Grantham*.
Soil. A red sand.

Cul-

Culture. A rood tranfplanted in rows, two feet six inches, in *March* 1767, I found it over-run with weeds. Two acres, three roods, broad caft, feven years old. Cleaned by harrowing.

Product. The tranfplanted cut once in 1767, and twice or thrice in 1768. The broad caft always cut three times a year. Often made into hay, a load an acre at each cutting. An acre lafts three horfes at foiling the fummer through; this, at fix months the fummer, and 2*s.* 6*d.* a week *per* horfe, amounts to 9*l.* 15*s. per* acre. All forts of cattle fed with it, but none affect it fo much as horfes.

Mr. *Lyfter,* at *Bawtry.*
Soil. A light fand.
Culture. Drilled five years ago in rows two feet afunder.
Product. Ufed for foiling horfes, but inferior to clover or natural paftures.

Mr. *Turner,* at *Kirkleatham.*
Soil. A rich loam.
Culture. Half an acre drilled in 1765, in equally diftant rows ten inches afunder. Kept clean from weeds by hand-hoeing.
Product. In 1766 cut five times, in 1767 five, in 1768 four. Maintains at the rate of four cows *per* acre through the fummer, which, at fix months, and 2*s. per* week *per* cow, is 10*l.* 8*s. per* acre.

Mr. *Dalton,* at *Sleningford.*
Soil. Shallow loam on limeftone rock. Rent at 8*s.*
Culture. Drilled in 1765, equally diftant rows, fix inches afunder.

Product. Cut three times in 1765, the fame in 1766 and 1767. Not comparable to fainfoine, nor equal to clover.

Mr. *Scroope,* at *Danby.*
Soil. A cold wet gravel, and a rich black loam, at 25*s.*
Culture. Drilled half an acre in 1761, the firft foil; but the plants all died the fecond year. In 1766 drilled feven rows, containing one rood eleven poles, equally diftant four feet on the fecond foil. Twice horfe and twice hand-hoed each year.
Product. Cut twice the firft year. The firft maintained four coach horfes and five calves fix weeks; the fecond kept feven horfes a month. In 1767 it was cut three times, and maintained feven horfes from the middle of *May* to the end of *September.* In 1768, fix horfes the fame time. It faved 12*s.* 10*d.* a week in hay for thefe fix horfes: the proportion for the feven, laft year, is, therefore, 14*s.* 11*c.* and the average 13*s.* 10½*d.*
The product, therefore, of thefe two years is this:
Twenty weeks } 13*l.* 17*s.* 6*d.*
at 13*s.* 10¼*d.* }
This *per* acre is 43*l.* 8*s.* 11*d.* This is a prodigious product, and, I think, much higher than the culture was ever before carried to.

Mr. *Penny,* at *Bendfworth.*
Soil. Sandy loam, at 21*s.*
Culture. Two acres drilled in 1761, in equal diftant rows, twelve inches afunder. Hand-hoed

hoed well for three or four years, and afterwards breast-ploughed twice a year.

Produce. In foiling horses, 16*l.* 12*s.* per acre.

Expences. Hand-hoeing, 40*s.* per acre. Breast ploughing, 5*s.*

From these several minutes we must, in the next place, draw an average of the whole. The product is the principal point.

	l.	*s.*	*d.*
Mr. *Middlemore,* per acre,	9	15	0
Mr. *Turner,*	10	8	0
Mr. *Scroope,*	43	8	11
Mr. *Penny,*	16	12	0

Average 20*l.*

This is a vast product, and certainly proves, in a very clear manner, the surprising excellencies of this vegetable.

The soil it requires to be in perfection appears clearly in the above table, for that of the latter three is very rich and deep; and Mr. *Scroope*'s, which yields so much the superior product, one of the blackest, richest, moist, crumbling loams I ever met with——the true *putre solum.* The great importance of an extreme rich soil to the culture of lucerne is, therefore, extremely evident; and it is equally plain that no use can pay better, if so well, as applying it to lucerne. Considering the smallness of the expences, Mr. *Scroope*'s crop far exceeds the profit of most hop-gardens.

In respect to manner of sowing, the broad cast is the least crop: Mr. *Scroope*'s four feet rows the greatest, Mr. *Penny*'s and Mr. *Turner*'s much the same, viz. one foot and ten inches. But the superiority of Mr. *Scroope*'s soil prevents our concluding absolutely that his distance is the most beneficial.

[Our ingenious and very industrious author has, in another work, given a regular detail of his own experiments upon this plant, in almost every degree and manner of cultivation; together with accurate estimates of the expence, the produce, and the profit: we shall conclude this article with an extract from it, which will shew the great benefits that may arise from a proper culture of lucerne.]

The effects of the rich manurings of former years, here appears clearly enough. The product is amazingly great; and the profit no less considerable. I know of no crop from which such great advantage is reaped that requires so little trouble; for the lucerne cannot be ranked with meadows and pastures, fed with cattle, in the small degree of attention requisite to them; yet, being a perennial crop, it spares the cultivator the round of various trouble demanded by annual ones. And as the culture bestowed on this noble grass is extremely similar every cutting and every year, it does not require that anxious attention which must be given to all sowings, &c. of annual crops. Any gentleman could better conduct the culture of 100 acres of lucerne, and with infinitely less probability of being cheated, than of 10 acres of corn.

This produce maintained at the rate of four horses 200 days; and a fifth 172 days. This is a greater produce than I should have conceived possible from one acre of land. Gentlemen who feed large coach-horses will not find such a produce in *time of keeping,* because

cause my horses are the small Suffolk ones, about 14¼ hands high: but their profit will be the same, as they must reckon a higher price per week.

In this experiment I have reckoned the cutting, made into hay, in the proportion of price as the others, having no rule to value the hay by; but I should observe, that lucerne seems much better adapted to feeding cattle with, mown green, than to making into hay; for it has not the quality of natural grass, of yielding good hay, notwithstanding some showers of rain. Common hay is often very good that has received no slight quantity of rain, providing it was made in a judicious manner: in this respect lucerne resembles clover, which is much more damaged by rain in making; or tares, which in very fine weather makes the finest of hay for hard working horses, but with a small quantity of rain becomes worse than straw. Now I would not be understood to think, that lucerne is so totally spoiled with a little rain: I know the contrary by experience; but, at the same time, it certainly will not bear the wet weather near so well as natural grass. This is no great objection to it; for the profit of it, in feeding horses, is so extremely great, that it would be extravagance to expect any thing farther.

In the product of this season, the increase from 1766 is very great, which shews what vigour the plants enjoyed from the preceding manuring. I complained

last year of the smallness of the profit owing to the expence of manuring, but the crops of this have amply repaid it. Reason must tell one, that a grass which is five times mown in full growth, in one season, must pay excellently for manure; and that it is very difficult to lay on too much.

The average profit upon the four first years, when the preparation is a fallow, and when two rich manurings are given, we find is but trifling: this evidently shews that lucerne should never be cultivated under the expectation of immediate payment; and that, being a perennial crop, an account of the three or four first years is the most disadvantageous light in which it can be viewed. Would to heaven I had it in my power to lay before the reader a register of twenty years! I feel the amazing profit which would then appear from lucerne.

Those who would form a true idea of the nature of this plant, should consider the first years as *preparation.* In fallowing land for any crop, the farmer does not expect that each ploughing should repay the expence, but looks forward two years for a reimbursement: in the case of this grass, the first years of it, when much is spent on it and little received, it should be the same; and the expectation of profit removed, till it is of a certain age, and well fixed in fertility and cleanness. In this way of considering the crop, the following division is the properest idea of the case.

PREPA-

PREPARATION.

	Expences.			Profit.			Lofs.		
	£.	s.	d.	£.	s.	d.	£.	s.	d.
1764,	7	0	4	0	0	0	5	7	4
1765,	2	19	11	3	5	1	0	0	0
1766,	8	11	5	2	4	11	0	0	0
	18	11	8	5	10	0	5	7	4
				5	7	4			
				0	2	8			
Average,	6	3	10	0	0	10			

CROP.

1767, — — 2 18 10   10 18 1

The year 1766, it is true, produces a vaft quantity; but as it is manured very richly, the expences ate out the profit, and fhould confequently be confidered as preparatory to the following years. The product of the three firft years we find juft pays the expence. After that year the annual profit would, beyond all doubt, continue very confiderable. That of 1767 is a noble beginning, and an earneft of great future profit.

But here it fhould farther be remembered, that, lucerne is not in perfection the fourth year.—I have already fhewn that there is at leaft a great probability of the fifth year being fuperior to the fourth: this is a circumftance that gives us reafon to fuppofe the regular permanent profit would not be inferior to this fourth year.

A profit of 10l. per acre gained from a perennial vegetable, I will venture to affert, exceeds any thing in hufbandry, *for gentlemen*. Hops, madder, liquorice, potatoes, and fome other crops, certainly exceed it, on fome foils, in the amount of profit; but fome of them are annuals, and others laft not above three years. Hops are, in particular, the moft troublefome culture that is known in the world fugar alone excepted. Now cro that laft but a year generally re quire to be fhifted from one fiel to another: if a man would ha annually fifty acres of potatoes, h muft farm, according to common management, 200 acres of land and thofe which are renewed a the end of two or three years a under the fame predicament, *ac cording to fome writers*; befides th cultivator having a perpetual roun of all that minute trouble whic attends the renovation of fuc crops.

But with lucerne the cafe is ve different: after it is once fowed, lafts many years; much longe from the beft accounts, than ar modern experiments refolve. attention it requires is very regu lar, and the operations to be per formed on it remarkably fimilar cuttin cutting as often as requisite, one horse-hoeing after each cutting, and a hand-hoeing when any weeds appear. No buying of seed, sowing, ploughing, harvesting, selling of corn, &c. &c. which render agriculture so troublesome to gentlemen. The product is open to no casualties; none of the misfortunes to which corn is liable; nor any of those evils that so regularly attend hay-making; but is all converted to the feeding of cattle, a business of the easiest kind.

If it be objected that the preceding experiments prove no more than the use of lucerne to horses, and that consequently a gentleman who undertook to cultivate it could extend his plantation no farther than the quantity requisite for his horses; in answer to this I should observe, that any food which is a good one for horses is also good for most other sorts of cattle. It is idle to suppose that a food which will fat a horse will not agree with a working ox—or a fat heifer—or feed cows or sheep, &c. &c. Reason (were experiment wanting) would be sufficient to make known these truths. Let any gentleman, therefore, cultivate lucerne to an extent, it is evident enough that he can never want a market for its produce, as long as he has money to buy cattle with.

Now can any gentleman wish for a better employment of his time and money than to expend in three years (according to this experiment) 18*l. per* acre in preparing for lucerne, the whole of which expence to be repaid him within that time, with an after annual profit of 10*l. per* acre. Such accurate elegant husbandry is an amusement; and in respect of profit, what more desirable than to enjoy 1000*l.* a year from 100 acres of land! To speak of 10,000*l.* a year from 1000 acres would sound like a great exaggeration; but yet it is a mere matter of multiplication, indubitably possible, and even easy.

Of SAINFOINE.

THIS grass is a common crop in many counties of this kingdom; but as several of the articles of intelligence concerning it are experimental, I shall treat of it here as I have done with the preceding grasses.

Mr. *Hewett* at *Bilham*.
   Soil. Fine hazel mould on limestone.
   Culture. Sow it with half a crop of barley after a fallow, or turneps, four bushels of seed *per* acre. Lasts twelve or fourteen years.
   Product. After the first year always mow the first growth for hay, 50 *cwt. per* acre, at 30*s.* a ton.

Sir *George Strickland*, at *Boynton*.
   Soil. Light wold land, at 2*s.* 6*d.*
   Product. Improves the land to 22*s.* 6*d. per* acre.

Sir *Digby Legard*, at *Ganton*.
   Soil. Light thin wold land, at 1*s.*
   Culture. Drilled one foot asunder.
   Product. A ton an acre of hay: improved to be well worth 10*s. per* acre.

Mr. *Dalton*, at *Slening ford*.
   Soil. Thin loam on a limestone, at 8*s.*

Culture. In 1764 fowed twelve acres after turnep, alone—and carefully weeded.

Product. Mows it once every year; it produces as much hay *per* acre as any three of natural grafs in the neighbourhood.

About *Benfington*.
Soil. Light chalk.
Culture. Sow a fack full of feed *per* acre; laft fifteen years.
Product. Mown once every year: 55 *cwt.* of hay *per* acre; the fecond crop fed off with lambs.

These trials all prove the great excellency of this grafs. The great improvement made by it on the poor wold lands by Sir *George Strickland*, and Sir *Digby Legard*, is a ftriking inftance; Mr. *Dalton*'s is alfo worthy of much notice. The products in weight are

	Tons	Cwt.
Mr. *Hewett*,	2	10
Sir *Digby Legard*,	1	0
About *Benfington*,	2	15

Average, 2 *tons*, 1 *cwt.*

From this ftate of the fainfoine culture, I cannot help remarking, how much the vaft tracts of poor light dry foils in this kingdom call for fo cheap and great an improvement: there are many very extenfive waftes in the north of *England* admirably adapted to this culture, and yet how few have the fpirit to fet about even this cheap and eafy improvement! The poor foils, on which this grafs is the greateft improvement, are not worth cultivating in any other manner: the common wold hufbandry is a proof of this. The yielding food for fheep is not a comparable produce to rich crops of excellent hay, and after feed; but nothing fpeaks this clearer than their letting only from 1*s*. to 4*s*. an acre, and being raifed by fainfoine to 10*s*. and 25*s*.

On the Number of Draught Cattle ufed in Tillage; from the fame.

THIS view of the ftate of tillage, throughout the counties I travelled, throws the whole matter into a very clear light: the refult is certainly furprizing. I never had any conception that a juft proportion would be found between the nature of the foil and the ftrength employed to till it; but that all common fenfe would be put fo totally to the blufh, was what I had little notion of. The equality of the draughts, on fuch different foils, is ftrange: the clay land takes no greater force than the loam; and the fand, within a feventh part as much as either of them. This fhews clearly, that cuftom alone has been the guide of the farmers in the number of draught cattle they ufe; a piece of abfurdity, which muft be attended with wretched effects on their profit, and fatal ones to the good of the kingdom at large.

Had the average draught of all foils been no greater than requifite, the evil would not have been fo great; but three and a half is more cattle than neceffary for any foil in *England*, provided the hufbandry is good. If fallows are broke up at the feafon they univerfally ought, two horfes, or two ftout oxen, are fufficient for the ftrongeft of all foils, alone excepting fuch as are on very fteep hills; and even in that cafe the courfe of ploughing ought

ought ever to be across the slope, which reduces the labour nearly to that of a level. Thus the grand average is near double the requisite strength. That of clay is the same as the general average: what, therefore, must be the excess of sand?

No farmer can urge the effect of long experience to this remark: his instancing the custom of his neighbours, and the prescription of ages, is of no avail; since nothing can be clearer than that custom and that experience are the effect of chance; not the result of reason, of knowledge, or experiment. No demonstration in mathematics can be clearer than the plain assertion, that clay requires a greater strength to work it than sand; which strength may as well lie in the quantity performed in a day, as in the number of cattle. This maxim every farmer will agree to; but they have no notion of the result of a general average.

But we find a yet greater equality in the quantity ploughed than in the number of cattle; nothing, therefore, is more certain, than the whole œconomy of tillage being quite a matter of chance. One cannot view a light sandy country ploughing with more than as many cattle as would till the strongest clays, without their performing more in quantity; one cannot think of such a course of business without indignation: thousands of families are deprived of half their subsistence; and the kingdom feeds millions of horses instead of industrious subjects. It is an object of infinite importance, and calls for attention from those who have it in their power to remedy so great an evil. The legislature certainly *might* interfere in some way which seemed most consistent with the delicacy of so free a people: but if nothing of that sort should be thought adviseable or, rather, if, among numerous other mattters, of equal import, overlooked or despised, to save time for ⸺ I cannot but recommend it to all landlords, to endeavour to remedy, on their own estates, such mischievous customs: there can be no doubt of its being in their power; all that is wanting is resolution: the moment a business is firmly resolved by a man who has money in his pocket, it is half executed. Prizes, rewards, bounties, &c. must be given, not only to farmers, but to ploughmen: both farmers and servants should be procured, that have been used to good customs, at any expence. It is well worth a landlord's thought; for he cannot introduce a cheap, and at the same time good method of culture, into a country, so as to make it common, without virtually raising his rents; besides the satisfaction which, I am confident, numbers must feel at being serviceable to their country.

In several of the richest and best cultivated parts of *Essex*, particularly between *Braintree* and *Hockerill*, by *Samford* and *Thasted*, the farmers do not keep above four or five horses *per* hundred acres of arable, which consequently perform all the work of the grass besides. Ten to a farm of two hundred arable, and one hundred grass, are reckoned a very complete allowance; and yet it is observable that the soil is a strong clay, strong enough to yield great crops of beans; and that many of the farms have

have much arable on the sides of hills, which makes the work pretty stout; yet they plough their land very well, and never use more than two in a plough, although they do not break up their stubbles till after barley sowing. Through the best cultivated parts of *Suffolk* it is the same: but as to nine horses to every hundred acres, it is a monstrous allowance: considering that it includes light loams and sands, it is at least five too many; so that more than double all the horses employed through this tract of country are kept to no purpose. When good husbandry and extraordinary tillage are the consequence of numerous teams, the objection is answered; but we very well know that is not the case, by clay farmers keeping no more than sand ones, and by the depth of stirring being the same in all. It is custom, not good husbandry, that occasions any variations at all. To reflect, for one moment, that half the horses employed in husbandry, through so considerable a part of the kingdom, are useless, is a very melancholy consideration: that useless horses are pernicious to the public good, is a fact indisputable. In no light whatever are they beneficial; they have nothing to do with the exportation of horses, supposing it a trade ever so beneficial; for it is consuming the commodity one's-self, which, in a commercial view, ought to be converted into money. It prevents the culture of a vast quantity of exportable corn. It takes great tracts of grass from fattening beasts, which yield plenty of butchers' meat, and consequently enables us to export the more corn, but gives no profit in return. No article of useful consumption is promoted by such extra horses; no industrious hands employed by them: in short, in every light the object can be viewed, the keeping such numbers of useless horses is a most pernicious conduct to agriculture, to the landlord, and to the public.

MISCEL-

MISCELLANEOUS ESSAYS.

Anecdotes of the Court of Peterſburg, *in the Reign of the Empreſs* Anne; *from General* Manſtein's Memoirs *of* Ruſſia.

THE Empreſs, though taken up with ſo expenſive and bloody a war, had, however, a mind to conclude the marriage which had been projected for many years between her niece, Princeſs Anne of Mecklenburgh, and Prince Anthony Ulrick of Brunſwick, who had reſided at the court ever ſince the year 1733.

The Marquis of Botta, who had ſucceeded to Count Oſtein, in quality of miniſter of the court of Vienna, took the character of ambaſſador; and, in a public audience, demanded, in the name of the Emperor, the Princeſs Anne in marriage for Prince Anthony Ulrick, nephew to the Empreſs of the Romans.

The eſpouſals were ſolemnized a few days after this audience, and on the 14th of July (1739) they were celebrated with all poſſible magnificence.

The equipages and dreſſes that were to appear at this ceremony had been preparing for a twelve-month before.

The Archbiſhop of Novogorod pronounced the nuptial bleſſing in the church of the Holy Virgin of Caſan, and made on this occaſion a ſermon much admired, that was printed.

When the Empreſs Elizabeth aſcended the throne, it was ſuppreſſed, there being ſeveral ſtrokes in it that were not reliſhed.

On the day of that ceremony no one imagined that the union of the Prince and Princeſs would one day produce their greateſt misfortune, as well as that of many perſons of diſtinction. The Princeſs Anne was then looked on as the preſumptive heireſs of the crown; I am perſuaded, too, that ſhe could not have failed of it, if the Duke of Courland had not oppoſed it.

Theſe nuptials, however, furniſh me the hint of giving an idea of the magnificence of the court, and of the Empreſs's uſual manner of living.

The Duke of Courland was a great lover of pomp and ſplendid ſhow: this was enough to inſpire the Empreſs with a deſire to have her court the moſt brilliant of all Europe. Conſiderable ſums were ſacrificed to this intention of the Empreſs, which was not, for all that, ſo ſoon fulfilled. The richeſt coat would be ſometimes worn together with the vileſt uncombed wig; or you might ſee a beautiful piece of ſtuff ſpoiled by ſome

some botcher of a tailor; or, if there was nothing amifs in the drefs, the equipage would be deficient. A man richly dreffed would come to court in a miferable coach, drawn by the wretchedeft hacks. The fame want of tafte reigned in the furniture and neatnefs of their houfes. On one fide you might fee gold and silver plate in heaps, on the other a fhocking dirtinefs.

The drefs of the ladies corresponded with that of the men; for one well-dreffed woman you might fee ten frightfully disfigured: yet is the fair fex in Ruffia generally handfome; that is to fay, they have good faces enough, but very few have fine fhapes.

This incongruity of Ruffian finery and fhow was almoft univerfal: there were few houfes, indeed, efpecially in the firft years of the reform, where every thing was of a piece. Little by little, others imitated the example of thofe who had tafte. But, not even the court, nor Biron, fucceeded at the firft in getting every thing into that order and arrangement which are feen elfewhere. This was the work of years. Yet muft it be owned, that, at length, every thing grew to be well regulated, except that the magnificence ran into excefs, and coft the court immenfe fums. It is incredible how much money went out of the empire upon this account. A courtier that did not lay out above two or three thoufand rubles, or from four to fix hundred pounds a year in his drefs, made no great figure. One might very well apply here the faying of a Saxon officer to the late King of Poland, advifing him to widen the gates of the town to let in the whole villages that the gentlemen carried on their backs. In Ruffia, all thofe who had the honour to ferve the court hurt their fortunes by over-dreffing, the falaries not being fufficient to afford the making fuch a figure. It was enough for a dealer in the commodities of luxury and fafhion to remain two or three years at Peterfburgh to gain a competency for the reft of his life, even though he fhould have begun the world there with goods upon credit.

The Emprefs's ufual manner of life was very regular. She was always up before eight in the morning. At nine fhe began to difpatch affairs with her fecretary and minifters. At noon fhe dined in her chamber with the Biron family. It was only in the great folemnities that fhe ate in public. When that happened, fhe was placed in a throne, under a canopy, with the two Princeffes, Elizabeth, fince Emprefs, and Anne of Mecklenburgh. On this occafion the high-chancellor waited at table. Here was commonly alfo a great table in the fame hall, for the firft noblemen and ladies of the empire, for the clergy and foreign minifters. But in the laft years of the Emprefs's life fhe did not any longer eat in public, nor were the foreign minifters treated at the court. In the greateft feftivals, Count Ofterman invited them to dinner with him.

In fummer the Emprefs took a good deal of exercife in walking; and in winter with playing at billiards. She made light fuppers, and went early to bed, between eleven and twelve.

The court ufed to pafs the beft part of the fine feafon at a fummerhoufe, mer-house, which Peter I. had built about seven leagues distance from Petersburgh, called Peterhoff. It is one of the most pleasant situations that can be imagined. It stands on the sea side; whence you may, on the left side, see Cronstadt, and the whole fleet; on the right there is a prospect of Petersburgh, and over against it are the coasts of Finland. There is a spacious garden to it, and magnificent *jet d'eaux*, but the house is no great matter: the apartments are extremely small and low.

The rest of the summer, the Empress resided at her summer palace at Petersburgh, which is far from being a good building, on the banks of the Neva: the garden to it is very large, and well enough kept in order.

The Princess Anne caused a new house to be set about, the old one falling almost to ruins, but had not time to finish it. It was reserved for the Empress Elizabeth to see the last hand put to it.

There was deep play at court: many made their fortune by it in Russia, and many others were ruined. I have myself often seen as far as twenty thousand rubles lost in one sitting at *quinze* or at *pharaoh*.

The Empress did not much love play; if she did play, it was only to lose. She then held the bank; and none were allowed to punt but those to whom she called. The person that won was immediately paid; but as they played with counters, she never received the money of those who lost.

She was fond of public entertainments and music, and sent for from Italy all that was necessary for that purpose. Comedies, acted both in Italian and in German, pleased her extremely. In 1736, the first opera was played at Petersburgh, and very well executed, though less liked than comedy, and the Italian interludes.

In the time of Peter I. and in the following reigns, drinking had been much practised at court; it was not so in the time of Anne: she could not bear to see any one drunk. There was nobody but Prince Kourakin that had free permission to drink as much as he pleased. But that the habit of it might not be entirely lost, the 29th of January (Old Style), being the day of the Empress's accession to the throne, was consecrated to Bacchus. Then every one was obliged to toss off a great bumper of Hungary wine, with one knee on the ground, in the presence of her Majesty. This reminds me of another singular enough ceremony. On the eve of the great festivals, the courtiers, and officers of the guards, had the honour of paying their compliments to her Majesty, and of kissing her hand: her Majesty at the same time presented each a glass of wine on a salver.

Towards the end of the year 1739, the Empress gave a comic entertainment. Prince Gallitzin was the occasion of it. Though above forty years of age, and even having a son serving in the army, in the rank of lieutenant, he was made at once page and buffoon of the court, by way of punishment for his having changed his religion. His first wife being dead, the Empress told him he ought to marry again, and that she would be at the expence of the wedding. He accepted the proposal; and, pitching

upon

upon a girl in low life, acquainted the Empress of his choice, and claimed her promise. The Empress, in giving this entertainment, had a mind, at the same time, to see how many different kinds of inhabitants there, were in her vast dominions. Accordingly, she caused orders to be dispatched to the governors of the provinces to send up to Petersburgh several persons of both sexes. These being arrived, they, at the expence of the court, were new dressed, each in the habit of his respective country.

Monsieur de Walinsky was appointed manager of the arrangements for this wedding, and winter was the season chosen for the celebration of it. The Empress, to make it the more completely extraordinary, had a house built wholly of ice: it consisted of two chambers, in which every thing of furniture, even the bed-place on which the new-married couple were to lie, was to be of ice. There were four small cannon and two mortars, made of the same matter. The cannon were fired several times, with half an ounce of powder in each, without bursting; and little wooden grenades were thrown out of the mortars without their being damaged.

On the wedding-day that the feast was to be celebrated, all the guests were assembled in the court-yard of Walinsky: thence the procession sat out, and passed before the imperial palace, and through the principal streets of the town. There was a great train, consisting of more than three hundred persons. The new-married couple were placed upon an elephant, in a great cage. The guests, two and two, were in a sledge, drawn by all kinds of beasts, as rein-deer, dogs, oxen, goats, hogs, &c. Some were mounted on camels. After the procession had gone the round prescribed to it, it was brought into the Duke of Courland's riding-house, where a flooring of planks had been laid for the purpose, and where there was a dinner prepared for them on several tables. Each was treated according to the manner of cookery in his own country. After the repast, there was a ball: each nation had its own music, and its own way of dancing. When the ball was over, the bridegroom and bride were conducted into the house of ice, where they were put into a dismally cold bed, with guards posted at the door, that they might not get out before morning.

In the month of August, the court ordered the seizure of Monsieur de Walinsky, minister of the cabinet: of the Count Mouschkin-Pouschkin, president of the college of trade; of the privy-counsellor Chroutschew; of the superintendant of the board of works, Jerepkin; of the private secretary of the cabinet, Eichler; and of another secretary, called Sowda. There were several crimes laid to Walinsky's charge; but his greatest crime was, the misfortune of having incurred the Duke of Courland's displeasure.

During some days of coolness between the Empress and her favourite the Duke, Walinsky had given this Princess a memorial, in which he accused the Duke of Courland, and several others, who were about her Majesty. But he particularly aimed at infusing into her suspicions of the Duke, and advised the Empress to dismiss him.

This

This Princess having made it up with her favourite, had the weakness to put this memorial into his hands, in which there were but too many truths. The Duke had no sooner read it than he resolved the ruin of his secretary; and as Walinsky was a man extremely haughty, impetuous, and often imprudent in his talk, and even in his actions, the other soon found the occasion he was seeking.

He was tried, and convicted of having often been guilty of speeches too free, and too disrespectful against the Empress and her favourite; so that he was condemned, first to have his hand cut off, and then his head. The sentence was executed. The privy-counsellor Croutschew, and Jerepkin, were also beheaded, because they were his friends and confidants. The Count Moufckin Pouschkin had his tongue cut out; Eichler and Sowda underwent the knout, and were sent to Siberia. All the estates of these unfortunate persons were confiscated, and given to others, who did not possess them long after them. In this manner it is, that, in Russia, not only money, but even lands, houses, and moveables, circulate quicker than in any other country in Europe. I have seen lands change masters at least thrice in the space of two years.

Walinsky was one that had wit, but a boundless ambition, a great deal of pride, vanity, and indiscretion. He was fond of forming cabals, and was all his life-time reckoned a turbulent spirit. Notwithstanding these faults, which he did not even know how to conceal, he had raised himself to the first posts of the empire. He had begun by serving in the military, where he had arrived at the rank of major-general. Having quitted the army, he was employed in the affairs of the state. Already, under the reign of Peter I. he had been sent as minister into Persia; he had been second of the embassy at the congress of Nemirow; and Count Jagousinsky dying towards the end of the year 1736, he had, two years after, the post of minister in the cabinet, where he could not keep himself long, before he had disputes with Count Osterman, who naturally did not love parts or wit in his colleagues: having, besides, drawn upon himself the resentment of the Duke of Courland, he could not well avoid coming to an unfortunate end.

[To these anecdotes we shall add the assassination of Major Sinclair, an instance of the detestable politics which at that time prevailed in the court of Petersburgh.]

I have precedently observed, that there was a talk of a treaty between Sweden and the Porte. Monf. de Bestuchoff, who resided at Stockholm, in quality of minister of Russia, gave advice to his court, that Major Sinclair had been sent to Constantinople, whence he was to bring back the ratification of this treaty. Upon this news, Marshal Munich, by order of the cabinet, sent certain officers, accompanied by some subalterns, into Poland, who were to disperse themselves into different places, and try to carry off Sinclair on his return from Constantinople; to take away all his letters and dispatches, and even to kill him, in case of resistance. The officers, as they could not be every where, employed some Jews, and some of the poorer Polish gentlemen, to get information of the

the arrival of Sinclair, so that the danger was divulged before he set his foot on the territories of Poland; and he had warning from the governor of Chockzim to take care of himself, for that there were lying in wait for him several Russian officers, particularly at Lemberg or Leopol, by the way of which he had proposed to pass. Upon this, Sinclair changed his rout, and the Bashaw of Chockzim gave him an escort that saw him safe to Broda, where the crown-general of Poland was, who gave him another escort, with which he got safe into Silesia. There he thought himself safe; but having been obliged to stop a few days at Breslaw, the Russian officers, who learnt by their spies the road he had taken, pursued, and overtook him within a mile of Newstadel. There they stopped him, took away his arms; and, after having carried him some miles farther, massacred him in a wood. After this noble stroke, they took his cloaths and his papers, in which, however, nothing of consequence was found. The court of Russia having had them examined, sent them some months afterwards by the post to Hamburgh, whence they were forwarded to Sweden.

The Empress disavowed this execrable action, protesting solemnly her having no knowledge of it. Her ministers presented memorials to all the courts, to remove all suspicion that might have been entertained of that of Russia; and that the assassins themselves might not be able to betray the secret, they were all seized and sent to Siberia, where they spent some years in dungeons, till the Empress Elizabeth, ascending the throne, released them, and had them placed in garrison regiments in the innermost parts of the country.

Those employed in this affair were, the secretary Kuttle, native of Silesia, the lieutenants Lesowitzky and Wesselowsky, both subjects of Russia, each of whom had two subalterns to assist them. The two first committed the assassination; the third remained in Poland, but underwent, nevertheless, the same treatment as the others.

Certain it is, that the Empress did not know the orders that were given to the officers about Sinclair, and that a great part of these proceedings was concealed from her even after the assassination. All this affair was juggled up among the Duke of Courland, Count Osterman, and Marshal Munich.

[We shall conclude this article with an account of the manner in which the election of Count Biron to the dutchy of Courland was conducted, and some anecdotes of the consequent government of that country.]

It was in the year 1737, that Count Biron was elected Duke of Courland. The Duke Ferdinand, of the house of Kettler, died at Dantzick, by which demise all the male line was extinct. The court of Petersburgh, on receiving advice of this, instantly ordered General Bismark, governor of Riga, to enter that dutchy with the troops under his command, to support the election of a new duke. The nobility of Courland having, in the mean while, assembled at Mittaw, repaired to the cathedral, where, after having sung the *Veni Creator*, Ernest John de Biron was elected Duke of Courland by a majority of votes. Here it is to be observed, that the General Bismark had posted
some

some companies of horse in the church-yard of the cathedral, and in the town, so that the election could not fail. The nobility of Courland, which had been very splendid, and had enjoyed great liberty under the government of the preceding dukes, saw itself all on a sudden in quite another situation. No one durst open his mouth without incurring the risk of being seized, and sent to Siberia. For executing this, a most particular mode of procedure was used. The party who had given offence by speaking, was, in the moment he the least thought of it, laid hold of by persons in masks, who threw him into a covered carriage, and conveyed him to the remotest provinces of Russia. There were several of these seizures attended with spiriting away in that manner, during the three years that the Duke Ernest John reigned, but one, among others, so singular and so comic, that I cannot well resist the temptation of inserting it here.

A gentleman, whose name was Sacken, standing one evening before the door of his country-house, was carried off and thrown into one of these covered carriages. He was for near two years carried about several provinces, without suffering him to see any human creature, not even his conductors themselves ever appearing before him barefaced. At the end of that time, one night the horses were taken out of the carriage, and he was left to lie in it. There he remained quietly till the morning, in the expectation of being made to continue his journey as usual. Broad day-light came on, without any one's coming to him, and all on a sudden he heard persons talking in the Courland language, near his carriage; upon which he opened it, and finds himself at the door of his own house. He made his complaints to the Duke, who did not fail of acting the farce of representing his grievance to the court of Russia; whence an answer came, that, if he could point out the persons who had done this action, he would take care to have them rigorously punished.

Three Letters, supposed to have been written by the celebrated M. Montesquieu.

LETTER I.

To M. Le Chevalier de BRUANT.

I WAS not at *** when your letter came; you embarrass me greatly: I shall only answer you for the pleasure of entertaining myself with a man who is much better able to resolve the doubts which he proposed, than the person to whom he sent them.

I am not of your opinion with regard to despotism and despotic princes. It appears to me horrible and absurd, to the last degree, that a whole people should blindly subject themselves to the caprice of one, even if he were an angel. For my own part, I would not live under him a single day. This angel may become in a moment a monster, thirsting after blood. Despotism is to me the most abominable and disgustful of all bad governments: a man is perpetually crushed, debased, and degraded, by it. Look into history, antient and modern, if ever there

there was one upon earth that was not an insult on mankind, and the disgrace of human nature. Monarchy would, doubtless, be the best of governments, if it was possible to find such kings as Henry IV.: the only one who ever deserved the homage and veneration of his subjects. Kings should always be brought up in a school of affliction, as this great man was: such alone are truly great, and the lovers of mankind. Before we can feel for the misfortunes of others, we must ourselves have been unfortunate. But, on the other hand, the hearts of princes, corrupted by prosperity, and the slaves of pride and folly, are inaccessible to pity, and insensible of true glory.

I am not at all surprised, that, in monarchies, and especially in our own, there should be so few princes worthy of esteem. Incircled by corruptors, knaves, and hypocrites, they accustom themselves to look upon their fellow-creatures with disdain, and set no value on any but the sycophants who caress their vices, and live in perpetual idleness and inactivity. Such is generally the condition of a monarch: great men are always scarce, and great kings still more so. Add to this, that the splendor of a monarchy is short and transitory. France is already sunk into misery and disgrace: an age more will annihilate her, or she will fall a prey to the first intrepid conqueror.

The English government has nothing to support it but a delusive outside, extremely flattering to the people, who fancy themselves the sole governors. I do not know any country where it is more easy to create such open dissensions as may overthrow the state. A man of sense and generosity may, in ten years time, erect himself into a despotic prince with more safety at London than Moscow: remember Cromwell. Money alone is sufficient to corrupt the whole parliament.

The great, ever fond of riches and power, and prostrate at the feet of fortune, who always attends the throne, will promote the views of their master; and the great, once gained over, this phantom of liberty, which appeared at intervals in the convulsive motions of the commons, which awakens, shakes itself, and soon vanishes, will be totally annihilated at the first signal given by the supreme ruler.

I know, indeed, of no monarchy that is fixed, constant, and perfect: the wisest kings oppress their subjects to arrive at despotism. Adieu, my friend; live in freedom and obscurity. Solitude will procure you the best and truest pleasure,—self-content. The foolish and the wicked, seen afar off, will only excite your compassion: to look nearly upon them would raise your contempt and indignation.

I write this in haste: we will treat this matter more fully in the free intercourse of guiltless friendship.

'LETTER II.

YOU ask me in what country a man may enjoy the most perfect liberty? In every place, my dear Philinthus, where there are men and laws. The wise man is free even in the court of a tyrant, because his happiness depends on himself. Reason and conscience

conscience are the throne of his liberty. It is not in the power of fortune, injustice, or any thing else, to unhinge his soul, or disturb his repose. He rejoices in himself, and his joy is always calm, permanent, and delightful.

Would you, my friend, because you see violence and iniquity every day committed by wicked ministers, by the rich and great, by almost every man in place and power; would you, therefore, entirely banish yourself from that society to which you are indebted for every thing, and for which every honest and good member of it should yield up all, without repining at the injuries which he suffers from it? because a prince buries himself in sloth and debauchery; because he persecutes, oppresses, and destroys, shall you become an exile from your country, leave your friends, and desert the poor and afflicted, who apply to you for relief, and rend your heart with their complaints? No, my friend; you have too much sensibility. Despise the unjust and cruel prince, but love mankind; and, above all, the unfortunate and distressed. Avoid the impetuous whirlwinds of a court: forget, if possible, that your king is surrounded with perverse, wicked, and oppressive men, who laugh at his ignorance, and avail themselves of his weakness. Fly to retirement, in search of that repose, friendship, and felicity, which are never to be found in the seats of power and grandeur, or in the dangerous and delusive tumults of a noisy metropolis. Bring with you a few friends, as worthy and sensible as yourself. Read Plato, Montagne, Charron, and Rabelais; exercise yourself in acts of kindness to the poor labourers, the only creatures upon earth who are always miserable, perpetually toiling to supply the necessities of nature, and victims to the cruel rapacity of the farmers-general, who grind and oppress them.

Thus will you enjoy the most delicate and lively of all pleasures, —the pleasure of doing good, the only consolation that can reconcile us to the miseries of human life. When once you are habituated to a country life, joy and peace will revive in your disquieted and uneasy mind, which will grow strong and great, raising itself by degrees to the celestial regions of genius and philosophy. There, free as the air you breathe, throw out your thoughts as they arise: your soul will then shoot forth such divine flames as shall warm and enlighten even the cold and ignorant. When you have filled your paper, arrange and correct the whole, and I will tell you with the utmost freedom my opinion of it. Adieu, my dear friend: with a heart of such delicate sensibility as your's is, youth, health, and a tolerable fortune, you must be happy, if happiness is the portion of virtue.

LETTER III.

YOU are right, my dear Philintbus, in believing and asserting to all your friends that education makes the man. That alone, is the parent of every virtue; it is the most sacred, the most useful, and at the same time the most neglected thing in almost every country, and in every station of life. But too many vague and impracticable rules have been laid down

down on this important subject. Even the wise Locke, the great instructor of mankind, is sometimes mistaken, like other writers. All education should have an eye to government, or we lose our aim. The man of patience and understanding will consider well the mind he has to form and instruct; he will infuse by little and little maxims adapted to his age, and suited to his genius, rank, and capacity. I know that there are some soils barren and ungrateful, and which will never answer the labour of the cultivator. But besides that such are very uncommon, I am inclined to suspect, that frequently the tiller has neither strength nor skill enough to dig into and improve it as he ought.

There is one radical vice in France, which may, perhaps, never be extirpated, because it comes from the women, who, amongst us, interfere in every thing, and in the end ruin, and destroy every thing. A child is soon spoiled in their hands, from two years old to six; when he is delivered up, without consideration, to a man whom he has neither seen nor known. The tutor, perhaps a fellow of no character, takes charge of him, not from inclination, but merely from his own interest. For ten succeeding years he vegetates in the narrow circle of a college, or in the unimproving converse and society of prating females of quality. These tutors are generally appointed by the women, who seldom look any farther than the outside; never considering personal merit, which they have not sense enough to distinguish, having never habituated themselves to reflect one moment on any thing serious or useful.

Another circumstance highly prejudicial to education, and which disgusts and deters men of merit from engaging in it, is the little regard paid to the tutor or preceptor, who ought to be respected as a father, whose place he is, in a great measure, intended to supply: he to whom is intrusted the heir of an illustrious name and family; he who is to form the worthy citizen, and the good subject; who is to do honour to his rank and character, and become the glory of his country. Such are the men, charged as they are with so important an office, who, in the fashionable world, are so often despised and ill-treated, and even sometimes suffered to perish for want. Such abuses, if they become general, must point out a shameful and universal depravity of manners. Our nobility, indeed, are free from this reproach: if they pay but indifferently, they make amends by the weight of their interest, and a thousand engaging civilities, for the small appointment which their fortune will permit them to allow. Your rich financiers, on the other hand, who are naturally morose, proud, and ostentatious, seldom pay a man without affronting him: having nothing but money to give, they gorge you with it.

In France the women ruin every thing, because they think themselves fit for every thing, and the men are weak and childish enough to humour their caprice. Nature, notwithstanding, made them but to obey, and the weakness of their constitution every day points out to us the weakness of their sex. With regard to education, it is worse at court than in any other place: the governor having a despotic power over his pupil, suffers

him

him to grow up in ignorance and idleness, fills his head with the nonsense of fashion, and puffs him up with the notion of his own rank, and a contempt of the insignificant creatures that crawl beneath him. Every thing around him is to be made subservient to his pleasure or advancement. Every thing is to fall down before him on the first notice. He never talks to him concerning the royal virtues that adorn a throne, justice, courage, beneficence, intrepidity, and the love of glory; therefore it is, that, amongst our kings, we never see a great man; for I call not the conqueror by that name, but rather consider him as the terror, scourge, and disgrace of humankind; one whom the people are bound by their own interest to destroy, as soon as the flame of his ambition breaks forth in projects of slaughter and oppression.

Lewis XII. was honest and just, but weak and ignorant. Francis I. a vain boaster, cruel, and a pretender to wit. Henry IV. brave and magnanimous; but too much given to women ever to become a philosopher. Lewis XIV., at once the greatest and meanest of mankind, would have excelled all the monarchs in the universe, if he had not been corrupted in his youth by base and ambitious flatterers. A slave during his whole life to pride and vain-glory, he never really loved his subjects, even for a moment; yet expected at the same time, like a true arbitrary prince, that they should sacrifice themselves to his will and pleasure. Intoxicated with power and grandeur, he imagined the whole world was made but to promote his happiness. He was feared, obeyed, idolized, hated, mortified, and abandoned. He lived like a sultan, and died like a woman. His reign was immortalized by the lowest of his subjects.

It is, therefore, my dear Philiathus, impossible there should ever be a great man amongst our kings, who are made brutes and fools of all their lives by a set of infamous wretches, who surround and beset them from the cradle to the grave.

Letter from Voltaire *to the Duke of* Valiere; *from* Voltaire's *Letters, lately translated by Dr.* Franklin.

YOU resemble, my Lord, the heroes of antient chivalry, by thus exposing your own person in defence of your faithful followers, when in danger; but the little error which you led me into has been the means of displaying your profound erudition. Few grand falconers would have delivered the *Sermones Festivi*, printed in 1502. Raillery apart, to put yourself in the breach for me, was an action worthy of your noble heart.

You told me, in your first letter, that Urceus Codrus was a great preacher; your second informs me he was a great libertine, but no Cordelier. You ask pardon of St. Francis, and all the seraphic order, for the contempt into which I am fallen. I join with you, and put on my penitentials; but it still remains true, that the mysteries represented at the Hotel de Bourgogne were more decent than most of our modern sermons. Place who we please in the room of Urceus Codrus,

Codrus, and we shall yet be in the right. There is not a word in the mysteries offensive to piety and good manners. Forty people would never agree to write and act sacred poems in French, that should disgust the public by their indecency, and of course oblige them to shut up their doors. But an ignorant preacher, who works by himself, and is accountable to none for what he does, who has no idea of decorum, may very probably advance some ridiculous things in his sermon, especially when he delivers it in Latin. Such, for instance, are the discourses of the Cordelier Maillard, which you undoubtedly have in your large and valuable collection. In his sermon on the Thursday in the second week of Lent, he addresses himself thus to the lawyers' wives that wore gowns embroidered with gold.

"You say you are cloathed according to rank: go to the devil, ladies, you and your rank together. You will tell me, perhaps, Our husbands don't give us these fine gowns; we earn them by the industry of our own sweet bodies: thirty thousand devils take your industry, and your bodies, too."

I will not put you to the blush, by quoting any more passages from brother Maillard; but if you will take the trouble to look into him, you will find some strokes worthy of Urceus Codrus. Brother Andrew and Minot were likewise famous for their filthiness. The pulpit was not indeed always polluted by obscenity: but for a long time sermons were little better than the mysteries of the Hotel de Bourgogne.

It must be acknowledged, that the members of what they call the reformed church in France were the first that brought reasoning and argument into their discourses. When we want to change the ideas and alter the principles of men, we must make use of reason; but this was still very far from eloquence. The pulpit, the bar, the stage, philosophy, literature, theology, every thing we could boast of in those times, some few particulars excepted, were beneath the common pieces exhibited at a country fair.

True taste was not established amongst us till the reign of Lewis XIV. It was this which long since determined me to attempt a slight sketch of that glorious æra; and you must have observed, in that history, the age is my hero more than Lewis himself, what respect and gratitude soever may be due to his memory.

It is true, indeed, that, in general, our neighbours made no greater figures than ourselves. How happened it that men could preach for ever, and yet preach so badly! and that the Italians, who had so long before shook off their barbarity in other respects, with regard to the pulpit were but so many harlequins with surplices on! Whilst at the same time the Jerusalem of Tasso rivalled the Iliad, and Orlando Furioso surpassed the Odyssey, Pastor Fido had no model in all antiquity, and Raphael and Paul Veronese actually performed what was only imagined of Zeuxis and Apelles.

You must certainly, my Lord, have read the council of Trent. There is not a peer in the kingdom, I suppose, who does not peruse

peruse some part of it every morning. You remember the sermon at the opening of the council by the Bishop of Bitonto.

'He proves, first, that the council is necessary, because several councils have deposed kings and emperors. Secondly, because, in the Æneid, Jupiter assembles a council of the gods. Thirdly, because, at the creation of man, and the building of Babel, God attended to it in the manner of a council. He insists on it, a little after, that the council should reduce themselves to thirty, like the heroes in the Trojan horse. And, finally, asserts, that the gate of Paradise and the gate of the council was the same thing. That living water flowed from it, with which the holy fathers should sprinkle their hearts, which were as dry lands; or, in lieu of this, that the Holy Ghost would open their mouths like the mouths of Balaam and Caiphas.

This, my Lord, was preached before all the general states of Christendom. The sermon of St. Anthony of Padua to the fish is still more famous in Italy than that of the Bishop of Bitonto; we may excuse, therefore, our brother Andrew, brother Garasse, and all the Giles's of our pulpits in the sixteenth and seventeenth centuries, as they were but on a level with our masters the Italians. What could be the cause of this gross ignorance, so universally spread over Italy in the time of Tasso; over France in the days of Montagne, Charron, and the Chancellor de l'Hospital; and over England in the age of Bacon? How happened it that these men of genius did not reform the times they lived in? We must attribute it to the colleges where youth were educated; to that monkish theologic spirit which finished the barbarism that the colleges had introduced. A genius, as Tasso was, read Virgil, and produced the Jerusalem. A merchant read Terence, and wrote Mandragora: but what monk or curate, at that time of day, read Tully or Demosthenes? A poor and wretched scholar, grown half an ideot by being obliged, for four years together, to get John Despautere by heart; and half a madman by supporting a thesis *de rebus & partibus*, on thoughts and categories, received his cap, and his letters of recommendation, and away he went to preach to an audience, three parts of whom were greater fools, and worse educated, than himself.

The people listened to these theological farces with outstretched necks, fixed eyes, and open mouths, as children do to stories of witches and apparitions, and returned home perfect penitents. The same spirit that made them give ear to the nonsense of a foolish mother, led them to these sermons, which they attended the more diligently, as it cost them nothing. It was not till the time of Coeffeteau and Balzac that some preachers began to talk rationally; though at the same time they were very tiresome. Bourdaloue, in short, was the first man of any eloquence in the pulpit. Of this, Burnet, Bishop of Salisbury, bears testimony, in his Memoirs; where he tells us, that, in travelling through France, he was astonished at his sermons; and that Bourdaloue reformed the preachers of England, as well as those of France.

Bourdaloue might be styled almost the Corneille of the pulpit, as Massillon became afterwards the Racine of it. Not that I mean to compare an art, half profane, to a ministry wellnigh holy; nor, on the other hand, the little difficulty of making a good sermon to the great and inexpressible one of composing a good tragedy. I only say, that Bourdaloue carried the art of reasoning as far in preaching as Corneille did in the drama; and that Massillon studied to be as elegant in prose as Racine was in verse. True indeed it is, that Bourdaloue was reproached as well as Corneille for being too much of a lawyer, for preferring argument to passion, and sometimes producing but indifferent proofs. Massillon, on the other hand, chose rather to paint than to affect; he imitated Racine as much as it was possible to do it in prose: not forgetting, at the same time, boldly to assert, that all dramatic authors would be damned. Every quack, you know, must cry up his own nostrum, and condemn those of others. His style is pure; his descriptions moving and pathetic. Read over this passage on the humanity of the great.

" Alas! if any of us have an
" excuse for being morose, whim-
" sical, and melancholy, a bur-
" then to ourselves and all about
" us, it must be those miserable
" wretches, whom misfortunes,
" calamities, home-felt necessity,
" and gloomy cares, perpetually
" surround. They might be for-
" given, if with mourning, bit-
" terness, and despair, already in
" their hearts, the marks of it
" should sometimes appear in their
" external behaviour. But shall
" the great and happy of this
" world, whom joy and pleasure
" accompany, whilst every thing
" smiles around them; shall these
" pretend to derive, even from
" their felicity, an excuse for their
" churlishness and caprice? Shall
" they be melancholy, disquieted,
" and unsociable, because they
" are more happy? Shall they
" look upon it as the privilege of
" prosperity to oppress with the
" weight of their ill humour the
" poor and unfortunate, who al-
" ready groan beneath the yoke of
" their power and authority?"

Recollect, at the same time, these lines in Britannicus:

Tout ce que vous voyez conspire
à vos desirs,
Vos jours toujours serins coulent
dans les plaisirs
L'empire en est pour vous l'in-
épuisable source,
Ou si quelque chagrin en inter-
rompt la course.
Tout l'univers, soignant de les
entretenir
S'empresse a l'effacer de votre
souvenir.
Britannicus est seul, quelqu' en-
nai qui le presse,
Il ne voit dans son sort que moi
qui l'interesse,
Et n'a pour tous plaisirs, seig-
neur, que quelque pleurs
Qui lui font quelquefois oublier
ses malheurs.

Whate'er thou seest conspires to
make thee happy,
Serene thy days in endless pleasures flow,
From the wide empire's unex-
hausted spring;
Or if intruding sorrow, for a
while,
Breaks in upon thy joys, the
world itself,
Still anxious for thy good, with
ardour strives
To blot out every painful, sad
idea,
And

MISCELLANEOUS ESSAYS. 147

And give thee peace again.—
Britannicus,
Mean time, is left alone: when cares oppress,
I, only I, participate his griefs,
And all his comfort is the tears I shed,
Which sometimes makes the wretch forget his sorrows.

In comparing these two passages together, I perceive the scholar, as it were, contending with his master. I could shew you twenty more examples of the same nature, but that I am afraid of being tedious.

Massillon and Cheminais knew Racine by heart, and disguised the verses of that divine poet in their pious prose. In the same manner several preachers learned the art of declamation from Baron, and corrected the gesture of the comedian by that of the sacred orator. Nothing can be a stronger proof than this, that the arts at least are brothers, though the artists themselves are far from being so.

The worst of sermons is, that they are only so many declamations pro and con. The same man who affirmed last Sunday that there was no felicity in grandeur, that crowns are thorns, that courts are full of nothing but illustrious wretches, and that joy is spread over the faces of the poor, will tell you, the Sunday after, that the lower part of mankind is condemned to misery and sorrow; and that the rich and great must one day pay for their dangerous prosperity.

They will inform you, in Advent, that God is perpetually employed in removing all the wants and necessities of mankind; and, when Lent comes, assure you, that the earth is barren and accursed. These common places, with a few flourishing phrases, carry them on from one end of the year to the other.

The preachers in England follow another method, which would not suit us at all. The deepest book of metaphysics which they have is Clarke's sermons* : one would imagine he had preached only to philosophers, who perhaps, too, at the end of every period, might have required of him a long explanation; and the *Frenchman at London, to whom nothing could be proved*, would soon have left the preacher there. His discourses, however, make an excellent book, which very few understand. What a difference there is between ages and nations! and how far off are brother Garasse and brother Andrew from Massillon and Clarke!

From my study of history I have at least learned, that the times we live in are certainly of all times the most enlightened, in spite of our bad books; as they are also the most happy, in spite of some casual misfortunes: for what man of letters can be ignorant that good taste was brought into France about the time of Cinna, and the *Provincial Letters?* or where is he, who has any knowledge of history, that can point out a period of time, from the days of Clovis, more happy than what has passed since the æra when Louis XIV. began to reign by himself, down to the present moment? I defy the most

---

* Clarke's sermons are by no means, as Mr. Voltaire here asserts, all metaphysical: those, indeed, on the being of a God, &c. are certainly so; but there are withal as many excellent, plain, practical discourses in this collection, as in any of our best writers.

L 2 malevolent

malevolent to tell me what age he would prefer to our own.

We muſt do juſtice; we muſt acknowledge, that. at preſent, a geometrician of four-and-twenty knows more than ever Deſcartes did; and that a country vicar preaches more ſenſibly than the grand almoner of Louis XII. The nation is better inſtructed, our ſtyle in general is much improved, and conſequently the minds of men greatly ſuperior now to what they were formerly.

You will ſay, perhaps, that our age is at preſent on the decline, and that we have not ſo much genius and abilities among us as we had in the glorious days of Louis XIV. Genius, I grant you, decays; but knowledge is increaſed. A thouſand painters, in the time of Salvator Roſa, were not worth a Raphael, or a Michael Angelo; but the thouſand painters formed by Raphael and Michael Angelo compoſed a ſchool infinitely ſuperior to that which thoſe two great men found eſtabliſhed. We have not, indeed, at the cloſe of our fine age, a Maſſillon or a Bourdaloue, a Boſſuet or a Fenelon: but the pooreſt of our preſent preachers is a Demoſthenes, in compariſon with all thoſe who preached from the times of St. Remi to thoſe of brother Garaſſe.

There is more difference between the worſt of our modern tragedies and the pieces of Jodelle than between the Athaliah of Racine and the Maccabees of La Motte, or the Moſes of the Abbé Nadal. Upon the whole, in the productions of the mind our artiſts fall ſhort of thoſe who flouriſhed in the dawn and meridian of our golden age; but the nation itſelf is improved. We are over-run indeed with trifles, and mine always adding to the number: theſe are but ſo many inſects, which denote the abundance of fruits and flowers; yet ſee none of them in a barren ſoil. You will obſerve, that in theſe little pieces that are perpetually coming out, deſtroyed one by another, and all of them, in a few days, condemned to eternal oblivion, there is often more taſte and delicacy than you will find in all the books written before the *Provincial Letters*. Such is our affluence in wit, when compared to the poverty of twelve hundred years paſt.

If you examine into the preſent ſtate of our manners, laws, government, and ſociety, you will find my account ſtrictly juſt. I date from the moment Louis XIV. took the reins into his own hand, and would aſk the moſt exaſperated critic, the graveſt panegyriſt of times paſt, whether he durſt compare the preſent period with that when the Archbiſhop of Paris went to parliament with a poignard in his pocket? Or would he prefer the preceding age, when the firſt miniſter was ſhot, and his wife condemned to be burned for a witch? Ten or twelve years of the great Henry IV. appear happy, after forty of abominations and horrors, that make one's hair ſtand an end; but whilſt the beſt of princes was employed in healing our wounds, they bled on every ſide. The poiſon of the league infected every mind; families were divided; the manners of men harſh and diſagreeable. Fanaticiſm reigned univerſally, except at the court. Commerce, indeed, began to increaſe; but was not, as yet, attended with any great advantages. Society had no charms, our cities no police; all the comforts, in ſhort,

MISCELLANEOUS ESSAYS.

short, and conveniences of life, were still wanting. Figure to yourself, at the same time, a hundred thousand assassinations committed in the name of God, amidst the ruins of cities laid in ashes. Even to the time of Francis I. you will see Italy stained with our blood, a king prisoner at Madrid, and the enemy in the midst of our provinces.

The name of *Pater Patriæ* was given to Lewis XII.; but this father had some very unfortunate children, and was so himself: driven out of Italy, duped by the pope, conquered by Henry VIII. and obliged to bribe him to marry his sister. He was a good king, over a poor uncultivated people, without arts or manufacture; the houses of his capital built with lath and plaister, and most of them covered with thatch. Who would not rather wish to live under a good king over a people opulent and wise, though dogmatical and mischievous?

The farther you go back into former ages, the more savage you will find them; which renders our history so disgustful, that we have been forced to make chronological abridgements in columns, where every thing necessary is inserted, and only that which is useless omitted, for the sake of those curious readers who are desirous of knowing in what year the Sorbonne was founded, and are in doubt whether the equestrian statue in the Gothic cathedral of Paris is of Philip of Valois, or Philip the Fair.

To say the truth, we have not really and properly existed above six score years. Laws, police, military discipline, trade, navigation, the fine arts, magnificence, taste, and genius, all began in the time of Lewis XIV. Some of them are ripening to perfection in our own age, which I meant to insinuate, when I advanced, that every thing heretofore was rude and barbarous, and the pulpit amongst them. Urceus Codrus most certainly was not worth talking so long about; but he has furnished me with reflections which may not perhaps be entirely useless: we should endeavour to draw some advantage from every thing.

We insert the following Letter, merely to shew the degree of Credit due to Voltaire's *History of* Peter the Great.

To Mr. ROUSSEAU[*], of Toulouse, Director of the Encyclopédian Journal, printed at Bouillon, concerning a Letter inserted in the St. James's Chronicle, July, 1762.

SIR, Ferney, Oct. 10, 1762.

IN answer to your's of August 14, for which I am greatly obliged to you, I must inform you, that the Duke of Grafton, who has been in my neighbourhood for some time past, shewed me, in the *St. James's Chronicle*, a letter attributed to me; but apparently the produce of Grub-street, or the Charnel-house of St. Innocent. I must be obliged, out of regard to my character, to contradict this impertinent rhapsody in all the English papers. Men of sense and candour know what credit is to be given to

---

[*] There were at this time at Paris three Rousseaus: Mr. Rousseau of Toulouse; the celebrated John Baptist Rousseau, an eminent poet; and the famous John James Rousseau of Geneva, equally distinguished for his extraordinary abilities, his ingenious paradoxes, and the persecutions which he has suffered from bigotry and enthusiasm.

idle reports of this kind, which the public is over-run with, and heartily tired of.

With regard to the German critique on my *History of Peter the Great*, I shall be glad to see it in your Journal. Those remarks, which are sensible and judicious, will be of service to me in the second volume. I may very probably be mistaken in some points, though I have followed as nearly as I could the memoirs sent me from.* Petersburgh.

There was a gross error in the manuscript concerning religion: the patriarch Nicholas was mistaken for the patriarch Photius, who lived an hundred years before him. This has been corrected in several copies. In another place, Apraxin is put for Narifkin. As to matters of fact, if they are contested, the archives of Petersburgh must answer for me. My *History of Charles* XII. was severely criticised: the criticisms are forgotten; the history remains.

An Account of the noble Aqueduct of Alcántara, by which Lisbon is supplied. From Barretti's Journey.

OUR author, after describing the Arsenal, proceeds as follows:

But I went to see another of another kind in the afternoon, which surpasses it by far in point of bulk as well as magnificence. I mean the *Aqueduct* in the valley of *Alcántara*, by which *Lisbon* is supplied with almost all the water that is used by the inhabitants.

That valley is sunk between two rocky and barren declivities. The Aqueduct, for about a quarter of a mile, which is the breadth of the valley, runs transversely over it, from the summit of the western declivity to the opposite summit of the eastern. A long range of square pillars supports it; and, to give you an idea of these pillars, it is enough to say, that one of their sides measures near twelve, and the other near thirteen times the length of my sword, which was the only instrument I had to take such measures; and the space between the two middle-most pillars is such, both in breadth and height, that a fifty-gun ship with her sails spread might pass through without obstruction. However, all the pillars are not of equal dimensions with the two central. They grow lower and lower, and the spaces betwixt them diminish gradually on either side the valley, as the ground gradually rises on either side.

The pillars support an architrave whose middle is formed into a canal, through which the water runs; and there is room enough left for three or four men to walk a-breast along the architrave on each side the canal, which is vaulted the whole length, and adorned from space to space with *Lucarnes* made in the form of little temples, each of which has a door or aperture large enough for a man to get at the water and clean the bottom of the canal in case of necessity.

The whole of this immense fabric is of fine white marble, dug out of a quarry not a musket-shot

---

* The French editor tells us, in a note on this passage, that Mr. Voltaire's *History of Peter the Great* is nothing but a Gazette, and that it was written by him merely to conciliate the favour of the court of Russia.

distant:

distant: and I am told, that about a league farther off there are some other parts of it, which have their share of grandeur, though by no means comparable to what is seen in this valley. The earthquake had spoiled it in two or three places; but the damage proved inconsiderable, and was easily remedied. And, indeed, I wonder not if it withstood the shocks. A concussion violent enough to effect its destruction would shatter the whole kingdom of Portugal.

When a man has once seen such a structure as the Aqueduct of *Alcántara*, there is no danger of his ever forgetting it, as it is the nature of grand objects to force remembrance. As long as I live I shall preserve the image of it, along with that of the valley which is rendered so conspicuous by it.

An Account of the Manner in which the Punishment of the Knout was inflicted on the celebrated Madam Lapoochin, *at* Peterburgh; *with some Observations on the* Russian *Punishments, and the Effects they produce; and several curious Particulars relative to the Banishment of Count* Lestoc *and his Lady into* Siberia. *From Mr.* L'Abbé Chappe D'Auteroche's *Journey into* Siberia.

SINCE the accession of the Empress Elizabeth to the throne of Russia, the punishments are reduced to two kinds, the *padogi*, and the *knout*.

The padogi are considered in Russia merely as a correction of the police, exercised on the soldier by military discipline, by the nobility on their servants, and by persons in authority over all such as are under their command.

I saw this punishment inflicted at my return from Tobolsky to St. Petersburgh. I looked out of a window, on hearing somebody cry out in the yard, where I saw two Russian slaves pulling a girl of fourteen or fifteen years of age by the arms: she was tall, and well made. By her dress, she appeared to belong to some good family: Her head, dressed without a cap, was reclined backwards; her eyes, fixed on one person, pleaded for mercy, which her beauty should seem to have insured her, independent of her tears. Nevertheless, the Russians led her into the middle of the yard, and in an instant stripped her to the waist; they then laid her prostrate on the ground, and placed themselves on their knees, one of them holding her head tight between his knees, and the other the lower part of her body: rods were then brought, which they continued constantly applying on the back of this girl, till some one cried out, *Enough*. This unfortunate victim was then raised, so disfigured that she was scarcely to be known; her face and her whole body being covered with blood and dirt. This severe punishment led me to imagine, that the young girl had been guilty of some very flagrant offence: some days after I learned, that she was a lady's waiting-maid; and that her mistress's husband had ordered her to be punished in that manner, on account of some neglect. In any other part of the world, she might perhaps have been turned away, if her mistress had happened to be in an ill humour. The Russians think themselves obliged to punish their servants thus, in order to make them faithful. These unhappy slaves, finding so many petty tyrants in their masters, are obliged on this account to live in perpetual mistrust; so that, even in the midst of their families, they are under a necessity of being constantly on their guard with every person who comes near them.

I never saw the punishment of the knout inflicted; but as I was going over to St. Petersburgh with a foreigner, who conducted me to see all the curiosities in the city, we stopped upon the spot where Mad. Lapouchin had suffered this punishment. The foreigner had been present on this occasion; and was still so much affected with the affair, that he gave me a particular account of it on the very spot. I shall relate the incident as he told it me, and as I found it in my journal.

Every body who has been at St. Petersburgh knows that Mad. Lapouchin was one of the finest women belonging to the court of the Empress Elizabeth: she was intimately connected with a foreign ambassador, then engaged in a conspiracy. Mad. Lapouchin, who was supposed to be an accomplice in this conspiracy, was condemned by the Empress Elizabeth to undergo the punishment of the knout. She appeared at the place of execution in a genteel undress, which contributed still to heighten her beauty. The sweetness of her countenance, and her vivacity, were such as might indicate indiscretion, but not even the shadow of guilt; although I have been assured by every person of whom I have made inquiry, that she was really guilty. Young, lovely, admired, and sought for at the court, of which she was the life and spirit; instead of the number of admirers her beauty usually drew after her, she then saw herself surrounded only by executioners. She looked on them with astonishment, seeming to doubt whether such preparations were intended for her: one of the executioners then pulled off a kind of cloak which covered her bosom; her modesty taking the alarm, made her start back a few steps; she turned pale, and burst into tears: her clothes were soon after stripped off, and in a few moments she was quite naked to the waist, exposed to the eager looks of a vast concourse of people profoundly silent. One of the executioners then seized her by both hands, and, turning half round, threw her on his back, bending forwards, so as to raise her a few inches from the ground: the other executioner then laid hold of her delicate limbs, with his rough hands hardened at the plough, and, without any remorse, adjusted her on the back of his companion, in the properest posture for receiving the punishment. Sometimes he laid his large hand brutally upon her head, in order to make her keep it down; sometimes, like a butcher going to slay a lamb, he seemed to sooth her, as soon as he had fixed her in the most favourable attitude.

This executioner then took a kind of whip called knout, made of a long strap of leather prepared for this purpose: he then retreated a few steps, measuring the requisite distance with a steady eye; and, leaping backwards, gave a stroke with the end of the whip, so as to carry away a slip of skin from the neck to the bottom of the back: then striking his feet against the ground, he took his aim for applying

plying a second blow parallel to the former; so that in a few moments all the skin of her back was cut away in small slips, most of which remained hanging to the shift. Her tongue was cut out immediately after, and she was directly banished into Siberia. This incident is known to all persons who have been in Russia. In 1762, she was recalled from banishment by Peter III.

The ordinary punishment of the knout is not disgraceful, because every individual under this despotic government is exposed to incidents of the same nature, which have often been the consequence merely of court intrigues.

Russians who have committed crimes with regard to society, are condemned to the great knout. This punishment is generally used on the same occasions as racking on the wheel in France. The great knout differs only in some particulars from the common knout: the criminal is raised into the air by means of a pulley fixed to a gallows, and a cord fastened to the two wrists tied together; a piece of wood is placed between his two legs, also tied together; and another of a crucial form under his breast. Sometimes his hands are tied behind his back; and, when he is pulled up in this position, his shoulders are dislocated.

The executioners can make this punishment more or less cruel: they are so dexterous, that, when a criminal is condemned to die, they can make him expire at pleasure, either by one or several lashes.

Besides the punishment of the knout, that of breaking on the wheel was in use before the reign of the Empress Elizabeth. Sometimes criminals were impaled through the side: sometimes they were hanged by the ribs upon hooks; in which situation they lived for several days: as did women who were buried alive up to the shoulders, for the murder of their husbands. Beheading was a punishment equally inflicted on the common people as on the nobility.

It appears evidently, from the example of the kingdom of Russia, that neither the death of criminals, nor the severity of their corporal punishments, do contribute to reform mankind.

The Empress Elizabeth has kept up the punishment of the knout only, as I have before observed; criminals are even seldom condemned to this: banishing of the nobility; confiscating their property, and putting the common people to public labour, have been substituted instead of it. I have known several persons, who blamed the conduct of the Empress Elizabeth in this respect, considering these punishments as too mild.

There may be some reason for this opinion with regard to crimes of a peculiar nature; but it is evident that such persons were little acquainted with the nature of banishment as practised in Russia.

All criminals condemned to public labour are treated in the same manner: they are shut up in prisons surrounded by a large piece of ground, inclosed with stakes fifty or sixty feet high; in bad weather they retire within side the prison, and when the season permits they walk about in the inclosure. They have all chains to their feet; and are kept for a very trifling

trifling expence, being generally allowed nothing but bread and water, or, according to the place they are in, some other food instead of bread. They are guarded by a certain number of soldiers, who lead them to the mines, or other public labours, where they are treated with the utmost severity. This punishment in many instances is not adequate to the crimes: it has not that effect on the minds of the Russians as one might expect, because they are slaves. It would certainly have a very different effect on a free and civilized nation, where a perpetual punishment of this kind would prove a more powerful restraint on the people than the fear of death. Some villains even look upon that moment as the end of all their sufferings; to which circumstance we may impute the resolution with which some of them have behaved on the scaffold: but I believe it might be very dangerous to expose such criminals, as they do in Russia, to the public view. The habit of seeing these unhappy people at length destroys sensibility; and this sentiment is of such importance to society, that every method ought to be taken to preserve it among people who are already possessed of it, or to excite it in the breasts of those who are yet strangers to it. I am persuaded, that the disagreeable sight of such a number of wretches in chains as are met with in most of the towns in Russia has contributed much to produce that ferocity and savageness of character so remarkable among the inhabitants of this realm.

Persons condemned to banishment are not all treated in the same manner; some are shut up, and others allowed a little liberty. Count Lestoc, after having placed the crown on the head of the Empress Elizabeth, was banished with his lady. Lestoc was arrested first, and shut up in the fort of St. Petersburgh. His wife was a native of Livonia, of one of the most noble families: she was maid of honour to the Empress before she married Count Lestoc; and, though living at court, had still preserved the noble pride inspired by that liberty which the province of Livonia, conquered by Peter I. still enjoys. The Countess of Lestoc, being arrested, took off all the diamonds belonging to her dress, as well as her watch, and other trinkets, and, throwing them at the feet of those who took her up, told them to lead her to the place they were ordered to conduct her to: she was shut up in the same castle with her husband, but in a separate apartment: all their effects were put under seal, in expectation of the sentence of the private court of chancery. These illustrious prisoners, given up to this odious tribunal, the judges of which were avowed enemies to Count Lestoc, especially M. de Bestucheff, the first minister[*], looked

---

[*] I have read in some manuscript notes on Russia, that in 1741 the Empress Elizabeth had abolished the secret chancery on her accession to the throne, and had referred to the senate all the matters which used to be tried there; but it does not appear that this order was ever carried into execution. Count Lestoc and his peers have never been judged by the senate, nor by any real court of justice.

upon

upon their ruin as inevitable, and therefore did not endeavour to offer much in their defence. Leſtoc had received a ſum of money from a foreign power in alliance with Ruſſia, and it was to this power that the Empreſs Elizabeth was indebted for the crown. The receiving of this preſent was the great charge brought againſt Count Leſtoc: on being queſtioned, he owned he had received it; but his judges having aſked him the value of the ſum, his anſwer was, *I do not recollect; but if you are deſirous of knowing, the Empreſs Elizabeth can tell you;* and, indeed, he had informed this princeſs that this ſum had been offered to him, on account of the favours ſhe ſhewed him; and the Empreſs had allowed him to accept of it.

The Counteſs of Leſtoc, as fully convinced of the ſentence that would be given as ſhe was of her own and her huſband's innocence, only begged one favour of the judges, that ſhe might be beheaded, but that they would ſpare her ſkin; that is, that ſhe might not receive the puniſhment of the knout.

Notwithſtanding all the contrivances of Beſtucheff, the Empreſs Elizabeth would never conſent that theſe priſoners ſhould be condemned to the knout: all their eſtate was confiſcated; they were baniſhed into Siberia, ſhut up in different places, and not allowed to correſpond with each other.

The Counteſs of Leſtoc had but one room to live in; her furniture conſiſted of a few chairs, a table, a ſtove; and a bed, without curtains, made of ſtraw, with one coverlet: ſhe got clean ſheets but twice in the firſt year. Four ſoldiers conſtantly watched her, and lay in her chamber; from whence ſhe was not allowed to ſtir, even for the common neceſſities of life: ſhe had only a few ſhifts to change now and then. Leſtoc gave out, at his return, that his wife had been ſurpriſed that the vermin, the neceſſary conſequence of the filth ſhe was obliged to live in, had not alone been ſufficient to deſtroy her. She uſed to play at cards with the ſoldiers, in hopes of getting four or five-pence to diſpoſe of as ſhe pleaſed, which however was not always allowed. Being one day out of humour with the officer who commanded, he ſpat in her face, and afterwards made her captivity ſtill harder.

Count Leſtoc was ſtill more unhappy, becauſe the vivacity of his diſpoſition made him very impatient of the leaſt contradiction; and he was only indulged in the liberty of walking about his room, on condition that he avoided coming near the window.

The Empreſs Elizabeth, however, had allowed Leſtoc, as well as his wife, twelve French livrés *per* day, which was very favourable treatment in Ruſſia; but theſe exiles were not permitted to touch the money allotted to them, leſt they ſhould have employed it in bribing their guards: the officer of the guard, therefore, was treaſurer; he was ordered to procure them all neceſſaries, and he let them want for every thing.

A few years after, Count Leſtoc and his lady were ſuffered to live together: they had then ſeveral apartments, and a ſmall garden at their diſpoſal: the Counteſs of Leſtoc worked in the garden, fetched water, brewed, baked, waſhed,

washed, &c.——Sometimes even the officer of the guard introduced company to them: one of his friends, who had conducted a party into Siberia, desired to see the Count. This officer, having contracted a kind of intimacy with him, proposed a party of play. Lestoc won four hundred French livres; this sum was a fortune for the two exiles: they were soon after informed, that it belonged to the party this officer conducted. The Countess fell at her husband's feet, intreating him to return the money to this imprudent soldier: Lestoc raised her up, and sent the money to the nearest village, to be distributed among the poor.

After the banishment of M. de Bestucheff, Count Woronzoff, the High Chancellor, attempted several times to have Lestoc recalled, as he was thoroughly persuaded of his innocence; but the Empress Elizabeth would never listen to his intreaties on this point: she was however particularly attentive in giving orders to have wine sent to him from time to time, knowing he was very fond of it.

Lestoc and his lady were at length recalled by Peter III. after fourteen years exile. Lestoc came to St. Petersburgh in the dress of the lower sort of people, which is commonly made of sheep skin*. All the noblemen of the court, and all foreigners, flocked eagerly to see him, endeavouring to make him forget the time he had passed in exile. The friendly proffers he received were sincere, because every body knew he was innocent: the Empress Elizabeth never had a subject more firmly attached to her; and he had constantly maintained his allegiance during his exile: he declared that M. de Bestucheff had been the cause of it, and that the Empress had only given way to the importunities of this minister.

Count Lestoc, though seventy-four years old, still preserved all that firmness which had been so necessary to him when he placed the Princess Elizabeth on the throne. He used to give a circumstantial account of this event, and of his banishment, in public company; although he knew very well that the story was highly disagreeable to the Russians, and that he thereby exposed himself daily to be banished again; nor were the admonitions of his friends of any weight with him in this matter. Peter III. having done him the honour of admitting him to his table, Lestoc spoke to him in the following terms: " Sir, my ene-" mies will not fail to do me all " the mischief they can, but I hope " your Majesty will permit an old " man, who has but few days to " live, to prate on, and die in " peace." He claimed all the effects that had been taken away from him when he was arrested: they had been already distributed among several private persons, according to custom. He declared he would take possession of them wherever he found them. He also demanded, that an account should be given him of his jewels, and of the money the officers of the guard had received during his exile. Count Lestoc himself acquainted me with every thing I have mentioned concerning his banishment, and furnished me also with the par-

* In the original, *habit de mousic*.

ticulars

ticulars of the revolution by which the Empress Elizabeth was fixed on the throne.

Count Munic, equally great as a courtier and as a general, acted in a different manner. He never complained. Both Russians and foreigners had the greatest respect for him.

General Munic was of the tallest size: though advanced in years, and extremely thin, he had preserved, in the midst of his misfortunes, a most agreeable countenance. He engaged all hearts by his politeness, and the gentleness of his disposition.

Account of a Debauch at the present King (then Prince) of Pruffia's Court, at Rheinsberg. From Baron Bielfeld's Letters.

THUS, Madam, our days here pass tranquilly away, and enlivened by every enjoyment that can please a rational mind. Royal cheer, wine for the gods, the music of angels, delicious pastimes, in the gardens, in the woods, upon the waters; the cultivation of letters and the polite arts, and a refined conversation, all concur to spread their powers over this enchanting palace. But as there is no felicity that is absolutely perfect, so the pleasures that I have enjoyed at Rheinsberg have been dashed with bitterness by a singular accident, of which, Madam, I shall here give an account; as you will soon see me return to Hamburgh, with two wounds on my forehead, a sable eye, and a cheek covered with all the colours of the rainbow: it is proper that I apprise you of this catastrophe. We seldom fail to see the effects of a debauch, and it was at a bacchanalian rout that I acquired all those ornaments. About a fortnight since, the Prince was in a humour of extraordinary gaiety at table. His gaiety animated all the rest; and some glasses of Champagne still more enlivened our mirth. The Prince, perceiving our disposition, was willing to promote it, and, on rising from table, told us he was determined we should recommence our jollity at supper, and in the same place where we had left off. Towards evening I was called to the concert; at the end of which the Prince said to me, *Go now to the Princess's apartment, and, when she has finished her play, we will sit down to table, and won't quit it till the lights are out, and we are somewhat enlightened with Champagne.* I regarded this threat as a pleasantry, for I knew that parties which are expressly intended for this purpose seldom succeed, but commonly become more dull than joyous. On entering the Princess's apartment, however, her highness convinced us that the affair was very serious, and prognosticated, with a smile, that I should not be able to defend myself against the Prince's attack. In fact, we were scarce seated before he began, by drinking a number of interesting healths, which there was a necessity of pledging. This first skirmish being over, it was followed by an incessant flow of sallies and repartees, by the Prince and the company: the most contracted countenances became expanded, the gaiety was general, even the ladies assisted in promoting our jollity. After, about two hours, we found that the largest reservoirs, by perpetually filling, might

might be overflown: necessity has no law; and the greatest respect could not prevent some of us from going to take the fresh air in the vestibule. I was one of the number: when I went out I found myself sober enough; but the air seized me, and, on entering the hall, I perceived a sort of vapour that seemed to cloud my reason. I had placed before me a large glass of water, which the Princess, opposite to whom I had the honour to sit, in a vein of mischievous pleasantry, had ordered to be emptied, and had filled it with sellery wine, which was as clear as rock water; so that, having already lost my taste, I mixed my wine with wine; and, thinking to refresh myself, I became joyous: but it was a kind of joy that leaned towards intoxication. To finish my picture, the Prince ordered me to come and sit by him: he said many very gracious things to me, and let me see into futurity, as far as my feeble sight was then capable of discovering; and at the same time made me drink bumper after bumper of his Lunel wine. The rest of the company, however, were not less sensible than I of the effects of the nectar, which there flowed in such mighty streams. One of the ladies, who was a stranger, and in a multiplying state, found herself as much incommoded as we were, and retired suddenly for a short time to her chamber. We thought this action admirably heroic. Wine produces complacency. The lady, on her return, was loaded with compliments and caresses: never was woman so applauded for such an expedition. At last, whether by accident or design, the Princess broke a glass. This was a signal for our impetuous jollity, and an example that appeared highly worthy of imitation. In an instant all the glasses flew to the several corners of the room; and all the crystals, porcelain, piers, branches, bowls, vases, &c. were broke into a thousand pieces. In the midst of this universal destruction, the Prince stood like the man in Horace, who contemplates the crush of worlds with a look of perfect tranquillity. To this tumult succeeded a fresh burst of mirth; during which the Prince slipt away, and, aided by his pages, retired to his apartment; and the Princess immediately followed.

For me, who unfortunately found not one valet who was humane enough to guide my wandering steps, and support my tottering fabric, I carelessly approached the grand stair-case, and, without the least hesitation, rolled from the top to the bottom, where I lay senseless on the floor, and where, perhaps, I should have perished, if an old female domestic had not chanced to pass that way, who, in the dark, taking me for a great dog belonging to the castle, gave me an appellation somewhat dishonourable, and at the same time a kick in the guts; but perceiving that I was a man, and, what was more, a courtier, she took pity on me, and called for help: my servants then came running to my assistance: they put me in bed, sent for a surgeon, bled me, dressed my wounds; and I in some degree recovered my senses. The next day they talked of a trepan, but I soon got rid of that dread; and, after lying about a fortnight in bed, where the Prince had the goodness to come every day to see me, and
con-

contribute every thing poſſible to my cure, I got abroad again. The day after this adventure the court was at its laſt gaſp. Neither the Prince nor any of the courtiers could ſtir from their beds; ſo that the Princeſs dined alone. I have ſuffered ſeverely by my bruiſes, and have had ſufficient to make many moral reflections.

Extracts from the Abbé Millot's *Elements of the Hiſtory of* England.

IT is well known that the Earl of Oxford (Mr. Harley) had greatly contributed to the diſgrace of the Duke of Marlborough. In 1712, after the change of the miniſtry, Prince Eugene came to London, and it was thought that the deſign of his viſit was to animate the whigs by his preſence and his intrigues. This great man treated Marlborough as if he had ſtill been in favour. Oxford, having invited him one day to dinner, congratulated him on having, at his table, the firſt general in Europe: *If I am*, replied the Prince, *I may thank you for it.* An eulogium the more ſeaſonable, as Marlborough's diſgrace was principally owing to Oxford.

[Similar to this was the Duke of Marlborough's own reply to Marſhal Tallard, after the battle of Blenheim; on the Marſhal's ſaying, that " he (the Duke) had defeated the beſt troops in Europe;" *I hope you except the troops that defeated them.* And ſuch alſo was the compliment paid by the Duke of Montague to the Duke of Marlborough, at Broughton in Northamptonſhire, on the latter admiring the waterworks there, and ſaying, " he thought them equal to thoſe of Lewis XIV. at Verſailles." *No, my Lord Duke, my waterworks are not equal, but your Grace's fireworks are much ſuperior to his.*]

" After the expulſion of the Stuarts, the royal prerogative was contracted within narrower bounds, the acts of arbitrary power were leſs common, civil liberty was better ſecured; but the ſovereign was ſcarce leſs powerful. He had always at hand thoſe reſources which work upon the paſſions. Having places and honours at his diſpoſal, he could bias that multitude of ambitious or venal ſouls who worſhip Fortune. A contagious corruption, produced by wealth and intrigue, infected from the time of William III. thoſe haughty people ſo jealous of their liberty. Two irreconcileable parties employed againſt each other the fatal art of ſeducing citizens, and purchaſing votes. In order to have a majority in parliament, they were not aſhamed of changing the principles of patriotiſm; and the court took care to profit by an evil that favoured its deſigns. It carried the point in filling the lower houſe with its partizans, of influencing their debates, and of drawing from thence enormous ſubſidies, more for its own intereſt than for the neceſſities of the ſtate. The act of triennial parliaments furniſhed the patriots with a reſource. They had hopes of ſoon gaining a ſuperiority. But ſince the duration of parliament was fixed at ſeven years, under George I. the nation ſeems expoſed to the attacks of deſpotiſm. In 1734, ſome vain attempts were made to reſtore matters to their antient footing.— There have always been in England

land those vigilant, zealous, incorruptible men, who have their country incessantly before their eyes, who struggle against the torrent of foreign interests, and who speak like citizens in the midst of the most corrupt assembly: A government where such men may freely speak their thoughts, where they speak them without fear, and without evasion, has in itself a grand principle of life and vigour. But since the crown has had a standing army, since it has had some interests which do not concern the nation, since it can depend on the votes of a long parliament, the balance of those powers which form the English constitution is become more difficult to support: some violent attacks on liberty would raise a rebellion among a people that are jealous and terrible in their fury. Corruption, by destroying principles, may one day, perhaps, occasion more mischief than the violence of despotism.

"Politeness had not yet softened that fierceness of manners which the English derive from their climate, from the form of their government, and from their situation in an island. Men accustomed to the sea, inflamed by the spirit of faction, proud of liberty and riches, addicted to party disputes, wholly engrossed by their interests, their systems; hot, fiery, less by fits than by principle, are so apt to disdain the art of pleasing, that they often transgress the bounds of good breeding. It frequently happens that the nobles themselves, intermixed with the people, partake of their heats, their riots, and excesses. Wealth levels rank; the great power of the commons elates the heart of the vulgar. Every one thinking himself of consequence, and fearing no man, the pride of all makes a kind of equality between all. Humour, whim, caprice, must necessarily prevail in a nation where most citizens are regardless of pleasing any one. *Most men of genius will be tormented by their genius itself*, according to the remark of M. de Montesquieu, *with a disdain or a distaste for all things: they will be miserable, though they have such abundant reason to be happy*. To this, doubtless, is owing the frenzy of suicide, of which there are frequent examples in England.

"Courage and politics, agriculture and industry, commerce and navigation, have exalted the power of the English to the highest point which it can probably attain. The sciences and polite literature have rendered their glory still more durable. No people surpass them in learned disquisitions. Their mathematicians, their philosophers, have opened an immense field to the human mind. It is sufficient to name Newton and Locke, geniuses the more wonderful, as they shut themselves up in the sphere of Nature, in order to dive into her mysteries, instead of losing themselves in fantastic systems to create new errors. Many philosophers in England have taken the false paths of impiety. But religion has found among the English some defenders without prejudices, and without fanaticism, no less powerful in their arguments, than respectable for the extent of their knowledge. The clergy, having lost their antient credit, have applied themselves to labours which procure them

them general esteem. They have very little influence in affairs, but they impress truth on the mind. Science conducts them to ecclesiastical dignities, and emulation nourishes talents which would be stifled under the empire of interest.

" In a country where the useful is preferred to the agreeable, researches and experiments which relate to the wants of society principally engage the attention of the public. Every one knows how much the English have laboured in this way, and what success they have had. In bringing to perfection agriculture and navigation, they have secured to themselves inexhaustible resources. By the inoculation of the small pox they have preserved some thousands of citizens. It is not for us to weigh the reasons for or against this practice. But in whatever point of view it is taken, the example of an intelligent nation is, in this way, the strongest of all proofs; and though an individual may be fearful of inoculation, the public ought to desire it.

" Learning is become, in this age, one of the principal ornaments in England: the celebrated authors that she has produced are at present too well known to make it necessary to name them. New ideas, deep reflections, refined thoughts, a manly emphatical style, often obscure for the sake of precision, characterize almost all of them. The English have enriched their theatre with the spoils of that of France, which they affect to despise; but they have taught us to think more closely, to put fewer shackles on genius, to diffuse useful truths even in frivolous writings, to change romances themselves into schools of morality. Let us do justice to their excellent writers; our own will not be less the delight of all Europe."

From this specimen, the English reader will doubtless be curious to see the whole, and will be glad to hear that his curiosity will soon be gratified by the ingenious pen of Mrs. Brooke.

Letter from the late Miss Talbot *to a new-born Child, Daughter of Mr.* John Talbot, *a Son of the Lord Chancellor.*

YOU are heartily welcome, my dear little cousin, into this unquiet world; long may you continue in it, in all the happiness it can give; and bestow enough on all your friends, to answer fully the impatience with which you have been expected. May you grow up to have every accomplishment, that your good friend the *Bishop of Derry can already imagine in you; and in the mean time, may you have a nurse with a tuneable voice, that may not talk an immoderate deal of nonsense to you.

You are, at present, my dear, in a very philosophical disposition; the gaieties and follies of life have no attraction for you; its sorrows you kindly commiserate; but, however, do not suffer them to disturb your slumbers, and find charms in nothing but harmony and repose. You have as yet contracted no par-

* Dr. Rundle.

tialities, are entirely ignorant of party diſtinctions, and look with a perfect indifference on all human ſplendor. You have an abſolute diſlike to the vanities of dreſs; and are likely for many months to obſerve the *Biſhop of Briſtol's firſt rule of converſation, Silence; though tempted to tranſgreſs it by the novelty and ſtrangeneſs of all the objects round you. As you advance farther in life, this philoſophical temper will by degrees wear off: the firſt object of your admiration will probably be a candle; and thence (as we all of us do) you will contract a taſte for the gaudy and the glaring, without making one moral reflection upon the danger of ſuch falſe admiration, as leads people, many a time, to burn their fingers. You will then begin to ſhew great partiality for ſome very good aunts, who will contribute all they can towards ſpoiling you; but you will be equally fond of an excellent mama, who will teach you, by her example, all ſorts of good qualities. Only let me warn you of one thing, my dear, and that is, do not learn of her to have ſuch an immoderate love of home as is quite contrary to all the privileges of this polite age, and to give up ſo entirely all thoſe pretty graces of whim, flutter, and affectation, which ſo many charitable poets have declared to be the prerogative of our ſex. Ah! my poor couſin, to what purpoſe will you boaſt this prerogative, when your nurſe tells you, with a pious care, to ſow the ſeeds of jealouſy and emulation as early as poſſible, that you have a fine little brother come to put your noſe out of joint. There will be nothing to be done then, I believe, but to be mighty good, and prove what, believe me, admits of very little diſpute (though it has occaſioned abundance), that we girls, however people give themſelves airs of being diſappointed, are by no means to be deſpiſed: let the men unenvied ſhine in public, it is we muſt make their homes delightful to them; and, if they provoke us, no leſs uncomfortable. I do not expect you, my dear, to anſwer this letter yet awhile; but as, I dare ſay, you have the greateſt intereſt with your papa, will beg you to prevail upon him, that we may know by a line (before his time is engroſſed by another ſecret committee), that you and your mama are well. In the mean time I will only aſſure you, that all here rejoice in your exiſtence extremely; and that I am,

My very young correſpondent,
Moſt affectionately your's,

C. T.

The pious and ingenious author of the above letter, who died Jan. 9, 1770, aged 48, was the only daughter of Mr. Edward Talbot, Archdeacon of Berks, and younger ſon of Dr. Talbot, Biſhop of Durham. There having been the moſt intimate friendſhip between him and the late Archbiſhop Secker, his widow and daughter lived as inmates in his Grace's family till his death, when he left the intereſt of 13,000l. to them, and the ſurvivor of them, and afterwards the whole ſum to charitable uſes.

* Dr. Secker.

Remarks on a Sentence in the Law, called Peine forte et dure.

Tom's Coffee-house, Devereux-Court, April 10, 1770.

SIR,

AS I was sitting this morning in the corner by the fire-side in the upper room of this house, two gentlemen entered, and took possession of the vacant chairs about the little round table, and one of them read a news-paper to his companion: when he came to the account of the shocking wretch who refused to plead to his indictment at Kingston *, the other expressed much astonishment at the folly of a man, who would submit to be dying for a week, in agonies inexpressible, rather than put himself upon his trial, by which means he would have a possibility, however slight, of avoiding punishment; and that, if he should be convicted, an easy death would be the utmost of his suffering in this world: his friend observed, that the fellow was lucky in not having been brought to trial on the last day of the assizes, for that, if the sentence had been passed upon him, and the commission of the judges expired, the sentence could not have been changed, and quoted some *dictum* of Lord Chief Justice Holt to that effect; and also said, that it had been objected by the King of Prussia, in some of what that Prince calls his Philosophical Works, Essays against the Existence of God, or Immortality of the Soul, &c.; that the *peine forte & dure* was to all intents and purposes the same as giving the question, as the French call it; or, in plain English, putting a man upon the rack.

I took the liberty to interpose with my opinion, that it could not be applied to putting a person to torture, in the usual meaning of the word, when applied to judicial matters, because the torture is given to make persons acknowledge their guilt; and the other is, on the contrary, to make men deny their guilt; but that still I thought it was a ridiculous and absurd regulation or institution, and that the law seemed in some measure to confess the folly of it; for in high treason, and petty larcenies, the prisoner, though he refused to

---

* The circumstance is as follows: A man who was charged with returning from transportation, being arraigned at the last assizes at Kingston, refused to plead to the indictment, unless the Judge would promise, that, in case he should be convicted, his sentence should not be transportation again: Mr. Baron Smythe remonstrated, and explained to him the impossibility of his complying with his demand; and also informed him, that, if he persisted in his silence, he must be sentenced to the *peine forte & dure*; that he must be laid naked upon the ground, with a considerable weight upon him, which would be gradually increased till his death; that he would be fed with a morsel of bread, and one draught of the next ditch water, daily; that he remembered two instances of men submitting for a little time to that punishment, but that neither persevered in their resolution. Upon which the wretch cried out, "You may die and be damned yourself." The Baron answered, in the spirit of an upright judge, "I am shocked for you, and pity you; but God forbid any thing you say should make me deviate from my duty with regard to you." The fellow, at last, pleaded, and was convicted; and, when he was carrying out of court, knocked down the hangman with a blow of his fist.

plead, is judged guilty, and has the ordinary sentence, in those cases, passed upon him. If this practice should be observed in any, why not in all cases, and whatever the offence may be which the prisoner is charged with?

To this question the gentleman returned for answer, that the law was particularly attentive to the preservation of landed property; that for this reason, upon a prisoner's standing mute in general, his landed property was saved to his family; but that in petty larcenies the offender could not be suspected of having any landed property; and in case he had, the law does not subject him to a forfeiture of it, upon his being found guilty upon pleading to his indictment; and, on the other hand, in case of high treason, a fact not likely to be committed but by men of high rank, or of high spirit, it was judged necessary to take away from them, for the sake of the public peace, that property in land, which in the hands of their posterity might be dangerous; and in order to make sure of succeeding in that prudent purpose, it was necessary to alter and take away, in that particular case, the common privilege that a person had by the common law, of preserving his estate in his family, by submitting to the *peine forte & dure*, which many persons of that property and spirit, which would qualify or dispose them to be guilty of high treason, would certainly submit to, and go through with, provided it would enable them to preserve their estates in their families.

He owned that this was rather an apology for the deviation from the common rule of the penalty of standing mute, in these two cases, than a good defence of the rule or practice itself; that, for his part, he thought that the best defence of it was the infrequency of its application; there having been, as he believed, but one instance of a person's having gone through with it since the last century, who was a master of a ship, charged with piratical practices, who had some landed property, and submitted to the penalty of standing mute, and persevered in it, and was pressed to death in Newgate in the press-yard there, so denominated from thence.

That was the last person, you say, Sir, I replied. The most remarkable person, as I believe, that ever submitted to that penalty, was Mr. Calverly, of a very great family in the North; who being a man of violent passion, conceived a jealousy against his wife, which by some unfortunate accident was turned to such a frantic rage, that early one morning he murdered her, by splitting her skull with his battleaxe, and forced seven children she had by him to leap off the battlements of his castle into the moat which surrounded it, where they all stuck fast in the mud, and were suffocated with the slime on the water: he then mounted his horse, and galloped towards a farmer's cottage, where one of his children, an infant at the breast, was at nurse. Whilst upon the road he was ruminating, in gloomy and horrid satisfaction upon the approach of the only matter wanting to the final completion of his zealous revenge, the moon on a sudden was darkened; he lost himself in the midst of a thick forest: the thunder of Heaven, which now stunned his ears, seemed to roll against

againſt him, and ſummon him to judgment; and the pale lightning appalling his ſoul, was, to his frantic imagination, the fire of hell preparing puniſhment intolerable, and tortures excruciating to millions of ages. He ſtopped, relented, repented, ſurrendered, and ſubmitted himſelf to juſtice. After having made his peace with Heaven, for the murder of his wife and children, he was agonized by the thought of having deprived the child, ſo reſcued from his dagger, even by the immediate interpoſition of Providence itſelf, as juſt related, of the eſtate and dignity of its anceſtors, and of leaving it, inſtead of its due inheritance, poverty, and the infamy of ſuch a father. He conſidered, that, when convicted, his eſtate muſt go to the crown. If he, with his own hand, ſhould anticipate the ſtroke of juſtice, he was informed, that the law gives the lands of ſuch wretches to the crown: he therefore ſtood mute upon being arraigned, and ſubmitted with ſatisfaction to the penalty attending that behaviour, and perſevered in bearing the moſt excruciating pain, with the patience of a proto-martyr.

His eſtate was preſerved for that child, which was a male, and from whom, if I am not entirely miſinformed, is lineally deſcended the preſent Sir Walter Calverly Blackett, a gentleman well known in the world, and of whom the world neither knows nor ſays any thing ill. This tragical tale likewiſe furniſhed the fable of the play called the Yorkſhire Tragedy, ſaid by ſome critics to be written by Shakeſpeare.

The gentlemen complimented me upon my ſtory, and, having nothing better to do, I have, by their deſire, ſent you this account of our tale and converſation.

EBOR.

Eſſay on Flattery.

SIR,

I HAVE the vanity to think myſelf a proficient in the art of *tickling*: by tickling, I mean, in plain Engliſh, *flattery*.—I here ſend you a ſketch of my hiſtory, which, if you are inclined to be lazy, or——; in ſhort, if you think proper, you are at liberty to publiſh: if you do not like it, you are at liberty to make it a preſent, either to the huſband of Venus, or to the venerable goddeſs Cloacina.

The firſt impreſſions, I have been told, are the deepeſt—I find it true by experience—the impreſſions I received at three years old are not effaced at forty.—How the diſtant ſcene riſes to my retroſpective view! Not to be tedious—my nurſe firſt taught me to flatter. The poor old woman never attempted to waſh my face, or to comb my hair, without the ſoothing expreſſions of, " There's a dear —Let me waſh its *pretty face*."— " There's a ſweet creature;" and numberleſs other endearing phraſes to the like purpoſe—When I grew a little older, I ſtill perceived that I never was ordered to do any thing without a little bit of flattery tacked to the command.—My ſchool miſtreſs bade me ſay. A by itſelf A, and always added, " There's a " good boy."—My father, my mother, my relations, all addreſſed me in the ſame ſtyle—My aged grandfather, too, how well I remember the hoary ſage! whilſt I was inno-

innocently asking him why he shook his head always, would often put his hand in his pockets, and give me a penny because I was a *brave boy.*—These praises, though they were only words of course, as I since learned, then gave me great pleasure; and I found myself always disposed to love the person that followed them on me.—I was artful!—I thought I might rule others by the same means by which others ruled me—nor was I deceived in the sequel—however, I had not then many opportunities to try the experiment.

I had an aunt, whose ill fortune it was not to be able to get a husband; and, therefore, as is usual, she was called an *old maid,* before time had made her an *old woman*—Old maids seldom despair till they have arrived at their grand climacteric—hence we often see ladies of fifty in the garb of sixteen.—My aunt was one of these—It happened one day, while I was playing near her toilette, and she was repairing the depredations which nature had made in her face, by the help of art, that I unmeaningly (it certainly must have been unmeaningly) cried out, " *La! aunty, what a pretty nose you have got! your hand is whiter than mine.*"—I had no sooner uttered these words, than she snatched me up in her arms and, almost stifled me with kisses—Every day, after that lucky moment, she continued to shew me new marks of her affection; spoke well of me; was continually saying, that I made sensible remarks, much above my years.—I was astonished at this alteration—She always before had looked on me with indifference and hatred—And, indeed, few old maids, I have since observed, are remarkably fond of children—However, as I did not want penetration, I soon discovered that it was my flattery which had gained her favour—And now it was that I resolved to make *flattery* the ruling principle of my conduct in future life.

When my father thought me of a proper age to go to school, he put me to one of those schools in which *youth are qualified* for—in short, every thing you can mention—A school I should not call it—The refined ideas of the master looked upon this as too gross an appellation; and therefore, to prevent mistakes, he had inscribed over the portal of his mansion, in large golden letters, " *The Academy.*"—To return from the digression: at my academy I soon found that the art of tickling was not unknown to my teachers—Whenever my cousin Tom, or my good aunt Deborah, came to see me, and to enquire, as the way is, how I went on, they were sure to hear, in the most extravagant terms, of all my good qualities—The usher observed, that " Master Billy was the finest young " youth that ever he set his eyes " on."—My mistress chucked me under the chin, and said, " It has " got a pretty face of its own, " bless it." My master, patting me on the head, and looking earnestly at me, used to cry, " It " really is surprising—Such a pro- " ficiency in so short a time! But " nature has been partial—And, " to be sure,—I take a great " deal of pains with him, that I " do; and the child takes vastly to " his book." These and many other encomiums were given to me whenever my friends paid me a visit—But, alas! after the vast ideas

ideas I had been taught to form of myself, my friends were no sooner gone, than, lo! I sunk to the condition of another boy—Notwithstanding my great talents, my beauty, and all the praises which had been lavished upon me, poor I underwent the correction of the rod, and was called dunce from morning till night—I comforted myself as well as I could—Nor indeed had I much reason to grieve, since my friends were pleased, though deceived; and I got half a crown, when otherwise I should have got but sixpence, and perhaps only a kiss and a farewel.

My master's flattery succeeded so well, that I was confirmed in the principle which I had been led into by my aunt, my nurse, &c. I therefore resolved to try my skill among my school-fellows—I soon found my schemes succeed to admiration; but then I was obliged to use a great deal of address in conducting them—My way was to discover their ruling passions and inclinations—I never commended the surly boy for his good nature; but I commended him for that which he took pride in, his *gravity* and *austerity*—I never praised the idle fellow for his diligence and learning; no: those he despised; but I praised him for his vivacity and gaiety—in a word, I always *tickled* the place which was most *ticklish*—Wherever I found vanity, I fed her plenteously—the advantages I enjoyed by this conduct were innumerable—Each individual looked upon me as his particular friend—Indeed, I had endeavoured by my flatteries to make him look upon me as such—Consequently, in all disputes, both parties readily consented to refer the points in controversy to my arbitration, each imagining I had a particular bias to himself—Thus I enjoyed a superiority over all my fellows, which gratified my pride not a little—I was beloved and caressed by all—No tales were told of me.—I must own that I learned a great deal of wisdom at school; not from my book—there, to my shame be it spoken, I was a dunce. —My wisdom was not the wisdom of the speculative philosopher, but that of the worldly-wise man.

I always considered a school as the copy of the world—All the vices and follies of the great original are there painted in miniature —Though the picture is small, the characters are drawn to the life— I was now at the eve of launching into the great ocean of the world; and I pleased myself with the thoughts of being possessed of a secret that would steer my little bark clear of every rock—I had been told from my cradle that I should be a soldier—Escaped from school, I thought the happy time was arrived at length—How transported was I with the thoughts of wearing a sword and a red coat!— But besides these, I had more substantial allurements—I thought the military profession would open to me the most ample field for the exertion of that genius for adventure which I perceived within me—In the midst of my anticipated bliss, O grief of griefs! my father bound me apprentice to a tradesman in Cheapside—After some time, however, I acquiesced in my condition—But how fallen was I! all the schemes which I had formed for the conduct of my life, and even my golden art of tickling, now—seemed to vanish—I had nothing

nothing now to do, I imagined, but plod behind the counter—I found myself wrong in these reflections—Flattery was grown natural to me, and nature will not be entirely stifled—Our customers consisted chiefly of females—This circumstance gave me some hope—Downright flattery from one in my station I knew would favour too much of familiarity; I was, therefore, obliged to act with great circumspection—While I was handing down a drawer or a box, I used to observe, in a faltering tone of voice, "That such a pattern, or such a colour, would be very pretty for a lady who wanted to set off a bad skin—but you, madam, are—How do you like this, ma'am?"— This never failed; the lady was tickled, turned towards the glass, adjusted her cap, stuck a pin, and bought the pattern on the strength of my recommendation. By such methods, I fixed fugitive customers, pleased constant ones, increased my master's trade, and did no harm to any body.

Seven years passed away in this manner—I forbear to relate every particular of my history during that space of time, as there would be very little variety in the relation—suffice it to say, that the *old trick* never failed—Just after the expiration of my apprenticeship, my aunt Deborah died, and left me a very pretty legacy, sufficient to set me up in trade—Thanks to my divine art!—I had almost forgot to tell you, she died an old maid, notwithstanding her *pretty nose* and *white hands*.

I took a shop, and furnished it—one piece of furniture was still wanting, without which, as the saying is, one is never rightly settled—in truth, I wanted a wife; and a wife I was resolved to have—In my amours, I must confess that I offered up incense to the shrine of Plutus as well as that of Cupid.—After some time, I got scent of a good wealthy widow—she was somewhat advanced in life—As for the lady's person, that was her least recommendation—However, I perceived, after a very slight acquaintance with her, that she was one of those who did not give a most implicit credit to looking-glasses. I knew how to proceed accordingly—I swore that her eyes were irresistible—that her cheeks were more blooming than the rose—I swore—but, to avoid prolixity, after a short courtship I won the lady and ten thousand pounds—I lived happily in my new state;—but cruel fate denies a long continuance of bliss—my wife died—Peace to her shade! I am married again, and to this day enjoy the company of my dear partner. I won my present deary's heart by praising her eyes—the conquest cost me my sincerity—but let that be a secret.

I pass over a million of adventures, in which I exerted my adulatory talent with success, to hasten to the last, and to me the most interesting: In the course of my trade, I scraped an acquaintance with an old square-toes, who was one of those rich men who accumulate immense sums, nobody knows how—I resolved to sound the breast of this new friend—there was no need of searching deep to discover that avarice had long swallowed up every other vice, passion, and appetite—This discovery gave me my cue—I raked

raked up all the remarks which I had heard, in sermons and in conversations with my brother tradesmen, on the subject of frugality and temperance—on these I declaimed on every occasion—I talked of the exorbitant price of every necessary of life, and complained of the luxury and extravagance of the age.—One day, as I was running on at this rate, he got up from his chair, and with a vehemence not common to men of that frigid disposition which it is necessary to have, in order to be a miser, slapped me on the shoulders, and swore " I was the honestest, prudentest, sensiblest fellow he ever met with."—In a few weeks the old hunks died, and bequeathed his fortune to me.

Thus, Sir, I have acquired an ample fortune—thus I have passed my life free from those animosities which an envious and contentious disposition never fails to foment—thus I have gained the love and esteem of all I knew—My art of tickling has made *me* happy, and, I flatter myself, it has made *others* so—I have increased the happiness of all who have fallen within the circle of my acquaintance, by gratifying their vanity—Whereever I was able, I have thrown an ingredient into the bitter cup of life, which never fails to sweeten it, namely, *self-applause*—Yet, I confess, I have often done this at the expence of truth—I confess—confession is a sign of repentance, and repentance claims forgiveness. Being now above dependance, to expiate my crime, I have taken the resolution to give the tribute of praise only where it *is* due—As a specimen of the justness of my commendation, I assure you, that I entirely approve of your design, and that none wishes success to it more ardently than

Your humble servant,
TICKLER.

The Adventures of Scarmentado; *a Satirical Novel by* Voltaire.

MY name is Scarmentado; my father was governor of the city of Candia, where I came into the world in the year 1600, and I remember that one Jro, a stupid and scurrilous poet, wrote a copy of doggrel verses in my praise, in which he proved me descended from Minos in a direct line; but my father being disgraced some time after, he wrote another poem, by which it appeared I was no longer a-kin to Minos, but the descendant of Pasiphae and her lover.

When I was 15 years old, my father sent me to Rome to finish my studies. Monsignor Profonde, to whom I was recommended, was a strange kind of man, and one of the most terrible scholars breathing: he took it into his head to teach me the categories of Aristotle, and I narrowly escaped his throwing me into the category of his minions. I saw many processions and exorcisms, and much oppression. Signora Fatelo, a lady of no rigid morals, was foolish enough to like me: she was wooed by two youthful monks, the Rev. Father Poignardini, and the Rev. Father Aconiti; but she put an end to the pretensions of both of them, by granting me her good graces; yet, at the same time, I narrowly escaped being excommunicated and poisoned.

poisoned. I left Rome exceedingly well pleased with the architecture of St. Peter's church.

I went to France, in the reign of Lewis surnamed the Just: the first thing I was asked, was, whether I chose to breakfast on a collop of the Marshal d'Ancre, whose body the public had roasted, and which was distributed very cheap to those that desired to taste it. This nation was at that time torn to pieces by civil wars, occasioned sometimes by ambition, sometimes by controversy; and those intestine broils had for the space of forty years deluged the most delightful country in the world with blood. Such were the liberties of the Gallican church: the French, said I, are naturally wise; what makes them deviate from that character? They are much given to joking and pleasantry, and yet they commit a massacre: happy that age in which they shall do nothing but joke and make merry.

From hence I set out for England; the same fanatical temper excited here the same furious zeal: a set of devout Roman Catholics had resolved, for the good of the church, to blow up the king, the royal family, and the parliament with gunpowder, and thereby free the nation from those heretics. I was shewn the spot where the blessed Q. Mary, daughter to Henry VIII. had caused above 500 of her subjects to be burnt alive. A pious Hibernian priest assured me, it was a very laudable action, 1st, because those they had burned were English; and, 2dly, because they were wretches who never took any holy water, and did not believe in St. Patrick.

From England I went to Holland, in hopes of finding more peace and tranquillity among a more phlegmatical people. At my arrival at the Hague, I was entertained with the beheading of a venerable old patriot, the prime minister Barneveldt, who was the most deserving man in the Republic. Struck with pity at the sight, I asked what his crime was, and whether he had betrayed the state? He has done worse, replied a preacher with a black cloak: he believes that we can be saved by good works, as well as by faith. You are sensible, that, were such systems suffered to prevail, the common-wealth could not long subsist, and that a severe law is necessary to check and refute such scandalous errors. A deep Dutch politician told me, with a sigh, that such commendable actions could not last for ever. Alas, Sir! said he, our people naturally incline towards toleration; some day or other they will adopt it; I shudder at the thought: believe me, Sir, pursued he, 'tis a mere chance that you actually find them so laudably and zealously inclined as to cut off the heads of their fellow-creatures for the sake of religion. Such were the lamentable words of the Dutchman; for my own part, I thought proper to abandon a country, whose severity had no compensation, and therefore embarked for Spain.

I arrived at Seville in the finest season in the year. The court was there, the galleons were arrived, and all seemed to proclaim joy, abundance, and profusion. I espied at the end of a beautiful alley, full of orange and lemon-trees, a vast concourse round an amphitheatre richly adorned: the king, the queen,

queen, the infants and infantas, were seated under a stately canopy; and over-against that august family, another throne, higher and more, magnificent had been erected. I told one of my travelling companions, that, unless that throne was reserved for God, I could not see the use of it: but these indiscreet words being over-heard by a grave Spaniard, I paid dear for having uttered them. In the mean time, I imagined we were to be diverted with a carousal, wrestling, or bull-baiting, when I perceived the grand inquisitor ascend that throne, and bestow his blessing upon the king and people. Then appeared an army of monks, filing off two by two: some were white, others were black, grey, and brown; some were shod, and some bare-footed; some had beards, and some had none; some were with cowls, and some without. Then came the executioner, followed by about forty wretches, guarded by a world of grandees and alguazils, and covered with garments, upon which were painted flames and devils. These fellows were Jews, who would not altogether be compelled to abandon the law of Moses; and Christians who had married their god-mothers, or perhaps refused to worship Nuestra Dama D'Atocha, or to part with their money in favour of the brothers Hieronymians. Prayers were said very devoutly, after which all those wretches were tortured and burnt, which concluded the ceremony, to the great edification of all the royal family.

The same night, while I was going to bed, two messengers from the inquisition came to my lodgings with the holy Hermandad. They embraced me tenderly, and, without speaking a word, carried me out of the house, and conducted me into a dungeon not incommoded by heat, adorned with a curious crucifix, and a mat instead of a bed. After I had been there six weeks, the father inquisitor sent his compliments, and desired to see me: I obeyed the summons. He received me with open arms, and, after having embraced me with more than paternal fondness, told me, he was very sorry they had put me in so bad a lodging, but that all the apartments happened to be full; it was impossible to give me a better; adding, however, that he hoped I should be better taken care of another time. Then he asked me very lovingly, whether I knew why I was put in there. I told the reverend father, I supposed it was for my sins. Well, my dear child, replied he, but for what sin? make me your confidant—speak. I did all I could to bethink myself of some misdemeanor, but in vain; upon which he made me recollect my imprudent words: in short, I recovered my liberty, after having undergone a severe discipline, and paid 30,000 reals. I went to take leave of the grand inquisitor: he was a very polite man, and asked me how I relished the holidays they had given me? I told him they were delightful, and at the same time went to press my companions to quit this enchanting country. They had time enough, during my confinement, to learn all the great atchievements of the Spaniards, for the sake of religion. They had read the memoirs of the famous Bishop of Chiapa, by which it appears, that

ten

ten millions of infidels were murdered in America to convert the rest. I imagined that bishop might exaggerate a little; but, suppose the victims were but half that number, the sacrifice was still admirable.

Notwithstanding the disagreeable adventures I had met with in my travels, I determined to finish my tour, and accordingly I embarked for Turkey, fully resolved never more to intermeddle with other people's affairs, nor give my judgment about public shows. These Turks, said I to my companions, are a set of unbaptized miscreants, and of course more cruel than the reverend fathers of the inquisition. Let us be silent among the Mahometans.

I arrived at Constantinople, where I was strangely surprized to see more Christian churches than in Candia; but much more so, to see also a numerous train of monks, permitted to offer their prayers freely to the Virgin Mary, and to curse Mahomet, some in Greek, others in Latin, and some in Armenian. How reasonable are the Turks! (exclaimed I) Whilst the Christian world stains a spotless religion with blood, these infidels tolerate doctrines which they abhor, without molestation or inhumanity. The Grecian and Latin Christians were at mortal enmity in Constantinople, and, like dogs that quarrelled in the streets, persecuted each other with the utmost violence. The Grand Vizir protected the Greeks, whose patriarch accused me before him of having supped with the Latins; and I was most charitably condemned by the Divan to receive one hundred blows with a lath, upon the sole of the foot, with permission, however, to be excused for 500 sequins. The next day the Grand Vizir was strangled; and the day following, his successor, who was for the Latin party, and who was not strangled till a month afterwards, condemned me to the same punishment, for having supped with the Grecian patriarch; and, in short, I was reduced to the sad necessity to frequent neither the Latin nor the Greek church. To make myself amends, I determined to keep a mistress, and pitched upon a young Turkish lass, who was as tender and wanton *tête à tête* as she was pious and devout at the mosque. One night, in the soft transports of her love, she embraced me passionately, calling out *alla, alla, alla.* These are the sacramental words of the Turks. I took them to be those of love, and therefore cried out, in my turn, *alla, alla, alla;* upon which she said, Heaven be praised! you are a Turk. In the morning the Iman came to circumcise me; but, as I made some difficulty, the Cadi of our quarters, a loyal gentleman, very kindly told me he purposed to impale me. I saved my foreskin, and my backside, with a thousand sequins, and flew into Persia, firmly resolved never to go to the Latin or Grecian mass in Turkey, nor ever more to say alla, alla, alla, at a rendezvous.

At my arrival at Ispahan, I was asked which I was for, white or black sheep? I answered, that the flesh of a white or black sheep was equal to me, provided it was tender. It must be known, that the factions of the white and black sheep still divided the Persians, who imagined I meant to laugh at both parties, insomuch that I had scarce entered the city gates, but I had a sad affair to extricate myself from, which I did however with a good number of sequins, by means of which I got safe out of the hands of the sheep.

I went as far as China with an interpreter, who informed me, that it was the only country where one might live freely, gaily, and peaceably. The Tartars had rendered themselves masters of it with fire and sword, and the reverend fathers the Jesuits on one side, and the reverend fathers the Dominicans on the other, said that they drew souls towards God every day, without any body's knowing it. Sure there never was a set of more zealous converters, for they persecuted one another by turns: they sent to Rome whole volumes of calumnies, wherein they reciprocally called each other infidels and prevaricators. There was particularly a terrible quarrel among them, about the method of making a bow. The Jesuits taught the Chinese to salute their parents after the manner of their country; and the Dominicans, on the contrary, held that they ought to bow to them after the manner of Rome. I happened to be taken by the Jesuits for a Dominican, and they told his Tartarian majesty, that I was the Pope's spy. The supreme council immediately ordered the prime mandarin, who ordered a sergeant, who ordered four guards to arrest and bind me, with all the ceremony used on such occasions. I was brought, after one hundred and forty genuflections, before his majesty, who asked me, whether I really was the Pope's spy, and whether it was true, that his holiness intended to come in person to dethrone him? I answered, that the pope was a priest, threescore and ten years of age; that he lived four thousand miles distant from his sacred Tartaro-Chinese majesty; that he had about two thousand soldiers, who mounted the guard with a parasol; that he never dethroned any body; and, in short, that his majesty might sleep in quiet. This was the last unfortunate adventure I met with in the whole course of my travels. I was sent to Macao, where I embarked for Europe.

I was obliged, in order to refit my ship, to put into an harbour on the coast of Golconda. I laid hold of that opportunity, to go and see the court of the great Aureng-zeb, so much renowned for its wonderful magnificence: he was then at Debli; and I had the good fortune to see him the day of that pompous ceremony, in which he received the heavenly present sent him by the sheriff of Mecca, viz. the broom with which they had swept the holy house, the Caaba, and the Beth alla. That broom is a symbol which sweeps away all uncleanness of soul. Aureng-zeb had no occasion for it, since he was the most pious man in all Indostan. 'Tis true he had cut his brother's throat, poisoned his father, and put to death, by torture, about 20 Rayas, and as many Omrahs; yet nothing was talked of but his devotion, which, they said, was without equal, except that of his most sacred majesty Muley Ismael, the most serene Emperor of Morocco, who never failed to cut off several heads every Friday after prayers.

To

To all this I spoke not a word: my travels and adventures had taught me to bridle my tongue; and I was very sensible, it was not mine to decide between the piety of the emperors of India and Morocco.

I had not yet seen Africa; but whilst I was debating with myself whether it was better to satisfy this last inclination, or sail for Italy, my ship was taken by the negroes, and I was, of course, carried thither. Our captain railed against the captors, asking them the reason why they thus outrageously violated the laws of nations? They replied, Your nose is long, and our's is flat; your hair is straight, and our wool is curled; you are white, and we are black; consequently we ought, according to the sacred and unalterable laws of nature, to be ever enemies.—You buy us on the coast of Guinea, as if we were not human creatures; then treat us like beasts, and with repeated blows compel us to an eternal digging into the mountains, in order to find a ridiculous yellow dust, of no intrinsic value, and not worth a good Egyptian onion: therefore when we meet with you, and are the strongest, we make you our slaves, and force you to till our ground, or else we cut off your nose or ears. We had nothing to say against so wise a discourse. I was employed to till the ground of an old negroe woman, having no inclination to lose either my nose or my ears; and, after a twelvemonth's slavery, I was redeemed by some friends I had written to for that purpose.

Having thus seen the world, and all that is great, good, and admirable in it, I resolved to return to Candia, where I married a little after my arrival. I was soon a cuckold, but plainly perceived it to be the most harmless and tolerable situation in life.

The most criminal not always the most unhappy. A moral tale; by the celebrated Helvetius.

WANT formerly assembled a number of men in the deserts of Tartary. Deprived of all, said one, we have a right to all. The law which strips us of necessaries to augment the superfluities of some Rajahs is unjust. Let us struggle with injustice. A treaty can no longer subsist, where the advantages cease to be mutual. We must force from our oppressors the wealth which they have forced from us. At these words the orator was silent; a murmur of approbation ran thro' the whole assembly: they applauded the speech; the project was noble, and they resolved to execute it; but they were divided about the means. The bravest rose first. Force, said they, has deprived us of all; it is by force we must recover it. If our Rajahs have by their tyrannic injustice snatched from us even what is necessary, so far as to require us to lavish upon them our own substance, our labour, and our lives, why should we refuse to our wants what the tyrants permit to their injustice? At the confines of these regions, the Bashaws, by the presents which they require, divide the profits of the caravans; they plunder the men, enslaved by their power and by fear. Less unjust, and more brave than them, let us attack

men

men in arms: let valour decide the victory, and let our riches be at least the price of our courage. We have a right to them. The gift of bravery points out those who should shake off the fetters of tyranny. Let the husbandman, without strength or courage, plow, sow, and reap. It is for us that he has gathered in the harvest.

Let us ravage, let us pillage the nation. We consent to all, cried those, who, having more wit and less courage, feared to expose themselves to danger; yet let us owe nothing to force, but all to imposture. We shall receive without danger, from the hands of credulity, what we shall in vain perhaps attempt to snatch by force. Let us cloath ourselves with the name and the habits of the Bonzes or the Bramins, and encompass the earth. We shall see every one eager to supply our wants, and even our secret pleasures.

This party appeared base and cowardly to those who were fierce and courageous. Being divided in opinion, the assembly separated: one party spread itself into India, Tibet, and the confines of China. Their countenances were austere, and their bodies macerated. They imposed on the people; they divided families, caused the children to be disinherited, and applied their substance to themselves. The people gave them lands, built them temples, and settled great revenues upon them. They borrowed the arm of power, in order to make the man of understanding bow to the yoke of superstition. In short, they subdued all minds by keeping the sceptre carefully concealed under the rage of misery, and the ashes of penance.

During this time their old brave companions retired into the deserts; surprized the caravans; attacked them sword in hand, and divided among themselves the booty.

One day, when doubtless the battle had not turned to their advantage, the people seized one of these robbers: they conducted him to the next city, they prepared the scaffold, and they led him to execution. He walked with a firm step, till he found in his way, and knew again, under the habit of a Bramin, one of those who had separated from him in the desert. The people respectfully surrounded the Bramin, and conducted him to his pagod. The robber stopped at seeing him: Just Gods! cried he, though equal in crimes, what a difference is there in our destiny! What do I say!—Equal in crimes? In one day he has, without fear, without danger, without courage, made more widows and orphans sigh, and deprived the empire of more riches, than I have pillaged in the whole course of my life. He had always two vices more than I, cowardice and falsehood: yet I am treated as a villain; he honoured as a saint: they drag me to the scaffold; him they lead to his pagod: me they impale; him they adore.

A Fortune with a Wife no ungenerous Demand in a Husband.

I HAVE frequently heard my brother bachelors reflected on for mercenary views in their matrimonial pursuits; and every girl with little or no fortune is sure to stigmatize

matize the man who requires money with his wife, as a downright *fortune-hunter*, in the odious sense of the word. But, under the shelter I now write, I dare tell these pretty disinterested maidens, that the man who is under a legal obligation to provide for his family is no such unreasonable monster in expecting a wife to furnish something besides her fair person; and, even when he has the name of receiving what is called a fortune with his wife, the affair is so managed after he is entangled by affection, that he has generally very little to boast of; and is extremely well off if the interest of this fortune indemnifies him for the extraordinary charges a family brings upon him.

But I will not let these blooming accusers off quite so easy; the tables may be fairly turned upon them; and if *some* men are rendered cautious by outliving their boyish attachments, and are hence charged with mercenary views (for I speak not of professed adventurers), it may justly be said that the *generality* of girls are real fortune-hunters, in the utmost latitude of the word. How many base parents are in specious circumstances, who drop artful hints of what they will do for a daughter, and, when an advantageous offer appears, will encourage a young man until they think he has swallowed the bait, and then discountenance the connection: when the young lady co-operating, a private match takes place, and the enraged papa or mama declares they will not give what they never had to bestow! The poor dupe, in such case, has no remedy but to take home the wife of his bosom, and make the best he can of his bargain: if he makes a good husband, it argues a generosity of temper, and a regard for his own peace and domestic happiness, which are not often found. Indeed, if the girl is as innocent as himself in the affair, none but a brute will consider her answerable for the trick; and if the marriage proves unfortunate, much, very much, has such a parent to answer for.

But, in a more general view, young ladies are too often the dupes of their own or their parents ambition. If miss has a tolerable face, and her father can give her five hundred or a thousand pounds, her first expectations extend at least to a carriage; and on this side thirty, which period she procrastinates as long as she decently can, she turns up her pretty nose at the plain tradesman behind a counter. If her fortune extends to fifteen hundred or two thousand pounds, she sets her cap at a coronet; and, because some such prizes have now and then turned up in the lottery of matrimony, her expectations seldom descend to a reasonable pitch, until she has no reason to hope for any thing: she has no remedy then in reserve but to rail at all mankind, and grow grey in protesting against matrimony.

Such, indeed, are the high motions and habits of dissipation that young ladies are ridiculously educated in, which their untutored understanding is seldom able to stem in the hoity-toity hey-day of life; so that it is equally dangerous for a sober thinking man, whom they generally undervalue and despise, to take a wife either with or without money. A tinsel

sop

fop beft fuits their eyes; they fly into the arms of fuch, and hence matrimony comes into difgrace by their being treated according to their deferts. Hence alfo arifes that habit of celibacy, which (profligates being out of my view) is very unjuftly charged to the account of the men.

Again; a father who can barely live, inftead of fending an able girl of a daughter out to fervice, or putting her in fome induftrious track of life to maintain herfelf, if he can but raife a filk gown or two for her, with a few ribbons, he too often depends himfelf, and teaches her to depend, upon enfnaring the affections of fome filly boy or other of property, by whom, though her cloaths are all her portion, fhe is to be fupported in a genteel character, which fhe has no juft claim to. If the fcheme fails, I am fhocked at reprefenting the confequences! Yes, ye unwife, ye cruel parents, this ftimulation of female vanity is the grand fource of proftitution: more unhappy girls walk the ftreets from this, as the firft caufe, than merely from the feduction of worthlefs men: which, if you acted a parental part in giving your daughters a fuitable fober education, they would in general be fortified againft. But I am tired of a difagreeable fubject: unwelcome truth will be conftrued into intended invective againft a fex which I honour, in general, though with which, unhappily, from fcrutinizing perhaps too narrowly, I have never been able to form a particular attachment; a point which was always in view, without being yet accomplifhed

But I have traced my fubject farther than I firft intended, which was only to obviate the accufation which difappointed fair ones are continually bringing againft the men for not marrying: this, in general terms, they are continually urging us to; but, in fo gay and luxurious an age, the follies of which women ever take the lead in, they either do not underftand, or defpife, the proper means of effecting. They may chufe the alternative, but either cafe renders them very unfit helpmates for thofe who are qualified to make *good* hufbands. This is found reafon, which all the wit and ridicule of a female pen, or tongue, however well pointed, cannot put to fhame.

A Dehortatory Speech, *by a wellaffected* Tanner, *to the County of* Berkfhire, *met at* Abingdon, *the 2d of* April, 1649, *for the Election of* Pembroke *to the Knight of the Shire.*

Honeft Friends,

YOU that are of the free-borne people of this land,—I fpeak to none elfe,—and lovers of the army, and the true Englifh intereft, all men elfe have forfeited their freedomes. I am full of anguifh and trouble for your fakes, when I behold this day. I fear you are in a way to ruine yourfelves, unleffe the Lord be merciful to you. The thing you meete for troubles me not a little: 'tis to choofe a knight. Truly, I hoped, and I hope we all hoped, to have done making knights by this time. The *thing* you meete to choofe troubles me more. This fellow that was a lord, this Pembroke, this Montgomery, this Herbert,

Herbert, this what shall I call him? call him what you will: we were promised a representative to begin on June next, and this parliament to end the last of this month; if so, why should we send this fellow thither to make mouthes for three weekes, and talke of dogs and hawkes? I say; let us have the representative, or we are cheated. But if we must make one knight more, let it not be Pembroke: he is no way fit for it. Consider him as a lord, and none of the wisest lords neither; and then consider how many wiser and fitter persons we have for parliament-men than ever a lord of them all: and what a brand it will be to us and our country to choose a lord, such a lord; and surely, unlesse you are fooles and madmen, you will not choose him. Againe; consider him as a lord, and so he is no free-borne commoner, and so not capable of our election. Is there not an act against king and lords? if there is, then let us have no lords; unlesse you intend to have a king too.

Let us be wise; we may see a designe in this lord as plain as the nose on his face. He was alwayes false; false to the king that loved him, false to the lord that sate eight yeares with him; and doe you not think he will be false to the commons too? I warrant you. Is not Michael Oldsworth, this lord's man, a parliament-man?— Are not his and other lords' sonnes parliament-men? If he get in too, the time will come, when the house of commons will be all lords, and lords' sonnes, and lords' servants, and then lords will be voted up againe, and king be in request againe, which if we live to see againe, we have spun a fair thread.

If all this which I have said be true, as it is impossible it should be otherwise, why should we not look on this turn-coat lord as a cheat, as one that comes to betray and undoe the free-borne people, and switch him out of the country?

I have done: if we must choose a knight, let him not be a lord: we doe not read in all the scripture of any lord was ever chosen knight of the shire for Barkshire. But rather let us choose none at all, and unanimously petition the parliament to dissolve, that the representative may succeed, and none but ourselves have any share in the gubernation and government of this commonwealth.

A godly Speech, spoken by Philip Herbert, late Earl of Pembroke, &c. as it was heard with much Content without an Oath.

Gentlemen,

IT was not the old fashion to make speeches before you chose your knights; but I hope you like it the better for not being old, I am sure I doe; give us old fashions againe, we must have king and lords, our old religion, and old lawes, and a hundred things older than Adam. I hate any thing that's old, unlesse it be an old man; for Adam was an old man, and so am I; and I hate myself for being an old man, and therefore will love you, if yu'le make me a new knight. The gentleman that spake before me, I know not where to have him, he is an *individuum vagum.* He is angry the representative goes not on: he is angry the

the parliament goes not off; he is angry I am a lord; he is angry I would be none; he is angry I seek to be your knight, and he would have me of that sort of seekers, who neither seeke nor finde: and he concludes, I am not to be chosen because no free-borne commoner. I fear he is a Jesuite by his subtle arguments; but though I have no logick, I hope I have reason to answer him, and satisfie you.

I answer, I am a free-borne commoner. All those three words fit me. First,

I am borne.

Else how came I hither into the world?

I am free.

My accounts for last yeare's expence came to six and twenty thousand pounds: that's faire you'l say; and when you have chosen me your knight, I'll carry you every mother's son, the whole county, into Wiltshire, and we'll be merry, and hunt, and hawke, and I'll be as free as an emperor. So I am free-borne.

I am a commoner.

Have I been so often at common councels, and common halls, to be accounted no commoner? Are not the lords all turn'd a grazing? Was not I a common swearer before I went to lectures, and a common sleeper ever since, and am not I chancellour of Oxford, where all are commoners? So I am a commoner.

I am no lord.

If I am, why should I come hither to be knight of your shire? but though I am a lord, is not Fairfax so? and yet he is a parliament-man; and is not Bradshaw Lord President? But I am no lord; for, I am for the parliament; I am for voting down the house of lords. And to tell you truth, I never loved the King since he was dead, and those that are lords goe in black for him; but I keep my old blue still, and my diamond hatband, though the crown jewels are sold. Therefore you may choose me well enough.

You must choose me.

Why came I hither else? why did Cromwell bid me come hither? and I bid my steward come hither to lay in provision, and gather voyces. If my steward's bill be right, every throat that votes for me costs me twenty pound.

Choose me, if you would have a representative. I that have been Lord of Pembroke and Montgomery, two counties may well represent one.

Choose me, if you would have no representative. For I'le doe and vote what you list; and so choosing me, you choose yourselves. So that, whether you would have a representative or no, the best way is to choose me.

But let me tell you by the way, now the parliament is fallen into the happy way of making acts of parliament, let them continue. This is one of the advantages you have by losing the King: you may have an act of parliament for what you please; and that's better than ordinance, and lasts longer; for an ordinance of parliament was good no longer than this parliament, which though it last for ever, an act lasts longer, because that lasts for ever, whether the parliament last or no.

For my religion.

Who questions it? I never changed it: I was for bishops when there were bishops; and I was for visitors

viſitors when there were none. It is well known I am an independant, and had beene ſo twenty yeares ago, had it not been for Michael Oldſworth, and will be ſo as long as the parliament pleaſe: I have been an old courtier, and that's an old court, and the higheſt court, and old courtiers always love to follow new faſhions. That religion is in faſhion now.

I am a chancellour of Oxford, which is hard by, therefore chooſe me: ſome of you have ſonnes and cozens there: all that are a kinne to any that give their voyces for me, ſhall be heads of colledges, and canons of Chriſt Church, though there be a hundred of them. The reſt of you ſhall have the leaſes of all the univerſity lands amongſt you: what, am not I chancellour?

The place I ſtand for, is knight of the ſhire. None but kings can make knights; make me your knight, you are all kings: and it will be an honour to me, and my poſterity, to have it recorded, I was the firſt lord that was knighted by ſo many kings.

I know, now, you cannot but chooſe me: I knew ſo before I came hither, and therefore I thank you beforehand, and invite you home.

I will conclude with that very exordium, wherewith a famous gentleman that was of this parliament concluded his ſpeech upon the like occaſion: "Behold your "knight."

Eſſay on good Humour.

HUMAN nature ever was, and ever will be, the ſame. It only takes different methods of diſplaying itſelf, according to the genius of the people, the auſterity or licentiouſneſs of time and place, &c. Thus a nymph of the Hottentots, who breaks the griſtle of her child's noſe, and anoints it with greaſe and ſoot, is equally as well pleaſed with the contrivance to increaſe what they think beauty, as our delicate European dames are when they ſpoil their own and their children's complexions by waſhes and paint. Fancy and imitation are the guides of taſte: why, then, may not the tawny mother admire her ſooty ſon, and bleſs his goggling eyes, his blubber lips, his woolly head, and delicate complexion? Why not laugh as heartily at our want of diſcernment as we do at their's? The reaſon is every whit as obvious to them, on their ſide the queſtion, as it is to us on our's. Black teeth, and extravagant long nails, are the greateſt ornaments of the Siameſe: painted bodies, and jewels dangling from their lips and noſes, is the fine taſte of the Americans. "Oh, odious creatures!—Ridiculous taſte!" ſays a London or Pariſian Belle.—And why ſo, my pert miſſes? Had it been your fate to have been born even in this polite iſland ſome two thouſand years ſooner, you might have been as great adepts in plaiſtering your bodies as you are now at daubing your faces. A ſtar on your arm might have had as fine an effect in thoſe days, as Bruſſels or Mechlin has in theſe. A creſcent painted on your forehead might have been eſteemed equal to a French fly-cap; and the meridian ſun diſplayed in full luſtre on your delicate naked boſoms might have had more at-

tractive

tractive powers than the dazzling glare of a modern birth-day diamond stomacher. But to be serious—Say, my pretty fair one, would you wish to please? Would you have your lover adore you? Nay, what is of far greater consequence than either, would you wish to be happy?—"Yes." Then study to make every person around you so. You will find far more satisfaction giving pleasure to another than in receiving it yourself. There is a kind of benignity in conveying happiness to another, which only experience can give you any idea of. Your own felicity depends, in a great measure, upon the proper exertion of this principle.

Flavia was left to the care of her own fortune at the age of seventeen. Her mother, knowing her innate virtue and solid principles, thought these her properest guardians. She thought right. Flavia's beauty and fortune, which were both considerable, drew crowds of fluttering fops and fortune-hunting rakes to her shrine. The rakes imagined so much youth and innocence could never resist their refined arts; the beaus depended upon the striking charms of their powdered paper-skulls. Had Flavia been so disposed, here was an ample field before her, in which she might have fully indulged the vanity of her age and sex, and coquetted away, at once, both her innocence and happiness. She, however, gave all these their answers as fast as they came, but with so much sweetness and sensibility, that she awed the rakes, and delighted the fools.

She was in her twentieth year when first young Lovemore paid his addresses to her. This youth was of a very different complexion from any of her former humble servants: he loved her heartily for her beauty; but he loved her more for her good humour and good sense. He saw how completely happy the man must be who gained so rich a prize; and the bare thought of a possibility of losing her gave him more real uneasiness, while it lasted, than it is in the power of beauty alone to create. She perceived his merit, and observed how respectfully he admired her. As it was contrary to the goodness of her heart to keep any one in a state of suspence, she was no sooner assured of the equity of his intentions, but she made him both easy and happy, by giving her hand where her heart dictated. Those maxims which preserved her in her youth, continued and increased her happiness in an advanced age.

Her husband is for ever extolling the darling of his heart, and expatiating on her virtues; indeed, every one that knows her admires her, and blessings flow from every tongue on the head of the good, the benevolent Flavia.

On the Origin of Signs denoting Trades.

AS, with respect to signs at least, London is become a kind of New Jerusalem, in which "old things are done away, and all things are become new," let me, before the remembrance of them also is gone, record something concerning them that may become an object of learning to posterity, as the symbols of Egypt and the coins of Palmyra are to us.

It is highly proba e, as others have

have observed, that signs were originally symbolical representations of certain trades, which the artificer or dealer hung out, to intimate, by a kind of universal language, what particular necessaries he sold or made. With this view, the woollen-draper hung out a woolpack; the retailers of linen tied up a few yards by way of festoon, the representation of which is still seen over the windows of their shops; the barber exposed a head, since converted to a long stick, because that also is called a *pole*; the ironmonger a frying-pan, before we were poisoned by copper; the shoemaker a last; and the vintner a tun.

But as luxury increased, and trades multiplied, imagination was soon exhausted in devising symbols, or, if symbols could have been contrived to express them in all their varieties, they would no longer have been generally understood. To discover the trade by the sign, would have become as difficult as to discover the sentiments of a hieroglyphic, in which the wings of an eagle are added to the body of a lion, and the tail of a serpent, to express the virtues of a prince who possessed courage, activity, and wisdom. Another insuperable objection would also very soon have arisen, from the complication of various things in a symbol or hieroglyphic: it would want a name, and for that reason could never be a direction to the house at which it should be set up as a sign. As it was necessary, therefore, that a sign should be some mark affixed to a house, of which a perfect idea was connected with its name, and by which any particular house might be distinguished from all others in the same street or district, signs soon became representations of some sensible object, as a dog, a horse, a bear, or a lion, without any regard to the trade or profession carried on in the house before which they were hung up.

As it was necessary to vary the sign oftener than new objects could easily be found, a very convenient diversity was introduced, by representing the same objects of different colours: thus had we blue boars, green dragons, black horses and white horses; and lions, black, white, golden, and red. It is something extraordinary, that when art had so far departed from nature as to give fictitious colours to one animal, she did not, for the same convenience, give fictitious colours to all; yet we have no blue horses, or green boars; nor did I ever hear of the red bear, or the white bull. It is also remarkable, that though all our lions, which are painted yellow, are called golden lions, we never should have exalted the white lion to a silver one. In Calais, however, there is an inn called the silver lion: does national genius differ even in the denomination of a sign! But signs, in whatever light they are considered, were certainly the effect of a general want of literature, and therefore can no longer be thought necessary, without national disgrace. It is very well known, that there was a time when an act was made for the encouragement of learning, or, as it is generally called, *for the benefit of the clergy*, which, when a felon was condemned to be hanged, gave him his life if he could read a verse in the Bible, opened at a venture, which was therefore called his

neck-

neck-verse. Thus was the fond parent induced to give his child good learning, not that he might with more advantage be an honest man, but that with less danger he might be a thief. How it came that our wise ancestors thought fit to encourage learning and larceny together, and thus sow tares with their wheat, we may as well not enquire; we are happy that so good a crop has been produced of the wheat, and we must get rid of the tares as we can. But it is equally certain, that, when it was thought expedient to make such a law for increasing the number of those who could read, it was necessary to distinguish houses by pictures, instead of writing, and that, now, houses may be distinguished better by writing than pictures. There is at present scarce a child among the poorest of the people, who at seven or eight years old cannot read a man's name and trade upon his door, or window shutter; and therefore we want the sign-painter no more.

Be it known, however, to posterity, that, long after signs became unnecessary, it was not unusual for an opulent shop-keeper to lay out as much upon a sign, and the curious iron-work with which it was fixed to his house, so as to project nearly into the middle of the street, as would furnish a less considerable dealer with a stock in trade. I have been credibly informed, that there were many signs and sign-irons upon Ludgate-Hill which cost several hundred pounds; and that as much was laid out by a mercer on a sign of the queen's head, as would have gone a good way towards decorating the original for a birth-night.

I remember to have seen three angels, not far from Somerset-house, in the Strand, which by the thumbs and noses I knew to be the work of a celebrated artist, who, to borrow a word from the present fashionable cant, *figures* in the exhibition. And there was not long since, in Paternoster Row, a head of Mr. Pope, by another artist not less eminent, who upon that occasion condescended to oblige his friend; but if I am glad that one opportunity of silly extravagance is taken away from our fine gentlemen of the shop, I am sorry that a set of industrious artificers have lost their trade: it is always very hurtful to turn money into a new channel: to take away an annual profit from those who have been accustomed to it, does more mischief than giving it to those who have not been accustomed to it can do good. He that has lived without it, can live without it still; but he cannot live without it, to whom habits of life long contracted have made it necessary.

But I shall now take notice of some strange corruptions, which, by change of customs, by the gradual obscurity which time throws round unrecorded events, and the inaccuracy of all oral language, have happened with respect to signs.

It is well known, that, among other signs which were lately taken down, there was the bull and mouth, and the bull and gate: how a bull and a gate might come together, it was very easy to conceive; but what should join a bull and a mouth, sure no mortal can guess:

guess: yet a monstrous pair of lips and a bull have been many years hung up, painted together upon a board, as a sign for an inn, so considerable, as to give name to the street where it stands.

Those who are at all acquainted with English history know, that one of our princes was born at Bologne in France, and was therefore distinguished by the name of Henry of Bologne. In compliment to this prince, one Roger du Bourg, after having himself been many times in France, took a house just within the old wall of the city near Alderfgate; and, converting it into an inn, put up the sign of the *mouth* or *harbour* of *Bologne*, which was called the *Bologne Mouth*, as we call the harbours on our coast Portsmouth, and Plymouth. What the success of du Bourg was, we cannot certainly tell, but probably it was considerable, for it produced a rival not far distant, who, as he could not put up the same sign, put up one that might easily be confounded with it;—the *gate*, instead of the *harbour*, of the town which was called the *Bologne Gate*.

There is an inn in the Borough still standing, which is known to have been the house from which the pilgrims set out to pay their devotions to St. Thomas à Becket, at Canterbury, whose tales have been recorded by our old poet Chaucer. This inn was formerly distinguished by the sign of a herald's coat without sleeves, called a *Taberd*. At that time, when our processions were by cavalcade, and when tilts and tournaments were held on every public occasion, a herald and his office, and his coat, were well known. But the name of his coat survived the remembrance of it, and the house, like other houses, long retained the name of the sign, after the sign was destroyed: when, upon some occasion, it was thought necessary to put up a new sign for the Taberd inn, nothing was known by a name any thing like *Taberd*, but a kind of spotted dog, with long ears, which was called a *Talbot*; a spotted dog, therefore, with long ears, was painted upon a board, instead of the herald's coat, and the inn continued, under a different symbol, to be distinguished by the same name.

But the present method of writing the name and the trade of our citizens over their doors, however explicit, is, like all other sublunary things, subject to error and inconvenience.

Not long ago, as I was walking along the Strand, I cast my eyes upon one side of a window which projected in half an octagon from the house, and I read the words *Hanging Warehouse*, written in large gold letters: *hanging*, thought I, is an operation that used to be performed among us too rarely to support a reputable house-keeper in a warehouse, which attracts the notice of passengers by its splendid appearance in one of our principal streets. I went on, and over the window of a corner house near Golden-square, I read in letters equally conspicuous, *Children made here*.

This shop, said I to myself, may probably get more customers than a *hanging warehouse*; but, surely, thus publickly to advertise the making of children is a most flagitious breach of public decency. As I came back, however, looking up at at the fame fhop in the other ftreet, I read, *Hofe for men, women, and* (to which I found the reft of the fentence) *children made here*, regularly followed upon turning the corner. When I came to read the middle line of my femi-octagon at the warehoufe, I found the man's name; and, upon looking back, I found that it ftood between the words, *The paper*, and thofe which I had read before, *hanging warehoufe*. Surely our houfe-keepers fhould fo divide the words which exprefs their name and their trade that any part of them may necefsarily imply that there are more, and not betray fome Frenchman, whom a bookfeller may hire to run through England, that he may publifh his travels when he goes back, into the affertion, that we publickly advertife the making of children, and a convenient warehoufe for the accommodation of the multitudes who in our dark weather go out of the world in a ftring. Abfurdities as grofs as we have feen, and do ftill fee, in the accounts of our country by foreigners, and of foreign countries by the natives of our own.

It has long been the cuftom of fome of our artificers, who keep a fhop where they fell what they make, to ufe a kind of mixed writing, partly literal, and partly hieroglyphic. The commodity is expreffed by a fymbol or a fample, and we are laconically informed, that it is *made* as well as fold, by the artificer's name placed before the word *maker*: thus Mr. *Day* hangs out a hat, and infcribes his door-way with *Day-maker;* and Mr. *King* does the fame by a *ftocking*. An inhabitant of India, therefore, to whom thefe words, and others of the fame kind, fhould be conftrued, might be tempted to think that he was not in another kingdom only but in another planet, among beings of a fuperior order, the makers of kings, popes, tempefts, dew, and daylight.

A diligent obferver, however, of thefe civic infcriptions will often be amufed by the happy union of profeffions with names, and of different names with each other in partnerfhip. Who but muft have noted the happy junction of *Young* and *Wife*, in Ludgate-ftreet, and of *Spinnage* with *Lamb*, *Sage* with *Gofling*, *Bowyer* with *Fletcher*, and many others, in different parts of the town, but particularly *Long* and *Short*, in High Holborn; a conjunction which muft produce that medium which has been celebrated by philofophers and poets in all ages and countries. Between *Bowyer* and *Fletcher*, perhaps all my readers may not know the relation; it is therefore neceffary to acquaint them, that, before the invention of fire-arms, two trades concurred in the making an arrow. One formed and feathered the fhaft, who was called a *flechiere*, from the French word *fleche*, an arrow; and the other prepared and fixed on the point, who was called an arrowfmith. *Flechiere* was eafily corrupted into *Fletcher*, and *arrowfmith* has become a proper name, without alteration. Every one alfo muft have obferved, that Mr. *Sharp* is a *furgeon*, that Mr. *Littlefear* is an *apothecary*, and that Mr. *Goodluck* keeps a *lottery-office*. Of Mr. Sharp, and Mr. Littlefear, I fhall fay nothing; but, in juftice to Mr. Goodluck, I muft relate an anecdote but little known.

Every

Every body remembers, that, some years ago, a person publickly advertised, that he would go into a quart bottle, at the Little Theatre in the Hay-market, which has ever since procured him the name of the Bottle-Conjuror. Many persons repaired to the house at the time, and among others Mr. Goodluck: by some fortunate accident he got into the green-room, when the conjuror was practising with a bottle, previous to his exhibition upon the stage; and, watching his opportunity, when the operator had just got his head below the rim of the bottle, he clapped a cork into it, and brought him away. It is supposed that Mr. Goodluck had a view to his future advantage in this bold attempt; but, however that be, it is certain that the bottle-conjuror is now in his possession, and has made the calculation which has so much astonished the world in Mr. Goodluck's advertisements. By this calculation Mr. Goodluck avers, that particular numbers have been ascertained, among 600 of which there will certainly be as many prizes as among 700 promiscuously chosen.

Mr. Goodluck has been severely censured for disappointing the company at the Hay-market, and confining a person, who, if not an Englishman, was at least under the protection of English government; and it is insinuated, that if his calculator should by any means escape from the bottle, he may recover such damages for false imprisonment as Mr. Goodluck will find it difficult to pay.

It must, however, be acknowledged, that Mr. Goodluck has given us a remarkable instance of disinterestedness, and even generosity, in distributing among his customers, at common prices, those fortunate numbers, by the private selection of which for himself he might have amassed an immense fortune.

I know it has been said, that it is ridiculous to suppose Mr. Goodluck to have any view in multiplying his customers but increasing his gains; and therefore it must be inferred, that he gets more by selling his tickets than by keeping them, which, if they were lucky numbers, that have more than an equal chance, could not be the case: but this is reasoning upon common principles, which may enable us to account for the actions of common men, but not to investigate the motives of One who keeps a conjuror in a bottle.

Your's, &c.
AMBULATOR.

The Folly of Self-Tormenting.

MR. Addison says, that when people complain of weariness or indisposition in good company, they should immediately be presented with a night-cap, as a hint that it would be best for them to retire. I own, I am one of those who have no idea of carrying either my cares or my infirmities out of my own habitation, except in such instances as I am sensible they can receive relief or mitigation.—Why should I unnecessarily wound the good nature of my friend, or make myself contemptible to my enemies?—If the communication of my grievances really interrupts the satisfaction of those amongst whom I am cast, I have hurt them without benefitting myself;

self; and, on the contrary, if they only dissemble with me, it is a species of ridicule which my mind is not calculated to sustain;—but you will allow me to observe, that I confine myself on this occasion to the valetudinarian, and the magnifier of trifles into calamities—for to deny the severely attacked, whether mentally or corporeally, the relief of complaining, would be to strike at the root of humanity, and forfeit the characteristics of our nature.

To come, however, more immediately to the point, I must tell you, that I have perhaps the most curious set of relations you ever heard of.—My mother, poor woman, her affections are sanctified by their poignancy and sincerity—the loss of the man she loved, and a consequential decay of constitution;—but then I have an aunt that is evermore upon the rack of her own imagination: not a change of weather, or a change of situation, that does not produce some present or prospective agony. If the day is fine, her corns inform her that we shall have rain to-morrow—if the sun is tolerably powerful, she expires with heat; or if temperate, she anticipates the inconveniencies of approaching winter:—if she perceives a cloud, she is for running into an obscure corner to preserve her eyes from lightning—and when she beholds a clear horizon, trembles for the consequences of a drought. Not a melancholy intimation is dropped in her hearing, but she instantly recollects a thousand dreadful disasters she has either experienced or escaped; and when she is told of any extraordinary piece of good fortune's reaching people unexpectedly, she repines at the ungraciousness of her stars, that withholds every such blessing from falling to her share.

A brother of this lady's, consequently an uncle of mine, who had met with a cruel disappointment in love at a very early period of his life, was so morose as to insist upon it, that women were universally unworthy, and universally unfaithful:—tell a story to their advantage, and he was petulant; mention them with severity, and you apparently tear open his old wounds:—if he was treated respectfully by them, they were deceitful; and if they behaved coolly, he complained of being despised. When the younger part of his relations were disposed to be merry, his head ached; and when they were serious, they treated him as if he was a bug-bear: when he was consulted what he would chuse for dinner, he was teazed; and when unconsulted, he was neglected.—But to sum up all—after years of assiduity and attention on the part of all his relations, excepting your humble servant, whose independent spirit frequently incited him to raillery, he died, and left me every shilling of his fortune as a reward for my sincerity.

A young fellow, who stands in the relationship of cousin-german to me, is what may justly be entitled a constitutional self-tormentor—for he was so from his infancy. When a school-boy, whatever was in another's possession was always considered by him as much better than his own:—his top never spun so well, nor his marbles rolled so dexterously, as those of his companions—his task was always harder than any body else's, and his repetition of it listened to with prejudiced ears by our master.

On

On entering into life, this strange humour increased upon him: he conceived every dinner he was not a partaker of much more excellent than the one he participated.—Every tailor, if he changed a dozen times in a month, was smarter than those he employed; and every estate he heard of happier situated, and better improved than his own, though the rents were absolutely inferior to what he was in the receipt of. He attached himself to a fine accomplished girl, but soon found out that her sister was much more charming. The sister had a young friend who had as much the advantage of her, and that friend a relation that surpassed them all—— His strange humour and inconsistency soon marked him for an object of contempt; and however, out of respect to his family, he is to this day received in some few houses, he is tolerated, not approved; pitied, not honoured, notwithstanding his birth, education, and estate.

I have a sister, which is the last oddity I introduce to you at this period, that is evermore labouring under some imaginary disease—— She sits down to table without an appetite, it is true—but then she has been eating all the morning: her complexion is extremely fine—but the bloom of nature is called a hectic: her voice, that is naturally sweet, is changed into an affected whine; and her nerves are so delicate, that one of my honest laughs is sufficient to throw her into hysterics. I have taken great pains to convince her of her folly; but if I attempt to rally, she bursts into tears, and I am hurried out of the room as the greatest of all barbarians. I make daily resolutions to renounce all connection with so ridiculous a groupe of wretches; my resolutions, nevertheless (barbarian as I am), are dissolved by their applications to return to them, though the infallible consequence of our re-union is an abrupt separation.

Is it not astonishing, Sir, that people in no degree deficient in understanding, and blessed with affluence, would be such enemies to their repose, that, instead of attending to the distresses of others, which they have the power so amply to relieve, they thus defeat all the gracious purposes of Providence, where their own happiness is concerned, and neglect all the opportunities of doing good that lie before them?

Your humble servant,
GEORGE GOODFELLOW.

An original Letter which was written by the celebrated Sir Walter Raleigh *to Prince* Henry, *eldest Son of* James *the First.*

May it please your Highness,

THE following lines are addressed to your Highness from a man who values his liberty, and a very small fortune, in a remote part of this island, under the present constitution, above all the riches and honours that he could any where enjoy under any other establishment.

You see, Sir, the doctrines that are lately come into the world, and how far the phrase has obtained of calling your royal father, God's Vicegerent; which ill men have turned both to the dishonour of God, and the impeachment of his Majesty's goodness. They adjoin vicegerency to the idea of being all-
power

powerful, and not to that of being all-good. His Majesty's wisdom, it is to be hoped, will save him from the snare that may lie under gross adulations; but your youth, and the thirst of praise which I have observed in you, may possibly mislead you to hearken to those charmers who would conduct your noble nature into tyranny. Be careful, O my Prince! Hear them not; fly from their deceits: you are in the succession to a throne, from whence no evil can be imputed to you, but all good must be conveyed from you.

Your father is called the Vicegerent of heaven: while he is good, he is the vicegerent of heaven. Shall man have authority from the fountain of good to do evil? No, my Prince: let mean and degenerate spirits, which want benevolence, suppose your power impaired by a disability of doing injuries. If want of power to do ill be an incapacity in a Prince, with reverence be it spoken, it is an incapacity he had in common with the Deity. Let me not doubt but all pleas, which do not carry in them the mutual happiness of Prince and People, will appear as absurd to your great understanding as disagreeable to your noble nature.

Exert yourself, O generous Prince, against such sycophants in the glorious cause of liberty; and assume such an ambition worthy of you to secure your fellow-creatures from slavery; from a condition as much below that of brutes, as to act without reason, as less miserable than to act against it. Preserve to your future subjects the divine right of being free agents, and to your own royal house the divine right of being their benefactors. Believe me, my Prince, there is no other right can flow from God. While your Highness is forming yourself for a throne, consider the laws as so many common places in your study of the science of government: when you mean nothing but justice, they are an ease and help to you. This way of thinking is what gave men the glorious appellation of Deliverers and Fathers of their country: this made the sight of them rouse their beholders into acclamations, and mankind incapable of bearing their very appearance, without applauding it as a benefit. Consider the inexpressible advantages which will ever attend your Highness, while you make the power of rendering men happy the measure of your actions. While this is your impulse, how easily will that power be extended!

The glance of your eye will give gladness, and your very sentence have a force of bounty. Whatever some men would insinuate, you have lost your subjects when you have lost their inclinations. You are to preside over the minds, not the bodies of men: the soul is the essence of the man, and you cannot have the true man against his inclinations. Choose, therefore, to be the King or the Conqueror of your people; it may be submission, but it cannot be obedience that is passive.

I am, SIR,

Your Highness's

most faithful servant,

WALTER RALEIGH.

London, Aug. 12, 1611.

The History of a popular Character in France very much mentioned, but very little known in England (from the Account of the Characters and Manners of the French).

WHILE taking notice of the domestic and familiar intercourse subsisting between the clergy and the fair sex in France, it were unpardonable to omit a being of which we simple Protestants entertain no sort of idea.

This being is what they call here an *Abbé*, a term not to be rendered in our language, as their existence is posterior to the reformation, and no such character was known among the Romanists till about a century and a half ago, and scarce even then. Their origin, like that of some nations, is hardly discernible; though one may venture to assert, that France has the best right to claim the merit of having produced them.

Their first appearance seems to have been about the commencement of the last century, as before that æra it is presumed the title of Abbé is not to be met with, unless in the monastic sense (in which it is very antient), or to denote a person possessed of those revenues of an abbey that fell to the department of the abbot; but as to the now common and almost burlesque denomination of *Abbé*, it is of the recent date above-mentioned.

It is, however, a very convenient word to signify what could not otherwise be comprised in one; as an *Abbé*, according to the strictest definition, is a person who has not yet obtained any precise or fixed settlement in church or state, but most heartily wishes for and would accept of either; just as it may happen. There is no deviation, it is to be hoped, from truth in representing them in this light.

In the mean while, their privileges are many. They are admissible in all companies, and no degradation to the best, notwithstanding they are sometimes found in the worst. Their dress is rather that of an academic, or of a professed scholar, than of an ecclesiastic; and never varying in colour is no incumbrance on the pocket. Their society is far from avoided; as numbers of them are genteel, sensible, well-bred, and enlightened men, fit for the conversation of any whose pursuit is either entertainment or instruction.

It should also be remembered, that the title of *Abbé* is not only applicable to those we have been describing, but likewise to ecclesiastics of the highest rank, cardinals and bishops only being above it, in the usual mention of churchmen; all degrees of whom it is otherwise promiscuously annexed to, and neither hurts nor benefits any body's character.

And really it is some comfort to a poor gentleman, as well as scholar, that he can produce himself to the community under the shelter of some decent appellation. That of gentleman becomes ridiculous, when the means of supporting it are apparently wanting; and that of scholar would be rather vain and affected.

These *Abbés* are very numerous, and no less useful. They are, in colleges, the instructors of youth; in private families, the tutors of young gentlemen: and many procure a decent livelihood by their literary and witty compositions of all kinds, from the profoundest philo-

philosophy to the most airy romances. They are, in short, a body of men that possesses a fund of universal talents and learning; and is incessantly employed in the cultivation of every various branch of literature and ingenuity. No subject whatever escapes them; serious or gay, solid or ludicrous, sacred or profane, all pay tribute to their researches; and as they are conversant in the lowest as well as the highest topics, their fame is equally great in the learned and in the scribbling world.

An essential article would be wanting in this description of the *Abbés*, were we to pass by their devotion to the fair sex, whose favourites, in return, they have the honour of being in the fullest and most enviable degree. The wit and smartness for which they are usually remarkable are just the very things that suit the ladies; to please whom, all must labour in vain who are not abundantly provided with this grand *desideratum*, in France, where it is more in request, and less willingly dispensed with, in all who aim at ingratiating themselves with the sex, than in any other country whatever. *De l'esprit & de la vivacité*, a lively and facetious disposition, is the only passport which, among the French ladies, will ensure the party a gracious reception. Whoever has it not, is far from being acceptable in the generality of French companies; where, as the ladies sit umpires, they who are deficient in what they deem the most necessary requisite will make but a very indifferent figure.

Hence though we serious, grave Englishmen, are by no means undervalued among the French gentlewomen, who know how to set a full and proper estimation on our respective merit, yet they are ever accusing us of being perpetually plunged in a reverie, from which nothing can totally extricate us.

Their accusation, however, falls erroneously on numbers of our countrymen, who are as jocund and airy as the merriest and most lively of their own. But then the gaiety of an Englishman is only occasional; the *toujours gai* is peculiar to a Frenchman: and it is worth observing, that such a disposition is so very far from being congenial to the former, that an affectation of it is the great *pierre d'achoppement*, the sure stumbling-block of our young English travellers; as an Englishman, indeed a man of any nation, always appears to the best advantage when he shews himself as he really is, and seeks not to set himself off by foreign airs unnatural to his temper and inclination; and which only lay him open to ridicule, by the awkwardness of his endeavours to imitate originals, of which nature never designed him for a copy.

To return to our *Abbés*: they are, like Gay's universal apparition, present every where; the reason of which is obvious, being sought after by most people, on various accounts, as they are equally men of business and pleasure, not less expert in the most serious transactions, than fond of enjoying their share of whatever occupies the gay world. Hence they diligently frequent all public spectacles, which are thought incomplete without them; as they compose the most intelligent part of the

the company, and are the moſt weighty approvers or condemners of what paſſes in almoſt all places.

Certain it is, that they are, in many reſpects, not only the inſpectors but the cenſors-general of the land, and that the judgments which flow from their tribunals are commonly very deciſive; more perhaps than ſome perſonages of very elevated ſtations would ſuffer them to be, if their power extended to the controlment of the underſtanding.

Diſſertation on the Virtues and Abilities of Caligula's *Horſe.*

WHEN I read over our own hiſtory, as well as that of other nations, I feel a kind of reverence riſe in my ſoul for the memories of ſeveral emperors, kings, princes, and ſovereign dukes, for the wiſdom, as well as excellent taſte, they have ſhewn in the judicious choice of ſuch perſons as they thought worthy to be placed at the helm of government.

When one conſiders that the prince has it in his power to chuſe out of millions of his ſubjects, and among whom there are no doubt both wiſe men and fools; when we ſee him hit on one in whom virtue and wiſdom are ſo equally conſpicuous, that all the world agrees there was not his fellow left, it muſt fill one's mind with wonder and ſurprize.

What a happineſs (for example) muſt it have been to live under the auſpicious reign of the Emperor Caligula, who had ſo great a regard to merit wherever he found it, and took ſuch a fatherly care in providing for the happineſs of his people, that he made his horſe a miniſter of ſtate! Yet there was not wanting a factious and ſeditious party at that time in Rome, who took liberties with the Emperor himſelf, only for making choice of ſo uſeful an animal to ſhare with him the burthen of governing the world, who, after all that could be ſaid of him, was certainly a moſt able miniſter.

I doubt not but he had his friends and flatterers, as well as other miniſters have had ſince; but it would move the indignation of every loyal heart to read with what contempt, and even ſcurrility, a perſon ſo highly in truſt and favour with the Emperor was treated by the malcontents of thoſe times.

There is a period to prejudice itſelf; the prejudice againſt this great miniſter is long ſince dead; and I don't doubt but the preſent age will think more favourably of him than that in which he lived. For I think the time might be pointed out, when a nation for near ten years' ſpace had reaſon to envy Rome for having even a *horſe for a miniſter.*

I am ſorry hiſtory ſhould be ſilent in reſpect to ſome things very material to be known; I mean thoſe relating to his birth, family, and education.—Methinks I am curious to know, whether this great miniſter was a coach or a cart-horſe,—a hunter, or a pad;— to ſpeak in the Newmarket ſtyle, whether he had blood in him.

I am not ignorant that the world has long run away with a notion that he was the worſt horſe in the ſtable; which notion I take to be built upon a general maxim which is known to have prevailed in the courts of ſome of thoſe wretched empe-

emperors: "That in a government to be supported by corruption, any beast may serve for a minister."

For my own part, I am willing to do justice to his memory, according to the best lights I am able to collect from history:—nay, I find in myself an inclination to believe, that he owed his high preferment to his merit.

Whether I have read or dreamed the following story, I can't recollect;—that the Emperor being one day on his back (bye-the-by, no man in the empire rode so ill), with his whole court about him, these obsequious gentlemen, perceiving how awkwardly he managed the reins, took occasion from thence to flatter him upon his being a most excellent horseman; upon which the horse immediately threw him, only to let him see what a parcel of rascals he had about him. The Emperor, perceiving that the horse was the only person about the court that had either truth or honesty in him, took a resolution from that moment to raise him to those high honours to which he afterwards arrived.

Be this as it may, it is certain many virtues shone on him after his rise. In the first place, he did not shew the least alteration of behaviour on this sudden change of good fortune:—he was the same creature as before;—he gave himself no overbearing airs upon it, as is common with those raised above their element.—He was the only person about court who seemed no way conscious of his having a superiority over others.

He did not by any mean arts engage the attention and confidence of the Emperor, nor did he misrepresent the good intentions of his subjects, nor did he prevail on him to turn a deaf ear to their complaints, or to reject their petitions; nor did he engross the power of all the great employments in the empire, although he had full as good a right to such power (if parts and abilities can give a right) as some that have usurped it since.

"He did not presume to erect himself into a dictator in the senate; nor did he either directly, or indirectly, bribe or command the senators to say black was white, green, blue, yellow, or any colour he was pleased to call it. He was not so insolent as to cause men of the first nobility in the empire to wait his pleasure for access to his person, nor did he ever send men of the patrician order on footmen's errands."—As corrupt as the patricians were grown at that time, if he had given himself those airs, some one amongst them would certainly have bestowed upon him the discipline of the horse-whip.

As he was no flatterer himself, he took no pleasure in the flatteries of others; of consequence he did not squander away the public treasure in pensions to prostitute fellows to sound his praises.—He had more sense, as well as more modesty, than to expose himself to the ridicule of the world by so preposterous a piece of vanity.

He was content with the fair and honest appointments belonging to his office, without multiplying perquisites, or turning every public thing into a job; nor was he eternally *eserbsing* more and more to his own family; and although he might have as stupid and indigent kindred

kindred as some other ministers have had since,——he neither took them from the plough nor the cart to disgrace his country abroad, nor to spoil the public business at home.

He was so remarkable for his temperance, that, if he had his belly full of oats in the morning, he never craved for more that day.—A rare instance of moderation in a person of so much power!

History is not only silent with respect to his family, but we cannot so much as learn from it whether this great minister was a stone-horse or gelding. Some will have him the latter, because there is nothing recorded of his amours. All that we know is, that he did not make himself ridiculous that way; if he had, it would not have escaped notice.

It is difficult to be particular in speaking of one of whom so little is recorded; but although authors have been silent as to his virtues, we may be sure he is free from all those vices with which he is not taxed; for the vices of those who are suddenly raised to high preferment are seldom buried in oblivion; and upon the whole I conceive, that notwithstanding for so many centuries past he has been treated as a stupid and ignorant minister, yet his parts would make no contemptible figure either in the arts of peace, or the management of war, when compared to those of other ministers who have lived since. Add to this, his temperance and modesty, and, above all, that honest and disinterested mind which kept him within such bounds, that though he lived upon nothing but hay and corn, he never stole any.

Whoever considers all these things with an unprejudiced judgment, must differ from the common opinion with respect to this favourite; and, upon an impartial comparison with some other modern favourites, will be obliged to own, that the horse was not only the honestest, but by far the wisest minister. I am, &c. CENTAUR.

Subject of a Picture, now painting by Sir Joshua Reynolds.

HAVING lately seen a paragraph in the public papers, relative to a picture now painting by Sir Joshua Reynolds, it may not be disagreeable to our readers to be made acquainted with the subject, which the admirable Dantè has introduced in his Inferno, and which is not sufficiently known. Ugolino, a Florentine Count, is giving the description of his being imprisoned, with his children, by the Archbishop Ruggeri.—" The hour approached, when we expected to have something brought us to eat. But instead of seeing any food appear, I heard the doors of that horrible dungeon more closely barred. I beheld my little children in silence, and could not weep. My heart was petrified! The little wretches wept, and my dear Anselm said, ' Father, you look on us! what ails you?' I could neither weep nor answer, and continued swallowed up in silent agony all that day, and the following night, even till the dawn of day. As soon as a glimmering ray darted through the doleful prison, that I could view again those four faces in which my own image was impressed, I gnawed both my hands, with grief and rage.

rage. My children, believing I did this through eagerness to eat, raising themselves suddenly up, said to me—'Father, our torments would be less, if you would allay the rage of your hunger upon us.' I restrained myself, that I might not increase their misery. We were all mute that day and the following. The fourth day being come, Gaddo, falling extended at my feet, cried, 'My father, why do you not help me?' and died. The other three expired one after the other between the fifth and sixth day, famished as thou seest me now! and I, being seized with blindness, began to go groping upon them with my hands and feet; and continued calling them by their names three days after they were dead. Then hunger vanquished my grief."

Translation of a Letter from the Empress Queen to the Dauphin of France, on his Marriage with the Archduchess her Daughter.

YOUR consort, my dear Dauphin, has just taken her leave of me. As she was my delight, I hope she will be your happiness. I have trained her up in full confidence that she would one day share in your fortune. I have inspired her with love to your person, and duty to your will; with tenderness to soften your cares, and with the desire of seeking every occasion of pleasing you. I have earnestly recommended to her most serious thoughts a fervent devotion to the King of Kings, under a firm persuasion that those who neglect their duty towards him, in whose hands are the sceptres of kings, can never promote the true interest of the people over whom they are allotted to govern. Be mindful, I say, my dear Dauphin, of your duty to God; and I repeat the same to the princess my daughter. Be mindful of the good of the people over whom, whenever it happens, you will govern too soon. Reverence the king your grandfather: be good as he is good; and render yourselves accessible to those who labour under misfortunes. It is impossible, in carrying yourself in this manner, but that you must share in the general happiness. My daughter will love you, I am sure she will, because I know the inward sentiments of her heart; but the more I make myself answerable for her love and her endearments, the greater reason I have to expect that you will preserve for her an inviolable affection. Farewell, my dear Dauphin; all happiness attend you: my eyes overflow with tears.

Extract from the Records of the Town of Arundel.

A FEW months before the abdication of the dastardly tyrant James II. Lord Chancellor Jeffries, of detested memory, went to Arundel in Sussex, in order to influence an election. He took his residence at the castle, and went the day fixed for the election to the town-hall, where Mr. Peckham, who was then Mayor of Arundel, held his court. Jeffries had the impudence to shew his bloody face there: the Mayor ordered

dered him to withdraw immediately; and, in cafe of refufal, threatened to have him committed. " You," faid he, " who ought to be the guardian of our laws, and of our facred conftitution, fhall not fo audacioufly violate them. This is my court, and my jurifdiction here is above your's." Jeffries, who was not willing to perplex ftill more the King's affairs, and to enrage the populace, retired immediately. The next morning he invited Peckham to breakfaft with him, which he accepted; but he had the courage to fcorn to take a place, which the mercilefs executioner offered him.

POETRY.

POETRY.

Extract from The Deserted Village, *a Poem, by* Dr. Goldsmith.

SWEET Auburn! parent of the blissful hour,
Thy glades forlorn confess the tyrant's pow'r.
Here, as I take my solitary rounds,
Amidst thy tangling walks, and ruined grounds,
And, many a year elapsed, return to view
Where once the cottage stood, the hawthorn grew,
Remembrance wakes with all her busy train,
Swells at my breast, and turns the past to pain.
  In all my wanderings round this world of care,
In all my griefs—and God has given my share—
I still had hopes my latest hours to crown,
Amidst these humble bowers to lay me down;
To husband out life's taper at the close,
And keep the flame from wasting by repose.
I still had hopes, for pride attends us still,
Amidst the swains to shew my book-learned skill;
Around my fire an evening groupe to draw,
And tell of all I felt, and all I saw;
And, as an hare whom hounds and horns pursue,
Pants to the place from whence at first she flew,
I still had hopes, my long vexations past,
Here to return—and die at home at last.
  O blest retirement, friend to life's decline,
Retreats from care that never must be mine,
How happy he who crowns in shades like these
A youth of labour with an age of ease;
Who quits a world where strong temptations try,
And, since 'tis hard to combat, learns to fly!
For him no wretches, born to work and weep,
Explore the mine, or tempt the dangerous deep:
No surly porter stands in guilty state,
To spurn imploring famine from the gate;
But on he moves to meet his latter end,
Angels around befriending virtue's friend;
Bends to the grave with unperceived decay,
While resignation gently slopes the way;
And all his prospects brightening to the last,
His heaven commences ere the world be past!

Sweet was the found, when oft, at evening's close,
Up yonder hill the village murmur rose;
There as I past with careless steps, and slow,
The mingling notes came softened from below;
The swain responsive as the milk-maid sung,
The sober herd that lowed to meet their young,
The noisy geese that gabbled o'er the pool,
The playful children just let loose from school,
The watch-dog's voice that bayed the whispering wind,
And the loud laugh that spoke the vacant mind;
These all in sweet confusion sought the shade,
And filled each pause the nightingale had made:
But now the sounds of population fail,
No cheerful murmurs fluctuate in the gale;
No busy steps the grass-grown foot-way tread,
For all the bloomy flush of life is fled.
All but yon widowed, solitary thing,
That feebly bends beside the plashy spring:
She, wretched matron, forced, in age, for bread,
To strip the brook with mantling cresses spread,
To pick her wintry faggot from the thorn,
To seek her nightly shed, and weep till morn;
She only left of all the harmless train,
The sad historian of the pensive plain.

Near yonder copse, where once the garden smiled,
And still where many a garden flower grows wild;
There, where a few torn shrubs the place disclose,
The village preacher's modest mansion rose.
A man he was, to all the country dear,
And passing rich with forty pounds a year:
Remote from towns he ran his godly race,
Nor e'er had changed, nor wished to change, his place;
Unpractised he to fawn, to seek for power,
By doctrines fashioned to the varying hour;
Far other aims his heart had learned to prize,
More skilled to raise the wretched than to rise.
His house was known to all the vagrant train,
He chid their wanderings, but relieved their pain;
The long-remembered beggar was his guest,
Whose beard descending swept his aged breast;
The ruined spendthrift, now no longer proud,
Claimed kindred there, and had his claims allowed;
The broken soldier, kindly bade to stay,
Sate by his fire, and talked the night away;
Wept o'er his wounds, or tales of sorrow done,
Shouldered his crutch, and shewed how fields were won:
Pleased with his guests, the good man learned to glow,
And quite forgot their vices in their woe;

Careless

Careless their merits or their faults to scan,
His pity gave ere charity began.
 Thus to relieve the wretched was his pride,
And even his failings leaned to Virtue's side;
But in his duty prompt at every call,
He watched and wept, he prayed and felt for all.
And, as a bird each fond endearment tries
To tempt its new-fledged offspring to the skies,
He tried each art, reproved each dull delay,
Allured to brighter worlds, and led the way.
 Beside the bed where parting life was layed,
And sorrow, guilt, and pain, by turns dismayed,
The reverend champion stood. At his control,
Despair and anguish fled the struggling soul;
Comfort came down the trembling wretch to raise,
And his last faltering accents whispered praise.
 At church, with meek and unaffected grace,
His looks adorned the venerable place;
Truth from his lips prevailed with double sway,
And fools, who came to scoff, remained to pray.
The service past, around the pious man,
With steady zeal each honest rustic ran;
Even children followed with endearing wile,
And plucked his gown, to share the good man's smile.
His ready smile a parent's warmth exprest,
Their welfare pleased him, and their cares distrest;
To them his heart, his love, his griefs, were given,
But all his serious thoughts had rest in Heaven.
As some tall cliff that lifts its awful form,
Swells from the vale, and midway leaves the storm,
Tho' round its breast the rolling clouds are spread,
Eternal sunshine settles on its head.
 Beside yon straggling fence that skirts the way,
With blossom'd furze unprofitably gay,
There, in his noisy mansion, skill'd to rule,
The village master taught his little school:
A man severe he was, and stern to view;
I knew him well, and every truant knew.
Well had the boding tremblers learn'd to trace
The day's disasters in his morning face;
Full well they laughed, with counterfeited glee,
At all his jokes, for many a joke had he;
Full well the busy whisper, circling round,
Conveyed the dismal tidings when he frowned;
Yet he was kind, or, if severe in aught,
The love he bore to learning was in fault;
The village all declared how much he knew;
'Twas certain he could write, and cipher too;

Lands he could meafure, terms and tides prefage,
And even the ftory ran that he could gauge.
In arguing, too, the parfon own'd his fkill,
For e'en though vanquifhed, he could argue ftill ;
While words of learned length and thund'ring found,
Amazed the gazing ruftics rang'd around ;
And ftill they gazed, and ftill the wonder grew,
That one fmall head could carry all he knew.

But paft is all his fame. The very fpot
Where many a time he triumph'd is forgot.
Near yonder thorn, that lifts its head on high,
Where once the fign-poft caught the paffing eye,
Low lies that houfe where nut-brown draughts infpir'd,
Where grey-beard mirth and fmiling toil retired ;
Where village ftatefmen talk'd with looks profound,
And news much older than their ale went round.
Imagination fondly ftoops to trace
The parlour fplendours of that feftive place ;
The white-wafhed wall, the nicely-fanded floor,
The varnifhed clock, that click'd behind the door ;
The cheft contrived a double debt to pay,
A bed by night, a cheft of drawers by day ;
The pictures placed for ornament and ufe,
The twelve good rules, the royal game of goofe ;
The hearth, except when winter chilled the day,
With afpen boughs, and flowers and fennel gay ;
While broken tea-cups, wifely kept for fhow,
Rang'd o'er the chimney, gliftened in a row.

Vain tranfitory fplendours ! Could not all
Reprieve the tott'ring manfion from its fall!
Obfcure it finks, nor fhall it more impart
An hour's importance to the poor man's heart ;
Thither no more the peafant fhall repair
To fweet oblivion of his daily care ;
No more the farmer's news, the barber's tale,
No more the wood-man's ballad fhall prevail ;
No more the fmith his dufky brow fhall clear,
Relax his ponderous ftrength, and lean to hear ;
The hoft himfelf no longer fhall be found
Careful to fee the mantling blifs go round ;
Nor the coy maid, half-willing to be preft,
Shall kifs the cup to pafs it to the reft.

ODE

ODE for the NEW YEAR, 1770.
By WILLIAM WHITEHEAD, Esq.

FORWARD, Janus, turn thine eyes,
 Future scenes in prospect view,
Rising as the moments rise
That form the fleeting year anew.
Fresh beneath the scythe of Time,
 Could the Muse's voice avail,
Joys should spring, and reach their prime,
 Blooming ere the former fail;
And ev'ry joy its tribute bring,
To Britain, and to Britain's King.

Suns should warm the pregnant soil,
 Health in every breeze should blow;
Plenty crown the peasant's toil,
 And shine upon his cheerful brow.
Round the throne whilst duty waits,
 Duty join'd with filial love,
Peace should triumph in our gates,
 And ev'ry distant fear remove;
Till gratitude to Heaven should raise
The speaking eye, the song of praise.

Let the nations round in arms
Stun the world with war's alarms;
But let Britain still be found
Safe within her watery bound.
Tyrant Chiefs may realms destroy:
Nobler is our Monarch's joy;
Of all that's truly great possest,
And, by blessing, truly blest.

Tho' comets rise, and wonder mark their way
 Above the bounds of Nature's sober laws,
It is the all-cheering lamp of day,
 The permanent, the unerring cause,
By whom th' enliven'd world its course maintains!
By whom all nature smiles, and beauteous order reigns.

ODE to the Hon. Miss YORKE (afterwards Lady Anson), on her copying a Portrait of Dantè by Clovio. By her Brother, the late Hon. Charles Yorke, Esq.

FAIR artist! well thy pencil has essay'd
 To lend a poet's fame thy friendly aid;
Great Dantè's image in thy lines we trace;
And, while the Muses' train thy colours grace,

The Muse propitious on the draught shall smile,
Nor, envious, leave unsung the gen'rous toil.
   Picture and Poetry just kindred claim,
Their birth, their genius, and pursuits the same;
Daughters of Phœbus and Minerva, they
From the same sources draw the heav'nly ray.
Whatever earth, or air, or ocean breeds,
Whatever luxury or weakness needs,
All forms of beauty Nature's scenes disclose,
All images inventive arts compose;
What ruder passions tear the troubled breast,
What mild affections soothe the soul to rest,
Each thought to Fancy magic numbers raise,
Expressive picture to the sense conveys.
Hence in all times with social zeal conspire,
Who blend the tints, and who attune the lyre.
See! in reviving Learning's infant dawn,
Ere yet in precepts from old ruins drawn,
Sham'd the mock ornaments of Gothic taste,
New artists form'd, each Grecian bust replac'd;
Ere Leo's voice awak'd the barbarous age,
Oppress'd by monkish law, and Vandal rage:
See! Dantè, Petrarch, thro' the darkness strive,
A * Giotto's pencil bid their forms survive!
When now maturer growth fair Science knew,
† Titian her favour'd sons ambitious drew;
Not half so proud with princes to adorn
His tablets, as with wits less nobly born,
Ariosto, Aretine, yet better skill'd
On letters and on virtue fame to build:
These in their turn instruct the willing song,
The painter's fading glories to prolong.
In latter times, hear Waller's polish'd verse
The various beauties of Vandyke rehearse;
And Dryden, in sublimer strains impart
To Kneller praise more lasting than his art.
   Friendships like these from time receive no law,
Contracted oft with those we never saw;
In ev'ry art who court an endless fame
Thro' distant ages catch the sacred flame:

---

* Giotto was the scholar of Cimabue, and the first painter of any genius that appeared in Italy. He worked at Florence; was the contemporary of Dantè and Petrarch, whose pictures he drew, and with whom he lived in friendship.

† Titian drew more portraits of kings and princes than any painter that ever lived. Ariosto and Aretine were his friends and contemporaries, of whom he made pictures.

See * Zeuxis, warm'd by Homer's rage divine,
With rapture read, and what he reads design!
See † Julio, bred on the Parnassian soil,
With Virgil's grandeur dignify his toil!
‡ Clovio, perhaps, like aid to Dantè ow'd;
Intent his figure on the canvas glow'd:
To Dantè's fame the grateful colours flow,
And wreaths of laurel bind his honour'd brow.

Thou, too, whom Nature and the Muse inspire,
List'ning the poet's lore hast caught his fire;
With so much spirit ev'ry feature fraught,
Clovio might own this imitated draught;
And Dantè, were he conscious of the praise,
Would sing thy labours in immortal lays:
His melancholy air to gladness turn'd,
No longer his unthankful Florence mourn'd;
Fair § Beatrice's charms would lose their force,
No more her steps o'er heaven direct his course;
To thee the bard would grant the nobler place,
And ask thy guidance thro' the paths of peace.

Oh! could my eloquence, like his, persuade
To leave the bounded walks by others made,
Thro' nature's wilds bid thy free genius rove,
Copy the living race, or waving grove;
Or, boldly rising with superior skill,
The work with heroes or with poets fill;
Then might I claim deserv'd the laurel crown,
My verse not quite neglected or unknown;
Then should the world thy glowing pencil see,
Extend the friendship of its art to me.

* Zeuxis is said to have studied Homer with particular attention. He always read such parts of his poems, as were best suited to the subject he had in hand, before he took up his pencil.

† Julio Romano, the disciple and favourite of Raphael, was said to have a peculiar majesty in his compositions. He was the best scholar of the modern painters, and a diligent reader of Virgil, and the greatest poets.

‡ Julio Clovio lived 200 years after Dantè. The portrait of Dantè, here mentioned, represents him in a melancholy posture in the fore-ground, looking back on Florence, from whence he was banished during the commotions in that state, in which he bore the highest offices. Clovio's great work is a book of drawings, to be seen at this day in the Florentine gallery, the subjects of which are all taken from Dantè's poem on hell, purgatory, and heaven.

§ Beatrice, the mistress of Dantè in his youth, who died many years before him, and of whom he speaks with great affection. She is represented in the poem as the guardian angel who leads him through heaven, as Virgil and Statius do their heroes through hell and purgatory.

To a Lady with a Present of Pope's *Works. By the Same.*

THE lover oft, to please some faithless dame,
    With vulgar presents feeds the dying flame;
Then adds a verse, of slighted vows complains,
While she the giver and the gift disdains.
These strains no idle suit to thee commend,
On whom gay loves with chaste desires attend;
Nor fancied excellence, nor amorous care,
Prompts to rash praise, or fills with fond despair:
Enough, if the fair volume find access;
Thee the great poet's lay shall best express.
Thy beauteous image there thou may'st regard,
Which strikes with modest awe the meaner bard.
Sure had he living view'd thy tender youth,
The blush of honour, and the grace of truth,
Ne'er with Belinda's charms his song had glow'd,
But from thy form the lov'd idea flow'd:
His wanton satire ne'er the sex had scorn'd,
For thee, by Virtue and the Muse adorn'd.

Stanzas in the Manner of Waller: *occasioned by a Receipt to make Ink, given to the Author by a Lady. By the Same.*

IN earlier times, ere man had learn'd
    His sense in writing to impart,
With inward anguish oft he burn'd,
    His friend unconscious of the smart.

Alone he pin'd in thickest shade,
    Near murmuring waters sooth'd his grief;
Of senseless rocks companions made,
    And from their echoes sought relief.

Cadmus, 'tis said, did first reveal
    How letters should the mind express,
And taught to grave, with pointed steel,
    On waxen tablets its distress.

Soon was the feeble waxen trace
    Supply'd by Ink's unfading spot,
Which to remotest climes conveys,
    In clearest marks, the secret thought.

Blest be his chymic hand that gave
    The world to know so great a good!
Hard! that his name it should not save,
    Who first pour'd forth the sable flood.

'Tis this consigns to endless praise
    The hero's valour, statesman's art;

Hiftoric truth and fabling lays,
  The maiden's eyes, the lover's heart.

If ftill oblivion's Lethe live
  Immortal in poetic lore,
What honours fhall the ftream receive
  Sacred to mem'ry's better pow'r!

Who now from Helicon's fam'd well
  The drops celeftial would requeft,
When by Ink's magic he can fpell
  The image of his faithful breaft?

This kindly fpares the modeft tongue
  To fpeak aloud the pleafing pain;
Aided by this, in tuneful fong
  Fond vows the virgin-paper ftain.

Tho' ftain'd, yet innocent of fame,
  No blufh th' indignant reader warms,
If well exprefs'd the poet's flame,
  Infpir'd by fair Maria's charms.

AMINTA. *An* ELEGY. *By* JOHN GERRARD, *Curate of* Withycombe in the Moor, Devon.

Flete meam, fylva, dilectaque rura, puellam
Non iterum tenero, rura, terenda pede!   RELAND.

AN o'ergrown wood my wand'ring fteps invade,
  With furface mantled in untrodden fnow;
Dire haunt, for none but favage monfters made,
  Where frofts defcend, and howling tempefts blow.

Here, from the fearch of bufy mortals ftray'd,
  My woe-worn foul fhall hug her galling chain;
For, fure, no foreft boafts too deep a fhade,
  No haunt too wild for mifery to remain.

O my Aminta! dear diftracting name!
  Late all my comfort, all my fond delight,
Still writhes my foul beneath its tort'ring flame,
  Still thy pale image fills my aching fight!

When fhall vain mem'ry flumber o'er her woes?
  When to oblivion be her tale refign'd?
When fhall this fatal form in death repofe,
  Like thine, fair victim, to the duft confign'd!

Again the accents falter on my tongue;
  Again to tear the confcious tear fucceeds:
From fharp reflection is the dagger fprung,
  And nature, wounded to the center, bleeds.

Ye

Ye bitter skies! upon the tale descend——
Ye blasts! tho' rude your visits, lend an ear——
Around, ye gentler oaks, your branches bend,
    And, as ye listen, drop an icy tear.

'Twas when the step with conscious pleasure roves,
    Where round the shades the circling woodbines throng,
When Flora wantons o'er the enamell'd groves,
    And feather'd choirs indulge the am'rous song.

Inspir'd by duteous love, I fondly stray'd,
    Two milk-white doves officious to ensnare:
Beneath a silent thicket, as they play'd,
    A grateful present for my softer fair.

But, ah! in smiles no more they met my sight,
    Their ruffled heads lay gasping on the ground:
Where (my dire emblem) a rapacious Kite
    Tore their soft limbs, and strew'd their plumes around.

The tear of pity stole into my eye;
    While ruder passions in their turn succeed:
Forbid the victims unreveng'd to die,
    And doom the author of their wrongs to bleed.

With hasty step, enrag'd, I homewards ran,
    (Curse on my speed) th' unerring tube I brought;
That fatal hour my date of woe began,
    Too sharp to tell—too horrible for thought!—

Disastrous deed!—irrevocable ill!——
    How shall I tell the anguish of my fate!
Teach me, remorseless monsters, not to feel;
    Instruct me, fiends and furies, to relate!

Wrathful behind the guilty shade I stole,
    I rais'd the tube—the clam'rous woods resound—
Too late I saw the idol of my soul,
    Struck by my aim, fall shrieking to the ground!

No other bliss her soul allow'd but me;
    (Hapless the pair that thus indulgent prove)
She sought concealment from a shady tree,
    In amorous silence to observe her love.

I ran—but, oh! too soon I found it true!—
    From her stain'd breast life's crimson stream'd apace;
From her wan eyes the sparkling lustres flew—
    The short-liv'd roses faded from her face!

Gods!—could I bear that fond reproachful look,
    That strove her peerless innocence to plead!
But partial death awhile her tongue forsook,
    To save a wretch that doom'd himself to bleed.

While I distracted press'd her in my arms,
  And fondly strove t'imbibe her latest breath;
" O spare, rash love," she cry'd, " thy fatal charms,
  " Nor seek cold shelter in the arms of death.

" Content beneath thy erring hand I die.
  " Our fates grew envious of a bliss so true;
" Then urge not thy distress when low I lie,
  " But in this breath receive my last adieu!"—

No more she spake, but droop'd her lily head!
  In death she sicken'd—breathless—haggard—pale!—
While all my inmost soul with horror bled,
  And ask'd kind vengeance from the passing gale.

Where slept your bolts, ye ling'ring lightnings, say;
  Why riv'd ye not this self-condemned breast;—
Or why, too passive earth, didst thou delay
  To stretch thy jaws, and crush me into rest?—

Low in the dust the beauteous corse I plac'd,
  Bedew'd and soft with many a falling tear;
With sable yew the rising turf I grac'd,
  And bade the cypress mourn in silence near.

Oft as bright morn's all-searching eye returns,
  Full to my view the fatal spot is brought;
Thro' sleepless night my haunted spirit mourns;
  No gloom can hide me from distracting thought.

When, spotless victim, shall my form decay?
  This guilty load, say, when shall I resign?
When shall my spirit wing her cheerless way,
  And my cold corse lie treasur'd up with thine?

An Epistle from an unfortunate young Gentleman to a young Lady. By the Same [*]

THESE, the last lines my hands can write,
  These words, the last my dying lips recite,
Read, and repent that your unkindness gave
A wretched lover an untimely grave!
Sunk by despair from life's enchanting view,
Lost, ever lost to happiness and you!—
No more these eye-lids show'r incessant tears,
No more my spirit sinks with boding fears;
No more your frowns my suing passion meet,
No more I fall submissive at your feet:
With fruitless love this heart shall cease to burn,
Life's empty dream shall never more return.

[*] Occasioned by a catastrophe well known in the West.

Think

Think not, that, lab'ring to subdue your hate,
My artful soul forebodes a fancied fate;
For ere yon sun descends his western way,
Cold shall I lie, a lifeless lump of clay!
　Tir'd of my long encounters with disdain,
Peaceful my pulse, and ebbing from its pain;
Each vital movement sinking to decay,
And my spent soul just languishing away;
Ere my last breath yet hovers to depart,
I prompt my hand to pour out all my heart;
The hand, oft rais'd compassion to implore;
The heart, that burns with slighted fires no more!
　Relentless nymph! of nature's fairest frame,
Unpitying soul, and woman but in name;
Angelic bloom the coldest heart to win,
Without, allurement, but disdain within;
Regard the sounds which seal my parting breath,
Ere the vain murmurs shall be hush'd in death.
Let pity view what love disdain'd to save,
And mourn a wretch sent headlong to the grave.
　Profuse of all an anxious lover's care,
To urge his suit, and win the list'ning fair;
Try'd ev'ry purpose to relieve my woe,
My soul chides not, for innocent I go;
Save when soft pity bids my gentler mind
Shrink at your fate, and drop a tear behind.
　How oft and fruitless have I strove to move
Unfeeling beauty with the pangs of love;
As rose your breast with captivating grace,
And heighten'd charms came blushing to your face;
Insulting charms! that gave a fiercer wound,
Fond as I lay, and prostrate on the ground.
Heav'ns! with what scorn you strove my suit to meet,
Frown'd with your eyes, and spurn'd me with your feet!
To bleeding love such hard returns you gave,
As barb'rous rocks that dash the pressing wave.
O could your looks have turn'd my hapless fate,
And frown'd my short-liv'd passion into hate,
Then had no scattering breeze my sorrows known,
Nor vale responsive had prolong'd the moan;
Then had those lips ne'er learnt their woful tale,
Nor death yet cloath'd them in eternal pale.
　Oft to the woods in frantic rage I flew
To cool my bosom with the falling dew;
Oft in sad accents sigh'd each prompting ill,
And taught wild oaks to pity and to feel;
Till with despair my heart rekindled burns,
And all the anguish of my soul returns.

Then restless to the fragrant meads I hie,
Death in my face, distraction in my eye;
There, as reclin'd along the verdant plain,
My grief renews her heart-wrung strains again:
Lo! pitying Phœbus sinks, with sorrow pale,
And mournful night descends upon the tale!
When tir'd, at length, my wrongs no more complain,
And sighs are stifled in obtuser pain;
When the deep fountains of my eyes are spent,
And fiercer anguish sinks to discontent;
Slow I return, and, prostrate on my bed,
Bid the soft pillow lull my heavy head.
But, oh! when downy sleep its court renews,
And shades the soul with visionary views,
Illusive dreams, to fan my slumb'ring fire,
And wake the fever of intense desire,
Present your softer image to my sight,
All warm with smiles, and glowing with delight:
Gods! with what bliss I view thy darling charms,
And strive to clasp thee melting in my arms!—
But, ah! the shade my empty grasp deceives;
And as it flits, and my fond soul bereaves,
The transient slumbers slip their airy chain,
And give me back to all my woes again:
There wrapt in floods of grief I sigh forlorn,
The constant greetings of unwelcome morn.
But should oblivion reassume her sway,
And slumbers once more steal my woes away;
When the short flights of fancy intervene,
Your much-lov'd image fills out ev'ry scene.
But now no more soft smiles your face adorn,
Lo! o'er each feature broods destructive scorn;
Suppliant in tears I urge my suit again,
Sullen you stand, and view me with disdain:
Your ears exclude the story of my smart,
Your baleful eyes dart anguish to my heart.
I wake—glad nature hails returning day,
And the wild songsters chaunt their matin-lay;
The sun in glory mounts the crystal sky,
And all creation is in smiles but I.
Then, sink in death, my senses!——for in vain
You strive to quench the phrenzy of your pain;
Break, break, fond heart!—her hate thou canst not tam
Then take this certain triumph o'er thy flame.
'Tis done!——the dread of future wrongs is past——
Lo! brittle passion verges to its last!
'Tis done!——vain life's illusive scenes are o'er——
Disdainful beauty shakes her chains no more.

Come, peaceful gloom, expand thy downy breast,
And soothe, O soothe me to eternal rest!
There hush my plaints, and gently lull my woes,
Where one still stream of dull oblivion flows.
No lab'ring breast there heaves with torture's throes,
No heart consumes her daily hoard of woes;
No dreams of former pain the soul invade,
Calmly she sleeps, a sad unthinking shade!

But e'er from thought my struggling soul is free,
One latest tear she dedicates to thee.
She views thee on the brink of vain despair,
Beat thy big breast, and rend thy flowing hair.
Feels tort'ring love her sable deluge roll,
Weigh down thy senses, and o'erbear thy soul.
In vain your heart relents, in vain you weep,
No lover wakes from his eternal sleep.
Alas! I see thy frantic spirit rave,
And thy last breath expiring on my grave.
Is this the fortune of those high-priz'd charms?
Ah! spare them for some worthier lover's arms.
And may these bodings ne'er with truth agree,
My grief and anguish be unknown to thee.
My bitter mem'ry ne'er recount with pain,
That e'er you frown'd, or I admir'd in vain.

No more——my spirit is prepar'd to fly,
Suppress'd my voice, and stiffen'd is my eye.
Death's swimming shadows intercept my view;
Vain world, and thou relentless nymph, adieu!

A Translation of Dr. King's *Latin Epistle, entitled* Antonietti's *Advice to the* Corsicans, *concerning their Choice of a King. By Mr.* Russell.

THO' Phœbus kindly should inspire
    Such strains as dwelt on Virgil's lyre,
With all the strength and ease polite
That poets wish for when they write,
Nor battles should my verse employ,
Nor kings who conquer—to destroy.
Bavaria's sons might crowd the plain,
And Gallia war with neighb'ring Spain,
While Britons, careless of their own,
Invade the peace of lands unknown.
Whate'er I had of skill or fame
My countrymen alone should claim;
And you, ye Corsi, brave and free,
Ye sons of arms and liberty!
Your fame should raise my willing voice,
Your prudent sires—your beardless boys,

Your

Your monks who honour's influence feel;
And change their hoods for caps of steel.
But now my once poetic rage
Consumes and languishes in age:
The muse who once my lays inspir'd,
In youth appear'd, with youth retir'd;
Yet still my country's love remains,
And triumphs in my aged veins;
My thoughts from long experience rise,
I've prov'd whatever I advise:
Thro' distant nations as I stray'd,
Both kings' and people's taste I weigh'd:
Attend! and freedom, (long pursu'd
In hostile plains and seas of blood)
Shall pleas'd vouchsafe a cheering smile,
And dwell for ever on our isle.
In me combin'd with rev'rence view
A poet and a prophet, too;
And tho' my numbers you despise,
Revere the gods who bid them rise!
Still undisturb'd shall Gallia pour
Her hostile legions on our shore;
Our isle her native worth defends:
On that her pow'r, her state depends;
Propp'd by her hero's matchless fame,
And honour'd with a kingdom's name,
Still may that name its force maintain,
And treason ply her schemes in vain.
But since our king seeks lands unknown,
And you're in doubt to fill his throne,
And, stead of him, would chuse a new,
As worthy Corsica and you,
A prince shall rise, in solemn state,
If not as active, full as great,
(Let my instructions but take place)
An offspring of an antient race,
Free all his days from loose delights,
And chaste and sober all his nights:
From foreign conquests still averse,
And careful of the public purse.
Our peace his views shall ne'er embroil,
Contented in his native soil:
His hands, from all corruption pure,
Your gold (if you have gold) secure:
His breach of faith shall ne'er surprize
His cheated subjects, or allies;
For kings, still practis'd to betray,
(Forgive, ye thron'd ones, what I say)

Kings have I known, for state intrigues,
Forget their oaths, and break thro' leagues:
A fairer prince than him I mean,
For shape and limbs, was never seen,
If our Alcimedon but know,
With cautious art to form him so;
Nor does his skill to his submit,
Of whom the Mantuan poet writ:
Alcimedon, whose skill could teach
To mock ev'n life, the sculptur'd beech,
In bowls, for which the swains contended,
By thee, O matchless bard, commended.
When first this monarch shall appear,
Salute his reign with joy sincere:
A wooden king! the crowds shall cry,
A wooden king! the groves reply.
Nor shall he (heav'n forbid he should!)
Be form'd of coarse and common wood;
Some timber mocks the artful tool,
Too hard to carve, not fit to rule.
Unnumber'd oaks adorn our land,
And still in safety let them stand;
In sullen state resist the storm,
But never bear a monarch's form!
Ne'er shall my int'rest strive to bring
A tattling Dodonæan king——
At pleasure to destroy and kill
By only saying, 'tis my will!
Oft, too, the sacred forest-maids
In silence dwell beneath their shades;
And when the tree receives a stroke,
With various ills revenge their oak.
Nor durst we do so rash a thing,
T'affront the gods—to cut a king!
But most beware to form his grace
Of that alluring glitt'ring race:
Of which an oak, in days of old,
Stretch'd out a branch of blooming gold;
From good Æneas, as befell,
A token to the god of hell.
One of this race would still incline,
Bright, like his ancestor, to shine;
Uneasy till his acts unfold
His ample branches with your gold.
Of this the Germans, France, and Spain,
Opprest and helpless, too complain:
And now, ye muses, lest I seem
To dwell too long upon my theme,

Whatever

Whatever skill you have bestow it
Both on the carpenter and poet!
Direct indulgently the tool
To form a king in peace to rule;
A king who much belov'd shall be,
Obey'd by all, and sung by me!
About it, skilful artist, seize
The pond'rous axe, and hew the trees!
But first adore with suppliant pray'r
The gods who oft inhabit there.
Of oaks, and elms, and all the rest
Of various timber, box is best:
Box! pliant wood, is turn'd with ease,
Alike is form'd for war or peace;
In box the royal form display,
And let him Corsica obey!
Then heav'nly peace, and arts shall smile,
Health, honour, riches bless the isle!
The Fauns secure, their haunts retain,
The fields shall wave with rip'ning grain;
The sailor safely cross the seas,
And bards grow old in learned ease.

   For motives, too, of nature strong,
This kingdom should to box belong:
Box! which for ages long has stood,
By all allow'd a regal wood!
Carv'd out in box, our moderns stand,
The work of some ingenious hand.
Secure shall box enjoy its fame,
Nor even malice wounds its name!
While patient gamesters leisure give
To chess, or Vida's poems live;
Where sacred walls the nations raise,
Around whose altars diamonds blaze;
The maid to whom the name is giv'n,
Of star of earth, or queen of heav'n,
In box carv'd out, is plac'd on high,
And view'd with reverential eye:
Oh, let not then my native land,
While thus ador'd her form shall stand,
Another kind of wood prefer,
To that which bears the name of her!
To prize ev'n angels more were wrong,
Such honour does to box belong:
But when the native woods it leaves,
And royal form the trunk receives;
When heav'n itself approves the choice,
And crowds lift up th' assenting voice;

Then will we bring our monarch home,
And place him in a marble dome:
A throne and sceptre we'll prepare,
Form'd by Alcimedon with care,
Cut from the individual tree
From whence he hew'd his majesty.
His front with laurel wreaths we'll bind;
A purple robe shall trail behind:
The bay, or ivy, round his head,
Shall their verdant foliage spread:
For, thus, as history allows,
The brave and witty bind their brows:
And sure they'll not improper be
To crown a prince so sage as he:
So shall he stand, our island's wonder,
Secure from faction, flames, and thunder!

And now a proper number chuse,
Who bend to public good their views,
To these the gen'ral power commit,
The sov'reign judges let them fit;
The temples, cities, laws protect,
And war or peace at will direct:
To envoys speak whate'er they please,
And combat with the Genoese;
Let this preside in ev'ry cause,
Defend, and execute the laws:
To these the gen'ral weight convey,
Of civil and of martial sway.

But when, to make offenders tremble,
In public counsel you assemble,
Bring out your wooden king, and place
On throne sublime his silent grace:
Beneath his name to make decrees,
And make him say just what you please.
Wise Venice thus discreetly rules,
Her dukes are necessary tools
Of wood, or wooden-like they reign:
The senators, the laws explain:
Decree, resolve, relinquish, claim,
Their princes do but lend a name;
And yet in royal domes they dwell,
Against their peace no crowds rebel:
In pompous robes adorn'd appear,
And wed the ocean ev'ry year;
And while to others' skill they trust,
Are neither tyrants nor unjust.
Their subjects active, rich, and wise,
Could even papal wrath despise:

But

But far, my countrymen, from hence,
Be still remov'd, a martial prince;
For kings who arm in time of peace,
Can only mean their realms to fleece:
With force to ratify their will,
Heav'n keep from us so great an ill!
Our monarch known, his country's friend,
One beauteous nymph shall still attend,
And still to her employment just
With care to brush him clean from dust;
That neither worms may breed within,
Nor spiders weave beneath his chin.
A naiad let the damsel be,
For none can be so fit as she;
And while the muses ('tis my due,
For counsels useful thus to you)
To distant times transmit my name,
Oh! nymph, to you an equal fame!
Who to this office dost succeed,
Shall be, and justly, too, decreed!
Forgive your gen'ral and your poet,
If my advice (since good I know it,
With prov'd success and truth replete)
Again with freedom I repeat:
For whether 'tis an idle tale,
Or that my own conceits prevail;
Or that the muse is better able
To give her sanction in a fable;
But in my mind a wooden king
Will freedom, peace, and plenty bring:
And future bards, whose wit shall praise
His sober nights and harmless days,
His chastity, his temper e'en,
Shall still this prince, *deriv'd from heav'n*,
His gentle sway and mild command,
That title justly may demand.
What blocks are register'd by fame,
When honour'd with a royal name?
As rough as oak, as dull as clods,
Yet call'd the offspring of the gods:
Phædrus, to prove the worth of logs,
Shall tell the fable of the Frogs.

   The Frogs to heav'n their pray'rs addrest,
A king—great thund'rer we request!
A king who knows our taste and genius,
To settle all disputes between us.
If Bees! small insects! dare to claim
The honour of a royal name;

P 4

Say

Say why should Frogs, great Jove, remain,
Beseeching for a king in vain?
From Phœbus' self our birth we trace,
The friend, the author of our race.
The charms of voice to us belong,
From us was nam'd the comic song.
A poet, too, of Greece, they say,
Made us a chorus in his play:
Nor is 't on voice our fame depends;
Our valour Homer's self commends.
They spoke, and soon their mighty boast
To laughter mov'd the heav'nly host;
Great Jove himself could not forbear,
Yet smil'd compliance to their pray'r.
Not long considering he stood,
But threw them down a log of wood:
Souse, it plung'd down—away they scud,
And croak and tremble in their mud.
The water dash'd a murm'ring sound,
The waves unusual pressure found:
But soon the log in peace repos'd,
Around its sides the waters clos'd;
The Frogs their panic fears recover,
The surface smooth'd, and all was over.
Phisignathus, a chief, his head
First rais'd above the stream, and said,
" Approach, my friends—your monarch view!
I know his kind, and where he grew."
Fix'd in amazement, long they stood,
Then grinn'd, and scorn'd the royal wood!
Jump on him, and, t' increase their crime,
Bedaub his sides with dirt and slime.
Again the the gods the Frogs address'd,
Again their worth and parts express'd;
And begg'd them to regard their merit,
And send them soon a king of spirit.
Jove with contemptuous anger view'd
How close destruction they pursu'd:
" The prince," he cry'd, " you merit, take!"
He spoke, and hurl'd them down a snake.
Around the lake the monster stray'd,
And dreadful devastation made;
On mothers, fathers, sons, he fed:
This lost a limb, and that a head.
O'er all alike he stretch'd his way,
And made whole multitudes his prey!
In vain they leapt about the bog,
And wish'd in vain their old king *Log*.

Their

POETRY.

Their pray'rs they made; but Jove no more
Comply'd, indulgent as before:
With smiles their mis'ry he survey'd,
And to their vows this answer made:
" Ye wretches! to your int'rest blind,
Ungrateful, faithless, like mankind:
You view'd with scorn a peaceful throne:
Beneath a tyrant learn to groan!"

The POET and STRAW.

A FABLE.

ON *Richmond* Hill with doublet bare
  A hungry poet takes the air:
The air on *Richmond* Hill, tho' good,
And excellent Camelion food,
Is rather of too thin a nature
For a beef-loving, two legg'd creature:
Our poet stops, he looks around,
And murmurs thus in doleful sound:
" While plenty o'er the landscape reigns,
" Shall Bards alone feel meagre pains?
" Ah, what avails, if in the town
" My madrigals acquir'd renown;
" If, stranger to all-pow'rful coin,
" I seldom taste the rich sirloin;
" If for the produce of my brain,
" I meet from money'd fools disdain?——
" In vain the laurel crowns my brows;
" What crowns my pocket?——Not one sous:
" Of bay or laurel, where the use is?
" Nor bay or laurel fruit produces:——
" I've fame pursu'd, and, now I've caught her,
" She proves——mere moon-shine in the water;
" How happier th' unletter'd glutton,
" Who can indulge on beef and mutton!——
" How curst each servant of the Nine!
" I'd rather be a fool and dine."
He said, and to his great surprize
Beneath his feet a Straw replies:——
" Ah, hapless Bard, look down and see
" Thy striking emblem here in me:
" Despis'd by those to whom my head
" Furnish'd the staff of living——bread:
" That gain'd, behold me here cast down,
" Trod on by ev'ry sordid clown:
" Just so the bard, who from his brain
" The hungry mind can entertain,

"Is soon neglected and forgot,
"A barren praise his hapless lot;
"To fame becomes an empty bubble,
"Trod on by fools, like straw or stubble."

The TWO KINGS.

A Fable.

CROSSING the river *Styx*, with shoals
Of new departed motley souls,
Old *Charon* look'd confounded black,
Lest with the load his boat should crack;
Tho' souls, as souls, are lightsome freight,
Their sins oft prove a deadly weight;
And should their floating carriage fail 'em,
Not ev'n cork jackets would avail 'em.
His boat chuck-full,——such screaming rose
From nurses, misses, ladies, beaus,
That *Charon* rais'd his voice, and swore,
While echo answer'd from the shore,
" If they continu'd their damn'd tricks,
" He'd souse 'em ev'ry one in *Styx*,"
And ask'd 'em, with a face most grim,
If they had ever learnt to swim:——
In short, he soon becalm'd the riot,
And made 'em tolerably quiet:
He trimm'd his boat, and with a frown,
Damn'd 'em, and made 'em all sit down.
Order observ'd in some degree,
A ghost of high pomposity,
With courtly air, and scornful look,
Thus to his brother shadows spoke:
" Hence, reptiles, hence—your distance know—
" Due homage to a monarch show;
" Shall one of my illustrious birth,
" A king,————a deity on earth,
" Be crowded thus with the *Canaille*,
" Fellows who stink of beef and ale?
" You, *Charon*, with that dirty face,
" Depend on 't you shall lose your place;
" My brother sovereign *Pluto* soon
" Shall make you smart for what you've done:
" Reptiles, avaunt——at distance tend;
" Your touch, looks, manners, all offend."
Old *Charon* grumbling in his maw,
Damn'd him, and bid him *hold his jaw*;——
Whilst one, who, living, from the stage
Had often entertain'd the age,

With whim *Ceroantic* in his face,
First bowing, thus address'd his Grace :———
" All hail——great king, great monarch, hail!
" Frown not; I'm not of the *Canaille :*
" In me your Brother *Brentford* view,
" I've been a king as well as you;
" Like you have worn a pageant crown,
" And aw'd the millions with a frown ;
" Like you, too, brother *Phiz*, resign'd,
" And left my pageant crown behind :——
" But now,———— good Sir, be not offended—
" The curtain dropt, the farce is ended :
" Tho' fortune for the stage equipt us,
" Our wardrobe keeper, Death, has stript us,
" And the rich robes on earth possest
" Lie folded in the grave at rest :——
" Maugre the rank we living bore,
" Like these we 're shadows now———no more;
" All, brothers all——at least in this,
" We're but *Personæ Dramatis ;*
" Like them we 're bound to Critic-hall,
" By critic rules to rise or fall :
" Where kings, lords, beggars, all must stand,
" And undistinguish'd hold the hand,
" While critic *Minos* and his Jury
" ('Tis true, good brother, I assure ye)
" Will hiss or clap, just as they find
" We've play'd the characters assign'd ;
" Where birth and rank pass unregarded,
" And merit only is rewarded."
  He spoke———the monarch, sighing, swore,
" He never heard such truths before."

On our MODERN COMEDIES.

SHAKESPEARE and *Jonson* with the learned corps
  Of poets, much admir'd in days of yore,
From nature drew their characters like fools;
Our modern play-wrights follow wiser rules:
Pictures from life they scorn to let you see ;
Not nature—but what nature *ought* to be :
Your low-liv'd humour, wit, and such poor stuff,
In times of ignorance did well enough :———
In this *refin'd,* this novel-reading age,
They 've banish'd all such nonsense from the stage ;
No wonder play-wrights swarm in these blest days ;
Sermons, they find, are easier *made* than *Plays.*

BAC.

BACCHUS; *by the late Doctor* Parnell.

[*This Poem is not in* Mr. Pope's *Edition.*]

AS Bacchus, ranging at his leisure,
(Jolly Bacchus, king of pleasure!)
Charm'd the wide world with drink and dances,
And all his thousand airy fancies,
Alas! he quite forgot the while
His fav'rite vines in Lesbos isle.

The God, returning ere they dy'd,
Ah! see my jolly Fauns, he cry'd,
The leaves but hardly born are red,
And the bare arms of pity spread:
The beasts afford a rich manure;
Fly, my boys, to bring the cure;
Up the mountains, o'er the vales,
Thro' the woods, and down the dales;
For this, if full the cluster grow,
Your bowls shall doubly overflow.

So cheer'd, with more officious haste
They bring the dung of ev'ry beast;
The loads they wheel, the roots they bare,
They lay the rich manure with care;
While oft he calls to labour hard,
And names as oft the red reward.

The plants refresh'd, new leaves appear,
The thick'ning clusters load the year;
The season swiftly purple grew,
The grapes hung dangling deep with blue.

A vineyard ripe, a day serene
Now calls them all to work again.
The Fauns thro' ev'ry furrow shoot
To load their flaskets with the fruit:
And now the vintage early trod,
The wines invite the jovial God.

Strew the roses, raise the song,
See the master comes along;
Lusty Revel join'd with Laughter,
Whim and Frolic follow after:
The Fauns aside the vats remain
To show the work, and reap the gain.

All around, and all around
They sit to riot on the ground;
A vessel stands amidst the ring,
And here they laugh, and there they sing;
Or rise a jolly jolly band,
And dance about it hand in hand;
Dance about, and shout amain,
Then sit to laugh, and sing again.

Thus

POETRY.

Thus they drink, and thus they play
The fun, and all their wits away.
 But as an antient Author fung,
The vine manur'd with ev'ry dung,
From ev'ry creature ftrangely drew
A twang of brutal nature, too;
'Twas hence in drinking on the lawns
New turns of humour feiz'd the Fauns.
 Here one was crying out by Jove!
Another, fight me in the grove;
This wounds a friend, and that the trees:
The lion's temper reign'd in thefe.
 Another grins, and leaps about,
And keeps a merry world of rout,
And talks impertinently free,
And twenty talks the fame as he;
Chatt'ring, idle, airy, kind:
Thefe take the monkey's turn of mind.
 Here one, that faw the Nymphs which ftood
To peep upon them from the wood,
Steals off to try if any maid
Be lagging late beneath the fhade:
While loofe difcourfe another raifes
In naked nature's plaineft phrafes,
And every glafs he drinks enjoys,
With change of nonfenfe, luft, and noife;
Mad and carelefs, hot and vain:
Such as thefe the goat retain.
 Another drinks and cafts it up,
And drinks, and wants another cup;
Solemn, filent, and fedate,
Ever long, and ever late,
Full of meats, and full of wine:
This takes his temper from the fwine.
 Here fome, who hardly feem to breathe,
Drink, and hang the jaw beneath.
Gaping, tender, apt to weep;
Their nature's alter'd by the fheep.
 'Twas thus one autumn all the crew
(If what the Poets fay be true)
While Bacchus made the merry feaft,
Inclin'd to one or other beaft:
And fince, 'tis faid, for many a mile
He fpread the vines of Lefbos ifle.

The BEGGAR.

*———————— inopemque paterni
Et Laris, et Fundi——————— Hor.*

Pity the sorrows of a poor old man,
　Whose trembling limbs have borne him to your door,
Whose days are dwindled to the shortest span;
　Oh! give relief—and heav'n will bless your store.
These tatter'd clothes my poverty bespeak,
　These hoary locks proclaim my lengthen'd years;
And many a furrow in my grief-worn cheek
　Has been the channel to a stream of tears.
Yon house, erected on the rising ground,
　With tempting aspect drew me from my road,
For plenty there a residence has found,
　And grandeur a magnificent abode.
(Hard is the fate of the infirm and poor!)
　Here craving for a morsel of their bread,
A pamper'd menial forc'd me from the door,
　To seek a shelter in an humbler shed.
Oh! take me to your hospitable dome!
　Keen blows the wind, and piercing is the cold!
Short is my passage to the friendly tomb,
　For I am poor, and miserably old.
Should I reveal the source of ev'ry grief,
　If soft humanity e'er touch'd your breast,
Your hands would not withhold the kind relief,
　And tears of pity could not be represt.
Heav'n sends misfortunes—why should we repine?
　'Tis heav'n has brought me to the state you see:
And your condition may be soon like mine,
　—The child of sorrow—and of misery.
A little farm was my paternal lot;
　Then, like the lark, I sprightly hail'd the morn;
But, ah! oppression forc'd me from my cot,
　My cattle dy'd, and blighted was my corn.
My daughter—once the comfort of my age!—
　Lur'd by a villain from her native home,
Is cast abandon'd on the world's wide stage,
　And doom'd in scanty poverty to roam.
My tender wife—sweet soother of my care!—
　Struck with sad anguish at the stern decree,
Fell—ling'ring fell, a victim to despair,
　And left the world to wretchedness and me.
Pity the sorrows of a poor old man!
　Whose trembling limbs have borne him to your door;
Whose days are dwindled to the shortest span;
　Oh! give relief—and heav'n will bless your store.

To the King of PRUSSIA, *on his Recovery; by M. de* Voltaire. *Translated by Dr.* Franklin.

IN Pluto's dark abodes, the sisters three,
Who weave too fast the threads of destiny,
As 'long the Styx they took their ev'ning walk,
Had often heard the wand'ring spirits talk
Of Prussia's gallant deeds, the laws he made,
The wars he fought, the virtues he display'd.
As thus they trac'd the hero from his birth,
They took him for the oldest king on earth;
And as his wondrous acts they counted o'er,
Instead of forty, wrote him down fourscore.
Then Atropos, to kings a hateful name,
Dispatch'd by gloomy Dis, to Berlin came;
Her fatal shears prepar'd, expecting there
To find a poor old man, with silver hair,
And wrinkled forehead:—Great was her surprize,
To see his auburn locks, and sparkling eyes;
To see him wield the sword, to hear him play
On the soft flute his jovial roundelay.
She call'd to mind how once Alcides great,
And smooth-tongu'd Orpheus, brav'd the pow'r of fate;
She trembled when she saw, in Prussia join'd,
The voice of Orpheus, with Alcides' mind;
Affrighted, threw her fatal shears aside,
And, home returning, to her sisters cry'd,—
For Prussia weave a new and golden thread,
Lasting as that for god-like Lewis made.
In the same cause did both the heroes fight;
'Gainst the same foes with equal zeal unite.
Both gain'd by wondrous acts immortal fame;
The same their valour, and their end the same;
And both hereafter shall——but soft; the muse
No longer the unequal task pursues;
Two living monarchs aptly to design,
Requires an abler pen and stronger pow'rs than mine.

To the Marquis de VILLETTE; *by the same.*

HOW few are those who teach while they delight!
How few, like thee, who think as well as write!
But reason with the sister graces join'd,
To give thee perfect empire o'er the mind;
Thus with his lyre Apollo wins our hearts,
And kills the serpent Pytho with his darts.
'Tis the same great, the same all-pow'rful god,
Who quells the savage monsters of the wood,
As he whose active and enliv'ning ray
Gives warmth to nature, and lights up the day.
But more a god he is, when to the charms
Of love he yields, and sports in Daphne's arms.

OD

ODE *for his* MAJESTY'S BIRTH-DAY, June 4, 1770:

Written by William Whitehead, *Esq. Poet Laureat, and set to Music by* Dr. Boyce, *Master of the King's Band of Musicians.*

DISCORD hence! the torch resign—
   Harmony shall rule to-day.
Whate'er thy busy fiends design
   Of future ills, in cruel play
To torture or alarm mankind,
   Lead the insidious train away;
Some blacker hours for mischief find:
   Harmony shall rule to-day.

Distinguish'd from the vulgar year,
   And mark'd with heav'n's peculiar white,
This day shall grace the rolling sphere,
And ling'ring end its bright career:
   Unwilling to be lost in night,
   Discord lead thy fiends away:
   Harmony shall rule to-day.

Is there, intent on Britain's good,
   Some angel hov'ring in the sky,
Whose ample view surveys her circling flood,
   Her guardian rocks that shine on high,
   Her forests, waving to the gales,
   Her streams, that glide through fertile vales,
   Her lowing pastures, fleecy downs,
   Towering cities, busy towns,
Is there who views them all with joy serene,
And breathes a blessing on the various scene?

O, if there is, to him 'tis giv'n,
   (When daring crimes almost demand
   The vengeance of the Thunderer's hand)
To soften or avert the wrath of heav'n.
O'er Ocean's face do tempests sweep,
   Do civil storms blow loud,
He stills the raging of the deep,
   And madness of the crowd.

He, 'too, when heaven vouchsafes to smile
Propitious on his favourite Isle,
With zeal performs the task he loves,
And every gracious boon improves.

Blest Delegate, if now there lies
Rip'ning in yonder pregnant skies

Some great event of more than common good,
Though envy howl with all her brood,
   Thy wonted power employ;
Usher the mighty moments in
   Sacred to harmony and joy,
And from this æra let their course begin!

ODE on his MAJESTY's BIRTH-DAY.

Said to be written by a very great Lady on the 4th of last June.

I.

WHEN monarchs give a grace to fate,
   And rise as princes should,
Less highly born than truly great,
   Less dignify'd than good.

II.

What joy the natal day can bring
   From whence our hopes began,
Which gave a nation such a king,
   And being such a man!

III.

The sacred source of endless pow'r
   Delighted sees him born,
And kindly marks the circling hour
   That spoke him into morn.

IV.

Beholds him with the kindest eye
   Which goodness can bestow;
And shews a brighter crown on high
   Than e'er he wore below.

A Specimen of Saragon *Poetry, from* Aubalfidal Annales Moslemici.—

On a Cat killed in a Dove-house.

I.

SWEET puss, whom as a child I lov'd,
   And as a child now mourn!
From home, ungrateful, hast thou rov'd,
   Ah, never to return!

II.

Nor doubts you felt, nor fears exprest,
   Though creeping to your fate;
While on my fond presaging breast
   Unbidden bodings sate.

III.

Into the dove-cot soft and slow
  You steal your cautious way;
But once an entrance found, not so
  You seize your fluttering prey.

IV.

But in thy steps swift vengeance treads,
  And winds thee in her snare:
The hunter, where the toils he spreads,
  Himself should perish there.

V.

The tender dove with curious scent
  Say, wherefore you pursu'd;
Nor rested, wretched puss, content
  With mice, thy proper food?—

VI.

That ever food, of life the spring,
  Should be of life the bane!
Curst be such dainty feasts as bring
  Destruction in their train.

The HORSE and the OLIVE.

By the late Archdeacon Parnell, not yet printed in his Works.

WITH moral taste let antient wisdom move,
  Whilst thus I sing to make the moderns wise:
Strong Neptune once with sage Minerva strove,
  And rising Athens was the victor's prize.

By Neptune, Plutus (guardian pow'r of gain),
  By great Minerva, bright Apollo stood;
But Jove superior bade the side obtain
  Which best contriv'd to do the nation good.

Then, Neptune striking, from the parted ground
  The warlike horse came pawing on the plain,
And as it tost its mane, and pranc'd around,
  By this, he cries, I'll make the people reign.

The Goddess, smiling, gently bow'd her spear,
  And rather thus they shall be bless'd, she said:
Then upwards shooting in the vernal air,
  With loaded boughs the fruitful Olive spread.

Jove saw what gift the rural pow'rs design'd,
  And took th' impartial scales, resolv'd to show
If greater bliss in warlike pomp we find,
  Or in the calm which peaceful times bestow.

On Neptune's part he plac'd victorious days,
   Gay trophies won, and fame extending wide;
But plenty, safety, science, arts, and ease,
   Minerva's scale with greater weight supply'd.

Fierce war devours whom gentle peace would save;
   Sweet peace restores what angry war destroys;
War made for peace, with that rewards the brave,
   While peace its pleasures from itself enjoys.

Hence vanquish'd Neptune to the sea withdrew,
   Hence wise Minerva rul'd Athenian lands;
Her Athens hence in arts and honours grew,
   And still her Olives deck pacific hands.

From fables thus disclos'd, a monarch's mind
   May form just rules to chuse the truly great,
And subjects weary'd with distresses find,
   Whose kind endeavours most befriend the state.

E'en Britain here may learn to place her love,
   If cities won her kingdom's wealth have cost;
If Anna's thoughts the patriot souls approve,
   Whose cares restore that wealth the wars had lost.

But if we ask, the moral to disclose,
   Whom her best patroness Europa calls,
Great Anna's title no exception knows,
   And unapply'd in this the fable falls.

With her nor Neptune or Minerva vies;
   Whene'er she pleas'd, her troops to conquest flew:
Whene'er she pleases, peaceful times arise:
   She gave the Horse, and gives the Olive, too.

On throwing by an old black Coat.

OLD friend, farewell—with whom full many a day,
   In varied mirth and grief, hath roll'd away.
No more thy form retains its sable dye,
But, like grey beauty, palls upon the eye.—
That form which shone so late in fashion's bloom!
How fallen—ere while the glory of the loom!
Late, wrapt secure within thy woollen folds,
I brav'd the summer rains, and winter colds.
Fearless of coughs, catarrhs, which Eurus brings,
Or dark November, on his noisome wings:
Whistling a tune, like Cymon in the song,
Through filthy streets and lanes I've trudg'd along;

Nor heeded aught the Hackney Coachman's cries,
Though, *Coach, your Honour,* founded to the skies:
And shall I, then, forget thy brighter hue,
Sell thee a slave to yonder hoarse-mouth'd Jew?
Forbid it, gratitude—forbid it, shame—
That were a deed would blacken Clodio's name.
Thou poor old man, whose brow is streak'd with care,
Stretch'd on the clay-cold earth, thy bosom bare,
Had I but half that Clodio's shining store,
Thy breast should heave with misery no more:
Yet take the scanty pittance I bestow;
This coat shall shield thee from the drifting snow.

 But ere we part—indulge the moral lay;
Hear it, ye fools, who flutter life away:
Vain are the rich man's toils, the proud man's brags:
Men turn to dust—and broad cloth turns to rags.

The EXPOSTULATION. *To* DELIA, *by Lord* G.

I.
FOR ever, O! merciless fair,
 Will that cruel indifference endure?
Can those eyes look me into despair,
 And that heart be unwilling to cure?

II.
If I love, will you doom me to die,
 Or, if I adore you, upbraid?
Can that breast the least pity deny
 To the wretch which your beauty has made?

III.
How oft what I felt to disguise
 Has my reason imperiously strove,
Till my soul almost fell from my eyes,
 In the tears of the tenderest love!

IV.
Till render'd unable to flow
 By the torture's excess which I bore,
That nature sunk under the woe,
 Or only recover'd to more.

V.
Then, Delia, determine my fate,
 Nor let me to madness be drove:
But, O! do not tell me you hate,
 If you even resolve not to love.

The REPLY. *By Lady* MARY S.

I.
O! Cease to mourn, unhappy youth,
　Or think this bosom hard:
My tears, alas! must own your truth,
　And wish it could reward.

II.
Th' excess of unabating woe
　This tortur'd breast endures,
Too well, alas! must make me know
　The pain that dwells in your's.

III.
Condemn'd like you to weep in vain,
　I seek the darkest grove,
And fondly bear the sharpest pain
　Of never-hoping love.

IV.
My wasted day, in endless sighs,
　No sound of comfort hears,
And morn but breaks on Delia's eyes
　To wake her into tears.

V.
If sleep should lend her friendly aid,
　In fancy I complain,
And hear some sad, some wretched maid,
　Or see some perjur'd swain.

VI.
Then cease thy suit, fond youth, O cease,
　Or blame the fates alone;
For how can I restore your peace,
　Who quite have lost my own?

A PRAYER *to* INDIFFERENCE. *By Mrs.* G——.

Found in Richmond Garden.

OFT I 've implor'd the gods in vain,
　And pray'd till I 've been weary;
For once I'll strive my wish to gain,
　Of Oberon, the fairy.

Sweet airy being, wanton sprite,
　Who liv'st in woods unseen,
And oft by Cynthia's silver light
　Tripp'd gaily o'er the green;

If e'er thy pitying heart was mov'd,
　(As antient stories tell)
And for th' Athenian maid, who lov'd,
　Thou sought'st a wondrous spell;

Oh! deign once more t' exert thy pow'r;
　Haply some herb or tree,
Sov'reign as juice from western flow'r,
　Conceals a balm for me.

I ask no kind return in love,
　No tempting charm to please;
Far from that heart such gifts remove,
　Which sighs for peace and ease.

Nor ease, nor peace, that heart can know,
　That, like the needle true,
Turns at the touch of joy or woe,
　But, turning, trembles too.

For as distress the soul can wound,
　'Tis plain in each degree:
Bliss goes but to a certain bound;
　Beyond 't is agony.

Then take this treacherous sense of mine,
　Which dooms me still to *smart:*
Which pleasure can to pain refine,
　To pain new pangs impart!

Oh! haste to shed the sov'reign balm,
　My shatter'd nerves new string;
And for my guest, serenely calm,
　The nymph, Indifference, bring!

At her approach, see hope, see fear,
　See expectation fly;
With disappointment in the rear,
　That blasts the purpos'd joy.

The tears which pity taught to flow
　My eyes shall then disown;
The heart which throbb'd for other's woe
　Shall then scarce feel its own.

The wounds which now each moment bleed,
　Each moment then shall close;
And peaceful days shall still succeed
　To nights of sweet repose.

Oh,

Oh, fairy elf! but grant me this,
  This one kind comfort send:
And so may never-fading bliss
  Thy flow'ry paths attend!

So may the glow-worm's glimmering light
  Thy tiny footsteps lead
To some new region of delight,
  Unknown to mortal tread!

HENRY *and* SOPHY.

HENRY and Fortune now are friends,
  His many sorrows all are past;
Fortune, to make him full amends,
  Gives to his wishing arms, at last,

The long-lov'd Sophy; fairest maid
  That ever caus'd or felt love's smart;
In her most richly were display'd
  The loveliest form and truest heart.

Long had their friends, with souls severe,
  Oppos'd the lover's happy fate;
But, chang'd, they smiling now appear,
  And with them at the altar wait.

Deep in the maiden's roseate bloom
  Grief's canker-worm had wasteful fed;
To snatch his Sophy from her tomb
  Invited, love-lorn Henry sped.

The holy priest pronounc'd aloud
  The Gordian wonder-working spell;
While Love and Hymen both avow'd,
  " Shrin'd in their breasts they'd ever dwell."

" And art thou mine," the bridegroom cry'd,
  " With all thy wondrous truth and charms?"
She smil'd—she would have spoke—she sigh'd—
  And straight expir'd within his arms.—

Too weak to bear Joy's rushing flow,
  Her tender frame resigns her breath;
This moment in Love' arms—and now
  Enfolded in the arms of Death.

In vain, in vain you fly for aid—
  Life shall no more that form relume;
The marriage-bed, ill fated maid,
  For thee ordain'd, is a cold tomb.

While floods of tears, and piteous moan,
   A genuine sorrow testify,
Silent, poor Henry's seen alone—
   No tear bedews poor Henry's eye.

Homeward his Sophy's corpse he tends;
   Frantic his Sophy he enfolds:
That friendly night his sorrow ends:
   One grave the new-wed lovers holds!——

We grasp at joys within our reach;
   We grasp, and catch a wat'ry bow:
Lessons like these should mankind teach,
   True joy exists not here below.

To FEAR.

O THOU, dread foe to honour, wealth, and fame,
   Whose tongue can quell the strong, the fierce can tame,
Relentless Fear! ah! why did fate ordain
My trembling heart to own thy iron reign?
There are, thrice happy! who disdain thy sway:
The merchant wand'ring o'er the wat'ry way;
The chief, serene before th' assaulted wall;
The climbing statesman, thoughtless of his fall;
All whom the love of wealth or pow'r inspires,
And all who burn with proud Ambition's fires:
But peaceful bards thy constant presence know,
O thou, of ev'ry glorious deed the foe!
Of thee the silent studious race complains,
And Learning groans a captive in thy chains.
The secret wish when some fair object moves,
And cautious Reason what we wish approves,
Thy gorgon front forbids to grasp the prize,
And seas are spread betwixt; and mountains rise.
Thy magic arts a thousand phantoms raise,
And fancy'd deaths and dangers fill our ways;
With smiling Hope you wage eternal strife,
And envious snatch the cup of joy from life.
O leave, tremendous pow'r! the blameless breast,
Of guilt alone the tyrant, and the guest;
Go, and thy train of sable horrors spread
Where Murder meditates the future deed;
Where Rapine watches for the gloom of night,
And lawless Passion pants for others' right;
Go to the bad, but from the good recede,
No more the foe of ev'ry glorious deed.

Une

POETRY.

Une traduction est desirée.

FORTUNE the FOUNDATION of FAME.

Translated from Rousseau.

HOW, heav'ns! when Rome is on fire,
   Can I the mad Sylla admire?
Or can fierce Alexander be prais'd,
Who with fire every nation has blaz'd?

Shall I call that a virtuous rage
   Which can murderous valour infuse,
Which no cries, no distress can assuage,
   Which its steel in my bosom embrues?
Can I make my mouth speak 'gainst my mind,
   And force it to praise all the ravage
   Which is made by a hero, a savage
Who is born for the grief of mankind?

What horrible pictures I see!
Ye conquerors, deaf to pity;
Vows broken, and projects conceiv'd,
And kings of their kingdoms bereav'd.

City walls all encompass'd by fire,
   Men and stones to the flame fall a prey.
With blood all the conqu'rors perspire,
   And death sweeps a nation away;
Mothers, pale and disfigur'd with blood,
Snatch their daughters from infamy's hold,
From the arm of a soldier that's bold,
From a grasp that's inhuman and rude.

Magnanimous warriors, display
Your courage in full open day;
Let it quickly, ye warriors, be shewn,
How your hearts will sustain Fortune's frown.

When Fortune gives aid to your arms,
   You are conquerors great of the earth;
Your glory our reason disarms,
   Your glory like Phœbus breaks forth.
But should Fortune her succour deny,
   The mask falls from before your pale face;
   You seem then of but human race,
And the hero is fled from the eye.

The PETITION *of the* FOOLS *to* JUPITER.

A FABLE.

(Supposed to be written by David Garrick, *Esq. addressed to the Earl of* Chesterfield.)

FROM *Grecian* ÆSOP, to our GAY,
 Each fabulist is pleas'd to say,
That JOVE gives ear to all petitions,
From animals of all conditions;
Like earthly kings he *hears* their wants,
And like them, too, not always *grants*.
 Some years ago—the *Fools* assembled,
Who long at STANHOPE's wit had trembled,
And with repeated strokes grown sore,
Most zealously did JOVE implore,
That he would shield them from that wit,
Which, pointed well, was sure to hit:
'Twas hard, they said, to be thus baited,
That were not by themselves created;
And if they were to folly prone,
The fault, they hop'd, was not their own.
 JOVE smil'd, and said—Not quite so fast:
You were, indeed, made up in haste;
With little care I form'd your brain,
But never made you pert and vain:
STANHOPE himself would be your friend,
Did you not strive my work to mend,
And, wildly straying from my rules,
Make yourselves fops, whom I made fools:
But tell me how, for I am willing
To grant your wish, on this side killing,
And shield you for the time to come.—
" Strike CHESTERFIELD deaf, blind, and dumb."
" First, in his *Tongue*, such terrors lie,
" If that is stopp'd he can't reply:
" To stop his *tongue*, and not his *ears*,
" Will only multiply our fears;
" He'll answer both in prose and verse,
" And *they* will prove a lasting curse:
" Then stop, O sire of gods and men,
" That still more dreadful tongue, his pen:
" Spare not, good JOVE, his Lordship's *sight;*
" We ne'er shall rest, if he can write."
 Hold, hold—cries JOVE, a moment stay;
You know not, fools, for what you pray:

Your

Your malice, shooting in the dark,
Has driv'n the arrow o'er the mark.
Deaf, dumb, and *blind,* ye silly folk!
Is all this rancour for a joke?
Shall I be pander to your hate,
And mortals teach to rail at fate?
To mend a little your condition,
And grant one *third* of your petition;
He shall be *deaf,* and you be free
From his keen, brilliant repartée
Which, like high-temper'd polish'd steel,
Will quicker wound than you can feel:
With fear, with weakness we comply,
But still what malice asks, deny:
How would Apollo, Hermes, swear,
Should I give ear to all your pray'r,
And blast the man, who from his birth
Has been their fav'rite care on earth?
What, tie his tongue, and cloud his sight,
That he no more may talk and write!
I can't indulge your foolish pride,
And punish all the world beside.

An Answer in the Name of Lord Chesterfield.

GARRICK, I've read your *Fools' Petition,*
And thank you for the composition;
Though few will credit all you say,
Yet 'tis a friendly part you play;
A part which you perform with ease;
Whate'er you act is sure to please.
But give me leave, on this occasion,
To make one little observation:
Though no good reason is assign'd,
At least not any I can find,
Why I should be *deaf, dumb,* or *blind;*
Yet since it was resolv'd above
By this same fool-obeying Jove,
I must not speak, or hear, or see,
Surely, to soften the decree,
He might have left the *choice* to *me.*
Were that the case, I would dispense
With sight and wit, and eloquence,
Still to retain my fav'rite sense;
For grant, my friend, we should admit,
What some may doubt, that I have wit;

What are the mighty pow'rs of speech,
What useful purpose do they reach?
When vain and impotent you see,
E'en down from *Socrates* to *me*,
All the *bon mots* that e'er were said
To mend the heart or clear the head,
Fools will be fools, say what we will,
And rascals will be rascals still.

But rather I your case would be in
Say you, than lose the power of seeing;
The face of Nature will you say
Is ever cheerful, ever gay,
And Beauty, parent of delight,
Must always charm the ravish'd sight?

This choice perhaps I might commend;
But here, you have forgot, my friend,
That Nature's face, and Beauty's heav'n,
Lose all their charms at seventy-seven;
The brightest scenes repeated o'er,
As well you know, will please no more;
The prospect's darken'd o'er with age,
The Drama can no more engage,
We wish with *you* to quit the stage.

In short, it is a point I'm clear in,
The best of senses is our hearing;
Happy who keeps it still, and he
Who wants must mourn the loss like me;
For though I little should regret
The table's roar where fools are met,
The flatt'ring tribe who *sing* or *say*
The lies or tattle of the day,
Still have I' cause for discontent,
Still lose what most I must lament,—
The *converse* of a *chosen few*,
The *luxury* of—*hearing* you.

A WISH *to the* NORTH. *By a Lady.*

O Liberty? blest gift of heav'n,
 Why sighs my breast for thee in vain?
Alas! by tyrants far thou 'rt driven,
 And rude constraint usurps thy reign.
O wert thou mine, no more confin'd
 To doze out life in one calm dream,
Ye Surry vales I 'd leave behind,
 And ply my bark on Humber's stream.

Fair stream! transported would I view
  Thy fruitful vallies, blooming groves;
There would my ravish'd mind pursue
  Such scenes as contemplation loves.
Thy sumptuous dwellings, stately piles,
  Thy wealthy, ample, wide domains,
Where Amaltheas' bounty smiles,
  And swells the tribute of thy plains.
Or if to pensive thought inclin'd,
  I'd read thy mournful annals o'er,
And view the time when wars combin'd
  To chase those blessings from thy shore.
When thorny roses, ting'd with blood,
  Rais'd fierce commotion through the land,
And Victory suspended stood,
  And wav'd the laurel in her hand.
Ill-fated Henry! then I'd mourn
  The stormy tempest of thy reign!
Thy weeping consort left forlorn,
  Thy son, too, number'd with the slain!
A tear should blot the guilty page
  Where Rutland dies in early bloom,
Fell'd by the hand of savage rage,
  And doom'd by slaughter to the tomb.
And when from hist'ry's tragic stores
  I turn'd, to view these horrors cease,
I'd bless the pow'r that guards our shores,
  And suppliant ask eternal peace.
But cease, my Muse, these lays of art,
  Nor more prolong th' ambiguous plea;
Ah! Love forgive; my conscious heart
  Revokes the strain, and turns to thee!
Thine is the wish that fondly roves,
  That thus inspires th' enraptur'd theme,
That leads the Muse to Northern groves,
  And wafts her sighs to Humber's stream.

To a ROBIN, *which has lately taken up his Residence in the Cathedral at Bristol, and accompanies the Organ with his Singing.*

SWEET, social bird! whose soft harmonious lays
  Swell the glad song of thy Creator's praise,
Say, art thou conscious of approaching ills?
Fell Winter's storms—the pointed blast that kills?
Shunn'st thou the savage North's unpitying breath?
Or cruel man's more latent snares of death?
Here dwell secure; here, with incessant note,
Pour the soft music of thy trembling throat.

Here,

Here, gentle bird, a sure asylum find,
Nor dread the chilling frost, nor boist'rous wind.
No hostile tyrant of the feather'd race
Shall dare invade thee in this hallow'd place;
Nor, while he sails the liquid air along,
Check the shrill numbers of thy cheerful song.
No cautious gunner, whose unerring sight
Stops the swift eagle in his rapid flight,
Shall here disturb my lovely songsters rest,
Nor wound the plumage of his crimson breast.
The truant school-boy, who, in wanton play,
With viscid lime involves the treach'rous spray,
In vain shall spread the wily snare for thee,
Alike secure thy life and liberty.
Peace then, sweet warbler, to thy flutt'ring heart;
Defy the rage of hawks, and toils of art:
Now shake thy downy plumes; now gladlier pay
Thy grateful tribute to each rising day;
While crowds *below* their willing voices raise,
To sing with holy zeal *Jehovah's* praise,
Thou, perch'd *on high*, shall hear th' adoring throng,
Catch the warm strains, and aid the sacred song;
Increase the solemn chorus, and inspire
Each tongue with music, and each heart with fire.

Part of the LAST CHORUS *of the Second Act of* Seneca's Troades.

FRAIL is the state of visionary man,
His pleasures transient, and his life a span:
At morn he blooms, with conscious pride elate,
At eve he shrinks, and dreads impending fate.
So the gay flow'r that decks the woodland glade
Is doom'd to blossom, and is doom'd to fade.
When Fate demands our tributary breath,
Then say, O reas'ner! what thou dread'st in death?
Oft, on a dunghill, Virtue's left to rot,
Its worth neglected, and its charms forgot;
Whilst gaudy villains reap the wish'd-for prize,
And ill-got trappings strike our wond'ring eyes.
How round the heart the soft affections twine,
When the tear falls at injur'd Virtue's shrine!
But oft we stretch our aid to worth in vain,
And pity adds but to a life of pain.
The rose that scents the zephyr's balmy wing,
Beneath its leaves retains a poignant sting:
No real joys from wealth or fortune flow,
Nay, length of life is but protracted woe.

Then what is death? why should the name affright,
The empty bugbear of a winter's night?
Why should we shudder at this final blow,
Which soothes each care, and drowns the voice of woe?
Let minds which float on Fancy's airy wing
Paint fields Elysian and eternal spring;
Let sad enthusiasts form a dreary cave,
And feel the blast which curls Cocytus' wave:
Be mine the lot to pass unheeded through
Life's mazy path, and take a transient view
Of fleeting bliss, while now and then a smile
Plays on my lips, each sorrow to beguile:
Not over-fond of life, nor fearing death,
Content and tranquil I'll resign my breath;
For, though with airy joys our fancies teem,
Sure life and death are but an anxious dream.

FAME and his COMPANIONS.
A poetical Fable. By the Rev. Mr. R——.

IT happen'd once upon a time,
(A phrase made choice of for the rhyme)
Water and Fire agreed to stray
With Fame, the partner of their way.
Fire was a noisy, rattling blade,
Water, a bashful, gentle maid.
Nor let the wife with wonder read
That two such contraries agreed;
For greater opposites than these
The love of Fame unites with ease.

Through various realms they travell'd long,
Went often right, but oft'ner wrong.
Fire sometimes miss'd his proper road,
And in a miser's chimney glow'd;
Water, mistaking her design,
Intruded frequently on wine;
While Fame, deluded by the crowd,
Lodg'd with the crafty and the proud.

Thus, men of diff'rent taste in vain
Attempt one project to sustain;
For while they dream of doing wonders,
They lead each other into blunders.

At length, with various errors tir'd,
Their first design a change requir'd;
Water and Fire, to gain their ends,
Propos'd to part—but part as friends:
Each was to leave some mark behind him,
That t'other, at a pinch, might find him.

"Where-

Where fprightly verdure decks the ground,
(Says Water) " I fhall ftill be found:
" With wealth and pow'r fometimes I dwell,
" But oftener in the hermit's cell,
" Banifh'd from feafts by nobler claret,
" I feek the raptur'd poet's garret:
" Where trade prevails, my torrents flow;
" My ftreams where bending ofiers grow."
' Where circling clouds of fmoke afpire,
' You're fure to meet with me (fays Fire):
' Deep in the bowels of the mine,
' And in the ftars above, I fhine;
' In every houfe on winter nights,
' In every verfe the poet writes;
' Illuminate, as whims prevail,
' A city, or a glow-worm's tail.'
" Comrades, (fays Fame) I own I'm loth
" To tell my temper to you both:
" When lov'd and courted by my friends,
" My care their ev'ry ftep attends;
" When view'd with a neglectful eye,
" Stung with th' affront, at once I fly.
" Since this the cafe, from either fide
" It gives me forrow to divide;
" You, when you pleafe, by certain figns,
" When love or intereft inclines,
" Again may meet, tho' now you fever;
" But—whom I leave, I leave for ever."

Written by a Brewer's Daughter, on her Father's difcharging his Coachman for getting in Liquor.

HONEST William, an eafy and good-natur'd fellow,
Would a little too oft' get a little too mellow:
Body Coachman was he to an eminent Brewer;
No better e'er fat on a box, to be fure;
His Coach he kept clean—no Mother or Nurfes
Took more care of their Babes than he took of his Horfes:
He had thefe, ay, and fifty good qualities more,
But the bufinefs of *tippling* could ne'er be got o'er;
So his mafter effectually mended the matter,
By hiring a man who drank nothing—but water.
Now, William, fays he, you fee the plain cafe;
Had you drank as he does, you'd have kept a good place.
Drink water! quoth William;—had all men done fo,
You ne'er would have wanted a coachman, I trow;
For 'tis *Soakers* like me, whom you load with reproaches,
That enable you *Brewers* to ride in your Coaches.

WISDOM

WISDOM and HEALTH.

COME, roseate Health, my temples bind
  With thy celestial wreath;
And thou, blest Wisdom, on my mind
  Thy choicest odours breathe.

As dearest friends together live,
  Like them you pine apart:
Health gone, not Wisdom e'er can give
  Pure rapture to the heart.

If Wisdom fly the youthful breast,
  Not smiling Health can gain
To it the cordial balm of rest,
  A mind exempt from pain.

Come, then, twin-daughters of the skies,
  Here make your social stay:
The moment either from me flies,
  Death snatch my soul away.

On the DEATH of the MARQUIS of GRANBY.

WHAT makes the soldier's breast incessant sigh?
  Why fall the streaming tears from ev'ry eye?
The noble RUTLAND's brow, with sadness spread,
Proclaims that GRANBY, generous GRANBY's, dead!
To fate all must submit, the great, the brave,
The sage philosopher, and courtly slave;
And when pale death dissociates the soul
From her weak tenement, the mansion whole,
To native earth return'd, there mould'ring lies,
But virtue pure exists, and death defies:
Hence all thy ancestors, O, GRANBY! live;
Their noble deeds our faithful annals give:
Nor shall thy worth be less enroll'd with fame,
As great thy merit, and belov'd thy name.

T. L.

ANOTHER.

OF courage, honour, charity, the boast,
  Was noble GRANBY—but though early lost,
Though early mingled with the honour'd dead,
Each Muse a tear upon his hearse shall shed;
Shall strive the mem'ry of his worth to save,
And plant with laurels his distinguish'd grave.

An Account of Books for 1770.

A Journey from London to Genoa, through England, Portugal, Spain, and France. By Joseph Barretti, Secretary for foreign Correspondence to the Royal Academy of Painting, Sculpture, and Architecture. [In 4 vols. 8vo.]

THE author of these volumes (whom we have formerly had occasion to make favourable mention of as a writer, from his account of the customs and manners of Italy, published in the year 1768) is a foreigner; nor will the attentive reader want any proofs of it. Indeed, from the *general* purity and propriety of the diction, we should almost suspect that these little trips in the language were not undesigned; but were left by the author as a sort of mark, to prove his title to the work.

We have mentioned the propriety of the diction, but it were doing great injustice to this gentleman to confine his praise as a writer to mere propriety of diction: we must do him the honour of owning, that he has attained to that masterly command of the language, that would not discredit the very best of our own writers.

The work before us is the story of a journey, digested into letters; and in the character of epistolary writing, we have not, perhaps, in the language, any thing more to be commended. It preserves the true genius of that mode of composition; and we cannot but regret that the fourth volume is rather a diary, and consequently wants that engaging and interesting manner that characterize the three first volumes.

The author seems in his preface to apologize in some sort for his frequent egotism, and his venturing to make himself the hero of his own tale: but, in fact, the man who writes his own journey must be his own hero. Besides which, the circumstance of drawing his remarks on the customs and manners of the people from incidents of the journey, and thereby making them, as it were, part of a story, is a very happy and dexterous method of instruction. The *Fandango*, for one example out of a thousand, we all knew was a Spanish dance; but Mr. Barretti carries us with him, we find the people here and there, and every where employed in the dance; we make one in the party; and are more convinced of his opinion that the Spaniards are a lively people, than if he had spent an hundred pages to confute the vulgar notion of their unconquerable gravity. Though the scene is laid in Portugal, of some of the extracts that we shall make upon this occasion, yet as the dance and the manners in this instance are the same in both countries, and the actors here composed of both nations,

ACCOUNT OF BOOKS. 243

nations, the following account, while it includes the one, gives an expreffive description of the other.

Our author, giving an account of the mafks who danced in the ftreets at Eftremor, proceeds as follows:

"A number of them ftopped in a ftreet where fome ladies fat in a balcony, and there they began a dance. A young fellow amongft them fingularly attracted my attention, and indeed that of the whole company, with his nimble capers and graceful motions. I have already feen the Portuguefe dance in Lifbon, and, to give them their due, no nation (of thofe that I have feen at leaft) has any dance performed by two perfons fo exhilarating as their Fandango. The Trefcone of the Tufcans, the Furlana of the Venetians, the Corrente of the Monferrines, and the Minuet or the Aimable of the French, are flat performances in comparifon of that gallant one which I faw executed before that balcony, by that young man and a boy dreffed in woman's cloaths. But dances cannot be defcribed by words, nor can I convey to you any idea of the Fandango, but by telling you that every limb was in fuch a motion as might be called with propriety a regular and harmonious convulfion of the whole body. I have heard a French mafter in Lifbon blame it much, and fay it was no dance at all: but what dance will be approved by a Frenchman that is not a production of his country? He has no idea of gracefulnefs but what is practifed on the opera-ftage at Paris.

"The inhabitants of this country, as well as the Andalufians and the Granadans, were famous for dancing fo far back as the times of the Romans; and their young women ufed then to go and dance at Rome and in other parts of the Roman empire, where they eafily captivated the hearts of confuls and proconfuls, as the female dancers of France go now to Italy, Germany, and England, to enamour *Signors*, *Minheers*, and *Mylords*. Martial mentions, with fatirical peevifhnefs, the Betick and the Gaditan female dancers; and the eldeft Scaliger, fomewhere in his Poetics, fays fomething of the dancing antiently ufed in the provinces that lie this way. You are lucky, my brothers, that I travel without a *Martial* and a *Scaliger*. Had I their books, I would not let this opportunity flip without making as great a wafte of erudition as our Bartoli the antiquarian does fo often."

We fhall now attend our traveller to Elvas, where he fays:

"I was fhewn up ftairs into a kind of gallery, which opened into feveral rooms full of people. This gallery was fpread with men who flept wrapped up in their cloaks. As I advanced amongft them, I felt the floor fhaking; and as my head has been filled with earthquakes ever fince I reached Portugal, it occurred on a fudden that the ground was fhaking; but prefently was fenfible that the concuffion was caufed by my moving along that ill-conftructed floor.

"As I was walking and waiting for my fupper, fome young muleteers came out of the fide-rooms. One of them began to tickle his guitar, and another produced a fong to the tune. They had fcarcely gone on three minutes with their performance, when the fleepers ftarted up,

R 2 while

while more than thirty people came out of those side-rooms; and a dance was begun. A man cut a caper, by way of reverence, to a woman, and the woman advanced immediately to dance the Fandango with him. There is no possibility of conveying to you any just idea of their hilarity, nimbleness, and elasticity. There were four Spanish and six Portuguese females. Out of the ten I only took notice of three. One was a brownish girl called Terefuela, whom I soon found to be the best finger of them all. The other two were sisters: the younger so renowned in the towns around for a beauty, that she goes under the appellation of *la bella Catalina*. The elder is not so handsome, but has such eyes! What a pity the comparison of the stars is no more in fashion!

"The dresses of these women were all gaudy, especially the Spanish, who are come from Badajos with some male friends to see Elvas-fair. I must repeat it, that I have seen various dances from Parenzo in Istria to Derby in England; but none of them is comparable to what I saw here to-night. It is true that their gestures and attitudes are sometimes not so composed as one could wish; yet, if I was possessed of the abilities of Martial, instead of running down the Fandango and the Seguedilla, which I suppose were the dances he satirized, I would write a thousand epigrams in praise of them, of Terefuela, of Cataliua, and most particularly of Paolita, who has those eyes I mentioned! Oh, this Paolita!

"Both the Fandango and the Seguedilla are danced either at the sound of the guitar alone, or the guitar accompanied by the voice, which is an advantageous addition when the guitarist happens to have a good voice. Both men and women, while dancing, give a double clap with their thumbs and middle fingers at every cadence, and both dances (the Fandango especially) are rather made up with graceful motions, and quick striking of their heels and toes on the ground, than with equal and continued steps. They dance close to each other, then wheel about, then approach each other with fond eagerness, then quickly retire, then quickly approach again, the man looking the woman steadily in the face, while she keeps her head down, and fixes her eyes on the ground with as much modesty as she can put on.

"I had slept but poorly for three nights together, and was so much tired with this day's journey, performed a-foot for the greatest part, that I was just debating whether I should, or not, go supperless to bed. But this unexpected feast changed my thoughts instantly, and, instead of going to rest, I stood there gazing with my whole soul absorbed in delight.

"The fellows, who but a moment before were sleeping on that floor, without the least ceremony, or the least shame of their rags, danced away with the gaudy as well as with the dirty women (for some of them were dirty enough); nor did any of the company shew the least partiality to age, to dress, or to beauty, but all seemed to dance merely for dancing sake. I was a little surprized to see a shabby rascal take up so clean a girl as Terefuela, who was the finest of them

them all, and look sweeter upon her than any *petit maitre* would at Paris upon a rich and tender widow. This would not have been allowed in any of the countries I have visited, where the ill-dressed keep company with the ill-dressed, and the fine with the fine, without ever dreaming of such mixtures as are practised in this part of the world.

"In a corner of this gallery there is a large table. Upon the table the cloth was laid, and my supper placed. There I sat down to eat, without ceremony or shame, in my turn.

"Having almost done, Batiste put before me a large English cake, made by Madam Kelly. This cake I cut up into slices, and placing them pyramidically upon a plate, I went to present it round to the ladies, paying them a Castilian compliment that I had been a quarter of an hour in composing. Each of them, with the most disembarrassed countenance, picked up her slice; some with a bow, some with a smile, and some with a kind word.

"The cake being thus disposed, I turned to the gentlemen (muleteers, ass-drivers, and all), and, calling them Fidalgo's and Cavallero's, invited them to drink the health of the *amables Baylarinas (amiable she-dancers)*, which they all did with the noblest freedom and greatest alacrity; and much was the general joy increased by this sudden piece of outlandish manners. Several of them, who till then had scarcely deigned to look on the Estrangeiro, or seemed afraid to speak to him, now shook him by the hand, and each had something to say to me, either in Spanish or Portuguese.

"To the ladies, after the cake, I ordered glasses of water; because I knew that to offer them wine would have spoiled all the good I had done, and the offer construed into a gross affront: in such esteem is sobriety amongst these people. One of them, who was with child, sent to ask a slice of the ham, and her example was followed by the rest."

To fill up the picture, we shall now attend our author to Madrid, where, in the account he gives of the Carnival customs, we again meet the *Fandango*, as we do indeed upon many other occasions.

"The Carnival-customs have undergone some change at Madrid, as the King has built there a very grand hall, called *el Amphitheatro*, where thousands resort twice a week during the Carnival-time. Any body, masked, is admitted there for only twenty reals (not quite five shillings), and passes there the whole night with as much pleasure as such a place can afford. There the dancing place is spacious enough for three hundred couples to dance at a time, and there are seats round it, amphitheatrically disposed, with three large galleries over, which admit five or six thousand people more. The hall has four spacious stair-cases at the four corners, that lead up to the galleries, and to several large rooms, where people may have hot and cold suppers at choice, coffee, chocolate, lemonades, and other refreshments, every thing nearly as cheap as at home. A considerable number of waiters attend, all uniformly dressed in Pompadour-colour. Besides these conveniences, there are two large rooms with fur beds in each, one for the men,

R 3 the

the other for the women, who should happen to be taken suddenly ill; and there are physicians and surgeons regularly attending, as well as four dancing-masters to direct the country dances, and teach their various motions and evolutions to those who do not know them well. Nor must I omit to mention two small rooms with inscriptions over their doors. one *Jaula por los páxaros*, the other *Jaula por los páxaras*; that is, a cage for the cock-birds, a cage for the hen-birds: in plain language, a jail for the men, and a jail for the women. Should any body raise any disturbance, or behave with any indecency there, he would be shut up for the night by the guards attending at the entrance door.

"I have seen above six hundred people dance at once the Fandango in that amphitheatre; and it is not possible to give an idea of such a rapturous diversion. The enthusiasm that seizes the Spaniards the moment that the Fandango is touched, is a thing not to be conceived. I saw hundreds of them, at supper, quit instantly the tables, tumble precipitously down the stair-cases, throng promiscuously into the dancing place, face about for a partner that was found in an instant, and fall a dancing, both men and women, with such a vigour as to beggar all description. Was the place ample enough, there is not one of them that would remain a simple spectator, as many are forced to be. Those who are forced to it, stand gazing from the seats below or the galleries above, with sparkling eyes and limbs trembling, and encourage the dancers with clamour and clapping of hands. There is a small printed book, intitled *Bayle de Mascaras, &c.* printed at Madrid in 1763, that sets forth the laws to be observed at the amphitheatre. Should any body contravene any of those laws, he would instantly be thrust into one of the Jaulas. The band there consists of forty instruments, that play alternately twenty at a time, so that the dancing is never stopped so long as the night lasts; that is, from nine o'clock at night till six in the morning."

The great objects of travel, and what would draw the attention of the statesman, the lawgiver, or the commercial politician, were not to be comprehended in the short space of time that Mr. Barretti allowed himself to spend on his tour; he, however, spent that little time so agreeably to him and his readers, that we must regret that he did not afford himself more leisure. He went very fast indeed through Portugal, which does not appear to be his favourite country. He seems there to feel some of those national prejudices that we all complain of, are all ashamed of, and perhaps have all experienced more or less. But our author, for the most part, generously carries the antidote for the poison which he may have scattered in his haste.

In Spain, our author's prejudices (if he has any) are all on the good-natured side; and as this country had seemed to him an object more engaging to his affections, and more worthy of his attention, we regret that he did not sojourn a while longer in it. While his prejudices contribute to his satisfaction, and render him a kind spectator of what he saw, we are pleased

pleased to indulge his prepossessions; but when he blindly adopts the wild infatuated politics of an uninformed bigotted people, we are obliged to quit him, and to lament that he has rendered himself liable to objections that no other writer of this age is subject to: he is, indeed, the only man who, at this time, can find either good sense or good policy in the cruel treatment which the Moriscoes met with in that country. So neat a master in language could not, however, omit an attention to the various tongues that are spoken in that kingdom; and the reader may be curious to see an extract from his dissertation on the Biscayan language.

"The Biscayan language, or Bascuenza, as they call it, according to the idea that I have been able to form of it, must be divided at least into three dialects; of which the first, or mother-tongue, must be called Biscayan, the second Navarran, and the third Basque.

"The Biscayan dialect, or mother-tongue, I take to be that which is spoken through that part of Biscay, the inhabitants of which consider the town of Bilboa, or rather that of Orduna, to be their capital. The chief seat of this dialect, or tongue, I take to be that which is spoken in either of those towns, only six leagues distant from each other.

"The Navarran dialect I call that which is spoken through the best part of the little kingdom of Navarre: and, as Pampeluna is the capital of that kingdom, it is to be supposed that the purest Navarran is spoken at Pampeluna.

"The Basque dialect I term that which is spoken through that tract of country called Païs de Basque by the French, to whom it belongs. That Païs is chiefly formed by thirty-three villages, and their territories, all subject to the spiritual jurisdiction of the bishoprick of Bayonne. And as the most considerable of those thirty-three villages is San Juan de Luz, there, I suppose, the best Basque is spoken; the chief people of the Païs de Basque residing in that village, which the French term a *bourg* or *ville*, to give some pre-eminence over the rest of those villages.

"The most capital Bascuenze-work is, doubtless, the folio Dictionary, compiled by father Laramendi, a Jesuit. The dictionary bears the title of Trilingue, because it runs in Bascuenze, Castilian, and Latin. As it has been printed only once, it is now become so scarce, that I could not find a copy of it any where, much to my disappointment, as I am informed that its preface, though penned in a most turgid strain, contains a great deal of rare erudition.

"Next the Dictionary comes the Grammar, composed by the same author, and oddly intitled *El impossibile vencido, The impossibility conquered*. In that grammar the Bascuenze is explained by the Castilian. I am told it has gone through several editions. I have that which was printed at Salamanca in 1729, and have repeatedly looked into it: but not yet to any purpose. In the prologo, or preface, it is said, that *el Bascuenze es una lengua que congenia poco con las otras, The genius of the Biscayan bears no great affinity to that of other languages*; and my reader will easily

easily give credit to this assertion, when he is told, that you say in Spanish, for instance, that bread is good *para aquel que lo come*, "*for him who eats it ;*" which phrase is rendered in the Biscayan language by one word only: *jatenduenarentzat*. But, though this is only one word, says father *Laramendi*, we must consider it as a compound of several; as *jaten* stands for the verb *comér*; *du* for the accusative *lo*; *en* or *end* for the relative *que*; and *arentzat* for the pronoun *aquél* followed by the article *para*.

"How easily a language thus constructed is to be learned, this only specimen may possibly give an idea. But, were it ever so easy, no great proficiency could be made in it by studying it out of the country where it is spoken, as, besides *Laramendi*'s dictionary and grammar, the number of books printed in Bascuenze is, as I said, quite inconsiderable. Eleven small volumes of Spiritual Discourses and Pious Meditations, a translation of Kempis's Imitation of Christ, another translation of Scupoli's Spiritual Combat, a short Catechism, about half a dozen small Collections of Prayers in prose, and of Spiritual Songs in verse, are almost the only works to be found printed in this language. I leave my reader to judge whether it would be possible to learn it out of the country by means of the small portion of it that is contained in so limited a library. But, was it even possible, would it be worth the while?

"I remember to have once read in an English magazine an account of an Irish priest, who, travelling through Biscay, could make shift with his Irish tongue to understand the Biscayans, and be understood by them. But whether the author of that account imposed upon the public or not, let the reader determine by the help of the following transcription of the Lord's-prayer in Biscayan and Irish."

We must refer our curious readers to the original for this specimen, in which the Lord's-prayer is divided into sentences, and given in Latin, in Biscayan, and in Irish, and by which the two latter languages seem to have no connection or resemblance.

The Life of Edward *Lord* Herbert *of* Cherbury. *Written by himself.*

THE ingenious editor of this work, with all that just and natural admiration which an editor commonly bears to his author, admits that his hero had *perhaps* some *vanity, surely* some wrongheadedness: the admission is, indeed, not a forced one. But, allowing his vanity, and his wrongheadedness, which was very much the consequence of his vanity, he was, whether you consider him as a public or a private man, a person of considerable merit, which will induce the good-natured reader more to lament than condemn a sort of feminine vanity, that led him to a too solemn avowal of personal qualities, that are, as he says, indeed scarcely credible, and, if they were, are of no merit; and yet he calls God to witness to their truths, as of things in themselves excellent and praise-worthy.

We can scarce, however, agree with the ingenious editor, that the whole relation throws singular light on the manners of the age. The age he lived in does not seem to have considered our author as a much

much less singular person than we consider him at this day: Sir Edward Sackville, who was a man of as much rank and consideration as himself, declined to have any thing to do in his wanton quarrel with the Governor of Lyons. In all probability, he was in his own time considered, as he must be now, as a very troublesome and yet respectable member of society. Perhaps we have the advantage of our ancestors in this particular, as Lord Herbert is a much better character to read than to have lived with; but his life, and the life of every man who has at all stood in a conspicuous light, will be a pleasant and possibly an instructive entertainment who writes from his real feelings, as Lord Herbert certainly does: it is, in fact, the history of his servants and of his horses, as well as of himself, and thereby carries us most agreeably through all his scenes: we will therefore present the reader with his boar-hunt, which is told us in a natural and lively manner, and possibly the reader may find himself almost as much interested for the dogs as for the knight.

"One time also it was my fortune to kill a wild boar in this manner: the boar being rouzed from his den, fled before our dogs for a good space, but finding them press him hard, turned his head against our dogs, and hurt three or four of them very dangerously. I came on horseback up to him, and with my sword thrust him twice or thrice without entering his skin, the blade being not so stiff as it should be: the boar hereupon turned upon me, and much endangered my horse, which I perceiving, rid a little out of the way, and, leaving my horse with my lackey, returned with my sword against the boar, who by this time had hurt more dogs; and here happened a pretty kind of fight, for, when I thrust at the boar sometimes with my sword, which in some places I made enter, the boar would run at me, whose tusks yet by stepping a little out of the way I avoided; but he then turning upon me, the dogs came in, and drew him off, so that he fell upon them; which I perceiving, ran at the boar with my sword again, which made him turn upon me, but then the dogs pulled him from me again: while so relieving one another by turns, we killed the boar. At this chace Monsieurs Disancour and Mennon were present, as also Mr. Townsend, yet so as they did endeavour rather to withdraw me from than assist me in the danger."

Our next extract will give a pretty good idea of the work and of the man; as it is a sketch of his ministerial conduct, and a sample of his personal whims.

"And now I shall mention some particular passages concerning myself, without entering yet any way into the whole frame and context of my negotiation, reserving them, as I said before, to a particular treatise: I spent my time much in the visits of the princes, counsel of state, and great persons of the French kingdom, who did ever punctually requite my visits: the like I did also to the chief ambassadors there, among whom, the Venetian, Low Country, Savoy, and the united princes in Germany ambassadors did bear me that respect, that they usually met in my house, to advise together concerning the great affairs of that time; for as the Spaniard then was so potent that he seemed to affect an universal

universal monarchy, all the above-mentioned ambassadors did in one common interest strive to oppose him: all our endeavours yet could not hinder, but that he both publickly prevailed in his attempts abroad, and privately did corrupt divers of the principal ministers of state in this kingdom. I came to discover this by many ways, but by none more effectually than by the means of an Italian, who returned over by letters of exchange the moneys the Spanish ambassador received for his occasions in France; for I perceived that when the said Italian was to receive any extraordinary great sum for the Spanish ambassador's use, the whole face of affairs was presently changed, insomuch that neither my reasons, nor the ambassadors above-mentioned, how valid soever, could prevail; tho' yet afterwards we found means together to reduce affairs to their former train; till some other new great sum coming to the Spanish ambassador's hand, and from thence to the aforesaid ministers of state, altered all. Howbeit, divers visits passed betwixt the Spanish ambassador and myself, in one of which he told me that tho' our interests were divers, yet we might continue friendship in our particular persons; for, said he, it can be no occasion of offence betwixt us, that each of us strive the best he can to serve the king his master. I disliked not his reasons, tho' yet I cou'd not omit to tell him that I wou'd maintain the dignity of the king my master the best I cou'd; and this I said because the Spanish ambassador had taken place of the English in the time of Henry the Fourth in this fashion, they both meeting in an anti-chamber to the Secretary of State, the Spanish ambassador leaning to the wall in that posture that he took the hand of the English ambassador, said publickly, I hold this place in the right of the king my master, which small punctilio being not resented by our ambassador at that time, gave the Spaniard occasion to bragg that he had taken the hand from our ambassador. This made me more watchful to regain the honour which the Spaniard pretended to have gotten herein, so that though the ambassador in his visits often repeated the words above mentioned, being, in Spanish, Que cada uno haga lo que pudiere por su amo; let every man do the best he can for his master; I attended the occasion to right my master. It happened one day, that both of us going to the French king for our several affairs, the Spanish ambassador, between Paris and Estampes, being upon his way before me in his coach, with a train of about 16 or 18 persons on horseback, I following him in my coach with about 10 or 12 horse, found that either I must go the Spanish pace, which is slow, or, if I hasted to pass him, that I must hazard the suffering of some affront like unto that our former ambassador received: proposing hereupon to my gentlemen the whole business, I told them that I meant to redeem the honour of the king my master some way or other, demanding farther whether they wou'd assist me? which they promising. I bid the coachman drive on. The Spanish ambassador seeing me approach, and imagining what my intention was, sent a gentleman to me, to tell me he desired to salute me, which I accepting, the gentleman returned to the ambassador, who alighting from his coach attended me in the middle of the highway,

highway, which being perceived by me, I alighted alfo, when fome extravagant complements having paſt betwixt us, the Spaniſh ambaſſador took his leave of me, went to a dry ditch not far off, upon pretence of making water, but indeed to hold the upper hand of me while I paſt by in my coach; which being obſerved by me, I left my coach, and getting upon a ſpare horſe I had there, rode into the ſaid dry ditch, and telling him aloud, that I knew well why he ſtood there, bid him afterwards get to his coach, for I muſt ride that way: the Spaniſh ambaſſador, who underſtood me well, went to his coach grumbling and diſcontented, though yet neither he nor his train did any more than look one upon another in a confuſed manner: my coach this while paſſing by the ambaſſador on the ſame ſide I was, I ſhortly after left my horſe, and got into it: it hap'ned this while, that one of my coach horſes having loſt a ſhoe, I thought fit to ſtay at a ſmith's forge, about a quarter of a mile before; this ſhoe could not be put on ſo ſoon, but that the Spaniſh ambaſſador overtook us, and might indeed have paſſed us, but that he thought I would give him another affront: attending therefore the ſmith's leaſure, he ſtayed in the highway to our no little admiration, untill my horſe was ſhoed. We continued our journey to Eſtampes, the Spaniſh ambaſſador following us ſtill at a good diſtance.

"I ſhould ſcarce have mentioned this paſſage, but that the Spaniards do ſo much ſtand upon their pundonores; for confirming whereof I have thought fit to remember the anſwer a Spaniſh ambaſſador made to Philip the ſecond king of Spain, who finding fault with him for neglecting a buſineſs of great importance in Italy, becauſe he could not agree with the French ambaſſador about ſome ſuch pundonore as this, ſaid to him, Como a dexado una coſa di importancia per una ceremonia! How, have you left a buſineſs of importance for a ceremony; the ambaſſador boldly replied to his maſter, Como por una ceremonia? vueſſa majeſta miſma no es ſino una ceremonia: How, for a ceremony? your majeſty's ſelf is but a ceremony.

"Howſoever the Spaniſh ambaſſador taking no notice publickly of the advantage I had of him herein, diſſembled it as I heard 'till he cou'd find ſome fit occaſion to reſent this paſſage, which he never did to this day.

"I ſhall relate now ſome things concerning myſelf, which tho they may ſeem ſcarce credible, yet before God are true: I had been now in France about a year and an half, when my taylour, Andrew Henly of Baſil, who now lives in Blackfryars, demanded of me half a yard of ſatin to make me a ſuit more than I was accuſtomed to give, of which I required a reaſon, ſaying, I was not fatter now than when I came to France; he anſwered, it was true, but you are taller: whereunto, when I wou'd give no credit, he brought his old meaſures, and made it appear that they did not reach to their juſt places; I told him I knew not how this hap'ned, but howſoever he ſhou'd have half a yard more. and that, when I came into England, I wou'd clear the doubt; for a little before my departure thence, I remember William Earl of Pembrook and myſelf did meaſure heights together at the requeſt of the Counteſs of Bedford,

and

and he was then higher than I by about the breadth of my little finger: at my return, therefore, into England, I measured again with the same Earl, and, to both our great wonders, found myself taller than he by the breadth of a little finger; which growth of mine I could attribute to no other cause but to my quartan ague, which, when it quitted me, left me in a more perfect health than I formerly enjoyed.

"I weighed myself in ballances often with men lower than myself by the head, and yet in their bodies slenderer, and yet was found lighter than they, as Sir John Davers Knight, and Richard Griffiths, now living, can witness, with both whom I have been weighed: I had also, and have still, a pulse on the crown of my head: it is well known to those that wait in my chamber, that the shirts, waistcoats, and other garments I wear next my body, are sweet, beyond what either easily can be believed, or hath been observed in any else, which sweetness also was found to be in my breath above others, before I used to take tobacco, which towards my latter time I was forced to take against certain rheumes and catarres that trouble me, which yet did not taint my breath for any long time."

The following specimens of his conduct at the siege of Juliers will be sufficient to give an idea of his knight-errantry.

"One day Sir Edward Cecill and myself coming to the approaches that Monsieur de Balagny had made towards a bullwark or bastion of that city, Monsieur de Balagny, in the presence of Sir Edward Cecill and divers English and French captains then present, said, 'Monsieur, On dit, que vous êtes un des plus braves de vôtre nation, et je suis Balagny, allons voir qui faira le mieux;' They say, you are one of the bravest of your nation, and I am Balagny, let us see who will do best; whereupon, leaping suddenly out of the trenches with his sword drawn, I did in the like manner as suddenly follow him, both of us in the mean while striving who shou'd get foremost; which being perceived by those of the bullwark and cortine opposite to us, three or four hundred shot at least, great and small, were made against us. Our running on forwards in emulation of each other, was the cause that all the shots fell betwixt us and the trench from which we sallied. When Monsieur Balagny, finding such a storm of bullets, said, 'Par Dieu il fait bien chaud,' It is very hot here; I answered briefly thus, 'Vous en irez primier, autrement Je n'iray jamais;' You shall go first, or else I will never go; hereupon he ran with all speed, and somewhat crouching towards the trenches, I followed after leasurely and upright, and yet came within the trenches before they on the bullwark or cortine could charge again, which passage afterwards being related to the Prince of Orange, he said it was a strange bravado of Balagny, and that we went to an unavoidable death.

"I could relate divers things of note concerning myself, during the siege, but do forbear, least I should relish too much of vanity: it shall suffice that my passing over the ditch unto the wall, first of all the nations there, is set down by William Crofts Master of Arts, and soldier, who hath written and printed the history of the Low-Countries."

After

ACCOUNT OF BOOKS.

After relating a quarrel which happened between him and Lord Walden, he goes on thus:

"Being among the French, I remembered myself of the bravado of Monſieur Balagny, and, coming to him, told him, I knew how brave a man he was, and that as he had put me to one trial of daring, when I was laſt with him in his trenches, I wou'd put him to another; ſaying I heard he had a fair miſtreſs, and that the ſcarf he wore was her gift, and that I wou'd maintain I had a worthier miſtreſs, than he, and that I wou'd do as much for her ſake as he, or any elſe durſt do for his. Balagny hereupon looking merrily upon me, ſaid, if we ſhall try who is the abler man to ſerve his miſtreſs, let both of us get two wenches, and he that doth his buſineſs beſt, let him be the braver man; and that for his part he had no mind to fight on that quarrel: I looking hereupon ſomewhat diſdainfully on him, ſaid, he ſpoke more like a Paillard than a Cavalier; to which he anſwering nothing, I r id my ways, and afterwards went to Monſieur Terant, a French gentleman that belonged to the Duke of Montmorency, formerly mentioned; who telling me he had a quarrel with another gentleman, I offered to be his ſecond; but he ſaying he was provided already, I rode thence to the Engliſh quarters, attending ſome fit occaſion to ſend again to the Lord Walden. I came no ſooner thither, but I found Sir Thomas Sommerſet with 11 or 12 more in the head of the Engliſh, who were then drawing forth in a body or ſquadron, who ſeeing me on horſeback, with a footman only that attended me, gave me ſome affronting words, for my quarrelling with the Lord of Walden; whereupon I alighted, and, giving my horſe to my lackey, drew my ſword, which he no ſooner ſaw, but he drew his, as alſo all the company with him. I running hereupon amongſt them, put by ſome of their thruſts, and making towards him in particular, put by a thruſt of his, and had certainly run him through, but that one Lieutenant Prichard, at that inſtant taking me by the ſhoulder, turned me aſide; but I recovering myſelf again, ran at him a ſecond time, which he perceiving, retired himſelf with the company to the tents which were near, although not ſo faſt but I hurt one Proger, and ſome others alſo that were with him; but they being all at laſt got within the tents, I finding now nothing elſe to be done, got to my horſe again, having received only a ſlight hurt on the outſide of my ribs, and two thruſts, the one through the ſkirts of my doublet, and the other through my breeches, and about 18 nicks upon my ſword and hilt, and ſo rode to the trenches before Juliers, where our ſoldiers were."

A Sketch of the Philoſophical Character of the late Lord Viſcount Bolingbroke. By Thomas Hunter, *Vicar of* Weverham, *in* Cheſhire.

THE good intention as well as the good execution of this work will naturally recommend it to the friends of piety and religion, which are, we hope, ſo numerous a body, that the work may flatter itſelf with a general good reception.

The author has, it ſeems, had the misfortune

misfortune to lose his sight, which he modestly pleads as an apology for any defects the too discerning critic may see in his work. We however persuade ourselves, that the humane and candid reader will find himself prejudiced in the favour of a man, who, though deprived of the greatest blessing of our human state, can still exert his faculties for the good of human kind; and surely there cannot be a greater service to men than that of exposing the futility and falseness of those bold and bad reasoners, who, like the serpent of old, pretending to raise and ennoble our nature, and to teach us wisdom, carry us away from that humble path of simplicity and obedience wherein it has pleased God to permit and direct that poor creature man to look for his salvation.

While we give every praise to the intention, and allow the merit of the execution of this work, we have still our doubts whether these kind of writers, who dignify themselves with the style of freethinkers, are not, especially after a time, best answered with disdain: while the weakness of mankind, and their madness for novelty, give a kind of weight to these sorts of works, they seem to call for answers, lest a silence on the side of truth should give confidence to falsehood; but when the novelty is worn off, the less notice is taken of them, the less they are remembered.

In reality, our modern freethinkers have been but copiers; and it is some respect to truth, that, while she remains one and the same, the false reasoner, availing himself of the forgetfulness of mankind, gets a momentary credit by retailing, in somewhat perhaps of a new mode and garb, the forgotten errors and follies of past times, and then lies by himself unheeded and unregarded, till some new sophist, fed and fostered upon his exploded errors, glories in being a new seducer of the unwise and unwary: we cannot, however, quite agree with our author, that the noble writer usefully and handsomely employs his reason and his rhetoric in decrying school divinity, nor that his Lordship's testimony, added to the church of England writers, is any increase of strength to our cause: his Lordship's object was to destroy the reverence of our church as much as that of Rome, and we believe it were better to stand wholly on our own firm ground, than to accept the treacherous assistance of so profane an hand.

Our author, with all his zeal against the philosophical or irreligious writings of Lord Bolingbroke, seems almost of an opinion with his Lordship in his political works, which, however, are fallen nearly into as much disrepute as his philosophical, and possibly not without reason: there is, however, a pompousness of phrase, a show and affectation of learning, and a sort of glair of elocution, that seems at least to excuse, if not to justify, the admiration that his works once excited.

Our author, however, exempts from his praise the noble Lord's political works that were wrote for the ends of party, or to gratify passion, or feed resentment.—This is, indeed, such an allay, as we fear leaves the noble Lord very little matter of praise behind.

The following extracts will give an idea of our author's manner, and

and enable our readers to form a conclusion on the observations we have made.

"The knowledge of human nature was easy, and clear to a mind capacious and penetrating like Lord Bolingbroke's, and, like his, familiar by practice and theory, by conversation and reading, with the history of mankind:—this is the proper school of the passions, where they appear not delineated in the lifeless draught, and with the insipid formality of a recluse professor, or the vague or crude hypothesis of some new adventurer in moral philosophy, but in their causes and combinations, their workings and progress by immediate effects, or remoter consequences, cloathed with circumstances, and realized, and, as I would say, embodied by fact and experience: but he saw still farther not only the general current, but the particular turnings and windings of the human passions;—not only their simple uniform operation, but their effects when combined and complicated, or when operating upon particular parties, from particular principles or interests, or upon single characters and in singular circumstances; and how each, or all, contributed to the forming, in the views of human wisdom, that political crisis, which, according to his Lordship's deductions, influenced the subject of his present examination.

"We must except from this merit of his political works the essays that were written to serve the ends of a party, to gratify passion, and feed his resentment. In these he has practised some of that subtilty he condemns in the schoolmen. And after all the applause that is given, and is due to his great political sagacity, it must be acknowledged, that he has sometimes a refinement in his reflections, and in his deriving effects from remote causes, that would escape the observation of common sense, and will be found of little use to the common good; as his building so much—nay, the whole success on a prudence without piety, and a course of nature without providence, is the baseless fabric of a political vision! and which, civil history might have shewn his Lordship, had been by seeming accidents, to appearance the most trifling, demolished in a thousand instances.

"We may, perhaps, not without reason, apply to his Lordship the remark which Montaigne has made upon Guicciardini: ' I have observed,' says he, ' this of him, that ' of so many persons and so many ' effects, so many motives and so ' many councils, as he judges of, he ' never attributes any of them to ' virtue, religion, or conscience, as ' if all these were utterly extinct in ' the world.' — The Frenchman adds, ' This makes me suspect that ' his own taste was vicious; from ' whence it might happen, that he ' judged other men by himself.' I wish there was no reason to apply this to his Lordship: but his confessed admiration of Tacitus might easily lead him to, or at least confirm him in, both his scepticism concerning providence, and his ill opinion of mankind. He gives you a general but striking review of times past, just observations on present objects, and rational conjectures of future consequences: he states facts, balances different interests, and weighs opposite powers: the genius of the several nations, the temper of the court and of the people, are tranſiently, yet very expreſſively, preſented to the reader: he is preciſe, yet not minute, as he is general, yet not confuſed; ſpeculative yet practical, refined yet rational and juſt. He reaſons with ſtrength and calmneſs, debates with temper, contradicts with decency, cenſures with modeſty, and condemns with ſeeming juſtice and impartiality.

"But his excellencies as a writer are not confined to politics, and political ſpeculations: he has with much elegance repreſented, or rather expoſed, ſchool-divinity and metaphyſics: his reaſon and his rhetoric are both uſefully and handſomely employed upon this occaſion; and ſubtilties and nonentities exiſt no where ſo gracefully as in his Lordſhip's confutation of them. The ſcandalous corruptions of Chriſtianity by the church of Rome had been abundantly diſplayed by the proteſtant divines, by thoſe of the church of England in particular; yet his Lordſhip's teſtimony to thoſe corruptions, deduced from perſonal obſervation and hiſtorical records, and a particular develope of the intrigues of emperors and popes, is by no means contemptible or inconſiderable; as the Lord Bolingbroke had no party or paſſion to ſerve by his judgment on this ſubject, nor was prejudiced in favour of any particular communion of Chriſtians. His indignation is here proper; his figures magnificent, maſterly, and ſtrong; and if d'Holbein is a great original, my Lord is a copier or commentator, whom few can equal. If he is any where more happy, it is in the picture he has given us of the folly, foppery, ſuperſtition, and idolatry of the church of Rome: here we perceive he drew from the life, and had his ſubject clearly before him. The pencil plays its part in the moſt admirable manner: the features are ſtrong and ſtriking; the colours glow, and the figures move. The ſubject was indeed proper, and ſuited to his hand: ſpiritual truth was not to be expreſſed, but a gaudy and a pompous ceremonial to be deſcribed: a temple, where marble, gilding, imagery, architecture, make ſo principal a figure; rendering it a ſcene much more ſuited for the imagination of a painter than the habitation of a God. If his Lordſhip is warm, it here becomes him, and his reſentment is pious.

"He inveighs with propriety enough, becauſe with juſtice, againſt the licentiouſneſs of ſacred interpreters, and their arbitrary practice of giving ſo many different ſenſes to the ſame paſſages of the Bible. It muſt be farther confeſſed, that much truth has been ſaid by his Lordſhip, though invidiouſly enough, of the corruptions of the clergy; and as truth is always on the ſide of virtue, much good uſe may be made of his Lordſhip's labours on this ſubject: it may teach this venerable body, if at this day they had need of teaching, that, by a conduct contrary to their profeſſion, they give occaſion to the enemies of the croſs of Chriſt, and arm infidelity with the keeneſt weapons againſt that church, of which they are members and miniſters."

THE CONTENTS.

HISTORY OF EUROPE.

CHAP. I.

State of the belligerent powers. Ruſſia. Conduct of the neutral powers. Probable conſequences of the war. Turkey. Firmneſs of the Grand Seignior. Probability of a peace. Spain. Falkland's iſlands. Great Britain. Portugal ....p. [1

CHAP. II.

War on the Danube. State of the armies during the winter. Account of the countries that were the ſeat of the war. Battle at the River Larga, in which the Kan of the Tartars is defeated. Grand Vizir croſſes the Danube. Great battle fought between the Pruth and the Cahul, in which General Romanzow gained a complete victory. The Turks purſued to the Danube, and obliged to croſs that river with great loſs.........[11

CHAP. III.

Bender beſieged by Count Panin. Brave defence made by the garriſon and inhabitants. The Governor, in a fit of deſpair, poiſons himſelf: another choſen by the garriſon in his room. Globe of compreſſion; a kind of mine ſo called by the Ruſſians. The place taken by ſtorm, and burned: a great ſlaughter made. Budziac Tartars conclude a treaty with the Ruſſians. General Romanzow fixes his head quarters at Calpouk, near the Danube. Ibrailow beſieged. Kilia Nova taken. Bialogrod taken by Baron Ingleſtrom. Turks abandon the citadel of Ibrailow, after a long ſiege. The Turks being entirely driven beyond the Danube, the Ruſſian armies go into winter quarters. War in Georgia...................[20

CONTENTS.

CHAP. IV.

Russian expedition to the Mediterranean. Count Orlow arrives in the Morea. Insurrection of the Greeks; cruelties committed by them. Misitra, Arcadia, and other places, taken. Messalongi taken. Coron besieged. Navarino taken. Patras taken, and the castle besieged. Several other places ineffectually besieged. Greeks massacred at Patras, and the city burnt. Mainotes defeated. Turkish army arrives in the Morea. Execution of several of the principal Greeks. Modon besieged by sea and land: actions between the besiegers and a body of Turks and Albanians: the siege finally raised. Russians and Greeks totally separate: the latter retire to Navarino, and soon after abandon the peninsula. Admiral Elphinstone's squadron arrives from England. Engagements at sea. Turkish fleet destroyed in the harbour of Cisme. Captain Pacha beheaded. Levant trade ruined. Smyrna in danger. Castle of Lemnos besieged: relieved by Hassan Bey. Enormities committed by the runaway sailors and deserters. Plague at Constantinople. Revolution in Egypt. Aly Bey. [27

CHAP. V.

Unhappy state of Poland: the plague breaks out in that country. Germany. Conduct of the Emperor. Of the King of Prussia. Prussian troops enter the territories of Dantzick. Changes in the ministry at Copenhagen. Danish expedition against Algiers. Sweden. Difference between the States of Holland and the Elector Palatine .... [41

CHAP. VI.

France. Sufferings of M. de Chalotais. Prosecution commenced against the Duke d'Aiguillon, at Versailles. A bed of justice held, at which the King puts a stop to the prosecution by his letters patent. Conduct of the Princes of the blood. Arret of the Parliament of Paris against the Duke. The King issues an arret, by which that of the Parliament is annulled. Grand deputation from the Parliament to Versailles: the King's answer. Conduct of the other Parliaments. Deputation from the Parliament of Britany: two of its members sent to prison. The King arrives suddenly at Paris, and holds a bed of justice, at which all the papers relative to the prosecution are seized, and the decrees of the Parliament erased from the registers. Violent measures taken with the other Parliaments. Arret from the King's council of state. Distresses of the people from the scarcity of provisions. Corsica. Expedition to Tunis. State of Italy ..... [47

CHAP. VII.

State of affairs previous to the meeting of Parliament. General discontent upon the determination on the Middlesex election. Addresses: petitions the
consequence

CONTENTS.

consequence of the addresses. Parliament meets. Speech from the throne. Debates. Amendment proposed to the address: affair of the petitions violently agitated: amendment rejected. Resignations. Motion tending to define the jurisdiction in cases of contested elections: amendment to the motion. Motion in the House of Lords. Protest .... [56

CHAP. VIII.

Motion for disqualifying certain officers of the revenue from voting for the election of members of Parliament: opposition to it: the motion overruled. Civil list. Repeal of part of the late revenue act for imposing duties in the colonies: duty upon tea continued. Act for regulating the proceedings on controverted elections. London remonstrance. Great debates. Address to his Majesty 69*

CHAP. IX.

State of affairs in Ireland at the meeting of the new Parliament. Augmentation bill passed. Privy Council money-bill rejected. Supplies raised in the usual manner. Lord Lieutenant's speech and protest. Parliament prorogued. Consequences thereof. Motion made here for the Irish papers: rejected. Motion, and resolutions, relative to American affairs: over-ruled. Bill for reversing the adjudications relative to the Middlesex election. Debates on the answer to the remonstrance of the city of London. Resolutions proposed in the House of Lords relative to the colonies. King's speech. Parliament breaks up 85*

The CHRONICLE. [65

Births for the year 1770 .... [178
Marriages .... [179
Principal promotions .... [181
Deaths .... [186

APPENDIX to the CHRONICLE.

Two protests of the House of Lords .... [193
The humble address, remonstrance, and petition, of the Lord Mayor, Aldermen, and Livery of the city of London; with his Majesty's answer .. [199
The humble address, remonstrance, and petition, of the Lord Mayor, Aldermen, and Common Council of the city of London; with his Majesty's answer, and the Lord Mayor's reply .... [201
A letter from the Lord Mayor of the city of London to the Lords of the Admiralty .... [203
A letter from the Lords of the Admiralty to the Lord Mayor, in answer to the preceding .... [204

CONTENTS.

Copy of a letter transmitted by the Lords of the Admiralty to the Right Hon. the Lord Mayor .... [205
The humble address, remonstrance, and petition, of the Lord Mayor, Aldermen, and Commons of the city of London; with his Majesty's answer [ibid
Account of the proceedings at the county meeting at York .... [206
A letter of thanks from the freeholders of the county of York to Sir George Saville, Bt. and Edwin Lascelles, Esq.; and their respective answers [208
Account of the unhappy riot at Boston in New England .... [211
Case of Captain Thomas Preston .... [215
Account of the trial of Captain Thomas Preston 218
Account of the trial of Mungo Campbell, for the murder of Alexander Earl of Eglingtoun .... [219
Genuine copy of a letter sent by the Committee of the Supporters of the Bill of Rights to the Hon. House of Assembly of South Carolina, in answer to one from the Assembly .... [224
Abstract of an act to regulate the trials of controverted elections, or returns of members to serve in Parliament .... [226
Abstract of an act for the better preservation of the game .... [227
Abstract of an act for preventing the stealing of dogs .... [228
Abstract of an act for registering the prices at which corn is sold in the several counties of Great Britain .... [ibid
Abstract of an act to prevent delays of justice, by reason of privilege of Parliament .... [229
Extraordinary conduct of the Regulators in the back settlements of North Carolina .... [230
The Lord Mayor's queries in respect to the legality of press warrants [232
The humble address of the Lord Mayor, Sheriffs, Commons, and Citizens of the city of Dublin .... [ibid
Supplies granted by Parliament for the year 1770 .... [234
Ways and means for raising the supplies .... [239

STATE PAPERS.

His Majesty's most gracious speech to both Houses of Parliament, on Tuesday the 9th of January 1770; with the humble address of both Houses on the occasion, and his Majesty's most gracious answer .... [244
The humble address of the Right Hon. the Lords Spiritual and Temporal, and Commons, in Parliament assembled, presented March 23, to his Majesty; with his Majesty's answer .... [248
A proclamation for encouraging seamen to enter themselves on board his Majesty's ships of war .... [249
His Majesty's most gracious speech to both Houses of Parliament, on Saturday the 19th of May 1770 .... [250
The humble address of the Lord Mayor, Aldermen, and Commons of the city of London, in Common Council assembled, presented to his Majesty on Wednesday the 30th of May 1770, on the birth of another Princess; with his Majesty's answer .... [251

His

CONTENTS.

His Majesty's most gracious speech to both Houses of Parliament, on Tuesday the 13th of November 1770; with the humble addresses of both Houses on the occasion, and his Majesty's most gracious answer.... [252

CHARACTERS.

Of the Russians; from the account of a journey into Siberia, made by order of the King of France.................................... 1
Some account of the Tartars of Kasan, under the government of Russia. 16
An account of the Wotiaks 18
Some account of the life, misfortunes, and character of the celebrated favourite Prince Menzikoff...20
Some account of Count Biron, late Duke of Courland.................27
Of the Cossacks, and the singular customs of the Zaporavian Republic...29
Of the antient Scandinavians 32
Of Rollo, the Conqueror of Normandy 40
Some account of the Albigenses......................................43
The character of Constantine the Great.............................44
An account of the Circoncelliones, in Africa 50
Character of Lewis XIII. of France..................................51
A short character of the late Sir Joseph Yates 52
Genuine anecdotes of the life of the late Peter Collinson, F.R.S. ...53
Memoirs of the Rev. Mr. George Whitefield...........................58

NATURAL HISTORY.

An extraordinary case of three pins swallowed by a girl, and discharged at her shoulder...64
A letter from the Hon. Wm. Hamilton, his Majesty's Envoy Extraordinary at Naples, to Matthew Maty, M.D. F.R.S., containing some farther particulars on Mount Vesuvius, and other volcanoes in the neighbourhood.68
Extract of a letter from Mr. B. Gooch, Surgeon, of Shottisham, near Norwich, to Mr. Joseph Warner, F.R.S., concerning a cuticular glove; with the history of the case relative thereto.............................70
Of the different quantities of rain which appear to fall, at different heights, over the same spot of ground.......................................72
Experiments to prove that the luminousness of the sea arises from the putrefaction of its animal substances:...................................74
Of a singular disease with which two butchers of the Royal Hospital of the Invalids in France were seized..77
The case of the Rev. Mr. Winder, who was cured by lightning of a paralytic disorder 80
Account of the Needles, in the Isle of Wight 82
An account of the tailor bird, with a description of an Indian forest....83

ANTI-

CONTENTS.

ANTIQUITIES.

The thirty-second fable of the Edda, or the antient Icelandic mythology: Of the twilight of the gods 86
The thirty-third fable; or, the sequel of the conflagration of the world. 88
The Runic chapter, or the magic of Odin 92
Extracts from the ode of King Regner Lodbrog 93
Some account of the Arabic manuscripts at the Escurial; with a translation of some curious passages on Arabic poetry 96
Dress of the antient French 101
Clause in the Salic law 102
Case of the unhappy Chundon 103
Advantages which France derived from the antient monks .... ibid
State of trade in the eighth and ninth centuries 104
Specimen of the wit and satire of the middle ages 105
A dissertation on Joduta, the idol of Saxony, and of the Marche 106
Anecdote of Shakespeare, never printed in his works 107

USEFUL PROJECTS, &c.

A letter from Mr. J. Moult to Dr. Percival, of Manchester, F.R.S., containing a new manner of preparing salep 108
Some account of an oil, transmitted by Mr. George Brownrigg, of North Carolina: by William Watson, M.D. R.S.S. 109
Improvements and experiments in agriculture:—of potatoes, and the amazing crops which they produce by a proper culture 111
    Of cabbages 116
    Of carrots 123
    Of lucerne 124
    Of sainfoine 129
On the number of draught cattle used in tillage 130

MISCELLANEOUS ESSAYS.

Anecdotes of the court of Petersburgh in the reign of the Empress Anne. 133
Three letters, supposed to have been written by the celebrated M. Montesquieu 139
Letter from Voltaire to the Duke of Valiere 143
A letter from M. Voltaire to Mr. Rousseau, of Toulouse, concerning a letter inserted in the St. James's Chronicle of July 1762 149
An account of the noble aqueduct of Alcantara, by which Lisbon is supplied 150
An account of the manner in which the punishment of the knout was inflicted on the celebrated Madame Lopouchin, at Petersburgh; with some observations on the Russian punishments, and the effects they produce; and several curious

CONTENTS.

curious particulars relative to the banishment of Count Lestoc and his Lady into Siberia 151
Account of a debauch at the present King (then Prince) of Prussia's court at Rheinsberg 157
Extracts from the Abbé Millot's Elements of the History of England .. 159
Letter from the late Miss Talbot to a new-born child 161
Remarks on a sentence in the law called pein forte et dure 163
An essay on flattery 165
The adventures of Scarmentado; a satirical novel, by Voltaire 169
The most criminal not always the most unhappy: a moral tale 174
A fortune with a wife no ungenerous demand in a husband 175
A dehortatory speech by a well-affected tanner to the county of Berkshire, met at Abingdon the 2d of April 1649, for the election of Pembroke to be knight of the shire 177
A godly speech spoken by Philip Herbert, late Earl of Pembroke, &c. as it was heard with much content without an oath 178
Essay on good humour 180
On the origin of signs denoting trades 181
The folly of self-tormenting 186
An original letter which was written by the celebrated Sir Walter Raleigh to Prince Henry, eldest son of James the First 188
The history of a popular character in France, very much mentioned, but very little known in England 190
Dissertation on the virtues and abilities of Caligula's horse 192
Subject of a picture now painting by Sir Joshua Reynolds 194
Translation of a letter from the Empress Queen to the Dauphin of France, on his marriage with the Archduchess her daughter 195
Extract from the records of the town of Arundel .... ibid

POETRY.

Extract from the Deserted Village; a poem, by Dr. Goldsmith 197
Ode for the new year, 1770: by William Whitehead, Esq. 201
Ode to the Hon. Miss Yorke (afterwards Lady Anson): by her brother, the late Hon. Charles Yorke, Esq. .... ibid
To a lady, with a present of Pope's works: by the same 204
Stanzas in the manner of Waller; occasioned by a receipt to make ink, given to the author by a lady: by the same .... ibid
Aminta; an elegy: by John Gerrard, Curate of Withycombe in the Moor, Devon 205
An epistle from an unfortunate young gentleman to a young lady: by the same 207
A translation of Dr. King's Latin epistle, entitled, Antonietti's advice to the Corsicans concerning the choice of a king: by Mr. Russell 210
The poet and straw; a fable 217
The two kings: a fable 218
On our modern comedies 219
Bacchus: by the late Dr. Parnell 220

The

CONTENTS.

The beggar 222
To the King of Prussia, on his recovery: by M. de Voltaire; translated by Dr. Franklin 223
To the Marquis de Villette: by the same .... ibid
Ode for his Majesty's birthday, June 4, 1770 224
Ode on his Majesty's birthday. Said to be written by a very great lady on the 4th of last June 225
A specimen of Saragon poetry, from Aubalfedal Annales Moslemici. On a cat killed in a dove-house .... ibid
The horse and the olive: by the late Archdeacon Parnel 226
On throwing by an old black coat 227
The expostulation; to Delia: by Lord G. 228
The reply: by Lady Mary S—— 229
Prayer to indifference; by Mrs. G——: found in Richmond Garden . ibid
Henry and Sophy 231
To fear 232
Fortune the foundation of fame: translated from Rousseau 233
The petition of the fools to Jupiter: a fable 234
An answer, in the name of Lord Chesterfield 235
A wish to the north: by a lady 236
To a robin, which has lately taken up his residence in the cathedral at Bristol, and accompanies the organ with his singing 237
Part of the last chorus of the second act of Seneca's Troades . 238
Fame and his companions; a poetical fable: by the Rev. Mr. R—— . 239
Written by a brewer's daughter, on her father's discharging his coachman for getting in liquor 240
Wisdom and health 241
On the death of the Marquis of Granby .... ibid
Another on the same .... ibid

An Account of Books published in the Year 1770.

A journey from London to Genoa, through England, Portugal, Spain, and France: by Joseph Barretti, Secretary for Foreign Correspondence to the Royal Academy of Painting, Sculpture, and Architecture. 4 vol. 8vo. 242
The life of Edward Lord Herbert of Cherbury; written by himself ...248
A sketch of the philosophical character of the late Lord Viscount Bolingbroke: by Thomas Hunter, Vicar of Weverham in Cheshire 253

THE END.

KNIGHT AND COMPTON, PRINTERS,
Middle Street, Cloth Fair.

Lightning Source UK Ltd.
Milton Keynes UK
UKHW031839280119
336340UK00011B/873/P